This volume offers a thoughtful, constructive and practical resour grate the Sustainable Development Goals into their daily practice. It provides guidance on each of the goals while making the connections between them. It sets out creative lesson plans and projects that nurture awareness and agency. We share a responsibility to get the SDGs back on track to make our world more inclusive, sustainable, just and peaceful. This can happen through learning how to learn and how to care together.

Stefania Giannini, *UNESCO Assistant Director-General for Education*

The book is a masterclass on how to introduce the Sustainable Development Goals to Young people. The book illustrates beautifully the authors' dedication to teaching and learning while applying their craft to UNESCO's Transforming Education agenda. The authors carefully embed human and nature rights around scientific knowledge and learning. The agenda for transformative education outlined in this book will help students to understand how sustainable development for all life and the planet itself can be achieved.

Patrick Paul Walsh, *Professor, University College Dublin, Vice President for Education, Sustainable Development Solutions Network (SDSN), and Director, SDG Academy*

With a focus on hope and optimism, Anne brings readers on a journey to finding solutions for our planet – together through connections and solidarity. Climate change is now, and climate action can be us all! This is a great addition for every teacher's bookshelf!

Jennifer Williams, *Co-founder of Take Action Global and #TeachSDGs, Author Teach Boldly: Using Edtech for Social Good*

Sustainability is still an abstract concept for many people. The authors help us to connect the dots between climate, nature, global citizenship, and what sustainability means for us as individuals. If you are not sure where to start, start here. You'll be guided through how you can break down this complex topic making it accessible and exciting for your students.

Patrick Kirwan, *secondary science teacher at Ardscoil Na Mara in Tramore, and founder of Irish Schools Sustainability Network (ISSN)*

This book serves as an 'Atlas' to guide educators and school communities through the complex, intricate, and interconnected global issues which we must urgently prioritise and address.

Fergal McCarthy, *Principal, Kinsale Community School and Vice President of the European Federation of Educational Employers*

A welcome stimulus to thinking things through. Anne, and the authors she has worked with, makes the connections, engages with complexity, and highlights challenges from the 17 SDGs. Yet the book enables us to gain a professionally optimistic understanding of the value of such work to the core task of meeting educational needs. It highlights the need for a cross-curricular approach, and offers substance to core education challenges relating to hope, respect, empathy, and advocacy.

Scott Sinclair, *Chair Tide~ global learning. Co-editor, Elephant Times Magazine*

This book provides an important learning framework for young people to better understand and develop critical thinking about the complex and interconnected world we all share. The interactive format and diverse content anchored in the SDGs will strengthen the students 'ubuntu' and help prepare them for a rapidly changing and challenging world they will soon help to shape.

Bernadette Connolly, *Coordinator, Cork Environmental Forum*

Research suggests that teachers, and their students, yearn for learning and teaching as if the world matters, and as if their part in changing the world towards greater justice, greater human rights and human flourishing, greater sustainability, is intimately connected with what goes on in school classrooms and corridors, in school playing fields and lunch-breaks, on the way to and from school, at home and in youth clubs and in the local community. Global Education, which includes education for hope, empathy and engagement, is crucial to the lives of educators and young people and to our current and future survival.

At the same time, research also shows that many educators, while deeply engaged and wanting to teach as if people and planet matter more than points and profit, nevertheless, feel at times underqualified, or underprepared, to teach these issues. And we are, to a certain extent, all unprepared to teach issues that are increasingly complex, depend on increasing volumes of data, with outcomes that are increasingly uncertain, in a world that feels increasingly insecure.

That's why this edition, edited by the incomparable Anne Dolan, and with superb contributions by those who know how, couldn't have come at a better time. This book marries deep and necessary theory with pedagogical practice, and provides a clear and critical approach to key issues that need to be addressed. There is no shirking here – this book is not neutral. Important ethical issues – the eradication of poverty, the obliteration of hunger, the power of new sustainable communities to tell new stories of the end times, the need to sing a song of the movement of resistance to current economic models, the inadequacy of the SDGs themselves – though our best hope, perhaps, for a framework for the next 5 years – and the need to put Human Rights at the core – all these issues, and more, are dealt with in a way that will provide background information, up-to-date analysis, and accessible resources for educators grappling with issues of global justice and sustainability.

The Brazilian educator Paulo Freire once said that those who are not grounded in hope should get out of education. This book, truly grounded in hope, provides an antidote to that feeling of being overwhelmed by all that faces us, and a way forward for those educators who, faced with almost insurmountable global and local challenges, nevertheless, choose daily, in the words of Adrienne Rich, to "cast [their] lot with those who, age after age, with no extraordinary power, reconstitute the world".

Liam Wegimont, *Executive Director at Global Education Network Europe (GENE)*

Anyone who works with younger people recognises that their engagement with social and environmental issues is often marked by anxiety and despondency about the future, anger at prior generations and at inequalities, and by a sense of isolation in an apparently interconnected world. These chapters by Anne Dolan and her collaborators addresses how educators can work with young people on these issues with a sense of hope, respect, and empathy, and how we can help to develop their capacity for advocacy. The book is highly relevant for teachers of any discipline. It is accessible, practical and optimistic, without ever being naïve or simplistic – a wonderful combination.

Roland Tormey, *Senior Scientist in the Ecole polytechnique fédérale de Lausanne (EPFL), Switzerland*

Education is an essential enabler for all of the Sustainable Development Goals. Half way to 2030 we all need to accelerate our actions to reach these goals. This book will be an important resource for student teachers and teachers who are teaching the Sustainable Development Goals and contributing, through transformative education, to a better, more sustainable and more equal world.

Frank Geary, *Director of Irish Development Education Association*

Every good school has a staff library replete with publications - short and long - whose sole shared characteristic is that they stimulate teachers to think about either the purposes of schooling, or pedagogy or curriculum or learning or assessment. And the leaders of such schools are always on the lookout for additions to this treasure of intellectual stimulation for their staff.

This book is a 'must-buy' for all schools. The UN's 'Sustainable Development Goals' have rightly shifted the aims and purposes of schooling and to ignore them is to betray our next generation. This book will enable teachers and schools to think through their practice effectively and creatively to meet these changed urgent needs.

Sir Tim Brighhouse, *(RIP) Formerly Chief Education Officer of Oxfordshire and Birmingham and Commissioner for London Schools*

TEACHING THE SUSTAINABLE DEVELOPMENT GOALS TO YOUNG CITIZENS (10-16 YEARS)

With the current climate and economic crises, education for sustainability has never been more critical. This timely and essential book encourages readers to rethink our current values systems and to interrogate common assumptions about our world. Written for all educators with an interest in sustainability, chapters address several possible future scenarios for our planet, allowing readers to make more educated choices about sustainability and to transfer this knowledge to students within the classroom.

Each chapter focuses on a specific Sustainable Development Goal. Beginning with a brief historical and theoretical introduction to contextualise each Goal, chapters then showcase practical activities, case studies and exemplars that teachers can adopt when teaching. Topics explored include, but are not limited to:

- Poverty
- Renewable energy
- Climate change
- Peace and justice
- Human rights
- Access to education

This book is an essential classroom resource for any teacher or student teacher wishing to promote the Sustainable Development Goals and to teach for a better and brighter future.

Anne M. Dolan is a lecturer in primary geography with the Department of Learning, Society and Religious Education in Mary Immaculate College, University of Limerick, Ireland. She is the author of *Powerful Primary Geography* and editor of *Teaching Climate Change in Primary Schools*. Formerly a primary school teacher, Anne maintains a strong interest in creative and student-based pedagogies.

TEACHING THE SUSTAINABLE DEVELOPMENT GOALS TO YOUNG CITIZENS (10-16 YEARS)

A Focus on Teaching Hope, Respect, Empathy and Advocacy in Schools.

Edited by Anne M. Dolan

Routledge
Taylor & Francis Group

LONDON AND NEW YORK

Designed cover image: The front cover image was created by Senior Infants children (6 years of age) in St Vincent's National School, Coolarne, Galway under the guidance of their teacher Geraldine Whelan.

First published 2024
by Routledge
4 Park Square, Milton Park, Abingdon, Oxon OX14 4RN

and by Routledge
605 Third Avenue, New York, NY 10158

Routledge is an imprint of the Taylor & Francis Group, an informa business

British Library Cataloguing-in-Publication Data
A catalogue record for this book is available from the British Library

ISBN: 978-1-032-14026-1 (hbk)
ISBN: 978-1-032-14028-5 (pbk)
ISBN: 978-1-003-23200-1 (ebk)

DOI: 10.4324/9781003232001

Typeset in Interstate
by codeMantra

The content of this publication has not been approved by the United Nations and does not reflect the views of the United Nations or its officials or Member States. You may access the United Nations' Sustainable Development Goals website at: https://www.un.org/sustainabledevelopment/

Dedicated to my amazing, loving sister Marguerite Dolan, Larkin (RIP). Marguerite was a Public Health Nurse who worked tirelessly serving her local community, Eyrecourt in East Galway. She was the ultimate champion for SDG 3. Marguerite was a wife, mother, daughter, sister, neighbour, cousin and friend and she is missed by all those who knew her.

In memory of my friends Celia and Ann Donoghue (RIP) two sisters, two educators both committed to human rights, equality and justice.

All proceedings from this publication will be donated to Cancer Care West and Galway Hospice Foundation, Ireland.

CONTENTS

FIGURES

TABLES

EXEMPLARS

CASE STUDIES

CONTRIBUTORS

Nicola Broderick is an Assistant Professor in the School of STEM Education, Innovation and Global Studies, Institute of Education, Dublin City University (DCU). She works in the area of Initial Teacher Education (ITE) and Teacher Professional Learning. Nicola's main responsibilities include researching, developing and facilitating ITE and continuous professional learning in science education. Nicola has developed educational resources in science and published in the areas of teaching and learning in primary science, STEM education, Nature of Science, Education for Sustainable Development and teacher professional learning. Nicola recently completed her Doctorate of Education at DCU, which examined the impact of teaching primary science through socioscientific issues on children's scientific literacy.

Noirín Burke is the Director of Education at Galway Atlantaquaria Ltd, the National Aquarium of Ireland. Her job involves developing and delivering educational activities within the aquarium and through outreach. Noirin is part of the coordination team for the Marine Institute Explorers Educational Programme. She provides support to other Explorer Centres nationally, helps trial new materials and activities, and assists with teachers training through regional Education Centres, Mary Immaculate College and St Patricks Campus, DCU. She also works on Local Community Funded projects and the Discover Primary Science and Maths (DPSM) Programme. She is part of the secretariat for the Irish Ocean Literacy Network www.irishoceanliteracy.ie, on the board of the Irish Whale and Dolphin Group (IWDG) www.iwdg.ie for over 8 years, and is part of the European Association of Zoos and Aquaria (EAZA) conservation education committee.

Padraic Creedon is 'Leave No Trace Ireland's Education and Training Officer and a 'Leave No Trace' Advanced Trainer located in Mayo, Ireland. He is an avid enthusiast of all things marine. He is always keen to bring groups to our shores and coastlines to explore the ideas of Leave No Trace with regards to our largest and most important neighbour – the ocean. He never passes up an opportunity to visit the outdoors and when inland he particularly enjoys exploring our woodland habitats. Each 'Leave No Trace' course that he has been a part of has been a unique and fascinating experience and he always enjoys bringing groups outdoors to learn about our incredible environment.

Ann Devitt is a professor in language and literacy education at the School of Education in Trinity College Dublin (TCD). She is Academic Director for Learnovate, the Enterprise

Ireland-funded research and innovation centre focused on educational technology which is hosted in TCD. She is a member of the Royal Irish Academy Committee on Languages, Literature, Culture and Communication Committee. She has been involved for many years with the Ubuntu network as TCD representative and is committed through her work as a teacher educator to the integration of global education across the curriculum.

Fiona Dineen is a lecturer in Religious Education and a member of the Department of Learning, Society, and Religious Education at Mary Immaculate College, Ireland. She teaches on undergraduate and postgraduate Initial Teacher Education programmes and coordinates MEd in Religious Education. Her research interests and publications focus on Catholic education, school ethos, educational policy development, teacher identity, continuing professional development. She has a particular interest in the intersectionality of Citizenship, Values and Religious Education.

Anne M. Dolan is a lecturer in primary geography with the Department of Learning, Society and Religious Education in Mary Immaculate College, Ireland. She is the author/editor of *Teaching Climate Change in Primary Schools: An Interdisciplinary Approach* (published by Routledge in 2022), *Powerful Primary Geography: A Toolkit for 21st Century Learning* (published by Routledge in 2020) and *You, Me and Diversity: Picturebooks for Teaching Development and Intercultural Education* (published by Trentham Books/IOE Press in 2014). Anne is particularly interested in creative approaches to geography, inter-disciplinary collaboration and the use of the arts in geographical explorations.

Paula Galvin is a development education practitioner and former primary teacher in Clonburris Primary School, Dublin. She has researched children's understanding of global justice issues. She is the author of an Irish National Teachers' Union (INTO) commissioned report, 'An Evaluation of Primary School Teachers' Experience of Implementing Global Citizenship Education' (2018) She continues to promote GCE through her membership of the steering committee of Global Citizenship School as well as local community citizenship initiatives in Clondalkin.

Claire Glavey is the Project Officer for Global Village, a strategic partnership for Global Citizenship Education in primary schools between Irish Aid at the Department of Foreign Affairs and a consortium of Trócaire, Dublin City University, the Irish National Teachers' Organisation and the Irish Primary Principals' Network. Her role involves researching, designing and developing Global Citizenship Education opportunities for primary schools in Ireland. Claire is a primary school teacher with a particular interest in incorporating global themes, critical thinking, philosophy for children and reflective practice into the primary school curriculum and daily school life. Claire has developed educational resources in the areas of development education and human rights education and has taught and supervised research on Global Citizenship Education as part of Initial Teacher Education programmes.

Miriam Hamilton is a lecturer in education in Mary Immaculate College, Limerick, Ireland and a member of the Department of STEM Education. Having spent much of her career teaching at second level, she transitioned in recent years to teacher education, where she teaches science education to undergraduate and postgraduate pre-service teachers. Her research studies and publications span a variety of educational domains including; the social context of education, student experience, cultural pedagogy and reflective self-study enquiry. The writing of this chapter facilitates a new challenge with the exploration of storytelling as a pedagogy for teaching biological and climate change concepts.

Sara Hannafin is a lecturer at the University of Limerick. She is a former secondary teacher of geography and currently teaches undergraduate courses in human geography and in the pedagogy of geography for pre-service teachers. She has recently introduced a module on Sustainability to the BA course at UL and is a member of the Geographical Society of Ireland's working group on the proposed Leaving Certificate Course, Climate Action and Sustainable Development. Her research interests are in migration, the emotion people have for place and incorporating teaching about the local place into second-level geography teaching.

Tandeep Kaur is a research associate at the Centre for the Advancement of STEM teaching and learning (CASTeL), Dublin City University, Ireland. Tandeep has extensive national and international experience in teaching mathematics at all levels and is skilled in curriculum and content development enhancing rich classroom activities. Her research interests lie in the areas of initial teacher education, mathematics pedagogy, global education, adult numeracy and reflective practices. Tandeep has carried out research across a range of projects in the areas of STEM and STEAM education, development education and initial teacher education and is currently also a doctoral candidate at the Institute of Education, Dublin City University, Ireland.

Patricia Kieran is a British Foreign and Commonwealth Chevening Scholar who teaches Religious Education at Mary Immaculate College. She is a member of the Mid-West Interfaith Network and the Religions and Beliefs in Changing Times Research team as well as Director of the Irish Institute for Catholic Studies. She has co-written and edited books on a range of topics including Catholic theology, Religious Education in an Intercultural Europe, Children and Catholicism & Trends and Challenges in Education. Her most recent book *Connecting Lives: Inter-belief Dialogue in Contemporary Ireland* (2019) focuses on dialogue among belief diverse communities. She has published numerous chapters and articles on the subject of inter-religious education, Catholic education, Roman Catholic Modernism and gender.

Peadar Kirby is Professor Emeritus of International Politics and Public Policy, University of Limerick, and a visiting professor at the Universidad de Valencia, Spain. He has lived in Cloughjordan Ecovillage since 2009, where he was on the board of directors from 2015 to 2019 and is currently coordinator of the ecovillage's education programme. His most recent books are *Karl Polanyi and the Contemporary Political Crisis: Transforming Market Society in the Era of Climate Change*, with a Foreword by President Michael D. Higgins (Bloomsbury, 2021) and, co-authored with Tadhg O'Mahony, *The Political Economy of the Low-Carbon Transition: Pathways Beyond Techno-optimism* (Palgrave Macmillan, 2018). He is currently writing a book entitled: *Athrú Treo: An Ghaeilge sa Trasnú Iar-Charbóin*.

Jennifer Liston lectures in primary geography, global education and research methods with the Department of Learning, Society, and Religious Education at Mary Immaculate College, Ireland. She lectures on the MEd in Education for sustainability and global citizenship on the topics of Education for Sustainability, Outdoor Learning and Climate Justice. Her research has explored teacher education and climate change education and she has been involved with a number of school-based global education and sustainable development projects. Jennifer is passionate about the need to connect young people to nature as a way to contribute to a more sustainable future. In her community she is a director of the Maigue River Trust which works to educate and protect this Irish river. She was also a founding director of a local primary school which embeds forest school and nature-based pedagogical approaches in its daily practice.

Maeve Liston is a Senior Lecturer in Science Education at Mary Immaculate College. She has extensive experience in teaching science and science education at all levels in education (primary, second and third level). Maeve is also the Director of Enterprise & Community Engagement. In her role she manages, designs and delivers a wide variety of different STEM (Science, Technology, Engineering and Maths) and STEAM (Science, Technology, Engineering, Art and Maths) educational outreach initiatives promoting creativity, innovation and problem solving. She also runs several programmes in the areas of entrepreneurial education, 21st-century skills and careers, with a variety of key stakeholders in enterprise and industry.

Elaine Murtagh is a Senior Lecturer in Physical Education at the Department of Physical Education and Sport Sciences (PESS), University of Limerick. She is currently Course Director for the BSc Physical Education programme and also teaches on the PME physical education programme. Elaine leads the PESS Athena SWAN initiative and is a member of the Faculty of Education & Health Science's equality, diversity and inclusion committee. Her research interests are in physical education, physical activity and health. She is particularly interested in understanding and enhancing physical activity experiences for children and adolescents. Elaine is currently a member of the Steering Committee of the World Health Organisation's European network for the promotion of Health-Enhancing Physical Activity.

Tereza Mytakou is a PhD candidate at Trinity College Dublin, Ireland, funded by the postgraduate Ussher Fellowship. Her research explores the use of feminist pedagogy in English language education for students with refugee backgrounds. She has volunteered and worked with linguistic minorities in Greece and Ireland, and is passionate about inclusive education. She has taught a postgraduate course on Inclusive Education in Mary Immaculate College, Limerick, and has been delivering a course on gender stereotypes through the Scholars Ireland Programme, coordinated by Trinity Access Programmes and the NGO AccessEd. Her interests include the exploration of gender in education, critical pedagogy, feminist pedagogy and refugee education.

Sarah O'Brien is Lecturer in Education in Mary Immaculate College, Limerick. She is the author of two books: *Of Memory and the Misplaced: Irish Immigrant Life Writing in the United*

States (Indiana University Press, 2023) and *The Irish in Argentina: Linguistic Diasporas, Narrative and Performance* (Palgrave, 2018). She leads the BEd International Program in MIC and is also Co-Director of MIC's Oral History Centre.

Daniel O'Connell is a lecturer in Religious Education at Mary Immaculate College, Limerick. His research interests include the public significance of Christian spirituality, Catholic education and curriculum development. He is the Principle Investigator on the first national research project exploring the understanding of Catholic identity among stakeholders in primary and secondary schools in Ireland. He has co-authored religious education text books for use in Irish Catholic primary schools in Ireland and Catholic high schools in the USA. He is chair of the Global Researchers Advancing Catholic Education (GRACE) project.

Anne O' Dwyer is a member of the Department of STEM Education at Mary Immaculate College. She lectures in Science Education. She teaches undergraduate pre-service elementary teachers and teaches on the MA in STEM Education programme. Anne's research interest is in Science Education and facilitating professional development to support learners. She is interested in self-study as a methodology to understand and improve teaching practices.

Carol O'Sullivan is a former Head of Department and former lecturer in Social, Personal and Health Education (SPHE) in Mary Immaculate College, Limerick. She currently lectures on the MEd in Leadership of Wellbeing in Education in MIC. Her research interests include educational policy development and analysis, the implementation of the SPHE curriculum in Irish Primary Schools, Teacher Wellbeing, Citizenship Education, Innovation in Teaching, and Health Promotion in college settings. She has contributed to a number of research publications and conferences and to the development of programme materials in SPHE and Wellbeing.

Anna Quinn is a marine scientist who discovered her passion for educating people about our ocean while working at Galway Atlantaquaria Ltd, the National Aquarium of Ireland. During her time as Education Officer, she shared her knowledge and passion with students of all ages. As a facilitator for the Marine Institutes Explorers programme, she assisted with teacher training and student teacher training through regional Education Centres, Mary Immaculate College and St Patricks Campus, DCU. Having earned a further qualification in Early Years Education, she is now using her knowledge and experience to educate and inspire the next generation of ocean heroes.

Sandra Ryan lectures in sociology of education and educational disadvantage in the department of Learning, Society and Religious Education in Mary Immaculate College, Ireland (MIC). She is Chair of the Transforming Education through Dialogue (TED) Project at MIC and works with DEIS schools in the Limerick area. A former primary teacher, Sandra's research interests include social justice and inequalities in education (socio-economic/social class, race/ethnicity), parent and family engagement, the role of parents in supporting children's learning and development, teacher well-being in diverse contexts and educational research and evaluation.

Joe Usher is a lecturer in Primary Geography Education and Social, Environmental and Scientific Education in the Institute of Education in Dublin City University. He works in the area of Initial Teacher Education (ITE) and Professional Learning for teachers. Joe's research interests include exploring children's rights and participation in local decision making through primary geography (doctoral thesis completed in this area), using digital resources in the teaching of primary geography (including GIS, Google Earth, LEGO Education and Minecraft Education) and enquiry-based teaching and learning in primary geography. He has also carried out national and international research in the development of, and evaluation of, educational resources including textbooks for primary geography education.

FOREWORD

The UN's 2030 Agenda for Sustainable Development remains the most universal, ambitious and transformative agenda ever adopted by the international community. Its 17 global goals add up to far more than a set of targets and related policies. They entail a profound paradigm shift in our priorities, our mindsets, how we produce, consume and relate to each other and the planet.

Such a shift in mindsets starts with education. A specific target – 4.7 – in the global goal on education captures the transformational ethos of the entire 2030 Agenda, referring to the importance of education for global citizenship, sustainable development, the promotion of human rights and gender equality, and appreciation of cultural diversity.

The SDGs are an impetus to transform education, so that learners are empowered with the knowledge, skills, values and attitudes to care and act for the well-being of people and planet. As the leading UN agency on education, UNESCO has been at the forefront of promoting target 4.7 through Education for Sustainable Development and Global Citizenship.

This is not just an add-on but a transformative approach running through curriculum, pedagogy, course materials, schools and learning environments. Our education systems are far from future ready. A global teacher survey conducted with our partner Education International that involved close to 60,000 teachers found that that although 95% believed teaching climate change was important, fewer than 40% were confident in doing so. Nor do they feel equipped to teach about human rights and gender equality. Furthermore, our analysis of curriculum documents from 100 countries found that nearly half made no reference to climate change and only 20% to biodiversity. Gender stereotypes and biases are still rife in teaching materials, affecting study paths and career choices, especially for girls.

The good news is that there is growing momentum to transform education systems. UNESCO's Futures of Education Report, led by an International Commission chaired by the President of Ethiopia, called for a new social contract for education to repair past injustices and recast our relationships to others, the planet and technology. It highlights the need for curricula to emphasise ecological, intercultural and interdisciplinary learning, and for pedagogy to be organised around principles of cooperation, collaboration and solidarity. Transformative education puts learners at the centre, giving them space to think critically, claim their rights and take action. It connects cognitive, behavioural and socio-emotional learning. It nurtures respect, compassion and empathy. It encourages experiential and project-based learning, linked to the wider school and community environment.

The COVID-19 pandemic accelerated the urgency to transform education – both to recover dramatic learning losses and to better attune learning to the stakes of the green and digital transitions, and to the entire SDG agenda. In September 2022, the UN Secretary-General convened the Transforming Education Summit, bringing unprecedented political attention to the learning crisis and the imperative to change course. Commitments to make education systems more inclusive, equitable and relevant were made by 133 countries.

Teachers are at the centre of this transformation. They are the most influential force on learning. Teacher shortages must be countered by valuing the profession, raising the status of teachers and offering high-quality initial training and professional development opportunities. This includes the provision of teaching materials that help them to connect learning to local and global issues in an empowering way, giving agency and hope to students.

This volume offers a thoughtful, constructive and practical resource for teachers to integrate the Sustainable Development Goals into their daily practice. It provides guidance on each of the goals while making the connections between them. It sets out creative lesson plans and projects that nurture awareness and agency. We share a responsibility to get the SDGs back on track to make our world more inclusive, sustainable, just and peaceful. This can happen through learning how to learn and how to care together. The SDGs are underpinned by human rights, human dignity and values of solidarity and shared responsibility. I commend the authors for their engagement and expertise, and hope that this precious volume will be made widely available to teachers, principals and educators around the world.

Stefania Giannini, *UNESCO Assistant Director-General for Education*

ACKNOWLEDGEMENTS

Personally, it is an honour and privilege to write this note of appreciation to my colleagues and friends who participated in this important project. As teacher educators we are acutely aware of the importance of teaching about the Sustainable Development Goals. This book was written to help student teachers, primary and secondary teachers and all educators to teach about, through and for the SDGs in their classrooms. The contents are in line with the most recent research in curriculum, pedagogy and active enquiry-based learning.

The stunning artwork on the cover of this book was designed by talented six-year-old children from Coolarne Primary School, Galway under the guidance of their inspirational teacher Geraldine Whelan.

I am grateful to all of the authors who have journeyed with me for the last three years. Members of Faculty of Education from Mary Immaculate College include my friends and colleagues Daniel O' Connell, Patricia Kieran, Sandra Ryan, Carol O Sullivan, Maeve Liston, Jennifer Liston, Sarah O Brien, Miriam Hamilton and Fiona Dineen.

A special word of thanks is due to guest writers who joined us along the way: Tereza Mytakou, Ann Devitt and Tandeep Kaur Trinity College; Elaine Murtagh and Sara Hannafin, University of Limerick; Joe Usher and Nicola Broderick from Dublin City University; Peadar Kirby from Cloughjordan Eco Village; Claire Glavey from Global Village, primary school teacher Paula Galvin and the wonderful team from the Explorers' Programme and Galway Atlantaquarium.

A thoughtful foreword has been written by Stefania Giannini, UNESCO Assistant Director-General for Education. It is an honour to have such an esteemed contribution to this publication.

I am grateful to Routledge for agreeing to publish this book and in particular I would like to thank Bruce Roberts and Lauren Redhead for their professionalism, diligence and attention to detail.

Finally, thanks to my wonderful family, to my husband Padraic for his generous support, his love and patience, to my mother Margaret Dolan for always being a source of encouragement and my two wonderful daughters Emily and Laura.

Anne M. Dolan (Editor)

Introduction

The sustainable development goals

If you are a teacher of students from 10 to 16 years of age, if you are interested in education for sustainability or if you are simply interested in the future of our planet, this book is for you. Our planet is under unprecedented pressure. Unlimited economic development on a planet with finite natural resources and a growing population is not sustainable. Locally and globally, people face significant social, economic, environmental and political challenges. However, there is scope for hopefulness. In 2015, 193 United Nations (UN) member states adopted the 2030 Agenda for Sustainable Development and its 17 Sustainable Development Goals (SDGs) or Global Goals. The SDGs are a set of goals with targets (Appendix 1) aimed at making the world a better place. Focusing on extreme poverty, climate change and world inequalities, the 17 SDGs reflect economic, social and environmental dimensions of sustainable development. All the member states of the United Nations (UN) have committed to 17 SDGs which, if achieved, will make the world's environments, economies and societies significantly better by 2030.

Since their launch in September 2015, the UN's Sustainable Development Goals (SDGs) have been adopted by many schools around the world. As global competency becomes an increasingly important requirement for all citizens, the SDGs provide a unique educational framework for thematic teaching, education for sustainability and global citizenship education. The Sustainable Development Goals constitute a call for action by all countries (poor, rich and middle-income) to promote prosperity while protecting the planet. New ways of thinking and acting are required to achieve the ultimate goal of sustainable living. The SDGs provide unprecedented opportunities for countries and communities to work together for a sustainable and equitable world. SDG thinking recognises that tackling climate change and the biodiversity crises must go hand-in-hand with economic policies which address a range of social needs including education, health, social protection and job opportunities, in the context of monumental environmental challenges. While the SDGs are universal, it is recognised that each country faces its own unique challenges, threats and opportunities. Furthermore, there are different approaches, visions, models and tools available to each country in accordance with national circumstances and priorities.

DOI: 10.4324/9781003232001-1

Why should we teach the SDGs?

Education for sustainability requires that teachers and students address a number of possible scenarios for our future. This involves rethinking our current value systems and addressing common taken-for-granted assumptions about our world. Young people need to be able to think critically and creatively about approaches to sustainable living. They need to develop competencies which are transferable to current and future, certain and uncertain situations (Wals, 2011).

The SDGs provide a unique focus for work across the curriculum, supported by rich data and real-life scenarios around universal themes and current global issues. They open up debate around differing ways of tackling extreme poverty and inequality and alternative perspectives on equality and wealth. The importance of education is firmly recognised within the SDGs. Indeed, education is both a goal in itself (Sustainable Development Goal 4) and a means for attaining all the other SDGs. That is why education in general and education for sustainability and global citizenship (SDG 4.7) in particular represent an essential strategy in the pursuit of the SDGs.

As teacher educators we are acutely aware of our responsibility to teach education for sustainability and global citizenship. Using the framework of the Sustainable Development Goals, this book sets out an approach for teaching sustainability and global citizenship through the process of building hope, respect, empathy and advocacy in schools. This book is written for student teachers and teachers (primary and post-primary) who are interested in teaching the sustainable development goals. It aims to help teachers to remain faithful to sustainable solutions while not overwhelming their students.

The book is underpinned by the five crises of our times: climate change, a decline in biodiversity, pandemics such as COVID-19, inequality and war.

Climate change

At the Paris Climate Conference (the 21st meeting of the Conference of the Parties, otherwise known as COP21) in December 2015, 195 countries adopted the first-ever universal, global climate deal. An agreement to limit the temperature increase to 1.5°C above pre-industrial levels was the official outcome. This commitment marks an unprecedented international consensus on the need to transition from fossil fuels within the next few decades. While urgent action to halt climate change and deal with its impacts is integral to successfully achieving all Sustainable Development Goals (SDGs), SDG 13 deals specifically with climate action (Chapter 16).

Trees are often referred to as the 'lungs of the earth' due to their ability to absorb and store carbon dioxide from the atmosphere. Rainforests including the Amazon, the Congo Basin, New Guinea and the Sundaland play a significant role in mitigating climate change. Deforestation and forest fires are reducing our global forest footprint. Fewer trees reduces the Earth's capacity to store and sequester atmospheric carbon. While forest fires are a natural occurrence during the dry season, the devastating 2019 fires led to international concern about the fate of the Amazon forest, the world's largest terrestrial carbon dioxide sink.

Similarly, bushfires are a regular part of the Australian summer. Nevertheless, the scale and intensity of fires during the summer of 2019–2020 shocked and devastated local communities.

In 2023, wildfires caused by record heat, forced the evacuation of tens of thousands of people in Greece, Spain, Portugal and other parts of Europe. Unprecedented wildfires on the Hawaiian island of Maui displaced thousands of residents, destroyed parts of the historic town of Lahaina and killed over 100 people. Canada experienced its worst wildfire season ever. Thousands of people were evacuated from Yellowknife, one of the largest cities in Northern Canada. Smoke from Canadian wildfires drifted over several cities in North America including New York, Washington and Philadelphia breaking air quality records and threatening people's health. Apocalyptic type pictures of these smog-covered cities were broadcast around the world. The thick pollution cast an eerie, yellowish glow over the Big Apple's famous skyscrapers, delayed flights and forced the postponement of sporting events. We are facing an intractable challenge from climate change. An Australian study published in 2019 argues that 'climate change represents a near to mid-term existential threat to human civilisation' (Spratt et al. 2019:4). But there is still a tiny window of opportunity remaining for us to take action by slashing the burning of fossil fuels down to zero. This is the focus of SDG 13.

Biodiversity decline

Biodiversity refers to the variety of life that can be found on Earth including plants, animals, fungi and micro-organisms, the communities they form and the habitats in which they live. As climate change threatens the habitats of numerous species, biodiversity is in decline. Indeed, biodiversity is declining faster than at any point in human history, with wildlife populations falling by more than two-thirds in less than 50 years, according to the World Wide Fund for Nature (WWF, 2018).

The situation with insects is even more alarming. Insects are essential for the functioning of all ecosystems, as pollinators, food for other creatures and recyclers of nutrients (Milman, 2022). According to a longitudinal international study, the world's insects are moving towards extinction, threatening a 'catastrophic collapse of nature's ecosystems' (Sánchez-Bayo et al., 2019: 17). There has been a 40% decline of insect species and a third of the remaining insect population is endangered. Indeed, the rate of extinction is eight times faster than that of mammals, birds and reptiles. The total mass of insects is falling by a staggering 2.5% a year, suggesting they could vanish within a century (Sánchez-Bayo et al., 2019).

Our very existence is ultimately tied to biodiversity and a healthy planet. The air we breathe, the water we drink, the food we eat and the medicines needed to survive, all rely on the maintenance of a fragile ecosystem of living things. This means that if active steps are not taken to tackle biodiversity loss, many of our planet's most vital resources will soon be depleted. Biodiversity is important for our health, in terms of high-quality food and access to pharmaceutical raw materials. Healthy functioning ecosystems are also important for a healthy economy. Biodiversity supports diverse industries including agriculture, cosmetics, pharmaceuticals, horticulture, construction and waste treatment. Consequently, the loss of biodiversity threatens our food supplies, opportunities for recreation and tourism, and sources of food, medicines and energy (Dolan, 2022). SDGs 14 and 15 deal specifically with biodiversity loss on land and in the oceans (Chapters 17 and 18).

COVID-19 and other zoonotic diseases

The arrival of COVID-19 in late 2019 and early 2020 toppled our sense of invulnerability and reminded us that it is possible for our world to be capsized in ways we cannot control. Coronaviruses are zoonotic, meaning they are transmitted between animals and people. Human interactions with the environment are not benign as exhibited through an exploitative relationship with nature in general and animals in particular. As the population continues to grow and as we continue to encroach on wild spaces and impose unnatural conditions on other species, we are creating the ideal environments for viruses and pathogens to spill across species, mutate and spread. Successful COVID-19 communication campaigns may have important lessons for ecology and biodiversity scientists. The dangers posed by climate change together with a collapse of global biodiversity are potentially more severe than those threatened by COVID-19. If the Covid-19 health emergency was able to generate billions of dollars in response, why have similiar funds not been made available to combat climate change and a decline in biodiversity. The just transition to a zero carbon or carbon neutral society is now absolutely essential for our very survival, yet the messaging and communications around this issue remains confusing, unclear and sometimes contradictory. Both COVID-19 and climate change do not recognise geographical borders. COVID-19 affected rich and poor, powerful and powerless. Nevertheless, the burden of COVID-19 was more acute for poorer nations and the economically destitute within richer regions. The same is true in the case of climate change.

COVID-19 demonstrated the interdependence of our world with dramatic clarity. SDG 3 focusing on good health and well-being aspires to achieve universal health coverage and access to affordable, essential medicines and vaccines for all.

The pandemic illustrated the power of the virus to spread along the lines of our personal, social, local and global connections. To date, COVID-19 has presented the greatest threat to the progress of all SDGs in general and SDG 3 in particular. Ultimately, all goals will be affected by COVID-19 due to re-allocation of funding and re-negotiated priorities (Mukarram, 2020).

Inequality

In July 2021, in the midst of the COVID pandemic, one of the world's richest men launched himself and his friends into space in his luxury rocket, while millions were dying needlessly below him because they could not access vaccines or afford food. Billionaire Amazon co-founder and former CEO, Jeff Bezos thanked Amazon customers and employees for making the trip possible. In a post-flight press conference Bezos said the following:

> I want to thank every Amazon employee and every Amazon customer, because you guys paid for all of this. Seriously, for every Amazon customer out there, and every Amazon employee, thank you from the bottom of my heart very much. It's very appreciated.
>
> (Gilbert, 2021)

During the pandemic, the increase in Bezos' fortune alone could have funded the safe vaccination for every person in the world (Ahmed et al., 2022). Bezos' note of appreciation, the modern day version of Marie Antoinette's iconic 'let them eat cake', aptly captures the crisis of inequality in our world today.

Data from the World Inequality Report 2022 is stark (Chancel et al., 2021). Inequality is on the rise across the globe (Stiglitz, 2016). Over the past decade, inequality has taken centre stage in public debate as the wealthiest people in most parts of the world have seen their share of wealth soar, relative to that of others. As the poorest and most marginalised people slip further behind, inequalities have been pushed to new heights between and within countries.

Inequalities are not only driven and measured by income alone, but are determined by other factors – gender, age, origin, ethnicity, disability, sexual orientation, class and religion. These factors determine inequalities of opportunity, which continue to persist. Inequality in all of its manifestations is exacerbated and underpinned by structural systems of inequality, precipitated by global economics. Inequality is not an accident, it is essentially a policy choice. For instance, in nations where tax rates on high incomes are slashed, the rich significantly increase their share of national income.

The COVID-19 pandemic further exacerbated embedded inequalities and discrimination through access to vaccinations, health services and Personal Protective Equipment (PPE). A stark report published by Oxfam (Ahmed et al., 2022), aptly named *Inequality Kills*, illustrates how COVID-19 exacerbated inequality throughout the pandemic (Figure 0.1). According to this report inequality is 'deadly'. Unequal vaccine distribution left millions of people vulnerable to the deadly virus, while allowing even more deadly variants to emerge and spread across the globe. The decision by some nations to give already inoculated citizens a booster vaccine, rather than prioritising doses for unvaccinated people in poorer countries illustrated a gross unequal distribution of resources. The Oxfam report refers to 'vaccine apartheid' (Ahmed, 2022: 8) whereby millions of people would have survived COVID-19, if vaccinations were widely available. Countries from the Global South led by India and South Africa, along with hundreds of other nations, sought the right to manufacture the vaccines and therapeutics themselves. Predictably, objections were raised by pharmaceutical corporations, in an effort to protect intellectual property and profits. While power, profit and political nationalism characterised the global response to Covid-19, more co-operation and sharing of resources could have eliminated the worst effects earlier in the pandemic's time-line.

While dealing with inequality is integral to successfully achieving all Sustainable Development Goals (SDGs), SDG 10 deals specifically with inequality (Chapter 13).

War and conflict

Violent conflict is increasing in multiple parts of the world including Afghanistan, Yemen, Syria, Democratic Republic of Congo, Somalia, Libya, Mali and South Sudan. At the time of writing, Russia continues its invasion of Ukraine. An escalation in violence between the Israeli military and Hamas in Gaza has had a ripple effect around the world, with reports of several incidents fuelled by anti-Semitism and Islamophobia. Based on a fear of or hatred of Muslims, islamophobia is rooted in racism. Anti-Semitism (prejudice against or hatred of Jews),

INEQUALITY KILLS

The wealth of the 10 richest men has doubled, while the incomes of 99% of humanity are worse off, because of COVID-19.[1]

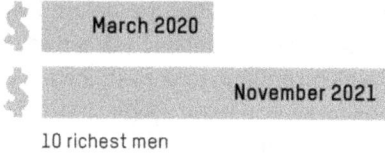

| | March 2020 |
| | November 2021 |

10 richest men

252 men have more wealth than all 1 billion women and girls in Africa and Latin America and the Caribbean, combined.

1BN

252

3.4 million Black Americans would be alive today if their life expectancy was the same as White people's. Before COVID-19, that alarming number was already 2.1 million.[4]

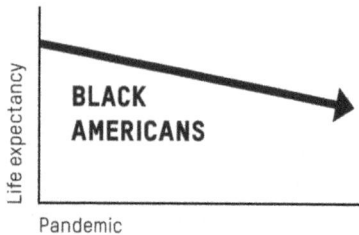

Life expectancy

BLACK AMERICANS

Pandemic

Inequality contributes to the death of at least one person every four seconds.[2]

COUNT THE SECONDS

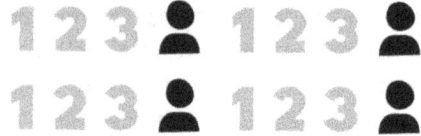

1 2 3   1 2 3

1 2 3   1 2 3

Since 1995, the top 1% have captured nearly 20 times more of global wealth than the bottom 50% of humanity.[3]

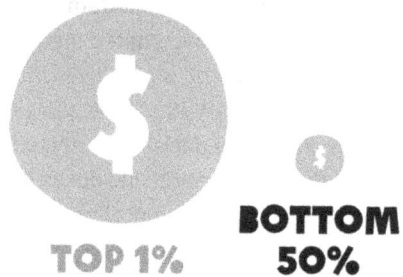

TOP 1%   **BOTTOM 50%**

Twenty of the richest billionaires are estimated, on average, to be emitting as much as 8,000 times more carbon than the billion poorest people.[5]

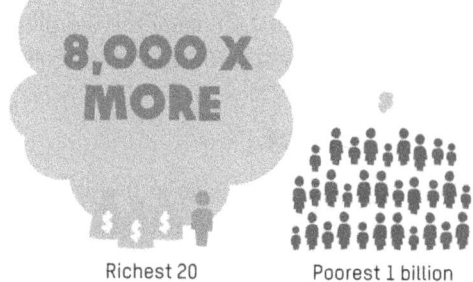

8,000 X MORE

Richest 20   Poorest 1 billion

Figure 0.1 Inequality Kills. (Source: Ahmed et al., 2022: 7).

often considered the world's longest form of hatred has existed for over two millennia. The onset of World War II brought accelerated persecution and deportation and later, mass murder, to Jewish people. During the systematic, state-sponsored genocide known as the Holocaust, six million Jewish men, women and children were murdered. Centuries of Jewish life in Europe and thousands of Jewish communities were destroyed. This unprecedented brutality, along with the enormous human and material cost of World War II, was the motivation behind the push to create the United Nations and a global rules-based system to render war a last resort.

Today, the post-war dream of a better world with universal human rights for all, is in danger of becoming obsolete. Hamas' October 7th (2023) attack on Israel, was followed by the Israeli offensive on Gaza, raising the fear of a wider war in the Middle East. As the world watched Israel's mass murder in Gaza, the wholescale destruction of entire areas, towns and cities and the mass displacement of nearly 2 million people, the post World War II mantra of 'never again' became redundant. The collective punishment of Palestinians is incomparable to any other conflict in recent memory. The murder of children and infants in both Palestine and Israel represents a catastrophic failure of politics, collective security and international law. It also represents a deeply rooted moral failure for which we are all responsible. There are no winners in war. This is the time to teach about peace initiatives and peace makers. This is the time to show solidarity with those who are suffering because of war. SDG 16 Peace, Justice and Strong Institutions (discussed in chapter 19) has never been more important.

Structure of the book

The book is divided into two sections. Section 1 provides an overview of the SDGs and discusses the importance of transformative education. It provides a model for teaching the goals based on hope, respect, empathy and advocacy. This model is informed by UNESCO's (2017) learning objectives. Finally, this section discusses the SDGs from a human rights perspective.

In Section 2, specific chapters address each Sustainable Development Goal providing teachers with theoretical and pedagogical advice for teaching the goals in an age-appropriate manner. The book also places the goals in the framework of hope, respect, empathy and advocacy, key elements in primary and post primary education. Thus education about the goals is not seen as an end in itself, but rather as a means of empowering young people in a manner that is empathetic and hopeful.

Dispositions such as respect, empathy, advocacy and hope are central tenets of primary and post primary education. The SDGs provide a unique opportunity for teachers to develop these core dispositions while learning about, through and in the midst of current challenges to sustainability. Informed by UNESCO (2017), each chapter includes a list of learning objectives, suggested topics for classroom exploration and learning activities. The interconnections between goals are addressed in every chapter. A list of children's literature, relevant resources, weblinks and related annual dates are also included for each goal.

An extensive online padlet is available with resources for teaching all of the SDGs: https://padlet.com/annedolan/o6rds38ylfy6a28h

Note about terminology

Despite significant development gains globally which have raised many millions of people out of absolute poverty, there is substantial evidence that inequality between and within the world's richest and poorest countries is widening. Terminology for capturing the complexity of political, social, historical and geographical reasons for inequality is problematic. Many terms have been used to denote poorer regions in the world. These include 'Global South', 'Periphery'; 'Less-developed', 'Developing', 'Underdeveloped' and 'Third World'. All of these terms are problematic as diverse economic, social and political experiences and positions are clustered into one overarching category. The homogenising nature of the terms obscures important differences between countries. Teachers need to be aware that each term has its own history and connotations and should be used on the basis of its limitations. Even so, teachers can explore the limitation of terminology with their students through use of glossaries, debates and critical thinking.

Global South - Global North

For some scholars and many non-governmental organisations (NGOs), the term Global South refers to countries classified by the World Bank as low or middle income that are located in Africa, Asia, Oceania, Latin America and the Caribbean. Its corollary, Global North refers to richer nations. These terms are a deliberate shift away from hierarchical terms such as First World/Third World or Developed/Developing. They are geographically problematic, however, with Southern Hemisphere countries Australia and New Zealand in the 'Global North', and Nouthern Hemisphere countries Haiti and Nepal in the 'Global South'. These terms are also apolitical, perhaps suggesting that poverty is an accident of geography rather than an outcome of exploitation. They are, however, overall less offensive than others and are widely used by international non-governmental organisations (NGOs).

Developing - developed

The 'Developing World' refers to low- and middle-income countries, and the 'Developed World' refers to high income countries. This terminology is easily recognisable and understood, and highlights disparities with regard to wealth. However, it implies that 'development' is linear; that all countries are on the same path, with some complete, and others lagging behind. This may perpetuate a stereotype of 'Developing' countries as being backward or less advanced. These terms also ignore the significant social and economic problems which still exist in all nations, including those considered 'developed'.

Third world - first world

This terminology, from the Cold War era, referred to the capitalist USA, Western Europe and their allies as the 'First World', and the communist Soviet Union and its allies as the 'Second World'. The 'Third World' referred to non-aligned nations, recently independent of colonial rulers and seeking a different way. Over time, the 'Third World' came to describe former colonies with high levels of poverty, and the 'First World' to refer to economically wealthier countries. Some view this terminology as outdated, while others maintain a strong connection with the idea of having a 'third way' to operate, independent of superpowers. These terms can give the impression of ranking countries in a way that portrays the First World as superior and more advanced than the Third World.

Notwithstanding its shortcomings, the terminology *Global South and Global North* is used throughout this publication.

References

Ahmed, N., Marriott, A., Dabi, N., Lowthers, M., Lawson, M. and Mugehera, L. (2022). *Inequality Kills: The Unparalleled Action Needed to Combat Unprecedented Inequality in the Wake of COVID-19*. GB: Oxfam https://www.oxfam.org/en/research/inequality-kills

Chancel, L., Piketty, T., Saez, E. and Zucman, G. (2021). *World Inequality Report 2022*. London: Oxfam https://wir2022.wid.world/www-site/uploads/2021/12/Summary_WorldInequalityReport2022_English.pdf

Dolan, A.M. (Ed.) (2022). *Teaching Climate Change in Primary Schools: An Interdisciplinary Approach*. London: Routledge.

Gibb, R., Redding, D.W., Chin, K.Q., Donnelly, C.A., Blackburn, T.M., Newbold, T. and Jones, K.E. (2020). Zoonotic host diversity increases in human-dominated ecosystems. *Nature*, 584(7821), 398–402.

Gilbert, B. (2021). Jeff Bezos thanks Amazon employees customers for paying for his jaunt to space: 'You guys paid for all of this'. *Business Insider Africa*. https://africa.businessinsider.com/tech-insider/jeff-bezosthanks-amazon-employees-customers-for-payingfor-his-jaunt-to-space-you/ldzyjxrMilman, O. (2022). *The Insect Crisis: The Fall of the Tiny Empires That Run the World*. London: Atlantic Books.

Mukarram, M. (2020). Impact of COVID-19 on the UN sustainable development goals (SDGs). *Strategic Analysis*, 44(3), 253–258.

Sánchez-Bayo, F. and Wyckhuys, K.A. (2019). Worldwide decline of the entomofauna: A review of its drivers. *Biological Conservation*, 232, 8–27.

Spratt, D., Dunlop, I. and Barrie, A.C., 2019. *Existential climate-related security risk. A scenario approach, breakthrough*. /https://docs.wixstatic.com/ugd/148cb0_a1406e0143ac4c469196d3003bc1e687.pdf

Stiglitz, J. (2016) *The Great Divide*. London: Penguin.

The Economist. (2021). The pandemic's true death toll. Accessed December 1, 2021. https://www.economist.com/graphic-detail/coronavirus-excess-deaths-estimates

UNESCO. Division for Inclusion, Peace and Sustainable Development, Education Sector. (2017). *Education for Sustainable Development Goals: Learning Objectives*. Paris: UNESCO.

Wals, A.E. (2011). Learning our way to sustainability. *Journal of Education for Sustainable Development*, 5(2), 177–186.

World Wildlife Fund. (2018). Living Planet Report. https://www.worldwildlife.org/pages/living-planet-report-2018

Section 1

1 You, me and mother nature

We are all connected

Anne M. Dolan

Introduction

Humanity faces the challenge of achieving a high quality of life for over eight billion people in a manner which will not destabilise the planet. Furthermore, the global population is expected to reach ten billion by 2050. Just imagine if the natural world was recognised in terms of its contribution to well-being, health, regulation of the climate and yes even economic benefits. A global stampede to regulate and protect nature and our natural environment would ensue. Yet, economic models of development fail to acknowledge the precarious condition of planet Earth. Our planet is under unprecedented pressure. Unlimited economic development on a planet with finite natural resources and a growing population is not sustainable. An unequal distribution of resources fuelled by greed is reducing the quality of life for everyone. The impacts play out unevenly, but across the world the poor and disadvantaged suffer the most. At a time when some people enjoy unprecedented wealth, millions go to bed hungry every night. This is further exacerbated by burning of fossil fuels, poverty, corruption and false promises from our politicians. A collective vision of 'progress' has been obscured resulting in unsustainable levels of corporate, financial and monetary gain built upon inequality, injustice and unfairness. The environmental cost has been staggering. The planet is now responding with various environmental shocks posing economic, social and political challenges.

A re-evaluation of how people live and the way wealth is distributed is required based on the connection between the natural world and the human story, past, present and future. The focus on gross domestic product (GDP), gross national product (GNP) and economic units of development as measurements of progress needs to be replaced with a model which prioritises ecological rather than economic sustainability. A model which facilitates progress for all, rather than riches for a few is now more important than ever. There is a need to shift from industrial growth to a life-sustaining model of development. In stark terms, we simply cannot continue to live beyond our means. 'Business as usual' is no longer an option. The United Nations Sustainable Development Goals, agreed by 193 member countries across the world were designed to meet the urgent environmental, political and economic challenges facing our world. This chapter sets the context for the SDGs in environmental, educational and societal terms. Specifically the chapter aims to

> explore the concepts of interconnectivity and interdependence
> discuss current ecological challenges

DOI: 10.4324/9781003232001-3

introduce the SDGs

provide an initial critique of the SDGs

outline some activities for introducing students to the SDGs.

Current ecological challenges

Planet Earth is now overstretched way beyond its regenerative capability. Problems related to the process of industrialisation such as biodiversity depletion, climate change and a worsening of health and living conditions, especially but not only in the Global South, are intensifying. As humans we need to recognise and acknowledge our role in contemporary, multiple ecological disasters. According to current consumption patterns, providing a healthy, fulfilling life to every person on the planet would require two to six times the natural resources that are actually available (O'Neill et al., 2018). Scientific evidence suggests that the living world is on course to collapse. According to Attenborough (2020: 105) 'everything we have come to rely upon – all the services that the earth's environment has always provided us for free-could begin to falter or fail entirely'.

Human beings have been on planet Earth for six million years, which represents less than .1% of the Earth's 4.5 billion years of existence. Yet, our impact on the planet is so great that scientists are proposing that this period in the Earth's history should be named the 'Anthropocene' – the age of humans. The current epoch, the Holocene began 11,700 years ago after the last major ice age. The word 'Anthropocene' derives from the Greek words *anthropo* (human) and *cene* (new). Scientists argue that humans have had such an impact on earth that a new epoch after the Holocene is required. A severe decline in biodiversity is now widely accepted. Only five times before in our planet's history has such devastation in biodiversity occurred. The fifth was when the dinosaurs were wiped out. This is why scientists and conservationists call what is happening now the 'sixth mass extinction'. Others have referred to the collapse in biodiversity in more dramatic terms as 'biological annihilation'.

Our accelerating growth simply cannot continue, as demonstrated by scientists who have studied the resilience of ecosystems. The Stockholm Resilience Institute identified nine planetary boundaries that regulate the stability and resilience of the Earth system (Rockström et al. 2009). The proposed boundaries include climate change, biodiversity loss, the nitrogen cycle, the phosphorus cycle, stratospheric ozone depletion, ocean acidification, global freshwater use, land use change, atmospheric aerosol loading and chemical pollution. Crossing these boundaries increases the risk of generating unacceptable environmental degradation and potential tipping points in Earth systems. A tipping point is a catastrophe involving thresholds beyond which there will be rapid transitions to new states which involve severe challenges to all biodiversity including humans. From a climate perspective, a tipping point is when a temperature threshold is passed, leading to unstoppable change in a climate system, even if global heating ends. The climate crisis has driven the world to the brink of multiple 'disastrous' tipping points (Armstrong Mc Kay et al., 2022). Today, the climate is 1.1°C warmer than the pre-industrial era and the impact of that change is being felt around the world. In 2015, at the UN Climate Change Conference in Paris, countries agreed to limit global warning to well below 2°C, preferably to 1.5°C, compared to pre-industrial levels. However, scientists suggest that the world is heading towards 2–3°C of global warming. Every fraction of a degree of warming matters. The greater the increase, the greater the anticipated and unanticipated tipping points. For instance, scientists now suggest that it is already too late to save summer Arctic sea ice (Kim et al., 2023). According to this research, even if greenhouse gas emissions are sharply reduced, the Arctic will be ice-free in September in coming decades.

The idea of planetary boundaries as developed by the Stockholm Resilience Institute has inspired University of Oxford economist Kate Raworth (2017, 2012). Using the metaphor of a doughnut, Raworth has developed a visual framework for sustainable development. Doughnut economics (Figure 1.1) presents a world where everyone has enough to meet their needs (the inside circle of the doughnut) while not exceeding the capacities of the biophysical world (the outside circle of the doughnut). The doughnut's inner ring represents the basic needs of a flourishing human society, which are not currently accessible to all. Representing the limits of planetary resource use which unfortunately are often overshot is the outer ring.

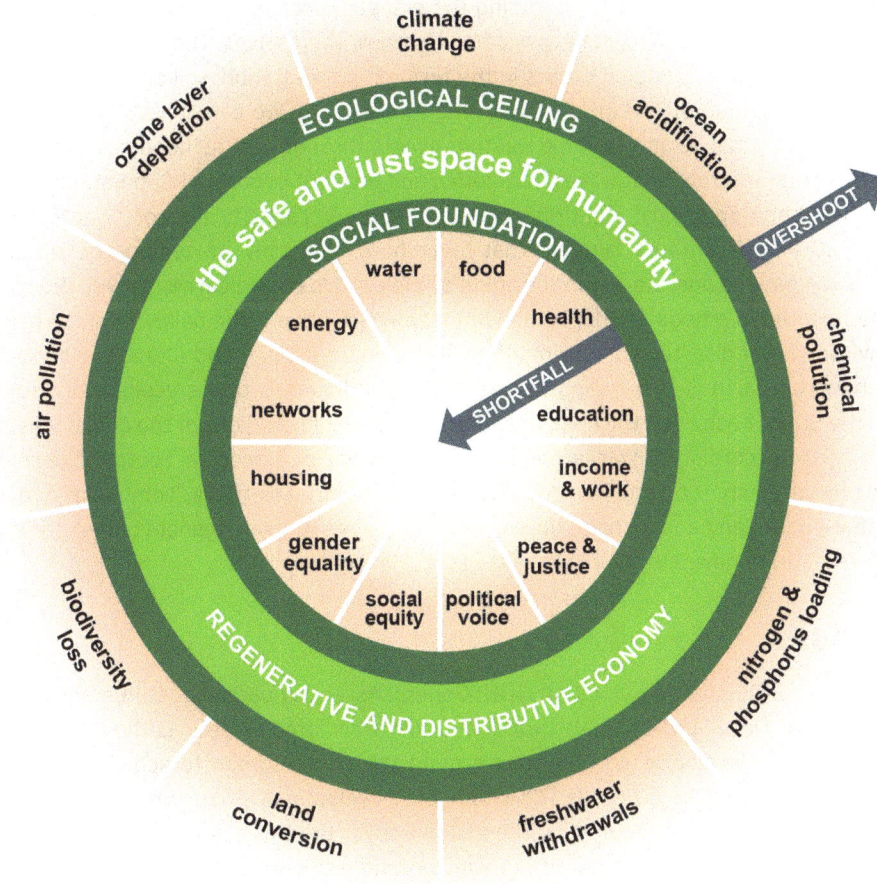

Figure 1.1 The Doughnut of Social and Planetary Boundaries. (Source: Doughnut Economics Action Lab, 2017).

Living sustainably is represented in the gap in-between the rings. This is the optimal zone for 'the safe and just space for humanity' (Raworth, 2012:1), powered by a regenerative and distributive economy.

Since the 1970s, we have been operating our life on Earth with an ecological deficit, often referred to as a global ecological overshoot. Earth Overshoot Day marks the date when humanity has used all the ecological resources and services that Earth regenerates during the entire year. The deficit is maintained by liquidating stocks of ecological resources and accumulating waste, primarily carbon dioxide in the atmosphere. The date, which varies from year to year depending on how fast such resources are exploited, is calculated by the Global Footprint Network (GFN), an international organisation that assesses humanity's ecological footprint. Humanity started to consume more than the Planet produces in the early 1970s and since then the deadline has been brought forward every year due to population growth and increased consumption on a global level. For instance, in 2022, Earth Overshoot Day fell on July 28th. It has been suggested that if everyone on the planet consumed as much as the average US citizen, four earths would be required (Butfield & Hughes, 2021). A date for Earth Overshoot Day is determined by assessing the planet's biocapacity and our ecological foot-print. Biocapacity is the ability of ecosystems to renew themselves. The resulting cost of our global ecological overspending occurs in the form of deforestation, soil erosion, biodiversity loss and the build-up of carbon dioxide in the atmosphere. We can literally see the results through climate change and extreme weather events through coastal flooding in Ireland, forest fires in the Amazon, heat waves in America and drought in parts of Sub Saharan Africa.

In their book *Ecological Footprint: Managing Our Biocapacity Budget* (Wackernagel & Beyers, 2019), the authors suggest that 'overshoot' can only be temporary. Ultimately, humans will have to operate within the limits of the Earth's ecological resources. The balance can be restored in a negotiated, planned manner. Alternatively, the balance will be restored by environmental disaster. Forest fires, flooding, climate change and ultimately death illustrate how the earth is responding to unsustainable demands on its ecological resources. While the SDGs if achieved will help, they are still insufficient in light of the challenges faced by the earth. According to Wackernagel (nd) co-inventor of Ecological Footprint (a science-based measurement tool) and founder of the Global Footprint Network, 'companies and countries that understand and manage the reality of operating in a one-planet context are in a far better position to navigate the challenges of the 21st century'.

The SDGs

In September 2015, the United Nations (UN) General Assembly passed a resolution identifying 17 Sustainable Development Goals (SDGs) and 169 associated targets as the '2030 Agenda for Sustainable Development'. Countries around the world agreed to achieve these Goals by 2030. On January 1st 2016, the 17 Sustainable Development Goals (SDGs) of the Agenda officially came into force (Figure 1.2). These Goals cover the three dimensions of sustainable development: economic growth, social inclusion and environmental protection. The 2030 Agenda acknowledges that different issues such as poverty, hunger, health, education, gender equality and environmental degradation are intertwined. As such, the 17 SDGs form an integrated system, i.e., they recognise that action in one area will affect outcomes in others

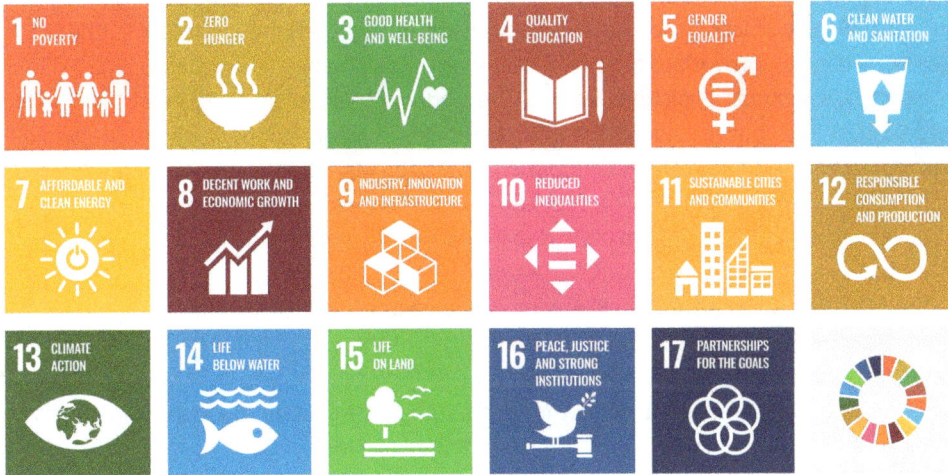

Figure 1.2 Sustainable Development Goals.

and that sustainable development must balance social, economic and environmental aspects (Nilsson, Griggs, & Visbeck, 2016). Collectively, the Goals are designed to achieve a sustainable, peaceful, prosperous and equitable life on earth for everyone now and in the future. The SDGs recognise key systemic barriers to sustainable development such as inequality, runaway consumption and environmental degradation. Characterised by universality and indivisibility, the Goals address all countries – from the Global South and the Global North.

Governments are required to develop national frameworks, policies and measures for the implementation of the 2030 Agenda. Political leaders are urged to plan for prosperity while protecting the planet in the interests of sustainable development. However, the SDGs are not just a programme of action for governments. They call on every individual and every group to play its part: governments, the private sector, civil society and every human being across the world. The transformative nature of the SDGs mean that groups, organisations, students and workers who have had no reason to work together before will now find themselves collaborating to bring about positive change for people and for the planet. National Implementation/ Action Plans have been drawn up in almost every country in the world with governments working with businesses, farmers, educators and civil society to bring about change for the common good. Each country must report on progress and challenges in bringing about change. With a strong focus on sustainability, the Goals have been described as a blue print for achieving a more sustainable future. Sustainability is defined as having enough resources for this generation while leaving enough for future generations based on the following 5 P's:

People: Living in Dignity and Equality
Planet: Protecting and Consuming Responsibility
Prosper: Enjoying Prosperous Lives

Peace: Peaceful and Inclusive Societies
Partnership: Working Together

The SDGs are communicated through brightly coloured visual icons (Figure 1.2). However the visual display of icons shows no interactions or connections, no curves or subtleties, no interdependencies or overlaps among 17 core elements of human living (Obura, 2020). There are other less common depictions such as the wedding cake version (Figure 1.3) which illustrate some of the implicit and explicit interrelationships within the Goals. The SDG 'wedding cake' shows the biosphere as the foundation of economies and societies and as the basis of all SDGs. Such a conceptualisation adopts an integrated view of social, economic and ecological development. This image depicts a departure away from the current sectorial approach where social, economic and ecological development are seen as separate entities.

The SDGs follow on from the Millennium Development Goals, which guided global development efforts in the years 2000–2015. As a result of the MDGs, there has been significant progress in poverty reduction, disease control and increased access to schooling and infrastructure in the poorest countries in the world. The SDGs seek to 'build on the Millennium Development Goals and complete what they did not achieve' (UN General Assembly, 2015: 1). Why do goals matter? The economist Jeffrey Sachs (2015) outlines four reasons for setting global goals. First, they are important for social mobilisation. Establishing and adopting goals helps people, communities and businesses to focus on what matters and to move in an agreed direction. Second, the goals serve to create peer pressure. Politicians have been

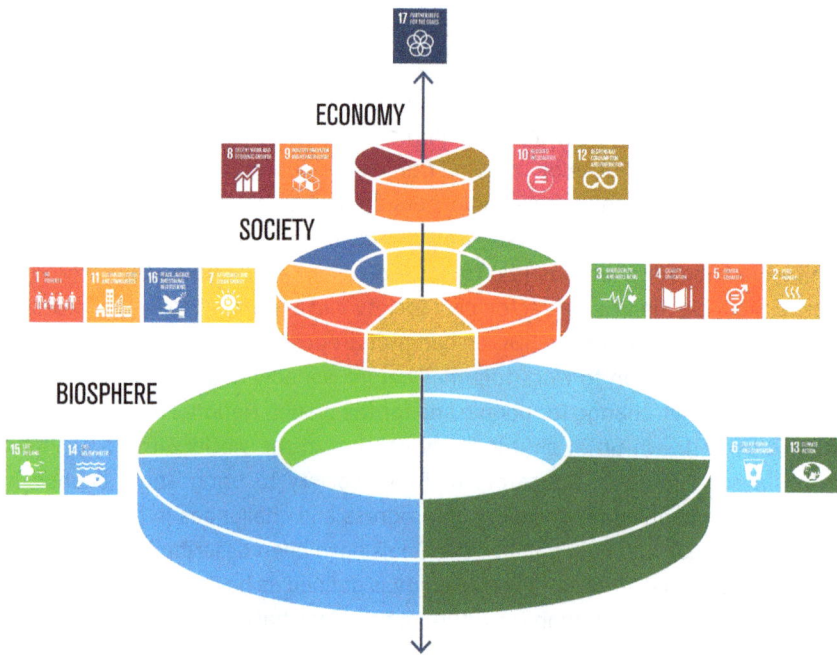

Figure 1.3 Wedding Cake Depiction of the SDGs. (Source: Azote Images for Stockholm Resilience Centre, Stockholm University).

asked to make national commitments in order to achieve the goals. Third, the goals serve to mobilise collective cross-sectoral expertise around sustainable development challenges and fourth, the goals mobilise stakeholder networks. In theory, community leaders, politicians, government ministries, the scientific community, leading non-governmental organisations, religious groups, international organisations, donor organisations and foundations are all motivated to come together for a common purpose.

Teaching 'about' and 'for' the SDGs

An engaging and effective way of framing global issues and questions for teachers and students lies within the SDG framework. The SDGs represent a useful framework for enhancing existing curricula and engaging the whole school community as well as for collaborating with other groups and organisations to consider the relationship between the local and the global. They provide multiple opportunities for embedding education for sustainability and global citizenship in the curriculum. (This is discussed in greater detail in Chapter 2.) Oxfam (2019: 5) differentiates teaching 'about' the Goals and 'for' the Goals. Education *about* the Global Goals can be addressed within curricular areas (for example, science and geography) and between curricular areas as thematic studies (for example, a focus on water or food). In order for the to be achieved, education *for* the Goals has to be part of the equation for every sector in society. Oxfam (2019) outlines benefits of studying the SDGs for students, teachers, schools, communities and the wider world (Table 1.1).

Ideally, schools would take a whole-school approach to the SDGs, embedding their themes across the curriculum and the life of the school, empowering young people to take action for them and supporting wider community engagement (Dolan, 2022, 2020, 2015). In the first instance however, teachers should introduce students to the aims, nature and context of the SDGs using introductory activities (Table 1.2). An alternative approach for introducing the SDGs is detailed in Exemplar 1 at the end of this chapter.

Critique of the SDGs

The year 2015 represented an historical episode of hope, solidarity and collaboration with the launch of the SDGs and the Paris Climate Agreement. However, progress has been mixed due to a myriad of political, economic and social factors. Many nations, including some of the wealthiest and most powerful, have reneged on their commitments. While the SDGs have been praised by some for being rights-based, universal and collaborative (Clarke, 2015), they have been criticised by others for reinforcing an unsustainable economic model and for failing to address the root causes of global poverty and inequality (Makwana, 2016). Several commentators have protested about the inherent contradictions within the aspirations of the Goals. Fourie, and O'Manique (2016: 277) suggest that the SDGs fail to question a growth model which exacerbates rather than moderates inequalities. They note a fundamental 'conceptual dissonance' whereby Agenda 2030 fails to challenge the major structural and systematic features of the global political economy which perpetuate inequality. Furthermore, the pursuit of economic growth and industrial development has environmental costs. Hence, some commentators such as Philip Alston, the former United Nations' (UN) Special Rapporteur on

Table 1.1 Benefits of studying the SDGs to learners, teachers, schools (adapted from Oxfam 2019: 6–7)

Benefits to learners

- Supports the acquisition of core skills and competences, especially those related to carrying out research, developing, presenting and responding to informed arguments; and building agency.
- The interdisciplinary nature of the SDGs helps learners to see the links between different subjects and skills, which, in turn, can support them to thrive in a fast-changing labour market.
- Motivates and enhances learning across the curriculum because the themes require creative and innovative engagement and are relevant to the real world.
- Acquaints learners with the systems used in national and global governance and the concept of international law (with its opportunities and limitations).
- Empowers learners to make sense of the diverse world and local communities in which they live; and to participate in and have a say in decisions that affect them.
- Deepens understanding of social science, scientific and mathematical concepts and processes by applying them to real-life contexts and data.
- Develops critical thinking and empowers learners to confidently challenge inaccurate or false assertions made by others – for example, in the media.
- Can support learners to feel that positive steps can be and are being taken to address global challenges and that everyone has a part to play in making progress.

Benefits to teachers and schools

- Provides a unifying, golden thread for schools that would like to place values, human rights and global competences at the very heart of learning. The wide-ranging, mutually supportive and interdependent nature of the SDGs make them an excellent tool for examining and developing whole-school curricula, school development plans and mission statements.
- Promotes a life-long approach to learning and the need for everyone to work together. Teachers and learners can discover more about the SDGs in partnership.
- Offers a useful tool for supporting primary–secondary or learning-stage transition – for example, through collaborative global learning projects.
- Can promote the value of diversity within and beyond the school.
- Supports schools to deliver on curriculum priorities.
- Provides opportunities to explore controversial issues, such as migration or religious tension, in appropriate ways
- Helps schools to deliver existing projects, programmes and awards (such as Fairtrade Schools and Green Schools) some of which have direct links to the SDG themes and targets.
- Supports linking with teachers around the world through SDG-focused projects, programmes and movements such as the #TeachSDGs movement and the World's Largest Lesson.

Benefits to communities and the wider world

- A framework for addressing controversial and complex local, national and international issues, especially those that present a global–local tension.
- Sharing learning about the SDGs can engage and strengthen relationships with parents, communities and businesses and between these different groups.
- Can provide a context for, and link with, local community or business engagement projects, such as zero-waste initiatives, refugee support groups and/or biodiversity action plans.
- Raises awareness of and support for local, national or global activities, such as pre-existing and ongoing community engagement, to achieve progress towards the SDG targets.

Extreme Poverty and Human Rights, recommends a 'recalibration' of the Goals. Alton posits that to 'avoid sleepwalking towards assured failure while pumping out endless bland reports' supporters of the UN Sustainable Development Goals (SDGs) need to focus on 'new strategies, genuine mobilization, empowerment, and accountability' (Alston, 2020: 20).

Table 1.2 Introducing students to the SDGs (Adapted from Development Perspectives 2020: 8–9)

Introducing Students to the SDGs	
Materials	One copy of the Sustainable Development Goals Cards for each group of students (Figure 1.2)
Learning outcomes	Learners will understand the 17 SDGs in a national and international context
	Learners will be able to critically analyse the SDGs and how they apply within their own country.
Learning activities	Start with the following warm-up questions:

• What do you think the world will look like in 2050?
• What would you like the world to look like in 2050?
• Do you think people in other parts of the world have different visions for their future?

Working either in small groups or in pairs, have learners prioritise (a pyramid shape works well or let them choose) the SDGs based on one of the following questions:

• Keeping in mind what you would like the world to look like in 2050, prioritise the SDGs according to which Goals are more important for realising this vision
• Which of the SDGs do you think are most relevant to your local issues?

Discussion Questions:

• Is there a difference between which Goals are most important locally and those that may be most important globally?
• Do you think the Goals are relevant to your country, i.e. is there work we should be doing at a national and local level to achieve the Goals? What would this work look like?
• Do you think there are any Goals missing? If so write up your own SDG.

The Goals are considered by some as over ambitious and vague. For others, the language of the SDGs is problematic. The terms 'sustainable', 'development' and 'education' are contested. Sustainability and sustainable development do not mean the same thing (Washington, 2015). Even the term 'sustainable development' itself is considered as somewhat of an oxymoron by some. Sustainability is the process of living within the limits of available physical, natural and social resources in ways that allow the living systems of the earth to thrive. The term 'sustainable development' was first adopted by the United Nations in the Brundtland Report (United Nations, 1987) defining sustainable development as a set of conditions that satisfy ' the needs of the present without compromising the ability of future generations to meet their own needs'. Nevertheless, the term 'sustainable development' remains a contested term. Commentators such as Clarke (2012: 22) believe that the concept of sustainable development is 'wedded to an industrial, economic growth model'. Clark believes the Goals are written with a post-colonial notion of economic development, which will actually take us in the wrong direction. Indeed, there is much evidence to suggest that this outdated mode has left our environment compromised and our financial system in tatters. It appears that we are married to the idea of one way forward and despite its failings we are afraid to digress to alternative routes. Our trajectory of development is and remains inherently unsustainable.

The SDGs have been critiqued for their 'neoliberal' credentials. Neoliberalism is a policy model that encompasses both politics and economics and seeks to transfer the control of economic factors from the public sector to the private sector. It views all human activity through the prism of economics. The prominent voice of economic growth within the SDGs ensures that obligations to the poor remain secondary to the market and big business. Fourie, and O'Manique (2016) argue that the 2030 Agenda for Sustainable Development equates sustainable development with pro-growth neoliberalism. Many neoliberal policies enhance the workings of free market capitalism and attempt to place limits on government spending, government regulation, and public ownership. They pitch people in competition with each other for resources, jobs, houses, relationships, happiness and control over the environment. Within a neo-liberal framework, the incompatibility of certain SDGs promoting economic growth and environmental protection is problematic. For instance SDG 13 (UN, 2015) demands 'urgent action to combat climate change and its impacts', while SDG 8 (UN, 2015) calls for 'sustained, inclusive and sustainable economic growth'.

McCloskey (2019: 152) suggests that the SDGs cannot succeed 'as long as they are fatally hitched to the broken neoliberal paradigm of development which is resulting in wealth concentration in fewer hands and growing social polarisation'. Other commentators argue that the Goals cannot be achieved through neoliberal policies of privatisation, trade liberalisation and reduction in government spending (Kumi et al., 2014). Furthermore, organisations such as Oxfam argue that some of the problems which the Goals are trying to address such as inequality, are ultimately caused and exacerbated by neoliberal policies and practices. According to an Oxfam report, the main driver of gender inequality, social injustice and wealth concentration is neoliberalism:

> Our economic rules have been written by rich and powerful men in their own interests. The neo-liberal economic model of today has made this worse – cuts to public services, cuts to taxes for the richest individuals and corporations, and a race to the bottom on wages have all hurt women more than men.
>
> (Oxfam, 2019a: 14)

While the term 'neoliberalism' is often used inaccurately, making it difficult to assess its actual influence, it continues to dominate ideas about economic and social change. Allocating environmental resources though mechanisms of the market is problematic. However, choices made by politicians and interventions by state agencies can counter the influence of neo-liberalism. EU social policies aiming to promote employment, improve living and working conditions, can provide adequate social protection and combat social exclusion. Government actions during COVID 19 demonstrated that prompt and decisive economic policies can support universal health, prevent commercial collapse and forestall unnecessary unemployment, waste and social suffering.

For others, the SDGs are problematic 'as issues of power and key political issues such as redistribution are totally absent from the Agenda' (Belda-Miguel et al., 2019: 2). The structural causes of poverty are ignored as the Goals support a managerialist and technical approach to development. For many commentators, the Goals will not succeed unless unfavourable power relations are addressed and an equal distribution of resources is placed at the heart of all SDG-related interventions (Kumi et al., 2014). The lack of specific and binding targets to determine what is nationally appropriate has also been noted. Fourie and O'Manique (2016: 276) highlight the absence of the term 'government accountability' in Agenda 2030. They also lament the lack of targets in several areas including: funding frameworks; regulatory frameworks; social protection measures; spending targets; access to credit; all public resources; international assistance; tax regimes; financial audits; all matters related to local governance; company reporting; company rules; consumer protection; capital market regulation and the share of family or household responsibilities. On a more fundamental level, commentators such as Obura (2020) highlight the esoteric nature of the Goals. While the SDGs have permeated international discourse, from biodiversity to climate change to health and human settlements, many citizens do not know anything about the Goals, do not question the Goals and do not relate them to their daily lives. Notwithstanding their limitations, Agenda 2030 and the Sustainable Development Goals constitute a collectively agreed pathway for local, national and international social, economic and political progress. An analysis of their progress and imperfections will generate much material for students in primary and post primary schools.

We are all interconnected: a focus on interdependence

Our destiny, or the future of the human story, is ultimately connected to the welfare of local and global ecosystems. For David Attenborough, we humans share the Earth with the living world 'the most remarkable life-support system imaginable' (2020: 121). It is no accident that the planet's stability is now in decline as biodiversity has collapsed. For Attenborough, restoring biodiversity is a crucial part of the solution and to do this we must rewild the world. Adopting a philosophy of sustainability in all things will help to improve the lives of all people while reducing our impact on the world. This challenge is immense but we can begin by learning from the living world itself.

David Attenborough has brought many carefully documented miracles of nature into our living rooms. The natural world has much to teach us about team work, collaboration and learning to live with threats posed by climate change. I recently watched one such documentary which beautifully illustrated the extraordinary behaviour of fire ants in the Amazon. Fire ants, named for the burning sting they use for defence, live in large colonies underground, meaning they're particularly at risk when the rain comes. Heavy rainfall destroys the ants' homes. To survive, the ants join their bodies together to construct a buoyant raft which allows them to safely float above the water's surface. This ingenious nautical solution is the ultimate example of collaboration. As many as 100,000 insects form a living raft which floats for weeks. The queen and larval young are kept in the middle for their own protection. Ants are covered in fine hairs that trap air against their bodies and this makes the mass of insects buoyant. The ants wait for the flood waters to recede, before making a new home under the earth. Biologists and engineers are continuously fascinated with this miracle of nature.

Human too have demonstrated great capacity to collaborate. *Meitheal* is an old Irish term that describes the rural tradition of neighbours coming together in times of need. A group of people (or a *meitheal*) came together to assist with farming work such as cutting hay, driving cattle to summer pasture, planting potatoes and harvesting crops. A term from the Irish language, the expression *Meitheal* indicates a team or a working group. Today, the phrase is recognised as an Irish expression of a community coming together in acts of mutually reciprocal support, solidarity and cooperative work.

While the term Meitheal demonstrates the benefits of community-based collaboration, the South African concept of Ubuntu is also based on the idea of a common and interdependent humanity. The African ethic of Ubuntu is exemplified in the Nguni saying 'Umuntu ngumuntu ngabantu', that is, 'I am because we are' or 'a person is a person through other persons' (Metz & Gaie, 2010; Shutte, 1993; Venter, 2004). With its roots in humanist African philosophy, Ubuntu is conceptualised in terms of humanness, where the idea of community is one of the building blocks of society. According to Tutu (1999: 31), it means, 'my humanity is caught up, is inextricably bound up, in yours. We belong in a bundle of life.... I am human because I belong, I participate, and I share'. Individual well-being and happiness are intimately linked to the well-being and happiness of others. Associated with human flourishing (Shutte, 1993), Ubuntu is 'a philosophy that promotes the common good of society and includes humanness as an essential element of human growth' (Venter, 2004: 150).

The person who possesses Ubuntu demonstrates respect, empathy, generosity, patience, hospitality, honour, cooperation and tolerance towards others in the community as well as caring for and helping others (LenkaBula, 2008; Metz & Gaie, 2010; Shutte, 2001; Venter, 2004). Tutu (1999: 31) further elaborates the relational aspect of ubuntu by noting:

> A person with ubuntu is open and available to others, affirming of others, does not feel threatened that others are able and good; for he or she has a proper self-assurance that comes with knowing that he or she belongs in a greater whole and is diminished when others are humiliated or diminished, when other are tortured or oppressed, or treated as if they were less than who they are.

The concept of human interdependence is beautifully articulated in the Irish Proverb: *Ní neart go cur le chéile*, which means there is no strength without unity. John Dunne's phrase 'no man is an island' conveys the idea that both women and men need to be part of a community in order to thrive. Furthermore, they do badly when isolated from others. Activities such as *The Web of Life Game* (described below) allow young people to explore the concept of interdependence in an ecological context.

Collectively our earth systems can be considered as a single, interconnected self-regulating entity, a notion that was originally popularised by James Lovelock in his Gaia theory. The web of life encompassing all of the planet's ecosystems is interconnected in so many ways. Nature, politics and the economy are connected. Seemingly unrelated events such as an international flight from London to Los Angeles and the severity of the hurricane season are links in the same chain of cause and effect. The consumer choices of a shopper from Dublin have an impact on farmers in Kenya. The idea of interconnectivity is complex but games such as *The Web of Life* allow young people to interrogate the concept in a meaningful manner.

Our local and global communities are now more interdependent and connected than ever before but they are also more vulnerable and susceptible to disasters and shock such as climate change, pandemics, financial crises and political conflict. In today's hyper-connected society, a catastrophe in one place can potentially disrupt affairs globally as illustrated after the Wall Street crash of 2008, the SARS epidemic of 2002 and Covid 19. This potential vulnerability has led communities to consider their own resilience through the development of small scale alternatives for food supply and energy generation (SDG 11) (discussed in Chapter 14). Rather than focusing primarily on individual environmental friendly behaviours alone, the possibilities for collaboration, co-operation and community based approaches have the potential to reap more long term and sustainable solutions.

THE WEB OF LIFE GAME

In an ecosystem, everything is connected, and the well-being of one can affect the well-being of all. It's important for students to understand this concept and recognise that as humans, our actions have effects on all sorts of living things found in the communities and environments in which we live. Games such as *The Web of Life* help illustrate how all living things are connected and, as a result, all living things are affected by one another. For example a decline in insects has a direct impact on the food supply for birds, reptiles, amphibians and fish. If this food source disappears animals will die. Students play this game to enhance their understanding about interconnections within the natural world (Figure 1.4).

Figure 1.4 Student Teachers Playing *The Web of Life Game*.

Materials

One ball of string (at least 20 metres long)
Approximately 15 pictures of one element/living thing within an ecosystem (plus some information about pictures). Sample information cards are included in Appendix 2.

Directions

1   Students stand in a circle facing inwards.
2   Each student is given a card with the name or image of one element or living thing within an ecosystem. For instance, a forest ecosystem includes the following: tree, seed, bat, sun, soil, mouse, fox, rain, owl, oak, insect, grass, water, rabbit, river, fly and bee. Cards based on any eco system can be used to play the *Web of Life* game. Each card should be clearly displayed. A card attached to a ribbon, which can be worn around the upper body is the best option. Older students can be given additional information about their image. Examples of cards for a forest eco system are available in Appendix 2.
3   One student (e.g. the soil) holds the end of the string then hands it to another student (e.g. a leaf). As the string is passed around, each student makes a statement about the nature of their relationships e.g. the soil may pass the string to leaves as the leaves decompose and become part of the soil. Some students may receive the string several times as their character has many connections. As the ball of string is passed around between students a web is created, the *Web of Life*. Students should take one or two steps backwards until the string is taut. By jiggling the string, students can feel the system's vibrations. NB: everybody needs to hold the string taut!
4   To demonstrate disruption in nature one element of the web can be removed or a piece of string can be cut. Any disruption to the eco system should be illustrated with a short narrative e.g. *the soil becomes poisoned due to use of illegal fertiliser* or *a tree is chopped* down for firewood.

Discussion

What does the web demonstrate about nature?
What plants and animals might you find in a healthy forest ecosystem? (Be sure to include mammals, insects, birds, reptiles, trees and other plants).
What might happen to the forest ecosystem if we remove an item from this list? What happens when we remove a link from the ecosystem? What might happen if humans are introduced to this ecosystem?
Discuss impacts which may be caused by climate change e.g. increases in temperature and flooding.

TEACHING THE SDGS IN SCHOOLS

Every chapter in this book contains ideas and resources for teaching the SDGs. An extensive online padlet is available with resources for teaching all of the SDGs: https://padlet.com/annedolan/o6rds38ylfy6a28h Exemplar 1.1 includes a simple activity for introducing the SDGs, and Table 1.3 outlines a cross-curricular framework for teaching the SDGs.

Table 1.3 Cross-curricular framework for teaching the SDGs

Literacy: Reading	*Whole school activity*	*Citizenship Education, Health and Well-being:*
Choose any book listed in the children's literature section for each Goal in this publication and discuss the story in the context of the SDGs. Use a wide range of stories and texts from around the world to showcase issues linked to the SDGs	Ensure the SDGs are on prominent display in the school building. Promote biodiversity on the school grounds. This could include tree planting, school gardens and wild meadows. An SDG week or day encourages the whole school community to pool resources and focus on SDGs collaboratively, creatively and comprehensively.	Consider the importance of setting goals and targets for each student (personal goals) and for the class (collective goals). Discuss the differences between needs, wants, rights and responsibilities. Explore the connections between our personal, physical and mental well-being and the environment.
Literacy: Oral language: Discussing the importance of setting goals and targets? Why are the SDGs important for us, for our community and for the world?	**Cross-curricular planning based on *the SDGs*** *Drama* Explore different perspectives and recognise the complexity of global issues by using role play or drama to convey SDG themes. For example, use hot-seating or freeze-frames to portray communities impacted by climate change or people forced to flee their homes by conflict.	**History** Study the positive and negative impacts of industrialisation on society. Explore the impact of public protest such as the Civil Rights Movement or the Anti-Apartheid Movement Examine significant moments in the history of gender equality e.g. the Suffragette Movement
Literacy: Writing Create a class/school newspaper based on the SDGs. Write a leaflet advocating action for one SDG. Informed by the SDGs, write a proposal to the town council or local authority proposing ideas for the care and enhancement of the local environment.	**Music** Music has always been used as a tool of resistance. From today's Black Lives Matter anthems; to protest songs of the '60s and political music collectives of the '80s; all the way back to coded spiritual songs of the slavery era; music has always played a pivotal role in giving voice to the voiceless, and resisting the status quo. Some of the genres and individual songs can be shared and discussed with students. Students can compose their own songs or raps in response to current contemporary issues.	
Literacy: Poetry Using haiku or acrostic formats, write a poem based one of the SDGs.		

(Continued)

Table 1.3 (Continued)

Art	Geography	Mathematics
Design an illustrated picturebook which explores the theme (s) of the SDGs. This can be in an A-Z or traditional illustrated format. The finished product should be available for local audiences and it can be sold to raise funds to support the students' choice of climate actions.	Take a walk in the local area. Assess evidence of biodiversity and local habitats. Indicate areas where improvements can be made. Write a letter to local council with maps, suggestions and a request for improvements.	Collect, interpret and discuss data representing progress towards the achievement of the SDGs such as mortality rates and access to education
Explore how some of the SDG themes are represented in art. Explore the potential of art for expressing opinions and ideas about the environment.	Conduct a survey with representatives from the local community to assess local opportunities and challenges linked to the SDGs. Decide on priorities for a local development plan and decide on personal and community based actions.	**Physical education** Discuss attributes which promote or inhibit team work. Examine the concept of 'fair play' sport exploring the issue of rules, inclusion and power. For instance how are rules decided and who makes decisions on behalf of players.
Ask students to create a new logo for each SDG and to explain their rationale.	Learn about the structure and importance of the United Nations. Using role play, set up a mock UN meeting to address specific challenges or problems.	*Science* Through scientific enquiry, students can explore core SDG topics such as climate change, energy conservation, food chains, food waste and ecosystems.

Exemplar 1.1 Introduction to the SDG's. Picking the most important SDG. Activity created by Padraic Creedon

Several years ago, when working for an environmental NGO in Dublin I was tasked with creating a set of workshops to introduce primary school students and post-primary students to the Sustainable Development Goals. My style of education is always based around games/activities and debates. I believe this stems from the fact that I am a complete board game fanatic. I love anything that resembles a game. So, if I am with a group of students, we are almost always playing something. I need to love what I am teaching; I think it's very important for the students to see that I love it as well. They will pick up on disinterest or feigned excitement in an instant and at that stage we have lost them.

So, from that starting point, I asked myself how could I introduce the 17 different SDGs to students while keeping them interested and entertained at the same time? There is no point in just listing them one after the other. I had tried something like that before with the SDGs' predecessors the Millennium Development Goals and the response I received was tepid to say the least. I did, however, have quite a bit of success in using moving debates with other topics. If you are unfamiliar with a moving debate, then let me quickly sum it up.

I have three different fruits, an orange, a banana and a pineapple and I want to know what is the best one and why? A simple vote from the room would tell me the most popular but it would be hard to determine exactly why that is? I want the group to really think about it, I want their reasons tested and their convictions shaken. So, I place each fruit at three different points in the room and I ask the group to stand up and walk to their favourite. They will have a few minutes in their favourite fruit groups to come up with a list of reasons why their fruit is the better than the others. Once time is up each group presents their arguments to the room. At any point during the debate, anyone may abandon their chosen group for another. This is often due to some very compelling arguments made by what I can only presume to be our future politicians and leaders. Once the debate part of the activity is over and the dust has settled, we can now see which fruit has come out on top as well as knowing exactly why that is. (Spoiler alert: it is the pineapple, always and forever. Try to change my mind.)

This style of debate is not only entertaining for almost everyone involved but it will force each individual to actually challenge their beliefs and question why they believe something rather than blindly sticking by their choices. The moving debate truly shines when the topic being covered is not as simple as favourite fruit. Give the group a set of equally compelling, difficult and grey-area choices and watch as more often than not, a series of well-crafted arguments and passionate pleas fill the room. It is a fantastic thing to witness when it gets going. Do not be alarmed if the arguments get a little heated. Real life debates are messy and so these should be too, also you will be there to calm things down if needs be.

This is where the moving debate becomes the perfect platform to introduce the SDGs to the students. I pick three goals at a time and tell the group that they can only choose one goal to succeed from the set. The goal with the highest number of supporters succeeds and the other two fail. For example, the group must choose between Goal 1: No Poverty, Goal 2: No Hunger or Goal 3: Good Health and Wellbeing. Not an easy choice by any measure, remember that the most popular goal succeeds, and the others fail. If you save the world from poverty you may still be dooming people to hunger and ill-health. You may be thinking "But, if we solve global poverty, surely the knock-on effects would improve the hunger and health problems". What I can say to that is "exactly"! The groups will delve into every nook and cranny of these goals in order to convince the room that their goal is best. They will present arguments you would never imagine. It is a fantastic display and I promise they will leave with more knowledge about the SDGs then any traditional explanation of the goals would give.

The fun of this activity does not end there. If you are so inclined you can collect some interesting data from the group, even more so if other classes in the school partake in this activity. As I travell from school to school with this workshop, I am able to see it play out many times over. Some goals are always more popular than others naturally, but it is fascinating to see how age and gender affects decision making. Goal 5 - Gender Equality is a personal favourite of mine. The popularity of this goal fluctuates madly depending on whether I in an all-girls school, an all-boys school or a mixed school. All-girls' schools consider that goal to be very important but not always number 1 on their list. All-boys' schools rarely have it high on their lists at all. But the mixed schools vary dramatically. Some have an almost unanimous support for it, with girls and boys flocking to it while a few stragglers support Goal 4 or Goal 6. At other times I see Goal 5 garner a small core group of support, with fierce and extremely well articulated arguments. The larger groups on the other goals are often browbeaten and shuffle over to Goal 5 in what might be their first realisation of true empathy..... or maybe just shame.

Anecdotally, I could go on and on with these stories, but I think you understand what I am trying to say here. The SDGs can be a deep, dividing and difficult topic to cover. But it is those very facts that make it so enjoyable a topic to engage with. Once each topic is discussed with its proper respect, you may be surprised to learn how much the students care when given the chance to truly express their opinions. I would highly recommend trying the activity described above and all going well consider the moving debate a tool at your disposal, to use on those murkier and deeper topics we sometimes discuss in the classroom. You can also whip out the moving debate to finally put an end to the never-ending mystery of "which fruit is the most popular in our class?"

Additional activities for promoting the SDGs

Conclusion

The SDGs have been developed to address the serious challenges facing us. While not perfect, the SDGs represent a collaborative, international response to local and global environmental, social and economic challenges. A force for sustainable development and peace, education has a crucial role to play in the potential achievement of all the SDGs. Every Goal in the 2030 Agenda requires education to empower people with the knowledge, skills and values to live in dignity, build their lives and contribute to their societies.

It is important to remember that we only have one Earth, this is ultimately the defining issue for human existence. Sustainability is not merely a noble cause, it is an essential condition for the well-being of people, profit and the planet. We need to re-assess our collective values and priorities while fully appreciating the critical importance of our natural environment. Successful delivery of the 2030 Agenda requires engagement from all sectors in society, but it is through thoughtful education that this engagement will be nurtured in an empathic, hopeful and effective manner.

Resources

Resources from the UN

1. The Sustainable Development Goals (SDGs) logo, including the colour wheel and 17 icons are available for use in the six official languages of the UN (Arabic, Chinese, English, French, Russian, Spanish)

    https://www.un.org/sustainabledevelopment/news/communications-material/

2. The World's Largest Lesson promotes use of the Sustainable Development Goals in learning so that students can contribute to a better future for all. All resources are free, open source and translated into over 30 languages. Along with partners including UNICEF and UNESCO, The World's Largest Lesson advocates for Education for Sustainable Development and encourages the widespread use of the Goals within formal education systems.

    https://worldslargestlesson.globalgoals.org/

3. Go Goals: A board game for students https://go-goals.org/

The SDG Academy: https://sdgacademy.org/about-us/

It is a non-profit educational initiative that creates free massive open online courses (MOOCs), educational videos, webinars and other educational resources on sustainable development and makes them available as a global public good.

Resources from Oxfam

The Sustainable Development Goals: A Guide for Teachers https://oxfamilibrary.openrepository.com/handle/10546/620842

    Useful teaching resources include: *Climate Challenge* (SDGs 7, 12 and 13), *Global Food Challenge* (SDGs 1 and 2) and *Everyone Counts* (SDG 10): www.oxfam.org.uk/education

Resources from Concern

Concern is an Irish based international NGO. Its mission is defined by one goal – ending extreme poverty, whatever it takes. Concern believes that no-one should have to live in fear that they won't have a home to sleep in or enough food to feed their children. Concern has created a resource collection with a booklet for each SDG along with easily adaptable activities and information to bring the issues alive for your students.

    https://www.concern.net/schools-and-youth/educational-resources

Software applications (Apps)

SDGs in Action app

The SDGs in Action app features:

- Detailed information about each of the 17 Global Goals, including targets, explanatory videos, key facts and figures, and suggestions for action

- The latest sustainable development news from around the world
- The ability to choose what Goals are important to you and receive notifications about those Goals.
- Access to the World's Largest Lesson explaining each of the Sustainable Development Goals.
- The ability to create locally based actions and invite others to join
- Support for the 6 UN official languages: Arabic, Chinese, English, French, Russian, Spanish.

The Concern app

An app created by Concern helps to bring the SDGs to life by exploring them through the lens of Concern's work with the world's poorest people.

https://www.concern.net/test-your-knowledge-our-concern-active-app

The Samsung Global Goals app

This app created in partnership with the United Nations Development Programme is increasing awareness of the 17 Global Goals and accelerating progress through individual acts of change. The education and donation-based app connects millions of users to critical information about each of the Goals and to easy and meaningful ways to make a difference.

The Samsung Global Goals app is pre-installed on all the latest Galaxy smartphones and is available for all Android users. Since August 2019, the app has reached 80M+ users worldwide and has raised over $1 million in donations. The funds have contributed to the UNDP's progress in improving the quality of education, combating climate change, and advocating for gender equality; including supporting the immediate crisis and the long-term recovery from COVID-19.

Samsung aims to build upon its impact by committing to future app investments which incorporate new educational content and devise new and simple ways to motivate their customers to learn, share and act together to help achieve the Global Goals by 2030.

The Earth Project app

This free app allows subscribers to monitor personal simple daily actions and the amounts of carbon avoided by taking those actions. The app allows students to take action and keep track of progress. This app supports advocacy in schools and teams can be created to collaborate for maximum impact. EarthProject app was created as part of Take Action Global's Climate Action Project (TAG). Launched in schools across 142 countries globally, TAG works with students, teachers, educational institutions and organisations to use climate education as a force for environmental action (https://www.takeactionglobal.org/).

Social media

@SDGoals
@connectSDGs
@UN_SDGs

@TheGlobalGoals
@GlobalGoalsUN
@SDGaction

Websites

Centre for Global Education: www.centreforglobaleducation.com

Development Education Resources: Development Education.ie

Eco-Schools: www.eco-schools.org.uk (England); www.keepscotlandbeautiful.org/sustainable-development-education/eco-schools (Scotland); www.keepwalestidy.cymru/pages/category/eco-schools (Wales); www.eco-schoolsni.org (Northern Ireland); https://greenschoolsireland.org/ (Republic of Ireland)

Earth Overshoot Day: https://www.overshootday.org/

Fairtrade Schools: https://www.fairtrade.ie/ schools.fairtrade.org.uk

Global Schools Programme resources: www.globalschoolsprogram.org

International School Award: schoolsonline.britishcouncil.org/about-programmes/internationalschool-award

Practical Action: practicalaction.org/schools

Take 1 Programme, Education for Sustainable Development in Post Primary Schools: https://www.take1programme.com/

Get Up and Goals: https://www.getupandgoals.eu/

Scotdec: www.scotdec.org.uk/resources

SDG Academy: sdgacademy.org

Stride Global Citizenship Magazine for Schools: www.stridemagazine.org.uk

Sustainability and Environmental Education (SEEd): https://se-ed.org.uk/

TeachSDGs movement: www.teachsdgs.org

Teacher Education for Equity and Sustainability Network (TEESNet): teesnet.liverpoolworldcentre.org

https://se-ed.org.uk/ Earth School https://ed.ted.com/earth-school

SDG Academy Library https://sdgacademylibrary.mediaspace.kaltura.com/

SDG Bookclub https://www.un.org/sustainabledevelopment/sdgbookclub/#list

TES Sustainable Schools Award: www.wwf.org.uk/get-involved/schools/tes-sustainableschools-award

UK National Association for Environmental Education: naee.org.uk UN Sustainable Development Goals Project: www.unsdgproject.com

UNICEF Rights Respecting Schools Award: www.unicef.org.uk/rights-respecting-schools

Worldwide Fund for Nature (WWF) Green Ambassadors: www.wwf.org.uk/get-involved/schools/green-ambassadors

References

Alston, P. (2020) *The parlous state of poverty eradication: Report of the special rapporteur on extreme poverty and human rights.* Geneva: Human Rights Council.

Armstrong McKay, D. I., Staal, A., Abrams, J. F., Winkelmann, R., Sakschewski, B., Loriani, S., Fetzer, I., Cornell, S. E., Rockström, J. and Lenton, T. M. (2022) Exceeding 1.5 C global warming could trigger multiple climate tipping points. *Science, 377*(6611), eabn7950.

Attenborough, D. (2020). *A life on our planet. My witness statement and vision for the future.* London: Witness Books.

Belda-Miquel, S., Boni, A. and Calabuig, C., (2019) SDG localisation and decentralised development aid: Exploring opposing discourses and practices in Valencia's aid sector. *Journal of Human Development and Capabilities, 20*(4), 386-402.

Butfield, C. and Hughes, J. (2021) *Earthshot: How to save our planet.* UK: John Murray Publishers.

Clarke, P. (2012) *Education for sustainability: Becoming naturally smart.* London: Routledge.

Clarke, J. (2015) 7 reasons why the SDGs will be better than the MDGs. *Guardian,* 26 September. Available: https://www.theguardian.com/global-development-professionals-network/2015/sep/26/7-reasons-sdgs-will-be-better-than-the-mdgs

Development Perspectives. (2020) *Stepping Stones for the Sustainable Development Goals: A workbook for community and education practitioners.* Available: https://www.developmentperspectives.ie/ResourcesPDFS/Stepping%20stones%20for%20SDGs.pdf

Dolan, A. M. (2015) Education for sustainability: An inclusive, holistic framework for teacher education. In A. O'Donnell (Ed.), *The Inclusion Delusion? Reflections on democracy, ethos and education* Oxford: Peter Lang, 133-149.

Dolan, A. M. (2020) *Powerful primary geography: A toolkit for 21st century learning.* London: Routledge.

Dolan, A. M. (Ed.) (2022) *Teaching climate change in primary schools: An interdisciplinary approach.* London: Routledge.

Fourie, P. and O'Manique, C. (2016) 'It sells, but it does not fly': An early assessment of the 2030 Agenda for sustainable development. *Development, 59* (3), 274-279.

Kim, Y. H., Min, S. K., Gillett, N. P., Notz, D. and Malinina, E. (2023) Observationally-constrained projections of an ice-free Arctic even under a low emission scenario. *Nature Communications, 14*(1), 3139.

Kumi, E., Arhin, A. A. and Yeboah, T. (2014) Can post-2015 Sustainable Development Goals survive neoliberalism? A critical examination of the sustainable development–neoliberalism nexus in developing countries. *Environment, Development and Sustainability, 16*(3), 539-554.

LenkaBula, P. (2008) Beyond anthropocentricity–Botho/*Ubuntu* and the quest for economic and ecological justice in Africa. *Religion & Theology, 15,* 375-394.

Makwana, R. (2016) #Globalgoals? The truth about poverty and how to address it. *Policy & Practice: A Development Education Review, 22,* Spring, 141-151.

McCloskey, S. (2019) The Sustainable Development Goals, Neoliberalism and NGOs: It's time to pursue a transformative path to social justice. *Policy and Practice: A Development Education Review, 29,* Autumn, 152-159.

Metz, T. and Gaie, J. B. R. (2010) The African ethic of *Ubuntu*/Botho: Implications for research on morality. *Journal of Moral Education, 39,* 273-290.

Nilsson, M., Griggs, D. and Visbeck, M. (2016) Policy: Map the interactions between Sustainable Development Goals. *Nature, 534*(7607), 320-322.

Obura, D. (2020) Getting to 2030 – Scaling effort to ambition through a narrative model of the SDGs. *Marine Policy, 117,* 103973.

O'Neill, D. W., Fanning, A. L., Lamb, W. F. and Steinberger, J. K. (2018) A good life for all within planetary boundaries. *Nature Sustainability, 1*(2), 88-95.

Oxfam. (2019) *The Sustainable Development Goals: A guide for teachers.* Available: https://policy-practice.oxfam.org/resources/the-sustainable-development-goals-a-guide-for-teachers-620842/

Oxfam. (2019a) *Public good or private wealth?* Available: https://www.oxfam.org.nz/sites/default/files/reports/Public%20Good%20or%20Private%20Wealth%20-%20Oxfam%202019%20-%20Summary.pdf

Raworth, K. (2012) *A safe and just space for humanity: can we live within the doughnut.* Oxfam. Available: https://www-cdn.oxfam.org/s3fs-public/file_attachments/dp-a-safe-and-just-space-for-humanity-130212-en_5.pdf

Raworth, K. (2017) *Doughnut economics: Seven ways to think like a 21st-century economist.* London: Random House.

Rockström, J., Steffen, W., Noone, K., Persson, Å., Chapin III, F. S., Lambin, E., Lenton, T. M., Scheffer, M., Folke, C., Schellnhuber, H. J. and Nykvist, B. (2009) Planetary boundaries: Exploring the safe operating space for humanity. *Ecology and Society, 14*(2). https://www.ecologyandsociety.org/vol14/iss2/art32/

Shutte, A. (1993) *Philosophy for Africa*. Milwaukee, WI: Marquette University Press.

Shutte, A. (2001) *Ubuntu: An ethic for a new South Africa*. Republic of South Africa: Cluster.

Tutu, D. M. (1999) *No future without forgiveness*. New York: Doubleday.

UN General Assembly. (2015) 'Transforming our world: the 2030 Agenda for sustainable development', Resolution adopted by the General Assembly on 25 September 2015. Available: http://www.un.org/ga/search/view_doc.asp?symbol=A/RES/70/1&Lang=E

Venter, E. (2004) The notion of *Ubuntu* and communalism in African educational discourse. *Studies in Philosophy and Education, 23,* 149–160.

Wackernagel, M. (nd) *Global footprint network*. Available: https://www.footprintnetwork.org/

Wackernagel, M. and Beyers, B. (2019) *Ecological footprint: Managing our biocapacity budget*. Canada: New Society Publishers.

Washington, H. (2015) Is 'sustainability' the same as 'sustainable development'? In H. Kopnina & E. Shoreman-Ouimet (Eds.), *Sustainability: Key issues* (359–376). New York: Routledge.

World Wildlife Fund. (2020) *Living planet report*. Available: https://www.worldwildlife.org/publications/living-planet-report-2020

2 Transformative education

Teaching hope, respect, empathy and advocacy in schools

Anne M. Dolan

Introduction

The UN's Sustainable Development Goals aim to end poverty, food insecurity, inequality, prejudice, exclusion and environmental degradation, while fostering among all humans the belief in global citizenship. The role of education is central in addressing this ambitious framework. However, many elements of our current education system were designed to meet the needs of a different generation in an unrecognisable historical context. Two decades ago for instance, students did not have to deal with social media, artificial intelligence and Tiktok. In the words of Sir Kenneth Robinson (2010: np)

> The current system of education was designed and conceived in a different age. It was conceived in the intellectual culture of the Enlightenment and in the economic circumstances of the Industrial Revolution...there is also built into it a whole series of assumptions about social structure and capacity.

Our current educational paradigm is underpinned by an outdated intellectual model which prioritises academic achievement. Built upon economic demands, it exacerbates multiple inequalities in terms of class, race and gender. Rather than making some minor adjustments to our education system, perhaps now is the time to redefine our educational priorities and redesign our systems of delivery in line with the SDGs.

Specifically, the chapter aims to discuss current issues with our education system and the role of transformative teaching and learning introduce the four Hs framework for a transformative pedagogy which underpins this book consider the rationale for the framework, a rationale which is based on teaching for hope respect, empathy and advocacy.

Twenty-first-century skills and global competences

Twenty-first-century students live in a globalised and interconnected world facing numerous environmental, economic, social and political challenges. Living in a competitive, globally connected and technologically intensive world requires students to become problem-solvers, critical thinkers and globally competent. For many years, educators have been engaged in

DOI: 10.4324/9781003232001-4

a reassessment of the knowledge, skills and dispositions young people need for success in today's rapidly changing and complex world. Large-scale assessment studies, most notably the Programme for International Student Assessment (PISA), triggered a rapid process of educational reforms aimed at increasing levels of students' competencies in various disciplines. Essentially, the term 'competency' combines skills, behaviours, knowledge, and abilities. However, the term's popularity across these differing domains varies, with different and sometimes conflicting meanings and intentions. The concept of 'competencies' has become part of popular education discourse (Glaesser, 2019). Closely associated with standards and testing, the term is commonly misunderstood. However, it is somewhat of a catch all phrase as illustrated by Norris (1991: 331).

> Everybody is talking about competence. It is an El Dorado of a word with a wealth of meanings and the appropriate connotations for utilitarian times. The language of competency-based approaches to education and training is compelling in its common-sense and rhetorical force. Words like 'competence' and 'standards' are good words, modern words; everybody is for standards and everyone is against incompetence.

Twenty-first-century competencies include critical thinking, problem-solving, communication, collaboration (teamwork), creativity and innovation, knowledge building (a growth mindset), resilience, citizenship and global competency (Colvin & Edwards, 2018; Schleicher, 2019; Trilling & Fadel, 2009: 50). These competencies are considered essential to help children and young people solve complex, messy problems including those that have yet to be encountered.

Since 2000, 15-year-olds have been assessed for their reading literacy, mathematical literacy and scientific literacy every three years. In 2018, the PISA Global Competence assessment measured students' capacity to examine local, global and intercultural issues, to engage in open, appropriate and effective interactions with people from different cultures, and to act for collective well-being and sustainable development. According to the OECD/PISA (2018: 4) 'globally competent individuals can examine local, global and intercultural issues, understand and appreciate different perspectives and world views, interact successfully and respectfully with others, and take responsible action toward sustainability and collective well-being' (Figure 2.1). Global competence is required: to live harmoniously in multicultural communities; to thrive in a changing labour market; to use media platforms effectively and responsibly; and to support the Sustainable Development Goals OECD/PISA (2018: 4).

Competencies are now featuring in sustainability discourses. The competencies required for a green transition have been set out in the EU's sustainability competence framework, Green Comp. These include, critical thinking, initiative-taking, respecting nature and understanding the impact everyday actions and decisions have on the environment and the global climate (Bianchi et al., 2022). Such sustainability competencies are designed to feed into education programmes, to help students develop knowledge, skills and attitudes that promote ways to think, plan and act with empathy, responsibility and care, for our planet and for public health.

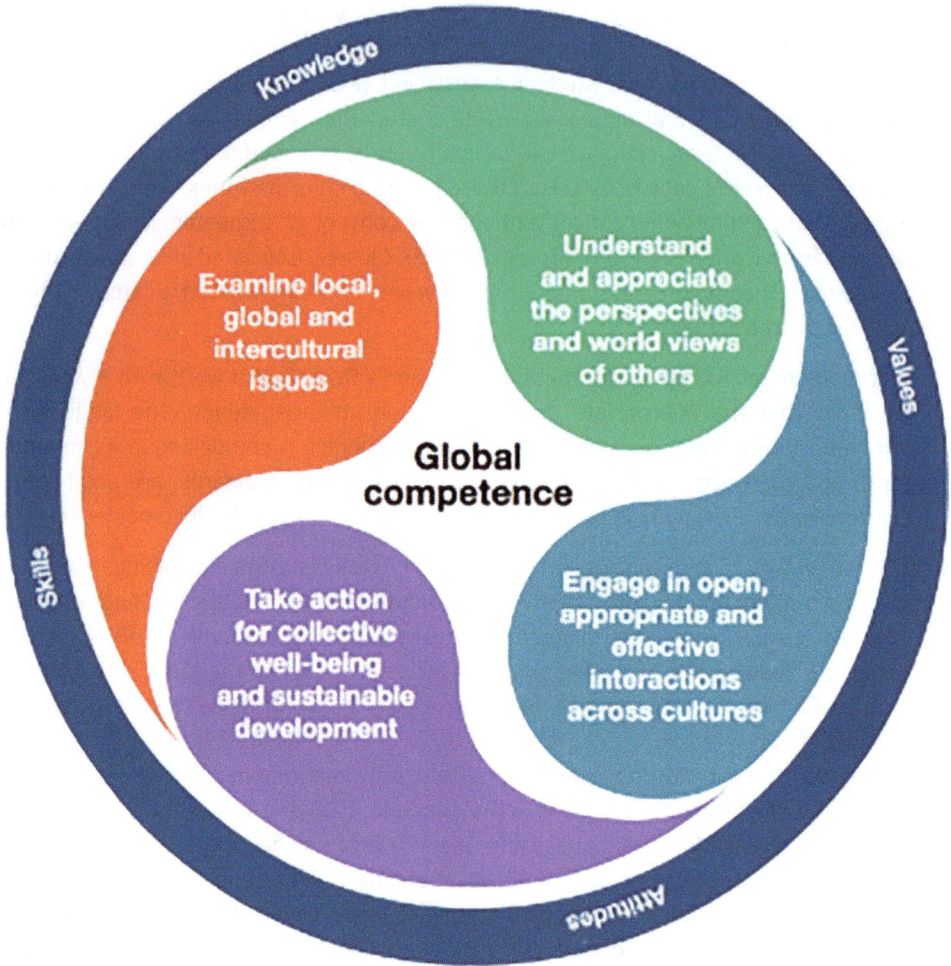

Figure 2.1 The Dimensions of Global Competence. (Source: OECD/PISA (2018: 11)).

Education for Sustainable Development or Education for Sustainability?

The UNESCO Roadmap for Education for Sustainable Development states that Education for Sustainable Development (ESD):

- empowers learners with knowledge, skills, values and attitudes to take informed decisions and make responsible actions for environmental integrity, economic viability and a
  just society empowering people of all genders, for present and future generations, while
  respecting cultural diversity
- is a lifelong learning process and an integral part of quality education that enhances
  cognitive, social and emotional and behavioural dimensions of learning
- is holistic and transformational and encompasses learning content and outcomes, pedagogy and the learning environment itself
- is recognised as a key enabler of all SDGs and achieves its purpose by transforming society (UNESCO, 2020: 8).

There are divergent views in respect of Education for Sustainable Development. Commentators such as Liddy (2012) argue that the discipline can be defined in both conservative and radical terms. Within Education for Sustainable Development, there is a continuum between weak, transmissive practice and transformative, participatory education. Hence, the need to build a bridge between Education for Sustainable Development and Transformative Education (Schnitzler, 2019; Sterling, 2011). Authors such as Corney suggest that much of the literature on ESD 'is based on rhetoric and exhortation' (2006: 224). Others such as Wade (2008) and Sterling and Huckle (2014) have proposed instead the term 'Education for Sustainability' as it reflects openness to alternative perspectives and radical viewpoints. Wade argues that the term Education for Sustainable Development is a Western construct on development which suggests a predefined path towards an elusive goal of development. Neo-liberal industrial-economic approaches to education perpetuate a system through which students are framed as consumers, reliant on continuous financial, economic and industrial growth and personal wealth. In other words, engaging in Education for Sustainable Development will not automatically assist policy makers, students and teachers to address the systematic environmental, social and political challenges facing society today.

Several commentators suggest that an Education for Sustainability (EfS) process offers an 'holistic approach through recognising the complex, interconnected nature of all aspects of the world around us from an individual to a global level' (Sterling, 2005: 23). Rather than developing positive attitudes and behaviours, Bonnett (2002) suggests that the aim of EfS should be the development of *a frame of mind* which requires teachers and students to be open and engaged with the complexity and meaning of political constructs in our multi-layered society, and engaged with nature through art, literature music and poetry. Instead of prioritising economic or instrumental values, Bonnett argues strongly for the role of the arts and humanities to include ecological, aesthetic, scientific, existential and spiritual values. Notwithstanding the debate about terminology (sustainability or sustainable development), there is widespread agreement that sustainability must feature more prominently in formal and non-formal education. Incorporating transformative teaching and learning approaches with a clear action dimension makes sustainability issues relevant, immediate and student-centred.

Education for global citizenship

Global citizenship refers to a sense of belonging to a broader community and common humanity. It emphasises political, economic, social and cultural interdependency and interconnectedness between the local, national and global. An increasingly globalised world raises questions about global learning, global citizenship and what constitutes meaningful citizenship. Citizenship education is firmly based on human rights and its associated values. According to Oxfam (2015: 5) a global citizen is someone who:

- is aware of the wider world and has a sense of their own role as a world citizen;
- respects and values diversity;
- has an understanding of how the world works;
- is passionately committed to social justice;
- participates in the community at a range of levels, from the local to the global; and
- works with others to make the world a more equitable and sustainable place.

Global citizenship education (GCE) aims to be transformative, building the knowledge, skills, values and attitudes (Table 2.1) that students need to be able to contribute to a more equitable, sustainable, inclusive, just and peaceful world. Global citizenship issues by their nature are controversial. To be globally competent one must engage with controversial issues (OECD/ PISA, 2018). Learning how to engage in dialogue with people who have different viewpoints and perspectives is central to the process of strengthening democracy and fostering a culture of human rights. Often considered too difficult to teach, controversial issues are those which generate strong feelings and divide opinions in communities and society at large. They vary from local issues such as community campaigns for fair trade (discussed in chapter 20) to global affairs, such as the challenges facing girls in Afghanistan (discussed in chapter 8).

While Global Citizenship Education (GCE) (originally referred to as development education) has a more radical origin than ESD, its degree of criticality and potential for transformation 'has been questioned. Bryan (2011: 2) raises the 'thorny' question of whether this adjectival education has been 'de-clawed' or stripped of its original radical underpinnings, based on the ideas of such radical thinkers as Paulo Freire'. Indeed Bryan (ibid.: 4) suggests that the term *Global Citizenship Education* could have de-radicalised what was considered 'as an essentially political, ethical and transformative project'. For some commentators, the term 'Global Citizenship Education' has been recognised by some scholars as a 'nodal point' or 'place of arrival' of other areas of education such as development education, global learning, environmental education, education for equality and sustainability education (Mannion, Biesta, Priestly & Ross, 2016). While this might be the case, the question remains where does the transformative agenda and critical interrogation now lie?

Drawing on post-colonial theory, Andreotti's (2006: 46–48) 'soft versus critical' framework presents a multi layered framing of Global Citizenship Education. In the soft approach, the potential benefits of GCED are 'greater awareness of some of the problems, support for

Table 2.1 Education for global citizenship – key elements as defined by Oxfam (2015: 8)

Knowledge and Understanding	Skills	Values and attitudes
Social justice and equity	Critical and creative thinking	Sense of identity and self-esteem
Identity and diversity	Self-awareness	Empathy
Globalisation and Interdependence	Reflection	Commitment to social justice and equality
Sustainable development	Communication	Respect for people and human rights
Peace and conflict	Cooperation and conflict	
Human Rights	Ability to manage complexity and uncertainty	Value diversity
Power and governance	Informed and reflective action	Concern for the environment and commitment to sustainable development
		Commitment to participation and inclusion
		Belief that people can bring about change

campaigns, greater motivation to help/do something, and feel good factor' and in the critical approach, the potential benefits are 'independent/critical thinking and more informed, responsible and ethical action'. Andreotti argues that soft approaches are eurocentric and tend to be characterised by passivism, paternalism and an uncritical engagement. While she recognises that soft Global Citizenship Education is appropriate for certain contexts, ultimately a critical lens is required. A gap between GCED's transformative intent and what is realised in practice has also been articulated. (Andreotti, 2006; Selby and Kawaga, 2011). For instance, within post-primary schools in the Republic of Ireland, the exam-driven focus of the curriculum has been identified as a major obstacle to the meaningful inclusion or in-depth exploration of development issues and global justice themes in schools (Bryan & Bracken, 2011).

Target 4.7

The aim of SDG 4 is to ensure inclusive, equitable and quality education and to promote lifelong learning opportunities for all. To encourage action and prepare young people for the future, Target 4.7 of SDG 4 states that we must

> Ensure all learners acquire knowledge and skills needed to promote sustainable development, including among others through education for sustainable development and sustainable lifestyles, human rights, gender equality, promotion of a culture of peace and non-violence, global citizenship, and appreciation of cultural diversity and of culture's contribution to sustainable development.
>
> (UN, 2015)

Target 4.7 is crucial for the promotion of Education for Sustainable Development (ESD) and seeks to ensure that all learners receive education and training that develops their knowledge and skills to act and respond to our unsustainable lifestyles. To achieve the aims of SDG 4 and Target 4.7 in particular, the importance of holistic and transformative approaches to education is recognised. Indeed, Target 4.7 of the SDGs recognises students 'as global citizens who require the knowledge and skills to build the sustainable futures of an increasingly interdependent world' (Tarozzi, 2023: 47). Furthermore, SDG 4.7 bridges the traditional gap between GCED and ESD highlighting how both fields struggle 'a lot but separately with questions of criticality' Khoo and Jørgensen (2021: 473). Target 4.7 brings international legitimacy to both Education for Sustainable Development and Global Citizenship Education.

The first indicator (4.7.1) for measuring the achievement of Target 4.7 is as follows:

> Extent to which (i) global citizenship education and (ii) education for sustainable development, including gender equality and human rights, are mainstreamed at all levels in (a) national education policies; (b) curricula; (c) teacher education and (d) student assessment).
>
> (UN Statistics, 2017: np)

While Target 4.7 represents many opportunities, it is important for practitioners to be mindful about critical and respectful dialogue; between the Global North and Global South; between policy makers and educators; between students and teachers; and between the different adjectival educations recognised within target 4.7.

Making connections: adopting systems thinking within education

Historically, shaped by the Industrial Revolution, several education systems continue to promote standardised testing rewarding memorisation and rote learning. Designed and conceived in a different age, the function and role of education needs to be examined, particularly in the context of current environmental, social and economic challenges. Underpinned by an outmoded intellectual model of the mind that values academic achievements, our education system is driven by economic agendas which are no longer valid. Sterling (2011) argues many education systems are transmissive and teacher centred, rewarding cognitive learning and memorisation. This focus on memorisation, fuelled by standardised testing, has obstructed learning, according to Linda Darling-Hammond (2012) of Stanford University, who argues that the acquisition of knowledge for its own sake is superficial, short term and lacks impact. She argues that if conceptual knowledge is applied or used to solve real world problems, students will enjoy a richer educational experience.

Education with a holistic perspective is concerned with the development of every person's intellectual, emotional, social, physical, artistic, creative and spiritual potentials. The fragmentation of knowledge delivered in schools, challenges our ability to consider issues holistically or from a number of perspectives. Many holistic thinkers identify this crisis of our time as an epistemological crisis. According to Laszlo (2012), a 'macroshift' is required from *logos* to *holos* thinking with a significant change in focus as illustrated in Table 2.2.

Sterling (2001) relates these debates to the education system, which he describes in mechanistic or ecological terms as illustrated in Table 2.3. Sterling maintains that mainstreaming Education for Sustainability within a mechanistic paradigm is pointless as it condones rather than challenges systems failures. Hence, there is a need to consider our education through a systems lens. Sterling draws on systems theory to argue for a paradigm shift in education from modern, mechanistic and reductionist forms to postmodern, ecological, expansive and holistic varieties. Such a lens emphasises contexts and connections in order to build up whole pictures of phenomena rather than breaking things into individual parts. It is a way of seeing which focuses on processes, patterns and dynamics.

Table 2.2 Macroshift from logos to holos

Logos	Holos
Reductionist thinking	Holistic thinking
Objective	Subjective
Competitive	Interdependent/collaborative
Individualistic	Community-based
'Head Oriented'	Whole being (head, heart, body, spirit)
Separate from nature	Connected with nature/ecological
Fragmented	Interconnected
Linear	Systems oriented

Table 2.3 Sterling's mechanistic and ecological perspectives on education (2001: 58-59)

Mechanistic View	Ecological View
Core Values	**Core values**
Preparation for economic life	Being/becoming
Competition	Cooperation
Curriculum	**Curriculum**
Prescription	Negotiation and consent
Fixed knowledge and truth	Provisional knowledge recognising uncertainty and approximation
Evaluation	**Evaluation**
External evaluation	Self-evaluation plus critical support
Teaching and learning	**Teaching and Learning**
Passive	Active
Meaning is given	Meaning is constructed

In Chapter 1, the interconnected nature of local and global issues is discussed. We live in a complex and dynamic world full of interconnected systems. An ocean is a system, so too are trees, forests and other ecosystems. Each human being is a complex system. Systems are often embedded in larger systems, which are embedded in yet larger systems. The earth's climate is a system comprised of the subsystems of our atmosphere, our oceans, the land, and human society. A systems thinking approach focuses on systems as a whole: how the parts interrelate and how interconnections create emerging patterns. A system is 'more than the sum of its parts'. It involves understanding that the social, economic and natural worlds are part of an interconnected system that is constantly changing, and that all humans are part of this dynamic system.

A systems thinking approach adopts a holistic, long-term perspective focusing on relationships between interacting parts, and how those relationships generate behaviour over time. Using a systems thinking approach allows students to see concepts, topics and themes as interconnected, rather than isolated. It provides the basis for deep rather than surface learning within well-planned integrated and cross curricular teaching. Systems thinking helps us to perceive phenomena as interconnected and dynamic. Systems thinking tools allow us to map and explore dynamic complexity including the anticipated and unanticipated impact of actions such as human behaviours or context such as environmental factors.

In the environmental domain, systems thinking is viewed as fundamental to understanding and addressing environmental problems such as climate change (Ballew et al., 2019). In our daily lives many activities are powered by fossil fuels or other sources of climate altering greenhouse gases. Every time we cook a meal, store data, heat our homes, these activities have an impact on the climate. Furthermore, everything that sustains our very existence and enriches our lives is affected either directly or indirectly by climate change. Access to clean water, the price of our food, national security, the health of ourselves and our loved ones, economic opportunities for this generation and those to come, all are placed in jeopardy by climate change. The complex nature of climate change requires solutions generated through a whole systems approach through new consumer practices, well informed individual and collective responses, new technologies, new policy frameworks, and most importantly, new ways of engaging with each other. There is no single silver bullet solution to stopping climate change. Exploring climate change within the frame of one curricular discipline in school such as geography or science is not sufficient. Using a cross-curricular or multidisciplinary approach to teaching climate change in schools allows students an opportunity to apply systems thinking to climate change in terms of its causes, impacts and solutions (Dolan, 2022).

Transformative teaching and learning

Transforming our world: the 2030 Agenda for Sustainable Development (UN, 2015) is a universal plan of action that calls upon every nation including all governments and citizens in the world, to take transformative measures to address the UN's 17 SDGs, which no country is yet fully accomplishing (Odell et al., 2020). To achieve the 2030 Agenda, the world as we know it, needs to change dramatically including changes in how we consume, travel, produce goods and interact with the environment. Such transformations require a radical shift in the way teaching and learning takes place. The goal of Education for Sustainability is 'to transform the environmental perspectives of the learners from viewing the environment as a commodity to a community, from consumer to conserver, from short-term reactor to long-term evaluator' (Singleton, 2015: 172).

Changing and expanding worldviews of learners is the goal of transformative learning (Mezirow, 1978; O'Sullivan, 2002; Taylor, 2007). Another perspective based on the work of Freire (1972) involves social transformation. Based on his concern for the oppressed in Brazil, Freire's programme of conscientisation was designed to achieve social change. It involved the identification and critical analysis of primary themes affecting the daily lives of the oppressed, with the purpose of creating a more equitable world. Based on Freire's work, O'Sullivan presents an ecological or planetary view which defines transformative learning as a profound shift in awareness that alters one's way of being in the world and one's view of the interconnectedness of self, the human community and the natural environment illustrated as follows:

> Transformative learning involves experiencing a deep, structural shift in the basic premise of thought, feelings and actions. It is a shift of consciousness that dramatically and irreversibly alters our way of being in the world. Such a shift involves our understand of ourselves and our self-locations; our relationships with other humans and with the natural world; our understanding of relations of power in interlocking structures of class, race and gender; our body-awareness, our visions of alternative approaches to living; and our sense of possibilities for social justice and peace and personal joy.

(O'Sullivan, 2002: 11)

Three different types of learning are identified in Table 2.4. including conformative, reformative and transformative learning. First order learning is concerned with effectiveness or efficiency or 'getting the right answer'. Second order learning involves asking questions and challenging the status quo. Third order learning (or epistemic learning) is concerned with transformative learning itself and aspires to help the learner to 'see things differently' (Sterling, 2011).

Transformative learning involving personal transformation, ultimately leading to social transformation. Hence, it is not just about a change in what we know and are able to do, it

Table 2.4 Levels of learning (Source: Sterling, (2011)

Orders of Change/Learning	Seeks/Leads to	Can Be Labelled As
First order change: *Cognition*	Effectiveness/Efficiency	*'Doing things better'* Conformative
Second order change: *Meta-cognition*	Examining and changing assumptions	*'Doing better things'* Reformative
Third order change: *Epistemic learning*	Paradigm change	*'Seeing things differently'* Transformative

involves a fundamental shift in how we come to know and how we understand ourselves in relation to others and the natural world (Mezirow, 2018, 1978). From an educational point of view, a fundamental shift is required 'from learning how to understand to learning how to act and transform' (Schnitzler, 2019: 243). Within a transformative education framework, the three interrelated dimensions of learning: the cognitive; social and emotional; and behavioural are seen as essential and interlinked components of Education for Sustainable Development and Global Citizenship Education (UNESCO, 2019) as follows:

> Cognitive: To acquire knowledge, understanding and critical thinking about global, regional, national and local issues, the interconnectedness and interdependency of different countries and populations, as well as social, economic and environmental aspects of sustainable development; Social and emotional: To have a sense of belonging to a common humanity, sharing values and responsibilities, empathy, solidarity and respect for differences and diversity, as well as feel and assume a sense of responsibility for the future; Behavioural: To act effectively and responsibly at local, national and global levels for a more peaceful and sustainable world.
>
> (UNESCO, 2019: 7)

Both Education for Sustainable Development (ESD) and Global Citizenship Education (GCE) have been adopted as global education agendas throughout the UN Sustainable Development Goals. While the origins and historical development of ESD and GCE differ somewhat, both share philosophical frameworks, theoretical underpinnings and pedagogical approaches. Both adjectival educations include themes such as climate change education, human rights, culture, peace, citizenship, inequality and justice. Both are underpinned by transformative ideas. In November 2022, the Global Education Network Europe (GENE, 2022: 2), launched its agenda for Global Education to 2050, which has become known as the Dublin Declaration. This declaration states:

> Global Education is education that enables people to reflect critically on the world and their place in it; to open their eyes, hearts and minds to the reality of the world at local and global level. It empowers people to understand, imagine, hope and act to bring about a world of social and climate justice, peace, solidarity, equity and equality, planetary sustainability, and international understanding. It involves respect for human rights and diversity, inclusion, and a decent life for all, now and into the future.

Arguing for a transformative approach to create peaceful, just and sustainable futures, (UNESCO, 2020) calls for a revisioning of the nature of relations between: men and women;

between human kind and the environment; and between humans and technology. Both GCE and ESD promote these ideas of interdependence and interconnections particularly between the social sphere and the biosphere. While the focus on a transformative approach is welcome, the nature and purpose of transformative education needs to be articulated. Education for Sustainability and Global Citizenship Education have much to offer this discussion. By making education encounters participatory, integrative, critical and reflective, education can help to shape a more sustainable, peaceful and just future. The following 4 Hs model is proposed as a model for transformative education.

The four Hs head, heart, hands and hope: a transformative pedagogy

Historically, humans have separated themselves from nature in many spiritual and intellectual philosophical traditions. This human/nature dualism positions humans as fundamentally outside nature. Children have a different relationship to nature. In a study conducted by Kalvaitis, and Monhardt (2015) children describe their relationship with nature as a friendship. This study (ibid:1) describes children's love of nature as; 'a positive deep-seated intellectual and emotional appreciation for nature based on 'experiences through' and 'affection for' nature'.

From an education perspective, young children's relationship with nature is a starting point for all future human interactions with the natural world, and has a direct impact on the future of the sustainability movement (ibid:2015). Building on a positive relationship with nature and the local environment, this book is not just about teaching the SDGs themselves, but rather using the Global Goals as a means of teaching hope, empathy, respect and advocacy. The warnings about the future of human civilisation as we know it, are extremely worrying. Authors such as Hicks (2018) argue that choices are now between 'managed collapse' and 'catastrophe'. While environmental problems and human responses are beyond serious, it is important not to overwhelm young people. To date, communicating information, statistics and the facts about environmental crises do not appear to have had much impact on individual and collective responses. Knowledge is simply not enough. Young people need to establish empathetic connections with the knowledge through a framework which recognises hope by facilitating young people's agency.

Informed by the ideas of Swiss educationalist and philosopher, Johann Heinrich Pestalozzi (1746–1827), Education for Sustainability and transformative learning are linked through an approach to education based on the framework of head, hand and heart. In this framework (Orr, 1992; Sipos et al., 2008), *head* refers to a cognitive understanding of sustainability and ecological principles. *Hands* refer to the psychomotor domain, whereby leaners engage in practical skill development and physical activities. *Heart* refers to the affective domain whereby values and attitudes are translated into behaviours. Informed by UNESCO (2017) learning objectives, this book presents a model for teaching the goals based on respect, empathy advocacy and hope. The four Hs model builds on the head, hand and heart framework by adding a fourth 'h': hope. This model for a transformative pedagogy built upon a pedagogy of hope (Figure 2.2) can be broken down as follows:

A pedagogy of hope, hopefulness and possibility (A holistic framework for teaching and learning: Hope)

A pedagogy of respect and understanding (Cognitive Learning Head): Teaching *about* the Goals

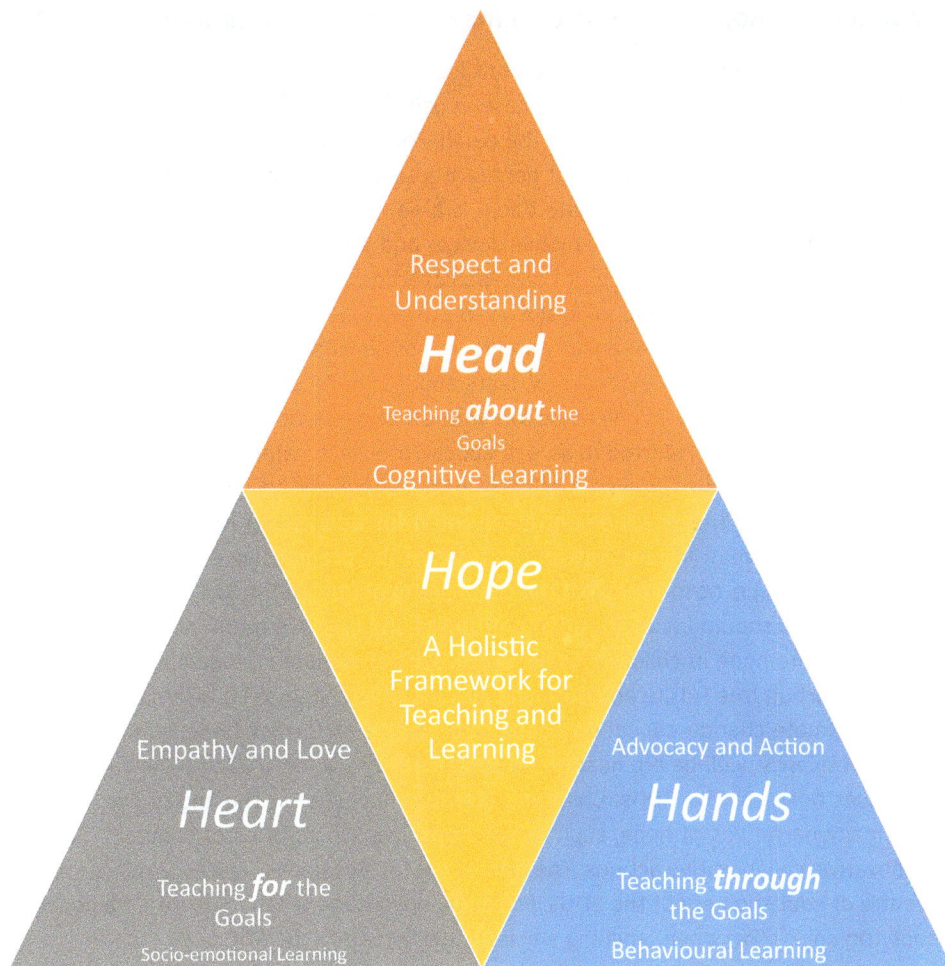

Figure 2.2 The Four Hs: A Model for Teaching the Goals Based on Respect, Empathy Advocacy and Hope.

A pedagogy of empathy and love (Socio-emotional learning: Heart): Teaching *for* the Goals

A pedagogy of advocacy and action (Behavioural Learning: Hands) Teaching *through* the goals

Each dimension in ESD and GCE teaching and learning needs to be emphasised vertically across education levels, and horizontally within each level across relevant subject areas – without however assuming that an equal level of focus and an identical approach to the three dimensions is necessarily the most appropriate across different countries, education levels and subject domains. However, less balanced ESD and GCE approaches such as a disproportionate focus on cognitive learning or addressing all three dimensions only at some education levels and not others may foster learners who will be less likely to alter their everyday actions and actively contribute to living in and building a more inclusive, just, peaceful and sustainable society.

A pedagogy of hope (A holistic framework for teaching and learning)

While global climate protests have generated increased awareness about climate change, there has also been a corresponding increase in psychological distress or 'eco-anxiety' otherwise known as fears for the future of the earth. Focusing on 'doom and gloom' scenarios make students feel helpless and do not generate a sense of agency. Indeed, commentators such as Mann (2021) claim that climate doom is a new form of climate denial. Twenty-four hour news cycles, alerts on personal mobile devices and social media feeds, collectively build a narrative of a bleak future. Much of the news coverage about environmental crises fail to discuss solutions. American psychologist Steven Stosny (2016) uses the term *headline stress disorder* to describe the state of anxiety and fear experienced by people in response to endless reporting of bad news. Consequently, fears about climate change and ecological uncertainty are so prevalent, they've given rise to a whole new genre of ecological-disaster themed entertainment commonly referred to as 'eco-apocalypse', 'eco-catastrophe' or 'climate porn'.

The environmental crisis is also a crisis of hope. Commentators such as Kelsey (2020) believe that hope for the environment is essential for addressing issues such as climate change. Indeed, as Freire argues, 'one of the tasks of the progressive educator... is to unveil opportunities for hope, no matter what the obstacles might be' (1994: 3). For instance, climate change education should focus attention on futures and possible pathways to a sustainable future to promote hope in children (Ojala, 2015). Part of climate change education involves imagining a carbon free future and outlining actions which need to be taken to achieve this. Therefore, climate change education needs to provide a forum for hope, informed by narratives of resiliency, well-being, health and sustainability (Dolan, 2022a). The same applies for all issues raised by the SDGs. Children's literature included at the end of every chapter include many narratives of hope, such as solutions, inspiring stories of community actions and innovative, collaborative actions. The framework for this book (Figure 2.2) places hope at the centre of education about the SDGs. I strongly encourage teachers to adopt a pedagogy of hope (Dolan, 2022a) when teaching any issue pertaining to the SDGs.

Hicks (2014) has an ongoing interest in how teachers and students can stay optimistic and hopeful in such difficult times. He makes a distinction between aspirational hope e.g. (hoping that we will have a day off school tomorrow) and more radical or active hope essential for survival in challenging circumstances. The latter is ontological in nature, it is what keeps us going in the most difficult of times. Hicks (2006) provides us with sources of hope which we may need to draw upon, when teaching challenging contemporary issues (Table 2.5).

The transformational power of hope has a political role to play in education (Tarozzi, 2023). Critical hope is required to dismantle social reality and re-imagine different futures. In the current era of neoliberalism and following the Covid 19 pandemic, young people are experiencing social, economic stresses and many feel disconnected from power structures in society. Insecurity in the labour market together with cost of living challenges framed by an environmental crisis ensure than many young people do not feel hopeful. Tarozzi (ibid.: 50) argues that 'education for global social justice must be able to nurture hope and optimism – always critical and never idealistic – for social transformation'. In this context hope is not optional, it is essential. In the words of Freire (2021: 1) hope is an 'ontological need' that allows us to challenge the dominant 'pragmatic discourse that would have us adapt to the facts of reality'.

Table 2.5 Key sources of hope. (Source: Hicks, 2015)

The natural world A source of beauty, wonder and inspiration which ever renews itself and ever refreshes the heart and mind	**Other people's lives** The way in which both ordinary and extraordinary people manage difficult life situations with dignity
Faith and belief May be spiritual or political. Offers a framework of meaning in both good times and bad	**Humour** Seeing the funny side of things, being able to laugh in adversity, having fun, celebrating together
Mentors and colleagues At work and at home who offer inspiration by their deeds and encouragement with their words	**Collective struggles** Groups in the past and the present which have fought to achieve the equality and justice that is rightfully theirs
A sense of self Being aware of one's self-worth and secure in one's own identity which leads to a sense of connectedness and belonging	**Relationships** The experience of being loved by partners, friends and family that nourishes and sustains us in our lives
Roots Links with the past, childhood, history, previous generations, ancestors, the need to honour continuity	**The Arts** The constant awe-inspiring upwelling of music, poetry and other arts-an essential element of the human condition.
Human creativity Both individual and community, music, song and dance, painting and sculpture, books, stories, poetry and utopia	**Visionaries** Those who offer visions of an Earth transformed and who work to bring this about in different ways

According to Popova (n.d) 'critical thinking without hope is cynicism. Hope without critical thinking is naïveté'. Incorporating both hope and creative thinking, radical hope as a philosophical and psychological concept has been discussed by different authors. Characterised by transformative power, radical hope provides a perspective for change. Radical hope can inform classroom practice through pedagogy and practice, through the formal and non-formal curriculum and most importantly through the relational experiences which occur on a daily basis in schools. Provide students with a scenario that sets a story from the beginning and ask them to write the ending. Discussions about characters, settings and plot can inspire discussions about agency, choice and power. By ensuring that all voices are valued, generating a pedagogy of hope in schools begins through daily encounters with students.

Drawing on psychological theories of hope, racial and ethnic studies and radical healing, Mosley et al. (2019: 4), have developed a multidimensional framework of radical hope (Figure 2.3). The center of the framework represents individuals and communities in the present moment, positioning themselves in a manner that acknowledges the two components of radical hope (i.e., collective memory; faith and agency) as well as all four orientations of radical hope (i.e., collective, individual, past, future). Separated based on the orientations, the two components create pathways that facilitate the development of radical hope including 'understanding the history of oppression along with actions of resistance; embracing ancestral pride; envisioning equitable possibilities; and creating meaning and purpose by adopting an orientation on social justice'. The authors suggest 'that a person who possesses radical hope is one who is, in the present moment, aware of both components (i.e., collective

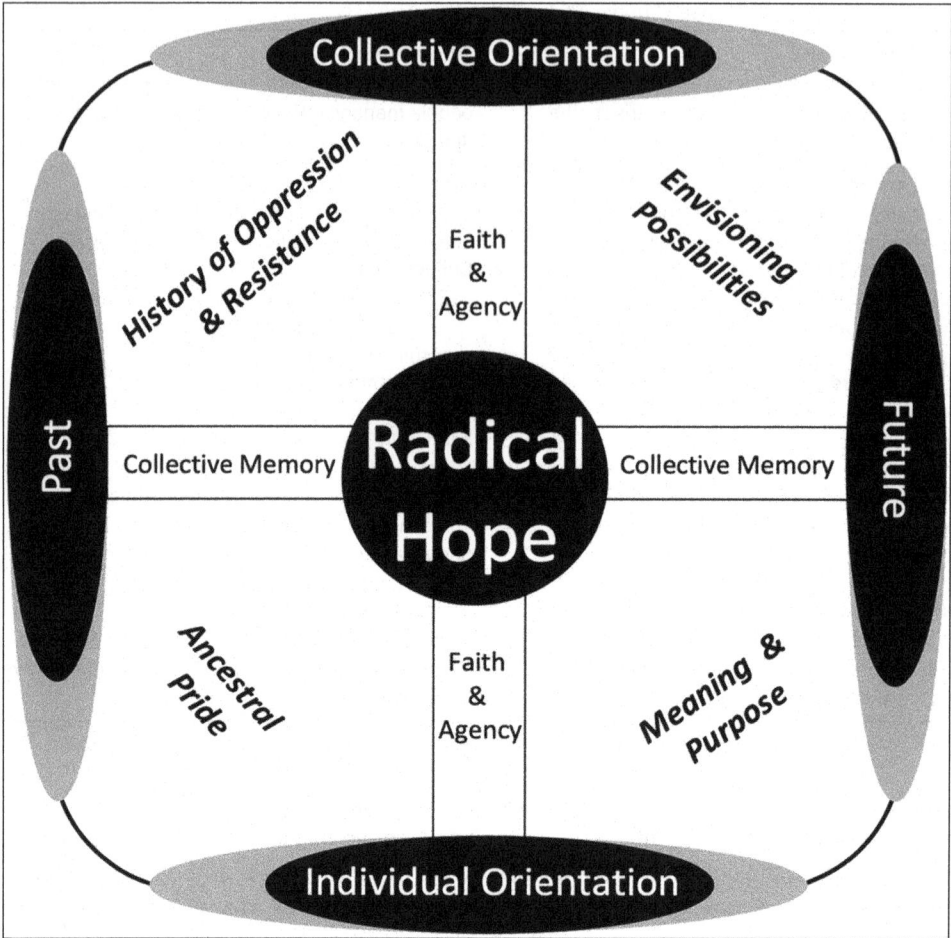

Figure 2.3 A Psychological Framework of Radical Hope, Mosley et al. (2019: 4).

memory, faith and agency) and simultaneously oriented (i.e., past, future, individual, collective) toward multiple pathways' (ibid.: 4). Furthermore, the ability to orient oneself in all directions, as depicted in Figure 2.3, is what differentiates radical hope from wishful thinking or false optimism.

One of the most inspirational writers about radical hope is Rebecca Solnit (2016: 4). Her writings speak to the transformative potential of global social justice in general and Target 4.7 in particular.

> Hope is not like a lottery ticket you can sit on the sofa and clutch, feeling lucky...hope is an axe you break down doors with in an emergency; because hope should shove you out the door, because it will take everything you have to steer the future away from endless war, from the annihilation of the earth's treasures and the grinding down of the poor and marginal. Hope just means another world might be possible, not promised, not guaranteed. Hope calls for action; action is impossible without hope

A pedagogy of respect and understanding: teaching *about* the goals

As teachers, we make choices about what to teach. Hence, the first step in developing a pedagogy for teaching the SDGs is to agree to teach the SDGs. Some teachers may be fearful about a perceived lack of conceptual knowledge. Others may believe that the SDGs are not a priority in their classroom. However, if you are reading this book, it is safe to assume that you are somewhat predisposed to the importance of the SDGs. Teaching is inherently a political task. Teaching about the SDGs is even more political in nature because it involves challenging the status quo, encouraging students to ask critical questions and imagining a variety of future scenarios. Focusing on respect and understanding is a good place to begin.

Respect is an integral part of the social and emotional fabric of human interaction. It can be defined as a noun, a feeling of admiration, a demonstration of 'high regard' or as a verb to admire someone because of their abilities, qualities or achievements (Dolan, 2014). Respect is a very important foundational factor in the development and maintenance of a healthy learning environment. Educational programmes promoting respect include self-respect and respect for others. In the context of interdependence (discussed in Chapter 1) learning to respect others is an important part of teaching the SDGs. Without respect, learning about the goals becomes an abstract exercise. Respect for the environment helps to nurture a holistic relationship with the natural world, whereby students learn to appreciate the hidden treasures in their local and global environments. Bonnett (2002) maintains we should conceptualise sustainability as a frame of mind that involves respect for human and non-human nature, seeking fulfilment through a process of co-evolution that people can encourage with appropriate technology (tools, institutions and ideas).

A pedagogy of empathy and love (socio-emotional learning): teaching *for* the goals

Empathy is a complex and multidimensional concept, and research into it spans multiple disciplines including biology, psychology, education, medicine, and neuroscience (Berardi et al., 2020). Psychologist Paul Ekman (2012) separates empathy into three different types: cognitive empathy (perspective taking, or imagining someone's feelings but not actually internalising the feelings themselves), emotional empathy (actually feeling others' feelings) and compassionate empathy (a balance of the two that usually leads to some action). Active empathy or compassionate empathy occurs when one is able to connect with another person's emotions, feel their pain so to speak, and take an appropriate action.

While the terms 'sympathy' and 'empathy' are often used interchangeably, they are not the same. Empathy means experiencing someone else's feelings. It requires an emotional component of really feeling what the other person is feeling. Sympathy, on the other hand, means understanding someone else's suffering. It's more cognitive in nature and keeps a certain distance. Empathy is the capacity not just for sympathy but an ability to understand another's circumstances and metaphorically to 'walk in their shoes'. Acts of empathy generally come from a place of love and understanding. Conversely, acts of anger and frustration are underpinned by a lack of empathy resulting in the reduction of chances for a positive resolution. Activities such as 'Walking in someone else's shoes' are useful for exploring empathy in the classroom.

Understanding of conceptual issues such as poverty, equality, sustainability, justice and related issues such as gender, climate change and educational access are core to the achievement of the SDGs. Understanding these concepts increases our ability to recognise the challenges that many people experience, including stereotyping, prejudice and discrimination. Not only can this help to ensure an empathetic approach, it can also help to mitigate potential bias and stereotyping on the basis of gender, background, religion, ethnicity, (dis) ability and family structure. From an intercultural perspective, it is important to acknowledge that we have all learned stereotypes and prejudice, and sometimes we too are uncomfortable with differences. Therefore, it is our role as teachers to become aware, unpack and address these issues for ourselves first, and then in the classroom setting. The SDGs can facilitate cross-curricular and integrated approaches to teaching and learning (see example Table 1.3, Chapter 1).

Clingan (2015) explores the concept of love as something that is present in all human lives as an emotional experience and as an intellectual idea as well. While love is central to our lives the word 'love' tends to be avoided in academic discourse. Clingan poses the question what might be possible if love were intentionally and specifically identified as a methodology, pedagogical practice, and valued in leadership, activism, and education. Indeed, Freire articulated the significance of love to both our pedagogical and political lives as he believed deeply in the transformative and emancipatory power of love. His is a concept of love not only meant to comfort or assuage the suffering of the oppressed, but also to awaken within us the historical thirst for justice and the political wherewithal to reinvent our world (Darder, 2014). So perhaps more investment in our socio-emotional learning through a pedagogy of love would assist students to build more sustainable relationships with each other and their local and global environments.

A pedagogy of advocacy and action (behavioural learning): be inspired by the activists

The Sustainable Development Goals will not be achieved without tangible actions and a radical change in our behaviour. For instance, climate action has been necessary for decades, but the latest generation of environmental advocates are collectively the loudest and most ambitious thus far. With the help of social media, their messages are able to travel faster and reach a wider audience. These activists are stepping outside of their comfort zones to show us all how to make a tangible difference in this world and in our future. In the infamous words of Greta Thunberg 'No-one is too small to make a difference'.

In November 2021, I had the privilege of attending *The Fridays For Future* protest in Glasgow. This was part of a series of demonstrations staged around the world, to coincide with the COP 26 climate negotiations. From small children waving their handmade picket signs, to older adults demanding a better future for those that will come after them, the COP 26 host city saw citizen activists in unprecedented numbers rallying to amplify their message.

Vanessa Nakate, a climate activist from Uganda spoke at the rally. She is a Fridays For Future climate activist in Uganda and founder of the Rise up Climate Movement, which aims to amplify the voices of activists from Africa. Nakate is no stranger to the world stage or being erased from the record, having attended another summit in Davos, Switzerland in 2019. While she was there she posed for a photo with other activists. She was the only black woman among the five who were photographed, and when *The Associated Press* published the photo, she was cropped out of the picture. After the photo was published Nakate tweeted: 'You didn't just erase a photo, you erased a continent, but I am stronger than ever'. Nakate, addressed the rally in Glasgow with the following words:

> Once again we are faced with another COP event. How many more of these (COP events) should they hold until they realise that their inactions are destroying the planet? Historically, Africa is responsible for only 3% of global emissions. And yet Africans are suffering some of the most brutal impacts fuelled by the climate crisis. But while the African continent, while the Global South, is on the front lines of the climate crisis, they're not on the front pages of the world's newspapers.

In her speech Greta Thunberg denounced global leaders over their promises to address the climate emergency, dismissing them as "blah, blah, blah". Thunberg (2021) said:

> They invite cherry-picked young people to meetings like this to pretend that they listen to us. But they clearly don't listen to us. Our emissions are still rising. The science doesn't lie.... We can no longer let the people in power decide what is politically possible. We can no longer let the people in power decide what hope is. Hope is not passive. Hope is not blah, blah, blah. Hope is telling the truth. Hope is taking action. And Hope always comes from the people.

A list of books about activism and advocacy including stories about Vanessa Natake and Greta Thunberg (suitable for all age groups) is included at the end of Chapter 16.

A pedagogy of advocacy and action (behavioural learning) teaching *through* the goals

There are opportunities for young people to be inspired by young activists and to design their own personal, class based or school based actions. Small scale simple actions can be identified through a version of Go Bingo in Appendix 2. More long term sustained action can be planned using templates such as the Worldwise Action Planning Framework (Figure 2.4). This book is ultimately about action and advocacy for the SDGs. It includes many stories of hope and case studies about school actions. Many individuals and organisations including the Goals Project (Case study 2.1) are spearheading excellent education programmes about the SDGs. Several videos, books and social media accounts document the inspiring activism of young people around the world. Chapters about each SDG include an extensive list of children's literature to facilitate further exploration of each Goal. These books can potentially inform class discussions, projects and action plans.

There are multiple examples of inspiring actions taken by young people in primary and secondary schools today. Students and teachers should share their innovative work with local and international audiences. By adopting the Four Hs model outlined in this book, teachers and students can plan and implement changes and actions which are age appropriate and

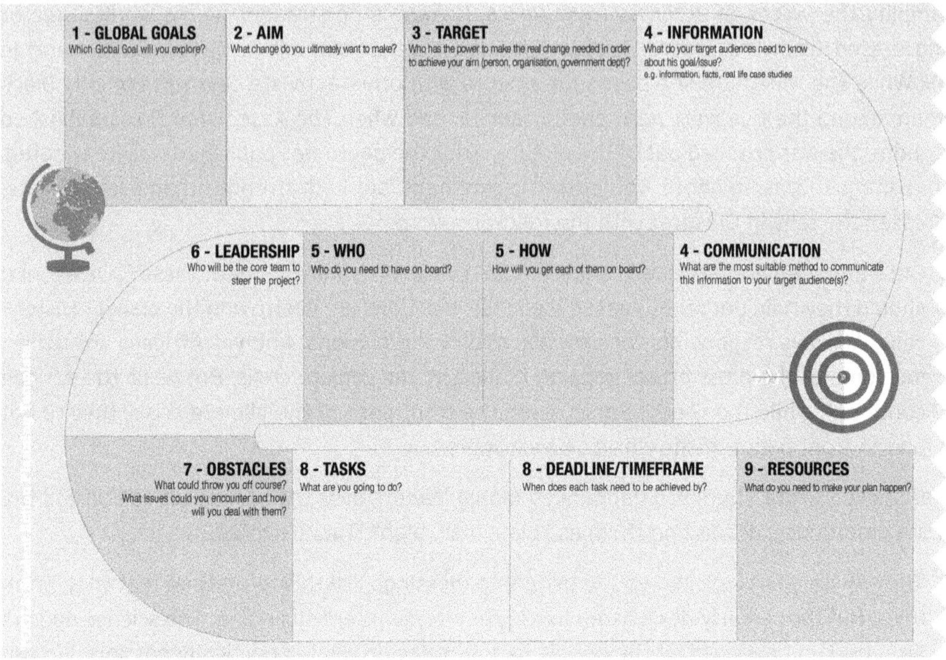

Figure 2.4 Student Action Planning Template. (Source: Worldwise Global Schools, 2020: 34).

which advance student agency now and in the future. By teaching hope, respect, empathy and advocacy though the SDG framework, students can engage with local and global issues in an informed, sustained and effective manner. Ultimately, this approach to education will make a difference.

Case study 2.1: The Goals Project https://www.goalsproject.org/

The Goals Project is an exciting new global learning initiative designed by Dr Jennifer Williams, educator, speaker, author and activist. To meet a universal call to action that ensured no one would be left behind, Jennifer set up #TeachSDGs a Global Goals Educator Task Force. Through this network teachers have pledged to #TeachSDGs by enabling students to connect to the global goals. With no more than a hashtag and a little determination, this project has established links with educators who were ready to mobilise and get to work in grassroots efforts to help reach these 17 Goals that hold a promise of transforming our world.

The Goals Project is a free global collaboration project for all classrooms of the world. The project provides opportunities for students (from 4 to 18 years), to work on a short project relating to a Sustainable Development Goals (SDG). Each participating class is assigned one of the SDGs and joins a team with 16 other classes from around the world. Global ambassadors provide support and inspiration. Classes collaborate on their small project locally and then have the opportunity to share their findings with the rest of their global team. As a result, each class learns something about all 17 Global Goals as well as learning something about their global team.

This work is supported through (1) global projects, (2) resources and publications, (3) world events, (4) advocacy and outreach, (5) communications and (6) partnership. An innovative approach to technology is the cornerstone of this project including the use of communication tools such as Twitter, Skype, Voxer, WhatsApp, Empatico and Flipgrid. The project has brought global educators together through Twitter chats, global games with Kahoot and global student learning experiences with The World's Largest Lesson (https://worldslargestlesson.globalgoals.org/).

Each participating class is invited to complete an enquiry based research project on one goal. Some classes may choose to create a presentation, a story, a video, a collection of photos, an art project, a song, an invention, a Minecraft world, a social campaign, a mock city, a garden, an eBook, and on and on! Classes are arranged in groups of 17 in line with the Goals. Final projects based on all 17 Goals are shared during the final week of the project through Form/Padlet social media by using the project hashtag #GoalsProject!

Through a six six-week global collaboration project, teachers and students have opportunities to meet international experts, work through enquiry and innovation, and collaborate with global classrooms through engaging with the Global Goals! A six week plan is set out as follows:

Week 1: Introduce the Sustainable Development Goals to your students. Highlight the Global Goal which will be the topic of investigation for this project.

Week 2: Research your SDG online, consider local and global needs, check out past projects for inspiration.

Week 3: Map out your class plan for your Class Goals Project.

Week 4: Create pathways for action.

Week 5: Package up your solution, share your impact.

Week 6: Share your solutions with the world!

Conclusion

This chapter presents the framework of The Four Hs: A model for teaching the Goals based on respect, empathy advocacy and hope. The SDGs provide a powerful planning framework for teachers and schools. This book is written as an aid for teachers to maximise the learning potential from the SDGs, to design appropriate school and locally based actions and most importantly to generate a sense of hope.

An extensive online padlet is available with resources for teaching all of the SDGs: https://padlet.com/annedolan/o6rds38ylfy6a28h

References

Andreotti, V. (2006) Soft versus critical global citizenship education. *Policy & Practice: A Development Education Review*, 3 (Autumn), 40-51.

Ballew, M.T., Goldberg, M.H., Rosenthal, S.A., Gustafson, A. and Leiserowitz, A. (2019) Systems thinking as a pathway to global warming beliefs and attitudes through an ecological worldview. *Proceedings of the National Academy of Sciences*, 116(17), 8214-8219.

Berardi, M.K., White, A.M., Winters, D., Thorn, K., Brennan, M. and Dolan, P. (2020) Rebuilding communities with empathy. *Local Development & Society*, 1(1), 57-67.

Bianchi, G., Pisiotis, U. and Cabrera Giraldez, M., GreenComp. (2022) The European sustainability competence framework. In Punie, Y. and Bacigalupo, M. (Ed.) EUR 30955 EN, Luxembourg: Publications Office of the European Union, ISBN 978-92-76-46485-3 (online), doi:10.2760/13286 (online), JRC128040.

Bonnett, M. (2002) Education for sustainability as a frame of mind. *Environmental Education Research*, 8(1), 9-20.

Bryan, A. (2011) Another cog in the anti-politics machine? The 'de-clawing' of development education. *Policy and Practice: A Development Education Review*, 12 (Spring), 1-14.

Bryan, A. and Bracken, M. (2011) *Learning to read the world? Teaching and learning about global citizenship and international development in irish post-primary schools*. Limerick: Irish Aid.

Clingan, J. (2015) A pedagogy of love. *Journal of Sustainability Education*, 9(2), 2151-2160.

Colvin, R.L. and Edwards, V., (2018) *Teaching for Global Competence in a Rapidly Changing World*. Paris: OECD.

Corney, G. (2006) Education for sustainable development: An empirical study of the tensions and challenges faced by geography student teachers. *International Research in Geographical and Environmental Education*, 15(3), 224-240.

Darder, A. (2014) *Freire and education*. London: Routledge.

Darling-Hammond, L. (2012) *Powerful teacher education: Lessons from exemplary programs*. New York: John Wiley & Sons.

Dolan, A.M., (2014) *You, Me and Diversity: Picturebooks for Teaching Development and Intercultural Education*. London: Trentham Books and IOE Press.

Dolan, A.M. (2022) Geography, global learning and climate justice: Geographical aspects of teaching climate change. In Dolan, A.M. (Ed.) *Teaching climate change in primary schools an interdisciplinary approach*. London: Routledge, 197-213.

Dolan, A.M. (2022a) Pedagogies of hope: Futures teaching for climate change. In Dolan, A.M. (Ed.) *Teaching climate change in primary schools an interdisciplinary approach*. London: Routledge, 284-304.

Ekman, P. (2012) *Emotions revealed: Understanding faces and feelings*. London: Weidenfeld & Nicolson

Freire, P. (1972) *Pedagogy of the Oppressed*. London: Sheed and Ward.

Freire, P. (1994) *A pedagogy of hope*. London: Continuum

Freire, P. (2021) *Pedagogy of hope: Reliving pedagogy of the oppressed*. London: Bloomsbury.

GENE (Global Education Network Europe). (2022) *The European declaration on global education to 2050: The Dublin declaration - A European strategy framework for improving and increasing global education in Europe to the year 2050*. Available https://static1.squarespace.com/static/5f6decace4ff425352eddb4a/t/636d0eb7a86f6419e3421770/1668091577585/GE2050-declaration.pdf

Glaesser, J., (2019) Competence in educational theory and practice: a critical discussion. *Oxford review of education*, 45(1), 70-85.

Hicks, D., (2014) *Educating for hope in troubled times: Climate change and the transition to a post-carbon future*. London: Trentham Books and Institute of Education Press.

Hicks, D. (2015) *Lessons for the future: The missing dimension in education*. London: Routledge.

Hicks, D., (2018) Why we still need a geography of hope. *Geography*, 103(2), 78-85.

Kalvaitis, D. and Monhardt, R. (2015) Children voice biophilia: The phenomenology of being in love with nature. *Journal of Sustainability Education*, 9 (March), 1-15.

Kelsey, E. (2020) *Hope matters: Why changing the way we think is critical to solving the environmental crisis*. Canada: Greystone Books.

Khoo, S.M. and Jørgensen, N.J. (2021) Intersections and collaborative potentials between global citizenship education and education for sustainable development. *Globalisation, Societies and Education*, 19(4), 470-481.

Laszlo, E., (2012).*Macroshift: Navigating the transformation to a sustainable world*. San-Francisco: Berrett-Koehler Publishers.

Liddy, M. (2012) From marginality to the mainstream: Learning from action research for sustainable development. *Irish Educational Studies, 31*(2), 39-155.

Mann, M.E. (2021) *The new climate war: The fight to take back our planet*. New York: Hachette.

Mannion, G., Biesta, G., Priestley, M. and Ross, H., (2016). The global dimension in education and education for global citizenship: Genealogy and critique. In *The political economy of global citizenship education*. London: Routledge, 134-147.

Mezirow, J. (1978) Perspective transformation. *Adult Education, 28*(2), 100-110.

Mezirow, J. (2018) Transformative learning theory. In Illeris, K. (Ed.) *Contemporary theories of learning*. 2nd ed. Oxon: Routledge, 114-128.

Mosley, D.V., Neville, H.A., Chavez-Dueñas, N.Y., Adames, H.Y., Lewis, J.A. and French, B.H. (2019) Radical hope in revolting times: Proposing a culturally relevant psychological framework. *Social and Personality Psychology Compass, 14*(1), e12512.

Norris, N., (1991) The trouble with competence.*Cambridge journal of education,21*(3), 331-341.

Odell, V., Molthan-Hill, P., Martin, S. and Sterling, S. (2020) Transformative education to address all sustainable development goals. In: W. Leal Filho, A.M. Azul, L. Brandli, P.G. Özuyar and T. Wall, eds., *Quality education*. Encyclopedia of the UN sustainable development goals. Cham, Switzerland: Springer International Publishing, pp. 905-916.

Ojala, M. (2015) Hope in the face of climate change: Associations with environmental engagement and student perceptions of teachers' emotion communication style and future orientation. *The Journal of Environmental Education, 46*(3), 133-148.

Orr, D. (1992) *Ecological literacy: Education for a post modern world*. Albany, NY: State University of New York.

O Sullivan' E. (2002) The project and vision of transformative education: Integral Transformative learning. In O'Sullivan, E. and Morrell, A. (Eds.) *Expanding the boundaries of transformative learning: Essays on theory and praxis*. New York: Palgrave Press, 1-33.

Popova, M. (nd) *Hope cynicism and the stories we tell ourselves*. Available https://www.themarginalian.org/2015/02/09/hope-cynicism/

Robinson, K. (2010) *Changing education paradigms*. Available https://www.youtube.com/watch?v=zDZFcDGpL4U

Schleicher, A., (2019) *PISA 2018: Insights and interpretations*. Paris: OECD.

Schnitzler, T. (2019) The bridge between education for sustainable development and transformative learning: Towards new collaborative learning spaces. *Journal of Education for Sustainable Development, 13*(2), 242-253.

Selby, D and Kagawa, F (2011) 'Development education and education for sustainable development: Are they striking a Faustian bargain?'. *Policy and Practice: A Development Education Review*, 12 (Spring), 15-31.

Singleton, J. (2015) Head, heart and hands model for transformative learning: Place as context for changing sustainability values. *Journal of Sustainability Education, 9*(3), 171-187.

Sipos, Y., Battisti, B. and Grimm, K. (2008) Achieving transformative sustainability learning: Engaging head, hands and heart. *International Journal of Sustainability in Higher Education*. 9, 68-86.

Solnit, R. (2016) *Hope in the dark: Untold histories, wild possibilities*. London: Canongate Canons

Sterling, S. (2001) *Sustainable education: Re-visioning learning and change*. Devon: Green Books.

Sterling, S. (2005) *Unit & study guide: Education for sustainability, education in change*. London: Distance Learning Centre, London South Bank University.

Sterling, S. (2011) Transformative learning and sustainability: Sketching the conceptual ground. *Learning and Higher Education, 5*, 17-33.

Sterling, S. and Huckle, J., Eds. (2014) *Education for sustainability*. London: Routledge.

Stosny, S., (2016) *Soar above: how to use the most profound part of your brain under any kind of stress*. Florida: Health Communications, Inc.

Tarozzi, M. (2023) Futures and hope of global citizenship education. *International Journal of Development Education and Global Learning, 15*(1), 44-55

Taylor, E.W. (2007). An update of transformational learning theory: A critical review of the empirical research (1999-2009). *International Journal of Lifelong Education, 26*(2), 173-191.

Trilling, B. and Fadel, C., (2009) *21st century skills: Learning for life in our times*. New York: John Wiley & Sons.

UN General Assembly. (2015) Transforming our world: The 2030 Agenda for sustainable development. Resolution adopted by the General Assembly on 25 September 2015. Available http://www.un.org/ga/search/view_doc.asp?symbol=A/RES/70/1&Lang=E

UN Statistics. (2017) Available https://unstats.un.org/sdgs/indicators/indicators-list/

UNESCO. (2020) *Education for sustainable development: A roadmap.* Available https://unesdoc.unesco.org/ark:/48223/pf0000374802

UNESCO (2017) *Education for Sustainable Development: Learning Objectives.* Paris: Author. *https://www.sdg4education2030.org/education-sustainable-development-goals-learning-objectives-unesco-2017*

Wade, R. (2008) Journeys around education for sustainability: mapping the terrain In Parker, J. and Wade, R. (Eds.). *Journeys Around Education for Sustainability*, London: South Bank University. 5–32.

Worldwise Global Schools. (2020) *A how to guide: Global citizenship education (2020–21).* Available http://www.worldwiseschools.ie/wp-content/uploads/2020/09/How_to_Guide_2020_1-web-size.pdf?x76647

3 A human rights-based approach to teaching the Sustainable Development Goals

Claire Glavey

Introduction

This chapter sets out a human rights-based approach to teaching the (SDGs). One of the key principles of the 2030 Agenda for Sustainable Development (comprising 17 SDGs and 169 associated targets), is a Human Rights-Based Approach (HRBA), which is 'well-recognized as an effective and essential way of putting people at the centre of development' (United Nations Sustainable Development Group, 2019: np). Taking a HRBA is both logical and essential, to fully reflect the origins and ambitions of the 2030 Agenda, when exploring the SDGs with students. This approach supports students to comprehend and critically reflect upon how the goals impact on human lives. Approaching the SDGs through a human rights lens emphasises our common humanity and lends further conviction to the need for solidarity and cooperation in addressing the many challenges faced by the global community.

By explicitly placing the SDGs within a human rights framework, we provide additional context to help students to better connect with, and make sense of, the aims and spirit of the 2030 Agenda. Young people connect readily with the concept of human rights, and there is historic and legal weight to key human rights documents and frameworks which underpin and strengthen the SDGs. These international human rights structures and laws provide the imperative for global solidarity, and responsible global citizenship. By emphasising rights and corresponding responsibilities, we are drawn away from an optional, charity-based approach to development, towards one of obligation and social justice (United Nations Sustainable Development Group, 2019). This strengthens our sense of empathy and responsibility towards one another, and our belief that a more equitable, just and peaceful future is possible.

This chapter aims to

discuss how human rights and human rights education evolved;

explore the human rights education framework of teaching **about**, **through** and **for** human rights;

examine human rights education in the context of the 4Hs model underpinning this book;

identify links between human rights and the SDGs; and

propose activities for teaching the SDGs through a human rights framework.

DOI: 10.4324/9781003232001-5

Development and human rights

Learning about how the fields of development and human rights evolved in parallel with one another in the 20th and 21st centuries, can help both teachers and students to better comprehend the significance of the SDGs and the importance of the underpinning HRBA.

Economic development

The Second World War provided the impetus for national leaders to unite and create a vision for a more peaceful, cooperative world. Development was conceptualised primarily in economic terms, with an underlying assumption that national economic growth would 'trickle down' to benefit all people, including those living in poverty (Daly and Regan, 2012). It was seen as a linear process, strongly linked to industrialisation, modernisation and ever-increasing Gross Domestic Product (GDP). As discussed in the introduction, terminology used to differentiate countries and regions on the basis of wealth, distribution of resources and equality is problematic. The terminology of 'developed' and 'developing' countries emerged from, and reflects, a problematic conceptualisation of development. Overall statistics and labels for countries and regions mask inequalities within countries. While rates of extreme poverty are much higher in certain regions of the world, there are vast inequalities and injustices to be found in every country, so the idea that any country is fully 'developed' is inherently flawed. From an educator's perspective, the oversimplifications, generalisations and stereotypes which arise from labels such as 'developing' and 'developed', 'first world' and 'third word', need to be grappled with in any exploration of the SDGs. From a human rights perspective, questions must be asked about how individual countries and governments are performing, with regard to achieving the SDGs and upholding human rights for all.

Poverty and inequality

Increases in overall GDP do not automatically reduce poverty. In order to see the impact of economic growth on poverty levels, we must analyse how the benefits of that growth have been distributed among the population of the country or region. Poverty is not merely about a lack of income and wealth, it is multidimensional. According to the United Nations Global Compact (2021, np), poverty 'has a range of different socioeconomic dimensions, including: the ability to access services and social protection measures and to express opinions and choice; the power to negotiate; and social status, decent work and opportunities'. Therefore, any analysis of the impact of economic growth on poverty must look not only at increases in income, which move people above the poverty threshold, but also at investment in education, health and social services, and the corresponding impacts on freedom and opportunities for people to live a full and meaningful life.

Treating economic development, rather than human well-being, as the end goal of development, has not, and does not, address deep inequalities and injustices within societies around the world. In fact, unfettered economic growth has gone hand in hand with a starker divide between wealthy and poor, within and between countries. According to Global Justice

Now (2015: 6), poverty is a result of a power imbalance; it is 'a direct consequence of others having too much power – ultimately too much control over resources'. Framing development in terms of human rights reminds us of the need to prioritise human well-being over economic growth. We must treat both extreme poverty and extreme wealth as part of the same picture of inequality and 'exploitation of people and the planet's resources' (Global Justice Now, 2015: 6).

Critiquing development

Development has strong political and ideological roots, linked to decolonisation, the Second World War and the Cold War. Some critics raise questions about the vested interests of development agendas, with concerns that they serve primarily to boost the political reputations and the economies of the Global North (Andreotti and de Souza, 2008). Others 'see development as the imperialism of knowledge, a continuation of colonialism, which imposes on the world a 'modernity' that it does not necessarily want' (Andreotti and de Souza, 2008: 9). These concerns are increasingly pertinent as humanity battles with climate change. Key questions must be addressed regarding our relationship with one another and with the natural world, our exploitation of people and of natural resources.

In exploring the SDGs with students, it is important to foster skills of critical thinking and questioning. Key questions to explore, include, what can be learned from different societies and ways of living, and how this fits, or not, with concepts of modernity and infinite economic growth. Much wisdom from indigenous communities has been disregarded and dismissed in the past, yet can teach us important lessons about how to live more sustainably with the natural world, and in greater harmony with one another.

Human development

There has been a shift towards human-centred development since the 1990s. The human development approach came about in response to the dominant focus on economic development and was led by the United Nations Development Programme (UNDP), and economists Amartya Sen and Mahbub ul Haq. Sen's (1999) conceptualisation of development as the expansion of human freedoms and choices, continues to be central to the UNDP's perception of human development. The SDGs are born of this human development approach, which 'is about expanding the richness of human life, rather than simply the richness of the economy in which human beings live. It is an approach that is focused on people and their opportunities and choices' (UNDP, 2021: np).

When exploring the SDGs with students, it is important to acknowledge the advances made by the human development approach, in redirecting the focus of development efforts towards human freedoms and choices. However, any critical exploration of the SDGs must also recognise and challenge the continuing global dominance of neoliberalism, which shapes the wider environment within which the 2030 Agenda is operating. The promotion and pursual of unlimited economic growth and profit must be seen for what it is – inherently unsustainable in a world of finite resources, and a process through which the divide between a wealthy, privileged minority, and a disadvantaged majority of the world's population, is exacerbated.

Connecting human development and human rights

Linking development to human rights strengthens the human development approach. The connection between the two has deepened over the past three decades. The first annual Human Development Report defined human development as 'a process of enlarging people's choices', and identified the most critical choices as 'to lead a long and healthy life, to be educated and to enjoy a decent standard of living' (UNDP, 1990: 10). Although central to each of these choices, human rights were merely identified on a list of 'additional choices'. By contrast, the topic of the 2000 report analysed the connection between human rights and human development, looking at 'human rights as an intrinsic part of development – and at development as a means to realizing human rights' (UNDP, 2000: np). The Human-Rights Based Approach (HRBA) being the first principle of the 2030 Agenda for Sustainable Development, demonstrates just how much progress has been made in integrating human development and human rights. This approach serves as a reminder to retain the human face of development in the pursuit of sustainable development.

Human rights declarations and laws provide a lens through which to analyse the impact of development agendas on individuals and communities. They provide the imperative for societies to be structured in such a way as to enable people to claim the freedoms and capabilities inherent in the human development approach, and the human rights enshrined in the Universal Declaration of Human Rights (Daly and Regan, 2012). Rather than waiting to see if development efforts will trickle down to those living in poverty in the future, human rights obligations implore us to ask, how are these development programmes affecting people, both positively and negatively, today? Furthermore, how might these actions have long-lasting effects on the rights of people in the future?

The essence of human rights means that they belong to all human beings, equally. As such, the fulfilment of one person's rights should not come at the expense of another person's rights. Applying a human-rights approach to an analysis of development agendas and programmes, means asking and investigating questions such as, what is the impact of development in one country on the people in another country? There are many examples within human history that could be used to illustrate this relationship and to develop critical thinking skills. For example, the slave trade, enabled huge economic growth and wealth accumulation in some countries, through the exploitation of many people with an extreme violation of their human rights.

Human rights

Human rights are what every human being on the planet is entitled to, by virtue of being human. They are 'standards that recognize and protect the dignity of all human beings' and they 'govern how individual human beings live in society and with each other, as well as their relationship with the State and the obligations that the State have towards them' (UNICEF, 2021: np). Human rights principles have been promoted by a broad range of philosophers and political leaders from different regions of the world since the beginning of recorded human history (Ward, 1995). The significance of the human rights movement of the 20th century in particular was that international laws and conventions were established, drawing together, and emphasising the ties of the international community and the concept of universal human rights.

Human rights are:

- Universal: human rights belong to all people in the world.
- Inalienable: human rights can not be given up or taken away.
- Indivisible: there is no hierarchy of human rights, they all have equal status and they are interdependent i.e. one set of rights can not be fully enjoyed without the fulfilment of the other rights (UNICEF, 2021).

On July 28th 2022, the UN General Assembly adopted a historic resolution declaring access to a clean, healthy and sustainable environment, a universal human right. The resolution recognises that the impact of climate change, the unsustainable management and use of natural resources, the pollution of air, land and water, the unsound management of chemicals and waste, and the resulting loss in biodiversity interfere with the enjoyment of this right - and that environmental damage has negative implications, both direct and indirect, for the effective enjoyment of all human rights. This follows a similar declaration by the UN Human Rights Council.

Human rights law

The Universal Declaration of Human Rights (UDHR), declared by the United Nations in 1948, is not itself legally enforceable, but it is the foundational document upon which legally binding international human rights treaties are based. As such, it is the starting point for exploring human rights in the classroom. It emphasises justice, equality and our common responsibility towards one another.

When it came to enshrining the UDHR into law, the political tension of the Cold War intervened. Because of this, two legally binding covenants were established, each focused on different sets of rights. The International Covenant on Civil and Political Rights, and the International Covenant on Economic, Social and Cultural Rights, were adopted in 1966, and entered into force in 1976. This split explains the limited reference to human rights in the earliest human development reports.

However, more recent human rights treaties, including the Convention on the Rights of the Child (1989), have abandoned this separation, and have returned to the roots of the UDHR, emphasising the interdependency and indivisibility of human rights (United Nations Human Rights Office of the High Commissioner, 2021). Once ratified, governments are obligated to protect human rights enshrined in these treaties, and rights holders have the opportunity to claim these rights. However, in order to truly achieve the human development vision of expanding individual freedoms and choices, people, particularly the most disadvantaged and marginalised in societies, must learn about their rights in order to be able to claim them. 'Learning about human rights is the essential first step towards respecting, promoting and defending those rights' (Amnesty International Ireland, 2012: 1).

The right to human rights education

The UDHR establishes the right to human rights education. Article 26, which proclaims the right to education, also identifies the purpose of education, including human rights education as follows:

> Education shall be directed to the full development of the human personality and to the strengthening of respect for human rights and fundamental freedoms. It shall promote understanding, tolerance and friendship among all nations, racial or religious groups, and shall further the activities of the United Nations for the maintenance of peace.
>
> (UN, 1948: np)

The Convention on the Rights of the Child (CRC), the world's most widely ratified human rights treaty, further solidifies the right to human rights education for children (people below 18 years).

Article 29: 1. States Parties agree that the education of the child shall be directed to:

a)   The development of the child's personality, talents and mental and physical abilities to their fullest potential;

b)   The development of respect for human rights and fundamental freedoms, and for the principles enshrined in the Charter of the United Nations;

c)   The development of respect for the child's parents, his or her own cultural identity, language and values, for the national values of the country in which the child is living, the country from which he or she may originate, and for civilizations different from his or her own;

d)   The preparation of the child for responsible life in a free society, in the spirit of understanding, peace, tolerance, equality of sexes, and friendship among all peoples, ethnic, national and religious groups and persons of indigenous origin;

e)   The development of respect for the natural environment (UN, 1989: np).

What is human rights education?

There are many definitions of Human Rights Education (HRE) available from a range of organisations working in the area. Amnesty International defines it as 'a process whereby people learn about their rights and the rights of others, within a framework of participatory and interactive learning' (Council of Europe, 2020: np). The United Nations World Programme for Human Rights Education defines it as 'education, training and information aimed at building a universal culture of human rights' and identifies knowledge, skills, attitudes and behaviours related to human rights (Council of Europe, 2020: np).

The Council of Europe identifies a consensus among key actors working in HRE and outlines a useful framework, which is used below to apply HRE theory to classroom practice.

> Learning **about** human rights, knowledge about human rights, what they are, and how they are safeguarded or protected;

Learning **through** human rights, recognising that the context and the way human rights learning is organised and imparted has to be consistent with human rights values (e.g. participation, freedom of thought and expression, etc.) and that in human rights education, the process of learning is as important as the content of the learning;

Learning **for** human rights, by developing skills, attitudes and values for the learners to apply human rights values in their lives and to take action, alone or with others, for promoting and defending human rights.

(Council of Europe, 2020: np)

Teaching about, through and for human rights

A human rights education framework to teach **about**, **through** and **for** human rights, when approaching the Sustainable Development Goals, is proposed here. This framework, advocated by many organisations and educators, provides a structure through which the connections between the SDGs and human rights can be readily made and explored with students. It ensures that the **knowledge** aspect of human rights education is included but is not the only focus of learning. Human rights are **brought to life** and **into action**. Underpinning this framework are four key principles: hope, respect, empathy and advocacy.

Hope

Human rights education is an inherently hopeful endeavour. It is grounded in what it means to be human, in the conviction of the UDHR, that 'all human beings are born free and equal in dignity and rights' (UN, 1948), and in the belief that education can be transformative. Education can bring about social change to address inequality and injustice. This belief echoes the work of Brazilian educator and philosopher, Paulo Freire, who advocated for 'problem-posing education', whereby 'students confront, explore, and act purposefully in a dynamic, ever-changing world' (Roberts, 2000: 56).

As students engage in critical thinking, dialogue, and analysis of the world around them, they come to realise that 'dominant ideas can be challenged and oppressive social formations transformed', and this brings a sense of 'hope that the world can change' (Roberts, 2000: 69). In the application of a human rights based approach to teaching about the SDGs, hope is evident in the conviction that human rights can be realised through practical actions linked to the SDGs.

This hope is not naïve to the enormity of the challenges faced by humanity. On the contrary, it is the type of hope that comes from seeking to understand the depth of inequality in our world, and from finding the courage to turn towards, rather than away from, injustice. It is this hope that pushes us to use the power we do have, to work for justice. In the words of Valav Havel (1990: 181–182),

Hope, in this deep and powerful sense, is not the same as joy that things are going well, or willingness to invest in enterprises that are obviously headed for early success, but rather an ability to work for something because it is good, not just because it stands a chance to succeed.

Respect

Respect is central to human rights education. It is about having regard and concern for the rights of others, as well as ensuring that our own rights are upheld. This respect comes from the recognition of our common humanity, and a belief in the equality of all human beings. It drives us to look beyond ourselves and our rights, to acknowledge and take interest in the rights of others, and to realise that the two are interconnected.

Essential in any human rights education programme is an exploration of both rights and responsibilities, and respect is key to this. At an individual level, it is about engaging students, to reflect upon and show respect for other people in their immediate environment. Collectively, it is about considering how different groups in society might work together to uphold the rights of one another – and particularly the rights of those who face exploitation, discrimination and injustice.

For example, students might explore the topic of migration, with a focus on refugees and asylum seekers, in a lesson on human rights and the SDGs. This learning could encompass an exploration of the main reasons people seek refuge and asylum in other countries. It could investigate the key frameworks in place to protect people, including the Geneva Conventions, which are the international treaties that set out to limit the impact of war, particularly on civilians (International Committee of the Red Cross, 2014). This could then be linked to students' own lives and actions, by considering how refugees and asylum seekers are treated by themselves and by others in their own communities.

Empathy

Human rights education is built upon a concern for the well-being and treatment of oneself and of other people. It seeks to develop empathy in students, so they can truly grasp the importance of human rights and the need to take an active role in challenging human rights violations.

When teaching about the SDGs, empathy is an essential skill for students to develop, so that they can understand and appreciate the perspectives of those most affected by the problems the SDGs set out to tackle, including poverty, climate change and gender inequality. Fostering empathy is key for students to truly connect with the essence of human rights 'as it is only through being able to view a situation from another's perspective that the universality of these rights will be valued' (Amnesty International Irish Section, 2003: 15).

Advocacy

Advocacy is a core dimension of human rights education. As per the UDHR, 'education shall be directed to... the strengthening of respect for human rights and fundamental freedoms' and 'shall promote understanding, tolerance and friendship among all nations, racial or religious groups' (UN, 1948: np). Human rights education involves encouraging and facilitating students to take a stance on human rights issues and to support actions to address human rights violations.

With regard to the SDGs, this element of human rights education calls for teachers and students to advocate for a human rights framework to be implemented with regard to each SDG, and any human rights violations or concerns related to the Goals to be resolved.

Teaching about human rights

This element of the framework focuses on the knowledge component of lessons. It is essential for students to develop a solid knowledge base regarding human rights and their relationship with the SDGs. Below are some examples of how this might be achieved in the classroom.

Activity: drawing connections between human rights and the Sustainable Development Goals

Step 1: Introduce the concept of human rights

Explain to students that human rights belong to every person in the world, regardless of who they are, where they come from, what they look like. Explain that human rights refer to everything a person is entitled to simply by virtue of being human. Show the Universal Declaration of Human Rights (UDHR), explaining that this is a list of human rights as set out and agreed by the international community.

Step 2: Introduce the Sustainable Development Goals

Explain that the goals are a commitment by the international community towards addressing many of the big challenges facing humanity. Show the 17 SDG icons (See Chapter 1, figure 1.2).

Step 3: Human rights/SDG ranking

The aim of this activity is to give students an opportunity to explore the UDHR and the SDGs. In small groups, they read, discuss and rank human rights and SDGs (in two separate lists) from what they consider to be the most important to least important.

Variation: rank human rights/SDGs from the perspective of different people - someone living in a refugee camp, someone from a small-island nation, someone living in poverty in India or someone wealthy living in Ireland.

Step 4: Human rights/SDG web

Everyone receives a slip of paper with a human right or SDG on it. Everyone stands in a circle. One person starts and reads aloud their human right or SDG. They hold a ball of string. Anyone else may identify a connection between that human right/SDG and the human right/SDG they are holding. The ball of string is passed to this person. People continue to make connections until the ball of string has been passed to each person, thereby creating a string web, showing how interconnected human rights and SDGs are with one another.

Step 5: Compare and contrast

Each group receives two sets of cards – the first with human rights as laid out in the UDHR, the second with the SDGs. Working together, they must match as many human rights as possible with relevant SDGs.

Activity: critical analysis of the SDGs from a human rights perspective

By analysing the SDGs from a human rights perspective, we emphasise a justice, rather than a charity perspective on inequality. The human rights framework challenges us to critically consider both the strengths and flaws inherent in the 2030 Agenda.

Step 1: Choose one of the SDGs and learn about the targets which make up this goal

Introduce the 17 SDGs to students. Provide information on each Goal, with a focus on the targets associated with those Goals. Working in groups, the students from each group choose one goal they are particularly interested in, and learn about that Goal and associated targets (See Appendix 1 for a full list of SDGs with their targets).

Step 2: Apply a human rights lens

Introduce/revise the concept of human rights. Provide a copy of the UDHR to each group and ask them to identify any rights which are related to the SDG they have been learning about. Ask them to consider both (a) how the SDG targets could contribute to the upholding of human rights; and (b) whether anyone might be excluded/forgotten by these targets and/or who might still not have their human rights met even if those targets are achieved.

Step 3: Debate – the SDGs are sufficient to uphold human rights

Allocate each student to a debate team and assign each team a stance in relation to any of the following motions or a motion chosen by the teacher and/or students:

- The SDGs are sufficient to uphold human rights
- Human Rights are more important than the SDGs
- Poverty should be eliminated in Ireland before we think about poverty in other countries
- The rights of refugees arriving in Ireland are more important than the rights of homeless people
- People should be encouraged to give more money to charitable organisations to help achieve the SDGs.

The proposition will argue in favour of the motion and the opposition will argue against it. A number of teams could be formed on each side of the debate, to present on different days or in smaller groups. Provide guidance on how to research the debate topic and put together a speech for each team member.

Teaching through human rights

This element of the framework concerns the overall approach taken in the learning environment to engage, include and respect all learners and to model human rights in action. Below are some tips on how this might be achieved in the classroom.

Creating a classroom charter

It is good practice to create a class charter before exploring human rights and the SDGs, and indeed at the start of any learning journey with a group of students. This 'can help to build trust in the compassion, empathy and sensitivity of the students themselves' (Donnelly, 2019: 7). A charter should be developed together with the students, asking them for their suggestions on how the class might best work together respectfully, collaboratively and inclusively. This shows students that their voice is valued and listened to, and that their cooperation in creating a rights-respecting environment, is essential. It gives them a practical experience of being recognised and respected as citizens in the classroom environment, and 'provides opportunities to practise and then develop skills which make people responsible citizens' (Fenney and Jarvis, 2002: 15).

Knowing your students and how to deal with sensitive issues

If some of your students are directly affected by a human rights or development issue being explored or discussed in your class, what can you do? Donnelly recommends that you 'maintain a focus on narrative within the broader society, rather than asking young people to state and defend their personal views on controversial issues (or those they might hear at home)' (2019: 7). Never expect or place pressure on individual students to share their own experience of an issue (Donnelly, 2019). Issues can be placed within a historic context, looking at how they were dealt with in the past, before addressing what is currently happening, to give students some distance and time to process their own beliefs, ideas and values regarding the issue (Donnelly, 2019).

Teaching through human rights includes making human rights education accessible to all. This involves differentiating teaching and learning activities and approaches and adapting lesson content for individual students who require additional support. The following groups may require lesson adaptations: younger children; older children; young people; students with additional needs; students with different learning styles; and gifted learners.

Building student self-esteem and well-being

Exploring big global issues through the SDG framework and a human-rights based approach brings many challenging questions and scenarios to the fore in the classroom setting. It can be worrying and disheartening for students to learn about complex problems faced by the global community. Therefore, it is important to be mindful of student well-being, and to emphasise examples of progress made towards the fulfilment of human rights, as well as facilitating opportunities for students to make a positive contribution to the wider world. Building student self-esteem and resilience is an important part of this approach, both for the well-being of the individual students, and for the collective benefit of the class and wider communities within which the students interact. According to Ruane, Horgan and Cremin (1999: 9), 'research suggests that children with a high self-regard are likely to be more altruistic, generous and sharing in nature. They will be more likely to exhibit positive attitudes towards others'.

Acknowledging your own stance as a teacher and being purposeful in how you use it

According to Freire, teachers are never politically neutral; we bring our own beliefs and stance on issues into our work in the classroom. Freire believed that teachers should be open and honest with students about their viewpoints, while at the same time avoiding imposing their views on students (Roberts, 2000). Furthermore, teachers should be open to their own viewpoints being questioned and should actively seek out and 'promote consideration of alternative views: to stimulate contrary discourses and invite critical appraisals of their own views' (Roberts, 2000: 75).

Conducting an audit of classroom materials, including textbooks

Many textbooks, story books and posters present challenging depictions of people and places around the world, particularly people and places on the African continent, which often feed into persistent stereotypes regarding poverty, famine and helplessness. Conducting an audit of classroom materials, including textbooks, through a human rights lens, will help to iden- tify these stereotypes. Some of these materials could then be used as the basis for a lesson on stereotypes, asking students to consider the perspective of the person in the images/ descriptions – if you were that person, would you be happy to come into this classroom and see your image/description of your life used as a representation of your entire community/ country/continent? With greater awareness of the types of depictions found in textbooks and other classroom materials, a teacher can make more informed decisions about the choice of classroom materials and pedagogical approaches.

Analysing the use of images and messages in the education setting

We are susceptible to reinforcing (unintentionally or otherwise), the message that develop- ment and poverty alleviation is about charity, rather than justice. Therefore, it is important for us to make use of guidelines available to support educators in the use of images and messages when exploring global issues linked to the SDGs and Human Rights. For example, if exploring a case study of how an SDG is being addressed in a particular community, ask your- self, are the images I am using clear, dignified, authentic and balanced? (Comhlámh, 2009: 2).
   Ruane, Horgan and Cremin (1999:10) propose some more tips for combating stereotypes in the use of images in particular:

- Present positive images to challenge stereotypes, counteract the acquisition of racist atti- tudes, and bring balance to the information they receive about other peoples and places;
- Use photographs in a range of contexts, mixing images of local and wider environments;

-   Choose photographs which highlight similarities as well as differences and which present a range of images of countries or large areas;
-   If images of poverty and disaster are discussed, the teacher should ensure that they are presented in context and as part of a range of images which emphasise the true diversity of every country.

Consciously choosing terminology

Make a deliberate and considered decision regarding the terminology you use when referring to countries, groups of countries and regions of the world. Be aware that each set of terminologies has its own history and connotations.

Using a diversity of maps

Check what kind of maps you are using in the classroom, and be aware of the impressions they give to students. Are they all Eurocentric? Do they accurately represent the relative geographic size and positioning of each continent? Many maps inaccurately show the Global North, (particularly Europe, the United States and Canada), as occupying much more space than it does in reality. This is a visual representation of global injustice and inequality. According to Galeano, (2001 cited in Daly and Regan, 2012: 38), 'the map lies. Traditional geography steals space just as the imperial economy steals wealth, official history steals memory, and formal culture steals the world'. There are many different maps available, which show different representations of power, wealth and geographic distribution around the globe. For instance, the Gall-Peters projection, commonly referred to as the Peters Projection World Map is a rectangular, equal-area map projection. This projection was popularized by Arno Peters, a 20th-century German historian, who was dissatisfied with the Mercator projection. Promoted by several human rights organisations, this map represents countries accurately according to their surface areas.

Challenging perspectives

Present students with a range of different perspectives on the SDGs. Stories and case studies are an ideal way to do this. Debating from a different stance to your own, role-playing from a new perspective, writing from a different point of view, are all strategies that can be used to 'develop perspective consciousness – the awareness that our own perspective shapes the way we view the world and that other opinions and perspectives can be equally valid' (Ruane, Horgan, Cremin, 1999: 4).

It is important to engage students in listening to real life stories of people living in situations where their human rights are being violated and threatened. Rather than merely imagining such situations without any concrete evidence or information, listening to the perspectives of real people, through video clips or written accounts, can go a long way towards fostering empathy and combating stereotypes and misconceptions. Doing this can avoid 'the uncritical reinforcement of notions of the supremacy and universality of 'our' (Western) ways of seeing, which can reproduce unequal relations of dialogue and power and undervalue other knowledge systems' (Andreotti and de Souza, 2008: 3).

Teaching for human rights

This element of the framework relates to incorporating action for human rights into teaching and learning. It involves facilitating action and advocacy opportunities for students to practice and defend human rights, within the context of the SDGs.

A human rights approach emphasises action based in social justice, rather than in charity. In the classroom setting, this involves moving away from a traditional focus on fundraising as a solution to inequality and poverty. Instead, identify ways in which students can challenge structural inequality and contribute to positive, systemic change.

This primarily involves emphasising collective rather than individual actions, and focusing on holding to account those with greater decision-making power and leadership roles in society. Students could, for example, write letters to those in positions of power demanding greater action on achieving the SDGs and emphasising the justice basis for these goals. Alternatively, they could join a campaign or attend a protest focused on systemic political, economic or consumer change. Within their own school community, students can get involved in awareness raising, educating other students about the SDGs and potential actions which could be taken within and beyond the school. For younger students, this could be particularly pertinent, as they could lobby adults to use their voting and wider political influence to demand greater justice. Students, teachers and parents can make lifestyle changes and join in local campaigns and activities, with an emphasis on how individual choices and engagement may connect to a wider collective movement, shifting towards more responsible living and active citizenship in the wider community.

Conclusion

Teaching the Sustainable Development Goals to Young Citizens involves encouraging and supporting them to grapple with big, complex, philosophical questions and dilemmas facing humanity. Learning through the framework of the Sustainable Development Goals (SDGs) provides students with the chance to connect with the concepts of common humanity and global citizenship. As educators, we have the opportunity to guide young people to explore and analyse these big issues, and to develop and apply their skills of empathy and advocacy to a range of situations they experience in their lives.

However, grappling with such big issues can bring with it a sense of helplessness, disillusionment, and anxiety in the face of the enormous problems facing humanity. It is also, therefore, our challenge as educators to facilitate learning within a framework of support and hope. It is essential that we do not focus exclusively on the global problems which gave rise to the need for the SDGs, but also on the work being done to achieve these goals, and the hope and solidarity inherent in local, national and international cooperation.

Approaching the SDGs through a human rights framework emphasises our common humanity and encourages greater empathy towards ourselves and one another. By recognising that we all have a shared set of human rights, arising from our shared humanity, we can draw hope that we have a common interest to work together and achieve a more sustainable, equitable future for all.

Resources for teachers

Amnesty International provides recommendations of human rights literature for different age ranges. https://www.amnesty.org.uk/education-resources-fiction-literature-poetry

Amnesty International Human Rights Education Resources. Available at: https://www.amnesty.org/en/human-rights-education/

Amnesty International Ireland Human Rights Education Resources. Available at: https://www.amnesty.ie/what-we-do/human-rights-education/

Amnesty International UK Human Rights Education Resources. Available at: https://www.amnesty.org.uk/resources

Andreotti, V. and de Souza, L. M. T. M. (2008). *Learning to Read the World Through Other Eyes: An Open Access Online Study Programme Focusing on Engagements with Indigenous Perceptions of Global Issues.* Derby: Global Education. Available at: https://developmenteducation.ie/media/documents/Learning_to_Read_the_World_Through_Other.pdf

Child Rights Connect and UNICEF. The United Nations Convention on the Rights of the Child – The Children's Version. Available at: https://www.unicef.org/media/60981/file/convention-rights-child-text-child-friendly-version.pdf

Comhlámh. (2009). *Images of the Global South: Guidelines for Primary Educators for Working With Photographs from Around the World.* Comhlámh. Available at: https://issuu.com/comhlamh/docs/images-of-the-global-south

Equality and Human Rights Commission Secondary Education Resources. Available at: https://www.ihrec.ie/download/pdf/equality_in_second_level_schools.pdf

Human Rights Watch Human Rights Education Resources. Available at: https://www.hrw.org/students-and-educators

Trócaire Development and Human Rights Education Resources. Available at: https://www.trocaire.org/our-work/educate/brighterfutures/

UNICEF Ireland Children's Rights Education Resources. Available at: http://www.unicef.ie/child-rights-education/

UNICEF Kahoot Quizzes Available at: https://create.kahoot.it/pages/32c22a99-b815-4a16-8bf1-ec29 15c82986?_=1571351723

UNICEF Short e-course: Child rights and why they matter. Available at: https://agora.unicef.org/course/info.php?id=11073

United Nations Human Rights Office of the High Commissioner Committee on the Rights of the Child: Information for Children. Available at: https://www.ohchr.org/EN/HRBodies/CRC/Pages/InformationForChildren.aspx

World's Largest Lesson. Available at: https://worldslargestlesson.globalgoals.org/

Children's literature

Picturebooks and Poetry

Amnesty International. (2008) *We Are All Born Free: The Universal Declaration of Human Rights in Pictures* Frances Lincoln Children's Books.

Amnesty International. (2015) *Dreams of Freedom* Francis Lincoln Children's Books.

Amson-Bradshaw and Broadbent, D. (illus) (2020) *We're All Equal* Franklin Watts.

Brooks, F. and Ferrero, M. (2021) *All About Diversity* Usborne Publishing Ltd

Butterfield, M. and Lynas, H. (2021) *Welcome to Our World: A Celebration of Children Everywhere!* Nosy Crow.

Chopra, A. and Tabaranza, J. (2021) *Know Your Rights or Have No Rights: Let's Know More About the UN Convention on the Rights of Children* EduMatch

Dalvand, R. (2023) *I Have the Right: An Affirmation of the United Nations Convention on the Rights of the Child* Scribble UK.

Davies, N. and Martin, M. (Illus) (2020) *Every Child a Song* Wren & Rook.

Harman, A. and Broadbent, D. (2020) *Human Rights, I'm a Global Citizen* Franklin Watts.

Hooks, G. (2017) *If You Were a Kid During the Civil Rights Movement* Scholastic.

Hope, J. (Ed.) *Our Rights! Stories and Poems about Children's Rights* Otter-Barry Books.

Hopkinson, D. and Gardiner, K. (illus) (2023) *Small Places, Close to Home: A Child's Declaration of Rights: Inspired by the Universal Declaration of Human Rights* Balzer & Bray/Harperteen.

Lewis, A. (illus) and Becker, H. (2023) *Eleanor Roosevelt: Her Path to Kindness* Little, Brown Young Readers.

Madison, M., Ralli, J. and Miller, S. (illus) (2024) *We Care: A First Conversation about Justice* Rise X Penguin Workshop.

Michelson, R. and Colón, R. (2008) *As Good as Anybody: Martin Luther King Jr. and Abraham Joshua Heschel's Amazing March Toward Freedom* Dragonfly Books.

Murray, M. an Kai, H. (illus) (2020) *Rights and Equality* (Children in Our World Picturebook Series) Wayland.

Riddell, C. (2021) *My Little Book of Big Freedoms, The Human Rights Act in Pictures* Buster Books.

Serres, A., Fronty, A (illus) and Ardizzzone, S. (translator) (2012) *I Have the Right to be a Child* Groundwood Books Ltd.

Spilsbury, L. and Newsome, T. (2021) *Human Rights* (Civil Rights Stories) Franklin Watts.

Tonatiuh, D. (2014) *Separate is Never Equal* Harry N. Abrams.

Turner, T. and Gilland, A. (illus) *We Are All Different: A Celebration of Diversity* Macmillan Children's Books.

UNICEF. (2000) *For Every Child: The Rights of the Child in Words and Pictures.* Red Fox in association with UNICEF.

Williams, M. (2019). *Children Who Changed The World: Incredible True Stories About Children's Rights!* Walker Books Ltd.

Winter, J. and Innerst, S. (illus) (2017) *Ruth Bader Ginsburg: The Case of R.B.G. vs. Inequality* Harry N. Abrams.

Children's novels

Amnesty International. (2017) *Here I Stand: Stories That Speak For Freedom* Walker Books Ltd.

Amnesty International. (2010) *Free? Stories About Human Rights* Candlewick Press.

Thompson, G. and Wolf, E. (Illus) (2004) Who Was Eleanor Roosevelt? Penguin.

References

Amnesty International in Council of Europe. (2020). *Compass: Manual for Human Rights Education with Young People.* 2nd Edition. Available at: https://www.coe.int/en/web/compass/introducing-human-rights-education

Amnesty International Ireland. (2012). *A Whole School Approach to Human Rights Education.* Amnesty International Ireland.

Amnesty International Irish Section. (2003). *The Right Start.* Amnesty International Irish Section, Amnesty International UK, Education International, Irish National Teachers' Organisation, Ulster Teachers' Union.

Andreotti, V. and de Souza, L. M. T. M. (2008). *Learning to Read the World Through Other Eyes: An Open Access Online Study Programme Focusing on Engagements with Indigenous Perceptions of Global Issues.* Derby: Global Education.

Comhlámh. (2009). *Images of the Global South: Guidelines for Primary Educators for Working with Photographs from Around the World.* Comhlámh. Available at: https://issuu.com/comhlamh/docs/images-of-the-global-south

Council of Europe. (2020). *Compass: Manual for Human Rights Education with Young People.* 2nd Edition. Available at: https://www.coe.int/en/web/compass/introducing-human-rights-education

Daly, T. and Regan, C. (2012) in Regan, C. (ed.) (2012). *80:20 Development in an Unequal World.* 6th Edition. Bray: 80:20 Educating and Acting for a Better World.

Donnelly, V. (2019). *Beyond Borders: A Toolkit of Creative and Participatory Approaches for Exploring Refuge and Migration Issues in Secondary School Classrooms.* Galway: Galway One World Centre.

Fenney, P. and Jarvis, H. (2002). *Time for Rights: Activities for Citizenship & PSHE for 9-13 Year Olds.* London: The Save the Children Fund and UNICEF.

Galeano, E. (2001) in Daly, T. and Regan, C. (2012) in Regan, C. (ed.) (2012). *80:20 Development in an Unequal World*. 6th Edition. Bray: 80:20 Educating and Acting for a Better World.

Global Justice Now. (2015). *The Poor Are Getting Richer and other Dangerous Delusions*. Available at: https://www.globaljustice.org.uk/resource/poor-are-getting-richer-and-other-dangerous-delusions/

Havel, V. (1990). *Disturbing the Peace*. Available at: https://www.vhlf.org/havel-quotes/disturbing-the-peace/

International Committee of the Red Cross. (2014). *The Geneva Conventions of 1949 and their Additional Protocols*. Available at: https://www.icrc.org/en/document/geneva-conventions-1949-additional-protocols

Roberts, P. (2000). *Chapter 3: Ethics, Politics, and Pedagogy: Freire on Liberating Education. In Education, Literacy, & Humanization : An Introduction to the Work of Paulo Freire*. Westport: Bergin and Garvey.

Ruane, B., Horgan, K. and Cremin, P. (1999). *The World in the Classroom: Development Education in the Primary Curriculum*. Limerick: Primary School Development Education Project

Sen, A. (1999). *Development as Freedom*. Oxford: Oxford University Press.

UNICEF. (2021). *What Are Human Rights? Human Rights Belong to Each and every One of Us Equally*. Adapted from: Introduction to the Human Rights Based Approach, UNICEF Finland, 2015. Available at: https://www.unicef.org/child-rights-convention/what-are-human-rights

United Nations. (1948). *Universal Declaration of Human Rights*. Available at: https://www.un.org/en/about-us/universal-declaration-of-human-rights

United Nations. (1989). *Convention on the Rights of the Child*. Available at: https://www.unicef.org/child-rights-convention/convention-text#

United Nations Development Programme (UNDP). (1990). *Human Development Report 1990: Concept and Measurement of Human Development*. Available at: http://hdr.undp.org/sites/default/files/reports/219/hdr_1990_en_complete_nostats.pdf

United Nations Development Programme (UNDP). (2000). *Human Development Report 2000: Human Rights and Human Development*. Available at: http://hdr.undp.org/sites/default/files/reports/261/hdr_2000_en.pdf

United Nations Development Programme (UNDP). (2021). *About Human Development: What Is Human Development?* Available at: http://hdr.undp.org/en/humandev

United Nations Global Compact. (2021). *Poverty*. Available at: https://www.unglobalcompact.org/what-is-gc/our-work/social/poverty

United Nations Human Rights Office of the High Commissioner. (2021). *Key Concepts on ESCRs - Are Economic, Social and Cultural Rights Fundamentally Different from Civil and Political Rights?* Available at: https://www.ohchr.org/en/issues/escr/pages/areescrfundamentallydifferentfromciviland politicalrights.aspx

United Nations Sustainable Development Group. (2019). *Integrating Human Rights, Leave No One Behind, and Gender Equality into UN Cooperation Frameworks*. Available at: https://unsdg.un.org/2030-agenda/universal-values

United Nations World Programme for Human Rights Education in Council of Europe. (2020). *Compass: Manual for Human Rights Education with Young People*. 2nd Edition. Available at: https://www.coe.int/en/web/compass/introducing-human-rights-education

Ward, M. (1995). *Yes, You Do Count: A Comprehensive Teaching Programme on Human Rights*. Dublin/Belfast: Churches' Peace Education Programme.

Section 2

4 Engaging with the causes and solutions of poverty (SDG 1)

Daniel O'Connell

Introduction

Poverty attacks dignity – it erodes and corrodes one's sense of self, one's sense of being a somebody. It is merciless in obliterating what is needed to live life to the full. It can do this in an obvious and brutal manner or in a way that is more subtle and less visible, but all the time undermining of dignity and sense of oneself.

This chapter explains the meaning and significance of terms such as 'extreme poverty' and 'relative poverty', all the time, keeping in mind the extent and impact of poverty on the lives of countless millions of people throughout the world. It describes some of the causes of poverty, along with work to reduce its impact. The chapter argues that information is not enough to change our behaviour, it is not enough to know the facts regarding the reality of poverty in the world. Our actions are not only shaped by what we know, they are also shaped by what we care about, what matters to us and what is in our hearts. Accordingly, attention is given to the importance of fostering values such as hope, empathy and advocacy in both ourselves as teachers and our students. Finally, the chapter concludes with some detailed, practical lessons that can be completed in class, with many references to resources and further education plans following these lessons.

What is poverty?

In thinking about poverty, it is important to differentiate between the sorts and levels of poverty in the world. While all poverty harms the dignity of the human person, it does this to varying degrees, in different parts of the world. It can manifest itself in conditions that make life precarious, where death is a distinct possibility. Or it can make itself felt in preventing someone from participating in a meaningful way in society, where a child is embarrassed to go to a friend's house, as her family can only afford second hand clothes. This is where terms such as 'extreme' and 'relative' poverty are helpful.

Extreme Poverty This refers to a condition characterised by severe deprivation of basic human needs, including food, safe drinking water, sanitation facilities, health, shelter, education and information. It depends not only on income but also on access to services. Extreme poverty is the term given to severe deprivation. It refers to an income below the international poverty line of $2.15 per person per day set by the World Bank (World Bank, 2023).

DOI: 10.4324/9781003232001-7

Relative Poverty People are living in relative poverty if their income and resources (material, cultural and social) are so inadequate as to preclude them from having a standard of living that is regarded as acceptable by society generally. As a result of inadequate income and resources, people may be excluded and marginalised from participating in activities that are considered the norm for other people in society' (Social Justice Ireland, 2021).

Sustainable development goal 1 – no poverty

SDG 1 calls for 'an end to poverty in all its manifestations by 2030'. The phrase 'in all its manifestations' is important. This refers to the many dimensions and impacts of poverty on people's lives. Traditionally, economists tended to think of poverty as simply a lack of adequate income, but poverty is more than that. It hinders, hampers and harms the life of human beings in countless ways.

Concern points out that in 2021, '193 million people in 53 countries faced acute food insecurity, meaning they were unable to consume enough adequate food, putting their lives or livelihoods in immediate danger. This is an increase of 40 million compared to 2020' (Concern, 2022). 785 million people drink unsafe water or have to travel more than 30 minutes to drink safe water (World Health Organisation, 2019a). More than 40% of the global poor live in economies affected by fragility, conflict and violence and that number is expected to rise to 67% in the next decade. (The World Bank, 2021). Poverty in Gaza and the West Bank has soared following Israel's war on Hamas. Around 368 million of the world's poor live in just five countries: India, Nigeria, the Democratic Republic of the Congo, Ethiopia and Bangladesh (The World Bank, 2019).

The effect of extreme poverty

It is difficult to appreciate the significance of these numbers and the dehumanising impact of living in poverty on the human person. People in extreme poverty are forced to live precariously on the edge of life, scrambling to survive, to get by on just enough. Their life is marked by insecurity and uncertainty. All the protections afforded to us in the Global North that help to shield us from hunger, violence, sickness, exploitation, poverty and displacement are stripped away for those who live and survive in extreme poverty. Those living in extreme poverty are vulnerable to the vagaries of life. So much of their time and energy goes to mere survival.

Living in extreme poverty is not just about a lack of money, rather, it is being exposed to all sorts of obstacles and limitations that hinder a person's ability to live a full life and provide for their family. If you live in extreme poverty, the pain it inflicts on you is not just physical. It is also emotional and moral. The World Bank says that it is humiliating, especially when people are forced to accept rudeness, insults and indifference when they seek help (World Bank, 2000). If you are poor, you have very little power and your voice does not carry very far. If you are poor, sometimes you have to make very difficult choices: will I pay the little I have to help a sick family member or use the money to feed the children. Living in extreme poverty is not just about material deprivation, it is much, much more than that. It corrodes a sense of self and enforces a sense of personal limitation. It constricts one's ability to be self-determining – a core characteristic of what it means to be human.

Children and poverty

Poverty impacts on the lives and wellbeing of children in a disproportionate manner. One billion children worldwide are living in poverty and 356 million children live in extreme poverty (UNICEF, 2018). The Borgan Project points out that the poorest 20% of the world's children are twice as likely as the richest 20% to be dead before their 5th birthday and to be stunted by poor nutrition (Borgan Project, nd). Figures from UNICEF (2018), suggest that 22,000 children die each day due to poverty. This is a staggering figure. Other poverty related statistics are as follows:

- 2.5 million newborns worldwide die within their first month of life (World Health Organisation, 2020);
- Almost 200 million children under the age of five in the Global South are underweight for their age (UNICEF, 2019);
- 19.4 million infants in the least developed countries are not protected from diseases by routine immunisation (Mantel & Cherian, 2019);
- 2.8 million children under the age of 19 currently live with HIV (UNICEF, 2020);
- 263 million children were out of school in 2015, with Sub-Saharan Africa having the highest out-of-school rates (UNESCO, 2016);
- One out of six children lives in extreme poverty (The World Bank, 2020a).

Relative poverty in Ireland

When we are talking about poverty in European countries such as Ireland, we are talking about relative poverty. Such levels of relative poverty in Ireland are illustrated in Table 4.1.
Some numbers:

How many people are poor in Ireland? 629,952 (Social Justice Ireland, 2021a);
How many children are poor in Ireland? 191,505 (Social Justice Ireland, 2021a);
How many people who are poor have a job? 15% (Social Justice Ireland, 2021a)

Table 4.1 Poverty levels expressed in numbers of people in Ireland (Social Justice Ireland, 2021a)

	2006	2009	2012	2019
Overall	719,597	639,209	776,335	629,952
Children under 18	250,418	223,084	232,124	191,505

The extent of poverty in Ireland is measured by identifying a poverty line (or lines) based on people's disposable income. Most European states, including Ireland, suggest a line, which is at 60% of median income, basically, the middle income in society. Those below the poverty line, generally do not have adequate resources for a standard of living considered 'acceptable' by Irish society.

As a consequence of being below this poverty line or being in relative poverty, people may not have access to adequate heating or own two pairs of strong shoes. They cannot afford a meal with meat, chicken or fish every second day or a warm waterproof coat. They are unable to buy presents for family members or any new clothes (these items are drawn from the 11 deprivation indicators used by the Central Statistics Office).

To understand the nature and impact of experiencing poverty and chaos in England and Ireland, Katriona O' Sullivan's (2023) memoir 'Poor: Grit, courage and life-changing value of self-belief' is a must read. This remarkable book charts the author's life in her own words from her poverty-stricken childhood as a child of addict parents to her journey through education, achieving a PhD in Trinity College Dublin. This book is an important contribution to our understanding of poverty and its impact on those who experience it. Her testimony reminds us of the insidious nature of poverty within a society divided by class in England and by socioeconomic status in Ireland. She speaks powerfully of poverty as follows:

> 'Being poor affects everything you do and everything you are. Thinking of poverty, we picture barefoot children in rags on the street. Of course, it is the lack of money and material possessions. For me it was those things: for so much of my life I literally had nothing. But 'poor' for me was also feeling like I had no worth. It was poverty of mind, poverty of stimulation, poverty of safety and poverty of relationships. Being poor controls how you see yourself, how you trust and speak, how you see the world and how you dream' (ibid:274).

The poverty of worth meant that the value of education as a 'gateway out of poverty' was hidden from her. O'Sullivan (ibid:273-274) also challenges the language of poverty. Her choice of a book title for her memoir was quite deliberate as the word 'Poor' 'cuts through a lot of jargon -words like 'disadvantaged', 'underprivileged', deprived', 'underclass'. Words that have their place but don't capture the visceral truth of what it is to grow up the way I did. The way thousands of children are growing up right now'.

What can be done?

It is interesting to note that in the past, the vast majority of the world's population lived in extreme poverty, however, it fell from 80% in 1800 to under 20% in 2014 (Beauchamp, 2014). In 1990 the figure had been 1.9 billion, in 2008 it was 1.2 billion, in 2015 it was 734 million. We can see significant progress in these figures. Over a billion people exited extreme poverty in the 15 years before 2015. The economist Max Roser (2017) pointed out in 2017, newspapers could have run a headline all over the world that said 'Number of people in extreme poverty fell by 137,000 since yesterday'. In China, over 500 million people exited extreme poverty in this time. Indeed, China has achieved the poverty reduction target laid out in the UN 2030 Agenda for Sustainable Development ten tears ahead of schedule. It is very important to see that things have improved a great deal in the past 200 years through industrial development and Chinese socialism.

In 2000, the UN published its Millennium Development Goals. The first goal was the Eradication of Poverty and Hunger. Part of the aim was to reduce the extreme poverty rate by half by 2015. This goal was realised five years ahead of schedule. The Millennium Development Goals have now been replaced by the Sustainable Development Goals and the first goal is to end extreme poverty, in all its forms, everywhere by 2030. Let us remember the extraordinary advances that have been made, despite the depth of poverty we face today.

While this reality can be overwhelming and induce a sense of hopelessness, it is important to look at where people and organisations are making a difference in the face of overwhelming odds. In order to help students connect with this issue, they need to relate and connect with the people who are suffering. As educators, we need to engage the imagination and get to the hearts of those we teach. The data won't be enough in and of itself to give rise to action. We need to tell stories of children, women and men, of their struggles for survival and their battle with poverty. It is through the use of story that we can engage the affect and desire of students to connect to those who are poor and find practical ways in which they can help.

In this short section, I want to highlight the work of one not-for-profit organisation, Trócaire based in Ireland. Trócaire (Irish for 'compassion') was founded in 1973 by the Irish Episcopal Conference in response to poverty and injustice in the Global South. It has five goals: defending human rights and promoting access to justice; climate and environmental justice; supporting women's and girls' protection, voice and leadership; saving lives and protecting human dignity and mobilising in Ireland to achieve global justice (Trócaire, 2022). For instance, in Sierra Leone (one of the poorest countries in the world) Trócaire gave agricultural support to 40,000 people, 22,000 people were supported through women's empowerment programmes and 1,000 people were supported through humanitarian aid (Trócaire, 2022a). It is important to showcase success for students by highlighting the positive contribution of aid efforts through government and non-government organisations. These sorts of achievements by Trócaire are replicated by groups such as Concern Worldwide, Goal, UNICEF Ireland, Christian Aid, Irish Aid and the Irish Red Cross.

We need to give students access to the human stories of success, to help them stand in solidarity and know that they too can make a difference. There are many examples of success stories detailed in the children's literature section at the end of this chapter.

In Table 4.2, the learning objectives for this goal, 'No Poverty', are outlined. It is split into three sections: the cognitive, the socio-emotional and the behavioural or, in other words, the head, the heart and the hands. Thus far, I have outlined some data regarding the nature and scope of poverty that speaks to the head. Below this table, I will outline some thoughts about the importance of engaging the heart of our students and finally, the chapter will finish with some detailed, practical suggestions to engage the hands and invite students to become advocates for change.

Table 4.2 Learning objectives for SDG 1 (Source UNESCO, 2017: 12)

Cognitive learning objectives Teaching **about** the goals: developing respect and understanding	1	The learner understands the concepts of extreme and relative poverty and is able to critically reflect on their underlying cultural and normative assumptions and practices.
	2	The learner knows about the local, national and global distribution of extreme poverty and extreme wealth.
	3	The learner knows about causes and impacts of poverty such as unequal distribution of resources and power, colonisation, conflicts, disasters caused by natural hazards and other climate change-induced impacts, environmental degradation and technological disasters, and the lack of social protection systems and measures.
Socio-emotional learning objectives Teaching **for** the goals enhancing empathy and love	1	The learner is able to raise awareness about extremes of poverty and wealth and encourage dialogue about solutions.
	2	The learner is able to show sensitivity to the issues of poverty as well as empathy and solidarity with poor people and those in vulnerable situations.
	3	The learner is able to identify their personal experiences and biases with respect to poverty.
Behavioural learning objectives Teaching **through** the goals Promoting advocacy and activism	1	The learner is able to plan, implement, evaluate and replicate activities that contribute to poverty reduction.
	2	The learner is able to publicly demand and support the development and integration of policies that promote social and economic justice, risk reduction strategies and poverty eradication actions.

Considerations for teachers – the heart

If we don't have any hope, any belief in a different kind of future, the status quo will remain in place. Hope is what engenders energy and effort, it is essential to action. If we are hopeful, we believe things can change. Hope is premised on a vision, a promise in the future that can start now. This is true in so many things in life. We might see ourselves being on a team, in a particular relationship, playing in a band, getting good grades or securing a job and as a consequence, this vision inspires us to put in the effort and make the necessary sacrifices to realise what we hope for, to make it happen. This is because we believe that the vision is realisable and that gives us hope. As Victor Frankl (2004) puts it in *Man's Search for Meaning*, if you have a good enough why, you will put up with any how. Such a hope is dynamic, it generates energy and sustains the effort in attaining one's goals. The challenge we face with the young people we teach is to engender hope with regard to reducing poverty in the world. The reduction of poverty needs to be a part of their vision for life, for the world in which we share. They need to believe that their actions can make a difference.

Regrettably, as I've pointed out earlier, we cannot simply 'think' our way into action. If as humans were defined by what we thought, then simply changing what we think and know would change how we act and what we do. Unfortunately, the human person is much more complex than that. Knowledge is not the issue. Instead, we need to appeal to the emotional, social, moral, spiritual and motivational dimensions of students. One of the ways to do this is through providing opportunities for them to develop empathy for the children, women and men who have to survive on so little in the world today. Is there a way for them to see and connect with families who suffer due to poverty? If young people don't care, they won't act. We need to help them to care. Stories are one of the ways we can do this (there is an extensive list of children's story books at the end of this chapter) – telling the stories of people who, through an accident of birth, live in places where it is so difficult to survive, never mind thrive in the world today. They need to see people afflicted by poverty, together with their courage, endurance, generosity, strength, laughter and most importantly their humanity. We need to speak to the heart of the people we teach – so that we move from an 'us' over here and 'them' over there, to a sense of 'all of us together'. Stories are a way to foster empathy and care. If we care about someone, we are more inclined to reach out and help.

While speaking to the heart of the young people, we also need to speak to their heads – to help them grasp intellectually what is happening. But we also want them to act – to use their hands, so that they can become advocates for the reduction of poverty in the world today. Young people will do this if they care, if they understand and if they believe they can make a difference. This belief in the power of their actions will be important for us to develop. They need to know that what they do matters and has a practical impact. It is also important that they appreciate and understand the balance between charity and justice. Both are needed. We must be careful not just to remain on the charity side of things, i.e. raising money. Students also need to appreciate the structural issues involved that force people to live in poverty in the first place. We need to challenge stereotypes that suggest poverty is the fault of those who are poor and notice our own role in sustaining such unjust structures in the world, i.e. perhaps in the clothes we buy. See Table 4.3 for some differences between these two different approaches.

It is important to remember that our actions shape who we are. In a way, we become what we do. For instance, if someone tells the truth a lot, they become an honest person. If they practice kindness, through lots and lots of small acts of kindness, they will become a kind person. There is a cumulative power in small actions. Over time, such action becomes second nature, a habit, automatic and almost done without thinking. In our attempts to help young people to act in reducing poverty, to become advocates, these actions can have an impact on their identity. If something is done repeatedly in your classroom, it becomes part of the

Table 4.3 Charity verses justice based responses to poverty

Charity	Justice
private, individual acts	public, collective
immediate need	long term
no change in causes	promote social change
no critical thinking	analysis
we do 'for' you	we do 'with' you
often feel good	not as immediately satisfying
alone	together
who and how	who, how and why?
relief	liberation
danger of dependency	inter-dependency
too soft	too hard
duty	rights
dignity	dignity

Table 4.4 Suggested topics for SDG 1 'no poverty' (Source UNESCO, 2017: 12)

Learn definitions of poverty
Cause and consequences of poverty
Global, national and local distribution of extreme poverty and extreme wealth and the reasons for this
To explore the interrelation of poverty, natural hazards, climate change and other economic, social and environmental shocks and stresses
Importance of equal rights to economic resources and access to basic services
Work conditions of those affected by poverty including child labour and modern slavery
Poverty informed policy solutions

Table 4.5 Suggested learning approaches and methods for SDG 1 'no poverty' (Source UNESCO, 2017: 12)

Plan and run an awareness campaign about poverty locally and globally
Conduct a case study on poverty and wealth in selected countries (through desktop research) or at the local level (through excursions, doing interviews, etc.)
Develop an enquiry-based project around: 'Is poverty increasing or decreasing?'

culture and can shape the student's outlook on the world. Just as information is important, so too is action, repeated action, in shaping the character and identity of the young people.

Tables 4.4 and 4.5 outline some of the topics, learning approaches and methods suggested in how to approach SDG 1 'No Poverty' by the UN. These can be helpful in framing your own approach, in how to work with your own students on this issue. They are followed by some detailed practical ideas and suggested resources to help engage the head, hands and heart of the young people in your classroom to reduce poverty in the world.

Practical ideas for the classroom

ACTIVITY 1: Reflecting about poverty

Learning Objectives: Students are able to identify their personal experiences and biases with respect to poverty

What is your own view about poverty?

Reflection (adopted from Andreotti & de Souza, 2008)

Put up the following statements in four separate places on the wall in your classroom and ask students to stand by the one (if any) that is most closely associated with their understanding of poverty:

> Wealthy people help alleviate poverty
> Wealthy people help create poverty
> Poverty is about a lack of financial resources
> Poverty is about a lack of principles or values

Ask in the groups, why they have chosen to stand by that statement

Journal

Write down your own definition of poverty and what can be done to reduce poverty in the world.

Further reflection

Take a few moments to reflect on the following:
Who would agree and not agree with your own definition?
What is the link between poverty and education? In what sorts of ways can education contribute to poverty alleviation?

Reflection

In groups, hand out the following sheet, each group is to agree on three of the following perspectives that they think represent the most prevalent attitude towards poverty in society today and give reasons for their selection.

Attitude towards poverty handout

Distribute statements about poverty (Table 4.6) to each group. Ask the students to discuss the statements and select their top three statements based on agreement within the group.

Table 4.6 Statements about poverty

1 'People are poor because they lack education, proper work habits and a good attitude towards life.'
2 'People are poor because they are exploited. They are made to work for low wages while their employers become rich.'
3 'You need money to make money. Those who are born in rich families have a much higher chance of success than those who are born into poor families.'
4 'If some poor people have managed to come out of poverty, why can't other poor people do the same? Some of them don't want to work very hard – they prefer to live on benefits.'
5 'Why would you want to participate in a game that is set to fail you and your children? You are payed less than others, you are perceived as ignorant, incompetent and in need of charity – at some point you give up. This happens when you realise that no matter what you do, you will never be good enough or meet the 'standards' set by other people.'
6 'Poverty is a consequence of social injustices, therefore overcoming poverty is not a gesture of charity, but of justice. It is the protection of a fundamental right, the right to dignity and a decent life. While poverty persists, there is no true freedom because there is no justice.'
7 'If everyone competed for their own interests, as everyone would be motivated to keep going, the good of all would be achieved. Competition creates wealth and brings benefits for all.'
8 'Competition is based on winners and losers. It cannot eradicate poverty. Where there is competition there will be those who have more and those who have less.'

Finally, in your group, what do you think this phrase means: 'One for all and all for one' shouted the elephants as they danced among the mice?

Activity 2: 5:50:500 exploring the structural injustice of poverty

Learning Objectives: Students know about the local, national and global distribution of extreme poverty and extreme wealth;
Students know about the cause and impacts of poverty such as unequal distribution of resources and power, colonisation, conflicts.

5:50:500 Structural issues

The basic idea behind 5:50:500 as set out in Tables 4.7 and 4.8, captures the degrees of magnitude involved in the unjust relationship between the 'Rich' and 'Poor' worlds.

How 5:50:500 works

While figures change from year to year, the ratio 5:50:500 has been adopted because it is on the conservative side of the estimates and because it graphically captures the degrees of magnitude involved in the unjust relationship between the 'Rich' and 'Poor' worlds. The 5 in the title refers to voluntary aid - that is, monies collected by the many charities and poverty/ development/aid non-governmental organisations (NGOs) across the globe. In recent years aid given to the Global South by non-governmental agencies (voluntary aid) has amounted to at least $5 billion. The 50 in the title refers to Official Development Assistance (ODA) as

Table 4.7 5:50:500

5	From 1997 to 2007, aid given to the Global South by non-governmental agencies (voluntary aid) has amounted to at least $5 billion. Estimates vary from a low of $5 billion to a high of $15 billion, so we have chosen the lower figure.
50	In the same period of time, aid given to the Global South by governments (official aid) has amounted to at least $50 billion. The actual figures vary considerably year by year from $50 billion in 2000 to $105 billion in 2007, so we have chosen the lower figure.
500	In the same period of time, the Global South lost an average of $500 billion as a result of the operation of the current unjust international economic system. The figure for 2007 was $792 billion, the estimate for 2008 was $895 billion, so we have chosen the lower figure.

Source: Developmenteducation.ie

Table 4.8 How 5:50:500 works

Each year:	
Interest payments on a total debt of some $375 =	$34 Billion Minimum
The cost to the Global South of unjust trade barriers =	$130 Billion Minimum
The cost of 'trade related intellectual property' issues =	$40 Billion Minimum
The cost of corruption and capital flight =	$193 Billion Minimum
The cost of the brain drain =	$100 Billion Minimum
Total	**$497 Billion Minimum**

the vast bulk of international aid to the Global South comes in the form of official govern-ment aid. ODA has grown significantly in monetary terms, from US$50 billion at the turn of the century to just over double that by 2007. However, the Global South loses a staggering figure of $500 billion as a result of our current unjust international economic system. So, in short, for every $55 billion transferred to the Poor World by the Rich World, $500 billion is transferred in the opposite direction.

We give $55 billion, we take $500 billion

Reflection

How do you think this impacts on efforts to reduce poverty in the Global South?
How does this impact on your own view of poverty looked at earlier?

Activity 3: The web of poverty (adapted from Concern, 2017)

Learning Objectives: Students know about the causes and impacts of poverty such as the unequal distribution of resources and power, colonisation, conflicts, disasters caused by natu-ral hazards and other climate change-induced impacts.

The following exercise will help students reflect on the causes of poverty. It will help point out the interconnectedness and complexity of poverty, moving away from a simple idea of poverty as just not having enough money. Figure 4.1 illustrates some of the root causes of poverty in our world today:

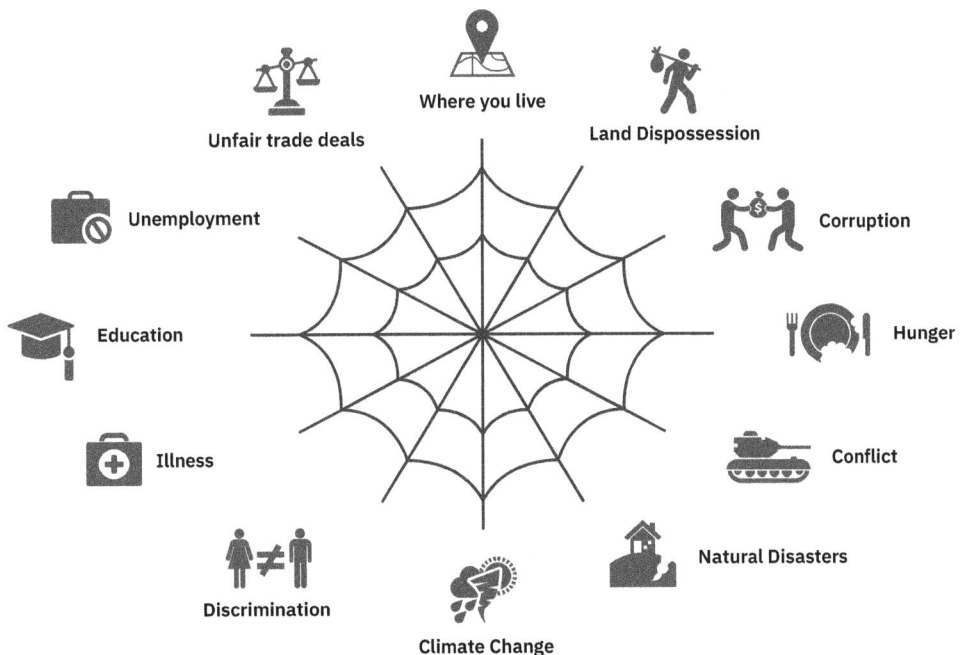

Figure 4.1 Web of Poverty (Concern 2017: 5).

Resources: *Causes of Poverty* information cards Table 4.9, scissors, balls of wool, camera to document

Instructions:

1. Divide the students into two groups. Distribute a set of *Causes of Poverty* information cards and a ball of wool to each group. Each student should pick an information card at random.

2. In their groups, encourage students to read their card and discuss.

3. Encourage each student to explain what is on their card to the rest of the group (in their own words).

4. Once everyone has shared the information on their card, invite the students to establish links between the causes of poverty. For example, if someone's livelihood was affected by extreme weather events (Climate change) they would have less money to buy food (Hunger).

Table 4.9 Causes of poverty information cards handout (source: Concern 2017: 6)

Education
If children cannot go to school it leaves them without literacy and numeracy skills required to further their careers. Their children, in turn, are in a similar situation years later, with little income and few options but to leave school and work.

Illness
Being very sick can prevent someone from going to school, work or enjoying life. The burden of caring is often taken on by a female relative, who may have to give up her education as a result, or take on waged work to help meet the household's costs.

Discrimination
Marginalised (socially excluded) groups and vulnerable individuals are often worst affected, deprived of the information, money or access to education, health services and jobs, or are not able to make their own choices about where they live.

Climate change
Rising temperatures and unpredictable rain makes it more difficult for farmers to grow key crops. They are unable to feed their families or earn a proper income.

Natural disasters
Floods, droughts and cyclones trigger infectious disease epidemics. Natural disasters destroy homes, schools and other infrastructures.

War and conflicts
Poverty increases the risk of civil war. During times of armed conflict, civilians are killed, infrastructures are destroyed and governance and economic performance is weakened, thus increasing the risk of conflict relapse.

Hunger
Very poor and vulnerable people may have to make harsh choices – knowingly putting their health at risk because they cannot see their children go hungry. Malnutrition effects development and many opportunities, such as going to school or work.

Corruption
The effects of corruption are personal and devastating. Corruption and bribery leaves families without healthcare, people without food and clean water, the elderly without security, and businesses without capital.

Land dispossession People who live and work on someone else's land are more vulnerable to evictions. Being landless makes it more difficult to earn money, plough and feed themselves or contribute to economic growth.

Where you live
Some families live in places where there is high unemployment and high drop out rates fro schools.

Unfair trade deals
Poor governments have to pay high taxes because of unfair trade deals. If taxes were lowered these governments could fund essential services such as education and healthcare for their people.

Unemployment
If someone does not have a job they are less likely to be able to purchase food, medicine or shelter.

5. Give groups 10 minutes to think and make a list of connections to their causes.

6. Make a large circle. Ask one student to choose another student whose cause is related to theirs.

7. Ask one member of the group to take the ball of wool. Have that person loop the wool around a finger, then toss it someone they believe whose cause is related to theirs. Each person, in turn, should catch the ball of wool, loop it around a finger, and then toss it to someone else. As the ball unwinds, it creates a web of interconnection. It's okay for students to get the ball of wool more than once.

8. Continue until everyone has received the ball of wool at least once and the web is nicely filled in (or you run out of wool, whichever comes first).

9. Remember to stop during the activity to discuss the range of causes.

10. Take a photo of the web and display it to highlight how interlinked the causes and consequences are.

Links with SDG 1 and other SDGs

Poverty is one of the central pillars in the transformative promise of the 2030 Agenda: leave no one behind. Ending poverty in all forms and everywhere is the first Sustainable Development Goal. Not only is the elimination of poverty important in its own right, it is fundamental for the success of other Goals, especially SDG 2 Zero hunger, SDG 3 Good Health and Well-being, SDG 4 Quality Education and SDG 6 Clean water and Sanitation. Furthermore, poverty poses as a central barrier to the implementation of all SDGs in the Global South (Filho et al., 2021). Figure 4.2 illustrates some of the links between SDG 1 and other goals. Links with SDG 8, 9, 10 and 13 are discussed in more detail.

Causes of poverty: decent work and economic growth (SDG 8)
(discussed in chapter 11)

Some major emerging economies have enjoyed relatively strong economic growth and diversification, while others have fallen further behind. Many regions underperform on measures of inclusive and sustainable economic growth. Despite much progress, not all sections of the workforce are enjoying decent well paid employment. Unemployment and underemployment levels in some regions continue to accentuate poverty levels. Moreover, poverty forces some groups including women and children into low paid exploitative and in some cases dangerous employment.

Causes of poverty: industry, innovation and infrastructure (SDG 9)
(discussed in chapter 12)

Industrialisation, including mining, manufacturing and construction are important drivers of employment growth and poverty reduction. While it is generally recognised that industrialisation can potentially be a powerful force for employment generation and poverty reduction, the magnitude of the employment and poverty impact may differ by stage of economic development. Take China, for example. Over the past 70-plus years, China has transformed from an economically challenged country into the world's second largest

SDG 16
Peace, justice and strong institutions

One of the effects of living in poverty is that one's voice is of little significance. It is rarely heard by those in power and it does not have much influence in the political or social systems of a society. And where people are poor, there is often a need for legislative protection from those who would exploit and abuse the vulnerable. Hence the importance of just institutions in a society that are available to all.

SDG 2
Zero hunger

Many in the world cannot afford to pay for food to feed their families and this contributes to hunger and malnutrition throughout the world, especially in the Global South. But more than that, being poor impacts on one's ability to produce food for one's family or for the market.

SDG 1
No Poverty

SDG 4
Quality Education

A good education is an essential dimension to reducing the reality and impact of poverty. However, where there is poverty, there can be an absence of schools, teachers and books. And even when these things are available, it can be difficult for people to participate in school, perhaps there is no transport system to the school or children need to work to survive and education is seen as something that will have to wait.

SDG 10
Reduced inequality
The reality of poverty perpetuates and fosters inequality, both at an individual and national level. Without financial, educational, social, political and cultural resources, it is very difficult to participate meaningfully and equally in a society with others who have access to such resources. Inequality in a society can lead to a 'culture of disparagement' towards those who are poor among those who are secure and safe.

SDG 13
Climate action

The effect of climate crisis is felt most acutely by those who are poor and unprotected from the impact of these events. Wildfires, droughts, hurricanes and floods all exacerbate the experience of living with very little resources and on the margins of society.

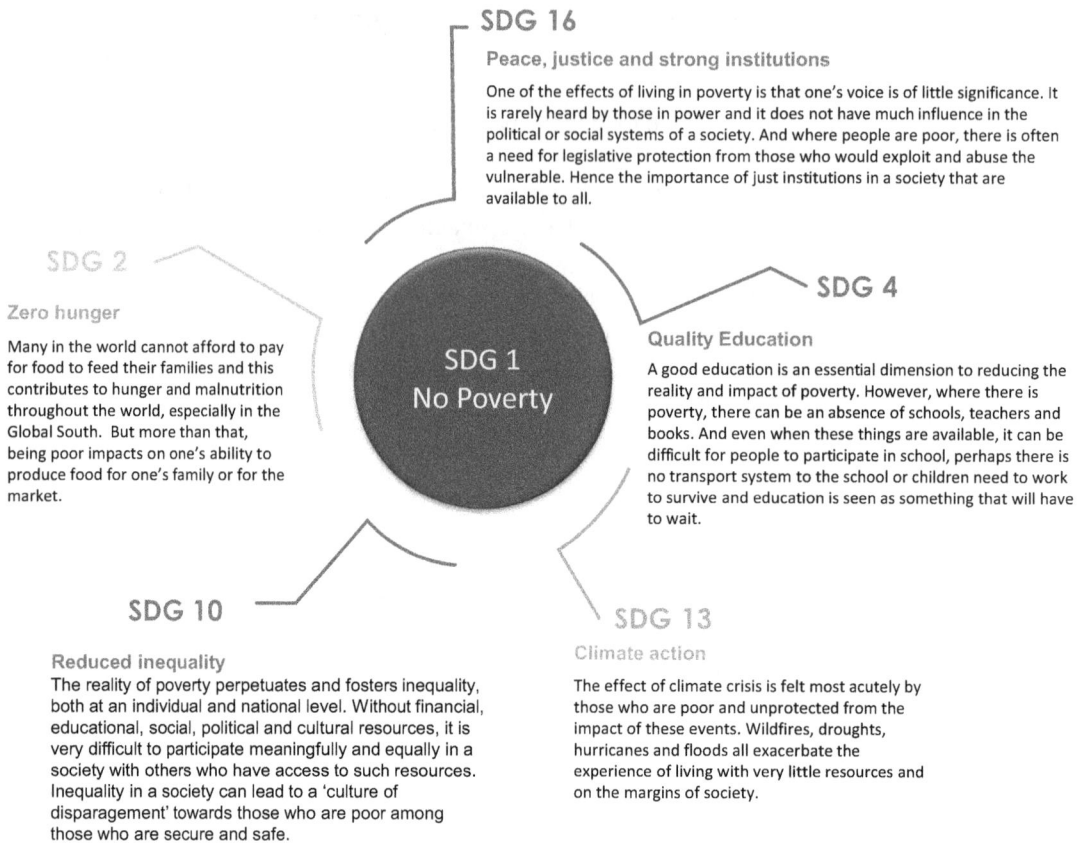

Figure 4.2 Links between SDG 1 and other SDGs.

economy. Political priorities and economic decisions were successful in moving more than 700 million rural people out of poverty (Shu, 2022). China's poverty alleviation programmes have been highly effective in combating poverty. Three defining features of China's poverty reduction include targeted support, effective governance and broad-based economic transformation (World Bank et al., 2022). Ultimately, poverty reduction is promoted as a national strategy inspired by the anti-poverty theory of the Communist Party of China's leadership. While industrialisation which is poorly managed and built upon systemic inequality and prejudice can exacerbate poverty in certain circumstances, the experience from China illustrates the direct link between industrialisation and poverty eradication.

Causes of poverty: inequality (SDG 10) (discussed in chapter 13)

Our world is deeply divided. Billionaire wealth has seen its biggest increase ever. Global economic structures perpetuate inequality. While many may disagree about economic policy, there is wide agreement that inequality between countries and within societies is not a good thing. Some of the key sources of growing inequality around the world are: the

Table 4.10 Juxtaposing inequalities (Oxfam, 2019)

Juxtaposing inequalities (Oxfam, 2019)

Mukesh Ambani ranks 19th in the Forbes 2018 billionaire list and is the richest Indian. His residence in Mumbai, a towering 570-foot building, is worth $1bn and is the most expensive private house in the world.

Pratima, who lives in a slum in Patna, eastern India, lost both her twins due to delays and scarce resources in her nearest clinic. Poor women like Pratima have to give birth without proper maternal healthcare, leaving them vulnerable to complications, neglect and stillbirth as a result.

Jeff Bezos, the founder of Amazon, is one of the richest men in the world, with a fortune of $112bn on the 2018 Forbes list. Just 1% of his total wealth is the equivalent of almost the whole health budget of Ethiopia, a country of 105 million people.

Zay is a shrimp processing worker in Thailand. The shrimp Zay peels is supplied to large retailers like Whole Foods supermarkets, now owned by parent company, Amazon. At the end of a shift, the exhaustion Zay feels after peeling shrimp for 12 or 13 hours can leave him almost immobile. "They are using the workers," says Zay. Zay is lucky if he earns more than $15 in a day.

lack of access to good primary and secondary education in many countries; a lack of public health care, like chronic disease that exacerbate income gaps; and social inequalities such as gender discrimination. The average income of people living in North America is 16 times higher than that of people in sub-Saharan Africa. In 2018, 26 people owned the same wealth as the 3.8 billion people who make up the poorest half of humanity, down from 43 people the year before (Oxfam, 2022: 5). The World Bank found that it is women who are among the poorest people in the world, especially during their reproductive years, due to the level of unpaid care work that they are expected to do. The World Inequality Report (2018) showed that between 1980 and 2016 the poorest 50% of humanity only captured 12 cents in every dollar of global income growth. By contrast, the top 1% captured 27 cents of every dollar. In any given day in 2018, 262 million children were not allowed to go to school and almost 10,000 people died because they could not access healthcare. According to Oxfam, the lesson is clear: 'to beat poverty, we must fight inequality' (Oxfam, 2019: 10). This inequality is illustrated well in the juxtapositioning of the very wealthy and the very poor in Table 4.10.

Causes of poverty: climate change (SDG 13) (discussed in chapter 16)

Along with inequality, climate change has a disproportionate effect on those living in poverty. Many of these families rely on agriculture and natural resources to survive. The increased frequency and intensity of events like hurricanes, wildfires and droughts impact on those depending on the land and the sea for survival. Over the past 40 years, almost 33 % of the world's arable land has been lost to erosion or pollution (Grantham Centre, 2015).

> In 2019, 396 [natural disaster] events – more than the annual average over the previous decade – affect 95 million people globally and caused £74 billion in economic losses. These damages can be nearly impossible for a family living in poverty to overcome.
>
> (MercyCorps, nd)

But more gradual changes, such as raising temperatures and lessening of rainfall also take their toll on people and their ability to survive. Those in the Global South are worst affected by droughts. Mercy Corps point out that

> Between 2008 and 2018, more than 80 percent of drought damage was absorbed by agriculture in low – and lower-middle-income countries, and the crop and livestock losses cause by all natural disasters in these countries during the same timeframe equated to enough calories to feed 7 million people per year.
>
> (Mercy Corps, nd)

As these situations grow more acute, families can be forced to leave their homes and even migrate to other countries – compounding their vulnerability and insecurity.

Addressing poverty through education: SDG 4 (discussed in chapter 7).

While the achievement of all SDG goals will cumulatively help to alleviate poverty, the role of education is especially important. In her memoir Educated (2018), American author Tara Westover recounts overcoming her survivalist Mormon family in order to go to college, and emphasizes the importance of education in enlarging her world. O' Sullivan's memoir discussed earlier in the chapter is also about the power of teachers and the transformative power of education. O' Sullivan (2023:280-281) challenges all educational institutions to do more to be inclusive of struggling students, to strive to promote diversity in schools as follows:

> Although the 'same' opportunities are open to people of all backgrounds, we live in a system where those coming from stable, secure childhoods do well and there is no allowance for the struggle of those who don't. We need equity in education, not equality. If someone can't see straight because the world is falling in around them, we need to raise them up to clearer skies...and the truth is, we are losing some brilliant minds in the trenches of poverty.

One of the most striking points made by O'Sullivan is that every single teacher can make a monumental difference in the life of a child and that quality education is crucial for breaking down barriers which keep people locked in poverty.

Conclusion

Eradicating extreme poverty for all people everywhere by 2030 is a pivotal goal of the 2030 Agenda for Sustainable Development. This chapter outlins the reality of extreme and relative poverty. It offers data for both and describes the destructive impact of poverty on the person. It seeks to bring a holistic approach to this issue. If we want our students to care about reducing poverty and act on it, then we need to do more than appeal to their heads and offer them information. While this is important, it will not be enough. We need to engage their imaginations and their hearts and find ways to ignite their hope, stir their empathy and help them towards action. We need to build on opportunities for them to link and connect with the lived experience of others who are poor, to reduce the distance between 'them' and 'us'. In this way, we move towards a world that is characterised by 'all of us together' – where there is a growing sense of a shared and common humanity.

Resources

An extensive list of resources, videos and case studies for SDG 1 is included in the SDG padlet accompanying this book: https://padlet.com/annedolan/o6rds38ylfy6a28h

Concern:	Primary https://www.concern.net/schools-and-youth/primary-education-programmes
	Secondary https://www.concern.net/schools-and-youth/secondary-education-programmes
Trócaire:	Primary https://www.trocaire.org/our-work/educate/peaceandjustice/primary/
	Secondary https://www.trocaire.org/our-work/educate/peaceandjustice/postprimary/
Development Education.ie	www.developmenteducation.ie
World Poverty Map	https://worldpoverty.io/map

Key dates

- **October 16th:** World Food Day
- **October 17th:** World Poverty Day

Children's literature (SDG 1)

(Picture Books)

Boelts, M. and Jones, N. Z. (illus) (2009) *Those Shoes* Logan, Turtleback Books.
Boelts, M. and Jones, N. Z. (illus) (2018) *A Bike Like Sergio's* Candlewick.
Bowen, J., Jenkins, G. and Kelley, G. (illus) (2015) *Bob to the Rescue* Red Fox Picture Books.
Brandt, L. and Vogel, V. (illus) (2014) *Maddi's Fridge* Brooklyn, Flashlight Press.
Bunting, E. and Castillo, L. (illus) (2015) *Yard Sale,* Candlewick Press.
Bunting, E. and Himler, R. (illus) (2012) *Fly Away Home Boston,* Houghton Mifflin Harcourt.
Burgos, H. E. and D'Alessandro, G. (illus) (2021) *The Cot in the Living Room* Kokila.
Campbell, M. and Luyken, C. (2018) *Arian Simcox Does NOT Have a Horse* Dial Books.
Christopher, L. and Tudor, N. (illus) (2023) *The Queen on Our Corner* Latana Publishing Ltd.
De la Peña, M. and Robinson, C. (illus) (2015) *Last Stop on Market Street* G. P. Putnam's Sons Books for Young Reader Second Story Press.
Footman Smothers, E. and Holyfield, J. (illus) (2003) *The Hard-Times* Jar Farrar, Straus and Giroux.
Fullerton, A. (2019) *Community Soup* Ontario, Pajama Press.
Gestalten, L., Wilkinson, R. and Kalorkoti, E. (illus) (2019) *Garbage Dog* Die Gestalten Verlag.
Gunti, E. and Meza, E. (illus) (2019) *A Place to Stay: A Shelter Story* Barefoot Books.
Gunning, M. and Pedlar, E. (illus) (2013) *A Shelter in Our Car* Children's Book Press.
Heine, T. and Gueyfier, J. (illus) (2014) *Chandra's Magic Light: A Story in Nepal* Barefoot Books.
Hood, S. and Wern Compart, S. (illus) (2018) *Ada's Violin: The Story of the Recycled Orchestra of Paraguay* Simon & Schuster Books for Young Readers.
Huddy, D. and Sutton, E. (illus) (2017) *The Christmas Eve Tree* Walker Books.
Javaherbin, M. and Alarcão, R. (illus) (2014) *Football Star* Walker Books.
Lee Stone, T. (2015) *The House that Jane Built: A Story About Jane Addams* Henry Holt & Company.
Milner, K. (2019) *It's a No Money Day* Barrington Stoke.
McBrier, P. (2004) *Beatrice's Goat* Aladdin Paperbacks.
McDonnell, C. and Tentler-trylov, V. (illus) (2022) *Sanctuary: Kip Tiernan and Rosie's Place, the Nation's First Shelter for Women* Candlewick Press.
O Brien, S. and Rogers, S. (2019) *How will Santa find us?* Gill Books.

O'Neill, D. and Magro, B. (illus) (2021) *Saturday at the Food Pantry* Albert Whitman & Company.
Parton, D. and Boynton-Hughes, B. (illus) (2016) *Coat of Many Colours*, Grosset & Dunlap.
Percival, T. (2021) *The Invisible,* Simon and Schuster.
Perkins, M. and Hogan, J. (illus) (2008) *Rickshaw Girl*, Charlesbridge Publishing.
Phi, B. and Bui, T. (illus) (2020) *A Different Pond* Oxford, Raintree.
Reeves Sturgis, B. and Linn, J. (illus) (2017) *Still a Family*: A Story about Homelessness Illinois, Albert
    Whitman & Company.
Roberts, J. (2018) *On Our Street: Our First Talk About Poverty* Orca Book Publishers.
Smith Milway and Fernandes, E. (illus) (2009) *One Hen: How One Small Loan Made a Big Difference*,
    A&C Black.
Soto, G. and Widener, T. (illus) (2002) *If the Shoe Fits* NY, Putnam Juvenile.
Spilsbury, L. and Kai, Hanane, K. (illus) (2017) *Poverty and Hunger* Wayland.
Upjohn, R. (2007) *Lily and the Paper Man* Second Story Press.
Watermeyer, S. and Williams, V. (2020) *Bernie The Chrismas Spirit* Nielsen.
Williams, V. B. (1998) *A Chair for My Mother* William Morrow.
Williams, L. E. and Orback, C. (illus) (2017) *The Can Man*, Lee and Low Books.
Yoshimi, K. Gaku, N. (Illus) and Wong, A. (Translator) (2020) *The World's Poorest President Speaks Out*
    Enchanted Lion Books.

(Chapter books 9–12 years)

Applegate, C. (2017) *Crenshaw* Macmillan.
Baptist, K.J. (2020) *Isaiah Dunn is My Hero* Bantam Dell Publishing Group
Bower, S. (2022) *The Dangerous Life of Ophelia Bottom* Pushkin Children's
Bauer, J. (2013) *Almost Home* Puffin Books.
Beauregard, Lute, R. and Valentine, L. (illus) (2020) *The Exceptional Maggie Chowder* Albert Whitman &
    Company.
Binns, B. (2022) *Courage* QuilTreeBk.
Blejwas, E. (2017) *Once you Know This* Random House Books for Young Readers.
Burg, A. E. (2015) *Serafina's Promise* Scholastic Press.
Carroll, S. (2017) *The Girl In Between* Simon and Schuster
Cruz, M. M. (2020) *Everlasting Nora* Macmillian.
Dee Ellis, A. (2018) *You May Already Be a Winner* Puffin Books.
Doherty, B. (2013) *Street Child* Harper Collins Children's Books.
Ellis, D. (2011) *No Ordinary Day* Groundwood Books Ltd.
Fox, J. (2021) *Carry Me Home* Simon & Schuster Books for Young Readers.
Gephart, D. (2020) *The Paris Project* Simon & Schuster Books for Young Readers.
Hill Long, S. (2020) *Josie Bloom and the Emergency of Life* Simon & Schuster.
Johnson, M. (2017) *Kick* Usborne Publishing Ltd.
Lewis Tyre, L. (2018) *Hope in the Holler* Nancy Paulsen Books.
Matheson, C. (2021) *Shelter* Random House Books.
Moore Fitzgerald, S. (2021) *All the Money in the World* Orion Children's Books
Munoz Ryan, P. (2002) *Esperanza Rising* Scholastic.
Ogle, R. (2021) *Free Lunch* Norton Young Readers.
Paterson, K. (2015) *The Same Stuff as Stars* Harper Collins.
Perera, A. (2011) *The Glass Collector* Penguin.
Pounder, S. (2020) *Tinsel* Bloomsbury Children's Books.
Raúf, O. and Paganelli, E. (illus) (2021) *The Great (Food) Bank Heist* Barrington Stoke.
Richard Jacobson, J. (2015) *Paper Things* Candlewick Press.
Savage Carlson, N. and Williams, G. (1989) *The Family Under the Bridge* HarperCollins.
Schmidt, G. (2013) *Okay for Now* Houghton Mifflin.
Schindler, H. (2014) *The Junction of Sunshine and Lucky* Dial Books.
Slater, K. (2014) *Smart: A Mysterious Crime, a Different Detective* Macmillan.
Sullivan, T. (2021) *Treasure of the World* Penguin Putnam Inc.
Summer, J. (2021) *Tune it Out* Atheneum Books for Young Readers.

Turner Stevenson, N. (2019) *Lizzie Flying Solo* HarperCollins.
Venkatraman, P. (2019) *The Bridge Home* Nancy Paulsen Books.
Yan Glaser, K. (2022) *A Duet for Home* Clarion Books.
Yang, K. (2019) *Front Desk* Arthur A. Levine Books.

(Chapter books 12 plus years)

Abani, C. (2014) *Graceland* St Martin's Press.
Armstrong, C. H. *Roam: Being a homeless teen is hard. Keeping it a secret is even harder.* Central Avenue Publishing.
Auxier, J. (2020*) Sweep: The Story of a Girl and her Monster* Harry N. Abrams.
Balliett, B. (2013) *Hold Fast* Scholastic Press.
Bird, J. (2023) *No Place Like Home* Feiwel & Friends.
Braden, A. (2018) *The Benefits of Being an Octopus* Sky Pony Press.
Cohn, E. (2021) *Birdie's Billions* Bloomsbury Publishing.
Cockcroft, J. (2021) *We Were Wolves* Andersen Press.
Curham, S. (2018) *Don't Stop Thinking About Tomorrow* Walker Books.
Devi, A. (2021) *Eve Out Of Her Ruins* Les Fugitives.
Doherty, B. (2009) *Street Child* Harper Collins Publishers.
Doherty, B. (2015) *Far from Home: The Sisters of Street Child* Harper Collins Publishers.
Elison, M. (2020) *Find Layla* Skyscape.
Ellis, Dee, A (2018) *You May Already Be a Winner* Puffin Books.
Faujour, Skelton, D. and Stallings, J. (2019) *Until the Sky Turns Silver* Sondiata Global Media Ltd.
Fox, J. *(2022) Carry Me Home* Simon & Schuster Books for Young Readers.
Jarman, S. and Burbridge, L. (2019) *Lela: Ashes of Childhood* Namuli-Hutchinson Books.
Haywood Leal, A. (2009) *Also Known as Harper* Henry Holt Books for Young Readers.
Landis, M. (2022) *Operation Final Notice* Dial Books.
Mauro de Vasconcelos, J. (2019) *My Sweet Orange Tree* Pushkin Children's Books.
McCormick, P. (2008) *Sold* Walker Books.
McCourt, F. (2005 *Angela's Ashes: A Memoir of a Childhood* Harper Perennial.
Mulligan, A. *Trash* Definitions.
Nielsen, S. (2018) *No Fixed Address* Andersen Press.
O'Connor, B. (2009) *How to Steal a Dog* Square Fish.
Pacton, J. (2020) *The Life and Medieval Times of Kit Sweetly,* Page Street Kids.
Padian, M. (2020) *How to Build a Heart* Algonquin Young Readers.
Pyron, B. (2013) *The Dogs of Winter* Andersen Press.
Pyron, B. (2019) *Stay* Katherine Tegen Books.
Rai, B. (2017) *The Harder They Fall* Barrington Stoke.
Reynolds Naylor, P. (2009) *Faith, Hope and Ivy* Random House.
Rhattigan, T. (2017a) *A Slice of Bread and Jam* Mirror Books.
Rhattigan, T. (2017b) *Boy Number 26* Mirror Books.
Richard Jacobson, J. (2017) *Paper Things* MA Candlewick Press.
Sarno, M. (2018) *Just Under the Clouds* Alfred A. Knopf Books for Young Readers.
Schroff, L. and Tresniowski, A. (2020) *An Invisible Thread* Simon & Schuster Books.
Sharp, C. (2018a) *The Girl in the Ragged Shawl* (Book 1) HarperCollins.
Sharp, C. (2018b) *The Winter Orphan* (Book 3) HarperCollins.
Sharp, C. (2019) *The Barefoot Child* (Book 2) HarperCollins.
Smyth, C. (2021) *Not My Problem* Andersen Press.
Stuart, D. (2020) *Shuggie Bain*, Pan Macmillan.
Sumner, J. (2020) *Tune It Out* Atheneum Books for Young Readers.
Thornburgh, B. (2019) *Ordinary Girls* HarperTeen.
Tressel, R. (2012) *The Ragged-Trousered Philanthropists* Grant Richards Ltd.
Venkatraman, P. (2021) *Born Behind Bars* Nancy Paulsen Books.
Voigt, C. (2012) *Homecoming* Atheneum Books for Young Readers.
Yan Glaser, K. (2022) *A Duet for Home* Clarion Books.

References

Andreotti, V. and de Souza, L. M. (2008) *Learning to Read the World Through Other Eyes*, Derby: Global Education, available: https://developmenteducation.ie/media/documents/Learning_to_Read_the_World_Through_Other.pdf

Beauchamp, Z. (2014) 'The world's victory over extreme poverty, in one chart', *Vox*, available: https://www.vox.com/2014/12/14/7384515/extreme-poverty-decline

Borgan Project. (nd) 'Global poverty 101', available: https://borgenproject.org/global-poverty/

Concern. (2017) *No Poverty, Educational Resource for Teachers and Educators*, available: https://developmenteducation.ie/app/uploads/2018/12/Concern-3.-No-Poverty-Resource.pdf

Concern. (2022) 'Hunger in 2022, the numbers are rising but the funding is failing', available: https://www.concern.net/news/hunger-2022-numbers-are-rising-funding-falling

Development Education.ie (nd) *Give and Take, Mostly Take?* Available: https://developmenteducation.ie/five-fifty-five-hundred/five-fifty-five-hundred-deciphered/

Government of Ireland. (2020) *Roadmap for Social Inclusion 2020-2025, Ambition, Goals, Commitments*, Dublin: Government of Ireland, available: file:///C:/Users/Daniel.OConnell/Downloads/46557_bf7011904ede4562b925f98b15c4f1b5%20(1).pdf

Grantham Centre. (2015) 'Soil loss: An unfolding global disaster – Grantham Centre briefing note', available: http://grantham.sheffield.ac.uk/soil-loss-an-unfolding-global-disaster/#:~:text=%E2%80%9CErosion%20rates%20from%20ploughed%20fields,in%20the%20last%2040%20years.

International Labour Organisation. (2020). *As Jobs Crisis Deepens, ILO Warns of Uncertain and Incomplete Labour Market Recovery*, available: https://www.ilo.org/global/about-the-ilo/newsroom/news/WCMS_749398/lang--en/index.htm

Leal Filho, W., Lovren, V. O., Will, M., Salvia, A. L. and Frankenberger, F. (2021) 'Poverty: A central barrier to the implementation of the UN Sustainable Development Goals', *Environmental Science & Policy*, 125, pp. 96-104.

Mantel, C. and Cherian, T. (2019) 'New immunization strategies: Adapting to global challenges', *Nature Public Health Emergency Collection*, available: https://www.ncbi.nlm.nih.gov/pmc/articles/PMC7079946/

Mercy Corps. (nd) 'The facts: How climate change affects people living in poverty', available: https://www.mercycorps.org/en-gb/blog/climate-change-poverty

O'Sullivan, K. (2023) *Poor: Grit, courage and life-changing value of self-belief* London: Penguin.

Oxfam. (2022) *First Crisis, Then Catastriphe*, available: https://oi-files-d8-prod.s3.eu-west-2.amazonaws.com/s3fs-public/2022-04/Oxfam%20briefing%20-%20First%20Crisis%20Then%20Catastrophe_0.pdf

Oxfam. (nd) 'News and stories', available: https://www.oxfamireland.org/blog/10-brilliant-questions-you-asked-about-oxfam%E2%80%99s-inequality-report

Rise up. (2017) *Facts about Poverty*, available: https://www.raiseup.org/blog/index.php/2017/06/24/facts-about-poverty/

Roser, M. (@MaxCRoser) (2017) Newspapers could have had the headline "Number of people in extreme poverty fell by 137,000 since yesterday", *Twitter*, 16 October 14:43, available: https://twitter.com/MaxCRoser/status/919921745464905728

Shu, D. (2022) 'China's uniquely effective approach to poverty alleviation', *Advances in Applied Sociology*, 12(6), pp. 205-218.

Social Justice Ireland. (2021) *Socio Economic Review 2021, Social Justice Matters, 2021 Guide to a Fairer Society*, Dublin: Social Justice Ireland.

Social Justice Ireland. (2021a) *Poverty Focus 2021*, Dublin: Social Justice Ireland, available: https://www.socialjustice.ie/sites/default/files/attach/publication/6489/2021-04-22-povertyfocusapril2021final.pdf?cs=true

Trócaire. (nd) *Food and Resources*, available: https://www.trocaire.org/our-work/food-resources-rights/

Trócaire. (2022) *Trócaire's Strategic Plan (2021-20250 Outlines Five Key Goal Areas*, available: https://www.trocaire.org/about/strategy/

Trócaire. (2022a) *Sierra Leone Overview*, available: https://www.trocaire.org/countries/sierra-leone/#overview

UNESCO. (2016) '263 million children and youth are out of school', available: http://uis.unesco.org/en/news/263-million-children-and-youth-are-out-school

UNESCO. (2017) *Education for Sustainable Development Goals-learning objectives* available: https://unesdoc.unesco.org/ark:/48223/pf0000247444

UNICEF. (2014) *Committing to Child Survival: A Promise Renewed*, available: file:///C:/Users/Daniel.OConnell/Downloads/ar049-progress-report-child-survival-pdf.pdf

UNCEIF. (2016) 'Nearly 385 million children living in extreme poverty, says joint World Bank Group – UNICEF study', available: https://www.unicef.org/press-releases/nearly-385-million-children-living-extreme-poverty-says-joint-world-bank-group

UNICEF. (2018) 'A child under 15 dies every five seconds around the world', Press Release, available: https://www.unicef.org/press-releases/child-under-15-dies-every-five-seconds-around-world-un-report

UNICEF. (2019) 'Poor diets damaging children's health worldwide, warns UNICEF', available: https://www.unicef.org/ghana/press-releases/poor-diets-damaging-childrens-health-worldwide-warns-unicef

UNICEF. (2020) 'Global and regional trends', available: https://data.unicef.org/topic/hivaids/global-regional-trends/

United Nations. (nd) *Goal 1: End Poverty in All its Forms Everywhere*, available: https://www.un.org/sustainabledevelopment/poverty/

United Nations Development Programme. (nd) *COVID-19 pandemic, Humanity Needs Leadership and Solidarity to Defeat the Coronavirus*, available: https://www.undp.org/coronavirus.

VPSJ. (2018) *Stories of Struggle, Experiences of Living Below the Minimum Essential Standard of Living*, Dublin: Society of St. Vincent de Paul.

The World Bank. (2019) 'Half of the world's poor live in just 5 countries', available: https://blogs.worldbank.org/opendata/half-world-s-poor-live-just-5-countries

The World Bank. (2000) *World Development Report, Attacking Poverty, 2000/2001*, London: Oxford University Press.

The World Bank. (2020) *Poverty and Shared Prosperity 2020, Reversals of Fortune*, available: https://www.worldbank.org/en/publication/poverty-and-shared-prosperity

The World Bank. (2020a) '1 in 6 children lives in extreme poverty, World Bank-UNICEF analysis shows', available: https://www.worldbank.org/en/news/press-release/2020/10/20/1-in-6-children-lives-in-extreme-poverty-world-bank-unicef-analysis-shows

The World Bank. (2021) 'Poverty overview', available: https://www.worldbank.org/en/topic/poverty/overview

The World Bank. (2023) 'Measuring poverty', available: https://www.worldbank.org/en/topic/measuring-poverty [accessed 6th March 2024].

The World Bank, China's Ministry of Finance and the Development Research Centre (DFC) of the State Council. (2022) Four Decades of poverty reduction in China Drivers, Insights for the World and the Way Ahead available: https://thedocs.worldbank.org/en/doc/bdadc16a4f5c1c88a839c0f905cde802-0070012022/original/Poverty-Synthesis-Report-final.pdf

Westover, T. (2018) *Educated* London: Windmill Books.

World Health Organisation. (2019) 'World hunger is still not going down after three years and obesity is still growing – UN report', available: https://www.who.int/news/item/15-07-2019-world-hunger-is-still-not-going-down-after-three-years-and-obesity-is-still-growing-un-report

World Health Organisation. (2019a) 'Drinking water', available: https://www.who.int/news-room/fact-sheets/detail/drinking-water

World Health Organisation. (2020) 'Newborns: Improving survival and well-being', available: https://www.who.int/news-room/fact-sheets/detail/newborns-reducing-mortality

5 Food for thought
Zero Hunger (SDG 2)

Patricia Kieran and Anne M. Dolan

Introduction

Ending world hunger is one of the greatest challenges of our times. The year 2022 marked an unprecedented year for a global food crisis due to conflict, Covid-19, the climate crisis and rising costs of food. According to the United Nation's State of Food Security and Nutrition Report (2022) up to 828 million people did not have enough food and 50 million people faced emergency levels of hunger. Almost 3.1 billion people could not afford a healthy diet in 2020. International targets for the reduction of hunger have largely failed, despite food production having grown faster than world population. Famine is not caused by a shortage of food, as there is more than enough food to feed every citizen on Earth. Our current food system is failing farmers, consumers and the environment. It is important to note that starvation is not inevitable. Famine and acute food insecurity are caused or exacerbated by human actions including political (in) actions, opportunistic investments, war, unequal distribution of resources, violation of human rights and simple indifference.

SDG 2 emphasises that access to a nutritious secure supply of food is a fundamental biological necessity and a universal human right. The term Zero Hunger signals emphatically that it is unacceptable for any human to be wasted, undernourished, malnourished or to die of hunger. SDG 2 Zero Hunger, represents a united global call to respond strategically to the enormous challenge of global hunger through sustainable food production, distribution and consumption. This chapter provides an overview of the key causes, manifestations, consequences and potential solutions to global hunger. It brings together a collection of educational ideas and resources based on SDG 2, so that educators can explore the complex causes, teach about the devastating effects and educate for transformative and collaborative action to support the elimination of hunger. These experientially based educational methodologies are designed to foster empathy, critical thinking and transformative action to end hunger.

Food security

Following the Russian attack on Ukraine, consequences for food security and famine were evident. As Russia and Ukraine together account for one third of global wheat exports, the war led to an acute wheat shortage in many dependent countries. Notwithstanding the consequences of this war, the global food crisis is a long-standing issue. International agencies have responded through increased agricultural production, financial support and the

DOI: 10.4324/9781003232001-8

provision of emergency food supplies. However, for decades there has been no systematic globally coordinated response to the food crisis and food security.

In the 1996 Rome Declaration on World Food Security, food security is defined as:

> Food that is available at all times, to which all persons have means of access, that is nutritionally adequate in terms of quantity, quality and variety, and is acceptable within the given culture (Madeley, 2002). Availability, access and affordability are all elements of food security, complex issues that encompass a wide range of interrelated economic, social and political factors.
>
> (Clover, 2003)

While war in Ukraine did contribute to a hike in the price of wheat and energy, the increase in global food prices was not simply an issue of supply and demand. The cost of energy, the growth of agrofuels, and underinvestment in sustainable agriculture together with climate change are all contributing factors. However, price increases are driven to a significant extent by excessive and insufficiently regulated speculation. Large institutional investors such as hedge funds, pension funds and investment banks, continue to enter food futures markets on a massive scale. While these investors are generally unconcerned with agricultural market fundamentals, their investment in the food futures markets was made possible because of deregulation in important commodity derivatives markets beginning in 2000 (De Schutter, 2010).

The injustice of hunger and famine

Although enough food is produced to feed everyone on this planet, the goal of a world with Zero Hunger, as set out in the 2030 Agenda for Sustainable Development and specifically in SGD 2, remains hugely challenging due to war, climate change, natural disasters and structural poverty and inequality. At the time of writing, regions in the Horn of Africa are facing unprecedented levels of famine. Five countries are experiencing catastrophic levels of hunger: Ethiopia, Somalia, South Sudan, Yemen and Afghanistan. Furthermore, war in Sudan is increasing political instability and causing migration as people flee the conflict to surrounding countries some of which are already experiencing food instability. Following four failed rainy seasons over a two-year period, the Horn of Africa is experiencing widespread crop failure and drought. With the native crops destroyed and spiralling fuel and food prices, people in Ethiopia, Kenya and Somalia can no longer afford the basic foodstuffs they need to survive.

The war in Ukraine has also been detrimental to the lives of families in the region. Somalia alone imports 92% of its wheat from Russia and Ukraine but supply lines have been destabilised due to war. In 2023, the Israeli military attack on Hamas used access to food and water as a weapon of war. During the offensive, the 2.3 million residents of Gaza had serious daily challenges in accessing food and water,

While the year 2022 has seen record breaking food prices across much of the world not everyone was equally affected. Corporations and the billionaire dynasties who control so much of our food system saw their profits soar. Oxfam's (2022) report *Profiting from Pain* states that billionaires involved in the food and agribusiness sector have seen their collective wealth increase by $382bn (45%) during the Covid 19 pandemic. 62 new food billionaires were created during the pandemic. This obscene inequality and injustice needs to be addressed as a contributing factor to world hunger.

Food production, consumption and waste: key issues in sustainability

Ensuring everyone in the world has access to a nutritious diet in a sustainable way is one of the greatest challenges we face. While there is enough capacity on this planet to feed everyone, the current system of food production is inefficient. For every 100 calories of crops fed to animals, we get 40 calories in the form of milk, 12 calories of chicken, and just 3 calories of beef. Arable crops, some of which are fed to farm animals, occupy 12% of the planet's land surface. But far more land (28%) is used for grazing, for pasture-fed meat and milk. Yet, across this vast area, farm animals that are entirely pasture-fed produce just 1% of the world's protein (Monbiot, 2022).

The global food system is the primary driver of biodiversity loss, causing deforestation, emptying our oceans and polluting waterways, leading to loss of eco-systems, insect collapse, and loss of plant and animal species. Industrial-scale monoculture farming is responsible for severe land and soil degradation. Agricultural land-use and food production account for around one third of global anthropogenic (human-caused) greenhouse gas emissions (GHGs). In the meantime, about one third of food that is produced globally is wasted, while over 800 million people go hungry. According to a report published in the Guardian (Butler:2023), UK shoppers spent £13.7bn on groceries in the run-up to Christmas. In anticipation of this spending splurge, major chains offered discounted items (bags of traditional vegetables were on sale for as little as 15p) to lure consumers into their stores

Our food system is broken. Sustainable solutions include a dramatic reduction in reliance on fossil-fuel fertilisers, chemical pesticides and herbicides through regenerative or agroecological practices. More space needs to be given to nature. We need to introduce more diversity and biodiversity on farms and transition away from diets high in animal products, which are the most resource-intensive and polluting, towards diets richer in plants. As consumers we need to think about what we are consuming, how much we are wasting and take immediate steps to prevent food waste in our homes. The issue of personal, community based and corporate food loss and waste needs to be addressed with immediate effect.

Introducing SDG 2 in the classroom

Teachers can raise students' awareness about the fundamental primacy of food and water as universal human rights central for sustaining human life. Three units for teaching SDG 2 focus on food, hunger and Zero Hunger (see Figure 5.1). These units foster respect, empathy, hope and advocacy by:

- Focusing on positive, healthy, sustainable food choices and production
- Analysing why hunger, wasting and malnutrition persist as cyclical realities for 10% of the world's population
- Challenging and transforming global injustice through fostering individual and communal action to eliminate the preventable reality of global hunger.

In all three units, it is understood that there are many different types of hunger and ways in which it is experienced in classrooms and communities across the globe. Hunger is not a quick-fix topic and teachers will be aware that it is also a potentially disturbing and deeply shocking topic.

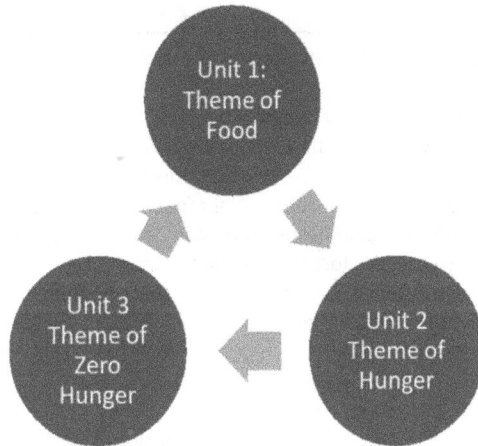

Figure 5.1 Three Units for Teaching SDG 2.

Education about Zero Hunger touches on disturbing issues e.g.

- Undernourishment & related illnesses
- Climate change
- Migration & food insecurity
- Natural disasters
- War
- Global inequality
- Maternal & child mortality
- Famine.

Food and hunger are highly charged, emotional, trigger-topics in a world where obesity, fat-shaming and body dysmorphia are not uncommon. Furthermore, there is a causal link between malnourishment and obesity. Indeed, communities and families with a history of food insecurity and malnourishment are at higher risk of obesity. According to the World Health Organisation's European Regional Obesity Study (2022) overweight (including obesity) is a common problem affecting 4.4 million children under five years of age, representing 7.9% of all children in this age group. Moreover, overweight and obesity affect almost 60% of adults in Europe.

In exploring global hunger, the learning objectives (see Table 5.2) of three units of learning deliberately focus on empathy, hope and advocacy and refrain from apportioning shame or blame and do not focus on body image. Their positive focus is on celebrating food and living healthy, sustainable, just lives where people's human rights are respected. Teachers can select and adapt materials appropriate to their unique learning contexts and students' individual learning needs. Teachers can extend their teaching about food and hunger by revising key terminology (Table 5.1) and incorporating some of the children's literature suggested at the end of the chapter.

Education, based on the four Hs of head (cognitive learning), heart (empathy and love), hands (advocacy and action) and hope has a vital role to play in eradicating hunger through increasing students' understanding, skills and attitudes (Table 5.2).

Table 5.1 Key terms associated with SDG 2

Anorexia nervosa an eating disorder characterised by markedly reduced appetite or total aversion to food.

Body dysmorphic disorder (BDD), or body dysmorphia, is a mental health condition where a person spends a lot of time worrying about flaws in their appearance.

Entomophagy refers to the consumption of insects as a source of nutrition by humans.

Famine is severe and prolonged hunger in a substantial proportion of the population of a region or country, resulting in widespread and acute malnutrition and death by starvation and disease.

Food security means having access to affordable, nutritious food.

Hunger is experienced when a person cannot obtain an adequate amount of food, even if the shortage is not prolonged enough to cause health problems.

Malnourishment is when a diet contains too much of the wrong types of food (poor nutrition) and too little of the right nutritious food (undernutrition) for a healthy life.

Obesity occurs when a person has too much body fat.

A **pescatarian** is a person who does not eat red meat or poultry, but does eat fish and other seafood.

Stunting is when a child has a low height for his/her age. A stunted child does not fully develop and stunting reflects chronic undernutrition during the most critical periods of growth and development in early life. Stunting is an important marker of childhood malnutrition.

Undernourishment means not having enough food to live a healthy life and to meet one's energy needs.

A **vegan diet** excludes all meat and animal products (meat, poultry, fish, seafood, dairy and eggs).

A **vegetarian diet** excludes meat, poultry, fish and seafood.

Wasting is a physical condition where the body becomes weaker as a result of reduced muscle mass and it leads to increased risk of death due to illness.

Table 5.2 Learning objectives for SDG 2 (adapted from UNESCO, 2017: 14)

Cognitive learning objectives Teaching *about* the goals: developing respect and understanding	1	The learner knows about the amount and distribution of hunger and malnutrition locally, nationally and globally, currently as well as historically.
	2	The learner knows the main drivers and root causes for hunger at the individual, local, national and global level.
	3	The learner understands the need for sustainable agriculture to combat hunger and malnutrition worldwide and knows about other strategies to combat hunger, malnutrition and poor diets.
Socio-emotional learning objectives Teaching *for* the goals enhancing empathy and love	1	The learner is able to collaborate with others to encourage and to empower them to combat hunger and to promote sustainable agriculture and improved nutrition.
	2	The learner is able to create a vision for a world without hunger and malnutrition.
	3	The learner is able to feel empathy, responsibility and solidarity for and with people suffering from hunger and malnutrition.
Behavioural learning objectives Teaching *through* the goals Promoting advocacy and activism	1	The learner is able to evaluate and implement actions personally and locally to combat hunger and to promote sustainable agriculture.
	2	The learner is able to take on critically their role as an active global citizen in the challenge of combating hunger.
	3	The learner is able to change their production and consumption practices in order to contribute to the combat against hunger and the promotion of sustainable agriculture.

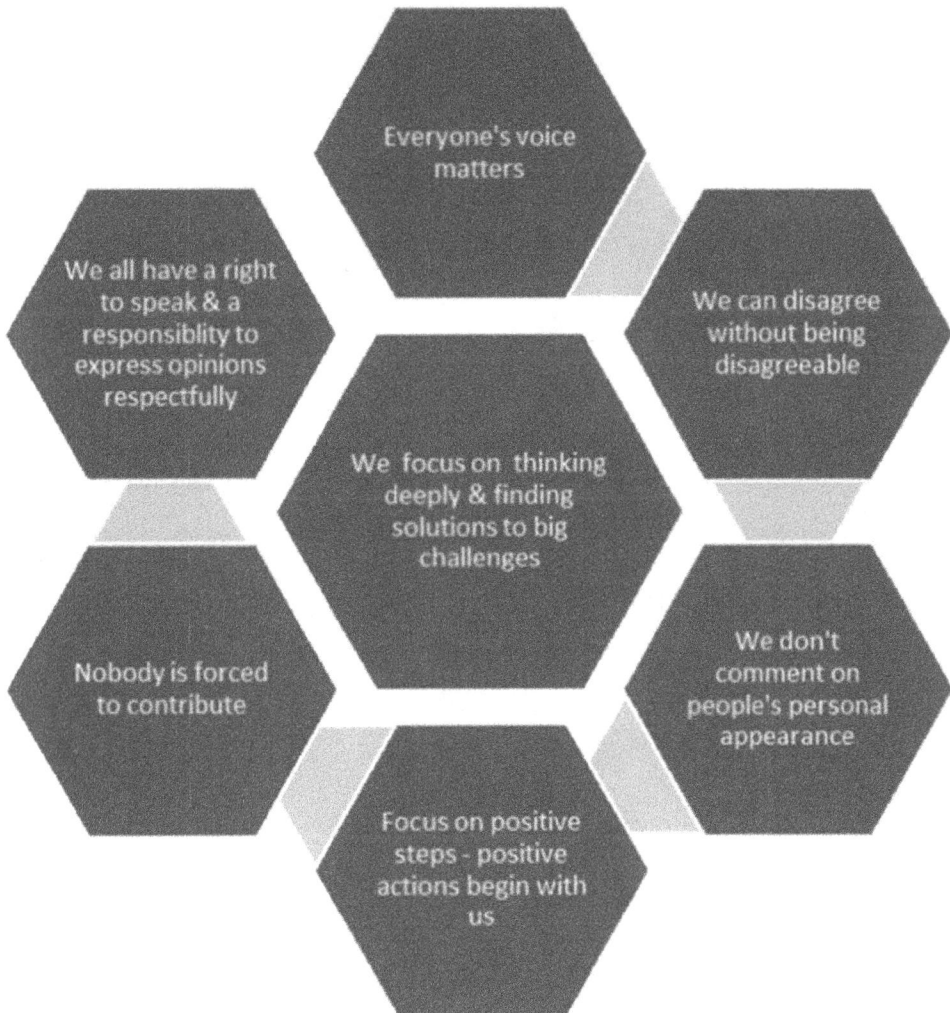

Figure 5.2 Sample Agreed Rules.

To create a safe, dialogical, positive classroom space for these three units, it is key to work collaboratively with students to draw up some agreed ground rules at the outset (see Figure 5.2).

Unit 1: Food

The unit begins with a celebration of the universal necessity of food as a healthy, enjoyable and vital human right. It focuses on students' diverse understandings and experiences of food. It overviews different types of food in the food pyramid, students' own food stories and the nutrients and health benefits of food. Only when students have explored this unit are they ready to progress to Unit 2 on Hunger as the absence of nutritious food.

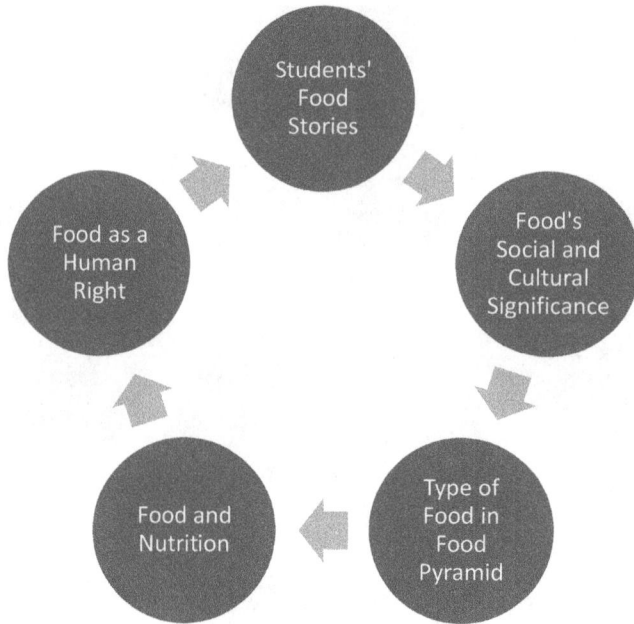

Figure 5.3 Potential Themes for Exploring the Concept of Food.

Objectives:

- Celebrate food as a vital and enjoyable ingredient in human life
- Identify key nutritional and health benefits of food
- Understand the significance of healthy food choices
- Appreciate the cultural, ethnic, religious and social significance of food
- Understand food as a human right.

Teachers might decide to select one or more food themes (see Figure 5.3).

Food's social significance

Food is much more than a physiological matter and has deep cultural, ethnic and religious significance in human communities where 'every mouthful, every meal can tell us something about ourselves and about our place in the world' (Bell & Valentine, 1997: 3). It can be fascinating to invite students to think and talk about the significance of food in their own lives and to listen to their peers' food stories. While creating a safe space for a variety of diets, tastes and attitudes in this discussion, teachers might sensitively iterate that to be different is to be normal and to be normal is to be different. Food manifests and expresses this difference as it has deep cultural significance by connecting people who often eat in a socially organised fashion involving specific food rituals (see Figure 5.4).

Abstaining from or eating certain foodstuffs to celebrate festivals (e.g. Chinese New Year, Ramadan, Christmas) or blowing out candles on a birthday cake, are very simple food rituals communicating deep meaning to particular social groups at particular moments in time. Individual and familial food stories and recipes can also be richly significant identity markers

Figure 5.4 The Way Food Is Eaten Is Often Part of a Complex Cultural Ritual Source: https://pixabay.com/photos/community-lunch-himachali-dham-4818317/

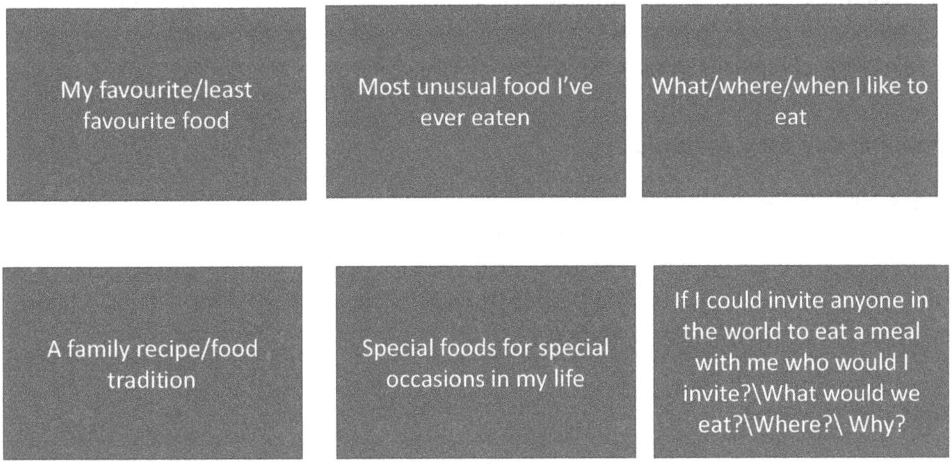

My favourite/least favourite food	Most unusual food I've ever eaten	What/where/when I like to eat
A family recipe/food tradition	Special foods for special occasions in my life	If I could invite anyone in the world to eat a meal with me who would I invite?\What would we eat?\Where?\ Why?

Figure 5.5 Listening to Each Other's Food Narratives.

and students benefit enormously from strategies that facilitate listening to each other's food narratives (see Figure 5.5). A food that one student loves may be detested by another. Vegetarian, vegan, pescatarian and entomophagy food choices may be practiced for a variety of cultural, religious, medical or ethical reasons among others. As an interculturally rich theme, the topic of food shows that despite students having vastly different tastes, preferences and traditions, they are all united in their need for food for survival.

Students' food stories

Building on Young People's Trust for the Environment lesson plans, packs and materials (Yip-pittee, Issue 2) students might use factsheets to investigate their favourite meals and discover what plants/animals/ingredients they contain. This discussion on students' favourite foods can expand from paired to group to whole-class discussion and interdisciplinary activities.

- **Drama** – Plan a family birthday party for a vegetarian family member
- **Geography** – Journey from farm to fork using media clips from the National Geographic's Food Education website
- **History** – Make a food timeline with famous foods from the past/food quizzes bringing the history of food to life e.g. bread and the French revolution/potatoes and the Irish famine.
- **Literature** – Explore stories based on food such as Roald Dahl's *Revolting Recipes* or *Charlie and the Chocolate Factory* or the short story *Janey Mary* by James Plunkett
- **Maths** – Vote and make graphs representing students' favourite/least favourite foods
- **Media** – Write a review of clips from the Seoul International Food Film Festival (SIFFF) or classic food films like Babette's Feast/Harry Potter's communal meals at Hogwarts
- **Oral language** – Discuss menus from around the world/a meal in a restaurant/buying local produce at a farmer's market
- **RE** – Learn about food rituals in religious traditions e.g. Passover/Harvest Festival/Last Supper/Eid
- **Science** – Explore where nutrients come from and how they contribute to good health – make a simple map or model of the human digestive system
- **Visual art** – Experiment with vegetable prints or still life inspired by Filippo Tommaso Marinetti's idea of food as art or Vincent Van Gogh's food paintings/Wayne Thiebaud's paintings of buns and cakes.

Shopping bag food pyramid

Bring a shopping bag into class containing a range of everyday food items. Students make their own food pyramid and classify the food items as carbohydrates, fats, proteins, vitamins, minerals and record/locate them on their food pyramid. Discuss the characteristic of the different types of food and watch the Safe Food Healthy Choices Food Pyramid video (https://www.youtube.com/watch?v=sTvJi3ndVOE).

What's in season?

Noting the time of year when the lesson takes place, invite students to identify locally grown and seasonal food produce (see Figure 5.6) as well as different ways of preparing/cooking/eating it. Identify the pros/cons of buying locally grown/organic produce at Farmers' markets as opposed to mass-produced international food products from a multinational supermarket chain.

Cooking is fun

Students contribute a favourite recipe for a class cookbook (see the example from Kinsale Community College in chapter 20). Identify the types of foods that are most popular. Reflect

Figure 5.6 Seasonal Produce at a Food Market. Source: https://pixabay.com/photos/market-vegetables-market-stall-3860952/

on the varieties of food in the cookbook (e.g. local, national, ethnic, religious, seasonal, vegetarian), noting their nutritional content and locating them on the food pyramid. Visit educational cooking websites and cook selected nutritious recipes with locally sourced ingredients (paying attention to safety and food hygiene). Research and explore different food traditions in the local community and from around the world that influence how and what students eat every day. Drawing on UNESCO's food culture resources (https://wander-lush.org/food-culture-unesco/) students might note different mealtime preparations and postures, the utensils people may or may not use, the incredibly diverse rituals around serving and receiving food, the places and times people eat and the various types of foods prepared for different occasions. The religious significance of food is explored by National Geographic in its resources on culture, food and ritual.

Food as a human right

A simple student-friendly way of exploring food as a human right involves examining the UN's (2002) book *For Every Child* in video form. Since food is essential for life, it is important to elicit why access to food is a 'universal' right that governments and states must uphold. Explore the right to good nutrition in the UN Charter and the Rights of the Child and what this might mean. Possible student activities might include writing letters to the UN Special Rapporteur on the right to food, stating whether they think this right is being upheld in their country and in other countries around the world.

Unit 2: Hunger

Hunger can be defined as a condition arising from insufficient access to food over a period of time to meet basic nutritional needs. The World Health Organisation (WHO) has identified hunger as the greatest threat to global health in a world where all humans have a right to an adequate supply of nutritious, safe, and culturally appropriate food. Hunger is a complex global challenge. It affects people of all ages in all countries and communities. It is present in the Global North and South, in affluent as well as poor communities, in urban as well as rural areas. In many countries after the outbreak of Covid-19, following mass unemployment, disrupted food supply, and lockdown, many families had severely reduced and insecure access to food. The World Food Programme (WFP, n.d.) report states that one in nine people do not get enough to eat each day and this is linked to extreme poverty, defined by the World Bank as living on $2.15 per person per day (World Bank, 2023). Poor people are often involved in a cycle of hunger as they spend between sixty and eighty per cent of their total income on food. Parents often skip meals while being forced to prioritise their children's education over food. Hunger can be both cyclical and intergenerational, and it can trap families into poverty. For instance, if mothers are undernourished, their children have less chance of living healthy lives. This point is key since globally, maternal and child undernutrition contributes to 45% of deaths in children under five.

Facts and figures -the global context

The Global Hunger Index (GHI) measures hunger in the world through the four main indicators of: (1) undernourishment in the whole population; (2) childhood wasting; (3) childhood stunting and (4) child mortality. Students might explore the World Map of Hunger and identify regions where people are more likely to experience hunger. Drawing on the National Agriculture in the Classroom Teacher Resources (https://agclassroom.org//), discussion might focus on why this is so and the causal factors behind the wealth and food disparity between countries through exploring the link between poverty and hunger. Students might begin to appreciate the connection between hunger and the percentage of the population living in extreme poverty. Using the picturebook *If the world were a hundred people* (McCann and Cushley, 2022), students can discuss global statistics in an accessible fashion.

The 'Jellybean Game' is a highly effective strategy to embody the impact of wealth and food disparity in a classroom setting. To play the game the teacher divides one quarter of the class into a Northerners group while three quarters of the students become Southerners. The Northerners are given 12 jellybeans each while the Southerners are given just three jellybeans each. Through discussion and groupwork, the teacher elicits students' thoughts, feelings and responses to this unequal situation while also facilitating students who make connections with global food inequality.

Game: who should get the fruit?

Srijit Mishra's apple game (Mishra, 2012) is designed around three hypothetical students and one piece of fruit. **Student 1** Zoe loves apples the most and really wants to eat the fruit. She has money to pay for the apple. The family of **Student 2** Michelle, grew the apple and it comes from a tree in her garden. Magnus, **Student 3** is undernourished and has insufficient access to food, especially fresh fruit. The teacher poses the question 'Who should get the fruit?' All three know that Zoe loves apples the most, that Michelle's family grew the apple. Yet neither Zoe nor Michelle are undernourished. In pairs, students decide who should get the fruit and provide reasons for their decision. Through whole class discussion, the teacher invites students to reflect on their choices and the rationale underpinning their decision making. This exercise gives students an opportunity to reflect upon ideas that influence them while thinking about money and privilege (Student 1), property rights (Student 2) and human rights (Student 3).

Causes of hunger

World hunger is caused by so much more than a shortage of food. Even in places where food is plentiful or can be grown, challenges like natural disasters, war, poverty, and inadequate infrastructure and storage facilities stop people from accessing sufficient food. It is important to explore the topic of hunger with sensitivity in a manner that appreciates the complexity of hunger and its many causes, manifestations and possible solutions. Students might begin by exploring the *Hungry Planet Family Food Portraits* (Menzel and D'Aluisio, 2007) of a week's worth of food for people around the globe. This highly effective visual strategy means that by looking at images, students can compare and contrast the quantity and nutritional quality of food available to families in different countries and continents.

It is vital that students do not become desensitised to the people behind the statistics or view them through stereotypical lenses. An excellent website from the *Dollar Street Framework* uses documentary photographs and income statistics as data to show different standards of living within and between countries. In her TED talk, Anna Rosling Rönnlund, the creator of Dollar Street, speaks about how photographs and videos can be used to challenge simplistic stereotypes. The Dollar Street website is a wonderful educational resource of 30,000 searchable photographs from 398 families in 65 countries. It presents a rich database of free images of typical household items organised around 135 themes including income, homes, kitchens, tables of food, fruit, vegetables, meat or fish, drinking water, grains, plates of food, stoves, cutlery, cooking pots, ovens, food storage and waste. These images and videos can be used to explore the varied ways in which people store, prepare, cook and eat food in their homes across the globe. This website facilitates higher order thinking and elicits comparisons and contrasts about people's access to, storage, preparation and consumption of food. The images are accompanied by short narrative texts and function as a springboard for curious engagement and group/paired discussion about the impact of wealth on food supply and consumption. Importantly, the database shows that there are significant similarities between the living conditions and diets of people on similar income levels in countries throughout the world. This shatters the notion that hunger is a distant reality disconnected from the country and region of any school across the globe.

What the world eats

The *National Geographic Hungry Planet:, What the World Eats* website provides a breakdown of calories and food groups eaten by the average person in a range of countries. Based on a book with the same title (Menzel and D'Aluisio, (2007), the Hungry Planet resources present images of what the average family eats in different countries in the course of a week, as well as their calorie intake and food costs. Teachers can use Visual Thinking Strategies (VTS) to scaffold students' responses to and discussion of selected images. VTS ask three key questions: 'What do you see? What do you think? What do you wonder?'.

As students begin to appreciate the range of diets, forms of food storage and preparation and calorie intake across the world, it is opportune to elicit students' ideas about the causes for the wide variation in food practice within and between countries. Linking with SDG 1 'No Poverty', students develop awareness that people in poverty generally spend between 60 and 80% of their income on food, forcing them to prioritise feeding their families over meeting other basic needs or reaching long-term goals. Further, if an illness or natural disaster or other emergency strikes, they may need to skip meals in order to cope financially, and so an inter-generational cycle of hunger continues.

Unit 3 Zero Hunger

It begins with me!

This unit is designed to engender hope not despair and to motivate students to act. It encourages students to think critically about the practical steps they might take in their schools, homes and communities to help eradicate hunger. It challenges a passive acceptance of hunger as a devastating global tragedy and searches for concrete multi-faceted solutions to this problem. Lessons aim to show that hunger is not an abstract, distant reality disconnected from students. The daunting task of achieving Zero Hunger is not only desirable and possible but it is achievable.

The ethics of food

Ethical issues are at the forefront of any exploration of food and hunger in the classroom. Our food choices can have an environmental impact that is negative or positive. How food is produced and marketed matters. How it is distributed and stored and who gets access to it is key. As part of eliminating global hunger, it is important to focus on ethical food production, sustainable farming, marketing, distribution and consumer practices. This unit reinforces the message for consumers to eat locally sourced sustainable food. The Global Goals Resource, *Every Plate Tells a Story* from the *World's Largest Lesson*, invites students to investigate the story behind their favourite dish. In pairs, students (age 9-14) are encouraged to work to make a plate pledge to help achieve SDG2. UNESCO provides a range of creative classroom-based practical materials for educators in early childhood, primary and post-primary contexts. Further, the World Café Method (Brown et al., 2005), is another strategy that might be used to encourage students to understand, problem-solve and offer solutions to global hunger.

Sustainable agricultural practices

Gender (SDG 5) is a key issue in sustainable farming in a world where half of the world's farmers are women who produce 60-80% of the food in the Global South. Shockingly, United Nations Development Programme (UNDP) reports that one in three women in the world of reproductive age are anaemic and one in three women have also experienced violence at some stage in their lives. This means that tackling violence against women is a key element in Zero Hunger. This links with SDG 5's pledge to improve educational opportunity for women and indigenous peoples. SDG 5 shows that increased educational opportunity for women not only improves their income, it also has a knock-on impact on health, housing and nutrition and contributes to global food security. It is important to remember that there are many global examples of woman leading the fight against hunger and child malnutrition. For instance, in Honduras, UNDP reports that women's activism has had a transformative impact.

For farmers, access to finance and technology can improve crop yields as well as tackle climate change and increase biodiversity. The UN SDG 2 website (https://www.un.org/sustainabledevelopment/hunger/) has interesting global case studies highlighting sustainable farming practice, fighting climate change, promoting biodiversity and restoring forests and small farms. Sustainable farming can help to prevent drought, famine and floods while protecting nature and farming livelihoods. Management of water resources and diversifying livelihoods as well as diversifying crop production is dependent upon farmers having access to education, technology, tools and skills.

Supporting sustainable food production – how far has it travelled?

Using an on-line food miles calculator (https://www.foodmiles.com/) students might calculate the distance travelled for food products from source to final distination. Alternatively, the class might calculate the food miles in students' and teacher's lunchboxes. The Climate Change and Food Security Challenge Badge (SIDA, 2009) provides a wide range of activity-based creative classroom activities encouraging young people to fight climate change and hunger and to make a difference. Students can compare and contrast the environmental impact of foodstuffs that have travelled long distances by road, boat and plane to locally sourced foodstuffs. In order to achieve SDG 2 Zero Hunger, supporting sustainable local food production is vital.

Biodiversity and eating more vegetables

Students might play the Veggie Trumps games, by using worksheets, crosswords and word searches to explore the nutritional value of fruit and vegetables. These activities explore why many people are deliberately turning to nutritious plant-based diets. A great activity involves students designing a colourful meat-free menu for a restaurant consisting of a range of starters, main courses and desserts. Students might opt to feature Fairtrade, local, organic, vegetarian, vegan or other types of produce in their menus. This interdisciplinary activity draws on graphic design, artwork, literacy skills, science, communication skills, information, maths, RE and technology. If students wish, they might include information on the health and environmental benefits and/or nutritional information about each dish on the menu.

It bugs me...

This lesson begins when the teacher introduces the term 'entomophagy' and invites students to guess its meaning. The teacher then elicits students' initial responses to eating insects

Figure 5.7 Insects Are a Nutritional Source of Food. Source: https://pixabay.com/photos/grasshopper-insect-red-animal-2655486/

as a sustainable food source (see Figure 5.7). The class might watch YouTube videos such as *Bugs for Breakfast* or *Insects the Food of the Future*. In pairs students might discuss their reaction to entomophagy. Drawing on the FAO (2013) *Edible Insects: Future Prospects for Food and Food Security* report, groups might research the benefits of entomophagy. For a debating activity, two teams might debate the motion 'Eating edible insects is better than eating meat'. The whole class might then discuss whether attitudes to foods are culturally conditioned, and if so how. During all stages of these activities, it is important not to promote stereotypical or simplistic binaries such as a 'yeuch' or 'yum' factor.

Waste not want not

With estimates that one third of all the fresh food produced in the world is wasted, the *Stop Food Waste* (https://stopfoodwaste.ie/) lesson materials provide a range of activities including questions, games quizzes, poster-design, on the 5 R's of Food Waste (Refuse, Reduce, Reuse, Repurpose, Recycle). The teacher might invite a farmer, chef or retailer into the classroom to discuss their experience of food waste in their work setting. After this the class might set up a task force to generate ideas on minimising waste in the school, in their homes and in the local community.

Planting ideas in the classroom

To reinforce the importance of sustainable and locally produced foods, students are introduced to the basics of growing plants and farming in a school garden, window box or recycled container. As they plant seeds and grow seasonal herbs, vegetables and fruit, students learn about agricultural literacy and sustainable agriculture. The idea of community gardens is discussed in greater detail in chapter 14.

Fishbowl debate on Zero Hunger

For this activity the class holds a fishbowl debate on the motion 'Zero hunger starts with me'. Students are given thinking time and an opportunity to prepare responses to the motion. As participants develop their arguments and listen to their opponents, the teacher might highlight particular targets such as displaying empathy, problem solving, presenting accurate information and ethical arguments. Two students stand in the inner centre of the 'fishbowl' and all other students stand in a circle around them. The students are given two minutes to present their perspective on the motion. The teacher encourages all students to listen for accuracy, before the class discuss their response and decide which speaker made the best points.

Bringing it all together: placemat activity

The Placemat Activity is a way of synthesising and documenting students' ideas, learning and written or graphic responses to the lessons on Food, Hunger and Zero Hunger. Groups are given a large blank A4 or Poster sheet and pens, pencils and markers. At the centre of the poster students draw a large rectangular 'placemat' (Figure 5.8) where the group's communal learning and response to the topic is collaboratively recorded. Lines are drawn from the rectangle shape at the centre to the edge of the page for the appropriate number of people in the group. To begin this activity each participant is given their own segment on the large poster sheet of paper where they simultaneously record their own learning and response to the topics.

Each student fills in their placemat outlining the story of their unique learning. Students are invited to reflect upon:

- What have you learned about hunger?
- What surprised you?
- Questions I have about Zero Hunger...
- What can others (e.g. governments/organisations etc.) do to end hunger?

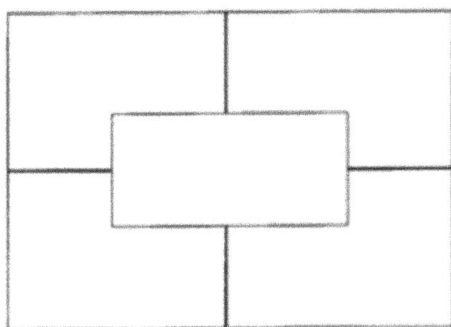

Placemat for 4 participants   **Placemat for 5 participants**

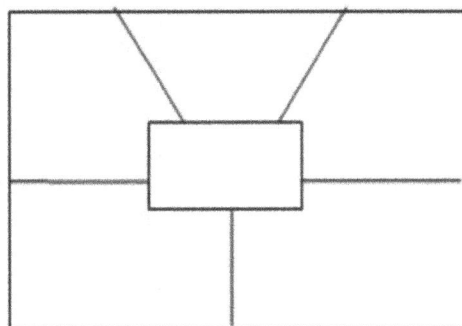

Figure 5.8 Placemat Templates.

- What can you do to make Zero Hunger happen?
- The most important thing I learned was…

When participants have completed their individual sections in the placemat, the group share their individual learning and key themes and ideas emerge. The group agree upon and list the key points of their shared learning and prioritise key actions for ending hunger. These are placed at the centre of the placemat. The groups' placemats are used as a scaffold for oral/visual presentation to peers where placemats function as a record of both individual and communal learning and collective action on the theme of Zero Hunger. They can be displayed, revisited and revised in the light of future learning.

Links to other SDGs

The multi-dimensional goal 'Zero Hunger' goal is closely connected to poverty elimination (SDG 1), food access, good health and well-being (SDG 3), and the need for clean drinking water (SDG 6). But beyond these, a broader set of socioeconomic SDGs supports the progress of SDG 2 and have been identified as key enablers (SDG 4, 5, 8, 10, 11, 12, 16, and 17). A sample of these links is illustrated in Figure 5.9. Ethical issues associated with the transportation, production, consumption and disposal of food are discussed in Chapter 15 (SDG 12).

The food we buy, eat, and throw away plays an enormous role in climate change. In turn, climate change threatens food security. It is a vicious circle: extreme weather events like heavy rainfall, flooding, droughts and wildfires caused by climate change directly impact food production, putting food supplies at risk. Intensive farming threatens the success of other SDGs including SDG 13 (Climate change). According to a study that was conducted by researchers at Oxford University and the Swiss Agricultural Research Institute Agroscope, a diet that is free from animal products can reduce personal emissions related to food by up to 73% (Poore et al., 2018). Yet, harmful agricultural practices continue to be supported by subsidies. For instance, in the European Union, the Common Agricultural Policy (CAP) continues to subsidise intensive production of alcohol, meat, dairy fats and sugars. Nonetheless, millions of people's lives depend on a dramatic reduction in the consumption of meat and dairy. Meat production requires a huge amount of land to sustain itself. Forests, particularly in South America, are burned every year to graze cattle and grow enough crops to feed billions of farmed animals. As global levels of hunger increase, this is morally wrong. Instead, that grain could be used to feed people directly and would help ensure everyone has enough food. By clearing forests, destroying habitats and using toxic pesticides to grow animal food, intensive beef farming is contributing to the extinction of thousands of species, many of which have not even been discovered yet.

We depend on a healthy environment for our own survival. The huge abundance and variety of the natural world (sometimes called biodiversity) is essential for food, clean water and medicines. Indeed, the rapid loss of biodiversity (which is the focus of SDG 15), largely driven by industrial farming is as significant a threat to our existence as climate change (SDG 13).

Further challenges are associated with an increasing global population. The European Union's new Farm to Fork Strategy calls for a 50% reduction in agricultural chemicals. While this means good news for insects and bees, it could also mean a reduction in food production at a time when we need to be producing more food on less land. So there are lots of opportunities for engaging debates about these issues in the classroom.

SDG 10

Reduce inequality

Food security is exacerbated by inequality. The fortunes of the world's richest 20 billionaires are greater than the entire GDP of Sub-Saharan Africa. This uneven distribution of hunger and malnutrition in all its forms is rooted in inequalities of social, political, and economic power. Therefore, the first step in tackling the inequalities of hunger is to understand how they are embedded in and magnified by the inequalities of power at work in the food system.

SDG 5

Gender Equality

Women and girls are more likely than men to suffer from hunger and malnourishment. Gender equality is essential for a world of Zero Hunger; where all women, men, girls and boys can exercise their human rights, including the right to adequate

SDG 2 Zero hunger

SDG 16

Peace, Justice and Strong Institutions

War and political upheaval are major contributing factors to famine, the impact being felt at household and national level. While famine is often a by product of war, it is also used as an instrument of war.

SDG 1

No poverty

Food insecurity and hunger are closely related to poverty and an inability to purchase food. Poverty causes hunger. Not every person living in poverty faces chronic hunger, but almost all people facing chronic hunger are also living in poverty.Hunger is the most severe and critical manifestation of poverty.

SDG 13

Climate action

The magnitude and frequency of extreme weather events is increasing. Higher temperatures, water scarcity, droughts, floods, and greater CO_2 concentrations in the atmosphere affect staple crops around the world. Corn and wheat production has declined in recent years due to extreme weather events, plant diseases, and a global water crisis.

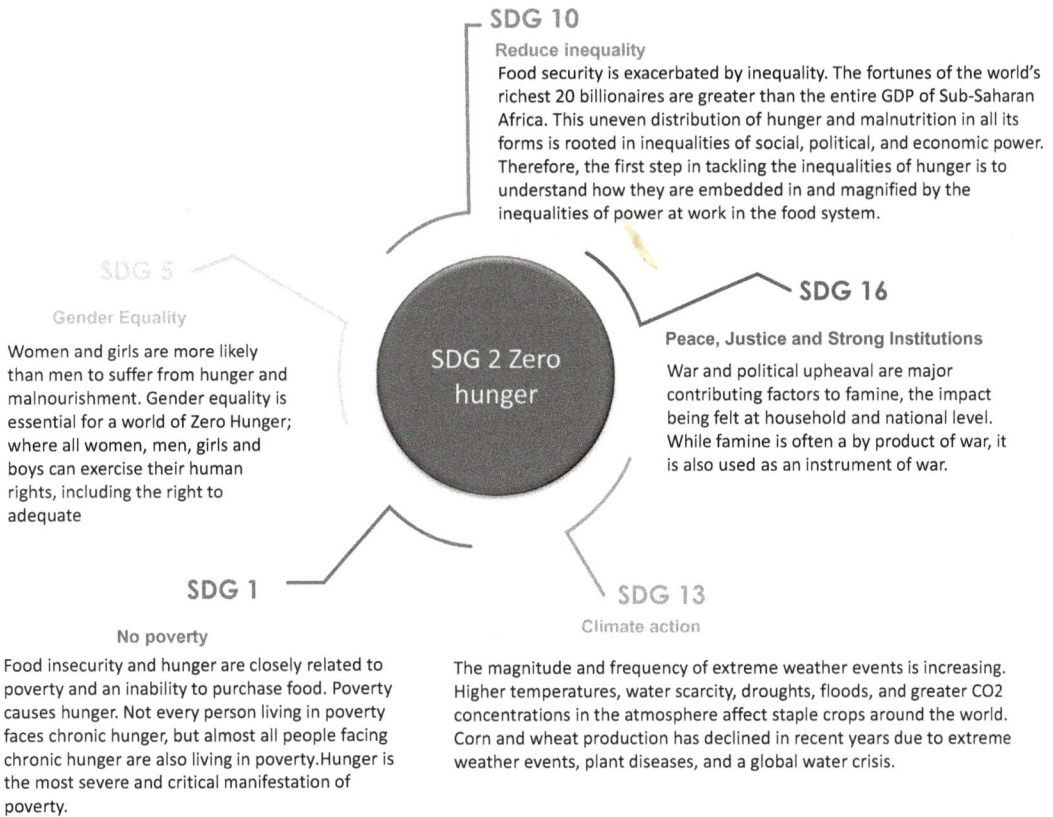

Figure 5.9 Interlinkages of SDG 8 with Other SDGs.

Conclusion

Teachers have a powerful role to play in educating students to make sustainable food choices that will last for their whole lives. Education can foster healthy food habits that promote fair trade, sustainable farming, and the just and secure distribution of food. Education has a pivotal role to play not just in raising awareness about inequitable access to a supply of nutritious food in the Global South and North, but in challenging and changing unjust practices that result in catastrophic illness and death arising from malnourishment, wasting, hunger and famine. The multifaceted political, medical, environmental, economic, cultural and ethical issues raised by hunger demands that we address it in an interdisciplinary, problem-solving manner. Zero hunger will only come about if we ensure that as a species, humans make urgent changes collaboratively so that we can live on a planet where farming is carried out sustainably, human rights are respected, food waste is eliminated and humans live respectfully in harmony with other species, the environment and the planet. Systemic factors and political decisions must also be recognised and named. On a positive note, there is enough food on the planet to feed everyone. Education about SDG 2 needs to acknowledge that the food crisis is a crisis of prices rather than availability. Beginning with this premise will ensure critical thinking and robust interrogation of the status quo.

Resources

An extensive list of resources, videos and case studies for SDG 2 is included in the SDG padlet accompanying this book: https://padlet.com/annedolan/o6rds38ylfy6a28h

Concern:	Primary https://www.concern.net/schools-and-youth/primary-education-programmes
	Secondary https://www.concern.net/schools-and-youth/secondary-education-programmes
Trócaire:	Primary https://www.trocaire.org/our-work/educate/peaceandjustice/primary/
	Secondary https://www.trocaire.org/our-work/educate/peaceandjustice/postprimary/
Development Education.ie	www.developmenteducation.ie
Dollar Street:	www.dollarstreet,org

Key dates

Veganuary: The idea behind Veganuary is that people who follow a non-vegan diet are encouraged to adopt a vegan diet throughout the month of January.

Shrove or 'Pancake Tuesday': is the day before Ash Wednesday (the first day of Lent) observed in many Christian countries.

Lent: begins on Ash Wednesday, six and half weeks before Easter and includes a 40 day period of fasting and abstinence

August 5: International Beer day

October 1: World Vegetarian Day

October 16: World Food Day

October 17: World Poverty Day

November 1: World Vegan Day

Last Thursday in November: Thanksgiving

December 25: Christmas Day

Ramadan: is the ninth month of the Islamic calendar, observed by Muslims worldwide as a month of fasting (sawm), prayer, reflection and community.

Eid al-Fitr: is a religious holiday celebrated by Muslims worldwide because it marks the end of the month-long dawn-to-sunset fasting of Ramadan.

Video

Eating Our Way To Extinction: https://www.youtube.com/watch?v=LaPgeO1NQTQ

Children's literature (Picture books) SDG2

Brandt, L. and Vogel, V. (illus) (2014) *Maddi's Fridge* Brooklyn, Flashlight Press.
Bromley, A.C. and Casilla, R. (2010) *The Lunch Thief* Tilbury House Publishers.
Carlson Berne, E. and Sordo, S. (Illus) (2018) *My Food, Your Food, Our Food (How We Are Alike and Different)* Cantata Learning; Illustrated edition.

Castaldo, N. and Hsu, G. (2020) *The World That Feeds Us: Discover How Our Food Is Produced in a Sustainable Way* Words and Pictures.

Chamberlin, M., Chamberlin, R. and Cairns, J. (illus) (2006) *Mama Panya's Pancakes* Barefoot Books.

Chancellor, D. and Ewen, D. (illus) (2019) *Don't Waste Your Food* Wayland; Illustrated edition.

Cho, T. (2018) *Rice From Heaven* Little Bee Books.

Crow, J. (2021) *Everybody Eats* Life's A Journey Publishing.

DeFelice, C.C. (2006) *One Potato, Two Potato* Farrar Straus Giroux.

Demi. (1997) *One Grain of Rice* Non Basic Stock Line.

Detlefsen, L.H. and Kurilla, R. (illus) (2021) *Right This Very Minute: A Table-To-Farm Book about Food and Farming*, Feeding Minds Press.

Gestalten, L. and Walrond, B. (illus) (2019) *A Taste of the World: What People Eat and How They Celebrate Around the Globe* Little Gestalten.

Heine, T. and Gueyfier, J. (2014) *Chandra's Magic Light: A Story in Nepal.* Barefoot Books.

Karmel, A. and Wilmore, A, (illus) (2022) *Where Does My Food Come From?* Welbeck Children's Books.

Marie, L. and Singh, P. (illus) (2019) *Mealtime Around the World* Beaming Books.

McBrier, P. (2004) *Beatrice's Goat* Aladdin Paperbacks.

Milner, K. (2019) *It's a No-Money Day* Barrington Stoke.

Mora, O. (2018) *Thank you Omu* Little Brown and Company.

Muth, J.J. (2003) *Stone Soup* Scholastic Press.

Naish, S., Jefferies, R. and Evans, M. (illus) (2017) *Rosie Rudey and the Enormous Chocolate Mountain* Jessica Kingsley Publishers.

Otoshi, K (2021) *Lunch Every Day* KO Kids Books.

Sala, F. (2019) *Lunch at 10 Pomegranate Street: A Collection of Recipes to Share* Scribble UK.

Staglioano, K. and Heid, K. (illus) (2014) *Katie's Cabbage* Young Palmetto Books.

Talkin, E. and Murray, S. (2020) *Lulu and the Hunger Monster* Free Spirit Publishing Inc.

Tamaki, J. (2020) *Our Little Kitchen* Abrams Books for Young Readers.

Waissbluth, D. and O' Byrne, C. (illus) *Teatime Around the World* Greystone Books.

Chapter books and informational texts 9-12 years

Berger Kaye, C. (2007) *A Kid's Guide to Hunger and Homelessness: How to Take Action* Free Spirit Publishing.

Craig, C. and Archer, J. (2016) *The Kew Gardens Children's Cookbook: Plant, Cook, Eat* Wayland

Clare, H. (2017) *Aubrey and the Terrible Ladybirds* Firefly Press.

Conlon-McKenna, M., Teskey, D. (illus) and Lynch, P.J. (1998a) *Under the Hawthorn Tree: (Children of the Famine)* O'Brien Press Ltd.

Conlon-McKenna, M., Teskey, D. (illus) and Lynch, P.J. (1998b) *Wildflower Girl (Children of the Famine)* O'Brien Press Ltd.

Conlon-McKenna, M., Teskey, D. (illus) and Lynch, P.J. (2006) *Fields of Home (Children of the Famine)* O'Brien Press Ltd.

Cottrell Boyce, F. and Lenton. S. (illus) (2022) *Noah's Gold* Macmillan Children's Books.

Fleischman, P. (2004) *Seedfolks* Harper Collins.

Harmon, A. (2020) *Poverty and Hunger* (Stand Against) Franklin Watts.

Lawrence, S. and Noy, V. (illus) (2022) *World of Food: A Delicious Discovery of the Foods We Eat* Templar Publishing.

Menzel, P. and D'Aluisio, F. (2007) *Hungry Planet: What the World Eats* Material World Books; Illustrated edition.

Mucha, L. Smith, E. and Lynas, H. (illus) (2023) *Welcome to Our Table: A Celebration of What Children Eat Everywhere* Nosy Crow.

Pierce, N. (2023) *In Between Worlds: The Journey of the Famine Girls* O'Brien Press.

Raúf, O. Q. (2021) *The Great Food Bank Heist* Barrington Stoke.

Smith Milway, K. and Daigneault, S. (illus) (2010) *The Good Garden: How: One Family Went from Hunger to Having Enough* Kids Can Press.

Smith Milway, K. and Fernandes, E. (illus) (2009) *One Hen How: One Small Loan Made a Big Difference* Kids Can Press.

Spilsbury, L. and Kai, H. (2018) *Poverty and Hunger* (Children in our world) Wayland.
Wenjen, M. and Sae-Heng, R. (illus) (2023) *Food for the Future: Sustainable Farms Around the World* Barefoot Books.

Chapter books (12 plus years)

Conlon-Mc Kenna, M. (2020) *The Hungry Road* Transworld Ireland.
Drinkwater, C. (2015) The Hunger (My Story) Scholastic.
Jozefkowicz, E. (2021) *The Cooking Club Detectives* Zephyr.
Ogle, R. (2019) *Free Lunch* W. W. Norton & Company.
Pierce, N. (2023) *In Between Worlds: Journey of the Famine Girls* The O Brien Press.
Pollan, M. (2015) *The Omnivore's Dilemma* (Young Readers Edition) Rocky Pond Books.
Rashford, M. (2021) *You Are a Champion: How to Be the Best You Can Be* Macmillan Children's Books.
Wilson, S.M. (2018) *The Extinction Trials* Usborne Publishing.

References

Bell, D. and Valentine, G. (1997) *Consuming Geographies: We Are Where We Eat.* London: Routledge.
Brown, Juanita, David Isaacs and the World Cafe Community (2005) *The World Cafe: Shaping our futures through conversations that matter.* San Francisco: Berrett-Koehler.
Butler, S. (2023) UK shoppers spent £13.7bn on groceries in run-up to Christmas. The Guardian https://www.theguardian.com/business/2024/jan/03/uk-shoppers-groceries-run-up-to-christmas?CMP=twt_b-gdnnews
Clover, J. (2003) 'Food security in Sub-Saharan Africa'. *African Security Review, 12*(1), 5-15.
De Schutter, O. (2010) *Food Commodities Speculation and Food Price Crises: Regulation to Reduce the Risks of Price Volatility Briefing Note 02.* www2.ohchr.org/english/issues/food/docs/Briefing_Note_02_September_2010_EN.pdf
FAO. (2020)*The State of Food Security and Nutrition in the World 2020. Transforming Food Systems for Affordable Healthy Diets.* https://www.fao.org/3/ca9692en/online/ca9692en.html
FAO (2013) *Edible Insects: Future Prospects for Food and Food Security* https://reliefweb.int/report/world/edible-insects-future-prospects-food-and-feed-security?gad_source=1&gclid=CjOKCQiAsvWrBhCOARIsAO4E6f_MpUUj9Qrqbz39kk3JboYDZV6XBRdW_Tc4OEprC1pqpjhCNZz6ABoaAhilEALw_wcB
Madeley, J. (2002) *Food for all: The Need for a New Agriculture.* London: Zed Books Ltd.
McCann, J. and Cushley, A. (2022) If the World Were 100 People.London: Red Shed
Menzel, P. and D'Aluisio, F. (2007) *Hungry Planet: What the World Eats.* Material World. https://www.menzelphoto.com/portfolio/G0000s3jj73.5TSs/I0000OfcnWWHU.Z8
Mishra, S. (2012) 'Hunger, ethics and the right to food'. *Indian Journal of Medical Ethics, 9*(1), 32-37.
Monbiot, G. (2022) *Regenesis: Feeding the World Without Devouring the Planet.* London: Allen Lane.
Oxfam (2022) *Profiting from Pain.* https://www.oxfam.org/en/research/profiting-pain
Poore, J. and Nemecek, T. (2018) 'Reducing food's environmental impacts through producers and consumers'. *Science, 360*(6392), 987-992.
SIDA (2009) *The Climate Change and Food Security Challenge Badge* https://www.fao.org/3/i1091e/I1091E.pdf
UN, (2002) *For Every Child* New York; Red Fox
World Bank. (2023) 'Measuring poverty', available: https://www.worldbank.org/en/topic/measuringpoverty [accessed 6th March 2024].
World Food Programme. (nd) https://www.wfp.org/ending-hunger
World Health Organisation (WHO) European Regional Obesity Report. (2022) https://apps.who.int/iris/bitstream/handle/10665/353747/9789289057738-eng.pdf
Young People's Trust for the Environment (Yippittee) https://ypte.org.uk/downloads/yippittee-issue-2-food-glorious-food

6 A time of hope, a time for empathy

Ensuring the health and well-being of students as they transition from primary to post-primary school (SDG 3)

Carol O'Sullivan and Anne M. Dolan

Introduction

Good health and well-being are vital for all people. While health and well-being are connected they are two separate concepts. In its 1948 (np) constitution, the World Health Organization defined health as 'a state of complete physical, mental, and social well-being and not merely the absence of disease or infirmity'. Taken together, physical and mental health affect everything we do. Well-being is a state of being comfortable, healthy or happy. It comes from a combination of factors such as physical health, emotions, feeling secure or safe and leading a life where a person can feel satisfied. Well-being is important for people everywhere as a lack of well-being can lead to physical and mental illness. Poverty, hunger, gender inequality and disaster (issues addressed by other SDGs) can have a negative impact on well-being, which, if not addressed, may cause long-term problems.

SDG 3 aims to ensure healthy lives and promote well-being for. This goal is underpinned by nine targets (see Appendix 1) that broadly fall into separate, but overlapping groups: reducing morbidity and mortality for vulnerable groups (mothers, newborns, the elderly and children); reducing communicable and non-communicable diseases; reducing risk factors (tobacco, substance abuse, road traffic injuries and hazardous chemicals and pollution) and providing universal health coverage and strengthening the health sector.

Through improved access to health care around the world, strong research, health finance and early warning systems, epidemics such as malaria, HIV/AIDS, mental health and cancer can be reduced. The importance of public health education was a key strategy in combatting the impacts of Covid 19. The pandemic also illustrated how health underpins all of the SDGs. While the educational aspirations of SDG 3 are broad and ambitious (Table 6.1), this chapter focuses on the promotion of good mental health and well-being during the transition between primary and post-primary school. This chapter is written with the understanding that not all students in the world progress to post-primary school. Nevertheless, for those that have this opportunity, the transition can be a time of uncertainty as well as hope.

DOI: 10.4324/9781003232001-9

Table 6.1 Key learning objectives for the promotion of mental health and well-being

Cognitive learning objectives Teaching *about* the goals: developing respect and understanding	1 The learner knows conceptions of health, hygiene and well-being and can critically reflect on them, including an understanding of the importance of gender in health and well-being.
	2 The learner knows facts and figures about the most severe communicable and non-communicable diseases, and the most vulnerable groups and regions concerning illness, disease and premature death.
	3 The learner understands the socio-political-economic dimensions of health and well-being and knows about the effects of advertising and about strategies to promote health and well-being.
	4 The learner understands the importance of mental health. The learner understands the negative impacts of behaviours like xenophobia, discrimination and bullying on mental health and emotional well-being and how addictions to alcohol, tobacco or other drugs cause harm to health and well-being.
	5 The learner knows relevant prevention strategies to foster positive physical and mental health and well-being, including sexual and reproductive health and information as well as early warning and risk reduction.
Socio-emotional learning objectives Teaching *for* the goals enhancing empathy and love	1 The learner is able to interact with people suffering from illnesses, and feel empathy for their situation and feelings.
	2 The learner is able to communicate about issues of health, including sexual and reproductive health, and well-being, especially to argue in favour of prevention strategies to promote health and well-being.
	3 The learner is able to encourage others to decide and act in favour of promoting health and well-being for all.
	4 The learner is able to create a holistic understanding of a life of health and well-being, and to clarify related values, beliefs and attitudes.
	5 The learner is able to develop a personal commitment to promoting health and well-being for themselves, their family and others, including considering volunteer or professional work in health and social care.
Behavioural learning objectives Teaching *through* the goals Promoting advocacy and activism	1 The learner is able to include health promoting behaviours in their daily routines.
	2 The learner is able to plan, implement, evaluate and replicate strategies that promote health, including sexual and reproductive health, and well-being for themselves, their families and others.
	3 The learner has the capacity to perceive when others need help and to seek help for themselves and others.
	4 The learner is able to publicly demand and support the development of policies promoting health and well-being.
	5 The learner is able to propose ways to address possible conflicts between the public interest in offering medicine at affordable prices and private interests within the pharmaceutical industry.

(Source UNESCO, 2017: 16)

Well-being is integrated throughout the Irish curriculum and is specifically addressed in Social, Personal and Health Education (SPHE) and Physical Education (PE). This chapter presents the *Wellbeing Policy Statement and Framework for Practice* (DES, 2019) as a response to the question of holistic implementation. This key document in current Irish education focuses on embedding well-being in both the formal and informal curriculum and in the broader school community. Also included in this chapter are activities in which students can engage as they negotiate the transition from primary to post-primary school. Specific consideration will be given to students who may have escaped from traumatic situations. At the time of writing this chapter, Irish schools welcomed hundreds of children and young people from Ukraine. Additional support is required for all newcomer children joining a new school in a new country.

It should be noted that the spelling of the term 'well-being' often gives rise to confusion thus demonstrating the complexity of the concept. In this article, the hyphen will be used, as in the SDG 3 goal, except in cases of direct quotations or references.

Well-being within a curricular framework

A key issue to bear in mind is that well-being should not be viewed simply as another curricular area. It may be easier to view the area as a discrete area on the school timetable, but this is to overlook the breadth and complexity of the area and the fact that it permeates all aspects of life. Figure 6.1 illustrates the broad ranging nature of well-being. In Ireland, the Junior Cycle Wellbeing Guidelines (NCCA, 2017) do much to illustrate that the area cannot be confined to one subject or to one timeslot. However, implementation literature demonstrates that there is still much to be done at both primary and post-primary levels to extend perceptions and understandings of this area (NCCA, 2008; DES, 2009; NicGabhainn et al., 2010; Mannix-McNamara et al., 2012).

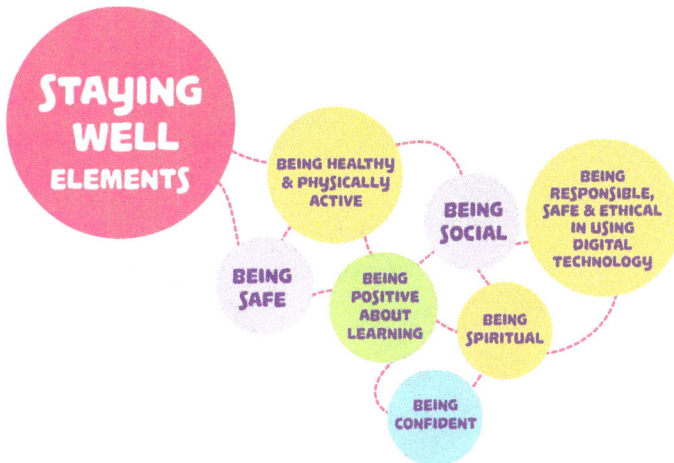

Figure 6.1 Staying Well Elements in Junior Cycle Wellbeing Guidelines. (NCCA, 2017: 23) (with permission from NCCA).

Key areas of well-being

The Wellbeing Framework for a whole school approach (DES, 2019) (Figure 6.2) comprises four key elements for a holistic approach to well-being promotion. These are as follows:

- Culture and environment
- Curriculum (Teaching and Learning)
- Relationships and Partnerships
- Policy and Planning

It should be noted that all dimensions have equal significance in the promotion and achievement of well-being in education.

Culture and environment

One of the first means of identifying the culture of a school is through reading its mission statement. This is usually seen in the entrance area of a school and on the home page of the school website. McClees (2016) proposes that school mission statements are a quantifiable rallying concept for faculty and staff while informing students and parents about the purpose of the school. He also highlights the importance of reviewing and changing the mission as necessary, so that it does not become an ineffective banner on the school's webpage. Fullan (1993) emphasises the importance of ongoing reflection on the school's mission statement, in order to preserve its relevance, particularly in the context of increased diversity. A good starting point for helping the transition to post-primary school, is for teachers of the senior classes of primary school to familiarise themselves with the mission statements of the chosen post-primary schools and to engage in active discussion with their post-primary colleagues in this regard. It is important that they encourage parents, and ultimately the

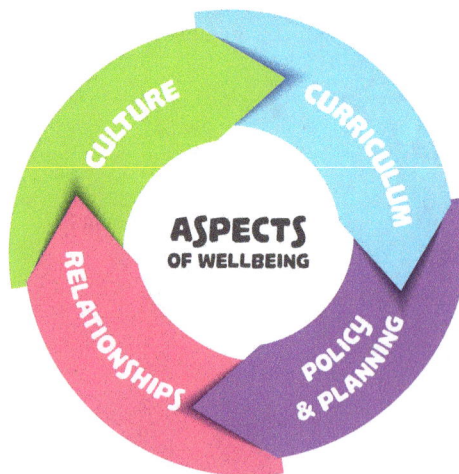

Figure 6.2 Four Key Elements for a Holistic Approach to Wellbeing Promotion. (NCCA, 2017: 26).

students themselves, to do likewise, thus enhancing cognitive engagement with the process. Slate et al. (2008) observe the need for the mission statement to acknowledge explicitly the need for partnerships with parents and other stakeholders, to ensure the success of the mission. The specific needs of asylum seeker and refugee families require active consideration here. Vaghri et al. (2019) lists the many and complex effects of flight on refugee students and their families. Hence, the engagement of refugee families with the mission statement may require additional facilitation. Engagement with the mission statements by all stakeholders will help students reach a greater understanding of, and empathy with, their current primary school and their future post-primary school.

The school classroom and environment is likely to be a much different experience for students beginning post-primary school. Van Rens et al. (2018) comment on the many changes that the new post-primary student encounters. These include a larger building, different teachers and a larger number of peers. Students also need to adjust to the geography of the school, following a timetable and being the juniors in the school environment. Visiting the chosen school in advance of commencement serves to allay some of the concerns of students in relation to their new environment and helps social-emotional and behavioural development. The Junior Cycle Well-being Guidelines (NCCA, 2017), for Irish post-primary schools, has some very practical advice on supporting students' adjustment to their new environment. There are a number of sample well-being programmes provided in the Guidelines. In each one, there is active recognition of the needs of first year students with a specific focus on the transition process. The importance of primary school teachers, particularly those in the senior classes, becoming familiar with the guidelines, as well as with the overall Junior Cycle Framework, becomes evident here. While this observation is made in the Irish context, the active engagement of teachers in the transition process is applicable internationally.

References to school and work environments tend to focus mainly on social interactions and dynamics. Vischer (2007, cited by O'Sullivan, 2019) observes that sometimes the physical aspects of the work environment (heating, lighting, ventilation, layout) can be sidelined in favour of the social aspects, but that both are important when considering well-being. These physical aspects have received a much greater focus during Covid-19, particularly in terms of ventilation. The sets of guidelines for Well-being in Primary Schools (DES/DoH/HSE, 2015) and Post-Primary Schools (DES/DoH/HSE, 2013) acknowledge the need for a warm, safe, well-maintained physical environment with access to plants and trees in order to promote and nurture well-being. This is of particular importance for traumatised students. The physical environment should not be overlooked in the context of transition to post-primary school. The first impressions of the new student are very likely to be influenced by their sensory responses and a welcoming, tidy, clean and colourful building may nurture hope while allaying fears and trepidation. This has a positive impact on mental health. Caring for the physical environment could be included as part of the role of the well-being coordinator in the school and, of course, there are particular links with the *Green Schools* initiative. The role of the school maintenance team is crucial here also and it may be relevant to invite a member of the team to staff meetings. Schools often have 'buddy systems' in place to care for and mentor younger students. Humphrey and Ainscow (2006) outline the benefits of the buddy system in helping students to negotiate their new environment. They outline how this system helps new students achieve a greater sense of connectedness and belonging thus promoting their mental health. Their social-emotional needs are actively addressed here. Assigning a designated task such as looking after the school plants may be an effective way of scaffolding the buddy system initiative. The buddy system is of particular significance in the context of refugee students who may need additional support in adapting to new circumstances.

Curriculum (teaching and learning)

Transitions and continuity are presented as one of eight key education principles in the Irish primary curriculum framework (NCCA, 2023). The importance of building upon prior learning is emphasised in the building of foundations for post-primary school. The sharing of information about learning and development at key transition points for students (pre-school to primary and primary to post-primary) is acknowledged and facilitated through *Mo Scéal* (meaning My Story) (pre-school to primary) and the Education Passport (primary to post-primary). The Education Passport provides a holistic view of the student at primary level, ensures continuity of learning and alerts the post-primary schools if additional support is required (NCCA, 2020). The importance of teacher collaboration is emphasised in the Junior Cycle Framework (DES, 2015) and the Primary Curriculum Framework (NCCA, 2023). However, these do not specifically acknowledge the importance of meetings between senior cycle primary teachers and junior cycle post primary teachers in order to discuss the transition process. This apparently simple suggestion maybe very difficult to achieve due to the many demands on teachers' time. Finding time to meet colleagues within one's own school setting can be challenging, thus organising a meeting with colleagues from another school may be even more problematic. Yet, this should be given consideration in the facilitation of transitions. Support from school leaders is key here. An additional consideration emerges when supporting refugee students whom might be joining a school from a context wherein education may not be valued or whom may previously have been denied education due to conflict. An Education Passport may not be possible for these students.

McCormack et al. (2014) observe that a significant proportion of post-transfer students in studies relating to academic transfer, did not see the post-primary curriculum as following on naturally from that at primary level. The authors signal a need on the part of post-primary teachers to make reference to students' prior learning. Hence, analysis of curriculum areas by both sets of teachers merits consideration. Transitions will be more seamless, if post primary teachers can demonstrate their familiarity with the relevant materials thus demonstrating the relevance of work completed in primary school. Students' cognitive development in terms of understanding health and health promotion is facilitated here. It is recognised that analysis of prior learning may sometimes be more difficult in the context of refugee students.

Relationships and partnerships

Much research indicates that it is in the area of relationships that well-being will flourish or flounder. Dooley and Fitzgerald (2012) demonstrate how the support of just one adult in the life of an adolescent is a significant protective factor for mental health. This is acknowledged in the *Junior Cycle Wellbeing Guidelines* (NCCA, 2017). Both the NCCA (2023) Primary Curriculum Framework, and the *Junior Cycle Wellbeing Guidelines* highlight the importance of relationships in the student's development and the links between positive relationships and academic achievement. The importance of positive affirming relationships was beautifully illustrated in Katriona O' Sullivan's (2023) memoir 'Poor' discussed in chapter 4. The transition between primary and post-primary school can unsettle a student's existing relationships and present them with many challenges in this regard. In many instances, students from one primary school go to different post-primary schools, resulting in the need to form new networks (Smyth et al., 2004; Smyth, 2016) while meeting more teachers each day often means a more formal relationship with school staff (Smyth, 2016). Students who have fled from conflict have been uprooted from their existing relationships and thus require additional care and empathy. Hence, it is very important that the building of relationships is not overlooked as other changes in the transition period are negotiated.

Partnerships also merit exploration and comment here. Partners are viewed by Cox-Petersen (2011) as anyone who is working towards the common good of the school. She observes that educational partnerships take time and effort to develop but once the time has been invested, the benefits are endless for all groups and individuals. Partnerships and collaboration between schools, families and communities enrich and extend students' learning by acknowledging and supporting their lives in and out of school (NCCA, 2020). Working in partnership comes into even sharper focus when looking at the transition stages of students. Coffey (2013) observes that assisting students to successfully navigate the journey from primary to is of import to educators, parents and policy-makers alike. She also notes that parents as well as students are forging new partnerships as their child moves to post-primary school. For refugee students, the move to post-primary school may be a new dimension in their lives which may not have been available previously. This will require new understandings and acceptance on the part of their parents. Partnerships should be meaningful, with each partner's role, including that of the student, accorded recognition. This is noteworthy in the research of Humphrey and Ainscow (2006) on transitions, wherein the students' viewpoints on this rite of passage are foregrounded.

Policy and planning

Even a cursory review of school policies will demonstrate that many of them address issues of mental health and overall well-being. The following school policies (or similar) emerge as being specifically relevant: Health and Safety; Cyber Safety; Anti-bullying; Relationships and Sexuality Education; Substance Use; and Healthy Eating. A useful activity for both primary and post-primary schools would be to examine how many of these policies acknowledge the transition stages in a student's life and the impact on their well-being. Policies are evolving documents and need ongoing monitoring. They also need effective implementation, which, in turn, requires effective planning.

A report by the DES (2009) in Ireland indicated that planning for Social, Personal and Health Education (SPHE) in Irish primary schools was less than optimal with approximately one-third of schools surveyed indicating insufficient planning for this area. There has been significant efforts to address this issue since then and planning for Well-being is now part of the School Self Evaluation (SSE) process. Time is often indicated as an impediment to effective individual and collaborative planning (Morgan and Nic Craith, 2015; Merritt, 2016). Collaborative planning is often facilitated through Professional Learning Communities (PLCs) (Merritt, 2016). Owen (2016) refers to shared vision, collaboration, engagement in practical activities, distributed leadership, professional growth and collegial learning as features of the PLC. Borko (2004) observes that key features of such communities include the establishment and maintenance of communication norms and trust, as well as the collaborative interactions which take place when groups of teachers work together. It may be worth considering the development of a specific PLC in the context of transition to post-primary school. Teachers from both primary and post-primary contexts could meet and plan for first-year students. It is acknowledged that there are practical concerns to be overcome here. Designated time for this activity is required. Teachers could opt to meet in clusters and in different school venues. This is of particular benefit to the post-primary teachers as they would become more familiar with the different schools from whence their first-year students have come. A more empathetic experience for the new students can then be formulated. School policies from both contexts could be reviewed and ideas shared in terms of their relevance to the transition to post-primary school.

Interconnections between SDG 3 and other SDGS

The importance of health and well-being is fundamental for the achievement of all goals. While SDG 3 targets do not specifically address the social elements of health and well-being, the importance of social factors, such as working conditions, income, education, and housing, is recognised within other SDGs. Indeed, the complex interconnections between SDG 3 and other SDGs is illustrated through the prism of COVID-19 (Figure 6.3). Waage et al. (2015) noted that achieving health and well-being for all relies not only on meeting the SDG 3 targets, but also on ending poverty (SDG 1), providing access to education (SDG 4), achieving gender equity (SDG 5), reducing inequality between and within countries (SDG 10), and promoting peace (SDG 16). Health and well-being also rely on adequate services and resources, including infrastructure (SDG 9), food security and agricultural production (SDG 2), decent work (SDG 8), sustainable consumption (SDG 12), provision of water and sanitation (SDG 6), access to energy (SDG 7) and resilient and inclusive cities that provide universal access to housing and transport (SDG 11). Health and well-being are also critically dependent on a safe and enabling environment, supported by mitigation of climate change (SDG 13) and sustainable protection and use of the oceans (SDG 14) and land (SDG 15). The broad interdependence between environmental and human health is also recognised in systems thinking discussed previously in chapter 2 and the focus on planetary health (Whitmee et al., 2015; Gatzweiler et al., 2017).

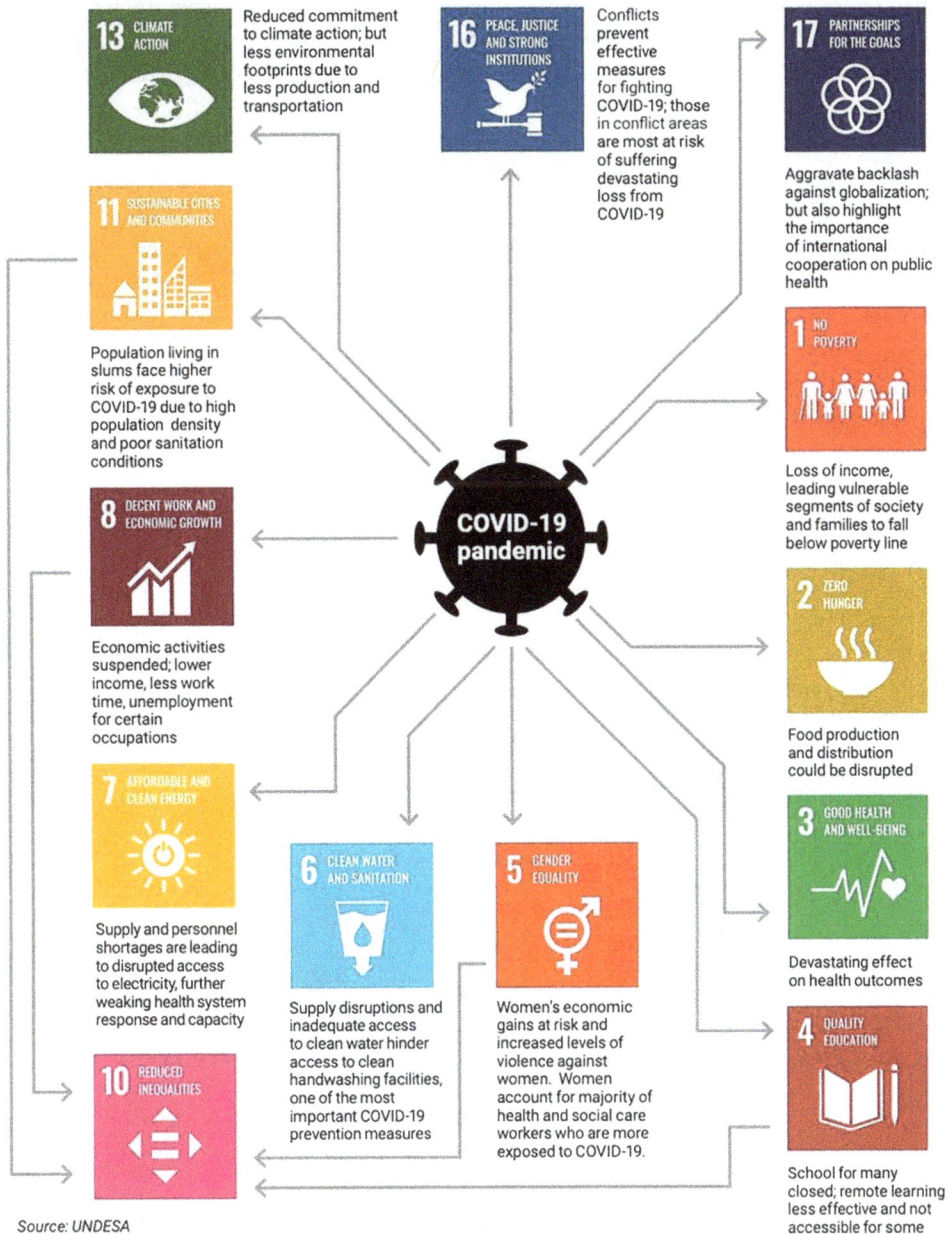

13 CLIMATE ACTION — Reduced commitment to climate action; but less environmental footprints due to less production and transportation

16 PEACE, JUSTICE AND STRONG INSTITUTIONS — Conflicts prevent effective measures for fighting COVID-19; those in conflict areas are most at risk of suffering devastating loss from COVID-19

17 PARTNERSHIPS FOR THE GOALS — Aggravate backlash against globalization; but also highlight the importance of international cooperation on public health

11 SUSTAINABLE CITIES AND COMMUNITIES — Population living in slums face higher risk of exposure to COVID-19 due to high population density and poor sanitation conditions

1 NO POVERTY — Loss of income, leading vulnerable segments of society and families to fall below poverty line

8 DECENT WORK AND ECONOMIC GROWTH — Economic activities suspended; lower income, less work time, unemployment for certain occupations

COVID-19 pandemic

2 ZERO HUNGER — Food production and distribution could be disrupted

7 AFFORDABLE AND CLEAN ENERGY — Supply and personnel shortages are leading to disrupted access to electricity, further weaking health system response and capacity

3 GOOD HEALTH AND WELL-BEING — Devastating effect on health outcomes

6 CLEAN WATER AND SANITATION — Supply disruptions and inadequate access to clean water hinder access to clean handwashing facilities, one of the most important COVID-19 prevention measures

5 GENDER EQUALITY — Women's economic gains at risk and increased levels of violence against women. Women account for majority of health and social care workers who are more exposed to COVID-19.

10 REDUCED INEQUALITIES

4 QUALITY EDUCATION — School for many closed; remote learning less effective and not accessible for some

Source: UNDESA

Figure 6.3 The Interconnections Between SDG 3 and other SDGs Through the Prism of COVID-19. (UN, 2020: 12).

Conclusion

This chapter has endeavoured to demonstrate the relevance of the *Wellbeing Policy Statement and Framework for Practice* (DES, 2019) in supporting the transition between primary and post-primary school. The transition process is accorded a defined holistic structure with a focus on cognitive, socio-economic and behavioural outcomes, aligning with the 4 Hs model which frames this entire book. There is acknowledgement that not all students have the opportunity to make this transition and that refugee students have very specific needs in this context. A key message in the chapter is that the process requires effective communication between primary and post-primary schools in advance of the students moving from one setting to the other. The nurturing of social as well as academic development emerges as key to a successful transition. Also, the issue of successful transitions should be incorporated into the overall curriculum and not confined to areas such as Social, Personal and Health Education. Familiarity with both primary and post-primary curricula on the part of teachers and other stakeholders is presented as being an obvious, yet possibly overlooked, element of success. Partnerships with the key stakeholders in the process are highlighted with the voice of the pupil being foregrounded. Recognition of the role of policy and the need for planning also emerges as the concern and business of all involved. Use of a structured approach is promoted as a means of creating empathy and maintaining the hope of students, as they navigate this new stage in their lives.

Activities for promoting well-being in the classroom

A sample of well-being activities is provided below. These activities can be used to reflect on well-being in general with senior primary and junior post-primary students, to explore the specific needs of refugee students and to assist students as they adjust to their new environment. These are easy to do and require limited resources.

Activity 6.1: well-being gifts

This fun activity (adapted from O'Sullivan, 2019) allows participants to enjoy giving and receiving gifts. It enhances positive relationships and is suitable for any age group. It would be a useful activity to help students to get to know each other.

Subject area: SPHE/Well-being

Time Allocation: (Two separate sessions): First session: Fifteen minutes for initial discussion, 30 minutes for art activity, Time to complete the gift bag (homework)

Second session: Fifteen minutes for distribution and reflection.

Materials: Plain paper carrier bags (available from most stationers), materials for design, small gifts.

Learning Outcomes: That the students will be enabled to:

- Reflect on the joy of giving and receiving gifts
- Realise that gifts do not need to incur a cost
- Enhance a classmate's day through giving a small gift.

Step one: introduction

Ask the students to reflect on giving and receiving gifts. List examples of when gifts may be given. Why do we exchange gifts? What influences our choice of gifts?

Step two: examples of gifts

Ask the students to provide examples of gifts that they would like to exchange with class-mates. Encourage them to reflect on gifts which may represent their culture/traditions. Intro-duce a monetary limit (€1) and ask the students what could they give as a gift with this limit. This helps the students to understand that giving gifts does not necessarily require spending money.

Gifts could include the following:

- Interesting article from newspaper or magazine
- Words of a favourite song/poem
- A tasty recipe
- An original drawing
- Sharing some words of a language other than English
- A photograph
- A small bar of chocolate
- A piece of fruit

Step three: choosing gift for a classmate

Distribute a slip of paper to each student. Invite them to write their names on the slip of paper and to fold it in two. Collect the names and place them in a bag. Each student then selects one name from the bag. They do not reveal the names.

Step four: distribution of plain paper bags

Distribute a plain paper bag to each student. Invite the students to suggest ideas for decorat-ing the bags and personalising them for their chosen classmate. Allow time for decoration.

For homework, the students are tasked with filling the bag with five small gifts to the maximum cost of €1. They should label the bag with the name of the recipient. Remind the students of why gifts are exchanged.

Step Five: (Session two). Distribution of gifts

Students bring their bags to school and leave them in a designated place. Each student is then presented with their gift bag. The gift givers remain anonymous. The recipients can try to guess the names of the gift givers (optional).

Each student is invited to express how they feel on receipt of their gift (focus on mental and emotional well-being).

NOTE: The success of this activity is contingent upon every student participating. It may be an idea to allow an interval between the first and second session to facilitate the participation of each student and to bring some additional gifts to school on the date of distribution to avoid any student being left out.

Possibilities for integration with other curricular areas
Visual Arts: Decoration of bags
Language and Literacy: Reading and writing a poem for inclusion in the bag; translation of words from another language
Maths: Estimating cost of items for bag

Activity 6.2: self-care calendar

This activity (adapted from O'Sullivan, 2019) will help the students to understand the importance of self-care at this time of transition in their lives. They are reminded of the need to take time to plan for self-care just as they would plan for other activities.

Subject area: SPHE/Well-being

Age group: 12–13 years (first year of post-primary school).

Time Allocation: 30 minutes

Materials: Copies of Self-care calendar

Learning outcomes:

That the students will be enabled to:

* reflect on the meaning of self-care
* understand the importance of planning for self-care
* complete a self-care calendar for one week

Step one: introduction

Conduct a brain storming session in relation to the meaning of self-care.
What does self-care mean? Do you think that people think about their own self-care?
Can you suggest some ideas in relation to self-care for your age-group? What would help you plan for your self-care?
Record some ideas on the board.

Step two: the self-care calendar

Show an example of the self-care calendar on the board (Table 6.2). Discuss the structure of the calendar. How is it similar to other calendars? How does it differ? How many spaces are there for self-care activities each day? Are more spaces needed?

Table 6.2 The self-care calendar

I Will Care for Myself /We Will Care for Ourselves By:						
Monday	Tuesday	Wednesday	Thursday	Friday	Saturday	Sunday
1						
2						
3						

Ask the students if they would be interested in completing the calendar for one week. Discuss the benefits of doing this activity individually/as a group. Invite the students to vote on which approach they will take.

Step three: completing the self-care calendar

Distribute a copy of the calendar to each student. Allow them time to record some self-care activities. Remind them that they can repeat some or all of the activities each day if they wish. Emphasise that their proposed activities must be realistic.

If the class has agreed to do a group self-care calendar for the week, discuss the individual ideas and negotiate agreement on what the class can do as a group. Record on a large copy of the calendar and display in the classroom.

Step four: conclusion

Invite ideas for making the calendar more relevant to themselves/to the class through illustration. Allow time for including illustrations on their calendars.

Possibilities for integration with other curricular areas:
Maths: Measurement/Time
Visual Arts: Illustrating the calendars
History: Origin of the Roman Calendar

Activity 6.3: as a team we keep our school clean

This activity (adapted from O'Sullivan, 2019) links with the observations on school environment in section one of this chapter. It also links with the whole-school approach to sustainability as outlined in the learning objectives for the SDGs (UNESCO, 2017: 53). The 4 Hs model framing this book are evidenced here in a very practical and inclusive manner.

Subject area: SPHE/Well-being.

Age Group: All (very helpful in relation to forming 'buddy systems' in a school)

Time Allocation: five-week initiative

Materials: Gloves, Litter pickers, Refuse sacks, Hand sanitisers, Bins, Brushes, Dustpans.

Learning Outcomes:

That all participants will be enabled to:

- Assess the physical environment of the school
- Draft a list of tasks to be shared among staff and students
- Acknowledge that a pleasant environment can be achieved through a joint effort
- Related the activity to citizenship education.

Step one: introduction

The issue of the physical environment of the school and its importance to well-being is tabled for discussion at a staff meeting. Teachers assigned to teams of students and each team is assigned to a specific area in the school. (Note: age-group of students to be mixed to facilitate 'buddy system' and leadership skills).

Step two: team meetings

A time for meeting with the teams is arranged and each team identifies 2–3 tasks to improve their assigned space. Procedure for the storage of communal resources in the school to be agreed. Students could be assigned the organisation and distribution of these resources when needed.

Step three: creating slogans

The importance of keeping the school clean and tidy is discussed by each team. Students are assigned the task of deciding a slogan relating to the organisation of their space and volunteers are sought in relation to designing a poster.

Step four: launch

A special school assembly is organised to launch the five-week campaign. Each team monitors their assigned space and encourages their peers to engage with the initiative. Best weekly improvement to be acknowledged at subsequent assemblies

Step five: conclusion of campaign

After the campaign, teachers and students in each team reflect on the process and the impact it had on their own physical and mental well-being and that of the school community.

Possibilities for integration with other curricular areas:
Visual Arts: Designing a poster
Music: Composing a 'Clean Up' song
Language and Literacy: Key words in the 'Clean Up' campaign
Science: Types of Pollution/Effects of Pollution on the Environment

Lesson 6.4: making connections in solidarity

This activity, along with activity 5, can be found in *Tidal: Educating the Heart* resource, published by Children in Crossfire (2017). It helps the students to develop a sense of empathy with others and awareness of the importance of community engagement. It also facilitates awareness of situations wherein solidarity may be lacking. Children in Crossfire (2017:25) define solidarity as follows: 'a feeling of Unity and Agreement – what affects some of us, affects us all. It is about supporting others and working with them to make positive change. It is about taking action for a fairer world'.

Subject area: SPHE/Well-being/Global Citizenship

Age Group: 11-13 years (final year of primary or first year of post-primary school)

Time Allocation: 45 minutes

Materials: Pens, Paper, Art materials

Learning outcomes:

That students will be enabled to:

- Understand the meaning of Solidarity
- Put the concept of Solidarity into action
- Promote the concept in the school/wider community

Step one: introduction

Ask students if they know what the word 'solidarity' means. This may require some discussion.
   Discussion Questions:

- Do you think solidarity is important? Why/Why not?
- Do you think solidarity is linked to kindness? Why/Why not?
- Do you think solidarity can help make the world a better place?
- Do you think it is possible for us as a class to do something in solidarity with the people who are working to make products, but not getting a fair wage or decent working conditions?
- What do you think we can do?

Step two: doing research

Explain to the students that we can do something in solidarity with organisations who are working to improve the working conditions for the people who make our products by doing some research. Divide the class into groups of four or five, and give each group one of the listed organisations below to research (alternatively, they might be aware of other organisations too)
   www.fashionrevolution.org
   www.cleanclothes.org
   www.fairtrade.ie
   www.fairtrade.org.uk
   www.labourbehindthelabel.org

Step three: presenting findings

Invite the students to think of creative ways to present their findings about the organisation and its work (Poem, Poster, Song, or News item).

Each group then provides a short presentation to their peers. Invite discussion and comment.

Step four: working in solidarity

Invite the students to identify an action they can take in solidarity with people who make their products e.g. sign one of the organisation's petitions, raise awareness through a school assembly, work to become a Fairtrade school.

Tip: Create an 'Action Wall' in the classroom where students can add their suggested actions. The teacher might wish to choose an action or a number of actions to complete as a class.

Possibilities for integration with other curricular areas:

Language and Literary: Developing a news item/writing a poem

Drama: Presenting the news item (simulation of radio/TV studio)

Music: Composing a song of solidarity

Visual Arts: Creating a poster

Geography: Research examples of unfair conditions for workers in other countries e.g. child labour

Activity 6.5: the mind jar

This lesson may help students to reach a state of calm and is useful when addressing traumatic situations.

Subject Area: SPHE/Well-being

Age group: 11–13 years (final year of primary or first year of post-primary school)

Time Allocation: 30 minutes

Materials: Glass jars with lids, Glitter Glue, Regular glitter, Hot water, Dish of soap or shampoo, Spoons, Measuring jug

Learning Outcomes:

That students will be enabled to:

- Develop skills for resilience and well-being
- Learn more about ways in which they can calm bodies and minds through breathing and other techniques
- Develop coping skills for responding to situations when things are not calm

Step one: introduction

Discuss with the students the impact of conflicting thoughts on their minds. Explain that they are going to make a 'Mind Jar'. (Note: this can be done as one Mind Jar for the class, or individual or group mind jars. Please bear in mind Health and Safety concerns when using hot water).

Step two: making the mind jar

Fill the jar with hot water – not boiling, but hot. Add a generous amount of glitter glue and stir it so it blends well with the water. Add regular glitter – encourage the students to choose colours that interest them. Add a few drops of dish soap or shampoo. Put the lid on it and give it a shake.

Step three: using the mind jar

When the mind jars have been made, explain to the students that their mind jar can help them to find focus and calm while paying attention to their emotions, feelings and thoughts.

Ask them to think of a time that they felt very frustrated or angry; they do not need to share that memory with anyone. When they have all thought of a time, ask them to shake their mind jars.

Explain that the glitter in the jar represents their emotions, feelings and thoughts. The act of shaking the jar demonstrates that our 'Thinking Brain' and 'Feeling Brain' are not communicating well. Ask the students to notice how the glitter is rushing and swirling about as they shake their jars. Ask them to notice how it is difficult to find a clear spot.

Then ask students to stop shaking their jars and put them down. Invite them to notice what happens when we stop shaking our mind jars and simply observe (the glitter should start to sink to the bottom and the water should soon become clear).

Step four: conclusion

Explain that when we give ourselves space and time to settle we can clear our minds. When we have cleared our minds, we are in a great position to feel good, to learn with and from each other, to have good friendships and to express ourselves in a healthy and happy way.

Invite the students to provide other suggestions for reaching a state of calm.

Possibilities for integration with other curricular areas:
Science: Floating and Sinking
PE: Calming activities
Visual Arts: Colour and Shape

The remaining activities will focus specifically on the transition between primary and post-primary schools.

Activity 6.6: comparing mission statements

This activity will help to develop the students' language and language and literacy skills as well as facilitating critical engagement and analysis of the mission statements of their current and new schools.

Subject area: Language and literacy

Age group: 11-12 years (final year in primary school)

Time Allocation: One hour

Materials: Copies of primary and post-primary school mission statements.

Learning Outcomes:

That the students will be enabled to:

- Compare the mission statements of their current and new schools
- Identify key words from each statement
- Analyse similarities and differences in each statement
- Make recommendations in terms of content

Step one: introduction

Discuss the meaning of mission and mission statement with the students. Ask them where the mission statement of their current school is located. Have they read the school mission statement? Who wrote it? How long is the statement? What are the most important words? Do they think about it? Is it important to their school lives? Why? What do they expect to read in the mission statement of their new school?

Mission: A specific task with which a person or group is charged (Merriam-Webster Online 2022)

Mission Statement: A statement of the purpose or goal of an organisation (Merriam-Webster Online 2022)

Step two: studying the mission statements

Divide the students into groups of four. Appoint a leader and a scribe. Distribute a copy of the current mission statement and the mission statement of their new school to each group. Allow time for the students to read each mission statement and to record the following:

-Five key words from each statement
-Two similarities in each statement
-Two differences in each statement
-The most important sentence in each statement
-Any additions that they would like to make to each statement (possibly in the context of supporting refugee students).

Step three: discussion of findings

When the groups have completed their analysis, invite a group member to present the observations of their respective group. Record the main conclusions on the board.

Step four: conclusion

Invite the students to write down their main learning from the activity. Are they more aware of mission statements now?

Remind them to look out for the mission statement of their new school.

Possibilities for integration with other curricular areas:

Geography: Mapping the location of the mission statement; identifying mission statements in other settings

History: Mission statements which shaped history

Visual Arts: Providing a pictorial representation of the mission statement.

Activity 6.7: a visit to the post-primary school

This activity will help students to become familiar with their new surroundings in advance of starting post-primary school. It needs careful planning between the final year of primary school teacher(s) and the first-year coordinator.

Subject area: Geography

Age group: 11-12 years (final year of primary school)

Time Allocation: 2 hours (This could be divided into 2x1 hour sessions).

Materials: Handouts for the field trip, clipboards, writing and art materials.

Learning Outcomes:

That the students will be enabled to:

- Map the journey from their primary school to their post-primary school. (Note: the focus will be on the post-primary school which the majority of the class will be attending).
- Identify eight key features of the post-primary school (including the school mission statement)
- Draw a picture of the post-primary school with the eight features included.

Step one: introduction

Discuss the impending transition from primary to post-primary school. Ask the students if they are already familiar with their chosen school. Do all students go to post-primary school? Are they aware of reasons why students may not get the opportunity to go to post-primary school? Invite descriptions of the school. Record the key words.

Step two: organisation of field trip

Organise the students into groups of three (leader, observer, scribe) distancing. Distribute the two handouts and one clipboard to each group.

Handout One: a blank page on which the students can draw a rough map of their journey to the post-primary school.

Handout Two: a list of key features to be found in the post-primary school.

Discuss the two handouts with the students and ensure that everyone understands what to do.

Outline all safety issues relating to the field trip. (Journey may be on foot or by bus).

Step three: field trip (this may take place on a separate day)

Lead the students on the field trip. Highlight any interesting features on the way. Encourage the students to take photographs as relevant, with permission being sought when photographs of people are taken.

On arrival at the school, meet with the first year coordinator or designated staff member. The tour of the school then begins. In their groups, the students are asked to note the locations of the eight key features on their handout. The tour should be of approximately 30 mins duration. At the end of the tour the students thank their guide(s) and present a thank you card signed by the class.

Step four: conclusion

Students then return to their own classroom, discuss their findings and draw an image of the school which they visited. These are displayed in the classroom. Ask the students if all schools are like the one that they have visited. Focus in particular on areas of the world affected by war, climate change or famine.

Tip: The tour of the school could be led by first year/second year students. This would enable the students to get to know some of their future peers.

Tip: Invite the students to take a photo of their field trip so that they can discuss the visit with their parents/guardians.

Possibilities for integration with other curricular areas:
Geography: Schools in other parts of the world
History: Research the history of the school and its former students
Maths: Distance to the school. Duration of journey.
Visual Arts: Drawing and presenting the picture of the school
Language and Literacy: Describing the key features

To do in advance of the field trip:
Meet with designated teacher in the post-primary school

- Prepare handouts
- Prepare thank you card
- Organise transport if necessary.

Activity 6.8: looking at timetables

This activity will help the students to become familiar with the timetable of their new school while comparing it with their current one.

Subject area: Maths

Age group: 11-12 years (final year of primary school)

Time Allocation: 30 minutes

Materials: Copies of current and first-year timetables

Learning Outcomes: That the students will be enabled to:

- Reflect on the role and importance of timetables
- Compare and contrast current and new timetables
- Engage with simple maths activities based on timetables

Step one: introduction

Ask the students to take out their copies of their current timetable. Invite them to reflect on its importance in the school day. Is it easy to understand? What do they think the main difference between their current timetables and their new timetables will be?

Step two: comparing timetables.

Distribute a copy of the first year timetable to each student and allow them time to study both timetables. Ask them to write down the main differences between both timetables and to discuss their observations in pairs.

Step three: short quiz on the first year timetable

Distribute the worksheet below to the students. Allow them 5 minutes to answer the questions. When the time is up, ask them to swap the sheet with another student and to correct the questions (Table 6.3).

Table 6.3 Sample questions about the new school

1   What time does school start in first year?
2   What time does school finish?
3   How much longer is the school day than in 6th class?
4   How many classes per day in first year?
5   How long does each class last?
6   Are there any double classes?
7   How long do the double classes last?
8   How long does lunch break last?
9   What is the total amount of time spent in class per day?
10 Do you think that all timetables are the same? What circumstances could have an impact on school timetables?

Step four: conclusion

Invite the students to share their learning from the activity. Focus on the fact that movement between rooms may be a key feature of the new timetable.

Possibilities for integration with other curricular areas:
Geography: Locating the different rooms in the school; using timetables in other contexts
Language and Literacy: Key words relating to timetables
Visual Arts: Designing a timetable

Activity 6.9: a big change in my life

This activity acknowledges that first year students experience many different feelings and allows them time to reflect on these feelings. It is an individual activity (Table 6.4) and could be completed prior to undertaking the group activity (Activity 6.10).

Subject area: SPHE/Well-being

Age group: 13 years (first year of post-primary school)

Time Allocation: 30 minutes

Materials: Copy of worksheet for each student (see below).

Learning Outcomes:

> That the students will be enabled to:

- Reflect on this key transition phase in their lives
- Engage with their new peers
- Record their observations

Step one: introduction

Acknowledge to the group that as they start secondary school, they are entering a new stage of their lives where there are big changes. They are making new friends, meeting new challenges and settling into a new environment.

Table 6.4 A big change in my life

A Big Change in my life
1   My name is...
2   The name of my new school is ....
3   The school principal's name is ....
4   The name of the person sitting on my on my right is...
5   The name of the person sitting on my left is..
6   My day so far has been...
7   At the moment I feel like the colour...............because...............
8   My hopes for my first year in secondary school are...
9   One key feature of my new school is ....
10 My hopes for my first week are:..

Step two: a time to reflect

Ask the students to close their eyes and to think about the main changes that are happening in their lives as they start post-primary school. Lead them through a guided meditation where they are focusing on moving into this new stage of life. Include appropriate music. Allow approximately 5 minutes for this reflection.

Step three: recording some key thoughts and learning

Distribute the worksheet to each student and allow them time (7–10 minutes) to complete the statements. Circulate the room and provide support as needed.
Invite the students to share their thoughts/new learning (if they wish).

Step four: conclusion

Ask the students to keep the worksheet in their SPHE/Well-being folder and to discuss with family members at home.

Possibilities for integration with other curricular areas:
Language and Literacy: Key words relating to feelings and changes
Visual Arts: Colour and mood
Music: Music and mood

Activity 6.10: discussing the changes

This activity can be found in the NCCA SPHE Resources for first Year students (NCCA, 2020). In these resources there is a specific focus on returning to school after their experience of extended absence due to Covid-19. However, many of the activities are relevant to the adaptation to post-primary school. It can be viewed as an extension/follow-up to activity 9 above.

Subject area: SPHE/Well-being

Age group: 13 years (first year of post-primary school)

Time Allocation: 30 minutes

Materials: Question cards (see NCCA, 2020).

Learning Outcomes: That the students will be enabled to:

- Understand that it is normal to experience many different feelings when moving to post-primary school
- Understand that others feel the same way
- Discuss their feelings and reactions with their peers

Step one: introduction

Refer to individual activity (A Big Change in my Life). Inform the group that today, they will do further work on this theme, this time, working in groups.

Step two: question cards (Table 6.5)

Divide the class into groups of 3–4. Give each group a set of questions on cards (facing down). Each person, in turn, picks up a card and answers the question. They can pass or pick up another card if they feel unable to answer the question on the first card they pick up.

Step three: class discussion

After the group work invite the class to comment on the activity. Did they feel confident about contributing to the discussion? Did the activity help them to express how they felt about starting post- primary school? Are there any changes that could be made to the activity?

Step four: conclusion

In conclusion, invite each student to choose a question and to illustrate their answer. Ask them to retain the picture in their SPHE/Well-being folders. (This may be done as a home-work activity).

Possibilities for integration with other curricular areas:
Language and Literacy: Oral language
Drama: Mime/Still images of primary school memories
Music: A song to show my feelings
Visual Arts: Illustration of responses to questions.

Table 6.5 Set of sample questions

What's the biggest change about being in post-primary school?	What's the best thing about being in post primary school?
What's challenging about being in post-primary school?	If a song could express how you feel right now, which one would you choose
What are you most looking forward to in your new school?	How has your day been going so far?
What's your happiest memory of sixth class?	What do you miss most about leaving primary school?

Resources

An extensive list of resources, videos and case studies for SDG 3 is included in the SDG padlet accompanying this book: https://padlet.com/annedolan/o6rds38ylfy6a28h

Weblinks

Children in Crossfire. (2017) *Tidal: Educating the Heart Pupil Programme*. Derry: Author. https://www.childrenincrossfire.org/wp-content/uploads/2019/10/Educating-the-Heart-Pupil-Programme.pdf

Concern Active Citizenship Unit. (2017) *Good Health and Well-Being: Resources for Teachers and Facilitators*. Dublin: Author. https://www.concern.net/schools-and-youth

National Council for Curriculum and Assessment. (2020) *SPHE Resources to Support 1st Year Students as They Return to School*. Dublin: NCCA. https://ncca.ie/media/4646/sphe-resources_1_final_24.pdf

O'Sullivan C. (ed.) (2019) *Teacher Well-Being and Diversity: A Manual for Teachers in Diverse Educational Settings*. Erasmus+ Project Number: 2016-1-NO 01-KA-201-022081. https://sites.google.com/view/teacherwellbeingdiversity/resources/classroom-manual?authuser=0

Key dates

February 4: World Cancer Day

March 14: World Kidney Day

March 24: World Tuberculosis day

April 2: World Autism Awareness Day

April 7: World Health Day

April 25: World Malaria Day

April 28: World Day for Safety and Health at Work

May 12: International Nurses Day

May 31: World No Tobacco Day

September 29: World Heart Day

October 10: World Mental health Day

October 16: World Food Day

December 1: World Aids Day

December 12: International Universal Health Coverage Day

December 27: International Day of Epidemic Preparedness

Children's literature for SDG 3

An extensive list of children's literature is available from the Professional Development Service for Teachers (Ireland):

PDST (2020) *Children's Books for Well Being: An Exploration of Picture Books and Novels Which May Support Teaching and Learning in SPHE* Dublin: PDST available on

https://www.pdst.ie/sites/default/files/Children%27s%20Books%20for%20Wellbeing%20.pdf

Picturebooks

Biddulph, R. (2019) *Odd Dog Out* HarperCollins.

Byers, G. and Bobo, K.A. (Illus) (2018) *I Am Enough* Balzer + Bray.

Christou, B. (2020) *Nervous Nigel* Templar Publishing.

Cook, J. and Dufalla, A. (illus) (2012) *Wilma Jean the Worry Machine* National Center for Youth Issues.

Cummings, B. and Svobodova, Z. (illus) (2019) *My Magical Choices* Boundless Movement LLC.

de la Peña, M. and Long, L. (illus) (2018) *Love* G.P. Putnam's Sons Books for Young Readers.

Evans, J. and Jackson, L. (illus) (2014) *How Are You Feeling Today Baby Bear?: Exploring Big Feelings After Living in a Stormy Home* Jessica Kingsley Publishers.

Fox, M. and Staub, L. (Illus) (2017) *Whoever You Are* HMH Books for Young Readers.

Garcia, G. and Hui Tan, Y. (Illus) (2017) *Listening To My Body* Skinned Knee Publishing.

Huebner, D. and Matthews, B. (illus) (2005) *What to Do When You Worry Too Much: A Kid's Guide to Overcoming Anxiety* Magination Press.

Ironside, V. and Rodgers, F. (illus) (2011) *The Huge Bag of Worries* Hachette Children's.

Jones, L. (2015) *The Princess and the Fog: A Story for Children with Depression* Jessica Kingsley Publishers.

Kelbaugh, G. (2002) *Can I Catch It Like A Cold?: A Story To Help Children Understand A Parent's Depression* Centre for Addiction & Mental.

Llenas, A. (2018) *The Color Monster: A Story about Emotions* Little, Brown Books for Young Readers.

Luyken, C. (2019) *My Heart* Dial Books.

Nhat Hahn, T. (2008) *A Handful of Quiet: Happiness in Four Pebbles* Plum Blossom.

Ortner, N., Taylor, A. and Polizzi, M. (2018) *My Magic Breath: Finding Calm Though Mindful Breathing* Harper Collins.

Percival, T. (2018) *Perfectly Norman* Bloomsbury Children's Books.

Percival, T. (2019) *Ruby Finds a Worry* Bloomsbury Children's Books.

Perry, L.M. (2016) *Skin Like Mine* G Publishing.

Perry, L.M. (2015) *Hair Like Mine* G Publishing.

Purtill, S. and Saha, A. (illus) *It's OK to be Different: A Children's Picturebook About Diversity* Dunhill Clare Publishing.

Verde, S. and Reynolds, P. (Illus) (2017) *I am Peace: A Book of Mindfulness* Abrams Books for Young Readers.

Chapter books and informational texts

Boyne, J. and Jeffers, O. (2014) *The Terrible Thing That Happened to Barnaby Brocket* Yearling.

Dunn Buron, (2013) *When My Worries Get Too Big! A Relaxation Book for Children Who Live with An Anxiety* Autism Asperger Publishing Co.

Gettern, K. and Douglas, S. (Illus) (2023) *Ada Rue and the Banished* Bloomsbury Books.

Haddon, M. (2004) *The Curious Incident of the Dog in the Night* Time Vintage Contemporaries.

O' Neill, P. (2018). *Don't Worry Be Happy* Vie Publishing.

Rosen, M. and Blake, Q. (2005) *The Sad Book* Candlewick; Library Binding edition.

Syed, M. and Triumph, T. (2019) *You Are Awesome: Find Your Confidence and Dare to Be Brilliant at (Almost) Anything* Sourcebooks Explore.

Williamson, L. and Bradley, J. (illus) (2023) *Best Friends Forever* Guppy Books.

References

Borko, H. (2004) 'Professional development and teacher learning: Mapping the terrain'. *Educational Researcher*, 33(8), 1-49.

Children in Crossfire. (2017) *Educating the Heart Pupil Programme*. Derry: Author. https://www. childrenincrossfire.org/wp-content/uploads/2019/10/Educating-the-Heart-Pupil-Programme.pdf

Cochrane Database of Systematic Reviews. (2014) Issue 4. Art. No.: CD008958. Oxford: Wiley and Sons Ltd. https://doi.org/10.1002/14651858.CD008958.pub2

Coffey, A. (2013) 'Relationships: The key to successful transition from primary to secondary school?' *Improving Schools*, 16(3), 261-271. https://doi.org/10.1177/1365480213505181

Cox-Petersen, A. (2011) *Educational Partnerships: Connecting Schools, Families, and the Community*. Thousand Oaks, CA: SAGE.

Department of Education and Science. (2009) *Social, Personal and Health Education (SPHE) in the Primary School*. Dublin: Author. www.education.ie

Department of Education and Skills. (2015) *The Framework for Junior Cycle*. Dublin: Author. www.education.ie

Department of Education and Skills. (2019) *Wellbeing Policy Statement and Framework for Practice*. Dublin: Author. www.education.ie

Department of Education and Skills, Health Services Executive, Department of Health. (2013) *Well-Being in Post-Primary Schools: Guidelines for Mental Health Promotion and Suicide Prevention*. Dublin: Authors. www.education.ie

Dooley, B. and Fitzgerald, A. (2012) *My World Survey 1: The National Study of Youth Mental Health in Ireland*. Dublin: Jigsaw and UCD School of Psychology.

Education Review Office, New Zealand. (2012) *Transition from Primary to Secondary School*. www.ero. govt.nz

Fullan, M. (1993) *Change Forces: Probing the Depths of Educational Reform*. London: Falmer Press.

Gatzweiler, F.W., Zhu, Y.-G., Diez Roux, A.V., Capon, A., Donnelly, C., Salem, G., Ayad, H.M., Speizer, I., Nath, I., Boufford, J.I., Hanaki, K., Rietveld, L.C., Ritchie, P., Jayasinghe, S., Parnell, S. and Zhang, Y. (2017) *Advancing Health and Well-being in the Changing Urban Environment: Implementing a Systems Approach*. Singapore: Springer.

Health Services Executive. (2013a) *Schools for Health in Ireland: Framework for Developing a Health Promoting School: Primary*. Dublin: Author.

Health Services Executive. (2013b) *Schools for Health in Ireland: Framework for Developing a Health Promoting School: Post-Primary*. Dublin: Author.

Humphrey, N. and Ainscow, M. (2006) 'Transition club: Facilitating learning, participation and psychological adjustment during the transition to secondary school'. *European Journal of Psychology of Education, 21*(3), 319–331.

Mannix-McNamara, P., Moynihan, S., Jourdan, D. and Lynch, R. (2012) 'Pre-service teachers' experience of and attitudes to teaching SPHE in Ireland'. *Health Education*, 112(3), 199–216.

McClees, E. (2016) 'School mission statements: A look at influencing behaviour'. *International Journal of Humanities and Social Science Review, 2*(1), 50–54.

McCormack, L., Finlayson, O. and McCloughlin, T. (2014) 'The CASE programme implemented across the primary and secondary school transition in Ireland'. *International Journal of Science Education, 36*(17), 2892–2917.

Merriam-Webster.com (2022) https://www.merriam-webster.com (17 January 2022).

Merritt, E. (2016) 'Time for teacher learning, planning critical for school reform'. *Phi Delta Kappan, 98*(4), 31–37.

Morgan, M. and NicCraith, D. (2015) *Workload, Stress and Resilience of Primary Teachers: Report of a Survey of INTO Members*. Dublin: INTO.

National Council for Curriculum and Assessment. (2008) *Primary Curriculum Review, Phase 2*. Dublin: Author. www.ncca.ie

National Council for Curriculum and Assessment. (2009) *Aistear: The Early Childhood Curriculum Framework*. Dublin: Author. www.ncca.ie

National Council for Curriculum and Assessment. (2017) *Guidelines for Wellbeing in Junior Cycle*. Dublin: Author. www.ncca.ie

National Council for Curriculum and Assessment. (2023) *Primary Curriculum Framework*. Dublin: Author. www.ncca.ie

National Council for Curriculum and Assessment. (2020) *SPHE Resources: To support 1st year students as they return To school*. Dublin: Author. www.ncca.ie

NicGabhainn, S., O'Higgins, S. and Barry, M. (2010) 'The implementation of social, personal and health education in Irish schools'. *Health Education, 110*(6), 452–470.

O'Sullivan, C. (ed.) (2019) *Teacher Well-being and Diversity: A Manual for Teachers in Diverse Educational Settings*. Erasmus+ Project Number: 2016-1-NO 01-KA-201-022081. https://sites.google.com/view/teacherwellbeingdiversity/resources/classroom-manual?authuser=00

O'Sullivan, K. (2023) Poor: Grit, courage and life-changing value of self-belief London: Penguin.

Owen, S. (2016) 'Professional learning communities: Building skills, reinvigorating the passion, and nurturing teacher wellbeing and "flourishing" within significantly innovative schooling contexts'. *Educational Review, 68*(4), 403–419.

Slate, J., Jones, C., Wiesman, K., Alexander, J. and Saenz, T. (2008) 'School mission statements and school performance: A mixed research investigation'. *New Horizons in Education, 56*(2), 17–27.

Smyth, E. (2016) 'Social relationships and the transition to secondary education'. *Economic and Social Review*, 47(4), 451–476.

Smyth, E., McCoy, S. and Darmody, M. (2004) *Moving Up. The Experiences of First-Year Students in Post-Primary Education.* Dublin: Liffey Press in association with the ESRI.

UN. (2020) *Shared Responsibility, Global Solidarity: Responding to the Socio-Economic Impacts of Covid-19.* New York: United Nations. https://unsdg.un.org/sites/default/files/2020-03/SG-Report-Socio-Economic-Impact-of-Covid19.pdf.

UNESCO. (2017) *Education for Sustainable Development: Learning Objectives.* Paris: Author. *https://www.sdg4education2030.org/education-sustainable-development-goals-learning-objectives-unesco-2017*

UNESCO. (2021) *Reimagining Our Futures Together: A New Social Contract for Education.* Paris: Author. ISBN 978-92-3-100478-0

United Nations (UN). (2020) *Sustainable Development Goals.* https://www.un.org/sustainabledevelopment/sustainable-development-goals

Vaghri, Z., Tessier, Z. and Whalen, C. (2019) 'Refugee and asylum-seeking children: Interrupted child development and unfulfilled child rights'. *Children,* 6(120), 1–16.

Van Rens, M., Haelermans, C., Groot, W. and Maassen van den Brink, H. (2018) 'Facilitating a successful transition to secondary school: (How) does it work? A systematic literature review'. *Adolescent Research Review,* 3, 43–56.

Vischer, J. (2007) 'The effects of the physical environment on job performance: Towards a theoretical model of workplace stress'. *Stress and Health,* 23(3), 175–184.

Waage, J., Yap, C., Bell, S., Levy, C., Mace, G., Pegram, T., Unterhalter, E., Dasandi, N., Hudson, D., Kock, R., Mayhew, S., Marx, C. and Poole, N. (2015) 'Governing the un sustainable development goals: Interactions, infrastructures, and institutions'. *The Lancet Global Health*, 3, e251–e252.

Whitmee, S., Haines, A., Beyrer, C., Boltz, F., Capon, A.G. and de Souza Dias, B.F., et al. (2015) Safeguarding human health in the anthropocene epoch: Report of The Rockefeller Foundation-Lancet commission on planetary health. *The Lancet,* 386(10007), 1973–2028.

World Health Organization. (1948) Preamble to the constitution of the world health organization. In: *Proceedings and Final Acts of the International Health Conference Held in New York from 19 June to 22 July 1946.* New York: World Health Organization, 100. *Official Records of the World Health Organization.* http://apps.who.int/iris/bitstream/handle/10665/85573/Official_record2_eng.pdf?sequence=1

World Health Organisation. (1986) *The Ottawa Charter for Health Promotion.* www.who.int

7 Education (SDG 4)
The building block for all SDGs

Sandra Ryan and Anne M. Dolan

Introduction

Education refers to any act or experience that has a formative effect on an individual's mind, character, or physical ability. In its technical sense, education is the formal process by which society, through schools, colleges, universities and other institutions, purposefully transmits its cultural heritage together with its accumulated knowledge, values and skills to the next generation and influences an individual's feelings, thoughts and actions (Mortimore, 2013). Education is valued because it helps develop citizens, builds social cohesion, fosters national identification and promotes the political development of nation-states (Pritchett, 2003; UNICEF and UNESCO, 2007). It builds human capital and thus contributes to individual earnings and the economic development of society (Burnett et al., 2013). Universal education is also a means to improving the quality and longevity of life, of enhancing human capabilities and freedoms (Sen, 2005), and contributing to sustainable social development (Kazeem et al., 2010). Education is a fundamental human right as identified in Article 26 of the Universal Declaration of Human Rights (United Nations, 1948). This right has been articulated repeatedly through the decades, through, for example, the UNESCO Convention Against Discrimination in Education (1960) and the Convention on the Rights of the Child (1989).

SDG 4 aims to 'ensure inclusive and equitable quality education and lifelong learning opportunities for all' by 2030 (UNESCO, 2015: np). Building education systems that are inclusive, equitable and relevant to all students requires political commitment, regional and global collaboration and government engagement as well as commitment from civil society, the private sector, the UN and other multilateral agencies. This chapter provides an overview of SDG 4 including a discourse on the right to education, an overview of relevant learning objectives and some sample practical learning activities.

SDG4 – quality education

Education in itself is an empowering right and one of the most important tools by which economically and socially marginalised children and adults can lift themselves out of poverty in a sustainable manner. SDG 4 was designed to promote lifelong learning opportunities for all through the provision of inclusive and equitable quality education. The right to education is one of the key principles underpinning Agenda 2030 in general and SDG 4 in particular. SDG4 (Quality education) aspires that all girls and boys complete free primary and secondary

DOI: 10.4324/9781003232001-10

schooling by 2030. It also aims to provide equal access to affordable vocational training, to eliminate gender and wealth disparities, and to achieve universal access to a quality higher education. Achieving inclusive and quality education for all reaffirms the belief that education is one of the most powerful tools for promoting a balance between environmental, economic and social demands.

Every child has the right to access safe, quality education as a basic human right. The commitment to this right is reflected in the Education for All (EFA) movement – a global commitment to provide quality basic education for all children, youth and adults. At the World Education Forum in Dakar in 2000, 164 governments, including Ireland, pledged to achieve EFA by 2015. Some progress has been made. According to UNESCO's Institute for Statistics (nd), on any given school day, over one billion children around the world attend formal tuition in a school setting Today, more children and adolescents are enrolled in pre-primary, primary and secondary education than ever before. The number of children who are out of school has declined in all world regions. Globally, this share has halved. Two decades ago, 16% of children were not enrolled in schools. This number has been reduced to 8% of children today. Yet, 57 million primary-aged children remain out of school, more than half of them in sub-Saharan Africa (UNESCO's Institute for Statistics, nd).

Despite improvements in school enrolments, levels of illiteracy remain high. For many young people, schooling does not lead to learning – and this was before COVID-19 disrupted learning across the globe, creating an urgent need to reimagine education. A lack of trained teachers, inadequate learning materials, makeshift classes and poor sanitation facilities make learning difficult for many children. Others come to school too hungry, sick or exhausted from work or household tasks to learn successfully. The consequences are grave: an estimated 617 million children and adolescents around the world are unable to reach minimum proficiency levels in reading and mathematics, even though two thirds of them are in school (UNESCO, 2017). This learning crisis is the greatest global challenge in preparing children and adolescents for life, work and active citizenship.

Overcrowded classrooms and poorly trained teachers create a very difficult learning environment. A significant proportion of teachers are untrained at both primary and secondary levels. Not all teachers have access to systematic information about their students' learning. Many teachers in the Global South do not have national assessments or standardised tests to monitor learning progress and may also have limited skills in forming their own evaluations of student progress. Attracting qualified people into the teaching profession, retaining them and providing them with the necessary skills, support and supervision is a critical part of improving quality and access to education. While there is much ongoing debate about the nature of quality education, there is broad consensus that national assessments have a role in improving quality and designing effective strategies to target children at risk. There is a real risk that significant investments that have been made in persuading parents and communities of the value of education and convincing them to send their children to school will be wasted unless serious efforts are made to address the quality of teaching and learning.

The current status of education is illustrated through a number of indicators including literacy levels, number of enrolments in primary and secondary schools and data relating to

Table 7.1 Key statistics for SDG 4 indicators (Source UNDP, https://www.undp.org/)

Indicator	Key Figure	Data at Time of Writing 2022 (this needs to be Updated in Line with Changing Data).
Enrolment in primary schools	91%	Enrolment in primary schools in the Global South has reached 91%.
Number of children out of primary school	57 million	57 million primary-aged children remain out of school, more than half of them in sub-Saharan Africa
Number of girls not attending school	25%	one in four girls are not in school in developing countries
Number of children living in conflict affected areas	50%	About half of all out-of-school children of primary school age live in conflict affected areas
Youth illiteracy	103 million	103 million youth worldwide lack basic literacy skills, and more than 60% of them are women.

the participation of girls in education (Table 7.1). Reliable, up to date data is available from the following sources:

Our World Data https://ourworldindata.org/
OECD Education at a Glance: https://www.oecd.org/education/education-at-a-glance/
Human Development Reports: http://hdr.undp.org/
UNESCO's Institute for Statistics: https://uis.unesco.org/

SDG 4: a foundational goal for all other goals

Education is central to the realisation of the 2030 Agenda for Sustainable Development. It has a well-recognised role as an enabler for several SDGs including gender, poverty and jobs. Conversely, progress in other areas may affect education in many ways. The links between SDG 4 and other SDGs have been mapped in Figure 7.1 (Vladimirovaa et al., 2015). In an extensive analysis of United Nations publications, the authors documented a number of links between education and other SDG areas. Figure 7.1 illustrates the relationship between SDG 4 and other SDGs by placing SDG 4 in the centre with one link to and from each SDG (Vladimirovaa et al. 2015: 21). This graphic illustrates how education can act as a catalyst for many other goals. For instance, education is fundamental for the achievement of goals such as poverty reduction (SDG 1), elimination of hunger (SDG 2) and gender equality (SDG5). Progress on some of the SDGs (including a shift to sustainable production patterns) places a requirement on education systems to increase their focus on education for sustainability. For most of the SDGs (with the exception of SDG 14 and SDG 17), causal links are identified in both directions, from education to other goal areas and vice-versa. The most emphasised connections are those between education and growth (SDG 8) as well as gender (SDG 5). By contrast, links with energy (SDG 7), water (SDG 6), cities (SDG 11), sustainable consumption and production (SDG 12) and climate change (SDG 13) receive much less attention in UN publications.

VALUES, NORMS, EMPOWERMENT

Changing norms help achieve

Health SDG3

LABOUR PRODUCTIVITY

Raises · alleviates

helps decrease

Improves

shapes

Gender equality SDG5

Poverty SDG1

Peaceful societies SDG16

Both general and health education improve health outcomes

Growth and jobs SDG8

Builds people's capacities and mobilizes them to fight for their rights

Contributes to society's demand for

Gender norms and discrimination leaves more girls out of school than boys

The poor have lower access to quality the education system

Higher GDP means more resources for education

Stimulates

Inequality SDG10

Transmits

CONFLICTS

Mobilizes people to fight for their rights

Human settlements SDG11

Inequality negatively affects education outcomes

Vital role of cities In transmitting ideas

disrupt

Education

ECONOMIC SHOCKS

Industrial transformation SDG9

disrupt

Sustainable consumption and production SDG12

Changes demand for skills

Creates demand for skilled labor

Facilitates

Builds disaster preparedness

Raises

Helps changing consumption behaviours

Negatively affects

Undernutrition negatively affects education outcomes

Helps transition to nonagricultural occupations

INNOVATION CAPACITY, ENTREPRENEURSHIP

Creates

TIME POVERTY

Disrupts

Food and agriculture SDG2

Access to electricity needed for schools

ENVIRONMENTAL DEGRADATION

AWARENESS

Lack of access creates

Access to water and sanitation is important, especially for girls education

Helps increase farm productivity and agricultural incomes

Facilitates energy transition

Energy SDG7

Lack of access creates

Water stress contributes to

climate change SDG13

Creates

Helps improve access to drinking water and reduce water stress

Water and sanitation SDG6

Ecosystem conservation SDG15

Key pillar in building climate-smart economy

Helps change harmful lifestyles and behavior

Improve ecosystem management

SPECIALIZED SKILLS for sustainable management

Increases adaptation capacity

Facilitate energy transition

Help achieve integrated water resource management

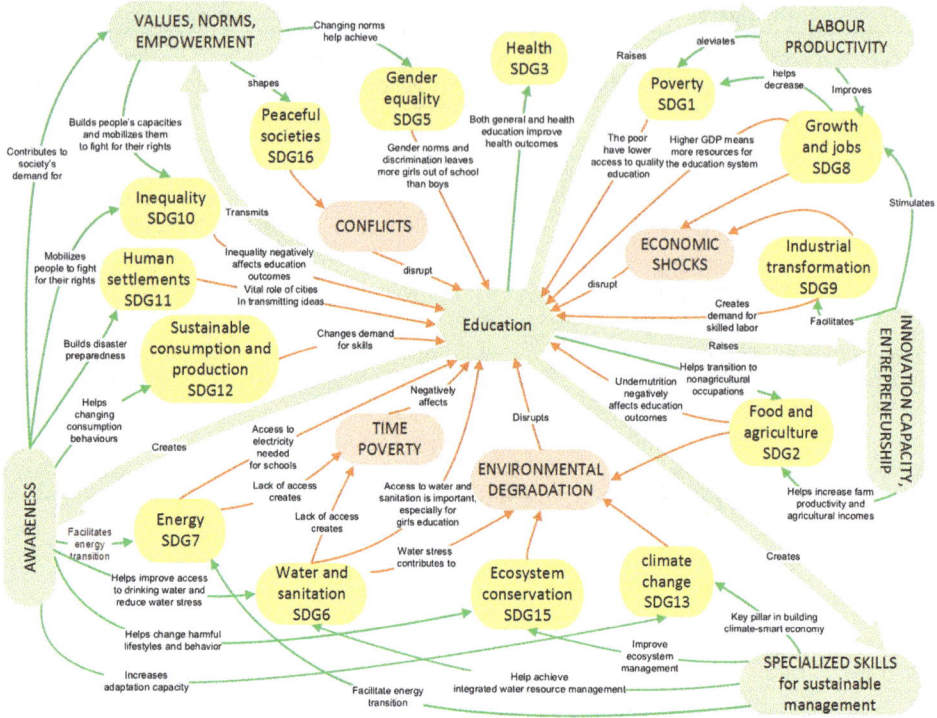

Figure 7.1 Links between Education and other SDGs Through the SDG Targets. Source: (Vladimirovaa et al. 2015:21).

Teaching about, through and for SDG 4

As participants in the 'education' project (for those who have access to formal education), it may appear somewhat strange to vicariously step outside the classroom setting to think about education in general and SDG 4 in particular. Teaching about, for and through the Goals is a good place to begin this process. Table 7.2 sets out learning objectives for SDG 4 using the framework proposed in Chapter 2. Potential topics and learning approaches are listed in Table 7.3. Through Target 4.7 (discussed in Chapter 2), SDG 4 formally recognises the role of education for sustainable development (ESD) and global citizenship education (GCED), which includes peace and human rights education, as well as intercultural education and education for international understanding. This target has been welcomed by those advocating for education for sustainability and global citizenship for decades (Dolan, 2014). Many innovative learning approaches and methods recommended for teaching SDG 4 have been developed by those involved in global citizenship education (Bourn, 2020).

Barriers to education

In many regions around the world where schools are available, enrolment rates continue to be low. Socio-cultural barriers constitute some of the factors why children fail to attend

Table 7.2 Learning objectives for SDG4 (adapted from UNESCO, 2020)

Cognitive learning objectives Teaching **about** the goals: developing respect and understanding	1 The learner understands the important role of education and lifelong learning opportunities for all (formal, non-formal and informal learning) as main drivers of sustainable development, for improving people's lives and in achieving the SDGs. 2 The learner understands education as a public good, a global common good, a fundamental human right and a basis for guaranteeing the realisation of other rights. 3 The learner knows about inequality in access to and attainment of education, particularly between girls and boys and in rural areas, and about reasons for a lack of equitable access to quality education and lifelong learning opportunities. 4 The learner knows about the nature and purpose of the SDGs. 5 The learner understands that education can help create a more sustainable, equitable and peaceful world.
Socio-emotional learning objectives Teaching **for** the goals enhancing empathy and love	1 The learner is able to raise awareness of the importance of quality education for all, a humanistic and holistic approach to education, ESD and related approaches. 2 The learner is able to raise awareness about the SDGs in general and SDG 4 in particular. 3 The learner is able to recognise the intrinsic value of education and to analyse and identify their own learning needs in their personal development. 4 The learner is able to recognise the importance of their own skills for improving their life, in particular for employment and entrepreneurship. 5 The learner is able to engage personally with Education for Sustainability.
Behavioural learning objectives *Teaching **through** the goals* Promoting advocacy and activism	1 The learner is able to contribute to facilitating and implementing quality education for all, ESD and related approaches at different levels. 2 The learner is able to promote gender equality in education. 3 The learner is able to publicly demand and support the development of policies promoting free, equitable and quality education for all, ESD and related approaches as well as aiming at safe, accessible and inclusive educational facilities. 4 The learner is able to promote the empowerment of young people. 5 The learner is able to use all opportunities for their own education throughout their life, and to apply the acquired knowledge in everyday situations to promote sustainable development.

Table 7.3 List of possible topics, (Source: UNESCO, 2020: 19)

Suggested topics	Examples of learning approaches and methods for SDG4
Education as a fundamental human right and a basis for guaranteeing the realisation of other rights	Develop partnerships between schools, universities and other institutions offering education in different regions of the world
Innovative and successful case studies about the power of education from around the world.	Plan and run a quality education awareness campaign
The relevance of inclusive and equitable quality education and lifelong learning opportunities for all (formal, non-formal and informal learning, including the use of ICT) and at all levels for improving people's lives and sustainable development	Conduct a case study on the education system and access to education (e.g., enrolment in primary education) in selected communities or countries
Barriers to education (e.g., poverty, conflicts, disasters, gender inequality, lack of public financing of education, growing privatisation)	Plan and run an ESD project at a school or university, or for the local community
Global attainment of literacy, numeracy and basic skills	Celebrate UN World Youth Skills Day (15 July), International Literacy Day (8 September) or World Teachers'
Diversity and inclusive education	Day (5 October); or take part in Global
Basic skills and competencies needed in the 21st century	Action Week for Education (last week in April)
Knowledge, values, skills and behaviours needed to promote sustainable development	Organize ESD days at local, regional and national level
Education for sustainable development including whole schools approaches	Develop an enquiry-based project: "What is a sustainable school?"
Promotion of the agency of young people and marginalised groups.	

primary school. For instance, some parents, particularly, those with low levels of education, undervalue education in general or they believe it is not suitable for certain children, such as girls and children with disabilities. Cultural barriers can also inhibit access to school for children belonging to a particular ethnic or religious group, social class, and/or sexual and gender minority. Various levels of child labour also affect rates of participation in schools. Furthermore, logistical issues such as distance from school affect students' attendance (UNESCO, 2015). Lack of progress with some SDGs, such as SDG 16 (peaceful societies) may also create barriers of access to education or to educational outcomes. Barriers to education are categorised in different ways in the literature. The graphic devised by Vladimirovaa et al. (2015: 21) (Figure 7.1) clusters barriers to education into four categories: conflicts, economic shocks, environmental degradation, and time poverty. The latter is caused by poverty-related issues including a lack of access to drinking water, nutritious food and energy.

Far too many of the world's children are subject to issues such as poverty, exclusion and pollution that affect their mental well-being, physical health and opportunities to achieve their potential. Prior to the Covid-19 pandemic, over 262 million children and youth were out of school and more than half of the world's children were not acquiring basic literacy and numeracy by age ten. School closures, implemented due to the pandemic worldwide, have further exacerbated existing inequalities. In response, UNESCO (2021) has put forward new methodological guidelines to accelerate progress towards more inclusive, resilient and effective education systems worldwide. Crises such as war, famine or natural disasters also have detrimental effects on the quality, management and equity of education systems and

SDG 4 Improving girls' access to education

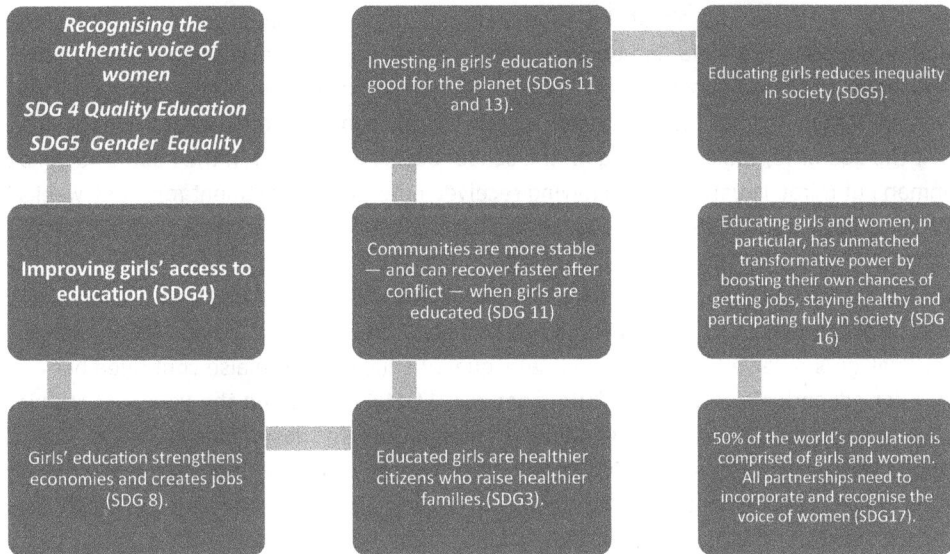

Figure 7.2 Investment in Girls' Education Has a Positive Impact on Several SDGs.

therefore on children's learning. Growing up in a war zone causes children and young people to be twice as likely to be out of school compared to those living in safe and stable environments (UNESCO, 2021/2022).

Failing to allow girls to finish their education bears a huge cost, including poverty, child marriage, early childbearing, and a lack of understanding of their rights and ability to access basic services. An increase in the investment in girls' education has a positive impact on several SDGs including SDG 4 (Quality Education) as illustrated in Figure 7.2.

Providing access to education for girls (SDG 4) is a question of rights as well as a question of gender equality (SDG 5). Evidence also shows that educated girls and women are healthier citizens who raise healthier families (SDG 3). Increased education for girls, who form half of the world's workforce, also strengthens economies and creates jobs (SDG 8) and is good for the planet (SDG 13). Having an education also increases girls' own opportunities for getting a job and participating more fully in society (SDG 16). Educated girls and women also contribute to more stable communities and help society to recover more quickly from conflict (SDG 11). Finally, the world's population is comprised of 50% women and their voice must be incorporated and recognised in a more just and equal world (SDG 17).

Gender as a barrier: the story of Malala Yousafzai

Malala Yousafzai became an international symbol of the fight for girls' education after she was shot in 2012 for opposing Taliban restrictions on female education in her home country of Pakistan. Through her incredible work and advocacy, she embodies the global struggle for gender equality (SDG 5) and female education. When Malala was growing up in Swat Valley in Pakistan, she was prevented from going to school by supporters of the Taliban, an extreme religious group who believe that women should not receive an education. Malala was a student at the school run by her father and believed that she and all other girls had a right to education. She spoke out about the issue even though it was dangerous to do so. In 2009, using a pseudonym, Malala had begun writing a blog about the increasing military activity in her home town and about fears that her school would be attacked. After her identity was revealed, Malala and her father Ziauddin continued to speak out for the right to education.

At the age of 15, while travelling on the school bus, she was shot in the head by a Taliban gunman but miraculously survived having received emergency treatment for many weeks in a UK hospital. It was too dangerous for Malala to return to Pakistan so she continued her education in the UK. The Taliban's attack on Malala received worldwide condemnation. Together with her father who ran a school for girls, she established the Malala Fund, a charity dedicated to giving every girl an opportunity to achieve a future of her choice. Her mission is to ensure all girls receive 12 years of free, safe, quality education. She also continued her campaign for education rights and in 2014, aged just 17, Malala became the youngest recipient of the Nobel Peace Prize. Secretary-General António Guterres designated Malala as a United Nations Messenger of Peace in 2017, to help raise awareness of the importance of girls' education. She has spoken at the United Nations and she is a powerful advocate for the SDGs. In 2013, on July 12th (the day of her birthday), Malala (aged 16) delivered an eloquent speech at the United Nations headquarters. She highlighted the need for worldwide access to women's education and called on all world leaders to reform their policies. The teenager received several rounds of standing ovations for her remarkable speech. The UN has declared July 12 as Malala Day to honour the young activist. In 2020, she graduated from Oxford University.

Malala travels to many countries to meet girls fighting poverty, wars, child marriage and gender discrimination. The Malala Fund is working to highlight their stories around the world. The Malala Fund's Education Champion Network supports educators and activists from the Global South. Malala's message and mission are universal in scope. From Niger to Malala's own Pakistan, girls are routinely deprived of education for a litany of reasons.

In Afghanistan, progress in girls' education has been decimated. When the Taliban were in charge from 1996 to 2001, they banned women and girls from school. After the United States-led invasion toppled Taliban rule in late 2001, female students began attending schools and universities as opportunities blossomed. Women were able to study for careers in business and government, and in professions such as medicine and law. In 2021 as the United States withdrew their forces from Afghanistan, the Taliban swept back into Kabul and seized power on August 15, and since then they have said they will impose their severe interpretation of Shariah law. Secondary schools were ordered to open only for boys which essentially involves a complete ban for girls. The Taliban have promised to uphold the rights of girls and women and they may be forced to do so in response to international condemnation. However, at the time of writing the future of girls' education in Afghanistan is bleak. Since the United States Military Forces completed their withdrawal from Afghanistan on 30 August 2021, girls' access to education has once again been denied. This is the time for every nation to use its political capital in solidarity with the women in Afghanistan. Malala's story has never been more relevant. Despite the obstacles, be they economic, cultural or social, everybody is entitled to a quality education as a basic human right.

Learning activities

Ranking exercise: exploring the barriers to education (Learning activity 1)

There are at least nine barriers to education experienced by children in many countries (Table 7.4). Each barrier can be discussed in terms of its definition, features and actions which can be taken to reduce associated impacts. The video *Educating at the Extreme* narrated by Meryl Streep (https://www.youtube.com/watch?v=jrtIDU5zxq8) is a short documentary which presents the nine barriers to education.

Discussion points following the video are as follows:
What are some of the barriers to education described in the video? (e.g., family value of education, geographical location, gender, dis/ability, prejudice, family poverty, natural disasters, conflict).

Table 7.4 Barrier cards

Poverty
Three of the key ways in which poverty acts as a barrier to accessing and completing a full course of quality primary education are: Education Costs. Child labour and Economic Migration.

Challenging geographies
Most countries have geographic areas that are challenging. In some countries these areas are more numerous or vast than in others. The more economically developed a country, the better able to adapt to or overcome the challenges of its geographies it may be.

Conflict-affected situation, Insecurity and Instability
Conflict-affected situations insecurity and instability act as significant barriers today to children receiving a quality primary education.

Refugees
Child refugees have no access to the school system of the country from which they have fled. Some countries with refugee populations (host countries) make provisions for the education of refugee children while others do not.

Gender
Gender refers to the socially constructed roles, behaviour, activities and attributes that a given society at a given time and place considers appropriate for men and women, and boys and girls and the relationships between them.

Infrastructure
The world's poorest countries need almost four million new classrooms in rural and marginalised areas to accommodate those who are not in school. More classrooms will alleviate overcrowding, cut class sizes and reduce long travel distances.

Resources
Three kinds of resources are necessary for delivery of quality formal and non-formal primary education programmes; human resources such as teachers, material resources such as pencils, writing materials, books and financial resources such as salaries.

Quality
A conventional definition of quality education includes literacy, numeracy and life skills, and is directly linked to such critical components as teachers, content, methodologies, curriculum, examination systems, policy, planning, and management and administration.

Climate change
Climate change is a real threat to many people in the Global South, especially those living in small island states.

Are there other barriers that you can think of that were not described in the video? Students can discuss barriers to education using a ranking exercise or 'Diamond 9'. Distribute cards (one barrier on each card) to groups of students. Each group can discuss barriers to education and arrange their cards in the shape of a diamond. The most significant barrier (in the opinion of the group) is placed at the top of the diamond, the least significant barrier (in the opinion of the group) is placed at the base, and the others placed in between (Figure 7.3).

Following this ranking exercise, students can suggest ways in which the world can keep its promise to provide a quality primary education to every child.

Share stories about access to education (Learning activity 2)

Examples of children's literature listed at the end of this chapter provide multiple stories of hope, of people overcoming adversity and of possible solutions. While goals and indicators may be somewhat complicated or abstract for students, their core fundamental concepts can be powerfully conveyed through story. Furthermore, there are many pedagogical resources for encouraging children to critically engage with the SDG themes through children's literature.

Statistics about the SDGs such as those in Table 7.1 can be somewhat overwhelming for students. Instead of focusing on statistics, teachers can introduce a goal related topic through a story, project work or independent research. Take the following statistic: In 2018, nearly one fifth of the global population of school going age were still out of school (about 258 million children and youth) (UNESCO, 2020). Rather than focusing on the number, tell the story of children who do not have the opportunity to attend schools. Based on a true story from Columbia, *Waiting for the Biblioburro* (by Monica Brown and illustrated by John Parra) is a story about a girl called Ana who loves to read. Ana lives in a remote village, where her teacher moved away and books are in short supply. One day a man brings books on burros (donkeys) and the travelling library enables Ana to read new stories. Ana eventually becomes an author sharing her stories with other people in her community.

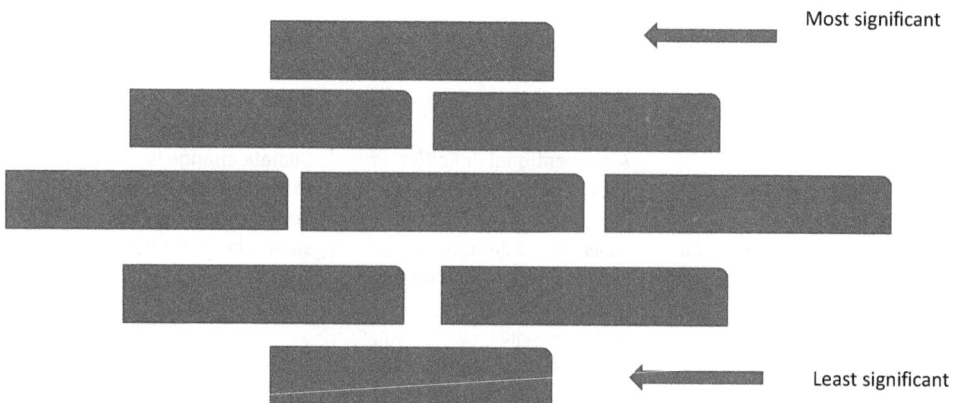

Figure 7.3 Template for Diamond 9 Ranking Activity.

Ask students to calculate one fifth of their school population and to imagine one fifth of their school population not attending school. Explain this is the reality around the world today. Table 7.5 indicates some stories which relate to each target for SDG 4. Further stories are listed at the end of the chapter. Throughout this book, a list of children's literature is included for each SDG. Once students have explored a topic and made their own connections, teachers can introduce data and statistics related to the issue. Data and statistics can also be sourced through student research. The reasons why high numbers of children do not attend school are complex and varied. However, picturebooks can make some of these reasons accessible.

Table 7.5 List of SDG 4 targets along with sample children's literature suitable for discussing each target in an accessible manner

Targets	Related books
Target 4.1. Free primary and secondary education	*Yasmin's Hammer* by Ann Malaspina and illustrated by Doug Chakra is the compelling story of a young Bangladeshi girl and her sister who work as brick chippers to realise their dream of going to school. *Yasmin's Hammer* offers insight into another culture and serves as an inspirational springboard for discussion at home and in class. Through her poetic prose, author Ann Malaspina highlights such themes as the value of hard work, perseverance, and, most of all, education.
Target 4.2 Equal access to quality pre-primary education	In *Beatrice's Goat*, illustrated by Lori Lohstoeter, Page McBrier tells the story of Beatrice, a little Ugandan girl whose family receives a goat from the Heifer Project International. Beatrice desperately wants to go to school, but her family cannot afford it. Instead, she spends her days caring for her younger siblings and helping in the fields on their small plot of land in a rural African village. Then one day, Beatrice's family receives a precious gift from a charity--a goat! In time, the goat provides milk to sell as well as baby goats, and soon the family has earned enough money so Beatrice can go to school.
Target 4.3. Equal access to affordable technical, vocational and higher education	The book *Running Shoes* features Sophy, a young Cambodian girl with a secret wish of attending school if only she had a pair of shoes. The census man notices Sophy, whose family is very poor, admiring his running shoes. When a pair of running shoes arrive for Sophy a few weeks later, she is delighted, because this means that she can run to the school eight kilometres away. When the numbers man returns the next year, Sophy has a gift for him: she can read and write.
Target 4.4 Increase the number of people with relevant skills for financial success	Inspired by true events, *One Hen* tells the story of Kojo, a boy from Ghana who turns a small loan into a thriving farm and a livelihood for many. After his father dies, Kojo leaves school to help his mother collect firewood to sell at the market. When his mother receives a loan from some village families, she gives a little money to her son. With this tiny loan, Kojo buys a hen.

(Continued)

Table 7.5 (Continued)

Targets	Related books
Target 4.5. Eliminate all discrimination in education	*Nasreen's Secret School* by Jeanette Winter is the true story of a young girl living in Afghanistan during the Taliban reign. After her father is taken by soldiers and her mother disappears Nasreen stops speaking, waiting and hoping her parents will return. Worried for her granddaughter, Nasreen's grandmother enrols her in a secret school for girls.
Target 4.6. Universal literacy and numeracy	Set in Guatemala, *Elena's Story* by Nancy Shaw and illustrated by Kristina Rodanas is about one girl's longing for education. Elena, who speaks the Mayan language at home, struggles to practice reading and Spanish for school, while helping with the family chores. When she shares a picture book with her little brother, her mother gives Elena the job of being a reader.
Target 4.7 Education for sustainable development and global citizenship	*'Change the World Before Bedtime'* by Mark Kimball Moulton, Josh Chalmers, and Karen Hillard Good is a call to arms for social justice. The book follows a group of children throughout their day as they eat and play and recycle. The children take cupcakes to sick friends and have a yard sale to build a well in Uganda. Each page of this book allows for learning and discussion about actions for an ethical life including recycling, visiting old and sick people, farmers' markets and planting trees.
Target 4A: Build and upgrade inclusive and safe schools	*Rain School* by James Rumford narrates the story of an eager Thomas, who follows the older children to school, hoping to receive a notebook, pencils and some lessons. But when he arrives at the schoolyard, he finds the school building is missing. However, there is a teacher and hope. "We will build our school", she says. "This is the first lesson". In *Rain School,* through Thomas, we experience the pain and joy of millions of children who long for education. As is summed up by the author himself –' Come September, school will start over. Thomas will be a big brother then, leading the children on their first day to school. They will all stand in front of their smiling teachers, ready to build their school again'.
Target 4B: Expand higher education scholarships for developing countries	*Ten Cents a pound* by Nhung N. Tran-Davies and Illustrated by Josée Bisaillon showcases the struggle that some working families have in finding the time and resources to pursue higher education.
Target 4C: Increase the supply of qualified teachers in developing countries	Based on a real life story, *Listen to the Wind: The Story of Dr. Greg and the Three Cups of Tea* by Greg Mortensen and illustrated by Susan Roth is about one man's effort to return a favour. Greg Mortenson stumbled, lost and delirious, into a remote Himalayan village after a failed climb up K2. The villagers saved his life, and he vowed to return and build them a school. The first school was in Korphe, a village so poor that children hitherto had no full-time teacher and had to write on the ground with sticks.

Learning about barriers to education through story (Learning activity 3)

Listed at the end of this chapter, there is an extensive list of children's literature dealing with the story of Malala Yousafzai. Simply reading these exquisite picturebooks is not enough. Students need to engage with the recommended books using many perpectives and approaches. Dolan's (2015) activity framework of *Respect-Understanding-Action (described below) and Roche's (2014) Book Talk and Critical Thinking support teachers to obtain maximum potential for discussion and reflection based on children's literature.* The picturebook *Malala's Magic Pencil* (Yousafzai and Kerascoët, 2019) is suggested here as an exemplar for curriculum making. As a child in Pakistan, Malala made a wish for a magic pencil that she could use to redraw reality. She would use it for good; to give gifts to her family, to erase the smell from the rubbish dump near her house. As she grew older, Malala wished for bigger and bigger things. She saw a world that needed fixing. Even if she never found a magic pencil, Malala realised that she could still work hard every day to make her wishes come true. This beautifully illustrated picture book tells Malala's story, in her own words, for a younger audience and shows them the worldview that allowed her to hold on to hope and to make her voice heard even in the most difficult of times. Using Dolan's (2015) framework of *Respect-Understanding-Action*, students can engage with the story of Malala through the picturebook *Malala's Magic Pencil*. While this story is used for illustrative purposes, the framework can be used for any picturebook,

Respect-understanding-action framework (Malala's Magic Pencil)

Respect

Respect 1: Reflecting on personal life stories. Students are invited to reflect on their experiences of learning (in school and beyond). A range of creative media can be used such as drawings, photography and poetry. Photographs from home can be shared with the class and scrapbooks or a montage can document learning stories. Students may be invited to document some of the highs and lows they have experienced. Personal reflections can be shared with the class in a respectful manner.

Respect 2: Reflecting on our reactions to the story. Ask half of the children in the class to stand up. Explain new rules have been introduced which mean that half of the class cannot attend school anymore. What would this mean for those who leave and those who are left behind?

Respect 3: Share the Picturebook: Read the story Malala's Magic Pencil and show the illustrations from the book. Ask students for their initial reactions.

Respect 4: Questioning the main character. Ask students to listen carefully to Malala's story again and to suggest a list of questions they would like to ask her.

Respect 5: Respond with drawings. Invite students to draw the events and characters from Malala's story. They could create a storyboard, drawing the sequence of events as they occur in the story.

Respect 6: Country Fact File. Ask students to conduct research about Pakistan, using headings such as 'population', 'economy', 'interesting facts', 'culture' and 'human rights'.

Understanding

Understanding 1: Create a sculpture. Ask for a volunteer to become a piece of clay to be sculpted. Explain that following directions from the class, students will create a sculpture of Malala. Together students decide which image of Malala from the story to sculpt and give instructions. This could be repeated by groups of students each working with a student to be sculpted. Each group presents its sculpture, justifying what has been created. This should be followed by class discussion about the representation of the sculptures, the decisions which informed their creation and the response of those viewing the sculptures.

Understanding 2: Create a photograph. Ask students to examine the photographs and illustrations in this picturebook and decide on a title. In groups, ask students to choose a scene from the story, e.g., Malala leaving her school, and invite leaners to role-play this moment. Instruct them to 'freeze' at a certain point to create their own still image from the story. Students can discuss what might happen next.

Understanding 3: Filmstrip. Ask students to identify the characters in the story such as Malala, her mum, dad and peers. Divide the class into pairs. One student in each pair is Malala and the other becomes one of the characters from the story. Each pair decides on one or two lines of dialogue and an appropriate action. They practice this and show it to the class. Discuss with the class the chronological order of these scenes, and create a sequence of scenes which illustrate the development of Malala's story. These scenes can come together as a virtual filmstrip, which is then performed for the rest of the class. It can also be recorded on a camcorder for further discussion and analysis.

Understanding 4: A role-play. Many educators have used role-play as a powerful medium for helping students to empathise with characters in a story and to consider the story from their own perspective.

Understanding 5: Hot Seating. Ask a volunteer to take on the role of Malala as the rest of the class ask questions about her life. This activity builds upon earlier questions (Respect 4: Questioning Malala), so questions should now be more critical, insightful and informed.

Understanding 6: Moving Debate. Place signs 'agree' and 'disagree' on opposite sides of the room. Read out debatable statements about Malala's story such as 'Malala should/should not be allowed to attend school'. Ask students to stand on the appropriate side of the room according to how they feel about the statement and to explain their decision. If students are unsure, or if they feel they do not have sufficient knowledge, then they can stand in the middle of the room. Each student must be able to articulate a reason for where they choose to stand.

Discuss with students any actions they would like to take in response to this true story.

Action

Action 1: Project work. Ask students to identify more information they would like to find out about Malala in particular and other children who have been denied access to education. Discuss how such information can be sourced. Share some of the conclusions from this project with other classes, with parents and with the local media.

Action 2: Write a letter. Write to Malala and/or to the author and illustrator, expressing personal reactions to the story. Authors and illustrators are generally interested in feedback from readers.

Action 3: Find out about organisations. Find out about organisations which provide services for children's rights and equality for girls. Create a poster for each of these organisations and display it in school corridors.

Action 5: Problem Solving. Ask students to create a list of problems identified in Malala's story and to suggest potential solutions.

Action 6: Personal reflection. Write about or discuss how different your life would be if one never went to school and never learned how to read and write.

Barriers to education: board game another brick in the wall (Learning activity 4)

This game created by Leah Murphy (age 15) and Sandra Ryan, is based on the concept of the traditional Snakes and Ladders game (Figure 7.4). The ten barriers to education (one additional barrier, disability, was added) are depicted using red squares – red means danger or STOP. When a player lands on a red square (snake) they must go to the bottom of the snake. The green squares – green means GO – are the UN targets for SDG 4. When a player lands on a green square (ladder) they advance more quickly in the game. Since SDG 4 Quality Education, is the heart of the SDGs and contributes to all 17 SDGs, each goal is listed within the game and players learn about all goals as they progress through the game.

The game can be adapted for different age groups.

Younger players (age 8–12)

Each red BARRIER square has an example of that barrier for players to read and discuss. For example, the barrier 'DISTANCE' says: 'Kamal has to walk 10 miles to school every day. Why is this a barrier?'

Similarly, the green TARGET squares each contain an explanation of the target for discussion. For example, the target 'GENDER EQUALITY' says 'Girls and boys are equal. Talk about what that means'.

As players progress in the game and land on the 17 SDG squares, these can also be explored and discussed. The SDG "NO POVERTY" says 'What is poverty? Give an example of poverty or Have you ever seen poverty?'

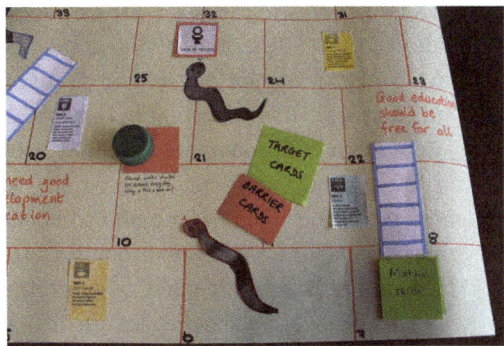

Figure 7.4 Home Designed Game: Just Another Brick in the Wall.

When players have finished the game, they have reached all 17 SDGs.

Young players and their parents/guardians could be challenged to design a game to teach a SDG.

Older players (age 12+)

Landing on a red BARRIER square requires a player to read that barrier. For example, the barrier 'DISTANCE' says: 'Kamal has to walk 10 miles to school every day. Why is this a barrier?' For older players, there is a separate BARRIER card with a question or challenge to be solved about the barrier of DISTANCE. 'How can education help solve the barrier of distance for Kamal?'

Landing on a green TARGET square requires a player to read an explanation of that target. For example, the target 'GENDER EQUALITY' says 'Girls and boys are equal. Talk about what that means'. For older players, there is also a separate TARGET card. The target GENDER EQUALITY asks players to give examples of inequality for boys and girls or men and women and to suggest solutions for how to address these inequalities.

As players progress in the game and land on the 17 SDG squares, these can be explored and discussed. Older players must also figure out how QUALITY EDUCATION contributes to each of the 17 SDGs. Hints are provided. By finishing the game, players have reached all 17 SDGs.

To provide an additional challenge for older players, the targets and barriers could also be moved around and players could decide priorities and arrange these on longer ladders/ snakes. Some (not all) of the barriers and goals also link together and players are awarded bonus points for making these connections.

Older students could be invited to design a game to teach any of the SDGs. Games are also discussed in chapter 16 (SDG 13) and chapter 18 (SDG 15).

Conclusion

This chapter outlines the concepts that are included in SDG 4: Quality Education. Each activity is linked to at least one of the SDG4 targets and, in some examples, to other SDG goals. The importance of developing empathy for others in more challenging circumstances also underpins the activities provided and students are encouraged to become active in developing and sharing awareness of the issues involved. An extensive list of children's literature is provided along with detailed activities for robust discussion and analysis based on SDG 4 Quality Education.

This chapter also focuses on the power of games for exploring SDG 4. While games can be used for all SDGs, students have their own bank of educational experiences which can provide much scope for debate and discussion.

In conclusion it is important to remember three underlying principles of SDG 4:

Education is a fundamental human right and an enabling right. To fulfil this right, countries must ensure universal equal access to inclusive and equitable quality education and learning, which should be free and compulsory, leaving no one behind irrespective of their gender, disabilities, social and economic situation.

Education is a public good, of which the state is the duty bearer. Education is a shared societal endeavor, which implies an inclusive process of public policy formulation and implementation, in which civil society, teachers and educators, the private sector, communities, families, youth and children have important roles. The role of the state is essential in setting and regulating standards and norms.

Gender equality is linked to the right to education for all. Achieving gender equality requires a right-based approach ensuring that boys and girls, women and men not only gain access to and complete education cycles, but are empowered equally in and through education.

Resources

An extensive list of resources, videos and case studies for SDG 4 is included in the SDG padlet accompanying this book: https://padlet.com/annedolan/o6rds38ylfy6a28h

Sources of further information

Facts, figures, info graphics useful to support learning about quality education are available on the following web pages:

UN Children's Fund: https://www.un.org/sustainabledevelopment/education/
UN Educational, Scientific and Cultural Organization (UNESCO): https://en.unesco.org/themes/education
Global Education First Initiative: http://www.unesco.org/new/en/gefi/home/?
Global Campaign for Education: https://campaignforeducation.org/en/
Social media: #OneBillionVoicesForEducation #EducationForAll @Cosydep @Ancefa Regional
UNICEF A better world: https://youtu.be/_F8nNLZIZrQ
Concern SDG resources: https://www.concern.net/schools-and-youth/educational-resources
UNESCO Teacher Resources for SDG4: https://en.unesco.org/sites/default/files/resources-sdg4.pdf
Oxfam Education: https://www.oxfam.org.uk/education/classroom-resources/
Concern: https://www.concern.net/schools-and-youth/educational-resources
Trócaire: https://www.trocaire.org/our-work/educate/all-education-resources/
National Youth Council of Ireland (NYCI): *SDGs Youth Resource Pack* https://www.youth.ie/wp-content/uploads/2018/11/SDGs_Youth_Resource-_Pack.pdf - Activity 10 Stand or Sit? Theme Education (Goal 4)
Malala Yousafzai on "Financing the Future: Education 2030" https://youtu.be/yzfPdn1xTKM
Malala Yousafzai on SDGs: http://webtv.un.org/watch/malala-yousafzai-un-messenger-of-peace-on-sustainable-development-goals/6192262490001/
UN SDG4 Infographic: https://www.un.org/sustainabledevelopment/wp-content/uploads/2019/07/E_Infographic_04.pdf
UNESCO Her Atlas. Atlas of girls' and women's right to education: https://en.unesco.org/education/girls-women-rights
UNESCO Observatory on the Right to Education: http://www.unesco.org/education/edurights/index.php?action=home&lng=en

Key dates

- **January 24:** International Day of Education
- **July 12:** Malala Day
- **July 15:** UN World Youth Skills Day
- **September 8:** International Literacy Day
- **October 5:** World Teachers' Day
- **Last week in April:** Global Action Week for Education (see https://campaignforeducation.org/en/gawe-2021/)

Children's literature

Picturebooks

Boston Weatherford, C. and Gregory Christy, R. (illus) (2017) *Dear Mr. Rosenwald,* CreateSpace Independent Publishing Platform.
Brown, M. and Parra, J. (illlus) (2011) *Waiting for the Biblioburro* Random House Children's Books.
Bunting, E. (2008) *Walking to School* Clarion Books.
Castle, C., Burningham, J. (illus) and UNICEF. (2001) *For Every Child: The UN Convention on the Rights of the Child in Words and Pictures* P. Fogelman Books.
Cohen-Janca, I. (2019) *Ruby, Head High: Ruby Bridge's First Day of School* Creative Editions.
Coles, R. (2010) *The Story of Ruby Bridges* Scholastic.
Cunxin, L. and Spudvilas, A. (2008) *Dancing to Freedom: The True Story of Mao's Last Dancer* Walker.
Elvgren, J. R. and Tadgell, N. (2006) *Josias, Hold the Book* Boyds Mills Press.
Fine, E. H., Josephson, J. P. and Sosa, H. (2007) *Armando and the Blue Tarp School* Lee & Low.
Henson, H. (2008) *That Book Woman* Atheneum Books for Young Readers.
Hughes, S. (2011) *Off to Class: Students and Schools Around the World* Turtleback Books.
Jordan-Fenton, C., Pokiak-Fenton, M. and Grimand, G. (illus) (2013) *When I Was Eight* Annick Press.
Kimball Moulton, M., Chalmers, J. and Hillard Good, K. (illus) (2018) (2nd ed.) *Change the World Before Bedtime* Schiffer Publishing Ltd.
Lipp, F. (2008) *Running Shoes* Charlesbridge Publishing.
Malaspina, A. (2016) *Yasmin's Hammer* Lee and Low.
Mcbrier, P. and Lohstoeter, L. (2004) *Beatrice's Goat* Aladdin Paperbacks.
Miller, W. (2000) *Richard Wright and the Library Card* Lee and Low.
Mora, P. and Colón, R. (2000) *Tomas and the Library Lady* Random House.
Newman, P. (2018) *Neema's Reason to Smile* Lightswitch Learning.
Paul, M. and Parra, J. (2019) *Little Libraries, Big Heroes* Clarion Books.
Rahman, B. and Grimard, G. (2021) *The Library Bus* Pajama Press.
Roth, S. (2010) *Listen to the Wind: The Story of Dr. Greg and Three Cups of Tea* Pearson.
Roth, S. L. (illus) and Abouraya, K. L. (2012) *Hands Around the Library: Protecting Egypt's Treasured Books* Dial Books.
Rumford, J. (2010) *Rain School* Houghton Mifflin Harcourt.
Ruurs, M. (2005) *My Librarian Is a Camel: How Books Are Brought to Children Around the World* Boyds Mills.
Ruurs, M. (2009) *My School in the Rain Forest: How Children Attend School Around the World* Boyds Mills Press.
Shaw, N. and Rodanas, K. (2012) *Elena's Story* Sleeping Bear Press.
Smith, P. and Shalev, Z. (2007) *A School Like Mine: A Unique Celebration of Schools Around the World* Dorling Kindersley.
Stamaty, M. A. (2004) *Alia's Mission: Saving the Books of Iraq* Knopf Books for Young Readers.
Suneby, E. and Vereist, S. (2020) *Razia's Ray of Hope: One Girl's Dream of an Education* Kids Can Press.
Tonatiuh, T. (2014) *Separate Is Never Equal: Sylvia Mendez and her Family's Fight for Desegregation:* Abrams Books for Young Readers.
Tran-Davies, N. N. and Bisaillon, J. (2018) *Ten Cents a Pound* Second Story Press.

Williams, M. and Christie, R. G. (2005) *Brothers in Hope: The Story of The Lost Boys Of Sudan* Lee & Low Books.
Winter, J. (2005) *The Librarian of Basra: A True Story from Iraq* Harcourt Children's Books.
Winter, J. (2009) *Nasreen's Secret School: A True Story from Afghanistan* Simon and Schuster.
Winter, J. (2011) *Biblioburro: A True Story from Colombia* Beach Lane Books.
Winters, K. L. and Taylor, S. (illus) (2014) *Gift Days* Fitzhenry & Whiteside.

Chapter Books

Palacio, R. J. (2014) *Wonder,* Corgi Childrens.
Rauf, O. (2018) *The Boy at the Back of the Class,* Orion Children's Books.

Children's literature about Malala Yousafzai

Picturebooks

Frier, R and Fronty, A. (2017) *Malala: Activist for Girls' Education* Charlesbridge.
Langston-George, R. (2017) *For the Right to Learn: Malala Yousafzai's Story* Capstone Press.
Maslo, L. (2018) *Free as a Bird: The Story of Malala* BalzerBray.
No author. (2022) *Malala Yousafzai: A Children's Book About Gender Equality, Civil Rights and Justice (Part of Inspired Inner Genius Series)* IIG Pub.
Noor Khan, H. and Petralucci, T. (Illus) (2019) *The Extraordinary Life of Malala Yousafzai* (Extraordinary Lives Series) Puffin.
Sanchez Vegara, M. and Mirza, M. (Illus) (2021) *Malala Yousafzai* (Little People, Big Dreams Series) Frances Lincoln Children's Books.
Yousafzai, M. and Kerascoët (illus) (2019) *Malala's Magic Pencil* Puffin.
Yousafzai, M. and McCormick, P. (illus) (2018) *Malala: My Story of Standing Up for Girls' Rights* Wren and Rook.

Chapter books for children aged 9–12

Galat, J. M. (2020) *The Story of Malala Yousafzai* (A biography series for new readers) Rockridge Press.
Langston-George, R. and Bock, J. (2016) *For the Right to Learn: Malala Yousafzai's Story* Capstone Pr
Yousafzai, M. and McCormick, P. (illus) (2015) *I am Malala: How One Girl Stood Up for Education and Changed The World* Orion Children's Books.

Chapter books for children 12 plus

Yousafzai, M. (2021) *We Are Displaced: My Journey And Stories from Refugee Girls* W&N.
Yousafzai, M. and Lamb, C. (2014) *I am Malala: The Girl Who Stood Up for Education and Was Shot by the Taliban* Little Brown and Company.

References

Bourn, D. (ed.) (2020) *The Bloomsbury handbook of global education and learning.* London: Bloomsbury Publishing.
Burnett, N., Guison-Dowdy, A. and Milan, T. (2013) *A moral obligation, an economic priority: The urgency of enrolling out of school children.* Doha: Educate A Child and Results for Development Institute. https://www.yumpu.com/en/document/view/26680433/a-moral-obligation-an-economic-priority-results-for-development-
Dolan, A. (2014) *You, me and diversity: Picturebooks for teaching development and intercultural education.* London: Trentham Books and IOE Press.
Educate a Child International. (2023) https://educationaboveall.org/#!/programme/educate-a-child

Gromada, A., Rees, G., Chzhen, Y. and Office of Research. (2020) *Innocenti UNICEF worlds of influence: Understanding what shapes child well-being in rich countries.* https://econpapers.repec.org/paper/ucfinreca/inreca1140.htm (accessed August 2021)Kazeem, A., Jensen, L. and Stokes, C. S. (2010) School attendance in Nigeria: Understanding the impact and intersection of gender, urban-rural residence, and socioeconomic status. *Comparative Education Review, 54* (2), 295–319.

Mortimore, P. (2013) *Education under siege. Why there is a better alternative.* Bristol and Chicago, IL: Policy Press.

Pritchett, L. (2003) *When will they ever learn? Why all governments produce schooling.* Cambridge, MA: JFK School of Government, Harvard University.

Roche, M., (2014) *Developing children's critical thinking through picturebooks: A guide for primary and early years students and teachers.* London: Routledge.

Sen, A. K. (2005) Human rights and capabilities. *Journal of Human Development, 6* (2), 151–166.

UNESCO. (2015) *Education for all 2000–2015: Achievements and challenges.* Paris: UNESCO.

UNESCO. (2017) More than one half of children and adolescents are not learning worldwide Fact Sheet No. 46 September 2017 UIS/FS/2017/ED/46. http://uis.unesco.org/sites/default/files/documents/fs46-more-than-half-children-not-learning-en-2017.pdf

UNESCO. (2020a) *Half of world's student population not attending school: UNESCO launches global coalition to accelerate deployment of remote learning solutions.* https://shar.es/afaYAl

UNESCO. (2020b) *Education for sustainable development goals: Learning objectives.* Paris: UNESCO https://www.unesco.de/sites/default/files/2018-08/unesco_education_for_sustainable_development_goals.pdf

UNESCO. (2021/2022) *Global education monitoring report.* https://unesdoc.unesco.org/ark:/48223/pf0000379875

UNESCO's Institute for Statistics (nd). https://uis.unesco.org/

UNESCO, UNICEF, UNICEF, the Global Partnership for Education, and the Foreign, Commonwealth & Development Office. (2021) (3rd ed.) *Education Sector Analysis: Methodological Guidelines.* https://unesdoc.unesco.org/ark:/48223/pf0000377738UNICEF & UNESCO. (2007) *A human rights-based approach to EFA.* New York: UNICEF.

United Nations (UN). (1948) *Universal declaration on human rights.* Geneva: United Nations.

United Nations Education Science and Culture Organisation (UNESCO). (2020) *Leading SDG4 – Education 2030.* https://en.unesco.org/themes/education2030-sdg4 (accessed July 2020).

United Nations Education Science and Culture Organisation (UNESCO). (2021) *From resilience to inclusion, new methodological guidelines to improve effectiveness in global education* http://www.iiep.unesco.org/en/protecting-education-during-crises-discover-new-education4resilience-platform-13929

Vladimirovaa, K. and Le Blanc, D. (2015) How well are the links between education and other sustainable development goals covered in UN flagship reports?: A contribution to the study of the science-policy interface on education in the UN system, October. https://sustainabledevelopment.un.org/content/documents/2111education%20and%20sdgs.pdf

8 Teaching about gender

Feminist hope and praxis for the future (SDG 5)

Tereza Mytakou and Elaine Murtagh

Introduction: the (continuing) need for gender equality

Gender Equality remains one of the most pressing issues in our time. Although significant progress has been made in women's rights issues, gender equality is still an ideal that societies are striving towards. Recent events globally have served to underline the pressing need for gender equality even further, and to expose the gender inequalities that are deeply rooted in our social systems. The recent increase in femicides in countries like Greece and Turkey, the #MeToo Movement which originated in the USA with the aim of exposing sexual harassment, the 2019 protests against rape culture which started from Latin America but quickly spread to the rest of the world, are all just a few examples of these events. They all point to the fact that women are still facing inequalities in everyday life, and that they are still fighting for basic rights and against gender-based violence.

In terms of facts and figures, global statistics confirm the above gender inequalities, whether those have to do with:

- Women's participation in the political sphere – representation of women in national parliaments is 23.7% globally (United Nations, nd)
- Girls' and women's access to education – more than two thirds of illiterate people globally are female (UN Women, nd)
- Gender-based violence – 750 million women and girls were married before the age of 18 and at least 200 million women and girls in 30 countries have undergone female genital mutilation (FGM) (United Nations, nd).

It is therefore clear that Gender Equality is still a goal which we need to work on, not only to eliminate the gender inequalities and harmful stereotypes that are embedded in our societies, but also to tackle the gender issues that are becoming even more prominent due to current circumstances, like the COVID-19 pandemic. As teachers, raising awareness about gender stereotypes and inequalities is the first and very crucial step that we can take, in order to strive for change.

This chapter will support teachers to navigate this sensitive and complex issue, and explore this SDG in an interactive, student-friendly manner. Students are encouraged to consider the issue of gender equality in local, national and international contexts. Case studies are drawn from countries scoring high and low on the Gender Inequality Index. We provide examples of actions taken around the world to address gender inequality: from

DOI: 10.4324/9781003232001-11

gender-responsive teaching in Ireland, to empowering girls through sport in Australia (as illustrated in Tables 8.2–8.4). We also propose some activities which will invite students to explore and deconstruct traditional gender stereotypes that are manifested in language use and popular culture. Throughout the chapter links are made to the other SDGs and we will highlight the relevance of Quality Education (SDG 4) to achieving the aims of the SDG on Gender. Finally, teachers are encouraged to reflect on their own practice in relation to their potential role as champions for gender equality in their schools and community. Terminology associated with gender-responsive teaching is set out in Table 8.1.

Below we provide definitions and explanations for terms that frequently encountered when reading and teaching about gender equality.

Key aspects of feminist pedagogy

Gender-responsive teaching, which we discuss further below, is largely based on the principles of feminist pedagogy, a method of teaching which seeks to provide education that is grounded in feminist thought and theory. As Crabtree, Sapp, and Licona (2009: 1) define it, feminist pedagogy is 'a movement against hegemonic educational practices that tacitly accept or more forcefully reproduce an oppressively gendered, classed, racialised, and androcentric social order'. The basic principles of feminist pedagogy can be summarised as follows:

Hierarchy/power

Feminist pedagogy is interested in breaking down traditional hierarchies in the classroom, and seeks to promote and build 'non-hierarchical relationships among teachers and students and reflexivity about power relations, not only in society but also in the classroom' (Crabtree et al., 2009: 5). Consequently, it departs from traditional conceptions of the teacher as expert'; the teacher is seen more as a 'facilitator', 'monitor' or 'group process manager', among others, whereas the student takes on the role of the 'negotiator' (Richards & Rodgers, 2015: 98-99).

Emphasis on feeling/emotion/personal experiences as valid ways of knowing

Feminist pedagogy disrupts widespread ideas that knowledge is solely based on logic, and acknowledges the feelings and lived experiences of students as equally valid ways of knowing and making sense of the world. According to feminist pedagogy, '[t]his integration of lived experiences means that emotions are also acknowledged as part of what it means to know and how we know' (Bostow et al., 2015: np).

Feminist praxis

Furthermore, feminist pedagogy is, as its name indicates, based on feminist theory, however it also places great emphasis on praxis. It calls for action and actual social change inspired by the theory. It expresses hope that the theory will inspire action, such as change in classroom practices and the materials taught, or even in the students' everyday lives.

Table 8.1 Terminology associated with gender-responsive teaching (Source: UNICEF, 2017) and LGBTI+ (lesbian, gay, bisexual, trans, queer, intersex, asexual and more)

Cisgender
When a person's gender identity and the gender they were assigned at birth are the same.

Gender
A social and cultural construct, which distinguishes differences in the attributes of men and women, girls and boys, and accordingly refers to the roles and responsibilities of men and women.

Gender equality
The concept that women and men, girls and boys have equal conditions, treatment and opportunities for realising their full potential, human rights and dignity, and for contributing to (and benefitting from) economic, social, cultural and political development.

Gender expression
How someone expresses their gender through clothes, hair, make up and some behaviours.

Gender identity
Our deeply felt internal experience of our own gender.

Gender norms
Accepted attributes and characteristics of male and female gendered identity at a particular point in time for a specific society or community. They are the standards and expectations to which gender identity generally conforms, within a range that defines a particular society, culture and community at that point in time. Gender norms are ideas about how men and women should be and act.

Gender stereotyping
The process of girls and boys, women and men learning social roles based on their sex, which leads to different behaviours and creates differing expectations and attitudes by gender.

Masculinities/Femininities
These are dynamic socio-cultural categories used in everyday language that refer to certain behaviours and practices recognized within a culture as being 'feminine' or 'masculine', regardless of which biological sex expresses them. These concepts are learned and do not describe sexual orientation or biological essence.

Non-binary
Someone who does not identify as either male or female but whose gender was assigned at birth.

Patriarchy
Social system in which men hold the greatest power, leadership roles, privilege, moral authority and access to resources and land, including in the family. Most modern societies are patriarchies.

Transgender
A term describing a person's gender identity that does not match their assigned sex at birth. This word is also used as an umbrella term to describe some groups of people who transcend conventional expectations of gender identity or expression.

Sex
Refers to the biological and physiological reality of being male or female.

Note: use of pronouns
She/Her/Hers is a set of gender-specific pronouns typically used to refer to women or girls.
He/him/his are gender-specific pronouns that are usually used to refer to men or boys.

Gender-neutral pronouns
Non-gendered or nonbinary pronouns are not gender specific and are most often used by people who identify outside of a gender binary. The most common set of nonbinary pronouns is they/them/their used in the singular.

Intersectionality

Intersectionality is a vital aspect of feminist pedagogy, and is termed as 'an explicit commitment to address the intersections of gender, race, ethnicity, class, and sexuality not only in the content of the discipline but also in the dynamics of the classroom' (Crabtree et al., 2009: 5). Therefore, feminist pedagogy strives to acknowledge intersecting forms of oppression in the classroom, noting how power structures in the classroom are shaped by the above factors, and how each student's lived reality differs according to them.

Feminism and gender diversity

Traditionally, Western society views gender as binary, with two gender categories: male and female. This categorisation has been influenced by societal understandings of gender, such as what it means to be male and female, and the idea that gender is determined by physical characteristics. The development of gender identity is influenced by many factors including family systems, community, culture and social norms, media and legal instruments.

Gender diversity expert Meg-John Barker (2019) offers a biopsychosocial understanding of gender (Figure 8.1), which shows how all aspects of our biology, psychology, and social context shape each other. Our bodies and brains are shaped by our gendered experiences, such as physical interventions (e.g. hormonal, surgical) and the gendered ways we navigate the world. This provides a different understanding, which disputes the common assumption that a person's biological sex determines their gender identity and experience (Barker & Iantaffi, 2019).

Although a binary way of thinking about gender has been prevalent in Western society, there are many non-Western cultures which have different gender systems. For example, in some Indigenous Native American[1] cultures they use the term 'two-spirit' to refer to a person who identifies as having both a masculine and a feminine spirit (Barker & Iantaffi, 2019). Gender does not operate in the same way across cultures, as it is a social construct tied to each particular cultural context. For many, the inclusion of transgender and intersex people is a key gender equality issue. Indeed, Agenda 2030 and SDG 5 in particular have been criticised for reifying a Western gender binary and hierarchy by omitting other cultural views of gender (Ongsupankul, 2019).

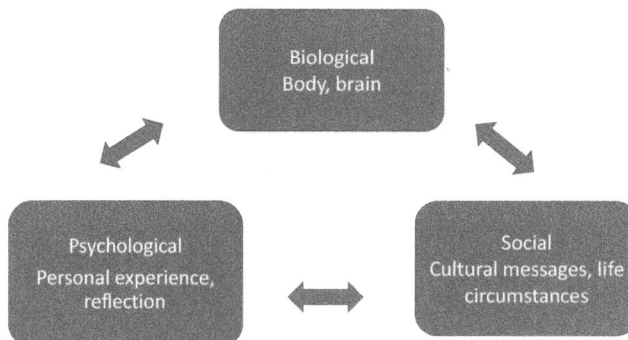

Figure 8.1 A Biopsychosocial Understanding of Gender.

In addition to traditional sexism (where men are viewed as more legitimate than women) there are other discriminative behaviours based on gender. The erasure of and discrimination against third gender and transgender identities is a feminist issue, as are the surgeries often performed on intersex children. Bodily autonomy and agency are key feminist issues that face cisgender women, transgender and intersex people alike. Lesbian, gay, bisexual, transgender and queer people around the world continue to face discrimination in their daily lives. For instance in 2023, the parliament in Uganda passed a controversial anti-LGBTQ+ bill, which makes homosexual acts punishable by death, attracting strong condemnation from rights campaigners. In 2022, a Florida committee advanced a bill that restricts discussions about sexual orientation and gender identity in schools. In Ireland, protesters have tried to remove LBGTQ+ books from public libraries.

Teachers encounter gender diversity all the time. It is important for teachers to adopt pedagogical approaches, which are democratic, non-hierarchical and focused on socio-emotional intelligence. 'Gender-facilitative classrooms' (Luecke, 2018) are welcoming environments for gender-diverse students.

Links with other sustainable goals

Gender equality is an enabler and accelerator for all the Sustainable Development Goals (SDGs). The gender-responsive implementation of the 2030 Agenda for Sustainable Development offers an opportunity to achieve not only SDG 5 (gender equality), but to contribute to progress on all 17 Sustainable Development Goals (SDGs).

Since gender is not a factor which exists in a vacuum, but is rather intricately related to other factors, such as social class, age, race, ethnicity, etc., it is useful to consider it in relation to the rest of the UN Sustainable Development Goals. Gender inequalities can be examined through the theoretical framework of what is termed 'intersectionality', in order for them to be understood more thoroughly. Intersectionality was coined by critical race theorist Kimberlé Crenshaw (1989) and has been used by black feminist scholars in order to draw attention to how gender and race intersect, and how these factors should be taken into account collectively when examining discriminations. It is no coincidence that insecurity, climate change and gender inequality intersect with women and girls bearing the brunt of the effects.

With that in mind, it is easy to see how gender equality is a goal that should not be achieved by its own, but should be considered in relation to other goals associated with, for example, quality education (SDG 4), or the protection of the environment (SDGs 11, 13, 14 and 15), or ending poverty SDG 1). The same applies to teaching about Gender Equality in primary or secondary classrooms. As Lewis (2020) confirms, teaching the sustainable goals should be based on 'the principles of interconnection and inclusion', a fact which makes it evident that 'we must teach about all the global goals in order to effectively teach about one' (2020: 22).

More specifically, one can draw links between Gender Equality and Quality Education (Goal 4), since education is one of the areas in which girls are still at a disadvantage throughout the world, whether that has to do with access to education, gender stereotyping in education, choice of subjects based on gender, or gender-based violence in educational settings (European Institute for Gender Equality, 2016). Discussed in the previous chapter, the issue of education for girls can be explored through case studies such as the story of Malala Yousafzai.

Furthermore, the link with all goals related to the environment is also quite strong, e.g. Climate Action (Goal 13), Sustainable Cities and Communities (Goal 11), Life Below Water (Goal 14), Life on Land (Goal 15), since women are usually the ones mostly affected by environmental issues (see Figure 8.2). Climate change for instance is not gender neutral. Of course, social class also comes into play here, since climate change primarily affects those in more dire economic conditions. According to the United Nation's website for Climate Change, 'Women commonly face higher risks and greater burdens from the impacts of climate change in situations of poverty, and the majority of the world's poor are women' (United Nations Climate Change, nd). This link between gender oppression and the exploitation of the environment has also been touched upon by ecofeminist critics who draw attention to how the exploitation of natural resources by patriarchal societies is similar to the exploitation of women, and how it affects women more than men.

When teaching about the Gender Equality SDG, it is fruitful to draw parallels with other goals and invite students to think critically about the links between them. How are gender inequalities experienced differently by different people? What other factors do we need to think of when thinking about gender issues? How does, for example, a white, cisgender, heterosexual girl experience gender inequality differently than a non-binary person of colour? How similar or different are the gender issues that exist in different countries, and what other factors come into play? These are the kind of questions that can inform our teaching in order for us to provide a more holistic view on gender issues.

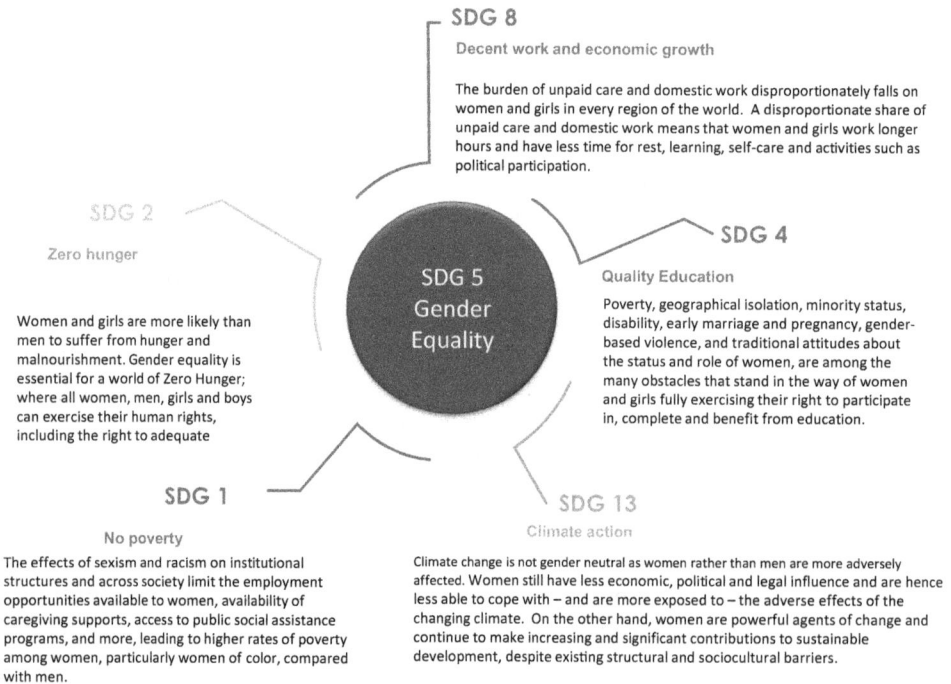

SDG 8

Decent work and economic growth

The burden of unpaid care and domestic work disproportionately falls on women and girls in every region of the world. A disproportionate share of unpaid care and domestic work means that women and girls work longer hours and have less time for rest, learning, self-care and activities such as political participation.

SDG 2

Zero hunger

Women and girls are more likely than men to suffer from hunger and malnourishment. Gender equality is essential for a world of Zero Hunger; where all women, men, girls and boys can exercise their human rights, including the right to adequate

SDG 5 Gender Equality

SDG 4

Quality Education

Poverty, geographical isolation, minority status, disability, early marriage and pregnancy, gender-based violence, and traditional attitudes about the status and role of women, are among the many obstacles that stand in the way of women and girls fully exercising their right to participate in, complete and benefit from education.

SDG 1

No poverty

The effects of sexism and racism on institutional structures and across society limit the employment opportunities available to women, availability of caregiving supports, access to public social assistance programs, and more, leading to higher rates of poverty among women, particularly women of color, compared with men.

SDG 13

Climate action

Climate change is not gender neutral as women rather than men are more adversely affected. Women still have less economic, political and legal influence and are hence less able to cope with – and are more exposed to – the adverse effects of the changing climate. On the other hand, women are powerful agents of change and continue to make increasing and significant contributions to sustainable development, despite existing structural and sociocultural barriers.

Figure 8.2 Interlinkages of SDG 5 with other SDGs.

Activities for exploring gender equality

Table 8.2 Taking action for gender quality! Example 1

Daughters and Dads Active and Empowered

A community-based programme that aims to engage fathers/father-figures to improve the physical activity behaviours, sport skills and social-emotional wellbeing of their primary school-aged daughters. It's led by Professor Philip Morgan and colleagues from the University of Newcastle, New South Wales, Australia.

The 8-week programme includes 'dads-only' information workshops, sessions for daughters and fathers and home-based tasks. The sessions combine theory and practical components that focus on a girl's physical and social emotional skills including resilience and critical thinking. Fathers are also taught positive parenting strategies and are empowered to become gender equity advocates for their daughters. The 'Daughters and Dads Active and Empowered' programme has been running since 2015 in Australia and since 2018 in England.

Table 8.3 Taking action for gender quality! Example 2

The 30% Club

The 30% Club campaign was founded by Dame Helena Morrissey and has since evolved to a global mission to reach at least 30% representation of women on all boards and on senior management globally. The campaign argues that gender balance encourages better leadership and governance, promotes diversity and inclusion as contributors to better all-round board performance and ultimately increases corporate performance for both companies and their shareholders.

The 30% Club campaign is working to bring about real transformation by:

- Encouraging and supporting Chairs and CEOs to appoint more women to their boards and senior management teams
- Providing information and supports for businesses trying to improve their diversity
- Harnessing public media support and leveraging social media
- Building on research to help governments, institutions and individuals make a difference in driving change
- Tracking progress towards the 30% target(s)

Founded in 2010 there are now chapters operating around the world: Australia, Brazil, Canada, Chile, East Africa, Middle East & North Africa, Hong Kong, Ireland, Italy, Japan, Malaysia, Southern Africa, Turkey, United Kingdom, United States www.30percentclub.org

The teacher's role in advancing gender equality

Self-reflexivity allows teachers to think critically about their practices in class, and how these serve to promote gender equality. It is important for teachers to reflect on their own *positionality* in class, that is, how your particular identity and background functions in the classroom, and how it shapes your beliefs, ideas and teaching. As Sarah Benesch puts it, it is important to acknowledge 'that teachers' and students' subjectivities are socially constructed. That is, *I* is a function of class, race, sexual preference, ethnicity, gender, history, and region' (Benesch,

Table 8.4 Taking action for gender quality! Example 3

Teaching Gender through the Scholars Ireland Programme

The course *He's a Boss, She is Bossy: Exploring Gender Stereotypes through Language, Literature and Culture* was delivered to post-primary school students at an all-boys school in Dublin. It was designed and taught by Tereza Mytakou, Ph.D. student at Trinity College Dublin (Figure 8.3). The course aims to provide students with the basic skills to analyse gender stereotypes and traditional gender roles, and to explore the following questions: *What is gender? How do language, literature and culture perpetuate or deconstruct gender stereotypes?* Students were given the opportunity to explore different cultural texts and examine the relationship between gender and language, gender in literature and gender in popular culture.

The course was delivered in Dublin, Ireland for four consecutive years (2019–2023).

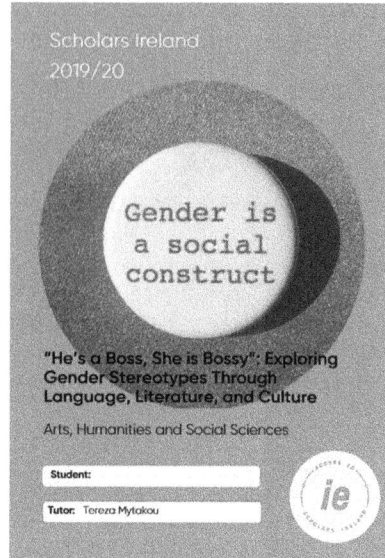

Figure 8.3 Gender Stereotyping.

1998: 103), and to take this into account when designing teaching activities. Awareness of your positionality can also help you to trace any prejudices you might have, and identify any sort of practices or behaviour that might be discriminating against certain students, and that you might not have noticed before. In particular, when reflecting on one's role as a gender equality champion, it would be useful to consider the reflection questions in Table 8.5.

Depending on your answers to these questions, you may already be adopting gender responsive practices in your teaching. We discuss this more in the following sections.

Gender responsive teaching

Gender responsive pedagogy refers to teaching and learning processes that pay attention to the specific learning needs of girls and boys through using gender-aware classroom processes and practices. These practices foster equal treatment and participation of girls and boys in the classroom and in the wider school community (Mlama et al., 2005). It is important to provide counter-stereotypical information, alternative role models, historical and global contexts and stories to challenge received norms which reinforce gender inequality but only if these are engaged with and made sense of through critical reflection, feminist pedagogy and dialogic enquiry. There are lots of ways in how and what we teach can contribute to positive or negative attitudes regarding gender. As teachers we should consider our decisions in relation to lesson planning (including teaching and learning materials and activities) and language use (Griffin, 2018).

Table 8.5 Reflection questions for teachers

Reflection questions

- What kind of wording do I use in class? Do I avoid traditional gender stereotypes?
- What kind of teaching methods do I use? Are they more teacher-centred or more student-centred? Do I allow students to take an active part during class, and move away from traditional classroom hierarchies that always present the teacher as the expert?
- When assigning team-work, do I split students into groups according to gender? If so, why? Can I modify this?
- Do the books/pictures/videos/songs I use in class reinforce traditional gender stereotypes? Do they include enough representation of women/girls and men/boys outside of stereotypical gender roles? Do they provide all the students with role models that they can identify with?
- Do I value equally the learning ability of both female and male students? Is everyone encouraged and praised using the same words?
- Do I facilitate both male and female students' abilities to learn, progress equally, and develop their potential to the fullest?
- Do I address potentially gender-biased attitudes that students may demonstrate towards their peers?
- Do I help students to question gender-biased attitudes in order to prevent them from happening in the future?
- Do I support students who demonstrate characteristics/behaviours resulting from social norms (e.g. shyness, arrogance, dominance, bullying, lack of confidence, fear of speaking in class) that may hinder academic learning and performance?
- Is behaviour managed in the same way for everyone? Do I have the same high expectations of behaviours from both boys and girls?

Questions adapted from Toliver and Sirtor-Gbassie (2018) and Gender Action (nd)

Lesson planning & delivery

Teachers are well used to planning lessons that take the different learning needs of the class into account. It is important to ensure that the lesson is gender inclusive. When planning teaching methodologies, consider how activities will allow equal participation of girls and boys. When assigning group projects ensure that both girls and boys are given leadership positions/roles. Critically review the teaching and learning materials with an eye for gender responsiveness (FAWE, 2020). If material contains gender stereotypes – e.g. pictures where surgeons or pilots are only depicted as men, or where teachers and nurses are only depicted as women, or texts that only profile famous men – plan how you will address this bias.

Language use & interactions

Language is one of the most powerful tools to define and reinforce gender relations and can be used to promote inclusion and gender awareness or to reinforce gender bias and stereotypes (Fisher et al., 2008). Some of the classroom activities in this chapter, demonstrate how language influences our perceptions of gender and gender stereotypes. Teachers can have an enormous influence on shaping the views of their students. It is important for teachers to examine their language use to eliminate choices that silence, stereotype or constrain others (FAWE, 2020).

Sexist phrases have unfortunately become common place in society. You will probably have heard comments such as 'boys will be boys', 'don't be such a girl', 'you throw like a girl', 'man up!', 'boys don't cry'. These comments imply that girls are not physically strong and that girls are emotionally weak. They also imply that boys need to be strong and stoic all the time. And that 'boys behave badly – it's just how they are'. These phrases are based on stereotypical beliefs about what it means to be a boy or a girl and how girls and boys should behave. Perpetuating these stereotypes can negatively affect all students. It is therefore very important that teachers choose their words carefully. The Gender Action schools programme in the UK supports a whole-school approach to challenging stereotype and encourages teachers to consider the impact of their actions. The above examples about sexist phrases are taken from their 'Gender stereotyping: Exploring bias and language' toolkit (see this website for further information: www.genderaction.co.uk).

Table 8.6 provides some guidance on appropriate language practices for the classroom. It also gives examples of both gender-biases and gender-responsive language.

Teaching through and about SDG 5: gender equality

SDG 5 aims to achieve gender equality and empower all women and girls. Nine targets have been set to stimulate action in relation to gender equality and thereby transform our world by 2030 (see appendix). It is possible to teach about Gender Equality from preschool through to secondary school. However, teachers will need to be cognisant of introducing age-appropriate content when discussing the SDG on gender. In providing SDG resources and guidance for educators, UNESCO (nd) advises that:

Table 8.6 Gender-neutral language practices. Adapted from Uworwabayeho et al. (2018)

Gender-Responsive Language Practices	Examples of Gender-Biased Language	Examples of Gender-Responsive Language
Use all pronouns: he, she, they; her, his, their.	When everyone contributes his own ideas, the discussion will be a success.	When everyone contributes her, his or their own ideas, the discussion will be a success.
Use the plural instead of the singular	If a student studies hard, he will succeed.	Students will succeed if they study hard
Recast a sentence in the passive voice	Each student should hand in his paper promptly.	Papers should be handed in promptly
Recast the sentence to avoid using the indefinite pronoun.	Does everybody have his book?	Do all of you have your books?
Create gender balance or neutrality in labels or titles	• Mankind	• Humanity, human beings, people
	• Man's achievements	• Human achievements
	• All men are created equal	• All people are created equal
	• The best man for the job	• The best person for the job
	• Chairman	• Chair, head, chairperson
	• Businessman	• Business executive, manager, businessperson
	• Congressman	
	• Policeman	• Congressional representative
	• Head master	• Police officer
		• Head teacher

At **Early Childhood Care and Education**, children should develop the ability to play positively both with girls and boys, and learn about sharing and being kind to everyone. Boys and girls should learn to value themselves and others.

In **Primary Education** children should be familiarised with the impact of gender roles on the identity and rights of girls and boys. They can learn to start thinking critically about socially constructed gender roles and stereotypes. They are thus able to unfold a de-gendered understanding of professions, sports, depictions in the media and politics, and family roles.

In **Secondary Education** children should acquire the understanding of the social construction of gender, including the gender dynamics in roles, professions, society and households. At post-primary level students should be encouraged to formulate strategies to overcome gender bias and to evaluate the role that socialisation plays in 'acceptable' emotional display. Students should be encouraged to challenge traditional gender roles, as well as gender-based violence and gender discrimination.

In their work to promote Education for Sustainable Development, UNESCO has identified indicative learning objectives, topics and learning activities for each SDG (UNESCO, 2017). These suggestions can be used as a guide when developing lesson and units of work about the SDGs (see Table 8.7). Teachers can select learning objectives and topics that are suited to the age-group of students in their classes. Later is this chapter we provide sample classroom activities for both primary and secondary school levels. At the end of the chapter, we provide a list with children's books that promote gender equality, as well as several helpful resources and websites for teachers.

Teaching about gender and the promotion of hope, empathy and advocacy

Through the discussion of the above theory, it can be concluded that teaching about gender is largely connected to promoting *hope, respect, empathy* and *advocacy* in the classroom. *Hope*, for a better future, in which gender inequalities in education will be obliterated, and in which the standard curriculum will encourage students to explore and celebrate gender diversity, while at the same time deconstructing harmful gender norms. Self-respect and respect for others are fundamental components of education about and for gender equality. By promoting respect, challenging stereotypes, building inclusive communities, and preventing discrimination, schools play a vital role in shaping a generation that values equality. Feminist teaching aims to sensitise students towards gender issues, and to help them develop e*mpathy* for one another through the sharing of feelings and lived experience. Finally, feminist pedagogy's ultimate goal is to inspire actual social change in the students' lives and in the wider community. It is therefore very much interlinked with promoting *advocacy* and praxis. These four key ingredients, *hope, respect, empathy*, and *advocacy*, were taken into account when designing the following classroom activities. They all aim towards educating students about gender, while at the same time developing their respect, and empathy, inspiring hope and encouraging them to become active advocates for gender equality.

Table 8.7 Learning objectives for SDG 1 (Source UNESCO, 2017: 20) and suggested topics/learning approaches (Source UNESCO, 2017: 21)

Learning Objectives

Cognitive learning objectives Teaching **about** the goals: developing respect and understanding	• The learner understands the concept of gender, gender equality and gender discrimination and knows about all forms of gender discrimination, violence and inequality and understands the current and historical causes of gender inequality. • The learner understands levels of gender equality within their own country and culture in comparison to global norms (while respecting cultural sensitivity), including the intersectionality of gender with other social categories such as ability, religion and race. • The learner knows the opportunities and benefits provided by full gender equality and participation in legislation and governance, including public budget allocation, the labour market and public and private decision-making.
Socio-emotional learning objectives Teaching **for** the goals enhancing empathy and love	• The learner is able to recognise and question traditional perception of gender roles in a critical approach, while respecting cultural sensitivity. • The learner is able to identify and speak up against all forms of gender discrimination and debate the benefits of full empowerment of all genders.. • The learner is able to reflect on their own gender identity and gender roles.
Behavioural learning objectives Teaching **through** the goals Promoting advocacy and activism	• The learner is able to take the measure of their surroundings to empower themselves or others who are discriminated against because of their gender. • The learner is able to evaluate, participate in and influence decision-making about gender equality and participation.

Suggested topics

Gender as a social and cultural construct.
Gender inequality, traditional gender roles and structural discrimination.
Gender equality and participation in decision-making.
Gender and education, including gender equality in achieving primary, secondary and tertiary levels of education.

Examples of learning approaches and methods

• Celebrate the International Day for the Elimination of Violence Against Women (November 25)
• Invite speakers who have experienced violence based on gender identity or sexual orientation
• Partner with groups from other parts of the world where the approach to gender may be different
• Explore how natural hazards and disasters affect women, girls, men and boys differently.
• Develop an enquiry-based project: *What is the difference between equality and equity and how does it apply to the world of work?*

Classroom activities

Primary students

Activity 1: gender inequality around the world

This activity is adapted from Concern (2019).
Aim: to introduce students to the need for the SDG on gender equality

Materials:

- Short video explaining the SDG goal (see suggestions below)
- Print out or use online link to the UN's gender inequality index

Suggested approach:

1   Use a video to introduce students to inequalities faced by women around the world. Following are a few suggestions:
    - ○   'Why striving for gender equality is important' on the Concern Worldwide YouTube channel (https://youtu.be/WvPuXHjOVh8)
    - ○   'The facts about gender equality and the Sustainable Development Goals' on the UN Women YouTube channel (https://youtu.be/K-oc4GOoWOl)
    - ○   There are several TED talks on gender equality
2   Ask students to share their initial reactions to the video.
3   With the students working in pairs, ask them to respond to the following questions:

    a)   Where does the country featured in the video (e.g. Malawi) rank on the UN's Gender Inequality Index?
    b)   What is the link between hunger and gender inequality for women and their communities?
    c)   Why do you think that women often have limited control over finances? Do you think this ever happens in Ireland?
    d)   Where does Ireland rank in the UN's Gender Inequality Index?

4   Invite pairs to share their responses with the rest of the class.
5   Ask students to consider what action they can take in their community on gender inequality.

Extension activity:
Watch the following video: #FromWhereIstand - Project for Gender Equality with Emma Watson on the Global Goals YouTube channel (1:14 minutes)

The lesson resources that Emma Watson refers to can be found at: https://worldslargest-lesson.globalgoals.org/ (select 'gender equality').

Activity 2: gender equality in the primary classroom

This activity is adapted from Trócaire (2007).

Aim: To carry out a gender audit in the school (this activity is suitable for a mixed gender school. In a single gender school, students could compile an audit for home).

Materials: Gender audit photocopied – enough for students to complete in pairs (Table 8.8).

Suggested approach:

1   Explain that the class is going to carry out an audit to examine how gender equal the school is.
2   Give each pair a copy of the audit form and invite them to complete it (alternatively you may wish to allocate each pair/group to a different topic).
3   Allow students to discuss and present their findings.
4   Invite suggestions for how the class could take action to address any inequalities that were noted.

Table 8.8 Sample gender equality audit

Our School Audit for Gender Equality

Organisation of students

Are girls and boys mixed when:
•   Lining up   Yes/No
•   Forming groups and teams in PE   Yes/No
•   Working in groups in the classroom   Yes/No

Use this space to write any notes about the above answers:

Organisation of space

Are boys and girls sitting together? Yes/No
  If no, how are they organised? _
Do girls and boys share the same play area? Yes/No
  If no, where do girls play and where do boys play? _
Are boys' and girls' work displayed equally? Yes/No
  If no, how are they displayed? _

Textbooks

Look at some of the textbooks to check who is doing tasks or taking on roles. Use this information to complete the table

Name of Textbook	*Tasks Done by Females*	*Tasks Done by Males*	*Tasks Done by Both Males & Females*

Organisation of tasks in the classroom
Fill in the following table by ticking the boxes to show who does certain tasks in our classroom (you can add other tasks to the list)

(Continued)

Table 8.8 (Continued)

Tasks	Boys	Girls	Both
Takes message to the principal or other classes			
Carries heavy items			
Cleans the classroom			
Tidies Up			
Waters the plants			

Are tasks shared equally between girls and boys? Yes/No
Give reasons for your answer: _

Solution Station!

Suggest changes that would make the organisation of your classroom more equal: _ _ _ _ _ _ _ _ _ _ _
_ _
_ _
_ _

Activity 3: our commitment to gender action

Aim: To develop a class-wide commitment to taking action for gender equality

Material: Sample gender action poster (see Table 8. 9)

Suggested approach:

1   Recap on the topics and learning from the previous activities.
2   Select one or two of the 'Taking Action for Gender Equality' examples that are provided
    in this chapter. Explain what the projects and initiatives aim to do and what they have
    achieved.
3   Introduce the concept of developing a class-level 'contract' for gender equality – this
    is an agreement of what the students in the class believe and commit to in relation to
    gender stereotypes.
4   Think-Pair-Share: Ask the students to think of two things they would like to see in the
    contract. Then ask students to share their ideas with a partner and discuss each one.
    Finally, ask pairs to share the key points raised with the whole class.
5   Collate the main ideas on the whiteboard or flip-chart paper. Display the gender action
    poster prominently in the classroom and refer it as the need arises (Table 8.9).

Post-primary students

Activity 1: riddles and myths

Aim: The aim of this activity it for students to think about how language influences our perceptions of gender and gender stereotypes.

Table 8.9 Sample gender action poster

Our Class Commitment to Gender Action
We believe that gender stereotypes should NOT limit our identities, experiences and life chances. In this classroom we: ✓ Know we all have different skills and abilities   ✓ Treat people as individuals and don't make assumptions   ✓ Believe all subjects, books, sports and colours are for everyone   ✓ Think about the words we use when talking to others   ✓ Speak up and challenge things we think are unfair

Adapted from Gender Action (nd)

Table 8.10 Can you solve this riddle?

CAN YOU SOLVE THE RIDDLE?
A father and son get in a car crash and are rushed to the hospital. The father dies. The boy is taken to the operating room and the surgeon says, "I can't operate on this boy, because he's my son."   How is this possible?   Answer: Discuss! What does this riddle show us about how language influences the way we think? What kind of stereotype is hidden in this riddle?

Materials: Riddle (Table 8.10, and a copy of 'Myth' by Muriel Rukeyser (1973)

Procedure: First, begin by telling the students that you will give them a riddle that they have to solve. Distribute handouts with the riddle (Table 8.10) and ask them to read the riddle individually and write down their answers.

Although the answer might seem pretty obvious, when this activity was carried out by one of the authors of this chapter in a classroom of 14-year-old students in Ireland, just one student managed to come up with the correct answer: the surgeon is the mother. The other students provided alternative options, some of which were the following: (a) the student has two fathers, (b) it's his grandfather, or even (c) it's God, because God is everyone's father. However, all the options presented referred to male characters, and not a single one was female (even God seemed to be a more likely option compared to a woman being a surgeon!). Therefore, this was a good opportunity to discuss with the students what this riddle shows about the influence of language on gender stereotypes. What kind of stereotypes are hidden in this riddle? Why do we immediately think of a man when we hear the word 'surgeon'? Does this mean that women can't be surgeons, or astronauts, or firefighters? What other examples of gender stereotypes can we see in the English language?

This activity can be used as a warm-up and can be combined with the reading and analysis of the poem 'Myth', by Muriel Rukeyser (the poem can be accessed online), which touches on gender inequality in language, and the generic use of the word 'man', which is used to signify and stand for not just men, but women too. For this activity, it would help to start off by gauging the students' previous knowledge on the myth about Oedipus and the Sphinx, and by giving a brief summary of the myth and the riddle that the Sphinx asked

Oedipus to solve. After reading the poem, possible discussion questions can include the following

- Why is the Sphinx dissatisfied with Oedipus' answer? Why does she claim that his answer is wrong?
- What is Oedipus' explanation?
- What does using the word 'man' for both women and men indicate about the role of men and women in the society we live in?
- How can the language we use affect gender roles?

Activity 2: gender stereotypes in advertising

Aim: For students to understand what traditional gender roles are, look critically at how these are reinforced in advertisements, and create their own non-sexist advertisements in response.

The purpose of this activity is for students to be able to trace the inherent sexism in the traditional 1950s advertisements, which portray certain ideas about the role of men and women in society. They reinforce stereotypes about women belonging to the domestic sphere, at home and in the kitchen, with the obligation of cooking dinner for their husbands and cleaning the house. In these advertisements, women are shown to be weak and simple-minded, and are supposed to be delighted with gifts that help them clean the house better, like a hoover. The recreations of the original advertisements by Rezkallah 'IN A PARALLEL UNIVERSE,' (2018), serve to expose and ridicule these stereotypes, simply by reversing the roles of the women and men portrayed in them, and thus bringing the audience's attention to these dominant assumptions about how men and women should behave.

Materials: Google images of sexist advertisements and their reversal (project by photographer Eli Rezkallah, which can be accessed at the following link: http://www.plastikstudios. com/inaparahlleluniverse)

Procedure:

1   Begin by introducing students to the concept of gender roles. Discuss the following questions with students: What are gender roles? What roles do women and men usually take in society? Think of what is expected of women and men in terms of obligations, behaviour, rights. Do you think these roles are starting to change?
2   Tell students that you are going to look at some original advertisements from the 1950s, as well as their recent recreations by photographer Eli Rezkallah, and discuss gender roles portrayed.
3   Present students with the advertisements and discuss the following questions: *What does the original advertisement show? Does it imply something about gender roles, and if yes, what? Do you agree with it or not? What is the purpose of the second advertisement and how does it achieve this? What techniques does the advertisements' language use to draw the audience in? Can you give some examples?*

After discussing these advertisements, this activity can be followed up by dividing students into groups and assigning each group another advertisement in which sexism is evident. The group then has to re-create the advertisement in a way which will reverse and deconstruct the gender stereotype that it portrays. All the groups will then present their advertisements in class, and discuss how their recreations subvert gender stereotypes.

Activity 3: exploring gendered oppression through drama

Aims

- For the students to be able to think about the gender inequalities and oppression that exist in society.
- For the students to be able to present this oppression through drama (a freeze-frame) and provide ideas about how an ideal society could be more gender equal and how oppression against women (and men) could be eliminated.

This activity is based on the work of drama theorist and theatre practitioner Augusto Boal on the *Theatre of the Oppressed* (Boal, 2002), a drama technique which is characterised by its liberatory aims, since its objective is to explore and undo different kinds of oppression. Through his 'Images of Transition' activity, Boal proposes a way for the students/actors to express how they experience different types of oppression that exist in society, to look at them through each other's depictions, and to think of ways in which these can change.

Materials: Google images of gendered oppression, handouts with instructions for the freeze-frame development

Procedure:

1   Start off by eliciting the theme of gendered oppression. This can be achieved by providing students with images that portray gendered oppression, whether that is the gender pay gap, the care work and housework that falls largely on women, or toxic masculinity and its effect on boys. The students can then be asked to give a definition of what gendered oppression is, and to provide more examples of it.
2   The next part of the lesson will be aimed at preparing the students for the drama activity. The students can be split into groups of four, and asked to think of a situation of gendered oppression at home/work/school, etc., as well as the basic elements of this situation: what is happening, the place and time in which it is happening, the characters involved in the scene, and how they are feeling.
3   Then, the students have to think of a way to show this with their bodies and without moving. They can use their facial expressions and posture, each student assuming a role, in order to create a 'freeze-frame', an image of this example of gendered oppression. For example, they might choose to portray a scene from family life, during which the mother has to do all the housework, while the father and children are not helping out with these tasks. Each group will have some time to prepare their freeze-frame, and will then present it to the rest of the class, who will try to guess what situation of gendered oppression it is depicting.

Table 8.11 Sample class commitment to gender action

Our Class Commitment to Gender Action
We believe that gender stereotypes should NOT limit our identities, experiences and life chances. In this classroom we: ✓ Know we all have different skills and abilities ✓ Treat people as individuals and don't make assumptions about who people are and what they are interested in ✓ Believe all subjects, books, sports and colours are for everyone ✓ Think about the words we use when talking to others ✓ Speak up – challenge biases and sexist behaviour

Adapted from Gender Action (nd)

4   Then, the class can be asked to modify this freeze-frame in order to set it right, and do away with the oppression that it depicts. What would have to change and what would the new image look like in an ideal world? How would the characters need to be positioned?

5   To conclude, ask the students to reflect on the creation of the freeze-frame, as well as the other images of gendered oppression that they saw, and how these can be corrected in real life.

Activity 4: our commitment to gender action

Aim: To develop a class-wide commitment to taking action for gender equality

Material: Sample Gender Action poster (see Table 8.11))

Suggested approach:

1   Ask students to share their key learning points from the earlier activities. Recap on the main topics that were covered.

2   Select two or three of the 'Taking Action' examples that are provided in this chapter. Explain what the projects and initiatives aim to do and what they have achieved.

3   Introduce the concept of developing a class-level 'contract' for gender equality – this is an agreement of what the students in the class believe and commit to in relation to gender stereotypes.

4   Working in small groups, ask students to think of items they would like to see in the class contract. Allow groups time to share ideas and collate ideas. Invite groups to present their ideas to the whole class.

5   Collate the main ideas on the whiteboard or flip-chart paper. Display the class commitment to gender equality prominently in the classroom and purposively refer it as the need arises.

Conclusion

This chapter has provided a summary of why Gender Equality (SDG 5) is still a topical issue which needs to be addressed and why teaching about gender is crucial in primary and secondary education. We have offered both a theoretical background, outlining the implications of gender in education, as well as a more practical guide with activities that teachers can use to introduce gender in their classroom and to make their practice more gender-equal. It is the aim of this chapter to inform teachers about the value of teaching about gender and using feminist pedagogy in the classroom. In this way, they can strive to inspire *hope* for a more gender-equal future, to develop the students' *empathy* for one-another and to help them become *advocates* of gender equality.

Resources

An extensive list of resources, videos and case studies for SDG 5 is included in the SDG padlet accompanying this book: https://padlet.com/annedolan/o6rds38ylfy6a28h

Further resources for teachers

Practice exemplar from a Scottish primary school

Find out about a gender quality project at Dalmellington Primary School, East Ayrshire. Their work led to the development of a toolkit to support embedding gender equality into school policy, ethos and curriculum.

https://education.gov.scot/improvement/practice-exemplars/gender-equality-for-primary-schools/

Gender action programme for schools

This award programme promotes and supports a whole-school approach to challenging stereotypes. Resources and support are provided.

https://www.genderaction.co.uk/

Gender Respect Education Project

The Gender Respect Education Project developed by the Development Education Centre South Yorkshire aims to help children and young people to understand, question and challenge gender inequality and violence in a local-global context.

https://genderrespect2013.wordpress.com/

International Women's Day

Oxfam has developed assembly and classroom resources that can be used to celebrate International Women's Day and explore gender equality with student aged 9-14 years.

https://oxfamilibrary.openrepository.com/handle/10546/620622

YouTube links

Gender Equality Now: https://youtu.be/4viXOGvvuOY

Key dates

February 6: International Day of Zero Tolerance to Female Genital Mutilation
March 8: International Women's Day
March: 31 International Transgender Day of Visibility
June 19: International Day for the Elimination of Sexual Violence in Conflict
July 12: Malala Day
October 11: International Day of the Girl Child
November 19: International Men's Day
November 25: International Day of the Elimination of Violence Against Women
December 10: Human Rights Day

Children's books

A detailed list of books about Malala Yousafzai Malala Yousafzai, the Pakistani female education activist and 2014 Nobel Peace Prize laureate is available in chapter 7.

Picturebooks

Allen, K. Allen, Z. and O'Brien, T. (illus) (2023) *My Brother George* UCLan.
Allen, K. Allen, Z. and O'Brien, T. (illus) (2023) *My Momma* Zo UCLan.
Baldacchino, C. and Malenfant, I. (illus) (2014) *Morris Micklewhite and the Tangerine Dress* Groundwood Books.
Beaty, A. and Roberts, D. (illus) (2013) *Rosie Revere Engineer* Abrams Books for Young Readers.
Beaty, A. and Roberts, D. (illus) (2016) *Ada Twist Scientist*. Abrams Books for Young Readers.
Beaty, A. and Roberts, D. (illus) (2019) *Sofia Valdez, Future Prez* Abrams Books for Young Readers.
Becker, H. and Phumiruk, D. (illus) (2019) *Counting on Katherine*: How Katherine Johnson Put Astronauts on the Moon Macmillan Children's Books.
Brannen, S. and Soto, L. (illus) (2021) *Uncle Bobby's Wedding* Hodder Children's Books.
Brown, P. (2021) *Fred Gets Dressed* Templar Books.
Cali, D. and Ramos, F. (illus) (2023) *Tourmaline* Tate Publishing.
Cheng Thom, K., Yun Ching, K. (illus) and Li, W. (illus) (2017) *From the Stars in the Sky to the Fish in the Sea* Arsenal Pulp Press.
Doyle, R. and Lindsay, A. (illus) (2020) *Dreams for Our Daughters* Andersen Press.
Doyle, R. and Lindsay, A. (illus) (2021) *Songs for Our Sons* Andersen Press.
Elliott, M. (2019) *The Girl With Two Dads* Farshore.
Estrela, J. (2022) *My Own Way: Celebrating Gender Freedom for Kids* Wide Eyed Editions.
Ewert, M and Ray, R. (illus) (2009). *10,000 Dresses* Seven Stories Press.
Fierstein, H. and Cole, H. (illus) (2014) *The Sissy Duckling* Little Simon.
Finch, M., Finch, P. and Davey, S. (illus) (2018) *Phoenix Goes to School: A Story to Support Transgender and Gender Diverse Children Jessica* Kingsley Publishers.
Frances, L. (2019) *My Awesome Brother: A Children's Book About Transgender* Mabel Media.
Frances, L. (2019) *My Awesome Sister : A Children's Book About Transgender* Mabel Media.
Gravel, E. and Blais, M. (2022) *Pink, Blue and You!: Questions for Kids about Gender Stereotypes* Anne Schwartz Books.
Hirst, J. and Bardoff, N. (2018) *A House for Everyone: A Story to Help Children Learn about Gender Identity and Gender Expression* Jessica Kingsley Publishers.
Jemp, A. and Ogilvie, S. (2010) Dogs Don't Do Ballet. Simon & Schuster Children's UK
Johnston, B. and Emberley, M. (illus) (2022) *Our Big Day* O'Brien's Press.
Lancet-Grant, J. and Corry, L. (illus) (2021) *The Pirate Mums* OUP Oxford.
Hall, M. (2015) *Red: A Crayon's Story* Greenwillow Books.

Hoffman, S., Hoffman, I. and Case, C. (illus) (2014) *Jacob's New Dress* Albert. Whitman & Company.

Hoffman, S., Hoffman, I. and Case, C. (illus) (2019) *Jacob's Room to Choose* Magination Press.

Hoffman, S., Hoffman, I. and Case, C. (illus) (2021) *Jacob's School Play: Starring He, She and They* Magination Press.

Latlip, K. and Wastyn, G. (illus) (2022) *Blink, Plue & Colorful You: A Story about Gender Expression and Acceptance* Rainbow Circus Publishing.

Locke, K. and Passchier, A.(2021) *What Are Your Words? A Book About Pronouns.* Little, Brown Books for Young Readers.

Love, J. (2019) *Julian is a Mermaid* Walker Books.

Love, J. (2021) *Julian at the Wedding* Walker Books.

Kilodavis, C. and DeSimone, S. (illus) (2011) *My Princes Boy* Simon and Schuster.

Madison, M., Ralli, J. and Passchier, A. (illus) (2021) *Being You: A First Conversation about Gender* Rise x Penguin Workshop.

Melvin, A. (2018) *My Day* Tate Publishing.

Moradian, A. and Bogade, M. (2018). *Jamie is Jamie: A Book About Being Yourself and Playing Your Way Free* Spirit Publishing.

Munsch, R. and Martchencko, M. (illus) (2018) *The Paper Bag Princess.* Annick Press.

Newman, L. and Mola, M. (illus) (2017) *Sparkle Boy* Lee & Low Books.

Newman, L. and Cornell, L. (illus) (2016) *Heather Has Two Mummies* Walker Books.

Newman, L. and Dutton, M. (illus) *Donovan's Big Day.* Tricycle Press.

McClintick, J and Medina, J. (2023) *'Twas the Night Before Pride* Walker Books.

Murray, B. (2022) *Gerald Wants to Wear Pink* Llama House Children's Books.

Pankhurst, K. (2018) *Fantastically Great Women Who Saved the Planet* Bloomsbury Children's Books.

Pankhurst, K. (2018) *Fantastically Great Women Who Made History* Bloomsbury Children's Books.

Pankhurst, K. (2018) *Fantastically Great Women Who Worked Wonders* Bloomsbury Children's Books.

Pankhurst, K. (2018) *Fantastically Great Women Who Made History* Bloomsbury Children's Books.

Pankhurst, K. (2016) *Fantastically Great Women Who Changed The World* Bloomsbury Children's Books.

Pearlman, R and Kaban, E. (illus) (2018) *Pink Is For Boys* Running Press Kid.

Pessin-Wheedbee, B. and Bardoff, N. (illus) (2016) *Who Are You? The Kid's Guide to Gender Identity.* Jessica Kingsley Publishers.

Roberts, J. and Robinson, C. (illus) (2022) *The Smallest Girl in the Class* Two Hoots.

Slade, B. and Soto, L. (illus) (2023) *Cinder and Ella* Owlet Press.

Stewart, J. (2017) *Tiny Dinosaurs* Oxford University Press.

Stowell, L. Barns, E. and Phelps, A. (illus) (2022) *ABC Pride* DK Children.

Stuart, S. (2020) *My Shadow is Pink* Larrikin House.

Stuart, S. (2022) *My Shadow is Purple* Larrikin House.

Stuart, S. (2021) *How To Be a Real Man* QUBM4.

Thorn, T. and Grigni, N. (illus) (2019) *It Feels Good to be Yourself: A Book About Gender Identity* Henry Holt and Co.

Tregoning, R. and Murphy, S. (Illus) (2023) *Out of the Blue: A heartwarming book about celebrating difference* Bloomsbury Children's Books.

Tregoning, R. and Curnick, P. (illus) (2023) *The Dress in the Window* OUP Oxford.

Tregoning, R. and Murphy, S. (illus) (2024) *A Fairy Called Fred* Bloomsbury Children's Books Walton, J. and MacPherson, D. (illus) (2016) *Introducing Teddy: A Gentle Story About Gender and Friendship* Bloomsbury USA Childrens.

Walton, J. and MacPherson, D. (2016). Introducing Teddy: A Gentle Story About Gender and Friendship. Bloomsbury USA Childrens.

Winslow, C. and Samels, R. (illus) (2022) *We Are The Rainbow* Sunbird Books.

Winter, J. (2009) *Nasreen's Secret School: A True Story from Afghanistan* Simon and Schuster.

Books recommended for students aged 8+ years

Adams, J. and Wright, L. (illus) (2018) *101 Awesome Women Who Changed Our World* Arcturus Editions.

Appleby, B. and Spilsbury, L. (2017) *What Is Feminism? Why Do We Need It? And Other Big Questions* London: Hachette Children's Group.

Ayala-Kronos, C. and Tirado, M. (illus) (2022) *The Pronoun Book.* Clarion Books.

Brami, E. and Billon-Spagnol, E. (illus) (2017) *Declaration of the Rights of Girls and Boys* Little Island Books.

Brooks, B. (2018) *Stories for Boys Who Dare to Be Different: True Tales of Amazing Boys Who Changed the World Without Killing Dragons* London: Running Press Kids.

Christina Gonzalez, M. (2017) *The Gender Wheel: A Story About Bodies and Gender For Everybody* Reflection Press.

Cummings-Quarry and Carter, N. A. (2021) *Grown: The Black Girls' Guide to Growing Up* Andersen Press.

Dale, L. K. and Qing Ang, H. (illus) (2022) *Me and My Dysphoria Monster* Jessica Kingsley Publisher.

Erickson, L. (2023). *Girls are amazing: Inspirational and Exciting. Short Stories for Girls about Love, Self-Awareness and Courage* Independently published.

Favilli, E. and Cavallo, F. (2017a) *Goodnight Stories for Rebel Girls* London: Penguin Books.

Favilli, E. and Cavallo, F. (2017b) *Goodnight Stories for Rebel Girls 2* London: Penguin Books.

Gino, A. (2022). *Alice Austin Lived Here* Scholastic.

Halligan, K. and Walsh, S. (illlus) (2018) *Her Story: 50 Women and Girls Who Shook The World* Nosy Crow Ltd.

Harrison, V. (2017) *Little Leaders: Bold Women in Black History* London: Penguin Books.

Harrison, V. (2020) *Little Leaders: Visionary Women Around the World* London: Penguin Books.

Love, J. (2018) *Julián Is a Mermaid.* Candlewick.

Pankhurst, K. (2016) *Fantastically Great Women Who Changed the World* Bloomsbury: Children's Books.

Pankhurst, K. (2018a) *Fantastically Great Women Who Worked Wonders* Bloomsbury: Children's Books.

Pankhurst, K. (2018b) *Fantastically Great Women Who Saved the Planet* Bloomsbury: Children's Books.

Pankhurst, K. (2018c) *Fantastically Great Women Who Made History* Bloomsbury: Children's Books.

Passchier, A. (2023) *Gender Identity for Kids: A Book About Finding Yourself, Understanding Others, and Respecting Everybody!* Little, Brown Books for Young Readers.

Russo, M. (2018) *If I Was Your Girl* Flatiron Books.

Sanders, J. and Gulliver, A. (illus) (2016) *No Difference Between Us: Teaching Children about Gender Equality, Respectful Relationships, Feelings, Choice, Self-Esteem, Empathy, Tolerance, and Acceptance* Educate to Empower Publishing.

Sanders, R. and Salerno, S. (illus) (2018) *Pride:The Story of Harvey Milk and the Rainbow Flag* Random House Books for Young Readers.

Singh, R. and Ferrer, M. (illus) (2020) *111 Trees: How One Village Celebrates the Birth of Every Girl* Kids Can Press.

Spanyol, J. (2016) *Clive and His Babies.* Child's Play International.

Spanyol, J. (2018) *Rosa Loves Cars* Child's Play International.

Stuart, S. (2020) *My Shadow Is Pink* Larrikin House

Stuart, S. (2022) *My Shadow Is Purple* Larrikin House

Taylor, A. and Stevens, L. (illus (2020) *The Big Book of LGBTQ+ Activities: Teaching Children about Gender Identity, Sexuality, Relationships and Different Families* Jessica Kingsley Publishers.

Walliams, D. and Blake, Q. (Illus) (2009) *The Boy In The Dress* Razorbill.

Watson, R. and Hagan, E. (2019) *Watch Us Rise* Bloomsbury.

Books recommended for students aged 12 + years

Andrews, A. (2014) *Some Assembly Required: The Not So Secret Life of a Transgender Teen* Simon & Schuster Books for Young Readers.

Atta, D. (2019) *Black Flamingo* Hodder Children's Books.

Backer, J. B. (2022) *Kisses for Jet* Nobrow.

Beam, C. (2012) *I am J* Little, Brown Books for Young Readers.

Brooks, B. and Winter, Q. (illus) (2018) *Stories for Boys who Dared to be Different: True Tales of Amazing Boys who Changed the World Without Killing Dragons* Running Press Kids.

Callender, K. (2021) *Felix Ever After* Faber and Faber.

Clyde, R. (2023) *Jay's Guide to Crushing* Scholastic.

Dawson, J. (2019) *What Is Gender? How Does It Define Us? And Other Big Questions. London:* Hachette Children's Group.

Dyer, H. (2021) *The Little Book of LGBTQ +: An A -Z Gender and Sexual Identities* Summersdale.

Easton, T.S. (2017) *Girls Can't Hit* Hot Key Books.

Ellis, R. and Sheridan, J. (illus) (2022) *Here and Queer: A Queer Girld's Guide to Life* Francis Lincoln.
Gail, L. (2021) *Extraordinary Women In History: 70 Remarkable Women Who Made a Difference, Inspired & Broke Barriers.* Independently published.
Gregory, J. (2021) *What Lovel looks like: Sometimes love turns up where you least expect* it Bloomsbury.
Jaigirdar, A. (2021) *The Henna Wars* Hodder Children's Books.
Laney, L. (2020) *The Little Book of Pride: The History, the People, the Parades* Dog 'n' Bone.
Mueller, D. (2023) *A Kids Book About Gender* DK Children.
Nicholls, S. (2018) *Things a Bright Girl Can Do* Andersen Press.
Oakes-Monger, T.C. (2023) *All the Things They Said We Couldn't Have* Jessica Kingsley Publishers.
O'Donoghue, C. (2021) *All Our Hidden Talents* Walker Books.
Peters, J.A. (2006) *Luna* Little, Brown Books for Young Readers.
Prager, S. and More O' Ferrall, Z. (illus) (2017) *Queer, There and Everywhere* HarperCollins.
Raum, E. (2019) *The Life of Ruby Bridges* Amicus Ink.
Reyes, S. (2023) *The Lesbiana's Guide to Catholic School* Faber & Faber.
Roehm Mc Cann, M. (2018) *Girls Who Changed the World* Simon & Schuster.
Russell, J. (2021) *Skywake Invasion* Walker Books.
Stoeve, R. (2021) *Between Perfect &Real* Amulet.
Trent, T. and Spivey, Gilchrist, J.S. (2016) *The Girl Who Buried her Dreams in a Can* Viking Books for Young Reader.
Wright, L. (2018) 101 *Awesome Women Who Changed our World.* Arcturus Editions.
Yolen, J. and Guevara, S. (illus) (2018) *Not One Damsel in Distress: Heroic Girls from the World Folklore* Clarion Books.

Note

1 While we chose the widely used term 'Native American' to refer to the indigenous people of the Americas, we would like to acknowledge that different cultural groups might prefer to be referred to by other terms, including their specific tribal name.

References

Barker, M.J. (2019). *Gender: A Graphic Guide*. London: Icon Books.
Barker, M. and Iantaffi, A. (2019). *Life Isn't Binary: On Being Both, Beyond and In-between.* London: Jessica Kingley Publishers.
Benesch, S. (1998). Anorexia: A Feminist EAP Curriculum. In Smoke, T. (Ed.) *Adult ESL: Politics, Pedagogy, and Participation in Classroom and Community Programs,* 101-114. Mahwah, NJ: Lawrence Erlbaum Associates.
Boal, A. (2002). *Games for Actors and Non-Actors* (A. Jackson, Trans.) (2nd ed.). London, New York: Routledge.
Bostow, R., Brewer, S., Chick, N., Galina, B., McGrath, A., Mendoza, K., Navarro, K., & Valle-Ruiz, L. (2015). *A Guide to Feminist Pedagogy: The Role of Experience and Emotions*. Vanderbilt Center for Teaching. https://my.vanderbilt.edu/femped/habits-of-head/the-role-of-experience-emotions/
Concern. (2019). Gender Equality, Resource for Teachers and Facilitators. https://www.concern.net/schools-and-youth/educational-resources
Crabtree, R.D., Sapp, D.A. and Licona, A.C. (2009). *Feminist Pedagogy: Looking Back to Move Forward.* NJ., The Johns Hopkins University Press.
Crenshaw, K. (1989). Demarginalizing the Intersection of Race and Sex: A Black Feminist Critique of Antidiscrimination Doctrine, Feminist Theory and Antiracist Politics. *University of Chicago Legal Forum, 1989*(1), 139-167. Accessed https://chicagounbound.uchicago.edu/cgi/viewcontent.cgi?article=1052&context=uclf
European Institute for Gender Equality. (2016). Gender Equality Training: Gender MainstreamingToolkit. Accessed https://eige.europa.eu/publications-resources/publications/gender-equality-training-gender-mainstreaming-toolkit
Forum for African Women Educationalists (FAWE), *Gender Responsive Pedagogy: A Toolkit for Teachers and Schools.* 2nd ed. (2020). Nairobi: Forum for African Women Educationalists.

Fisher, D., Frey, N. and Rothenberg, C. (2008). *Content-Area Conversations: How to Plan Discussion-Based Lessons for Diverse Language Learners*. Alexandria, VA: ASCD.

Gender Action. (nd). Gender Stereotyping: Exloring Bias and Language. https://www.genderaction.co.uk/gender-action-resources

Gender Action. (nd). Classroom Posters. https://www.genderaction.co.uk/gender-action-resources

Griffin, H. (2018). *Gender Equality in Primary Schools, A Guide for Teachers*. London: Jessica Kingsley Publishers.

IN A PARALLEL UNIVERSE. (2018). http://www.elirezkallah.com/inaparalleluniverse/

Lewis, V. (2020). Teaching and Learning about all the Sustainable Development Goals. *ETBI Journal of Education*, *2*(1), 21–26. https://www.yumpu.com/en/document/read/63575156/etbi-journal-of-education-vol-2-issue-1-june-2020

Luecke, J.C. (2018). The Gender Facilitative School: Advocating Authenticity for Gender Expansive Children in Pre-Adolescence. *Improving Schools*, *21*(3), 269–284. Doi: 10.1177/1365480218791881.

Mlama, P., Dioum, M., Makoye, H., Murage, L., Wagah, M. and Waskika, R. (2005). *Gender Responsive Pedagogy. A Teacher's Handbook*. Nairobi: Forum for African Women Educationalists (FAWE).

Ongsupankul, W. (2019). Finding Sexual Minorities in United Nations Sustainable Development Goals: Towards the Deconstruction of Gender Binary in International Development Policies. *LSE Law Review*, 5. 1–30.

Richards, J.C. (1–30). and Rodgers, T.S. (2015). *Approaches and Methods in Language Teaching* (3rd ed.). Cambridge: Cambridge University Press.

Rukeyser, M. (1973). Myth. https://murielrukeyser.emuenglish.org/2018/12/07/myth/

Toliver, M. and Sirtor-Gbassie, V. (2018). MCSP HRH Liberia Gender Responsive Teaching Methods, Facilitator's Guide. Accessed 1st September 2020, https://www.mcsprogram.org/resource/mcsp-hrh-liberia-gender-responsive-teaching-methods-facilitators-guide

Trócaire. (2007). Trócaire Lenten Campaign 2007. Primary School Teachers' Resource (Malawi – Gender Equality) https://www.trocaire.org/sites/default/files/resources/edu/malawi-gender-equality-lesson-plan-junior-primary.pdf

UNESCO. nd). SDG Resources for Educators – Gender. Accessed 1st September 2020, https://en.unesco.org/themes/education/sdgs/material/05

UNESCO. (2017). *Education for Sustainable Development, Learning Objectives*. UNESCO: Paris, France.

UNICEF. (2017). *Gender Equality, Glossary of Terms and Concepts*. Kathmandu, Nepal: Regional Office for South Asia.

United Nations. (nd). Goal 5: Achieve Gender Equality and Empower all Women and Girls. https://www.un.org/sustainabledevelopment/gender-equality/

United Nations Climate Change. (nd). *Introduction to Gender and Climate Change*. https://unfccc.int/gender

UN Women. (nd). *Facts & Figures*. Accessed 1st July 2020, https://www.unwomen.org/en/news/in-focus/commission-on-the-status-of-women-2012/facts-and-figures

Uworwabayeho, A., Bayisenge, J., Katwaza, E., Umutoni, J., Habumuremyi, J. and Rwabyoma, A. (2018). *National Gender-Responsive Teacher Training Package*. Rwanda, Ministry of Education.

9 Blue gold
Clean water and sanitation (SDG 6)

Anne O'Dwyer

Introduction

Water is one of the world's most precious resources and we simply cannot live without it. Access to clean water is now more challenging due to climate change, an increase in population, increased water consumption and urbanisation. Over two billion people live in countries which experience high water stress. This occurs when the demand for water exceeds the available amount during a certain period or when poor quality restricts its use. By 2050, global water demand is expected to increase by 20 to 30%, while supply of clean, safe drinking water will dwindle to a serious extent (WWAP, 2019). Currently, access to clean, safe drinking water is denied to many (Table 9.1). SDG 6 aims to ensure the availability and sustainable management of water and sanitation for all.

A sustainable and clean water supply can have a positive impact on food and energy production, and thus economic growth. Understanding and managing our water systems responsibly can help to preserve ecosystems and thus contribute to positive climate action. This chapter aims to help teachers focus on the importance of water, the science of water (including the water cycle), the management of water supplies (including sanitation facilities) and the need to conserve water. The ideas in this chapter help to support students' understanding that everyone needs clean safe drinking water, good sanitation, hygiene education and well-monitored water quality. The lesson ideas support students' development as responsible water users as they gain a better understanding of the water cycle, water pollution and treatment. Learning can be linked to everyday contexts by increasing awareness of ways to reuse our water and become more aware of improving our water management.

The importance of our water

Over 70% of the Earth's surface is covered with water with oceans accounting for over 96% of all Earth's water. Saltwater or seawater, the water in oceans and seas is unsuitable for human consumption. Freshwater is naturally occurring water that contains a low concentration of salts and other dissolved solids. Freshwater is vital for human and animal lives on Earth. However, only 3% of the water on Earth is freshwater. It is present in various water bodies such as lakes, ponds, reservoirs, rivers, wetlands, glaciers and icebergs. These sources include frozen and meltwater, natural precipitations, surface runoffs, as well as groundwater.

DOI: 10.4324/9781003232001-12

Table 9.1 Key statistics about water

771 million people globally don't have access to clean water. That's one in ten people.
A child dies every 2 minutes from a water related disease.
1.7 billion people globally don't have access to adequate sanitation. That's one in five people.
2.27 billion people globally don't have access to basic hygiene services. That's one in three people.

Source: (WHO, nd) https://www.who.int/news-room/fact-sheets/detail/drinking-water and Just a Drop (nd).

Indeed, as water scarcity increases, desalination plants are on the rise with the world's largest plants located in Saudi Arabia, United Arab Emirates and Israel.

In addition to our human need for water (for consumption and sanitation), water is necessary for plant growth, animal life, irrigation, hydropower, as well as residential, commercial and industrial use. As a premium resource, we need to understand where our water comes from. However, many people do not have access to clean water, adequate sanitation or basic hygiene services (Table 9.1). Furthermore, many people do not appreciate the significance of water as an essential resource for life.

The water cycle

Our water sources need to be replenished, purified and circulated for continued daily use, and nature helps to do this job, in a process called the water cycle. In this natural process, water moves through its three states of matter (gas, liquid and solid) in different layers of our Earth's atmosphere. The water cycle impacts on our weather as it creates precipitation e.g. rain or snow, it hydrates the Earth's surface and it transports many minerals. Through phases of evaporation, condensation and precipitation, water circulates through the Earth's atmosphere (Figure 9.1). The water cycle creates many geographical features, e.g. icebergs, rivers and lakes.

Unfortunately, climate change, natural disasters and human action have interrupted the natural water cycle resulting in shortages of water for many. Climate change affects the natural patterns of precipitation and evaporation, which impacts on water supply and availability on the Earth's surface. This has resulted in some areas experiencing increased water flow and flooding, while other areas may experience decreased water supply and drought. Furthermore, in some coastal areas the combination of increasing sea levels and groundwater levels will change the distribution of land and sea water, and thus impact on the volumes of freshwater and saltwater (Cliwat, 2008).

Water literacy

Water literacy is essentially knowledge about water sources, water management and water-related issues encompassing water knowledge, attitude and behaviour (Maniam et al., 2021), as shown in Figure 9.2. McCarroll and Hamann (2020: 2) define water literacy as the 'culmination of water-related knowledge, attitudes, and behaviors'. The cognitive, affective and behavioural domains are each important components of water literacy (see Figure 9.2).

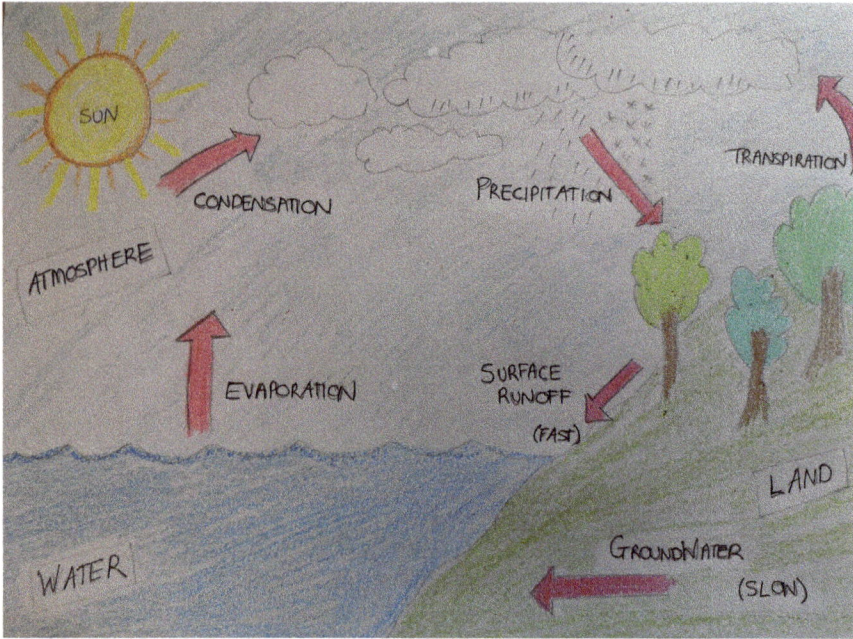

Figure 9.1 Drawing of the Water Cycle.

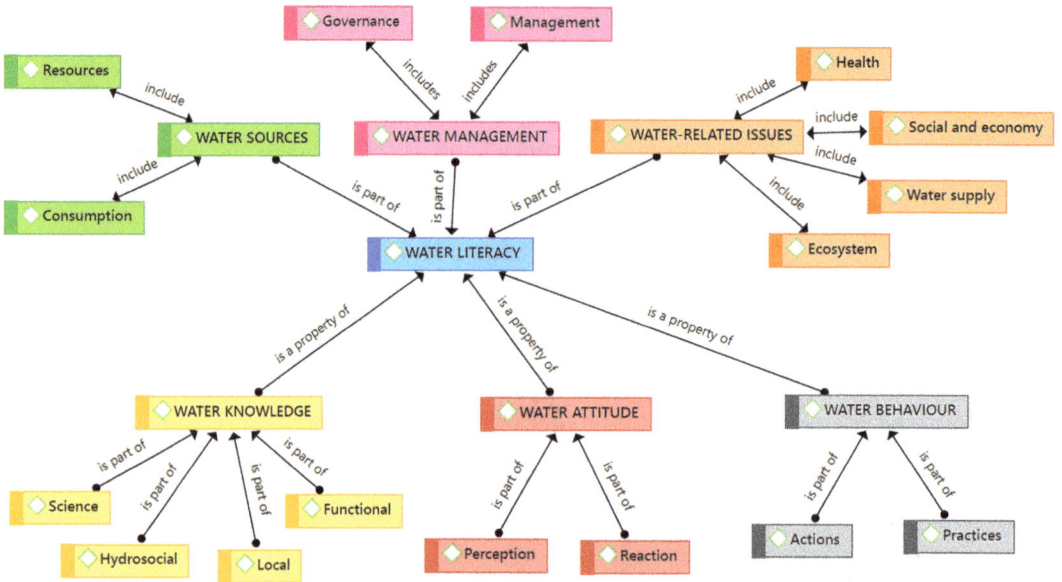

Figure 9.2 Water Literacy. (Source: Maniam et al., 2021: 2311).

However, research illustrates the limited opportunities for students to learn about water in a robust, holistic approach. Instead, learning opportunities about water tend to be disconnected and discipline specific, leading to a partial understanding of water (Mostacedo-Marasovic et al., 2022). While a cognitive understanding of water is regularly addressed in lessons about water, the affective domains together with its social and emotional components are somewhat neglected.

Many countries around the world are facing low to medium water stress. Indeed, the water situation in regions in the Global South has changed from one of relative abundance to one of absolute scarcity. As global temperatures rise due to climate change, prolonged heat waves place severe strains on local and national water supplies. Water literacy has a growing importance for improving water sustainability. Conventional water management strategies are no longer sufficient. As populations grow and rapid urbanisation occurs, the challenges to manage water and its resources will continue to increase. Innovative water management approaches will be required based on active public participation.

According to Maniam et al. (2021) public participation in water management is an amalgamation of (i) the understanding of water science, resources and the ecology environment; (ii) water attitude, which is a fusion of water appreciation, responsibility, and ethics; and last but not least, (iii) adoption of the pro-environmental behaviour. Active public participation is often limited due to water illiteracy.

Awareness of one's water footprint is critical for one to be more conscious of water usage and wastage. In the early 2000s, a Dutch professor named Arjen Hoekstra introduced the concept of a water footprint. The water footprint of a person is defined as the total volume of freshwater that is used to produce the commodities, goods and services consumed by that person. A water footprint includes direct water, i.e. the water which can be seen flowing from a tap or garden hose; blue water, i.e. surface or ground water; and grey water that which is used to make waste water safe for reuse. Every product produced has a water footprint and often consumers are unaware of the large volumes of water required for commodities purchased. A water footprint can reveal water-use patterns that can help individuals, businesses, and countries understand how they can become more water literate. Different countries have introduced schemes to promote an awareness of one's water footprint. In some Southeast Asian countries, the Water Efficient Product Labelling Scheme (WEPLS) is an initiative to educate the public about the level of water-efficiency of certain products such as water taps, flush toilets, urinal equipment, showerheads and washing machines. Products are rated according to the level of water-efficiency with one star being the least efficient and three stars being the most efficient (Maniam et al., 2021).

Clean drinking water and sanitation

A drinking water supply includes the abstraction, treatment, storage and distribution of water from the water source to the consumer's tap. The raw water sources, which are our rivers, lakes, springs and groundwater, can be a source of contaminants if the water is not properly managed and treated at all stages of the process. Although access to clean drinking water is a human right, 785 billion people remain without access to safe drinking water (UN, 2020). In many areas of the Global South, drinking water is contaminated by humans and animals. Contaminated and unsafe drinking water leads to illness and death. In many cases, the lack of clean drinking water is a result of poor water management and waste water treatment. Over 80% of wastewater from human activities is dumped into rivers or seas without any treatment (UN, 2020). This leads to pollution and contamination of water sources.

Some 40% of people worldwide do not have a basic hand washing facility with soap and water (UN, 2020). Sadly, water and sanitation-related diseases are the major cause of death for young children. More than 800 children die every day due to poor hygiene and sanitation. In addition, one in four health-care facilities worldwide lack basic drinking water services (UN, 2020). Almost 10% of the global population still practice open defecation (UN, 2020). According to regular reports from the Environmental Protection Agency in Ireland (2023), raw sewage from several towns and villlages continues to be discharged into nearby waters. Our waste and waste water needs to be treated and managed in a safe and appropriate manner. Water treatment systems and sewage treatment systems need to be appropriately resourced and managed to maximise water recycling and increase the safe-use of water globally. Sustainable water management contributes to public safety, food production and economic growth.

Promoting water literacy in schools

Learning objectives adapted from UNESCO (2017) are included in Table 9.2. The specific learning objectives aligned to each classroom activity are outlined in the description of each

Table 9.2 Learning objectives for SDG4 (adapted from UNESCO, 2020)

Cognitive learning objectives Teaching **about** the goals: developing respect and understanding	1. The learner understands water as a fundamental condition of life itself, the importance of water quality and quantity, and the causes, effects and consequences of water pollution and water scarcity. 2. The learner understands that water is part of many different complex global interrelationships and systems. 3. The learner knows about the global unequal distribution of access to safe drinking water and sanitation facilities. 4. The learner understands the concept of "virtual water" 5. The learner understands the concept of Integrated Water Resources Management (IWRM) and other strategies for ensuring the availability and sustainable management of water and sanitation, including flood and drought risk management.
Socio-emotional learning objectives Teaching **for** the goals enhancing empathy and love	1. The learner is able to participate in activities of improving water and sanitation management in local communities. 2. The learner is able to communicate about water pollution, water access and water saving measures and to create visibility about success stories. 3. The learner is able to feel responsible for their water use.
Behavioural learning objectives Teaching **through** the goals Promoting advocacy and activism	1. The learner is able to cooperate with local authorities in the improvement of local capacity for self-sufficiency. 2. The learner is able to contribute to water resources management at the local level. 3. The learner is able to reduce their individual water footprint and to save water practicing their daily habits. 4. The learner is able to plan, implement, evaluate and replicate activities that contribute to increasing water quality and safety. 5. The learner is able to evaluate, participate in and influence decision-making on management strategies of local, national and international enterprises related to water pollution

lesson idea. These help the students to develop respect, empathy and advocacy by learning through their heads, heart and hands.

It is important that these learning objectives are actionable and achievable. Linking these objectives to school curricula, classroom activities and students' learning makes them more tangible. The classroom activities that follow explore concepts that help students to achieve these objectives, and then to reflect on their own actions in seeing how global learning objectives can be relevant to local and everyday life.

Practical classroom activities

All students need to appreciate the importance of water as a global and natural resource in order to achieve UNESCO learning objectives (2019) listed in Table 9.2. An improved understanding of our water systems can lead to more responsible use and better water management. While the effects of water shortages and lack of appropriate sanitation are experienced more in the Global South, all students need to develop an awareness of these effects.

The terminology in Table 9.3 may be useful to scaffold classroom discussion during the activities and support students in developing their content knowledge. This box is not an exhaustive list, but is suggested as a guideline to scaffold learning in the activities that follow. The terminology in the box and the classroom activities that follow are not prescriptive for particular class levels. Rather, they are an outline of suggestive ideas that teachers could explore, in a manner appropriate to their own class level and ability.

Some of the learning approaches recommended by UNESCO (2017: 23) are included in the practical classroom activities outlined in this chapter:

- Calculate one's own water footprint.
- Develop a concept for local sustainable water use and supply.
- Organise excursions and field trips to local water infrastructures.
- Monitor water quality at school and home

Understanding the water cycle in action

- Objective: *The learner understands that water is part of many different complex global interrelationships and systems* (UNESCO learning objective (2017: 22)

Overview: It is important that students have an understanding of how our water is replenished, purified and circulated through the natural process of the water cycle. The water cycle is essential for almost all life on land and underwater, as it involves water on, above and below the Earth's surface. This hands-on investigation is worthwhile in supporting students' understanding of the water cycle. This lesson focuses on the properties of materials and their relationships, in particular the relationship between heat energy and the changing state of water. This demonstration addresses the common misconception that water molecules 'disappear' or 'break up' when it changes from a liquid to a gas. Testing the droplets (condensation) that form inside the top of the jar (using an agent such as anhydrous copper sulphate) confirms they are water. Also, carefully measuring and recording the volume of water at the beginning and at end of the activity confirms that all of the water is present, and simply circulated,

Table 9.3 Terminology about properties of water

Boiling point: The temperature that a liquid changes into a gas (100°Celsius for water). The strong hydrogen bonds between the water molecules are broken. The strong covalent bonds between the hydrogen atoms and oxygen atom within the water molecule are not broken.

Condense: To change from a gas to a liquid. This happens when there is a reduction in temperature.

Covalent Bonding: Strong intra-molecular bond within each water molecule, as electrons are shared between the oxygen and each hydrogen atom. This bond does not break when water boils or evaporates.

Desalination: the process of removing salt from sea water.

Evaporate: To change from a liquid to a gas. This happens when there is an increase in temperature.

Filtration: Process used to separate solids from a liquid (or a gas) using a filter that is too small to allow the solid to past though.

Flocculation: Process where a chemical agent is added to water to cause small particles to clump together.

Flooding: When a lot of water covers an area that is usually dry, due to a dramatic increase in rainfall.

Freeze: When a liquid turns hard and solid. This happens when there is a reduction in temperature (0°Celsius for water).

Fresh water: Water without salt in it, found in lakes and rivers.

Gas: Something that is neither a solid nor a liquid. The particles are separated and can move freely e.g. water vapour (steam) is a gas.

Hydrogen-bonding: Inter-molecular bond which forms in liquid water as the hydrogen atoms of one water molecule are attracted towards the oxygen atom of another water molecule.

In-soluble: Particles that do not dissolve in water. These can be removed by filtration.

Liquid: Something that is neither a solid nor a gas. The particles are close together and can move e.g. water is a liquid.

Melt: To turn from a solid to a liquid. This happens when there is an increase in temperature.

Molecule: Group of two or more atoms. Each water molecule is H_2O (two hydrogen atoms and one oxygen atom)

Particulate nature of matter: Anything that has a mass and occupies space is matter. Matter can exist in three states (solid, liquid, gas). Water is matter. The same H_2O molecule exists in each state.

Salt water: Water with salt in it, found in seas and oceans.

Sedimentation: Process where water is kept still in a tank, gravity causes suspended particles to naturally settle at the bottom of the tank.

Solid: Something that is neither a liquid nor gas. It has a fixed shape, particles are tightly packed e.g. ice is a solid.

Soluble: Particles that dissolve in water (these may be seen or unseen).

States of Matter: Three phases that microscopic particles can behave in; solid, liquid or gas. States of matter change as you add more energy e.g. heat.

Temperature: Measure of how hot or cold something is

Transpiration: Process of water movement through plants, evaporation from leaves, stems and flowers.

Water vapour: Water as a gas.

Water stress: This occurs when the demand for water exceeds the available amount during a certain period or when poor quality restricts its use.

through a change in state, as it does in the natural process of the water cycle. This is suitable as a teacher demonstration or as a student activity (depending on the age of the class, intended learning outcomes of the lesson and time available).

Resources: Large glass jar, measuring jug / cylinder, small aluminium plate (to cover the top of the jar), ice cubes, water, kettle.

In the classroom: Using the kettle or access to a hot tap, have hot water ready (not boiling). Half fill the jar with this hot water. Quickly place the aluminium plate on top of the jar (as a lid). Place some cubes of ice on top of the plate. Mark the level of the water on the side of the jar, observe and record the changes within the jar. Some of the water will evaporate (as a gas, steam). This steam is less dense than the liquid, so it rises to hit the foil plate at the top of the jar. The plate will be cold (as it is covered in ice). When the water vapour (gas) hits the cold surface, it condenses (to a liquid) and forms droplets on the bottom of the plate. The class may also observe and record condensation droplets on the inside of the jar. After some time, when the water cools, all of the evaporated water condenses (gets heavier) again and rolls down the inside of the jar to where it began.

This changing state of water and its movement provides a visual representation for students of how water changes state as it moves on our Earth's surface and in the atmosphere. Students could be encouraged to represent their observations of this classroom activity visually. This could be compared with a visual representation of the water cycle (refer to Figure 9.1).

The track to your tap

Overview: This activity supports students' appreciation for access to safe and affordable drinking water. It is important the students as citizens are aware of where their water supply comes from, and the process and infrastructure that support the supply system. Our tap water may come from lakes, rivers or groundwater, depending on where we are living. Students should research local watersheds (area of land that drains into a body of water such as a river, stream, lake or bay) and develop awareness of where their water supply comes from.

This lesson links to some of the UNESCO learning objectives (2017: 22):

- *The learner understands the concept of Integrated Water Resources Management (IWRM) and other strategies for ensuring the availability and sustainable management of water, including flood and drought risk management.*
- *The learner is able to communicate about water access.*
- *The learner is able to cooperate with local authorities in the improvement of local capacity for self-sufficiency.*
- *The learner is able to evaluate, participate in and influence decision-making on management strategies of local, national and international enterprises related to water pollution.*

Classroom Invitation: Teachers may invite a guest speaker from the local water authority to speak to the class. This may provide opportunities to learn more detailed information about the process of getting water to their own homes and school. Learning about local dams and/ or reservoirs for water storage can help students to develop a meaningful appreciation for where water in their homes comes from. A visit to a local water treatment plant is invaluable for understanding the stages involved in water treatment, the costs involved and the importance of water conservation. Although water is free from nature, the infrastructure needed to deliver it is expensive. The European Union Water Framework Directive requires EU member

States to achieve water quality of at least 'good status' in rivers, lakes, groundwater, estuaries and coastal waters, by 2027 at the latest. This legislation mandates public participation, (recognising the value of local knowledge) and community involvement in decision making processes. The Water Framework Directive is implemented through River Basin Management Plans (RBMPs) in three six-year cycles. Each cycle providing an opportunity to assess water conditions at different stages and set out actions to achieve water quality objectives. In Ireland, the Minister for Housing, Local Government and Heritage is responsible for implementation of the European Union Water Framework Directive

Class Debate 1: Occasionally local rivers, lakes and beaches feature in the news due to poor water quality. Students can explore a water related issue through research and role play. Various perspectives can be explored such as: local authorities; statutory agencies such as the Environmental Protection Agency; the relevant Government Minister; and key local people such as farmers, fishermen, swimmers and parents. Older students can become involved in drawing up their own River Basin Management Plans (RBMPs) which can be presented to the Local Council.

Class Debate 2: The context for this debate is situated in Ireland. However, similar ideas could be debated about urban and rural water supply and usage in many countries. Figure 9.3

Figure 9.3 Water Supply Project Eastern and Midlands Region. (Source: Uisce Éireann https://www.water.ie/projects/national-projects/water-supply-project-east-1/)

illustrates a proposal for a future Dublin Region Water Supply Project. This proposal involves linking the longest river in Ireland, the River Shannon (which has an estuary on the west coast), and its lakes, to Dublin, which is over 100 km away. Invite the class to debate the proposed water supply project. The following issues could be explored in the class debate: cost of building and maintaining such a long distance waterway, residential water charges, potential loss of water in leaks, metered water usage, impact on natural watersheds and flood plains

Class Debate 3: The context of this debate is centred around the cost of water, albeit a natural resource. This debate may follow the activity above. In discussing the source of our water, students may have argued for/against a water charge. In recent years, there has been much debate around proposed charges for water in Ireland. Invite the class to debate the introduction of public water charges. The following could be explored and researched as part of the class discussion and debate: sources of water through public mains supply; group water schemes or private wells; waste water treatments; household usage rates; and exemptions.

Water wars

Overview: This lesson idea aims to help students understand the reality of water stress and water scarcity in many countries, and the need to implement and integrate water resource management across boundaries. The three points for discussion are deliberately distinct to highlight that water problems and management are not just issues for the Global South, but for all countries. Many countries at northern latitudes and in the tropics are getting wetter, while countries at mid-latitude are running increasingly low on water (Goldenberg, 2014).

There are three points of discussion that could be taken individually (over a number of lessons). Through enquiry based approaches, students can communicate their research during class discussion, raising awareness about the availability of water and the implications water supply and flooding can have on different communities.

This lesson links to some of the UNESCO learning objectives (2017: 22):

- *The learner understands water as a fundamental condition of life itself, the importance of water quality and quantity, and the causes, effects and consequences of water pollution and water scarcity.*
- *The learner understands that water is part of many different complex global interrelationships and systems.*
- *The learner knows about the global unequal distribution of access to safe drinking water and sanitation facilities.*
- *The learner is able to communicate about water access and water saving measures.*
- *The learner is able to plan, implement, evaluate and replicate activities that contribute to increasing water quality and safety*

A war for 'blue gold'

Many of the water systems that keep ecosystems thriving and feed growing human populations have become stressed. Decades of bad management and overuse is leading to continued water shortages in many parts of the world. Ireland for instance has faced significant fines for not implementing EU rules on health and safety guidelines for septic tanks. Water shortages have caused major international disputes in many parts of the world, and have been the cause of crisis and war in some countries. It can become increasingly difficult when rivers cross country boundaries. In the Global South, water resources are of strategic concern, and a major cause of political conflict. 90% of countries in the world must share water basins or rivers with at least one or two other countries (The New Humanitarian, 2020). Human activity such as transportation, dams, and hydroelectric power stations interfere with surface and below surface water supplies.

For example, in addition to Egypt, the River Nile runs through or along the border of ten other African countries, namely, Burundi, Tanzania, Rwanda, the Democratic Republic of the Congo, Kenya, Uganda, Sudan, Ethiopia, and South Sudan. Natural flooding along the banks of the Nile deposits silt and sediment to fertilise the soil for agriculture. However, coastal erosion and construction of dams have interfered with this natural flooding. These floods are necessary to flush and clean the water of human and agricultural waste. As a result, the water is becoming more polluted (National Geographic, 2020a).

> **Activity**: There are a number of consequences of global water shortages. Choose one of these to research further- exploring causes and solutions. Consequences include increased global conflict and war, lack of access to clean water, lack of food supply, energy shortages and economic slowdown.

Fuelling the floods

An increase in winter precipitation (rain/ snow), Atlantic storms and climate change impacts have led to an increase in flooding in Ireland and Britain in recent years. Previous design of flood defences (in Ireland) in towns situated along the River Shannon, and other rivers such as the River Blackwater and the River Suir were based on historic weather records and assumed that the same patterns would continue. However, the changes we expect with climate change mean that many existing flood defences will not be able to provide the same level of protection as when they were built (Irish Academy of Engineering, 2009). The development of floodplains has been debated economically and environmentally. Developing these areas increases the numbers of industrial and domestic properties at risk of flooding. The combined effects of climate change and urban development mean that such flooding is likely to become a more common occurrence in Ireland (Environmental Protection Agency, 2003a).

> **Activity**: Find and collate local and national newspaper articles detailing flooding and the effects of flooding. Consider domestic, environmental, agricultural and economic effects of flooding.

California gold

California is one of the most productive agricultural regions in the world, however, the region is prone to severe drought (Cooley et al., 2015). Record lows in rainfall and highs in temperature experienced in California between 2012 and 2016 resulted in a severe drought (National Geographic, 2020b). Since 80% of California's water supply is used for agriculture, this drought has impacted the economy, in particular the agricultural sector. Water transfers were used as one approach to mitigate the impact of the drought. This meant that farmers with lower-value crops sold their water to farmers with higher-value crops, thereby reducing total losses in agricultural revenue. Other strategies used, included fallowing land and rotating crops. This acute crisis in the agricultural sector highlights the water management problems in the state. Vast pumping of groundwater is unsustainable. Severe over-drafting of groundwater supplies will have lasting and damaging consequences for local communities, ecosystems, and future generations (Cooley et al., 2015).

> **Activity**: Find and collate information online about California, its average rainfall and temperatures, its population and industries. Consider how a drought can cause a ripple effect on jobs and the local economy. For instance, planting, harvesting, production, and retail of agricultural produce are all affected by drought. Consider alternative solutions to the crisis that drought is placing on the agricultural industry.

Finding clear solutions to a problem

Overview: This activity supports an understanding of the processes involves in improving water quality, waste water treatment and safe reuse. Many students may have completed science experiments investigating filtration. Other text books may provide guidance on setting up a filtration system in the classroom e.g. using a large inverted bottle (with the base cut off), filled with layers of gravel, sand (large and small particles) to remove insoluble waste from a water sample. The ideas presented in Figure 9.4 are useful as they illustrate how innovative and creative ideas from young people can help to contribute to processes to improve our water quality. Lalita's idea uses the concept of separating insoluble particles by filtration. Jonathan's idea involves water evaporation and condensation to separate the contaminants.

This lesson links to some of the UNESCO learning objectives (2017: 22):

- *The learner is able to contribute to water resources management at the local level.*
- *The learner is able to plan, implement, evaluate and replicate activities that contribute to increasing water quality and safety.*

Group work activity: Working collaboratively for this task may help with creativity and sharing of ideas. Present both stories to the class (Figure 9.4). Further details for both are available in the resource list at the end of this chapter. Students could research either of these in further detail and/or research other simple and cheap innovations that have been used for water filtration and treatment. Students should then be encouraged to extend their desk-based research to a hands-on investigation to trial and test these and/or other simple ideas to remove impurities from water.

Every drop counts

Overview: These two activities help students to develop awareness and increase their water use efficiency.

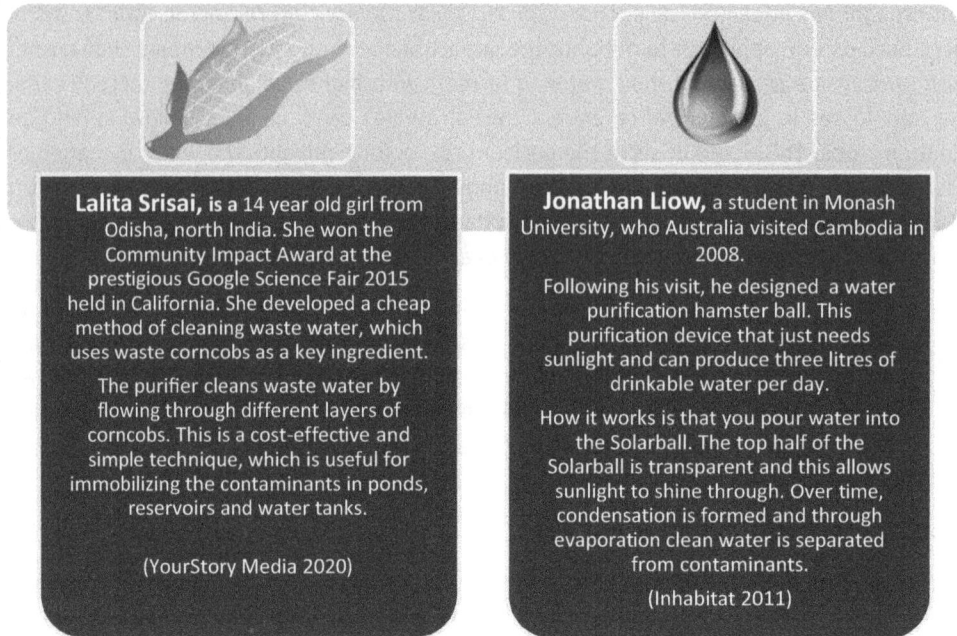

Lalita Srisai, is a 14 year old girl from Odisha, north India. She won the Community Impact Award at the prestigious Google Science Fair 2015 held in California. She developed a cheap method of cleaning waste water, which uses waste corncobs as a key ingredient.

The purifier cleans waste water by flowing through different layers of corncobs. This is a cost-effective and simple technique, which is useful for immobilizing the contaminants in ponds, reservoirs and water tanks.

(YourStory Media 2020)

Jonathan Liow, a student in Monash University, who Australia visited Cambodia in 2008.

Following his visit, he designed a water purification hamster ball. This purification device that just needs sunlight and can produce three litres of drinkable water per day.

How it works is that you pour water into the Solarball. The top half of the Solarball is transparent and this allows sunlight to shine through. Over time, condensation is formed and through evaporation clean water is separated from contaminants.

(Inhabitat 2011)

Figure 9.4 Cheap & Innovative Ideas for Waste Water Treatment and Water Reuse.

This lesson links to some of the UNESCO learning objectives (2017: 22):

- *The learner understands the concept of 'virtual water'*
- *The learner is able to feel responsible for their water use*
- *The learner is able to reduce their individual water footprint and to save water practicing their daily habits*

Classroom demonstration

This teacher demonstration is useful to stimulate and generate classroom discussion about efficient water use. You will need a small jar (to hold 50ml), basin, large measuring jug (or pipette if available in a secondary school) and two clear 2 Litre bottles (labels removed) filled with water. It is helpful to support students' observation by adding some droplets of food colouring to the water, so it is more visible in the bottles. Holding up one of the bottles of water, tell the class that this 2L bottle represents all of the water on our Earth. Using a think, pair share strategy, ask the class to predict what proportion of the water (2L) is available for human consumption. After allowing time for discussion, listen to and record the class feedback. This could be done by having students mark the proportion of water (available for human consumption) on the side of the bottle and or record their suggestions on the class whiteboard e.g. 1L, 1.5L or 750ml. Invite one student to assist you in the next part of the demonstration (if you wish). This student will be using the measuring jug. As you talk through each of the following points, the student helping with the demonstration can use a measuring jug (or pipette) to pour out the mentioned volume of water from the 2L bottle into the jar and basin. Older classes should calculate the volume of water when provided with the percentage values.

- 97% of our Earth's water is found in oceans- *remove 1950ml from the 2L bottle.*
- 3% of our Earth's water is fresh water- *pour the remaining 50ml into a small glass jar.*
- 70% of our fresh water is frozen in ice caps- *remove 35ml from the small glass jar.*
- 29% of our fresh water is in the air, soil and deep underground- *remove 14.5ml from the small glass jar.*
- Less than 1% of our fresh water is available for human consumption- *There should be just 0.5ml (two drops!) remaining in the small glass jar.*

Pour these two drops back into the empty 2L bottle. Concluding the demonstration, show the class both 2L bottles again, reminding them that one bottle (full 2L) represents all of the Earth's water and the other bottle (0.5ml) represents the amount of water available for human consumption. This memorable visual demonstration engages students and stimulates discussion about our efficient use of water.

Homework task

The availability of fresh water, safe for human consumption is a major environmental problem. Household water usage could be brainstormed together as a class. Students can complete a diary to record and calculate the average volume of water used in each of their homes over one week. Students may take individual tasks to research and/or calculate the volume of water for each itemised usage. Here are some approximations:

- Flushing a toilet-5 litres
- A 5 minute shower -25 litres (5 litres per minute)
- Dishwasher cycle-20 litres
- Washing Machine cycle-65 litres
- Average bath-80 litres
- Home car wash-300 litres

These approximations are subject to water pressure, age of appliances (e.g. some older toilets have larger cisterns) and alteration of settings (e.g. long/short cycles in washing machine). Students should design & organise a table to record daily water usage in their homes over one week (see example in Table 9.4). This class data could be collated to enable students to make observations and inferences about their water use. Developing awareness should encourage more sustainable and responsible use of our fresh water supplies.

Lesson extension

In addition to developing an awareness of the 'visible' volumes of water that students use in their everyday lives, UNESCO (2017) also suggests exploration and calculation of our 'invisible' water use. This includes the water required to produce our food and our clothes.

Table 9.4 Sample student water diary

Activity	Volume of Water (Estimated)	No. of Times Per Day	Daily Usage	Weekly Usage
Drink a glass of water	.25L	8	2L	14L
Having a Bath	80L	1	80L	160L
Five minute shower	25L	1	25L	150L
Flushing the Toilet	5L	5	25L	175L
Brushing teeth with tap off	1L	2	2L	14L
Using the washing machine	65 L	1	65L	130L
Running the Dishwasher	20L	1	20L	80L
Total			**219 Litres**	**723 Litres**

Perceptions of pollution

Overview: As students learn about protecting and restoring water eco-systems, this activity helps them to understand what water pollution is, what causes it and how it can be reduced, Water pollution occurs when any source of water (rivers, lakes, oceans) is mixed with substances harmful to living things. Living things refer to humans, animals and plants. While many examples of the water pollution explored in these two suggested activities include visible evidence of water pollution, it is important that students are also aware that we cannot always see water pollution. Two activities are outlined here; one suitable for a lesson within the classroom, and the other is suggested as a project outside of the classroom.

Research & Reshuffle: This in-class activity encourages students' independent research to inform their decision making. Students could work individually or in small groups. The teacher presents a list of sources of water pollution to the class. The class is tasked with ordering these pollutants, to determine which is most damaging. This activity should stimulate discussion and debate. To make informed decisions, students have to research and understand the causes and effects (long term/short term on plants/animals) of each source of pollution. A visual representation of these pollutants would be useful to present to the class. The following water pollutants could be included:

- Waste water and sewage waste is treated with chemicals and then released into the sea. Unfortunately, high level of the world's sewage finds its way into seas and rivers untreated.
- Agricultural and Industrial chemicals: The term eutrophication is the increase in chemical nutrients (including phosphorus and nitrates) in an ecosystem which results in excessive plant growth and decay. These chemicals can change the water colour and temperature. Other chemicals include lead, sulphur, mercury and asbestos. Eutrophication

can occur naturally, but more commonly this process is caused by a number of human influences such as the release of sewage effluent, and run-off from fertilisers.

- Oil pollution and burning of fossil fuels: The burning of fossil fuels, such as coal and oil, produces ash that is released into the atmosphere. The particles are toxic when they become mixed with water vapour in clouds causing acid rain. Occasional oil leakages also cause extensive environmental pollution.
- Plastic pollution: Much of the plastic pollution in the ocean comes from fishing boats, tankers and cargo shipping.
- Household waste: due to illegal and irresponsible dumping, some household waste is one of the causes of water pollution

Local clean up: Involving students in a local clean up or preservation project focused on a water source is a valuable experience. While many school groups participate in community litter clean ups they may not have as much experience or insight into preserving a local river, lake or seaside. Observation of health and safety guidelines is critical here. This activity could be enhanced through collaboration with a local environmental/community group. Members of this group may offer their expertise to the class and help guide and plan the clean-up initiative project.

Water is one of the core themes of the Green-Schools programme (Green Schools Ireland, 2020). The Green Schools programme also looks at a variety of issues that are connected to water; global citizenship, waste, the marine environment and biodiversity. The *Water* theme looks at developing awareness around water conservation and how to effectively manage this important resource in our schools and homes. There are many other resources available on the Green Schools webpage (link available with the listed resources at the end of the chapter).

Links with other goals

Water is a limited resource and there is an imminent need to be mindful around our water consumption behaviour. Goal 6 is one of the most interconnected goals (see Figure 9.5). Access to safe water and adequate sanitation is a basic human right and underpins success in development areas such as agriculture, energy, disaster resilience, human heath, the environment, and ultimately economic growth. In many countries, economic and population growth, as well as urbanisation, have increased water demand, while supply has remained unchanged or has even decreased due to climate change.

Sustainable Development Goal 6 recognises that sustainably managing water goes beyond simply providing a safe water supply and sanitation (Targets 6.1 and 6.2) to address the broader water context, such as water quality and wastewater management, water scarcity and efficient use, water resources management, and the protection and restoration of water-related ecosystems. There is huge scope for climate change mitigation in the way we use water at home.

The COVID-19 pandemic has demonstrated the critical importance of sanitation, hygiene and adequate access to clean water for preventing and containing diseases. Without access to clean water, targets from other SDGs will not be achieved (Figure 9.5).

SDG 11

Sustainable Cities and Communities

As our world is becoming increasingly urbanized, we need to carefully plan for safe and efficient supply of water as well as responsible waste water management.

SDG 3

Good Health & Well-Being

Improving water quality and access to hygienic sanitation will contribute to good health.

SDG 6
Clean
Water &
Sanitation

SDG 12

Responsible Consumption & Production

We need to develop awareness of responsible water and energy usage in our daily household and dietary habits. The Earth's water is required for food production so we need to be responsible in our purchasing and use of food products.

SDG 15

Life on Land

Nature and wildlife are dependent on water, as well as humans. As human activity increases, there are limited water and land resources available. We need to conserve and restore our water eco-systems.

SDG 14

Life Below Water

Marine life is essential to global health. Ensuring diversity of plant and animal life below water is essential. Responsible waste water treatment and sanitation systems are critical to avoiding pollution of our water systems.

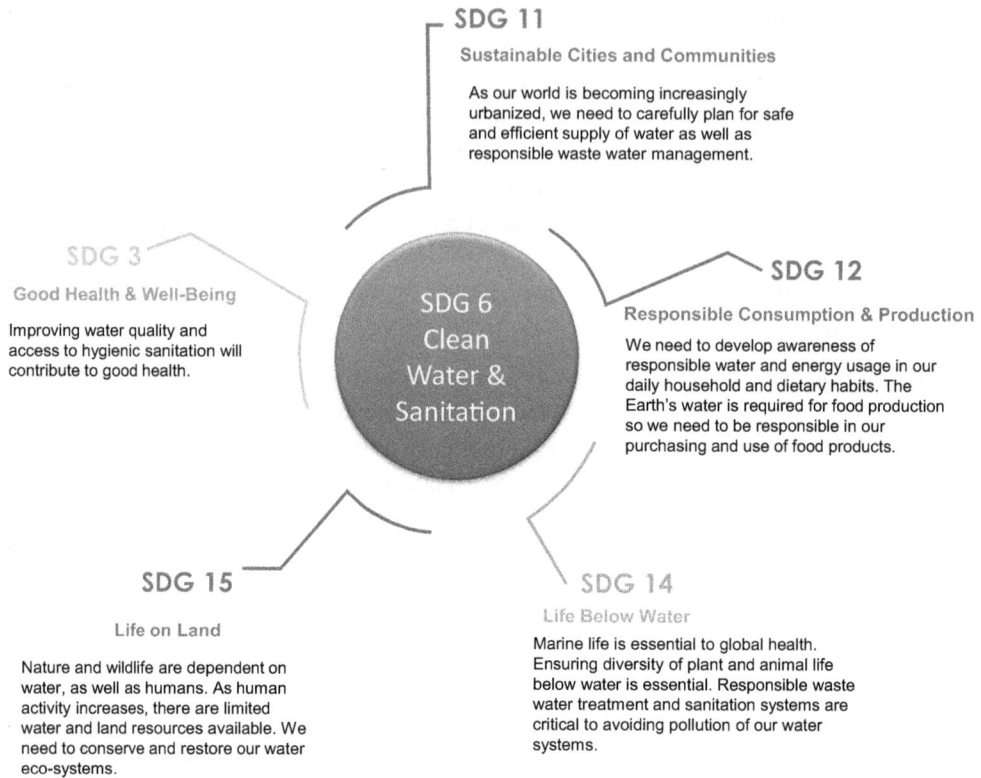

Figure 9.5 Interlinkages of SDG 6 with Other SDGs.

Conclusion

This chapter provides an overview of the concepts, conflicts and challenges related to SDG 6: Clean Water and Sanitation. The practical classroom activities are aimed at helping young people to develop empathy, respect and advocacy through developing a better understanding of clean water and sanitation. The cognitive, socio-emotional and behavioural learning objectives outlined for classroom activities are designed to develop hope and optimism among students. While students recognise the importance and relevance of responsible water use in their own everyday lives, they develop care and consideration for others who are living in different circumstance and contexts than themselves. The learning activities included in this chapter each link to other goals as well as SDG 6 to support students' holistic understanding of meaningful and integrated sustainable development. In addition, the lesson ideas encompass curricular learning, in particular geography and science knowledge and skills as well as communication, presentation and research skills. The variety of activities outlined are intended to enable students to become ambassadors for safe and responsible water usage and treatment beyond their classrooms; in their schools, homes and communities. In 1746, Benjamin Franklin wrote *"When the Well's dry, we know the Worth of Water"* (Labaree, 1961). Almost four centuries later, his words are as discerning as they were in the 18th century. It is hoped that education will help citizens worldwide to understand the poverty, inequality and environmental degradation caused by a lack of water supply, and thus be better informed to face these challenges.

Resources

An extensive list of resources, videos and case studies for SDG 6 is included in the SDG padlet accompanying this book: https://padlet.com/annedolan/o6rds38ylfy6a28h

Sources of further information

A variety of facts, figures, info graphics and other resources that would be useful in supporting learning about clean water and sanitation are available on the following web pages:

- **Action Aid** (Water Resources) https://www.actionaid.org.uk/school-resources/resource/water-teaching-resources
- **British Council:** Rivers of the World: The Story of Water Education Pack https://www.britishcouncil.org/sites/default/files/the_story_of_water_education_pack_0.pdf
- **Concern:** Clean water and sanitation-Educational resource for teachers and facilitators https://www.concern.net/schools-and-youth/educational-resources
- **Environmental & Protection Agency (EPA):** http://www.epa.ie/researchandeducation/education/educ/cleanwater/
- **Global Dimension:** https://globaldimension.org.uk/wllgoal/clean-water-and-sanitation/
- **Green Schools Programme:** https://greenschoolsireland.org/resources/
- **The National Water Forum:** https://thewaterforum.ie/
- **Trócaire:** Make every drop count Education Resource for Primary Schools https://www.trocaire.org/sites/default/files/education/lent2014/resource-pack-primary-schools.pdf
- **United Nations:** https://www.un.org/sustainabledevelopment/water-and-sanitation/
- **Water Aid:** https://www.wateraid.org/uk/get-involved/teaching/ks2-resources
- **Water Footprint Calculator:** https://www.watercalculator.org/educational-resources/for-teachers/

Key dates

February 2: World Wetlands Day
March 22: World Water Day
June 8: World Oceans Day

Students' literature

Younger students

Asch, F. (2000) *Water* Clarion Books.
Armson-Bradshaw, G. (2019) *The Water Cycle* (Geographics) Franklin Watts.
Bailey, J. and Lilly, M. (illus) (2004). *A Drop in the Ocean: The Story of Water.* Picture Window Books.
Baker-Smith, G. (2018) *The Rhythm of the Rain.* Templar Publishing.
Barnham, K. and Frost, *Maddie.* (illus) (2019). *The Great Big Water Cycle Adventure.* Wayland.
Barr, C. and Engel, C. (illus) (2023) *Water: How We Can Protect Our Freshwater* Candlewick.
Barr, C. and Engel, C. (illus) (2022) *Water: Protect Freshwater to Save Life on Earth* Otter-Barry Books.

Black, S. (2022) *The Water Cycle: Learn About Water* C. Press/F. Watts Trade.

Boulos, R. (2021) *Pearl the Raindrop: The Great Water Cycle Journey* Independent Publishing Network.

Carter, J. and Nomoco (illus) (2020) *Once Upon a Raindrop: The Story of Water* Caterpillar Books.

Ezra Stein, D. (2017) *Ice Boy* Walker Books.

Ghigna, C. and Jatkowska, A. M. (illus) (2012) *We Need Water (My Little Planet)* Picture Window Books.

Goldner, R. (2019) *Agent H20 Rides the Water Cycle* Dancing Ants Press

Gray, J. and Kolanovic, D. (illus) (2014) *The Little Raindrop.* Sky Pony.

Hale, C. (2018) *Water Land: Land and Water Forms Around the World* Roaring Brook Press.

Harrison, L. and Harrison, J. (illus) (2019) *Why Water's Worth It* World Environmental Federation.

Hegarty, P. and Clulow, H. (illus) (2018) *The River: An Epic Journey to the Sea* Caterpillar Books.

Herrington, L. M. (2022) *What Is Water?* C. Press/F. Watts Trade.

Hooper, M. and Coady, C. (2015) *The Drop in My Drink: The Story of Water on Our Planet* Lincoln Children's Books.

Johnson, T. and Allday, A. (illus) (2021). *Two Hydrogen One Oxygen A Children's Book about Water a Story of Oceans, Baths, and Swimming Pools* Tracey Johnson.

Lindley, J. (2021) *Where Does My Poo Go?* DK Children.

Lindstrom, C. and Goade, M. (illus) (2020) *We Are Water Protectors* Roaring Brook Press.

Locker, T. (2002) *Water Dance* Clarion Books.

Lyon, G. E. and Tillotson, K. (illus) (2011) *All the Water in the World* Atheneum/Richard Jackson Books; Illustrated edition.

Mace, C. and Yates, B. (illus) (2019) *The Terrific Trip of Douglas Drip* Curious Cat Books.

Mann, D. L. (2022) *How You Can Save Water (Learn About Water)* C. Press/F. Watts Trade.

Martin, M. (2017) *A River* Chronicle Books.

Mc Ginty, A. B. and Begay, S. (illus) (2021). *The Water Lady: How Darlene Arviso Helps a Thirsty Navajo Nation.* Anne Schwartz Books.

Messner, K. and Silas Neal, C. (illus) (2017) *Over and Under the Pond* Chronicle Books.

Mohan, D. and Aveira, H. (illus) (2020) *Chloe Cloud, Bring Me Some Rain! Nature Science for Kids- Water Cycle and Riverside* Habitat Candlewick.

Moon, E. K. (2021) *Drop: An Adventure through the Water Cycle* Dial Books.

Nofel, S. A. (2022) *Water: Exploring the Elements* Hearty and Free.

Olien, R. (2017) *The Water Cycle at Work (First Facts in Our World)* Raintree.

Park, L. S. and Pinkney, B. (illus) (2019). *Nya's Long Walk: A Step at a Time.* Clarion Books.

Paeff, C. and Carpenter, N. (illus) (2021) *The Great Stink: How Joseph Bazalgette Solved London's Poop Pollution Problem.* Margaret K. McElderry Books.

Paterson, J. (2018) *I am the Rain: A Science Book for Kids about the Water Cycle and Change of Seasons* Dawn Publications.

Paul, M. (2015) *Water Is Water: A Book about the Water Cycle* Macmillan USA.

Portis, A. (2021) *Hey Water!* Scallywag Press.

Rosinsky, N. M. and John, M. (Illus) (2002) *Water: Up, Down and All Around* Picture Window Books.

Salas, L. P. and Dabija, V. (illus) (2014). *Water Can Be...* Millbrook Press.

Senior, O. and James, L. (illus) (2013) *Anna Carries Water.* Tradewind.

Shaw Mc Kinney, B. and Maydak, M. S. (1998) *A Drop Around the World: The Science Of Water Cycles On Planet Earth For Kids.* Dawn Publications.

Sharratt, N. (2018) *Splash Day* Barrington Stoke.

Strauss, R. and Woods, R. (illus) (2007) *One Well: The Story of Water on Earth* Citizen Kid.

Thomas, I. and Morgan, P. (illus) (2016). *What on Earth? Water: Explore, Create and Investigate.* QEB Publishing.

Verde, S, Badiel, G. and Reynolds, P. H. (illus) (2016) *The Water Princess* (Based on the childhood experience of Georgie Badiel) G.P. Putnam's Sons Books for Young Readers.

Waters, E. and Fernandes, E. (illus) (2014) *Hope Springs* Tundra.

Older students

Bajaj, V. (2020) *Thirst* Nancy Paulsen Books.

Baron, A. and Davies, B. (illus) (2018) *Boy Underwater* Harper Collins.

Bethell, Z. (2018) *The Extraordinary Colours of Auden Dare* Piccadilly Press.

Canavan, R. and Antram, D. (illus) (2014) *You Wouldn't Want to Live Without Clean Water!* Franklin Watts

Clendenan, M. and Laughlin, J. (illus) (2022) *Fresh Air, Clean Water: Our Right to a Healthy Environment* Orca Book Publishers

Huddleston, T. (2019) *Flood World* Nosy Crow.

Ibbotson, E. (2014) *Journey to the River Sea* Macmillan Children's Books.

Johnson, M. (2022) *Spark* Orion Children's Books.

Mihaly, C. (2021) *Water: A Deep Dive of Discovery* Barefoot Books.

Mulder, M. (2022) *Every Last Drop: Bringing Clean Water Home* Orca Book Publishers.

Park, L. S. (2018) *A Long Walk to Water, Based on a True Story* Rock the Boat.

Sager, Weinstein, J. (2017) *The City of Secret Rivers* Walker Books.

Shusterman, N. and Shusterman, J. (2018) *Dry* Walker Books.

References

Cliwat. (2008). *Climate & Water* [online]. Available from: https://cliwat.eu/modelling/

Cooley, H., Donnelly, K., Phurisamban, R. and Subramanian, M. (2015). *Impacts of California's Ongoing Drought: Agriculture* [online]. Available from: https://pacinst.org/wp-content/uploads/2015/08/ImpactsOnCaliforniaDrought-Ag-1.pdf

Environmental Protection Agency. (2003). *Urban Water Treatment in 2002* https://www.epa.ie/publications/monitoring--assessment/waste-water/uww-report-2022.php

Environmental Protection Agency. (2003a). *Climate Change: Scenarios and Impacts for Ireland. RTDI Programme, 2000-2006.* Dublin: Environmental Protection Agency.

Goldenberg, S. (2014). *Why Global Water Shortages Pose Threat of Terror and War.* [online]. Available from: https://www.theguardian.com/environment/2014/feb/09/global-water-shortages-threat-terror-war [Accessed 2 June 2020].

Green Schools Ireland. (2020). *Working Together for a Sustainable Future* [online]. Available from: https://greenschoolsireland.org/ [Accessed 2 June 2020].

Irish Academy of Engineering. (2009). *Ireland at Risk, Critical Infrastructure Adaptation for Climate Change*. Dublin: Irish Academy of Engineering.

Just a drop: https://www.justadrop.org/why-water.

Labaree, L. W. (1961). *The Papers of Benjamin Franklin, vol. 3, January 1, 1745, through June 30, 1750*. New Haven: Yale University Press, pp.100–106.

Maniam, G., Poh, P. E., Htar, T. T., Poon, W. C. and Chuah, L. H. (2021). Water literacy in the Southeast Asian context: Are we there yet? *Water, 13*(16), 2311.

McCarroll, M. and Hamann, H. (2020). What we know about water: A water literacy review. *Water, 12*(2803), 28. https://doi.org/10.3390/w12102803.

Mostacedo-Marasovic, S. J., Mott, B. C., White, H. and Forbes, C. T. (2022). Towards water literacy: An interdisciplinary analysis of standards for teaching and learning about humans and Water. *Disciplinary and Interdisciplinary Science Education Research, 4*(1), 25.

National Geographic. (2020a). *Nile River* [online]. Available from: https://www.nationalgeographic.org/encyclopedia/nile-river/#:~:text=In%20addition%20to%20Egypt%2C%20the,%2C%20Ethiopia%2C%20and%20South%20Sudan.

National Geographic. (2020b). *The California Drought* [online]. Available from: https://www.nationalgeographic.org/media/california-drought/

The New Humanitarian. (2020). *Water Is Running Out: How Inevitable Are International Conflicts?* [online]. Available from: https://www.thenewhumanitarian.org/report/61029/global-water-running-out-how-inevitable-are-international-conflicts

United Nations (UN). (2020). *Sustainable Development Goal* [online]. Available from: https://www.un.org/sustainabledevelopment/sustainable-development-goals/

United Nations Educational, Scientific and Cultural Organization (UNESCO). (2017). *Education or Sustainable Development Goals: Learning Objectives* [online]. Available from: https://unesdoc.unesco.org/ark:/48223/pf0000247444

World Health Organisation WHO. (n.d.). https://www.who.int/news-room/fact-sheets/detail/drinking-water.

WWAP (UNESCO World Water Assessment Programme). (2019). *The United Nations World Water Development Report 2019: Leaving No One Behind*. France: United Nations Educational, Scientific and Cultural Organisation.

Your Story Media. (2020). *This 14-Year-Old Odisha Girl Has Developed a Cheap Method of Cleaning Waste Water* [online]. Available from: https://yourstory.com/2016/05/lalita-prasida-sripada-srisai?utm_pageloadtype=scroll

7 AFFORDABLE AND
CLEAN ENERGY

10 Powering our lives with secure, equitable and sustainable energy sources (SDG 7)

Maeve Liston

Introduction

Access to affordable, reliable, sustainable energy, derived from natural sources is the focus of SDG 7. This Goal is underpinned by three targets: ensuring universal access to energy services (7.1), increasing the share of renewables in the energy mix (7.2), and improving energy efficiency (7.3) (see Appendix 1 for complete list of SDG targets). At the time of writing, the ongoing energy crisis was exacerbated by the Russia–Ukraine War, with significant implications for energy security. Hence, transitioning to a net zero way of living is the dominant challenge facing citizens today, not only for environmental and economic reasons but also for the provision of access to secure, equitable and sustainable energy sources.

Science, Technology, Engineering and Mathematics (STEM) education involving the development of solutions for environmental issues through an empathetic lens, can be a very effective means for teachers and students to engage with the UN's Sustainable Development Goals (SDGs) in general and SDG 7 in particular. The interdisciplinary and transdisciplinary nature of STEM education requires the development of new knowledge, skills and attitudes that go well beyond any one subject area, in offering new ways of responding to environmental issues and problems. Integrating Education for Sustainability with STEM develops an affiliation between STEM and respect, STEM and empathy, STEM and advocacy and STEM and hope and it underpins the importance of STEM in achieving the SDGs.

The chapter provides examples of STEM teaching and learning experiences for students 'in the environment', 'about the environment' and 'for the environment', where students are empowered by their education to develop a more sustainable lifestyle and create solutions for addressing real-world problems. The author proposes a pedagogical approach to STEM education where an Engineering Design Process and a Design Thinking process are combined during engineering challenges in the classroom. This combined Engineering Design Process/ Design Thinking process emphasises the importance of empathy in STEM education, in allowing students to realise the impact of STEM on people and society. The STEM activities based on SDG 7 Affordable and Clean Energy featured in this chapter, incorporate Prensky's 'Better Their World' Paradigm, where students are empowered by their education to create solutions to real-world problems (Prensky, 2016).

DOI: 10.4324/9781003232001-13

Sustainable and renewable generation of energy

Access to sustainable energy sources is fundamental for human, social and economic development. At one time, humans were fuelled by the consumption of animals and plants and the burning of wood. Many tasks were completed through the assistance of their domesticated animals. Some additional energy was captured by windmills and waterwheels. The Industrial Revolution (which began around 1750) was powered by coal and eventually by oil and natural gas. Fossil fuels were formed from the remains of plants and animals layered under water from much earlier geologic times. During the 19th Century, industrialisation, particularly large-scale factories powered by steam created from the burning of large amounts of coal, changed the face of cities across the world. Since that time many humans have enjoyed, albeit unequally, the benefits of industrialisation from mobility to manufacturing, from travel to food production and from home heating to mass consumerisation. When fossil fuels are burned, they release energy, that has been stored for hundreds of millions of years. This process also results in the emission of carbon dioxide into the atmosphere. Building on research completed by John Tyndall in 1859, a Swedish chemist Svante Arrenius linked the average surface temperature of the Earth to the level of carbon dioxide in the atmosphere. Since the industrial revolution, the concentration of carbon dioxide in the atmosphere has risen from 275 parts per million (ppm) in 1750 to 415 ppm in recent times. The rate at which the carbon concentration is rising is also increasing. As a result, there is irrefutable evidence that our climate is changing a phenomenon (discussed in greater detail in Chapter 16 (SDG 13) which is raising serious challenges for local and global communities. Through the establishment of a link between burning fossil fuels, the release of carbon into the atmosphere and climate change, the focus has now turned to renewable sources of energy. This is a key point of interest for those involved in STEM education.

Addressing EfS in STEM education through SDG 7: renewable energy

Education for Sustainability (EfS) discussed in chapter 2 focuses on enabling participants to make decisions and carry out actions to improve our quality of life, without compromising the planet, not only exploring the here and now, but also focusing on long-term future-oriented thinking (Sterling, 2006). EfS is founded on principles of inquiry, problem-solving, participation, decision making and taking action, all of which are key features of STEM education. Real-world STEM projects based on solving real-world problems can contribute significantly in developing students' understanding of key environmental issues, socio-scientific concepts and sustainability (Straw et al., 2011). There are many environmental issues and socio-scientific concepts that students need to understand when addressing SDG 7: Renewable Energy in STEM lessons, some of which are included in Table 10.1 An explanation of renewable and non-renewable sources of energy is provided in Table 10.2.

STEM engineering activities based on relevant environmental, societal and industrial issues, such as those topics mentioned in Table 10.1, encourages exploration of new ideas, resourceful problem solving and risk-taking (Ramirez, 2013). Targets within SDG 7 (Appendix 1) refer to affordable, reliable, sustainable and modern energy for all. STEM activities

Table 10.1 SDG 7: Renewable energy: Environmental issues and socio-scientific concepts

Addressing EfS in STEM Education through the SDG 7: Renewable Energy.

- Different energy types
- Renewable energies such as solar, wind, water, geothermal and tidal
- Energy production, supply, demand and usage of different countries
- Energy efficiency and sufficiency in energy usage
- Greenhouse gases and global warming
- Centralised versus decentralised energy production; energy self-sufficiency, e.g. via local energy supply companies (LESCOs)
- Political, economic and social dimensions of energy and linkages to power constellations, e.g. in mega energy projects like large scale solar farms or dam projects – potential conflict of interests (political and economic power (across borders), rights of especially indigenous people)
- Environmental impacts and issues of energy production, supply and usage (e.g. climate change)
- The role of the public and private sectors in ensuring the development of low carbon energy solutions
- Peak of oil production and energy security – (over) dependence on non-renewable energies
- Bridging technologies and technology for a 'cleaner' use of fossil fuels
- Gender issues related to energy production, supply and usage

Adapted from UNESCO (2020: 25)

Table 10.2 Renewable vs non-renewable sources of energy

Term	Explanation
Non-renewable	Non-renewable energy resources include coal, natural gas, oil, and nuclear energy. Once these resources are used up, they cannot be replaced, which is a major problem for humanity as we are currently dependent on them to supply most of our energy needs.
Fossil fuels	Fossil fuels are materials, such as oil, coal, turf or gas. They were formed millions of years ago with the organic remains of animals and plants. They are nowadays burned to produce energy but when the existing reserve has been used up, fossil fuels will be gone forever. When fossil fuels are burned they gives off gasses such as carbon dioxide, which are released into the atmosphere. **Oil is a fossil fuel**. It is a black liquid normally found under the ground or under the sea. Oil is processed to make many products such as fuel for cars or even chemicals, paints and plastics. It can be very polluting and bad for the environment. Oil will eventually run out. It is therefore called a non-renewable energy source. **Coal** is a black or brown rock found under the ground and is very dirty. Coal is burned in power plants and turned into electricity. Burning coal is however extremely bad for the environment because when it burns, gasses such as carbon dioxide are released into the atmosphere. Coal will eventually run out. It is therefore called a non-renewable energy source.
Renewable Energy	is energy that is produced from everlasting sources like the sun, the wind, or the oceans. As the sun or the wind will always be available, renewable energy will never run out. In addition, renewable energy is clean and neither its production nor its use pollutes the environment

(Continued)

Table 10.2 (Continued)

Term	Explanation
	Solar Energy is the light and heat that come from the sun. The light and heat from the sun not only make plants grow, but can also be used by humans to produce electricity or to warm up the water in your house. **A Solar Panel** is a board generally placed on the roof of a house or in any other place that is exposed to sunlight. It soaks up the sunlight that is then converted to use as electricity. Solar panels can also be used to capture the heat from the sun and warm the water we need for our homes.
	Wind Power is the energy produced by the movement of the air. When the wind blows it generates movement that is captured by wind turbines and turned into electricity.
	A Wind Turbine is a huge tower with blades; when the wind makes the blades turn, this movement produces electricity.
	Ocean energy is energy from waves and tides
	Being an island has its advantages. Ireland is fortunate to be surrounded by the Irish Sea and the Atlantic Ocean. We can harness the energy in these ocean waters by using the movement of the tides and waves to generate electricity.
	Examples of ocean energy
	1. Wave energy
	Wave energy is energy from the perpetual motion of waves, which is caused by the wind blowing across the sea. Wave machines are used to capture the energy from waves and turn it into electricity.
	Wave energy depends on daily weather conditions – sometimes waves can be large and powerful and have lots of energy, but in calm weather there could be no waves at all!
	2. Tidal energy
	Tidal energy is energy from the horizontal motion of tidal currents in the sea, caused by the pull of the moon. All around Ireland's coast, the tide flows in and out twice per day, making this source of energy reliable.
	Tidal energy is very powerful, and can be harnessed by building tidal barrages across estuaries. These work like dams to capture the energy of moving water and turn it into electricity.
	3. Hydro energy is energy from flowing water
	The energy in flowing water, called hydropower, has been an important source of power in Ireland for centuries. Rivers and waterfalls have been used to drive waterwheels in mills for grinding flour and corn since early times. Today, we use hydropower to generate electricity, by pushing water turbines. The electricity made from hydropower is called hydroelectricity.

incorporating the SDG 7 targets, promotes the development of problem solvers, innovators and globally empowered students, making the world a better place for everyone to live in (Kennedy & Odell, 2014; Prensky, 2016; Huling & Speake Dwyer, 2018).

STEM activities should include the following features of EfS:

- positive;
- future-focused and change-oriented thinking;

- learner-centred and community connected;
- interdisciplinary and/or transdisciplinary with a focus on long-term and lifelong learning.

(Davis, 2010)

It is important when designing STEM activities and projects for students, based on environmental problems, that we not only focus on solutions to problems that we expect students and future generations to solve, but also on positive preventative measures that can be taken here and now to prevent major environmental issues such as climate change. It is not fair to pass responsibilities from adults to students, we should focus on positive actions and ideas. Therefore, STEM activities in the classroom should be categorised into two types: Developing solutions to deal with the impacts of climate change (adaptation) and developing innovations and prototypes to prevent climate change (mitigation) (Liston, 2022).

In the followings sections, I will provide details of how I as a STEM teacher educator try to include EfS in STEM teaching and learning through interdisciplinary, holistic and values-driven activities. I always try to instil in my undergraduate and postgraduate primary teachers an interest and love for learning about the world around them, while focusing on transformative learning experiences, including innovative pedagogies and activities going beyond the constraints of the curriculum (Sterling, 2011). I try to ensure that when teaching about environmental issues, such as renewable and non-renewable sources of energy and their effects on the environment, that I do not create a barrier between the topics and the student. In certain situations, I believe that educational exposure to environmental problems can result in students feeling hopeless and disempowered (Sobel, 1996). Examples of teaching and learning activities in this chapter are designed to prevent the development of 'Ecophobia' and to break down the barriers that can affect the development of environmental empathy among students.

STEM engineering activities

In this section we will explore how the Engineering Design Process can be used to incorporate Sustainable Development Goal 7: Affordable and Clean Energy into STEM education. STEM activities and lessons implement the Engineering Design Process as a means of approaching problems and designing solutions for those problems (Jolly, 2017). The Engineering Design Process provides a model that guides students from identifying a problem, to creating and developing a solution. The Engineering Design Process includes the following stages: Ask; Imagine; Plan & Design; Create; Test & Evaluate; Redesign/Improve and; Communicate (Table 10.3).

As a first step, the Engineering Design Process is a very effective teaching and learning strategy in developing students' understanding about different sources of energy (renewable and non-renewable, advantages and disadvantages, effects of burning fossil fuels, solutions to a cleaner environment and moving from non-renewable forms of energy to renewable energy sources). I begin the process of exploring renewable energy with students through prescribed engineering challenges such as:

- Design, build and cook using a solar oven.
- Design and build a solar water heater.

Table 10.3 Stages in the Engineering Design Process

Stage of Engineering Design Process	Activity
Ask/define the problem: introducing criteria and constraints	The specific challenge the children are to address. Q: *What is the problem you want to solve?* *What needs to be designed and who is it for?* *Were there any specific requests or requirements?*
Conducting research	Children carry out research (documentaries, news reports, etc.)
Imagine	Team members explore ideas through brainstorming informed ideas on how to solve the problem and come up with possible solutions. Q: *What is the end product?* *What are the overall goals?* *What are the project requirements and limitations?*
Plan & design	The team choose an idea and decide on how to design their prototype by sketching their design. Q: *What will you need?* *What steps will you take?* *Why did you design it this way?*
Create/build	Team members create the design and prototype they selected.
Test and evaluate	The teams test their design to check if it works as they expected and as per the criteria. They evaluate the design based on how well the design met the criteria and solved the problem. Q: *How will you test your design?* *Did it work as you expected?*
Redesign/ improve	The team decide if they need to change/alter/redesign the prototype in any way. Q: *Do you need to change or alter or improve your design in any way?* *Why?* *How will you do this?*
Communicate	The children present their prototypes to the class mentioning the problem, their design solutions and their results.

- Design and make your own solar panels to charge a mobile phone.
- Design and build a giant air blaster.
- Design and build a hovercraft.
- Design and build a wind powered instrument that can make music.
- Design and create a wind turbine for a power supply company using only recycled materials.
- Design and build a water turbine.
- Design and build a model watermill.
- Design and build a model of a geothermal power plant.
- Design and build a steamboat.

As previously mentioned, the Engineering Design Process allows for the integration and application of a deeper level of knowledge and understanding of science and mathematics concepts to create technologies and solutions for real-world problems (Jolly, 2017).

Students, through the above-mentioned activities, can develop an understanding about the differences between renewable and non-renewable sources of energy and the pros and cons to the different sources of energy available to us in the world. The Engineering Design Process can be further enhanced by adding a Design Thinking approach which promotes a focus on empathy.

Design Thinking and the Engineering Design Process

The term 'Design Thinking' (DT) refers to thinking skills or practices designers use to create new ideas and solve problems. DT is an innovative, creative and human-centred process, that employs collaboration in order to generate user-focused products, services or experiences. It is a pedagogical philosophy that places more emphasis on the process, rather than the product, and invites creativity, exploration, and collaboration into teaching. A pedagogical framework for Design Thinking designed at Stanford University d. School involves five stages; Empathy, Define, Ideation, Prototype, Test and Share (Table 10.4). An integrated model of the Engineering Design Process and Design Thinking can therefore bring the 4 H's (head, hope, heart and hands) into STEM.

Design thinking is a methodology for creative problem solving and if incorporated effectively in the classroom can help students generate 'big questions and provide opportunities for relevant research' (Morrin, 2022: 164). The following sections will describe a variety of teaching and learning strategies and resources that can be used during the 'empathy', 'conducting research' and the 'defining the problem' steps of the Engineering Design Process/ Design Thinking processes with students.

Table 10.4 Stages in the Design Thinking and the Engineering Design Processes

Stage of Engineering Design Process	*Stage of the Design Thinking Process*
	Empathise Collecting information: Empathising with the users, listening and observing and understanding their users, finding new ideas and further defining the design challenge
Ask/define the problem: Introducing criteria and constraints	**Defining the design challenge**
Conducting research: Observing, understanding and synthesising	**Empathise** Collecting information: Empathising with the users, listening and observing and understanding their users, finding new ideas and further defining the design challenge
Imagine: Brainstorming	**Ideate:** Brainstorming
Plan & design	**Prototype**
Create/build	**Prototype**
Test and evaluate	**Test**
Redesign/improve	**Iteration: what has been learned?**
Communicate	**Share**

Education about and through the environment: Empathising, conducting research and defining problems on renewable energy

Students should be provided with the opportunities to carry out research and learn about renewable sources of energy using Davis' (2010) three different types of learning experiences i.e. in the environment, about the environment and for the environment. In the environment, the natural environment is utilised as a medium for learning. Educators should provide as many opportunities as possible for students, not only to connect with the natural world, but also with the physical and human-made world. This provides an opportunity to link with STEM education outside the classroom. Education about and through the environment, involves students learning how natural systems function (see UNESCO's Cognitive Learning Objectives for SDG 7 (Table 10.5)). This helps students to appreciate the complexities of natural systems and the interconnectedness between humans and nature. Education for the environment encompasses UNESCO's Socio-Emotional and Behavioural Learning Objectives for SDG 7 (Table 10.7).

Throughout all activities in this chapter, it is important for students to use the terminology listed in Table 10.2. Using images or photographs, students are invited to sort and classify the energy sources as renewable or non-renewable forms of energy.

Questions to promote discussion

What do all of these things have in common? (they are sources of energy).
Which of these sources are renewable?
Which of these sources are non-renewable?
Can you explain what a renewable source of energy is?
Can you explain what a non-renewable source of energy is?
What advantages are there to using renewable/non-renewable energy sources?
Do you use any renewable/non-renewable sources of energy in your home?

Table 10.5 Cognitive Learning Objectives Adapted from UNESCO (2020: 24)

Cognitive learning objectives Teaching ***about*** the goals: developing respect and understanding	1. The learner knows about different energy resources – renewable and non-renewable – and their respective advantages and disadvantages including environmental impacts, health issues, usage, safety and energy security, and their share in the energy mix at the local, national and global level. 2. The learner knows what energy is primarily used for in different regions of the world. 3. The learner understands the concept of energy efficiency and sufficiency and knows socio-technical strategies and policies to achieve efficiency and sufficiency. 4. The learner understands how policies can influence the development of energy production, supply, demand and usage. 5. The learner knows about harmful impacts of unsustainable energy production, understands how renewable energy technologies can help to drive sustainable development and understands the need for new and innovative technologies and especially technology transfer in collaborations between countries.

Children's books

Picture books are an effective means of introducing 'Education about the Environment' into the classroom. Picture books provide students with a range of windows through which they can view the world (Dolan, 2014:2017). With diverse picture books, students can develop environmental empathy, through the exploration and discovery of peoples, plants and animals locally and around the world. For younger students, we should always begin by exploring their immediate and local environments and look at possible environmental issues to which they can relate to (Sanger, 1997). Global energy challenges and the effect of climate-change on our habitats may be too conceptually abstract for younger students and can cause the development of 'ecophobia'. One approach to prevent such reactions is to begin by fostering environmental empathy for their own natural environment, through books that use narrative to engage their interest (Mc Knight, 2010). As students grow older, we can then broaden their explorations and explore picture books from habitats around the world.

Once students have developed an appreciation for the world around them, they must then further develop their environmental awareness and empathy with others. Picture books on different renewable sources of energy, industry, peoples' experiences and reactions to environmental challenges can then be incorporated into teaching and learning activities in the classroom.

Looking at the world from afar

A strategy I find effective in developing students' environmental awareness and empathy, involves allowing students to look at the world from afar and exploring the world from a different angle to what they are used to. Allow students to explore books that include photographs of the Earth from space, where 'those spectacular, two-thousand mile views make you (them) a lot more aware of the big picture' (Hadfield, 2014).

> As we get farther and farther away, it (the earth) diminished in size. Finally, it shrank to the size of a marble, the most beautiful you can imagine. That beautiful, warm, living object looked so fragile, so delicate, that, if you touched it with a finger, it would crumble and fall apart. Seeing this has to change a man....
>
> James B. Irwin (1930–1991) Apollo 15 astronaut (cited in Bright & Sarosh, 2018)

Chris Hadfield's and Tim Peake's books *'You are here. Around the world in 92 minutes'* and *'Hello, is this planet Earth? My View from the International Space Station'* provide spectacular pictures of the world, demonstrating how fragile the world can be:

> It's impossible to look down on earth from space and not be mesmerised by the fragile beauty of our planet. I was struck by just how thin our atmosphere really is – that tiny strip of gas that sustains all life and differentiates our planet from the barren, hostile conditions of Mars or Venus.
>
> (Peake, 2016)

Students' immediate environment

Paren (2005) sets out five key elements for a lesson on environmental issues:

- Facts
- Seeing connections
- Seeing both sides of an issue
- Problems and solutions
- Involving students in school or community action.

As part of the Engineering Design Process/Design Thinking process, when students are researching they will find out facts about renewable sources of energy and begin to see connections between sources of energy and climate change, which leads them further onto exploring problems and solutions. It is important that during the empathising, conducting research and defining problems stages, students link what they are exploring in the classroom with their own immediate local environments. This is achieved through a variety of means:

- Experiment with renewable energy technologies.
- Reflect on and calculate their own energy usage through Energy Usage Audits.
- Reflect and evaluate their energy usage in terms of efficiency and sufficiency.
- Discuss with students their responsibilities around energy consumption.
- Conduct an energy saving campaign in their school or at home.
- Run a group project on how much energy is required to produce their daily needs (UNESCO, 2020: 26).
- Field trips in the community.
- Connecting STEM content with real people.

Field trips in the community and connecting STEM content with real people, will now be explored in further detail.

Field trips

Place based instruction has been used as a solution in addressing inadequacies of traditional STEM education by using the students' immediate environment (Avery & Kassam, 2011; Sobel, 2004). Field trips are an effective means of linking the formal with the informal and further reinforcing prior learning that has taken place in the classroom (Bell et al., 2009; Farmer & Wott, 1995; NRC, 2010). Organising field trips to different energy sites and industries, that use different sources of energy, is important for students to be able to compare and assess different models and to carry out ethical debates and discussions around the pros and cons of different energy types and projects (UNESCO, 2020).

Fieldtrips must be impactful and involve effective learning experiences, in-order for them to be worthwhile. When planning a field trip exploring the renewable and non-renewable sources of energy, always ensure that it provides students with the opportunity to develop their knowledge, skills and attitudes that will add value to and support their experiences in the classroom (Dillon et al., 2006). On one hand, field trips allow students to apply basic principles to determine the most appropriate renewable energy strategy, in a particular situation or project (UNESCO, 2020). On the other hand, it allows them to conduct scenario analyses for future energy production, supply and usage (UNESCO, 2020).

Educators have an important and difficult decision to make regarding their role in responding to local issues in their community (Biddle & Schafft, 2016). For example, STEM industries that are harvesting and/or burning non-renewable sources of energy may be having negative effects on an environment, but on the other hand, they may be providing much needed employment for many families in a local area and thus contributing to the economic development of the area. Therefore, educators are faced with the ethical dilemma when exploring the long-term effects of such an industry (Gruenewald, 2008).

Table 10.6 Building an Eco-Friendly House

STEM Project	Design and Build a Prototype of an Eco-Friendly House
Empathising with the users, listening and observing and understanding their users, finding new ideas and further defining the design challenge	Conduct interviews with builders and people of all ages and backgrounds in the community that have an interest in developing a more sustainable life style but have to work with their existing properties.
Defining the design challenge: Introducing criteria and constraints	Did you know? In Ireland more than 90% of our electricity is made from fossil fuels which are a non-renewable source of energy. If it could be properly harnessed, enough sunlight falls on the earth in just one hour to meet world energy demands for a whole year. There are 113 wind farms, in 21 counties on the island of Ireland. In Ireland, we use more than twice as many cars as we did just ten years ago.
Conducting research on renewable sources of energy	(1) Photo voltaic – these need strong sunlight and they convert the sun's light into electrical energy so they can be used to power electrical appliances in the house (2) Solar thermal – these harness the sun's heat and don't need strong sunlight so they are very suitable for Ireland. They can be used to heat the hot water in your house. Solar panels are made of a shiny metal and are usually placed on a roof to get maximum sun. Make solar panels on the house by adding small strips of silver foil or painted black panels on the roof of the house. Make sure they are well positioned to obtain maximum energy from the sun. Let's imagine this home is near a body of fast-moving water and harness the hydropower! – if the house is beside a river or waterfall you may be able to harness the power of the moving water to make electricity. The water has to be moving at speed so a lake, pond or slow stream won't do. Add a waterfall or fast running river beside the house with silver foil or painted card. Build a small dam over the water to capture the power – a small match box with holes in it (to let the water through) would represent a hydropower station.

(*Continued*)

Table 10.6 (Continued)

STEM Project	Design and Build a Prototype of an Eco-Friendly House
	Finally, let's go underground! Geothermal – Pipes are laid in the garden or yard under the ground for geothermal energy. Use straws, wool or pipe cleaners to demonstrate this in your model house.
Imagine and ideate	Brainstorming design ideas for an Eco-friendly house.
Plan & design	Questions to consider during the planning stage:
	Is there some material you could use to insulate your house Use old scrap material as carpet and curtains, and bubble-wrap as roof and wall insulation.
	Use laminated sheets of plastic or acetates as windows. Stick one on each side of the window hole to act as double glazing.
	Make rainwater collectors out of cardboard with straws as drainpipes.
	Think about large windows for natural light.
	Maximise the potential of your South facing aspect.
	Consider a green roof (or a roof top garden)
Create/build	They then build their prototype with as many eco-friendly materials and systems as possible.
Test and evaluate	They present their designs to a team of judges with set assessment criteria. For example: sustainable materials for construction and insulation, eco-friendly heating systems and sources of energy.
Redesign/improve	Iteration: what has been learned?
Communicate	Share their designs during a school STEM/EfS fair.

Fieldtrips to eco-villages and to eco-friendly designed buildings can be very informative and thought provoking for the students, questioning how people live and how we could live more sustainable lives. This includes sites such as Cloughjordan Ecovillage discussed in chapter 14 (case study 14.1). After a fieldtrip exploring sustainable living, you could engage your students in a STEM activity where they have to design and build a prototype of an eco-friendly house. An outline of this activity which incorporates the Engineering Design Process and Design Thinking is included in Table10.6. Further design opportunities are discussed in chapter 14 whereby students can work as energy engineers.

Connecting STEM content with real people: the head, heart, hope and hands

In-order to teach STEM education through an empathetic lens, we must connect STEM content with real people (Liu Sun, 2017). Students need to examine how the content relates to real people and what are the real-life issues that STEM content relates to. This is another means of incorporating the 4 Hs model into STEM. Bringing in guest speakers to the classroom such as members of a community, scientists and engineers can be an effective tool in developing students' understanding of a particular situation, helping them to empathise with people working in and or affected by the situation. Once students gain an understanding of the 'user' or the people their solution will affect, they will engage at a deeper level with the topic being explored.

There are also many news features and documentaries on how communities and societies are coping with the effects of harvesting and using renewable and non-renewable sources of energy, for example wind farms, solar farms, gas fields, mining and fracking. As a result of watching and listening to such documentaries, students can gain an insight into both sides of a situation. They must then analyse all the information they have gathered in order to come to a well-informed, unbiased decision.

There are number of international organisations and Non Governmental Organisations (NGOs) working on humanitarian energy access projects, transforming energy systems, in order to achieve a healthier, cleaner and more sustainable world. Students should be made aware of these organisations, when they are carrying out research during their STEM projects, as it will help them to further develop their understanding of the energy situation both the Global North and the Global South. Contacting representatives from such organisations and setting up virtual meetings woul help students to further develop their empathy with situations across the world.

Education for the environment: Empathising, conducting research and defining problems on renewable energy

Education for the environment is concerned with social action for change. This involves UNESCO's Socio-Emotional and Behavioural Learning Objectives for SDG 7 (Table 10.7).

Table 10.7 Socio-emotional and behavioural objectives adapted from UNESCO (2020: 25)

Socio-emotional learning objectives Teaching *for* the goals enhancing empathy and love	1	The learner is able to communicate the need for energy efficiency and sufficiency.
	2	The learner is able to assess and understand the need for affordable, reliable, sustainable and clean energy of other people/ other countries or regions.
	3	The learner is able to cooperate and collaborate with others to transfer and adapt energy technologies to different contexts and to share energy best practices of their communities.
	4	The learner is able to clarify personal norms and values related to energy production and usage as well as to reflect and evaluate their own energy usage in terms of efficiency and sufficiency.
	5	The learner is able to develop a vision of a reliable, sustainable energy production, supply and usage in their country
Behavioural learning objectives Teaching *through* the goals Promoting advocacy and activism	1	The learner is able to apply and evaluate measures in order to increase energy efficiency and sufficiency in their personal sphere and to increase the share of renewable energy in their local energy mix.
	2	The learner is able to apply basic principles to determine the most appropriate renewable energy strategy in a given situation.
	3	The learner is able to analyse the impact and long-term effects of big energy projects (e.g. constructing an off-shore wind park) and energy related policies on different stakeholder groups (including nature).

Table 10.7 (Continued)

	4 The learner is able to influence public policies related to energy production, supply and usage.
	5 The learner is able to compare and assess different business models and their suitability for different energy solutions and to influence energy suppliers to produce safe, reliable and sustainable energy.

STEM engineering activities on renewable energy

'Education for the Environment' can be incorporated into STEM education by using engineering projects that are based on socio-scientific issues. In-order for this to be achieved, STEM challenges provided to students should place an emphasis on social action for change. The Engineering Design Process/Design Thinking process allows students the opportunity to work collaboratively in trying to solve local and global issues through empathy, questioning, defining problems, creating and testing solutions.

Examples of 'big' engineering challenges I have used in the past to incorporate 'Education for the Environment' into the Engineering Design Process/Design Thinking process during STEM lessons, are as follows:

- How can we engineer a better more sustainable world?
- Design to improve community resilience through an on and off grid energy system.
- Design and test an energy-efficient model school.
- Design and test a sustainable home of the future.
- Design a model for generating electricity for the future.
- Design a system to make solar energy affordable.
- Design alternative fuel options.
- Design alternative power sources.
- Design new technologies where countries can collaborate with one another in developing a more energy-efficient world.
- Develop a vision of reliable, sustainable energy production, supply and usage in your country.
- Deign an affordable energy efficient electric car for countries in the Global South.

All of the above challenges need much more than just STEM knowledge and skills, students need to develop reasoning, listening, communication and empathy skills to understand the complex nature (naturally, socially, economically, scientifically) of sourcing and developing different forms of renewable energy. The examples of STEM activities, that I have included above, show that teaching about renewable energy does not always have to be negative, it supports students to be problem seekers and activists in their environments (Davis, 2010).

Links between SDG 7 and other SDGs

SDG 7 aims to ensure access to affordable, reliable, sustainable and modern energy for all by the end of the next decade. Energy itself however is at the heart of many of these Sustainable Development Goals (Figure 10.1). It is clear that the energy sector must be at the heart

SDG 9

Industry, innovation and infrastructure

As a renewable energy source, bioenergy is likely to form an increasingly important part of the energy mix. Commercialising bioenergy production could lead to the creation of agricultural and forestry jobs, as well as to higher wages and more diversified income streams for land-owners. Similarly, more investment in renewable energy projects including solar panels, wind farms and wave energy will generate more jobs and sustainable investment opportunities.

SDG 2

Zero hunger

Developing agrofuels could lead to higher global food prices (and thus reduced access to affordable food) as well as to competition between agrofuels and food crops over scarce agricultural land, water and energy for agrofuel production.

SDG 7 Affordable and clean energy

SDG 4

Quality Education

Quality education is an enabling factor in achieving SDG7. Energy is also a key element of science education; and better inclusion of energy in school curricula may foster better science literacy at all levels of society.

SDG 1

No poverty

The concept of 'energy poverty' includes 'fuel poverty'. While some communities in richer countries experience fuel poverty, the phenomenon is more acute within some communities in the Global South where access to to electricity, technologies and /or clean cooking fuels is limited. Ensuring the world's poor have access to affordable, reliable and modern energy services enables the goal of poverty eradication.

SDG 13

Climate action

An immediate up scaling of renewables and energy efficiency is strongly linked to keeping global warming to well below 2 °C above pre-industrial levels, the legally binding objective of the Paris Agreement.

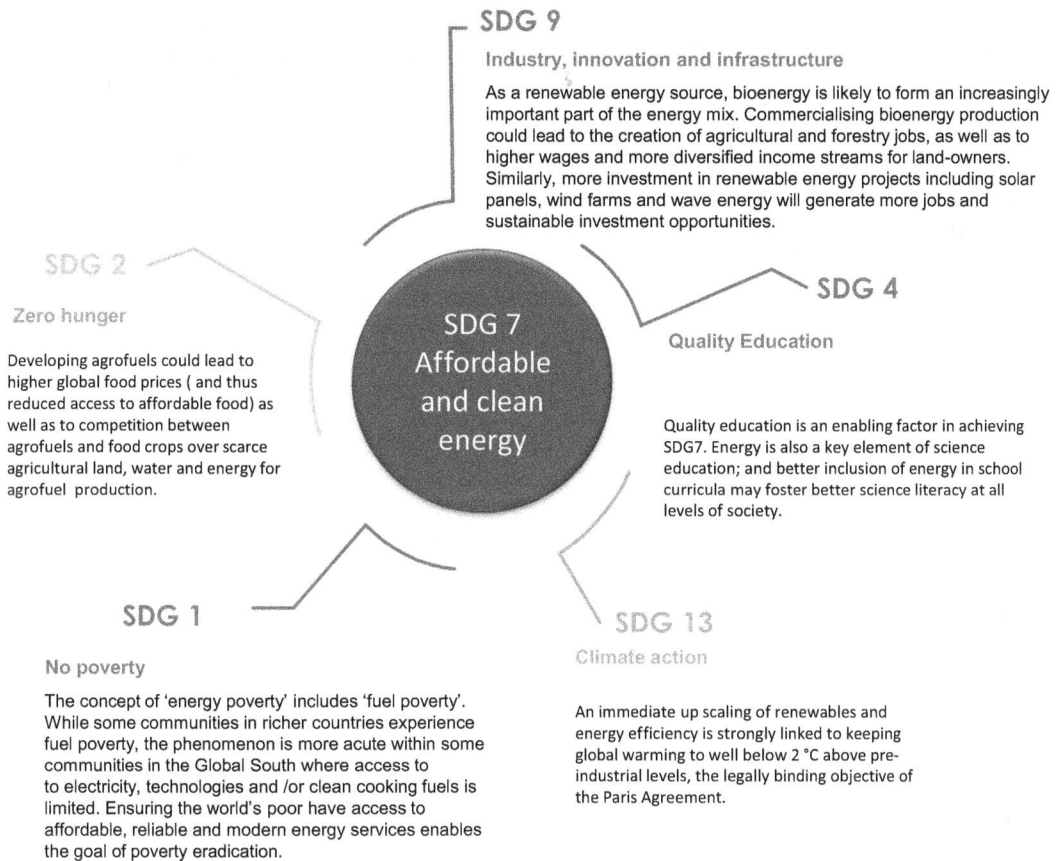

Figure 10.1 Links between SDG 7 and other SDGs.

of efforts to lead the world on a more sustainable pathway. The need to move to renewable sources of energy is even more pertinent in the wake of the Russian invasion of Ukraine and the associated surge in costs for energy.

As can be seen from the activities discussed in this chapter, when students are carrying out the challenges, they are not only considering SDG 7: Affordable and Clean Energy, but also many other interconnected goals such as, good health, quality education, good jobs and economic growth, sustainable cities and communities, responsible consumption, climate action, life below water and life on land. Therefore, inter-disciplinary and transdisciplinary education is very much needed in order for students to be able to view the bigger picture. We need to break down the barriers that traditionally exist between discrete subject areas and begin making meaningful linkages between STEM, EfS, geography and social studies in the classroom.

Conclusion

From my experience as a teacher educator in STEM education, at both pre-service and in-service level, I believe we need to rethink how STEM is taught. Traditionally engineering challenges being taught in classrooms around the world and activities included in a wide variety of educational literature are based on developing STEM knowledge and skills. However, educators should be trying to connect the scientific with the social. The human factor of socio-scientific issues will allow empathy to feature much more prominently in STEM education. Empathy in STEM lessons will allow students to realise the impact of STEM on people and society. I have proposed a process whereby the Engineering Design and Design Thinking processes are combined in STEM education, where there is a stronger emphasis placed on the empathising step when solving STEM challenges. This combined Engineering Design Process/Design Thinking process emphasises the importance of research and empathising with people affected by a particular situation. Such a process allows students to connect with the real lives of all. This chapter provides examples of teaching and learning experiences for students 'in the environment' and 'about the environment', such as children's literature, field trips and, connecting with real people. These strategies can be used at different stages of the Engineering Design Process/Design Thinking process and can be very effective in preventing the development of 'Ecophobia' among students , breaking down the barriers that can affect the development of their environmental empathy.

This chapter also provides many different examples of STEM engineering activities based on relevant environmental, societal and industrial issues. These activities place a focus on learning experiences 'for the environment'. Students that use the combined Engineering Design Process/Design Thinking process in solving these challenges will not only develop their understanding of key environmental issues and socio-scientific concepts, but will also place a focus on social action for change in the classroom.

Our future generations need be ready to tackle an array of global challenges. Education for Sustainability (EfS) and in particular education about affordable and clean energy should and can feature prominently as part of STEM education.

Resources

An extensive list of resources, videos and case studies for SDG 7 is included in the SDG padlet accompanying this book: https://padlet.com/annedolan/o6rds38ylfy6a28h

Weblinks

Sustainable Energy Authority of Ireland (SEAI) is Ireland's national sustainable energy authority. The organisation works with with householders, businesses, communities and government to create a cleaner energy future.

https://www.seai.ie

SEAI Primary Resources: https://www.seai.ie/community-energy/schools/primary-school/

SEAI Post Primary Resources: https://www.seai.ie/community-energy/schools/post-primary-school/

Examples of international organisations are as follows:

Synergie Solaire involves engineering companies supporting NGOs working on humanitarian energy access projects all over the world.

https://www.synergiesolaire.org/

International Renewable Energy Agency (IRENA) is an intergovernmental organisation dedicated to renewable energy. This concerns all forms of energy produced from renewable sources in a sustainable manner, which include bioenergy, geothermal energy, hydropower, ocean, solar, and wind energy. http://www.irena.org/

Power for All is an organisation dedicated to delivering universal energy access before 2030. http://www.powerforall.org/

Sustainable Energy for All (SE4ALL) brings together governments, business and civil society to achieve a transformation of the world's energy systems, for a prosperous, healthier, cleaner and safer world for this and future generations. http://www.se4all.org

The Commonwealth Sustainable Energy Transition Agenda helps member countries fast track an inclusive, just and equitable sustainable energy transition
https://thecommonwealth.org/our-work/commonwealth-sustainable-energy-transition-agenda

Key dates

January 26: International Day of Clean Energy
Third Friday in May: Bike to Work Day
June 3: World Bicycle Day
September 21: Zero Emissions Day
First Wednesday in October: Energy Efficiency Day
October 4: International E Waste Day

Children's Literature

Picturebooks

Brown, P. and O'Hanlon, M. (illus) (2015) *The Boy Who Switched Off the Sun* Fourth Wall Publishing.
Clark, S. and Beghelli. A. (illus) (2021) *Planet Power: Explore the World's Renewable Energy* Barefoot Books.
Drummond, A. (2016) *Green City How One Community Survived a Tornado and Rebuilt for a Sustainable Future* Farrar, Straus and Giroux (BYR).
Drummond, A. (2017) *Pedal Power: How One Community Became the Bicycle Capital of the World* Farrar, Straus and Giroux (BYR).
Drummond, A. (2020). *Solar Story: How One Community Lives Alongside the World's Biggest Solar Plant.* Farrar, Straus and Giroux (BYR).
Green, J. and Gordon. M. (illus) (2005) *Why Should I Save Energy?* Barron's Educational Series Inc.
Kamkwamba, W., Mealer, B. and Zunon, E. (illus) (2012) *The Boy Who Harnessed the Wind* Dial Books for Young Readers; Illustrated edition.
McDonald, R. and Mc Donald, J. (illus) (2019) *I am the Sun: A Book about the Sun for Kids.* House of Lore.
Spiro, R. and Chan, I. (illus) (2018) *Baby Loves Green Energy* Charlesbridge Publishing.
Sturmberg, B. and Stitzel, L. (illus) (2022) *Amy's Balancing Act: An Inspiring Tale About Clean Energy* Little Steps.
Suneby, E. and Green, R. (illus) (2018) *Iqbal and His Ingenious Idea: How a Science Project Helps One Family and the Planet* Kids Can Press.
Tyler, J. and Martins, E. (illus) (2021) *Energy Animated.* Familius.

Free online picturebooks and illustrated books

Bartosik, M. Nuttall Jones, P. and Zadeh, Z. (2019) *Let the Wind Blow* https://www.letthewindblow.org/

This picturebook tells the story of how renewable energies like wind will help lead the transformation to a cleaner, healthier world for everyone. The book is available free of charge online in over 30 languages.

Drummond, A. (2021a) *Roads to Clean Energy* Commonwealth Secretariat. https://production-new-com-monwealth-files.s3.eu-west-2.amazonaws.com/s3fs-public/2022-02/Roads%20to%20Clean%20Energy%202022.pdf

Drummond, A. (2021b) *Energy and Me* Commonwealth Secretariat. https://production-new-common-wealth-files.s3.eu-west-2.amazonaws.com/s3fs-public/2022-02/Energy%20and%20Me%202022.pdf

Drummond, A. (2021c) *The Energy Around Us.* Commonwealth Secretariat. https://production-new-com-monwealth-files.s3.eu-west-2.amazonaws.com/s3fs-public/2022-02/Energy%20Around%20Us%202022.pdf

Jacob, L. and Nolan, A. (illus) (2020). *Climate SOS* SEAI. https://www.seai.ie/community-energy/schools/climate-sos/Climate_SOS_ePub_PDF.pdf

Jacob, L. and Nolan, A (illus) (2021) *Guzzler's Party: Learn How to Save Energy* Sustainable Energy Authority of Ireland. https://www.seai.ie/guzzlers-party-book/Guzzler-Party-book-pdf.pdf

SEAI and Dillon, D. (illus) (2021) *Guzzler's Big Book on Energy* SEAI. https://www.seai.ie/community-energy/schools/schools-documents/GUZZLER_big_bookENG_LR.pdf

Information books

Bang, M. and Chisholm, P. (2014) *Buried Sunlight: How Fossil Fuels Have Changed the Earth* Blue Sky Press

Brundle, H. (2020) *Renewable Energy (Climate Change)* The Secret Book Company.

Brearley, L. (2018) *Solar Power: Capturing the Sun's Energy* Children's Press.

Brearley, L. (2018) *Geothermal Energy: The Energy Inside Our Planet* Children's Press.

Brearley, L. (2018) *Water Power: Energy from Rivers, Waves and Tides* Children's Press.

Cinami De Cristofano, C. and Medeiros, G. (illus) (2018). *Running on Sunshine: How Does Solar Energy Work* Harper Collins.

Dickman, N. (2019) *Renewable Energy* Wayland.

Diehn, A. and Li, Hui. (illus) (2018a) *Energy: Physical Science for Kids* Nomad Press; Illustrated edition.

Diehn, A. and Li, Hui. (illus) (2018b) *Forces: Physical Science for Kids* Nomad Press; Illustrated edition.

Diehn, A. and Li, Hui (illus) (2018c) *Matter: Physical Science for Kids* Nomad Press; Illustrated edition.

Diehn, A. and Li, Hui (illus) (2018d) *Waves: Physical Science for Kids* Nomad Press; Illustrated edition.

James, A. and Allen, P. (illus) (2017) *See Inside Energy* Usborne Publishing Ltd.

Jacoby, J. and Vann, J. (illus) (2021) *Cool Engineering Filled With Fantastic Facts for Kids of All Ages* Pavilion Children's Books

Ziem, M. (2018) *Wind Power: Sailboats, Windmills and Wind Turbines* Children's Press

Books for older students

Mealer, B. and Kamkwamba, W. (2019) The Boy Who Harnessed the Wind (Young Readers Edition). Razorbill Fower, G. (2017) *Moondust: Out of Darkness We Shine* Chicken House.

References

Avery, L. M. and Kassam, K. A. (2011). Phronesis: Children's local rural knowledge of science and engineering. *Journal of Research in Rural Education*, 26(2), 1–18.

Bell, P., Lewenstein, B., Shouse, A. and Feder, M. (2009). *Learning Science in Informal Environments: People, Places, and Pursuits*. Washington, DC: National Academies Press.

Biddle, C. and Schafft, K. A. (2016). Educational and ethical dilemmas for STEM education in Pennsylvanian's Marcellus shale gasfield communities (Chapter 14, 205–214). In *Reconceptualizing STEM Education. The Central Role of Practices*. Editors Duschl, R. A. & Bismack, A. S. New York: Routledge.

Bright, M. and Sarosh, C. (2018). *Earth From Space. Epic Stories of the Natural World*. London: BBC Books, Penguin Random House.

Davis, J. (2010). *Young Children and the Environment. Early Education for Sustainability*. Australia: Cambridge University Press.

Dillon, J., Rickinson, M., Teamey, K., Morris, M., Choi, M. Y., Sanders, D. and Benefield, P. (2006). The value of outdoor learning: Evidence from research in the UK and elsewhere. *School Science Review*, 87(320), 107–111.

Dolan, A. M. (2014). *You, Me and Diversity: Picturebooks for Teaching Development and Intercultural Education*. London: Trentham Books.

Dolan, A. M. (2017). Engaging with the world through picture-books. Chapter 3. In *Teaching Geography Creatively*. Editor Scoffham, S. London: Routledge.

Farmer, A. J. and Wott, J. A. (1995). Field Trips and follow up activities: Fourth graders in a public garden. *The Journal of Environmental Education*, 27(1), 33–35.

Gruenewald, D. A. (2008). The best of both worlds: A critical pedagogy of place. *Environmental Education Research*, 14(3), 308–324.

Hadfield, C. (2014). *You Are Here. Around the World in 92 Minutes*. London: Macmillan.

Huling, M. and Speake Dwyer, J. (2018). *Designing Meaningful STEM Lessons*. NSTA Press.

Jolly, A. (2017). *STEM by Design: Strategies and Activities for Grades 4–8*. New York: Routledge.

Kennedy, T. and Odell, M. (2014). Engaging students in STEM education. *Science Education International*, 25(3), 246–258.

Liston, M. (2022). Bringing climate change alive in the science classroom through science, communication and engineering STEM challenges (Chapter 9, 121–137). In *Teaching Climate Change in Primary Schools*. Editor Dolan, A. M. London: Routledge.

Liu Sun, K. (2017). The importance of cultivating empathy in STEM education. *Science Scope* (April/May 2017), 40(8), 6–8.

Mc Knight, D. (2010). Overcoming "ecophobia": Fostering environmental empathy through narrative in children's science literature. *Frontiers in Ecology and the Environment*, 8(6), 10–15.

Morrin, A. M. (2022). Do you see what I see? A visual lens for exploring climate change (Chapter 11, 152–167). In *Teaching Climate Change in Primary Schools*. Editor Dolan, A. M. London: Routledge.

National Research Council (NRC). (2010). *Surrounded by Science: Learning Science in Informal Environments*. Washington, DC: National Academies Press.

Paren, L. (2005). *Teaching Primary Environmental and Social Studies*. Oxford: Macmillan Publishers Ltd.

Peake, T. (2016). *Hello, Is this Planet Earth? My View from the International Space Station*. London: Penguin Random House Group.

Prensky, M. (2016). *Education to Better Their World. Unleashing the Power of 21st-Century Kids*. New York: Teachers College Press (Columbia University).

Ramirez, R. (2013). *Save Our Science: How to Inspire a New Generation of Scientists*. https://dukespace.lib.duke.edu/items/7c48df6f-1123-4ee2-8d95-8a4e26a5ab8a.

Sanger, M. (1997). Sense of place and education. *The Journal of Environmental Education*, 29(1), 4–8.

Sobel, D. (1996). *Beyond Ecophobia: Reclaiming the Heart in Nature Education*. Great Barrington, MA: The Orion Society and the Myrin Institute.

Sobel, D. (2004). *Place-Based Education: Connecting Classrooms & Communities* (1st Edition). Great Barrington, MA: The Orion Society.

Sterling, S. (2006). *Sustainable education: Revisioning learning and change*. United Kingdom: Green Books.

Sterling, S. (2011). Transformative learning and sustainability: Sketching the conceptual ground. *Learning Teachnologies for Higher Education*, 5, 17–33.

Straw, S., Hart, R. and Harland, J. (2011). *An Evaluation of the Impact of STEMNET's Services on Pupils and Teacher*. Slough: NFER.

UNESCO. (2020). *Education for Sustainable Development Goals: Learning Objectives*. Available at: https://unesdoc.unesco.org/ark:/48223/pf0000247444

United Nations (UN). (2020). *Sustainable Development Goal*. Available at: https://www.un.org/sustainabledevelopment/sustainable-development-goals/

11 Decent work and economic growth (SDG 8)

Jennifer Liston, Tandeep Kaur and Ann Devitt

Introduction

Work is a major aspect of our everyday lives, and it is important to learn about various features of working life such as fair wages, work conditions, job creation and economic sustainability. While work has a central place in society, throughout the world there are many versions of a working day. Issues of financial injustice, child labour and gender inequality in workplaces continue to hamper progress towards a fair and sustainable world. Progress is hindered so much so that in 2021 (the International Year for the Elimination of Child Labour), regrettably, an increase in child labour was recorded (The United Nations Children's Fund 'UNICEF', 2021). Children continue to be exploited for work and economic growth seems to have a negative impact on both human and natural environments. While child labour may be more prevalent in some localities, it is important to highlight this issue to students globally, particularly considering children's rights, and the injustice of child labour. Developing an understanding of decent work conditions and the economic impacts of workplace issues is instrumental to support student learning on achieving the goal of a fair and equitable society.

This chapter explores teaching SDG 8- *Decent work and Economic growth* with students in the age range 8–15 years across primary and secondary schools. Primary and secondary education plays a significant part in achieving SDG 8. UNESCO suggests for primary education students to develop their 'understanding of why people work, and the meaning of social enterprises' (UNESCO, 2020). The suggested focus is on considering the value of all different forms of work (for example, unpaid care work, artistic endeavour, corporate employment) and the importance of equality of access and opportunity for all. In secondary education, enterprise, cooperatives, workers' rights, social justice, and fair trade are key topics for developing the skills, to devise and evaluate innovative and sustainable approaches in relation to work. UNESCO also stresses the opportunities of fair trade and alternative models of ownership for the mutual benefit of their own communities' (UNESCO, 2020).

The main focus of the chapter is on topics of financial justice, equality and child labour. To situate the sample classroom activities in context, Section 1 examines some of the key issues to consider when teaching SDG 8. incorporating reflective tasks for teachers to consider their own perspectives on the theme. Reflective tasks are included to allow educators engage with the theoretical underpinnings of SDG 8 topics in order to ground and motivate the practical classroom approaches. Section 2 provides practical examples of classroom activities for SDG

DOI: 10.4324/9781003232001-14

Table 11.1 SDG 8 key terminology

Economic growth	an increase or improvement in the production and value of the goods and services produced by an economy over time.
Sustainable development	is a term for achieving economic growth goals while also sustaining the natural resources on which the economy and society depend.
Decent work	refers to the formal and informal sector and includes all kind of jobs, people and families that respects the rights of workers
Child labour	refers to the exploitation of children through any form of work that deprives children of their childhood, interferes with their ability to attend regular school, and is mentally, physically, socially and morally harmful
Labour rights or workers' rights	are legal and human rights included in national and international labour and employment law to protect workers

8 covering a range of areas including the use of statistics, investigating a product, immersion in forest school, understanding workplaces, balancing economic costs and creating entrepreneurial ideas. These activities provide opportunities for students to engage in rich classroom discussions, encouraging them to consider their role in sustainability and the elimination of child labour. Section 3 discusses how achieving SDG 8 may contribute to achieving other SDGs by highlighting the interlinkages between SDG 8 and other goals, thus facilitating an integrated approach to the SDGs. The chapter concludes by listing some helpful resources for teaching SDG 8 and relevant literature for children (ages 8–12 years) and young people (ages 12–17 years) respectively. Some key terminology relevant to SDG 8 is outlined in Table 11.1.

Section 1: understanding SDG 8- a theoretical context

SDG 8 aims to 'promote sustained, inclusive and sustainable economic growth, full and productive employment and decent work for all'. The goal recognises the importance of the eradication of all forms of forced labour, promotion of labour rights and safe and secure working environments. According to the International Labour Organization (ILO), in 2015, almost 204 million people were unemployed. The COVID-19 pandemic hit the global labour market significantly and led to increased rates of unemployment all over the world. The estimated number of unemployed people in 2021 was 214.2 million (ILO. 2022). The effects on inequality, poverty and child labour are also alarming. According to ILO and UNICEF's 2021 report on Child labour, as a result of the COVID-19 pandemic, the number of children in child labour grew to 160 million worldwide and nine million additional children were at risk of child labour by the end of 2022. Under these circumstances, it becomes more important than ever to educate youth about the SDGs and SDG 8 in particular.

A key dimension to understanding SDG 8 is that it requires holding in balance the potentially conflicting economic and sustainability imperatives. The overarching goal of SDG 8 is to have full and productive employment by 2030 while maintaining environmental and social justice imperatives. Frey (2017) critically examines SDG 8 from two perspectives – the business approach advocated by the International Organisation of Employers (IOE) and a human rights perspective. Frey's study concludes that SDG 8 is challenging as it presents both opportunities for advocating for human rights and accountability but also enhances legitimacy for the business/economic growth approach. These two perspectives are in constant tension. In fact, a financial justice approach is helpful in the interests of achieving balance between the needs of economic growth, decent work, and human rights.

The United Nations (UN, 2017) targets for SDG 8 (see Appendix 1) illustrate the delicate balance that must be struck between economic growth and sustainable models of work, for example, between targets 8.1 and 8.2 with 8.8 and 8.9, or within target 8.5.

Focusing on the education system and the settings in which educators work, can be a good starting point for becoming active in achieving SDG 8. Education policies throughout the world have been criticised for focusing on the purpose of education as serving the economy, being grounded in Cartesian rationalism and Western scientific knowledge and amplified by the rise of neoliberalism in a context of global capitalism (Lynch 2010; Lynch, Grummell & Devine, 2012). Hicks (2003) warns that such an approach is at odds with the need to work towards a more just and sustainable world. While the focus and purpose of education is largely a broader policy task, as educators we can reflect on our practice and consider who are we serving and for what purpose in our everyday work and decision making.

Ending child labour at the heart of SDG 8

During the Victorian Era in England, child labour was synonymous with slavery. Child labourers were forced to work in factories and workhouses at the insistence of their parents and workhouse guardians. In both his autobiographical and fictional writing, Dickens emphasizes the poor conditions of the factories that took advantage of child labour. The children he depicted in his novels are vulnerable and susceptible to exploitation. The novel *'David Copperfield'* highlights the miseries of David's life, the mistreatment of his stepfather, his life at boarding school and as a child factory worker. The story of *'Oliver Twist'* portrays the miseries and degradation of destitute children. Oliver's life is characterized by loneliness and lack of care. A victim of child labour, Oliver is sold to an undertaker, later escapes the horrid experience and goes to London where he is exposed to criminal activities of a gang led by Fagin. Two hundred years after Dickens, child labour continues to ruin the lives of millions of children. Today, children's literature explores this theme through historical, geographical, environmental, social justice and human rights persepctives. An extensive list of picturebooks and novels about child labour is listed at the end of this chapter.

An explicit target within SDG 8 is ending child labour in all its forms by 2025. There is a considerable difference between the types of work in which children are engaged. Hence the need to make a distinction between childhood chores and child labour. Children doing work that does not affect their health and personal development or interfere with their schooling, can often be regarded as being something positive. Child labour is a very different matter. The ILO defines child labour as 'work that deprives children of their childhood, their potential and their dignity, and that is harmful to physical and mental development' (2004: 16). This includes work that is dangerous or impacts negatively on their schooling and extends to the very worst forms including enslavement, family separation and abandonment from a very young age. This is an issue that requires consideration both locally and globally. For example, consider the cup of coffee you buy in terms of its origins. It might have come from a place where children work in agricultural lands to earn for their family and remain deprived of basic education rights. Not only do children work as farm labourers against their will, but they may also be victims of child slavery. In fact, the issues of child labour and child slavery may be so deeply embedded in the cultural and social settings of some localities, that a complete eradication of these issues remains a huge challenge. UNICEF's 2021 statistics suggest that more than 1 in 4 children aged 5–17 years, in the Global South are involved in child labour working in dangerous conditions. The economic implications of child labour are also considerable. Not only are children and their families affected, but it also affects nations' economic growth and development. Given that millions of children across the world are exploited for labour, efforts to eradicate child labour in all its forms are crucial. The activities provided in this chapter will enable students to consider these issues and reflect on how they can act as agents of change.

Teaching SDG 8: a balancing act

SDG 8 articulates a set of targets in tension where success can only be achieved through balancing diverse priorities. Teaching SDG 8 requires explicitly engaging with and considering the impacts of actions or decisions on this delicate balance of priorities. Financial Justice Ireland, for example, has many educational activities outlined on their website (https://www. financialjustice.ie/). Grounded in key concepts such as trade justice, tax justice and debt justice, these activities help students to devise solutions in light of the sometimes conflicting economic and human rights agendas (Financial Justice Ireland, 2020). In this chapter, we conceptualise this balance in line with the hands, heart, head and hope model (as discussed in Chapter 2) and as a pedagogy of empathy and advocacy acknowledging that a balanced understanding of the SDG 8 tensions entails engaging cognitively as well as emotionally with the themes. Understandings of empathy, hope and advocacy in education settings are often explicit in referring to the wellbeing, relationships and the whole school culture of schools. What is often implicit is how empathy, hope and advocacy translate into the content we teach and how we teach it.

The activities in this chapter aim to translate the pedagogical ideologies of empathy, hope and advocacy into practice in teaching SDG 8. For example, in order to teach and learn about child labour, learning objectives which include information on child labour locally and globally are required but affective learning objectives which connect students with the experience of child labour are also required. Activity 3: 'A Day in my life', in this chapter aims to engage students with content knowledge and their feelings of empathy. Through discussion, a teacher could help students explore such feelings by clarifying the distinction between empathy and sympathy. The activity would then move towards hope and advocacy by asking students to consider consumption choices. Another example of how this chapter helps integrate empathy, hope and advocacy into teaching SDG 8 is within activity 4 'Forest conservation'. Within SDG 8, teachers are required to explore efforts to decouple production from the impact of natural hazards and environmental degradation. Freire (1990) suggests that education has to exist in the context of a profound love for the world. Activity 4 aims to both teach about forest conservation and indigenous forestry work practices while developing a love for forestry through application of the hand, heart, head and hope model (see Chapter 2). Baba Dioum (1968) suggests, 'in the end we will conserve only what we love, we will love only what we understand, and we will understand only what we have been taught' (nd).

UNESCO identifies a breadth of topics and learning outcomes associated with SDG 8 (see Table 11.2). Developing a sense of love, empathy, hope and advocacy is required in addressing this wide-ranging list of topics from entrepreneurship to slavery. SDG 8 topics require consideration in terms of ensuring that both ends of the spectrum (in terms of economy and care) are included in teaching. It must be noted that choosing certain aspects to teach within the topics may lead to conceptual gaps. For example, teaching entrepreneurship often focuses on product and profit, but teaching the topic in terms of SDG 8 requires examining the impacts of the enterprise on society and sustainable development. Achieving a balance of economic growth and sustainable models of work is a challenging matter for policymakers and companies all over the world and this balancing act transfers into teaching SDG 8. In order to achieve such a balance, a range of learning objectives, as listed in Table 11.3, are required to allow for knowledge, application and affective engagement when teaching SDG 8.

Table 11.2 SDG 8 topics adapted from UNESCO (2020)

- The contributions of economies to human well-being, and the social and individual effects of unemployment
- Economic ethics
- Theoretical assumptions, models and indicators of economic growth (GDP, GNI, HDI)
- Alternative economic models and indicators
- Financial systems and their influence on economic development
- Labour force
- Gender equality in the economy and the (economic) value of care work
- Inequalities in the labour market
- Formal and informal labour, labour rights, especially for migrants and refugees, forced labour, slavery and human trafficking
- Entrepreneurship, (social) innovation, new technologies and local economies for sustainable development

Table 11.3 SDG 8 learning objectives adapted from UNESCO (2020)

Cognitive learning objectives	The learner understands
Teaching **about** the goals: developing respect and understanding	1 the concepts of sustained, inclusive and sustainable economic growth, full and productive employment, and decent work.
	2 has knowledge about the distribution of formal employment rates per sector, informal employment, and unemployment in different world regions or nations, and which social groups are especially affected by unemployment.
	3 understands the relation between employment and economic growth.
	4 understands how low and decreasing wages for the labour force and very high wages and profits of managers and owners or shareholders are leading to inequalities.
	5 understands how innovation, entrepreneurship and new job creation can contribute to decent work and a sustainability-driven economy.

(Continued)

Table 11.3 (Continued)

Socio-emotional learning objectives Teaching **for** the goals enhancing empathy and love	The learner is able to
	1 discuss economic models and future visions of economy and society critically.
	2 collaborate with others to demand fair wages, equal pay for equal work and labour rights.
	3 understand how one's own consumption affects working conditions of others in the global economy.
	4 identify their individual rights and clarify their needs and values related to work.
	5 develop a vision and plans for their own economic life.
Behavioural learning objectives Teaching **through** the goals Promoting advocacy and activism	The learner is able to
	1 engage with new visions and models of a sustainable, inclusive economy and decent work.
	2 facilitate improvements related to unfair wages, unequal pay for equal work and bad working conditions.
	3 develop and evaluate ideas for sustainability-driven innovation and entrepreneurship.
	4 plan and implement entrepreneurial projects. develop criteria and make responsible consumption choices.

So, how can teachers plan for teaching SDG 8 while maintaining the balance between the potentially competing priorities of sustainable work? It is helpful for teachers to reflect on their ideological thinking on matters which may arise in the classroom in advance. To that end, three reflective tasks are suggested for teachers. Reflective task 1 offers opportunities to unearth assumptions about SDG 8 including potentially conflicting conceptions of growth and success at local, national and global levels. Reflective task 2 challenges teachers to look at their immediate work setting and consider the values noted there. In order for teachers to maintain a balanced perspective in the classroom, it is necessary first to articulate and consider the balance of their own priorities. Reflective task 3 asks teachers to consider their own understanding of children's rights and how they enact this in their classrooms.

REFLECTIVE TASK 1

To what extent do you agree or disagree with the following statement:

> 'Economic growth accompanied by worsening social outcomes is not success. It is failure.'

New Zealand Prime Minister Jacinda Ardern

REFLECTIVE TASK 2

Reflecting on your school mission statement, what messages regarding the purpose of education are present? Do these messages reflect in the school life and in your class-room? (Note: school mission statements are discussed in detail in chapter 6).

REFLECTIVE TASK 3

Have you completed the programme below or an equivalent?
https://www.tusla.ie/children-first/childrenfirst-e-learning-programme/
When you were in school, how did you experience the use of authority by adults (teachers/school leaders)? Think about the power dynamics in your classroom: What is the balance of power, authority and respect between adults and students?

When approaching SDG 8 in the classroom, it is important to offer students opportunities to adopt alternative and competing perspectives and to solicit and amplify the resonance of empathy within the classroom. Activities such as debates, devil's advocate, comparing and contrasting data or stories can enhance perspective-taking. More activities for exploring unconscious bias from a gender perspective are detailed in chapter 8. Role plays, walking in another's shoes and experiential learning can support affective learning objectives and engage students with empathy. These capacities can be further deepened by creating the time and space for individual and collective reflection. The example activities below illustrate how the delicate balance inherent in SDG 8 can be examined and explored. Some tasks that could extend or enhance the activities in the chapter include:

- Compare and contrast statistics related to gender gaps in the Global North and Global South countries **(SDG 5)**
- Use the census data to look at gender differences in work in the local context **(SDG 5)**
- Run an entrepreneurial project **(SDGs 8 and 9)**
- Do an internship **(SDGs 8, 9 and 11)**
- Interview employers and employees to compare experiences **(SDGs 8 and 9)**
- Compare workers' rights and workplace discrimination in different industries or coun-tries **(SDGs 8 and 9)**
- Organise a Fairtrade day in your own school **(SDGs 8 and 17)**
- Research your school's Fairtrade footprint by examining the products in the canteen and shop **(SDGs 8 and 17)**
- Collect statistical data from ILO's website for ten countries with highest rates of child labour and present the data in the form of a bar graph. **(SDGs 8 and 9)**
- Read the surgeon's dilemma and find out more about implicit bias here: https://atchub.net/diversity/the-surgeons-dilemma-a-test-for-unconscious-bias/ **(SDGs 5 and 10)**
- Produce an infographic that presents the economic and health costs of the Covid-19 pandemic. **(SDG 3)**

Section 2: practical examples

Activity 1: mind the pay gap

SDG target: 8.5
Age: 12–15 years

Overview

This activity asks students to manipulate, represent visually and evaluate how men and women in one company (company X) are paid for their work and whether the company meets the target of having equal pay for work of equal value. It also requires students to consider the idea of what 'work of equal value' means. Table 11.4 provides information from company X's monthly report.

Table 11.4 Company X's monthly report

Staff No.	Job Designation	Name	Age	Gender	Monthly Salary in Euros	Education	Experience
1	Chief technical officer	Philip	42	M	5,500	Master's	Fifteen years
2	Senior Web developer	William	45	M	4,000	PHD	Five years
3	Senior web developer	Paula	38	F	2,900	Master's	Four years
4	Junior web developer	Liam	29	M	2,800	Bachelor's	Six years
5	Business analyst (senior)	Cormac	35	M	3,600	Bachelor's	Five years
6	Business analyst (junior)	Oliver	42	M	3,800	Master's	Six years
7	Senior technology analyst	James	29	M	2,800	Master's	Six years
8	Junior technology analyst	Iza	35	F	2,400	Bachelor's	Six years
9	QAA	Nimisha	27	F	2,600	Bachelor's	Four years
10	UX designer	Dillon	28	M	3,200	Bachelor's	Four years
11	Junior analyst	Ethan	31	M	2,600	Master's	Three years
12	Research analyst (senior)	Aidan	35	M	2,900	Bachelor's	Four years
13	Research analyst (junior)	Jenny	34	F	1,800	Master's	Two years
14	Public relations officer	Benjamin	36	M	3,300	Bachelor's	Three years
15	Chief executive officer	Daniel	45	M	4,600	Master's	Five years
16	IT executive (senior)	Ryan	39	M	4,100	Bachelor's	Five years
17	HR manager	Bert	37	M	2,800	Bachelor's	Ten years
18	Creative content writer (senior)	Jordan	26	M	2,500	Master's	Five years
19	Creative content writer (junior)	Meabh	24	F	2,200	Bachelor's	Three years
20	Administrative assistant	John	32	M	2,500	High school	Five years

Suggested questions

What is the ratio of male and female employees in the company?

Present the company pay data visually (bar/pie charts), line graph of salaries, integrate data on gender, age, experience, etc.

How many senior positions are male/female?

From your calculations is there a 'gender pay gap' in the table above?

What can you say about the company in terms of SDG 8? (consider differences in pay)

Critical thinking

Read and discuss the following with students.

Differences in pay are as a result of many possible dimensions, including worker education, experience and occupation. When the pay gap is calculated by comparing all male workers to all female workers – irrespective of differences along these additional dimensions mentioned above – the result is the 'raw' or 'unadjusted' pay gap. When the gap is calculated after accounting for underlying differences in education, experience, etc., then the result is the 'adjusted' pay gap (https://ourworldindata.org/six-facts-pay-gap)

Considering this, ask students to reconsider their answers/statements and make changes if they wish.

Make changes in the sheet to present an equitable scenario if you found any inequalities. Considering SDG 8 and the indicator 8.5.1, what should be done to change the situation?

Discussion/debate leading to interlinkages of SDGs

1   Discuss- 'Companies that embrace gender equality in the workplace are more likely to have high financial returns'. (Link with SDG 5)

2   How important do you consider the role of education in achieving the goal of 'equal pay for equal work'? (Link with SDG 4)

Activity 2: from farm to your cup

SDG target: 8.3
Age: 10-15 years

Overview

This activity focuses on Fairtrade through examining the real costs of consumption and distribution of income within a value chain, in particular looking at coffee.

'Coffee is booming – but farmers are earning less than a dollar a pound for their beans.... While the global coffee industry now generates more than $200 billion per year, the average farmer's income has not changed in the past 20 years' (https://www.fairtrade.net/news/we-love-coffee-are-we-willing-to-pay-the-price)

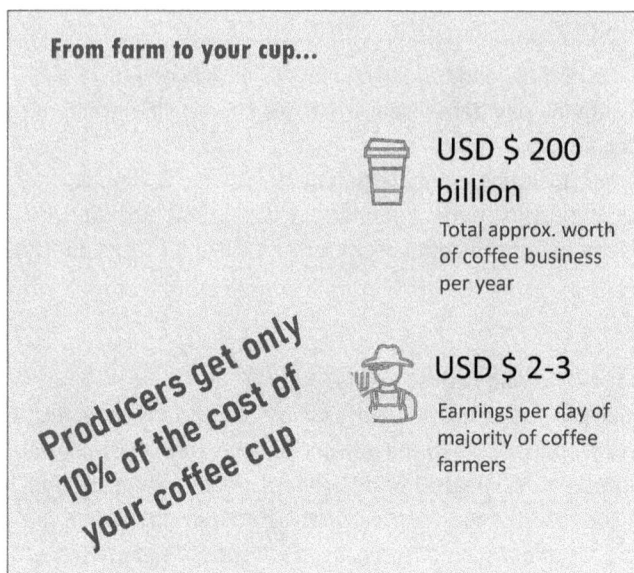

Figure 11.1 From Farm to Your Cup. (Source of information: https://www.fairtrade.net/news/we-love-coffee-are-we-willing-to-pay-the-price).

The infographic shown in Figure 11.1 can be used as a prompt to stimulate class discussion (the following may serve as additional prompts to begin)

- Do teachers in your school drink coffee? (try to estimate number of teachers who drink coffee in the staff room)
- How much does a single cup of coffee cost?
- How many cups of coffee (on average) does a teacher in your school drink per day?
- What is the approximate amount the school spends on coffee per day?
- Could you guess the breakdown for cost of one cup of coffee for all the stages from its production to distribution?

Suggested questions

- Why is such a small amount earned by the producers (farmers)? Whose work is most demanding?

  (Discussion leads to...

  ○ lack of access to all the equipment to turn harvested cherries into a cup of coffee.
  ○ the remote locations of the farmers
  ○ dependence on one crop)
- What could be the impact when farmers get a low income to survive?

  (For example, farmers may take their children out from schools to assist them on farms for extra earnings... connects to child labour.)
- What could be the implications of low income for coffee farming families?

  (Examples include: increased child and forced labour, food insecurity, higher emigration rates, lower coffee quality, decreased environmental stewardship and an impact on school going children.)

Critical thinking and discussion leading to interlinkages of SDGs

- How can we contribute?
- Have you seen the Fairtrade mark on any product you buy?
  Helpful links to know more on Fairtrade:

    http://www.fao.org/3/x6938e/x6938e05.htm,
    https://www.fairtrade.ie/
    https://www.fairtrade.net/

- What is Fairtrade?
- How will it benefit farmers? (for example, access to equipment, direct link with buyers etc.)
- What is the impact of Fairtrade on sustainability? (Economic, Environmental, and societal)
- What are the benefits of Fairtrade to the whole community?

Discussion leads to exploring interconnection of SDGs, e.g. SDG 1 (no poverty), SDG 2 (zero hunger), SDG 4 (quality education) and SDG 17 (partnership). The issue of Fairtrade is discussed in greater detail in chapter 20.

Extension

The average price of a cup of coffee you buy is $ 3.50 - $ 4.50. Figure 11.2 shows the cost breakdown of one cup of coffee. Find the total cost from the figure and evaluate the net profit % to the cafe owner for a cup of coffee sold (Total cost per cup: $ 0.80 - $ 1.00; Net Profit per cup : 300% -400%). See Table 11.5 for additional background information.

Takeaway cup
$0.10 – $0.20

Labour $0.20

Milk $0.20

Coffee
$0.30- $0.40

Figure 11.2 Cost Breakdown for a Cup of Coffee. (Source of data: https://www.cafe-coach.com.au/the-secret-to-real-profits-in-a-cup-of-coffee/).

Illustration: Harman Malhotra

Table 11.5 Fact box

- Globally, over 21 million families make a living from coffee.
- Brazil is the world's largest coffee producer.
- The world's second largest coffee producer is Vietnam.
- Every year October 1 is celebrated as International Coffee Day
- The International Coffee Organization (ICO) is the main intergovernmental organisation for coffee. Its member governments represent 98% of world coffee production and 67% of world consumption.

Activity 3: a day in my life

SDG target: 8.7
Age: 10-13 years

Overview

Millions of children in the world work in harsh circumstances and sometimes lose their right to education. This activity helps students to compare a typical day in the life of a child labourer with their own daily life. Read the following story to your students.

Hamid's story

Hamid is 11 years old. He lives in a small village in South Africa. He gets up at 6 a.m. every morning and goes with his father to work at a gold mine where they both work till 8 p.m. every evening. Sometimes he works with his father to dig or crush pebbles in the scorching heat. On other days, he works in an underground gold mine. He must pick heavy tools and instruments which make him very tired. Hamid's mother packs his lunch box everyday which he eats in his work break at 12.30 p.m. During his one-hour lunch break, he sits with his friends who also work at the same gold mine. He gets paid an equivalent of $2 every day.

Hamid likes to play football and wants to be a national level player. He wants to go to school but his parents cannot afford school fees and other expenses. He has four younger siblings (two brothers and two sisters).

Ask students to fill the given template and compare a typical day in their life with Hamid's day (Table 11.6).

Suggested questions

- Compare your answers with that of Hamid. What are your thoughts on Hamid's quality of life?

    Discussions can be extended to

    ○ other forms of child labour e.g. salt mining, stone quarrying, agricultural work
    ○ exploring feelings regarding the activity, particularly feelings of empathy and sympathy and helping students identify a distinction between those feelings,

Table 11.6 Activity template: A day in my life

Hamid's Day	My Day
Name: Hamid **Age**: 11 years **Country of origin**: Africa **Education**: Hamid does not go to school. **About**: Hamid works at a gold mine. He works in the underground tunnel and mineshafts. He wants to play football and go to a school to study.	**Name**: **Age**: **Country of origin**: **Education**: **About**:
Number of hours worked: 11 **Number of meals taken**: Two (lunch and dinner) **Amount earned in a day**: $ 2 equivalent	**Number of hours worked**: **Number of meals taken**: **Amount earned in a day**:

- the 'danger of the single story' concept – discuss wealth distribution in South Africa e.g. Do all children in South Africa live similarly?
- local history- discuss child labour in industrial schools and on farms in Ireland in the past)
- Are there any health and safety hazards related to Hamid's work? For example, poor health due to toxic gases and dust in mines, inadequate supply of oxygen in mines, risk of explosions and/or tunnel collapse, and malnutrition due to improper meals. This connects to SDG 3: Good health and well-being.
- What are the wider consequences of child labour?
- Explore the countries where child labour is most prevalent. What could be the causes of child labour in different forms? (See chapter 4 for a discussion on poverty and SDG 1). What impact has child labour on education? (See chapter 7 for a discussion on education and SDG 4).
- Explore national and international organisations working to improve the quality of life for children. How can you contribute to this?

Critical thinking

Discuss the statement: 'Participation of children in non-hazardous activities (e.g. some agricultural activities) is not always child labour'. Do you agree?

Highlight distinction between 'light duties which do not have any negative effect on a child's life' and 'child labour which affects their health and personal life'. Some tasks completed by children which do not affect their education can be a part of their normal life. Such activities contribute to the transfer of skills, improved confidence, and self-esteem in children (International Labour Organization). UNICEF's standard indicator for child labour includes the following:

- Age 5 to 11 years: At least 1 hour of economic work or 21 hours of unpaid household services per week.
- Age 12 to 14 years: At least 14 hours of economic work or 21 hours of unpaid household services per week.
- Age 15 to 17 years: At least 43 hours of economic work per week.

See Table 11.7 for additional background information.

Table 11.7 Fact box

• More than 200 million children today are child labourers. Approximately 120 million are engaged in hazardous work. • Forced labour is thought to generate around $150 billion a year in illegal profits. • Most of child labour takes place in agriculture, which includes fishing, forestry, livestock herding and aquaculture. • 48% of all victims of child labour are aged 5–11 years. • The highest number of child labourers is in sub-Saharan Africa. • Causes of child labour include poverty, barriers to education, cultural practices, market demand, and the inadequate/poor enforcement of legislation and policies to protect children. • June 12 is recognised globally as the World Day Against Child Labour.

Link activity

Children as young as eight years old are working on Indonesian palm oil plantations. Watch the video *Indonesia: Fruits of Their Labour* (https://www.youtube.com/watch?v=a3ip-iJQjmw). While watching the video, ask students to answer the following questions:

1   What are the main problems for people working in palm oil plantations identified in the video?
2   What is the name of the palm oil production company mentioned in the video?
3   In what country are the palm oil plantations featured in this video?
4   How are women workers discriminated against on the palm oil plantations?
5   Why are toxic chemicals used in producing palm oil?
6   What are the risks to people working with those chemicals?
7   How old are the children who work on the palm oil plantations?
8   Name six products that contain palm oil.
9   Name four companies that use palm oil in their products.
10 What is Amnesty International asking people to do to help fix the problems for the people who work on palm oil plantations?

(Sourced from https://www.amnesty.org.au/wp-content/uploads/2017/01/Child-Labour-Lesson-Plan.pdf)
See chapter 15 (SDG 12) for more activities relating to responsible consumption and production.

Activity 4: forest conservation

SDG target: 8.4
Age: 8–12 years

Overview

Understanding forest dependent livelihoods is an important topic to consider when studying deforestation, conservation and sustainability. Forest dependent people vary widely as do their relationships with the forest. Often the role of indigenous people in forest conservation

Figure 11.3 Student at a Forest School.

is overlooked. The forest school approach is used to support the connection between students and the natural world. Forest schools can take place in a woodland, natural environment, or a local park (see Figure 11.3). Some countries have organisations to support forest school education for students and professional development courses for teachers. For example: https://irishforestschoolassociation.ie/about/

Activity

Pre-requisite: Students should have an understanding of deforestation (the causes and effects) and some knowledge of the characteristics of indigenous communities.

Read the following extract with students (teachers trained in forest school leadership can do this activity by the campfire).

> 'Indigenous communities have a strong spiritual relationship with their land, and feel responsible for keeping it healthy, for themselves and future generations. *'We take care of our forests, we know much more than the loggers, we are not going to hurt our forests,'* explains Diana Rios, Community Leader of Alto-Tamaya Saweto in Peru. *"We know that people will be hungry, that there will be no water, if we don't protect our forests."* Indigenous communities are very successful at keeping rates of deforestation low in their territories and keeping water sources clean. They are the rainforest's best protectors, and their knowledge will be endangered if indigenous communities do not have access to education that values their perspectives and knowledge'.
>
> Source: https://rainforestfoundation.org/education/

Suggested questions for discussion

Ask students to spend some time exploring the forest and using a notepad, try to explore the following questions:

What is to love about the forest? How do we take care of forests? Why do we take care of forests? What happens if we don't?

Forest conservation and woodland management

Provide opportunities for students to engage with some traditional forest conversation activities e.g.

- Planting
- Monitoring species
- Managing dead wood
- Habitat creation e.g. boxes and habitat piles
- Techniques such as coppicing, pollarding, thinning.

Coppicing and pollarding were traditionally used to harvest juvenile shoots off the same trees for fuel and craft materials. The concept is simple: by cutting a deciduous tree when it is dormant, you allow it to send up fresh shoots in the spring. Willow is ideal for this exercise. Seek permission from the relevant organisation (local authority/ forestry management organisation) before engaging in these activities.

Extension activity

Research and compare woodland management activity in different kinds of forests – e.g. rainforests, Siberian larch forest, deciduous oak forests.

Activity 5: SDG 8 and Covid-19

SDG target: 8.1
Age: 12-15 years

Overview

The infographic shown in Figure 11.4 is used as a prompt to stimulate class discussion about how to balance economic costs with other costs, in this case costs to public health. The class is first asked to produce an equivalent infographic on the public health outcomes of Covid-19. The class is divided in two for a debate on *'Which costs should be minimised – economic costs or health costs?'*

Activity 6: design for decent work

SDG target: 8.3
Age: 8-12 years and 12-15 years

Overview

This activity aims to introduce students to a key part of innovation and entrepreneurial activity – design thinking (discussed in chapter 10). The *Foil Challenge* for primary students and *Redesign the School Lunch* experience for middle and high students from Stanford University d. School takes students through a simplified design cycle to create a novel eating utensil. The 5-step design process illustrated in Figure 11.5, can then be applied to other contexts that require innovative and sustainable solutions.

The element of SDG 8 that relates to entrepreneurial activity emphasises the potential of individual agency when it comes to creating decent work. This can be linked to SDG 12 on responsible consumption in relation to appropriate materials to use (See chapter 15).

Suggested questions for discussion

1   What have we learned about innovation from going through this process?
2   What choices do we need to make during the design process to make sure our product is sustainable?

Link activity

Evaluate the cost of the design and its production and determine a reasonable price for the product.
Estimate how many utensils you would need to sell to earn a decent wage for this innovation.

8 DECENT WORK AND ECONOMIC GROWTH

PROMOTE SUSTAINED, INCLUSIVE AND SUSTAINABLE ECONOMIC GROWTH, FULL AND PRODUCTIVE EMPLOYMENT AND DECENT WORK FOR ALL

GLOBAL ECONOMIC RECOVERY
—— IS HAMPERED BY: ——

NEW WAVES OF COVID-19

RISING INFLATION

SUPPLY-CHAIN DISRUPTIONS

POLICY UNCERTAINTIES

LABOUR MARKET CHALLENGES

GLOBAL ECONOMIC RECOVERY IS
FURTHER SET BACK BY THE UKRAINE CRISIS

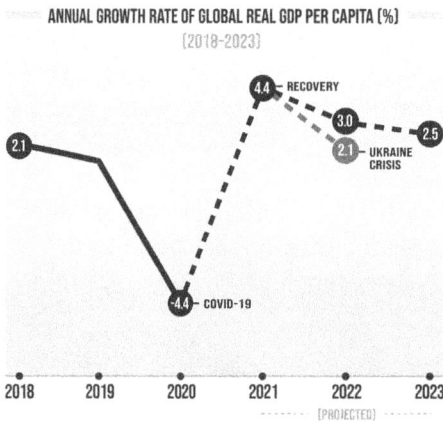

ANNUAL GROWTH RATE OF GLOBAL REAL GDP PER CAPITA (%)
(2018–2023)

2.1

4.4 RECOVERY

3.0

2.1 UKRAINE CRISIS

2.5

-4.4 COVID-19

2018   2019   2020   2021   2022   2023
------- (PROJECTED) ------

GLOBAL UNEMPLOYMENT
TO REMAIN ABOVE PRE-PANDEMIC LEVEL UNTIL AT LEAST **2023**

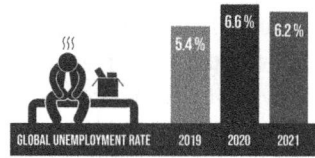

GLOBAL UNEMPLOYMENT RATE

5.4% — 2019
6.6% — 2020
6.2% — 2021

1 IN 10 CHILDREN ARE ENGAGED
IN CHILD LABOUR WORLDWIDE

160 MILLION TOTAL CHILDREN (2020)

WORKER PRODUCTIVITY HAS REBOUNDED,
BUT NOT IN LDCs

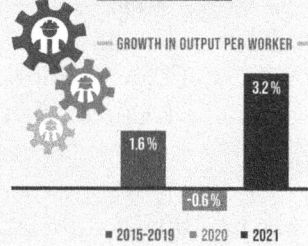

GROWTH IN OUTPUT PER WORKER

1.6%

-0.6%

3.2%

■ 2015-2019   ■ 2020   ■ 2021

THE SUSTAINABLE DEVELOPMENT GOALS REPORT 2022: UNSTATS.UN.ORG/SDGS/REPORT/2022/

Figure 11.4 Implications of Covid-19. (Source: https://unstats.un.org/sdgs/report/2020/ The-Sustainable-Development-Goals-Report-2020.pdf)

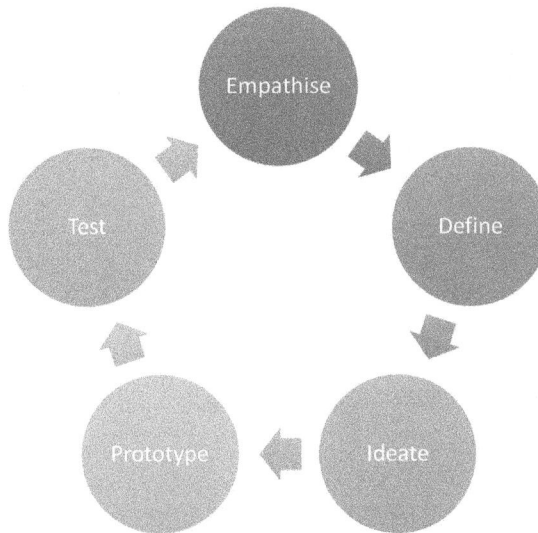

Figure 11.5 Five Step Design Process.

Section 3. Interconnections of SDG 8 with other SDGs

SDG 8 aims to 'promote sustained, inclusive and sustainable economic growth, full and productive employment and decent work for all' (UN, 2015). Progress in SDG 8 impacts the achievement of many other sustainable development goals and the progress in other SDGs can impact SDG 8. The integrated nature of the SDG framework is certainly important for the progress of SDG 8 as it provides a holistic approach to sustainable development (Coopman et al., 2016; Le Blanc, 2015; Nilsson et al., 2016; UN DESA, 2019; UN HLPF, 2019). For instance, full and productive employment is directly linked to SDG 1 (No Poverty). Inclusive and sustained economic growth will result in greater employment opportunities for all and therefore help in achieving the goal of poverty eradication. Reduced levels of poverty through income-generating employment opportunities will help tackle the challenges of youth unemployment and issues such as child labour, slavery and human trafficking. Figure 11.6 shows the interlinkages between SDG 8 and some other sustainable development goals.

Lack of nutrition and poor health conditions are the underlying causes of many diseases and premature deaths. Increased income will foster food security and improved health of individuals, thereby alleviating hunger problems (SDG 2) and contributing to their good health and well-being (SDG 3). Safe and decent working conditions also lead to improved mental and physical health. This ensures higher levels of productivity and improved economic growth.

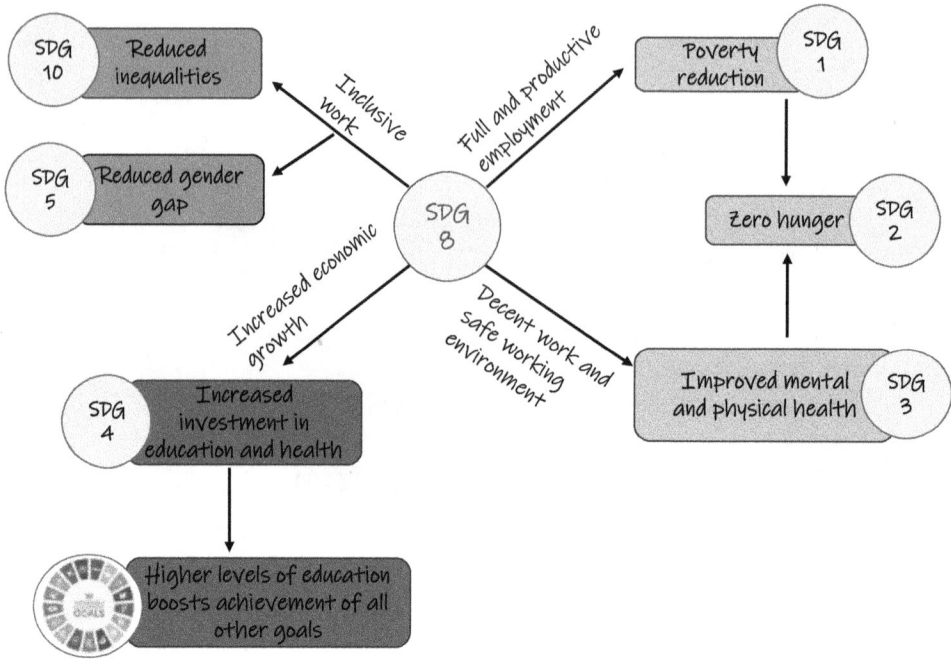

Figure 11.6 Interlinkages between SDG 8 and other SDGs.

Equality at the workplace, reduced poverty and decent employment opportunities help to reduce social inequalities creating more equitable societies (SDG 10). Inclusive and safe working conditions will create more employment opportunities for women and empower them to become independent (SDG 5).

Increased economic growth and improved national wealth will help governments invest more in education and health facilities. Access to quality education will promote youth entrepreneurship and create more job opportunities. Greater levels of educational attainment will also result in increased understanding and awareness of challenges related to sustainable development (SDG 4). This helps individuals to make informed decisions and promote resilience among individuals. Quality education can be leveraged to make positive progress in all other SDG including SDG 8.

Conclusion

This chapter provides an overview of context and some practical examples for teaching SDG 8. The practical activities are aimed at helping young people to understand the targets related to SDG 8. Overall, the chapter aims to support the work of educators in order to teach SDG 8 successfully. The reflection exercises require teachers to consider aspects of SDG 8 alongside their own practice in classrooms and whole school practice. This brings us to the final reflection activity for this chapter.

REFLECTIVE TASK 4

What are you doing already that supports teaching SDG 8? What other individual or whole school practices are teachers in your school already doing? What opportunities are there for linking with other school subject teachers and/or other whole school initiatives and/or local communities to strengthen teaching SDG 8 in your school?

Helen O'Connor, Deputy Principal of Abbey Community College, Waterford, Ireland (2020: 35) recalls the journey her school has undertaken to integrate the SDGs. She describes how they began by 'reflecting on what we were already doing', from this reflective task they choose to focus on SDG 8 as it was felt student voice and justice were already central aspects of their school culture. The school focused on topics such as human trafficking, women's suffrage and gender inequalities, unemployment, and employment rights. Engagement in these areas in a way which linked in with what the school was already doing and enhancing the school's strengths even further was deemed to successfully start the schools SDG integration journey and raise awareness of SDG 8 topics. Using such an integration approach and engaging with the suggestions and resources mentioned in this chapter supports engagement with SDG 8 in your classroom and school.

Helpful resources

Topic	Link
Supporting children's rights through education, the arts, and media (SCREAM): Education Pack	https://www.ilo.org/ipec/Informationresources/WCMS_IPEC_PUB_1559/lang--en/index.htm
ILO's Global music against child labour initiative	https://www.ilo.org/colombo/info/pub/pr/WCMS_730785/lang--en/index.htm
Song on child labour- *Till everyone can see*	https://www.youtube.com/watch?v=qHNgfStLwNc
Advocacy- World day against child labour	https://www.ilo.org/ipec/Campaignandadvocacy/Youthinaction/WCMS_113843/lang--en/index.htm
Children rights – Various activities and lesson plans	http://gc2000.rutgers.edu/GC2000/MODULES/CHILD_RIGHTS/reorganizing.htm
Simulation activities	https://www.worldvision.com.au/docs/default-source/school-resources/simulation-and-activities.pdf?sfvrsn=0 https://www.tutor2u.net/economics/reference/economic-growth-key-word-chop-activity
Interactive game	https://developmenteducation.ie/resource/the-paper-bag-game/
Role play activities	https://children.salvationarmy.org.nz/sites/default/files/files/lesson3-poverty-simulation-game-and-resources_0.pdf

(Continued)

(Continued)

Topic	Link
Fairtrade in Ireland	https://developmenteducation.ie/blog/2015/03/top-10-facts-about-the-fairtrade-movement-in-ireland/
SDG 8 resources for educators	https://en.unesco.org/themes/education/sdgs/material/08
Global goals – useful Websites	https://worldslargestlesson.globalgoals.org/global-goals/good-jobs-and-economic/
	Global Goals: *www.globalgoals.org*
	World's largest lesson: *www.tes.com/worldslargestlesson*
Lesson plans for teachers	https://earthbeat.sk.ca/pdf/lessonplan/worldbeat/2013/10/Child-Labour-Activity-2-Complete.pdf
	http://tve.org/reframing-rio/schoolresources/pdf/meethechildrenofrio_41.pdf?static=1
	https://www.amnesty.org.au/wp-content/uploads/2017/01/Child-Labour-Lesson-Plan.pdf
	https://www.socialstudies.com/pdf/ZP865TG.pdf
	https://www.loc.gov/classroom-materials/child-labor-in-america/#procedure

Children's literature for SDG 8 (8–12 years, primary students)

Adler, D. A. and Miller, E. (illus) (2016) *Prices! Prices! Prices! Why They Go Up and Down* Holiday House Inc; Illustrated edition.

Baccelliere, A. and Ale & Ale (illus) (2017) *I Like, I Don't Like* Eerdmans Books for Young Readers.

Berlak, A. (2015) *Joelito's Big Decision/ La Gran Decisión de Joelito* Hard Ball Press.

Brown, D. (2004) *Kid Blink Beats The World* Roaring Brook Press.

Brown, M. and Cepeda, J. (Illus) (2010) *Side by Side: The Story of Dolores Huerta and César Chavez* HarperCollins.

Cohn, D. (2005) *¡Si, Se Puede!/Yes, We Can! Janitor Strike In L.A.* Cinco Puntos Press.

Cronin, D. (2003) *Click, Clack, Moo Cows That Type* Simon & Schuster.

Deitz Shea, P. and Morin, L. (Illus) (2003) *The Carpet Boy's Gift* Tilbury House Publishers.

Ellla Lyon, G. and Cardinale, C. (illus) (2011) Which Side Are You On? The story of a song Cinco Puntos Press.

Faye Duncan, A. (2018) *Memphis, Martin, and the Mountaintop: The Sanitation Strike of 1968* Calkins Creek Books.

Hernandez Madrigal, A. (2001) *Earndi's Braids* Putnam Publishing Group, U.S.

Hinrichs, A.S..D., and Garland, M. (illus) (2021) *The Travelling Camera: Lewis Hine and the Fight to End Child Labor* Getty Publications.

Hopkinson, D. and Caldwell, K. (illus) (2020) *Thanks to Frances Perkins: Fighter for Worker's Rights* Peachtree Publishing Company.

Howard, G. and Kirk Noll, C. (illus) (2002) *A Basket of Bangles: How a Business Begins* Millbrook Press.

Khan, R. and Himler, R. (illus) (2004). *The Roses in My Carpets* Fitzhenry & Whiteside.

Kulling, M. (2016) *On Our Way to Oyster Bay: Mother Jones and her March for Children's Rights* Kids Can Press.

Malaspina, A. and Chayka, D. (illus) (2016) *Yasmin's Hammer* Lee and Low.

Markel, M and Sweet, M. (illus) (2013) *Brave Girl: Clara and the Shirtwaist Makers' Strike of 1909* Harper Collins.

Smith Milway, K. and Fernandes, E. (illus) (2009) *One Hen* Kids Can Press.

Whelan, G. and Milelli, P. (illus) (2009) *Waiting for the Owl's Call* Sleeping Bear Press.

Winter, J. and Carpenter, N. (illus) (2020) *Mother Jones and Her Army of Mill Children* Schwartz and Wade

Yoo, P. and Akib, J. (illus) (2014) *Twenty-Two Cents: Muhammad Yunus and the Village Bank* Lee and Low Books.

Young people's literature for SDG 8 (12–17 years, post-primary students)

Auxier, J. (2018) *Sweep: The Story of a Girl and her Monster* Abrams Books.

Burgan, M. (2011) *Breaker Boys: How a Photograph Helped end Child Labour* Compass Point Books.

D'Adamo, F. (2005) *Iqbal* Aladdin Paperbacks.

Dee Humphreys, J., Chikwanine, M. and Dávilla, C. (illus) (2015) *Child Soldier: When Boys and Girls Are Used in War* Franklin Watts; Illustrated edition.

Dickens, C. (1992) *David Copperfield* Wordsworth Editions.

Doherty, B. (2009) *Street Child* HarperCollins Children's Books

Ellis, D. (2008) *I am a Taxi* Groundwood Books Ltd.

Fernandez Prados, E. (2016) *Economics Through Everyday Stories from Around the World* Create Space Independent Publishing Platform.

Fletcher, C. (2008) *Ten Cents a Dancer* Bloomsbury

Forchuk Skrypuch, M. (2019) *Making Bombs for Hitler* Scholastic.

Greenwood, B. (2007) *Factory Girl* Kids Can Press

Hall, S. and Wysocky, L. (2014) *Hidden Girl: The True Story of a Modern-Day Child Slave* Simon & Schuster Books for Young Readers.

Jacob, A. (2019) *The Courage of Elfina* Lorimer Children & Teens.

Jimenez, F. (1997) *The Circuit: Stories From the Life of a Migrant Child* University of New Mexico Press.

Johnson, M. (2017) *Kick* Usborne Publishing Ltd.

Kelly, L. (2012) *Chained* Farrar, Straus and Giroux (BYR).

Kirby, M. J. (2010) *The Clockwork Three* Scholastic.

Lynne, K. (2012) *Chained* Farrar Straus Giroux.

Marrin, A. (2015) *Flesh and Blood So Cheap: The Triangle Fire and Its Legacy* Random House Books for Young Readers.

McCormick, P. (2008) *Sold* Walker Books.

McCormick, P. (2013) *Never Fall Down* Corgi Childrens.

Nelson, S.D. (2014) *Digging a Hole to Heaven* Abrams Books for Young Readers; Illustrated edition.

Paterson, K. (2008) *Bread and Roses, Too* Clarion Books

Perkins, M. and Hogan, J. (illus) (2008). *Rickshaw Girl* Charlesbridge Publishing.

Polonsky, A. (2016) *Threads* Disney-Hyperion.

Porter, T. (2013) *Creekmore* HarperCollins.

Saeed, A. (2018) *Amal Unbound* Nancy Paulsen Books.

Sheth, K. (2011) *Boys Without Names* Balzer + Bray.

Sullivan, T. (2017) *Bitter Side of Sweet* Speak.

Williams, M. (2015) *Diamond Boy* Tamarind.

Winthrop, E. (2007) *Counting on Grace* Random House.

Yang, K. (2019) *Front Desk* Arthur A. Levine Books.

Key dates

First Monday of May: *Labour Day (International Workers' Day)*

June 12: *World Day Against Child labour*

August 9: *International Day of the World's Indigenous Peoples*

October 11: *International Day of the Girl Child*

December 2: *International Day for the Abolition of Slavery*

References

Coopman, A., Osborn, D., Ullah, F., Auckland, E. and Long, G. (2016). *Seeing the Whole: Implementing the SDGs in an Integrated and Coherent Way*. Research Pilot Report. Stakeholder Forum for a Sustainable Future. London.

Dioum, B. (1968). *Speech Presented at the International Union for Conservation of Nature*, New Delhi: India.

Financial Justice Ireland (2020). *Resources and Publications*, available at https://www.financialjustice.ie/resources/

Freire, P. (1990). *Pedagogy of the Oppressed*, New York: Continuum.

Frey, D. F. (2017). Economic growth, full employment and decent work: The means and ends in SDG 8. *The International Journal of Human Rights*, 21(8), 1164-1184.

Hicks, D. (2003). *Lessons for the Future: The Missing Dimension in Education*, London: Routledge.

International Labour Office and United Nations Children's Fund (2021). *Child Labour: Global Estimates 2020*, trends and the road forward, New York: ILO and UNICEF.

International Labour Organization (ILO) (2004). *Child Labour: A Textbook for University Students,* available at: http://www.ilo.org/ipecinfo/product/download.do?type=document&id=174

International Labour Organization (ILO) (2016). World Employment and Social Outlook: Trends 2016.

International Labour Organization (ILO) (2022). World Employment and Social Outlook – Trends 2022.

Le Blanc, D. (2015). *Towards Integration at Last? The Sustainable Development Goals As a Network of Targets*. United Nations Department of Economic and Social Affairs (UN DESA), Working Paper No.141

Lynch, K. (2010). Carelessness: A hidden doxa of higher education. *Arts and Humanities in Higher Education*, 9(1), 54-67.

Lynch, K., Grummell, B. and Devine, D. (2012). *New Managerialism in Education. Commercialisation, Carelessness and Gender*, New York: Palgrave Macmillan.

Nilsson, M., Griggs, D. and Visbeck, M. (2016). Map the interactions between sustainable development goals. *Nature*, 534, 320-322.

O'Connor, H. (2020). Sustainable Development Goals; Our journey so far. *ETBI Journal of Education*, 2(1), June 2020, 35-39.

UNICEF (2021a). *Child Labour Rises to 160 Million – First Increase in Two Decades*, available at https://www.unicef.org/press-releases/child-labour-rises-160-million-first-increase-two-decades (Accessed: 20 June 2021).

UNICEF (2021b). *UNICEF Data*, available at https://data.unicef.org/topic/child-protection/child-labour/ (Accessed: 29 April 2021).

United Nations (2015). *The UN Sustainable Development Goals*, New York: United Nations.

United Nations (2017). Resolution adopted by the General Assembly on 6 July 2017, Work of the Statistical Commission pertaining to the 2030 Agenda for Sustainable Development (A/RES/71/313).

United Nations (2019). *Review of SDG Implementation and Interrelations Among Goals*. United Nations High Level Political Forum on Sustainable Development, available at https://sustainabledevelopment.un.org/hlpf/2019 (Accessed: 22 July 2020).

United Nations (UN) (2020). *Sustainable Development Goals*, available at https://www.un.org/sustainabledevelopment/sustainable-development-goals/ (Accessed: 20 July 2020).

United Nations Department of Economic and Social Affairs (UN DESA) (2019). *An Expert Group Meeting in Preparation for HLPF (2019) Empowering People and Ensuring Inclusiveness and Equality.* https://sustainabledevelopment.un.org/content/documents/21441EGM_SDG_8_Concept_Note_15_Feb_2019.pdf

United Nations Educational, Scientific and Cultural Organisation (UNESCO) (2020). *SDG Resources for Educators - Decent Work and Economic Growth*, available at https://en.unesco.org/themes/education/sdgs/material

12 Building a better future through industry, innovation and infrastructure (SDG 9)

Sara Hannafin

Introduction

SDG 9 recognises the role of innovation and the importance of reliable and resilient infrastructure to support and develop sustainable industry and employment around the world. Zhang et al. (2019) describes it as the backbone for all the Sustainable Development Goals since appropriate industrial development has a direct impact on the economic growth of a country. A country with a healthy economy is more likely to be able to tackle poverty and to provide adequate education and healthcare and thus be able to reach the targets of a range of other Goals. Goal 9 recognises the need for employment which provides a living wage and links this with the development of infrastructure, such as transport, water supply, energy and information and communication technology. Despite some exceptions, economic growth has occurred at the expense of the environment and the health of people. By reframing thinking on industrial and infrastructural development to consider innovations which enhance well-being and sustainability, we acknowledge our responsibility to our fellow global citizens as well as to the generations to come.

Thinking about industrial growth and change, the development of infrastructure and the need for innovation around these might feel distant from students' lives. This chapter aims to bridge this gap and provide activities which help our students to consider the importance of innovative industrial and infrastructural developments for a healthy economy and society. It outlines why we may need to rethink the way we teach economic geography, how we can make more explicit links between industry and innovation and the role of reliable infrastructure in this. It suggests how looking at local, historical industrial developments can help students appreciate how their local area developed and understand how past industry has shaped their current places in ways that were previously unnoticed. The chapter raises awareness about often taken for granted infrastructure and its importance as part of a functioning economy. In this way, students can gain a sense of people's lives in the past and an insight into lives in the present. The chapter also introduces the idea of the circular economy (Ellen MacArthur Foundation), one which enables sustainable economic growth while also designing out waste and pollution. This is an innovative way of rethinking how our economy can continue to function without further environmental degradation and is key to enabling the success of SDG 9.

DOI: 10.4324/9781003232001-15

The three strands of SDG 9 – industry, innovation and infrastructure

Sustainable Development Goal 9 seeks to promote inclusive and sustainable industrialisation, through fostering innovation and building resilient infrastructure. This SDG encompasses three important aspects of sustainable development: industrialisation, innovation and infrastructure. Terminology associated with SDG 9 is set out in Table 12.1. Learning objectives associated with SDG 9 are listed in Table 12.2.

Table 12.1 SDG 9 key words

Industry: the production of goods or related services within an economy.
Innovation: a new idea, a new product or a new way of doing something.
Infrastructure: the facilities and systems which enable a place (country, city or small area) to function.
Circular economy: an economy in which materials move through a cycle of use and thereby waste and pollution are eliminated.

Table 12.2 SDG 9 learning objectives UNESCO (2020: 28)

Cognitive learning objectives Teaching **about** the goals: developing respect and understanding	1	The learner understands the concepts of sustainable infrastructure and industrialisation and society's needs for a systemic approach to their development.
	2	The learner understands the local, national and global challenges and conflicts in achieving sustainability in infrastructure and industrialisation.
	3	The learner can define the term resilience in the context of infrastructure and spatial planning, understanding key concepts such as modularity and diversity, and apply it to their local community and nationwide.
	4	The learner knows the pitfalls of unsustainable industrialisation and in contrast knows examples of resilient, inclusive, sustainable industrial development and the need for contingency planning.
	5	The learner is aware of new opportunities and markets for sustainability innovation, resilient infrastructure and industrial development.
Socio-emotional learning objectives Teaching **for** the goals enhancing empathy and love	1	The learner is able to argue for sustainable, resilient and inclusive infrastructure in their local area.
	2	The learner is able to encourage their communities to shift their infrastructure and industrial development toward more resilient and sustainable forms.
	3	The learner is able to find collaborators to develop sustainable and contextual industries that respond to our shifting challenges and also to reach new markets.
	4	The learner is able to recognise and reflect on their own personal demands on the local infrastructure such as their carbon and water footprints and food miles.
	5	The learner is able to understand that with changing resource availability (e.g. peak oil, peak everything) and other external shocks and stresses (e.g. natural hazards, conflicts) their own perspective and demands on infrastructure may need to shift radically regarding availability of renewable energy for ICT, transport options, sanitation options, etc.

(Continued)

Table 12.2 (Continued)

Behavioural learning objectives Teaching **through** the goals Promoting advocacy and activism	1	The learner is able to identify opportunities in their own culture and nation for greener and more resilient approaches to infrastructure, understanding their overall benefits for societies, especially with regard to disaster risk reduction.
	2	The learner is able to evaluate various forms of industrialisation and compare their resilience.
	3	The learner is able to innovate and develop sustainable enterprises to respond to their countries' industrial needs.
	4	The learner is able to access financial services such as loans or microfinance to support their own enterprises.
	5	The learner is able to work with decision-makers to improve the uptake of sustainable infrastructure (including internet access).

Industrial development and local area studies

Industry as a school topic has traditionally been taught in terms of primary, secondary, tertiary and more recently, quaternary, sectors. In this trajectory, 'work' moves from the gathering or extraction of raw materials and physical labour, such as farming or mining, to more service-based employment such as tourism, finance or research and development. Implicit in this is the assumption that all economies follow a similar trajectory and that as an economy develops and grows there is a decline in the primary or extractive industries and an increase in the service jobs in the tertiary or quaternary sector. Levels of economic development can therefore be measured by the percentages of people employed in the different sectors. This model applies particularly well to economic growth in 19th-century Britain following the Industrial Revolution and this may be a useful starting point for discussing SDG 9. In many of our villages, towns and cities it is possible to find evidence of previous industrial development (in the Irish context see Rynne, 2006, for detail) thus there is an opportunity for local area studies and use of old photographs, maps or fieldwork to investigate this further. In some parts of Ireland there were small scale mines for copper, lead, silver and coal. In other parts are disused grain stores and mills, typically built close to the crops which supplied them. In addition, old bridges, canals and railways are all evidence of the infrastructure which supported our industry. Investigating the local built heritage enhances the connection of students with their local place, helps them appreciate how and why places change over time and encourages them to think about how the growth or decline of industry may also impact people's lives in other places.

In Ireland, the website of the Heritage Council (heritagemaps.ie) provides a series of maps on which students can identify features of the local area and compare these with historical maps. This is a useful way of researching the industrial past of a place, especially where there may be little evidence of it in everyday life. It also introduces the basic use of Geographic Information Systems (GIS) to students. One example of where local industrial heritage can be evidenced through such map work can be found in the area around Arigna, Co. Roscommon. The historic 6 Inch map for the area was created by the Ordnance Survey in Ireland between 1829 and 1841 and shows coal pits and the Arigna Iron Works which were of major significance to the local economy. Subsequent maps, which can be layered over this map using heritagemaps.ie, show the coal pits and iron works as disused although coal continued to be mined in the area until 1990. Students can try to imagine what life might have been like in the area when the coal pits and iron works were active and how the place changed once they closed.

In some places, it is the case that the example of primary or secondary industry around which the place may have developed is now a tourist facility and thus is an example of tertiary sector employment. In Arigna, Co. Roscommon, investment aimed at preserving the mining heritage of the area and boosting the local economy enabled the establishment of the Arigna Mining Experience which was opened in 2003. Similar visitor attractions can be found all over Ireland from small scale examples, such as Foxford Woollen Mills in Co. Mayo and Blennerville Windmill in Co. Kerry to the Guinness Storehouse in Dublin.

Linking industry and innovation

The United Nations designated 21 April as World Creativity and Innovation Day, to raise the awareness of the role of creativity and innovation in all aspects of human development.

Achieving the 2030 Agenda for Sustainable Development and the 17 SDGs, the most ambitious development agenda in human history, requires both creativity and innovation.

While teaching about industry is often seen as part of the geography curriculum, SDG 9 offers a way of linking geography with the STEM subjects, humanities and business studies. SDG 9 recognises the importance of innovative and creative thinking in order to stimulate appropriate industrial development. This includes innovations which solve problems of past industrial development such as polluted soil or derelict buildings as well as innovations which foster future new industries. Having researched the industrial heritage of the local area, students could then consider the possible futures of the built environment thus further enriching their knowledge of and engagement with place. One aspect of the work of Historic England (historicengland.org.uk) is to protect, conserve and manage change in England's industrial and transport heritage and their website gives a number of examples of the successful repurposing of old industrial buildings and sites. This includes, for example, the conversion of *The Custard Factory* (the original site for the production of *Bird's Custard*) in Birmingham, into space for small businesses and the conversion of a former tobacco factory in Newcastle to residential use. The website provides examples of what they describe as 'heritage at risk' and projects which have rescued several old industrial buildings. In the classroom, the website could be used to search for former industrial buildings in the local area. They also give advice on how to save an old building which could be used to stimulate class discussions of the best use for abandoned industrial sites.

Innovative thinking is also essential to developing new forms of industry and infrastructure which support economic development and are also environmentally sustainable. It recognises the role of imagination in allowing us to see a problem from a different or new perspective or bringing into being, something which does not currently exist. The story of Jessica Matthews (myfounderstory.com) is an excellent example of using imaginative thinking to meet a need for innovation. While an undergraduate student in the US, she co-created the SOCCKET, an energy-generating soccer ball. This is a soccer ball that uses the kinetic energy created in its movement, converting it into a renewable and mobile energy source. For every thirty minutes of movement the *Soccket* can supply three hours of light, it can therefore meet the needs of those who have no permanent or constant electrical supply. Jessica's innovation was inspired by a visit to her family in Nigeria who regularly met power outages with a diesel generator. Since her initial idea, Jessica has gone on to develop her own company, *Uncharted Power,* which works towards developing sustainable infrastructure solutions in cities. Further examples of innovative thinking are described below with reference to the circular economy.

Infrastructure

Infrastructure refers to the systems and services a country needs in order to function properly. It includes the road and railway networks, water supply and sewage systems, electricity and gas supplies as well as telephone and internet connectivity. For many of us, infrastructure is something only noticed when it stops working properly and our taken-for-granted behaviours have to be adjusted in some way. In the classroom, students can try to imagine how different their school day would be if there was no electricity or water in the school or how different their journey to school might be without a reliable road or public transport network. The archives of the ESB in Ireland (esbarchives.ie) document the introduction of electricity across Ireland during the 20th century and can be used to investigate the changes that electricity brought to the country. As well as learning about how their local places have changed since the introduction of this vital infrastructure, researching this topic may also help students appreciate the lives of others around the world who have yet to receive a reliable electricity supply.

There are significant differences in the availability of key infrastructure around the world thus compounding global inequalities. More than 2.5 billion people lack access to basic sanitation, three in ten people do not have access to safe drinking water and 3.8 billion people do not have access to the internet (United Nations). Developing sustainable infrastructure is vital as it affects so much of our daily lives. It improves the well-being of the population and, with reference to SDG 9, it supports the success of sustainable industrial development.

One significant infrastructural necessity is that of access to information and communications technology. The increased demand, the speed at which it has been implemented and the way it has changed our lives can be equated to the spread of electricity infrastructure in the 19th and 20th centuries. Reliable access to mobile cellular services allows people access to global information flows and is now as important to economic growth as a reliable power or water supply. As well as information, access to internet services allows for increased mobile financial transactions and banking services. Hence, access to high-speed broadband, can make an important contribution to the economic status of individuals and families as well as to national economic growth. Writing in the E-magazine, *Africa Renewal,* Joel Macharia (2013) reports on the impact of fibre-optic cables connecting Africa with the Americas, Europe and Asia. This has enabled new business opportunities which benefit from being able to communicate globally and access online financial services. Internet use across the continent of Africa rose by over 3,000% between 2000 and 2012 and in Kenya by over 9,000% illustrating the demand which the fibre optic cable infrastructure met. However, uneven access endures on a more local scale with a continuing need to develop fibre-optic networks and connection within countries (Macharia, ibid). By investing in this technology, governments recognise that flows of information and communication improve life for all across a range of areas. A functioning infrastructure is therefore an essential element of SDG 9, enabling the growth of industry and employment across a range of scales.

New thinking on industrial and infrastructural development – the idea of a circular economy

A circular economy is one which involves extending the life cycle of an item by reusing, repairing, sharing, upcycling or recycling the product or its constituent materials. Economic growth has typically taken a 'take, make, waste' approach in which we are *consumers* and has been dependent on the exploitation of our natural resources with little consideration for the impact on the environment of the extraction process or of the waste created by our growing consumption. In contrast, the circular economy recognises the need to preserve the finite resources available to us by designing out waste. Instead of buying and consuming something there is increased use of leasing, renting or sharing and in this way the *consumer* is replaced with the idea of the *user* of a product. By using less and for longer the circular economy needs fewer raw materials, therefore the subsequent reduction in extraction also protects habitats and reduces pollution. The transition to a circular economy requires new ways of thinking. It requires innovation in how we use resources and what happens at the end of life of a product. One of the challenges of such a change is that it can be seen as a threat to the taken-for-granted ways in which we live, particularly in the wealthier countries. It is for this reason that we need to see such changes as improving lives for all. In teaching about lives in other places, we help students make connections with other people and recognise our global interdependence. In addition, it is important to acknowledge the complexities of moving to a circular economy. Some of the required changes may have negative impacts on employment, standard of living and the economy. Consequently, there is a need for innovative thinking to stimulate new economic opportunities which focus on reuse, refurbishing, remanufacture, recycling, anaerobic digestion and composting (Ellen MacArthur Foundation).

Increasingly, companies are recognising the need for circular thinking in developing their business models. In Vancouver, the website of *ChopValue* states that it aims, 'to make a difference one chopstick at a time'. It is a company which works to create a second life for used chopsticks and since its beginnings in 2017, the company has recycled over 32 million (Kassam 2021). These small, seemingly insignificant items are made from bamboo, travel 9,600 km from China to reach the restaurants of north western Canada and after 20–30 minutes of use, typically end up in landfill. *ChopValue* collects, cleans and repurposes the chopsticks into, for example, tiles, table tops and wall décor and resells them through a number of outlets in north America (see chopvalue.com). It is a good example of how making small changes and seeking creative solutions can cumulatively contribute to big improvements in the way we live. What everyday items do our students use both at school and at home which could be repurposed to extend their life and prevent them going to landfill? A class survey could promote some innovative thinking on items perhaps currently taken for granted.

In addition to the things we use, the circular economy is key to thinking on infrastructural developments. Infrastructure projects require large investments of capital, often from governments and therefore need to both support economic development and be sustainable in themselves over the long term. Building roads, rail networks, energy or water supply schemes all help support a growing population, but can also have negative impacts on the environment. Innovative approaches are needed to protect fragile habitats and species and to prevent further pollution of our ecosystems.

Infrastructure to support the recycling or reuse of resources is a key component of the circular economy. In the example above, the founder of *ChopValue* began by supplying local restaurants with chopstick recycling bins. On a larger scale, the separation of waste into plastic and paper for recycling is an established feature of waste disposal in many parts of the world. Water reclamation is a further example of how investment in infrastructure can protect water as a resource. Water reclamation involves obtaining wastewater from a range of sources, treating it and reusing it to water gardens or for toilet flushing. On a larger scale it can be used in industrial processes, environmental restoration, irrigation, and groundwater replenishment. This innovative solution to wastewater requires infrastructure such as new pipes and pumps to divert the grey water (used water from bathroom sinks, showers, baths, washing machines and some industrial process) away from sewers and into treatment sites, irrigation systems or toilet cisterns. It is one example of how infrastructure projects can contribute to protecting resources, reductions in waste and the circular economy.

The website of the Ellen MacArthur Foundation explores the circular economy in more detail. It explains the thinking behind it, gives many examples of its application and provides teaching resources. Figure 12.1 shows the Butterfly diagram which summarises how the circular economy works.

The diagram illustrates a continuous flow of materials in the economy. The diagram is divided into two parts, the left showing the cycle of biological materials and the right showing the cycle of technical materials. In the biological cycle, composting and anaerobic digestion encourage materials to biodegrade thus returning nutrients to the earth and allowing the land to regenerate and continue to produce biological materials. In the technical cycle the focus is on reuse, repair, remanufacture and recycling so that the component materials are kept in use and do not become waste.

Instead of focusing solely on individual citizens' actions, supporting a circular economy reminds us that it is businesses and corporations that create the very products that pollute the earth, thus leaving them with an immense responsibility to mandate sustainable production processes from beginning to end.

In line with the circular economy and the European Green Deal, the European Commission has introduced a new 'right to repair' for consumers. Up to now replacement has often been prioritised over repair whenever products become defective and insufficient incentives have been given to consumers to repair their goods when the legal guarantee expires. The proposal will make it easier and more cost-effective for consumers to repair as opposed to replace goods.

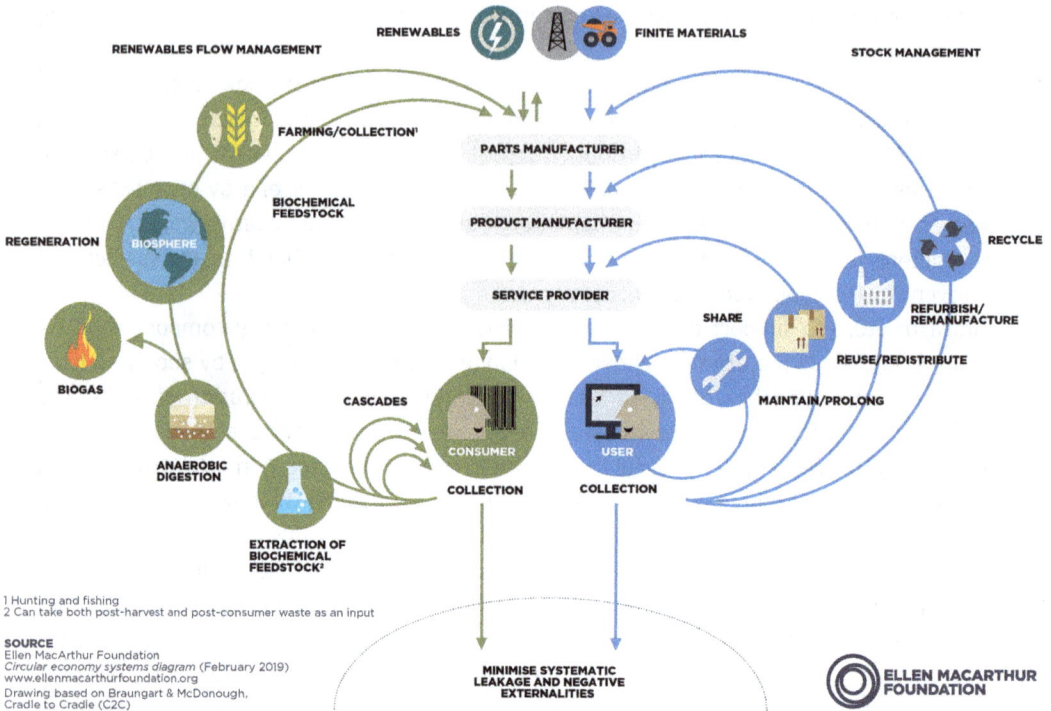

Figure 12.1 The Butterfly Diagram: Visualising the Circular Economy. (Source: Ellen MacArthur Foundation Source https://ellenmacarthurfoundation.org/circular-economy-diagram)

There are 8 rs (including repair) associated with the circular economy as follows:

Rethink: Consider how things are made including their environmental impact and if they really need to be purchased.

Repair: Our parents and grandparents had excellent skills in repairing different items. We need to re discover some of these skills.

Reuse: Repurpose and reuse items that you have

Reduce: Stop buying goods, only buy items were are needed. Just because an item is available at a good price, does not mean that it should be purchased for the sake of a bargain.

Refuse: Say no and re think. There is no need to buy new clothes every year. Children do not need massive mountains of plastic toys. Say 'no'.

Recycle: while it is important to recyle, this is only part of the overall solution

Recover: recover goods that are on their way to being discarded. A good example of this is the redirection of food (close to expiring) from stores to re-distribution sites.

Regift: think about the long term impact of gifts. Money is always an option. Your unwanted gifts might be very welcome for others. Don't let gifts pile up in a corner.

Biomimicry: Innovation inspired by nature

Biomimicry is the process of copying the natural world and its systems. Originating from the Greek word 'bio' meaning life, and 'mimesis' meaning to imitate, biomimicry is the study of how nature solves problems relating to living organisms. Biomimicry is the practice of applying lessons from nature to the invention of healthier, more sustainable technologies for people. It is a design approach that uses models and systems found in nature to create sustainable solutions. Biomimetic designers ('biomimics') focus on understanding, learning from, and emulating the strategies used by living things, with the intention of creating designs and technologies that are sustainable.

Janine Benyus (2002:2) co-founder of the Biomimicry Institute describes biomimicry as 'the conscious emulation of life's genius', that is:

- 'Conscious': being intentional
- 'Emulation': learning from living things, then applying those insights to the challenges humans want to solve.
- 'Life's genius': recognizing that life has arrived at well-adapted solutions that have stood the test of time, within the constraints of a planet with finite resources.

With biomimicry, we can develop new products, processes, and systems, or improve existing designs. It can help us to shift our perspective, see design problems and objectives differently, and uncover 'new' solutions to difficult problems.

Leonardo da Vinci, a visionary who merged art and design to perfection, is arguably the founding father of biomimicry. Today, there are many examples of innovation inspired by nature. Perhaps the most famous example of biomimicry is Velcro. In 1941, engineer George de Mestral was walking his dog when he noticed burrs) sticking to both of them. When he studied the burrs under magnification, he found their clinging property was the result of hundreds of tiny hooks. In London, the 30 St Mary Axe skyscraper, colloquially known as 'The Gherkin' – was inspired by a marine animal called a Venus Flower Basket. In Japan, the design of bullet trains has been inspired by the Kingfisher bird. There is infinite potential for us to learn from nature. As Benyus (2002:2) states 'unlike the Industrial Revolution, the Biomimicry Revolution introduces an era based not one what we can extract from nature, but on what we can learn from her'. In the classroom, just imagine what can happen when our students, inspired by the natural world, learn and work as biomimetic designers ('biomimics')!

Practical classroom activities

Inventions and innovators

Investigating innovation and innovators (Target 9.5)

Students investigate people who were innovative thinkers in their time as an individual, group or class activity and present their findings to the class or with a visual display. Encourage students to reflect on what stimulated the innovation and what supports were available to the individual they are researching. This is a way of highlighting the ongoing importance of investing in and supporting research. It is interesting to note that some of the innovations that have had the most impact on us were accidental discoveries. Alexander Fleming's discovery of penicillin is perhaps the most famous example. More relevant to the pencil cases and school bags in the classroom might be to investigate Velcro (discussed above). Some examples of people who led innovation in the past are given in Table 12.3.

Table 12.3 Innovators past and present

Research the work of the following people.	
Thomas Edison	Anthony Mutu
Patricia Bath	Albert Einstein
Margaret Knight	Maria Telkes
Alexander Fleming	Johan Van Veen
Walt Disney	Leonardo Di Vinci
Ada Lovelace	John Blume
Steve Jobs	Marie Curie
When and where did/do they live? What did they invent? Why was it needed? How has it changed our lives? How do we use it today?	

Innovation in the present (Target 9.1, 9.4, 9A, 9B)

Geographical mystery – what should be done with Seville's oranges? (Adapted from Burgen, 2021))

Mysteries are used in geography to address real world problem solving. They start with an enquiry question from which students are given a set of statements. Working in groups, the task is to digest and organise what can seem to be discrete sets of information (Table 12.4) and suggest a solution to a problem.

Instructions to students:

You are the head of Seville City Council in southern Spain. You need to decide what to do with the problems caused by orange trees in Seville. Locate Seville in your atlas and find out about the climate in this part of Europe. Read the statements below and identify the options for Seville. Explain what you think is the best solution. Present your decision to your fellow councillors orally or through a written explanation.

Table 12.4 Set of statements for geographical mystery – What should be done with Seville's oranges?

Seville smells sweet with orange blossom in the spring time.	Seville has 48 thousand orange trees which were originally introduced by the Arabs 1000 years ago.	If all the city's oranges were recycled and the energy put back into the grid, 73,000 homes could be powered.
The oranges are exported to Britain to make marmalade	The oranges taste bitter and local people don't eat them.	As the oranges ferment, they create methane which can be used to generate electricity.
On his way to school in Autumn, Pablo loves to look at the flies which gather around the rotting fruit.	The oranges look pretty on the trees and are an iconic feature of Seville.	1,000kg of oranges will produce enough electricity for five homes for one day.
The problem of rotting fruit on roads and footpaths would be solved if the trees were cut down.	Seville needs new investment in its water purification plants which use almost 40% of the energy needed to provide the city with drinking water and sanitation.	The oranges often end up in landfill.
The trees thrive in the climate of southern Spain.		When Pablo's teacher walks to school she finds her shoes are sticky from walking across the squashed fruit which has fallen.

The squashed tomatoes challenge (practicalaction.org)

This is a classroom activity created by Practical Action (practicalaction.org), an international development organisation which focuses on innovations to help people in poverty to develop solutions and create change. The Squashed Tomato Challenge is aimed at students aged 8-16 and is based on some of the problems faced by farmers in Nepal. It supports the teaching of the STEM subjects and could be used as a case study for Junior Certificate or GCSE geography students (13-16 years).

Background: In Nepal the many farmers who grow fruit and vegetables live in mountainous areas. The journey to sell their products at the local market takes them on a long and dangerous walk down the mountain after which time their products may be a bit squashed.

Activity: Design, build and test a way of moving tomatoes that won't squash them.

The challenge creates opportunities for team working, problem solving and presentation skills, it reinforces learning from the science and design technology curriculum and shows students how STEM can help solve global issues and achieve the Sustainable Development Goals.

Homework activity 1- innovation and everyday life (Target 9.5)

What has changed in the everyday lives of the student's parents and/or grandparents to make life better? For this homework activity, students ask parents and/or grandparents for examples of things that exist now that didn't exist when they were students and how that has changed and improved everyday life. If they could go back in time what would be the one thing they would not want to be without? Although mobile phones and the internet are obvious examples, encourage the students to find out about other ways life has changed. It could be something we barely notice nowadays but which was a big change at the time. They could also consider if some of the innovations they have experienced have not been positive ones. This could be followed up with a class debate 'All innovation is good'.

Homework activity 2- living without electricity (Target 9.1)

A nine year old student in Gaelscoil an Ráithín, Limerick made a list of all the things in her home which use electricity (Table 12.5).

The table highlights how essential electricity is to our lives with most items in constant or daily use. This can lead to a discussion of what life would be like without electricity either for a day or permanently. How would we store food, cook and clean? How would we wash and keep warm? What would we do for entertainment or relaxation? A realisation of the way our electrical supply is essential and taken for granted in our lives highlights the need to ensure all people have access to this infrastructure. Without electricity what would we do in the evening after it gets dark? For over 80% of the population of Uganda this is a reality (see caseforchange.com). Without electricity in the evening businesses cannot operate and students cannot study. *Case for Change* describes an innovative approach to this situation in which solar energy is generated in the daytime and can supply power for lights, radios and televisions in the evening.

Table 12.5 How do we use electricity at home?

How Often Is Electricity Used?	Constantly	Daily	Once/Twice Weekly
Television		✓	
Radio		✓	
Fridge/freezer	✓		
Oven		✓	
Kettle		✓	
Microwave		✓	
Washing machine			✓
Tablet charger			
Laptop	✓	✓	
Mobile phone charger			
Boiler	✓	✓	
Lights			
Toaster		✓	✓
Hairdryer			✓
Hoover			✓
Dishwasher		✓	
Cooker		✓	

How does SDG 9 link with the other SDGs?

By supporting the development of industry and employment SDG 9 facilitates the achievement of many of the other SDGs (Figure 12.2).

The links between SDG 9 and other SDGs can be illustrated through a case study on the People's Republic of China. The Beautiful China Initiative (BCI) is a major strategic idea and task proposed at the 18th National Congress of the Communist Party of China (CPC). The BCI is a plan for the sustainable development of the Chinese nation as well as for China to fulfill the United Nations' 2030 Agenda for Sustainable Development. In the broad sense, the Beautiful China Initiative refers to the implementation of the 'five-in-one' strategy of national economic, political, cultural, social and ecological progress in accordance with the principles of national sustainable socioeconomic development, of sustainable use of natural resources and of ecological and environmental protection. 'so as to achieve beautiful scenery, great wealth, harmony between humans and nature, the preservation of cultural heritage and political stability' (Fang et al 2020:692).

Currently, China stands in second position in the world in terms of its Gross Domestic Product (GDP) and China has been progressing rapidly when it comes to industrialisation and urbanisation. Eradication of poverty (SDG 2) has been a very clear political priority. Today 745 million fewer people are living in extreme poverty in China than were 30 years ago. China's achievements in poverty reduction are impressive. Rapid urbanisation and intensified agricultural production have brought greater prosperity and higher living standards, but they have also created high demand for energy and raw materials, increased pressure on ecosystems and related health problems (SDG 3). China's carbon emissions (SDG 13) remain

SDG 9 links to Goals 6, Clean Water and Sanitation, Goal 7, Affordable and Clean Energy and Goal 11, Sustainable Cities and Communities all of which refer to specific aspects of infrastructure.

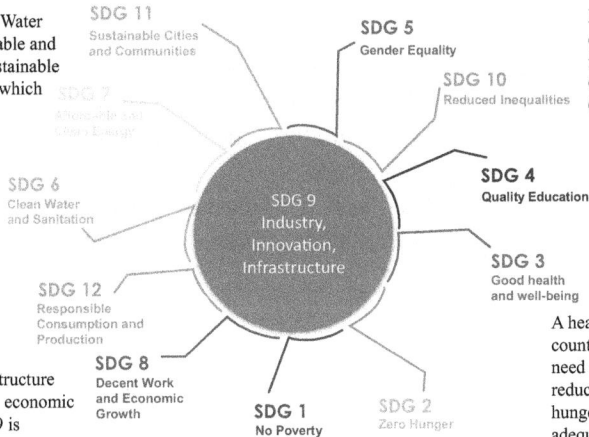

Investing in infrastructure contributes to addressing inequalities thus linking with Goal 5, Gender Equality and Goal 10, Reduced Inequalities.

SDG 11
Sustainable Cities and Communities

SDG 5
Gender Equality

SDG 10
Reduced Inequalities

SDG 7
Affordable and Clean Energy

SDG 6
Clean Water and Sanitation

SDG 9
Industry, Innovation, Infrastructure

SDG 4
Quality Education

SDG 12
Responsible Consumption and Production

SDG 3
Good health and well-being

SDG 8
Decent Work and Economic Growth

SDG 1
No Poverty

SDG 2
Zero Hunger

Industry, innovation and infrastructure are key to enabling sustainable economic growth in a country and SDG 9 is therefore closely linked with Goal 8, Decent Work and Economic Growth and Goal 12, Responsible Consumption and Production.

A healthy economy allows a country to invest in other areas of need and work towards the reduction of poverty (Goal 1), hunger (Goal 2) and to provide adequate healthcare (Goal 3) and education (Goal 4).

Figure 12.2 SDG 9 and the other SDGs.

high. The country remains the world's largest emitter of greenhouse gases accounting for a quarter of total CO_2 emissions, more than the US and the EU combined. However, emissions growth in recent years has decelerated sharply, underpinned by tighter environmental regulation and massive green investments including renewable energy and electric vehicle infrastructure. The SDGs have been criticised because of the clash between the aspiration of industrial growth and how this may impact on climate and environmental issues. However, China has committed itself to ecological conservation and to green, circular and low-carbon development. The Chinese example may therefore be one to learn from into the future in terms of sustainable growth.

Conclusion

This chapter has highlighted the importance of SDG 9: Industry, Innovation and Infrastructure in meeting the UN targets for sustainable development. Sustainable development of industry and infrastructure is essential to economic growth. This can potentially (subject to political decisions) ensure the reduction in poverty and allow for investment in health and education therefore contributing to improving quality of life for all. A focus on developments which consider the impact on the environment also considers the protection of habitats and prevents further loss of biodiversity. The case studies and activities in this chapter suggest approaches to teaching the significance of this goal in the classroom and link the need for the development of industry and infrastructure with investment which is sustainable in the long term.

Resources

An extensive list of resources, videos and case studies for SDG 9 is included in the SDG padlet accompanying this book: https://padlet.com/annedolan/o6rds38ylfy6a28h

Weblinks

Squashed Tomato: https://practicalaction.org/schools/squashed-tomato-challenge/
TED (2015) *The surprising thing I learned sailing solo around the world*. Available: https://www.ted.com/talks/dame_ellen_macarthur_the_surprising_thing_i_learned_sailing_solo_around_the_world [accessed 1 October 2020].
The Heritage Council. https://heritagemaps.ie/ [accessed 29 March 2021].
The Story of Stuff. https://www.storyofstuff.org/ [accessed 1 October 2020]

Key dates

January 26th: International Day of Clean Energy
February 11th: International Day of Women and Girls in Science
Second Friday in March: Solar Appreciation Day
April 21: World Creativity and Innovation Day
April 28: World Day for Safety and Health at work
June 30: Social Media Day
August 21: World Entrepreneurs Day
October 24-3th: Global Media and Information Week

Children's literature

Picturebooks

Beaty, A. and Roberts, D. (illus) (2007) *Iggy Peck, Architect* Abrams Books for Young Readers.
Beaty, A. and Roberts, D. (illus) (2016) *Ada Twist, Scientist* Abrams Books for Young Readers.
Beaty, A. and Roberts, D. (illus) (2013) *Rosie Revere, Engineer* Abrams Books for Young Readers.
Cornwall, G. (2020) *Jabari Tries* Candlewick.
Dillemuth, J. and Woods, L. (illus) (2019) *Camilla, Cartographer* Magination Press.
Fliess, S. and Tempest, A. (illus) (2021) *Sadie Sprocket Builds a Rocket* Two Lions.
Funk, J. and Palacios, S. (illus) (2018) *How to Code a Sandcastle* Viking Books for Young Readers.
Greder, A. (2021) *The Inheritance* Murdoch Books
Hood, S. and Wern Comport, S. (illus) (2018) *Ada's Violin:The Story of the Recycled Orchestra of Paraguay* Simon & Schuster Books for Young Readers.
Kamkwamba, A., Mealer, B. and Zunon, E. (illus) (2012) *The Boy Who Harnessed the Wind* (Picture book Edition) Dial Books for Young Readers.
Lewis, C. and Skaltsas, C. (illus) (2021) *My House in 2055* Lerner Publication.
Litton, J. and Mansilla, M. (2018a) *The Great Go Kart Race* QEB Publishing.
Litton, J. and Mansilla, M. (2018b) *The Backyard Build* QEB Publishing.
Paul, M. and Zunon, E. (2015) *One Plastic Bag: Isatou Ceesay and the Recyling Women of the Gambia* Millbrook Press.
Riggs, S. and Saleem. F. (illus) (2019) *Meet the Gears A Family of Engineers* Independently published.
Riggs, S. and Saleem. F. (illus) (2020) *Meet the Gears A Family of Engineers Career Day* Independently published.
Spires, A. (2013) *The Most Magnificent Thing* Kids Can Press.
Yolen, J. and Sheban, C. (illus) (2019) *What to Do with a Box* Creative Editions; Illustrated edition.

Informational picturebooks

Agrawal, R. and Hickey, K. (illus) (2021). *How Was that Built? The Stories Behind Awesome Structures* Bloomsbury Children's Books.
Amstutz, L. and Evans, R. (illus) (2021). *Plants Fight Back* Dawn Publications.

Ansberry, K. and DiRubbio, J. (2020) *Nature Did It First: Engineering Through Biomimicry* Dawn Publications.

Armstrong, S.(2015) *Cool Architexture: 50 Fantastic Facts for Kids of all Ages* Portico.

Barr, C., Williams, S. and Husband, A. (illus) (2020) *The Story of Inventions* Frances Lincoln Children's Books.

Clendenan, M. and Ryall Wookcock, K. (2021) Design Like Nature: Biomimicry for a Healthy Planet Orca Book Publishers.

Dorion, C. and Herba, G. (illus) (2021) *Invented by Animals:Meet the Creatures Who Inspired Our Every-day Technology* Wide Eyed Editions.

Lee, D. and Thompson, M. (illus) (2011) Biomimicry: Inventions Inspired By Nature Kids Can Press.

Isabella, J. and Shin, S. (illus) (2015) *The Red Bicycle: The Extraordinary Story of One Ordinary Bicycle* Kids Can Press.

Johanson, P. (2017) *Tech Industry, High Tech Industrial* Science Crabtree Pub.

Kaner, E. and Wiens, C. (2018) *Wild Buildings and Bridges Architecture Inspired by Nature* Kids Can Press; Illustrated edition.

Menu, S. and Walker, E. (illus) (2020) *Biomimicry: When Nature Inspires Amazing Inventions* Triangle Square.

Nordstrom, K. and Boston, P. (illus) (2021) *Mimic Makers: Biomimicry Inventors Inspired by Nature* Charlesbridge.

National Geographic Kids and Swanson, J. (2020) *Beastly Bionics: Rad Robots, Brilliant Biomimicry and Incredible Invetions Inspired by Nature* National Geographic.

Spray, S. (2019) *Awesome Engineering* Franklin Watts.

Wise, B. and Evans. R. (illus) (2020) *If Animals Built Your House* Dawn Publications.

Chapter Books -9-12 years

Kamkwamba, A., Mealer, B. and Hymas, A. (illus) (2016) *The Boy who Harnessed the Wind* (Young Reader's Edition) Puffin.

Books for older readers

Kamkwamba, A. and Mealer, B. (2010) *The Boy Who Harnessed the Wind* (Young Reader's Edition) William Morrow.

Sciezka, J. and Biggs, B. (2017) *Frank Einstein and the Electro-Finger,* Amulet Paperbacks.

Walker, E. and Menu, S.(2020) *Biomimicry: When Nature Inspires Amazing Adventures,* Triangle Square Press.

References

Benyus, J.M., (2002). *Biomimicry: Innovation inspired by nature.* New York: Perennial.

Burgen, S. (2021). *How Seville Is Turning Leftover Oranges into Electricity.* Available: https://www.theguardian.com/environment/2021/feb/23/how-seville-is-turning-leftover-oranges-into-electricity [accessed 23 February 2021].Case for Change. *Connecting Solar Energy Brings a New Dawn to Uganda.* Available: https://www.caseforchange.com/case-studies/connecting-solar-energy-brings-a-new-dawn-to-uganda

Ellen McArthur Foundation. (nd). *The Circular Economy.* Available: https://www.ellenmacarthurfoundation.org/circular-economy/what-is-the-circular-economy

Fang, C., Wang, Z. and Liu, H., (2020). Beautiful China Initiative: Human-nature harmony theory, evaluation index system and application. *Journal of Geographical Sciences, 30,* pp.691-704.

Historic England. *Sustainable Growth for Historic Places.* Available: https://historicengland.org.uk/advice/constructive-conservation/sustainable-growth-for-historic-places/

Kassam, A. (2021). *Chop, Chop: Meet the Innovator Who Recycled 32m Chopsticks.* Available: https://www.irishtimes.com/life-and-style/homes-and-property/interiors/chop-chop-meet-the-innovator-who-recycled-32m-chopsticks-1.4452357

Macharia, J. (2013). *Internet Access Is No Longer a Luxury. Africa Renewal.* Available: https://www.un.org/africarenewal/magazine/april-2014/internet-access-no-longer-luxury.

Rynne, C. (2006). *Industrial Ireland 1750-1930: An Archaeology.* Cork: Collins Press.

The World Bank, China's Ministry of Finance and the Development Research Centre (DFC) of the State Council (2022). *Four Decades of poverty reduction in China Drivers, Insights for the World and the Way Ahead.* China: World Bank Publications.

Zhang, Y., Khan, U., Lee, S. and Salik, M., (2019)The influence of management innovation and technological innovation on organization performance. A mediating role of sustainability. *Sustainability, 11* (2), p.495.

13 Bridging gaps though reducing inequality (SDG 10)

Sarah O'Brien and Anne M. Dolan

Introduction

Inequality is one of the defining issues of our time and a significant obstacle to the achievement of the SDGs. As discussed in the introduction, dealing with inequality is a fundamental part of the entire SDG project. Inequality is a relational concept that refers to differences between individuals or groups across different dimensions, such as economic or social. In Ireland, as elsewhere, inequality is related to gender, race, religious and ethnic status. Inequality is especially apparent among lone parent households, the Traveller community and asylum seekers (IHREC, 2021). Participation in the cultural life of Ireland for these groups is severely constrained due to their social profile, economic circumstances and in some cases low self-esteem (Watson, Kenny and MGinnity, 2017; Ndahiro and Osikoya, 2020; NCCA, 2023, 2019).

SDG 10 deals with inequality. Targets (outlined in Appendix 1) include 'empowering and promoting the social, economic and political inclusion of all' and 'eliminating discriminatory laws, policies and practices' (United Nations General Assembly, 2015: np). However, as Stiglitz and others argue, inequality is not *just* a problem of policy (Stiglitz, 2016). Rather, it is a problem of culture, and of culturally accepting that inequality is a natural part of living in a complex society. The aim of this chapter is to expand upon this culturally erroneous way of thinking, and to help students think along new lines when it comes to inequality.

When all 193 United Nations Member States adopted the 2030 Agenda for Sustainable Development, they made a pledge to ensure 'no one will be left behind', and to 'endeavour to reach the furthest behind first' (UN General Assembly, 2015). In practice, this means taking explicit action to end extreme poverty, curb inequalities, confront discrimination and fast-track progress for the furthest behind. People get left behind when they lack the choices and opportunities to participate in and benefit from development progress. All persons living in extreme poverty can thus be considered 'left behind', as can those who endure disadvantages or deprivations that limit their choices and opportunities relative to others in society. This chapter features case studies of inequality (The Traveller Community in Ireland) and case studies of equality movements (the Halaf community of Mesopotamia, and the Zapatistas of Mexico).

DOI: 10.4324/9781003232001-16

The United Nations Development Programme (UNDP) (2018: 3–4) has developed a framework with five intersecting factors for assessing who is left behind and reasons for this. The five factors illustrated in Figure 13.1 are as follows:

1   Discrimination: What biases, exclusion or mistreatment do people face based on one or more aspects of their identity (ascribed or assumed), including gender as well as ethnicity, age, class, disability, sexual orientation, religion, nationality, indigenous, and migratory status?
2   Geography: Who endures isolation, vulnerability, missing or inferior public services, transportation, internet or other infrastructure gaps due to their place of residence?
3   Governance: Where do people face disadvantage due to ineffective, unjust, unaccountable or unresponsive global, national and/or sub-national institutions? Who is affected by inequitable, inadequate or unjust laws, policies, processes or budgets? Who is unable to gain influence or participate meaningfully in the decisions that impact them?
4   Socio-economic status: Who faces deprivation or disadvantages in terms of income, life expectancy and educational attainment? Who has less chances to stay healthy, be nourished and educated? Compete in the labour market? Acquire wealth and/or benefit from quality health care, clean water, sanitation, energy, social protection and financial services?

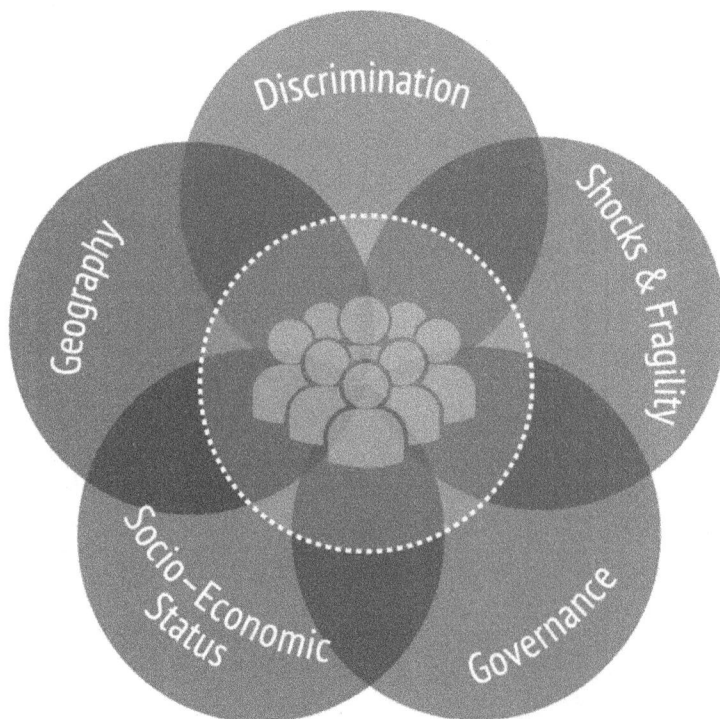

Figure 13.1 Who Is Being Left Behind and Why? Five Intersecting Factors (UNDP, 2018:10).

5   Shocks and fragility: Who is more exposed and/or vulnerable to setbacks due to the impacts of climate change, natural hazards, violence, conflict, displacement, health emergencies, economic downturns, inflation or other shocks.

This framework is useful for students for analysing dimensions of inequality in case studies, stories and contemporary events.

Inequality: let's begin by acknowledging it exists

The reduction of inequalities, both within and between countries, is a prerequisite for achieving the 2030 Agenda for Sustainable Development and the SDGs. When inequalities persist, especially in an extreme way, across economic, social, political or environmental dimensions, sustainable development and social cohesion will always be beyond reach. It is worth remembering that young people today inevitably know what inequality is all about. How could they not? It exists all around them. On their journey to school, they may see a wide disparity of living conditions: for some, 'home' is a large house with electric gates and a private garden; for others, it is an apartment block, underserviced and unclean (Ball, 2003). Some people have holiday homes at the seaside, while others are homeless. Such banal realities may become dangerously normalised to adults but, for young people, these realities are often quite perplexing.

Inequality is perhaps most visible in young people's school life (Vincent and Ball, 2006). The school that students attend will often classify them into a certain socio-economic group: 'privileged' students who attend private boarding schools will be socially distinguished from non fee-paying school students who go to free, local schools. Often, their entry into secondary school will tangibly reinforce the reality of class difference (Windle, 2016). Students, at the beginning of adolescence, will begin to make subconscious conclusions about who is 'elite' and who is 'poor', who is deserving and who is not. They will also be looking for reasons as to why social hierarchies exist, inside and outside of their classrooms. Is it a natural order for some to have more than others? Are those who have more entitled to their wealth? Do poor people deserve to be poor?

Evidence of inequality at a local level becomes even more apparent and systematic at macro level. While some countries have reduced the numbers of people living in extreme poverty, economic gaps have continued to grow as the very richest stockpile unprecedented levels of wealth. Economically, the gap between rich and poor has widened to a point never previously imaginable. According to Oxfam, the world's eight richest men now own the same amount of wealth as the poorest half of the world (Ahmed, et al., 2022). While the gap itself between rich and poor is increasing, so too is the rate of growth. Over the last 30 years growth in the incomes of the lowest 50% of earners has been zero, while the growth in income of the top 1% of earners stands at 300%. Investments in superyachts and mega yachts continue to soar (Spence, 2016). Such yachts host luxuries such as swimming pools, helicopter pads, saunas, beauty salons and gyms. A new $500 million yacht, currently known as Y721, is reportedly so big that the historic Koningshaven Bridge in the port city of Rotterdam may have to be temporarily dismantled just so the vessel can pass. Technology billionaires (including Mark Zuckerberg of META) are allegedly investing in bunkers to survive a societal collapse they helped create. Their extreme wealth and privilege serve only to make them obsessed with insulating themselves from the very real and present danger of climate change, rising sea levels, mass migrations, global pandemics, and resource depletion.

Meanwhile, levels of homelessness have increased dramatically across all cities. For millions of people, access to housing has become a grinding struggle, as property becomes a lucrative asset, snapped up by wealthy investors as an item to make profit on rather than a place of security and protection (Putnam, 2015; Hearne, 2020; O'Broin, 2019). Levels of poverty are exacerbated by gender and race. For instance, in many parts of the world, people of colour continue to suffer more social, medical, educational and economic injustice than white people (Obermeyer et al., 2019).

Let's not spend too much time, then, trying to explain the concept of inequality to students. Let's acknowledge that their lived experience is one of inequality and get to the more pressing question: why does inequality exist and what can be done to prevent it? Terminology associated with equality and inequality is set out in Table 13.1.

Table 13.1 Terminology associated with equality and inequality

Ageism can be defined as any attitude, action or institutional structure, which through its actions ends up making people subordinate because of their age (sees them as inferior, less, less important, less able…). Age discrimination occurs when a person is treated less favourably because of their age and particularly affects young and older people.

Anti-Semitism refers to hostility towards or discrimination against Jews as a religious, ethnic or racial group

Bullying can be defined as offensive behaviour which violates a person's dignity, or creates an intimidating, hostile, degrading or offensive environment, or which humiliates or undermines an individual or group. Bullying can take various forms, from name calling, sarcasm, teasing, and unwanted criticism, to threats of violence or actual physical violence. Such behaviour can be vindictive, cruel or malicious.

Disability is the disadvantage or restriction of activity arising out of how society regards people who have a disability, failing to make adjustments to enable disabled people to enjoy full and free access to all aspects of society and the environment. Disability is not caused by an individual's impairment but by the way society fails to meet their needs.

Diversity means the different backgrounds and beliefs of people we serve or work with. Diversity recognises that everyone is different in a variety of visible and non-visible ways, and that those differences are to be recognised, respected and valued.

Equal opportunities, or equality of opportunity, may be defined as ensuring that everyone is entitled to freedom from discrimination, where individuals have an equal opportunity to fulfil their potential.

Equality is about eliminating disadvantage, discrimination, deprivation and treating people fairly. Equity is where groups have parity.

Homophobia describes the aggressive or fearful feelings and behaviour directed at lesbians, gay men and bisexual men and women. This can range from jokes, graffiti, insults and threats, discrimination, to physical threats and violence.

Islamophobia is a form of irrational hatred or fear of people who follow Islam. It is often replicated as discrimination, harassment, abuse or hate crime towards people of Asian and Arabian origin, sometimes this will include people who do not follow Islam.

Prejudice refers to an unfavourable opinion or feeling, formed beforehand or without knowledge or awareness, based on partial knowledge or selective use of knowledge. It includes unreasonable feelings, opinions or attitudes, especially hostile ones.

(Continued)

Table 13.1 (Continued)

Race equality is equality based on ethnicity, race and national origin.

Racism is the negative behaviour towards people because of their ethnicity, race or national origin.

Sexism is discrimination based on sex. Traditionally such discrimination has operated against women by limiting employment and other opportunities, or by restricting rights such as voting rights.

Stereotyping refers to having a fixed mental impression about particular groups of people. Stereotypes have developed whereby large groups of people are labelled as having the same limited, usually negative, characteristics. Even though most of the people in the group are nothing like the stereotype, the characteristics of a tiny minority are used to maintain the stereotype.

Some activities for the classroom

Activity 1: four corners

A Four Corners debate requires students to show their opinion on a specific statement (*strongly agree, agree, disagree, strongly disagree*) by standing in a particular corner of the room. This activity elicits the participation of all students by requiring everyone to take a position.

Procedure

Step 1: Prepare the room Label the four corners of the room with signs reading *Strongly Agree, Agree, Disagree,* and *Strongly Disagree*. Generate a list of debatable statements relating to equality and inequality. Statistics about inequality such as those documented (Table 13.2) can be used as material to inform discussion. Statements that are most likely to encourage discussion typically elicit nuanced arguments (e.g. 'This might be a good idea sometimes, but not all of the time'), represent respected values on both sides of the debate, and do not have one correct or obvious answer.

    Step 2: Read each statement and ask students to move to the corner of the room that best represents their opinion. (Alternatively, students could be asked to write their views privately in preparation for the debate). Once students are in their places, ask for volunteers to justify their position. When doing so, they should refer to evidence from history, especially from material they have learned, as well as other relevant information from their own experiences. Encourage students to switch corners if someone presents an idea that causes them to change their mind. After a representative from each corner has defended their position, you can allow students to question each other's evidence and ideas. Before beginning the discussion, reiterate the ground rules to facilitate a respectful, open discussion of ideas.

    Step 3: There are many ways to conduct a debrief. Students can reflect verbally or in writing about how the activity changed or reinforced their original opinion. Some of their views may have been strengthened by the addition of new evidence and arguments, while others may have changed altogether. It is quite possible that some students will be more confused or uncertain about their views after the Four Corners debate. While uncertainty can feel uncomfortable, it is an important part of the learning process and represents an authentic wrestling with moral questions that have no clear right or wrong answers. To clarify ideas

Table 13.2 Statements for four corners discussion

- In our local area/country/world all children live in a world where their basic needs like health/education/housing are met.
- While gender equality in Ireland has improved much more has to be done.
- The phrase *A rising tide lifts all boats* describes the idea that when an economy is performing well, all people will benefit from it. Do you agree?
- I have never seen any evidence of racism (in my school/locality/country).
- The right to vote for (my age group) should be considered by the government.
- Out of all the SDGs dealing with topics such as climate change, poverty, gender and innovation, SDG 10 which deals with equality is the most important.

---

shared during the discussion, teachers can chart the main for and against arguments on the board as a whole-class activity.

Activity 2: introduction to global inequality through a rights based perspective

Procedure

Step 1: Take a bag of supplies that can be divided among the group (individually wrapped Fair Trade bars, bags of Maltesers or small bags of jellies work well).

Make sure you only give out enough for 60% of the class.

1   Hand out a large number of sweets or other types of objects to three participants (no one is to open them yet).
2   Hand pick a few people to come and select bags of sweets for themselves.
3   Ask half of the participants to come up and take sweets for themselves (no rules, they can grab more than one).
4   Offer the rest of the students the opportunity to come up and take any bags of sweets and to sit back down.
5   Participants can now open and eat their sweets, tell those who did not get sweets, to ask those that have them to share.

Step 2: Explore the following questions with the group (15-minutes).

- Who were given sweets? Does this represent a certain group of people in our society? (*inherited wealth*)
- Those that were hand-selected, who do they represent in our society? (*privileged classes, those that have access wealth, or a head start in life*)
- The middle group, who do you represent? (*average person, without privilege*)
- The last group, who do you represent? (*disadvantaged*) Was there much left for you? How did it feel asking for others to share? Were you dis-empowered? Did you feel you should have an equal right to the sweets?
- How did those who had sweets feel about being asked? Did you feel guilty that you had more? Would you have shared, if others were not visible and people didn't know you were asked?
- For those who received sweets or had easier access to them, did you deserve this over the others in the group?

- How would you divide the sweets with the group?
- Who in society would be the most vulnerable and unable access the sweets?
- Why are rights as opposed to charity important?
- Ask participants to think about this globally and ask which group they belong to?
- Who in society would be the most vulnerable and unable to get to the sweets in time?

Source: UNICEF Reduced Inequalities, For Every Child A Fair Chance https://www.unicef.ie/our-work/schools/global-issues/reduced-inequalities/#activity2

Chapter 3 contains more activities for exploring a rights based approach to equality.

Why does inequality exist?

Western society influences our young people to believe two paradoxical myths about inequality: first, that it can be overcome though labour; second, that it is natural (McGrath-Brookes et al., 2021).

Myth 1: inequality can be overcome through labour

Western society implants the idea that those who work hard, study responsibly and save carefully will inevitably achieve a 'respectable' position in society. This implies that the poor deserve to be poor because they are deemed to have failed in one or more of these areas. The notion of the 'American dream' is built on this very premise – on the idea that anyone can be successful if they are willing to work for it (Putnam, 2015).

Let's address this assumption head on. As teachers today, we will be aware of increased competition for jobs. It is not enough to just study: we are now competing with others who may have been able to afford a Masters' degree, or to attend a 'prestigious' university. Those who were able to afford to travel after school may have desirable international job experience on their CV, making them more appealing to employers. Such competition for jobs is being felt throughout the world and it forces workers to accept positions and wages that often barely cover the rising cost of living. Similarly, the privatisation of third level education in some jurisdictions, means that those who study in primary and secondary school may still not be able to access university education – now an essential prerequisite for most employment. Their families' increased struggle to make payments may also necessitate their entry into the work force as quickly as possible, to ease the burden on overworked parents. Given these realities, it becomes preposterous to uphold the idea of a 'meritocratic society', where hard work and study necessarily leads to success and equality (Markovits, 2020). Increasingly, it is the wealth of a person's family background that will decide their success in society. People's inability to save money has been further exacerbated by a global housing 'crisis'. In the last two decades, 'property' has become an important asset for wealthy investors (Hearne, 2020; O'Broin, 2019; Kenna, 2011). These investors make profits by buying up large tracts of housing and renting them at extremely high rates. This makes it impossible for most workers to buy their own house – for how can they compete with the prices paid by wealthy investors? It also means that most people are stuck in a cycle of paying rent, making saving and long term security an impossibility. How, in these combined set of circumstances, can we argue that inequality can be overcome through work?

Furthermore, for many it becomes more difficult to avoid inequality depending on one's race, ethnicity and country of origin. For centuries, white colonisers from Europe and North America systematically exploited vast tracts of Africa, Asia and South America, enforcing acute structural inequalities that persist into the present day. To argue that equality is attainable for people who have been historically subjugated is to deny the culpability that rests in the hands of European corporations and industrialists responsible for colonialisation and exploitation (Goodson, 2004).

Myth 2: inequality is natural

History has taught us to believe that social hierarchies have naturally emerged over time (Wengrow and Graeber, 2015). As societies became larger and more complex, it argues, humans began to require a system of management to manage its finite resources. Thus, we have governments to oversee the distribution of things like social welfare and we have large agricultural producers to supply sufficient amounts of food. Sounds fair, right?

Well, not exactly. By studying history, we begin to see that these kinds of top down systems very quickly increased inequality. Further, when people realised this system's flaws they consciously fought to develop and maintain egalitarian systems within their own communities that ensured fairness and dignity for all. Learning about these communities helps us to realise a number of things: first, that inequality is definitely not a natural precondition of modern society; second, that it is possible through collaboration and community to defeat the systems that perpetuate inequality.

Case study 13.1 A case study in inequality: Irish Travellers

Irish Travellers are an indigenous nomadic ethnic minority with a long established past in Irish history dating back to at least the 12th century. Today Irish Travellers constitute 0.8% of the population. The Equal Status Act 2000 defines the term 'Traveller community' as the community of people who are commonly called Travellers and who are identified (both by themselves and by others) as people with a shared history, culture and traditions including, historically, a nomadic way of life on the island of Ireland. (Equal Status Act, 2000. Section 'Exploring the Concepts of Equality and Inequality with Students' (1)). Traveller language, culture and traditions, are a vital part of Ireland's history. Shelta (widely known as Cant, Figure13.2) is a language spoken by Mincéirí (Irish Travellers) in Ireland and the UK. Traditionally, Travellers played an important role in an agrarian society, with niche roles as seasonal agrarian labourers, tinsmiths, poets, providing services as needed to a settled rural population. Traveller culture and traditions have survived in spite of oppression, racism and exclusion.

Figure 13.2 The STATUS (Supporting Travellers Advance Through Universal Services) Toolkit Poster. (Source Involve.ie).

For Travellers, belonging to a distinct ethnic minority means that they have a common ancestry, share fundamental cultural values and traditions, have a language and cultural heritage of their own and are seen by themselves and others as distinct and different. One of the strongest influences on Traveller culture is nomadism, which is possibly one of the most distinctive features of Traveller culture that differentiates between Traveller and the wider 'settled' Community. Travellers were nomadic for either part or all of the year, reflecting different family patterns and trades, but were characterised by their living in extended families. Although the vast majority of Travellers no longer practice a nomadic lifestyle, nomadism is still regarded as a vital part of Traveller identity, with McDonagh (1994: 95) asserting that the nomadic mindset continues to be a crucial aspect of Traveller culture even when Travellers are not practising nomadism.

The nomadic way of life of Travellers refers to the practice of some Travellers to travel from place to place, traditionally for commercial and cultural purposes; to buy and sell goods; to go to markets and fairs; and engage in new spaces. Travellers share common cultural characteristics, traditions and values which are evident in their organisation of family, social and economic life. Nomadism, in a range of forms, has been central to the development and expression of these characteristics, traditions and values (IHRC and Pavee Point, 2008: 9). As the Irish government has not provided a suitable number of appropriate halting sites, increasing the reliance on unauthorised and roadside halting sites, the culture of Travellers has essentially become diminished in social value, and the lack of provision for creating Traveller specific accommodation leans into assimilationist policies (Gilbert, 2004). Commentators such as McVeigh (2008: 100) describes the official response to Travellers as a state policy of 'assimilation and cultural genocide', including through the criminalisation of nomadism.

Travellers continue to constitute one of the most disadvantaged communities in Ireland. While the ethnicity of Travellers was formally recognised by the Irish State in 2017, this community continues to face discrimination and racism both in day to day living and on a systemic level (Joyce, 2018). Among the Irish public, anti-Traveller racism is deeply embedded, accepted and normalised. As a marginalised group, Travellers experience significantly poorer health status, lower access to education and greater levels of poverty than their counterparts in the settled community.

Research conducted by the European Union Agency for Fundamental Rights (2020) illustrates significant barriers to equality faced by Travellers. The report found that members of the Traveller and Roma community feel discriminated against because of their backgrounds as follows:

- **Employment** - Travellers in Ireland report lowest rates of employment in all countries surveyed at 15%.
- **Poverty and Social Exclusion** - 10% of Travellers (including children) surveyed report 'going to bed hungry' at least once in the last month from time of compiling the report, rising to a fifth in some countries surveyed.

- **Accommodation** – Over 90% of Travellers report that there is insufficient and inadequate accommodation available, including halting sites.
- **Racism and Discrimination** – Ireland had the second highest rate of reported discrimination within the countries surveyed – 68% of men and 62% of women reported experiencing discrimination. This is reflected in the general respondents surveyed with 46% stating they would feel 'uncomfortable with Roma and Travellers as neighbours'.
- **Education** – Ireland has the second highest rate of Traveller children participating in early childhood education (75%), however, it continues to lag behind that of the general population. There is a 70% rate of early school leaving among Irish Travellers, compared to 5% for the general population

Nevertheless, Traveller culture and traditions continue to survive in spite of, rather than with the support of, State policies. The persistence of Traveller culture underlines the strength and depth of the Community's connections and traditions.

How should we approach questions of equality and inequality in the classroom?

Children's literature feature in every classroom. The easiest way to discuss the complexities of inequality in an age appropriate manner is through story (Dolan, 2014). There are many excellent books available which include minority voices. While developing the traditional forms of literacy, reading and writing, strategies can also be used to promote critical literacies and intercultural education. Critical multicultural analysis of these children's literature examines the complex web of power in our society, the interconnected systems of race, class and gender and how they work together.

Radical writing has always existed from the beginnings of children's literature, contributing to cultural revolutions and campaigns of resistance. Slavery and racism have not disappeared, of course, meaning radical children's literature must continue to inform each generation of its pernicious effects in their own time. A notable example is *Journey to Jo'burg* (1985), by the South African-born writer, Beverly Naidoo. This tale of two black children living under apartheid graphically illustrates of the realities of the brutal injustices of that regime..

Other issues regularly featured in radical writing today include prejudice based on biological sex, sexual orientation, religion and age. Some of the most effective ways of bringing about change come from works that appreciate and celebrate difference. That said, the domain of radical writers and illustrators is wide. Other significant topics regularly addressed in radical children's literature include pacifism, access to health, education and opportunities, living conditions, children's rights, size, disability and caring for the planet. A detailed list of radical literature is included at the end of every chapter in this book.

Today many young adult books take race as a focus. Malorie Blackman's landmark series, *Noughts & Crosses (2001)*, created shockwaves with an incredibly simple yet highly effective premise; a race-switched version of today's world. It is set in Albion, an alternative Britain that was colonised by Africa, where the black population call themselves Crosses (as they are closer to God), while the white are Noughts (poorer, institutionally discriminated against). The first book, published in 2001, focuses on Persephone (Sephy) Hadley, the privileged Cross daughter of Albion's home secretary, and Callum McGregor, the Nought son of the Hadleys' housekeeper. Their romance is illicit and fraught: Sephy struggles to understand what Callum is facing in their deeply segregated world, while Callum comes to see violence as the only way to advance Nought rights.

In sequels *Knife Edge (2004)* and *Checkmate (2005),* Sephy's daughter with Callum, Callie Rose, becomes a teenager with more opportunities than her father. In *Double Cross (2008),* Callie and her Nought friend Tobey are involved in a racialised gang war. Then came Trump and Brexit, which prompted Blackman to write *Crossfire* (2019), in which Tobey becomes the first Nought prime minister. The final book in the series *Endgame (2021),* includes references to a pandemic and a Nought Lives Matter movement.

Children's literature provides a powerful tool through which SDG 10 themes can be explored. For instance, each of the topics suggested by the United Nations (Table 13.3) to explore SDG 10 can be explored by every age group through story.

Themes of inequality raised through children's literature can be further explored through enquiry based learning and independent investigation. Examples of learning approaches and methods for teaching SDG 10 Reduced Inequalities are set out in Table 13.4.

Table 13.3 Sample topics for exploring Goal 10, Adapted from UNESCO (20017: 31)

Inequality in my locality

- Case studies of inequality based on gender, race and class (refer to children's literature at the end of this chapter)
- Representation of different social groups in government/ influential institutions
- The amount and effects of international development aid
- Global trade systems and regulations
- Historic roots of inequalities
- Migration and mobility of people
- How inequality has been resolved in our society

Table 13.4 Examples of learning approaches and methods for teaching SDG 10, Adapted from UNESCO (20017: 31)

- Plan an awareness campaign directed at inequalities in global trading systems
- Analyse one's own personal history to explore times when one was privileged or discriminated against
- Develop an enquiry based project: 'How does inequality influence people's happiness?'
- Play distribution games to analyse the psychological effects of unfair or unequal treatment such as the trading game (https://www.christianaid.org.uk/get-involved/schools/trading-game)
- Interview a person who has experienced inequality, prejustice or racism
- Adapted from UNESCO (20017: 31)

Case studies of equality movements from across the world

To understand core concepts of equality and inequality students can explore contemporary local, national and international events and issues. The news is full of stories – including those on immigration policy, educational and income disparities and the struggle for gender equality. Large scale historic campaigns such as The Civil Rights movement and the Suffrage Movement can be explored through both historical and contemporary perspectives such as Black Lives Matter and #MeToo. When we think of the civil rights movement as an ongoing struggle, rather than as an event that reached its end in the 1960s, it is easier to identify its relevance today in current events.

Many campaigns for equality have roots in the civil rights movement. The Black Lives Matter movement was formed in 2013 to address institutional racism and violence towards black people. It is now a global movement, and in 2020 it became increasingly prevalent, meaning that many young people will have heard about it. Exploring Black Lives Matter in school ensures that students have a good understanding of the movement and how it relates to current and historic racism, institutional racism, and why racism must end. Children's literature cited at the end of this chapter and throughout this book provides much material for exploring individual champions and community collaborations in their successful and not so successful efforts to address inequality.

This chapter suggests approaching the topic of inequality through a narrative-based historical lens by examining case studies of communities that successfully campaigned for more equal and fair societies. In so doing the case studies and accompanying lessons that follow address the following learning objectives (Table 13.5).

Table 13.5 Learning objectives for SDG 10, Adapted from UNESCO (20017: 30)

Cognitive Learning Objectives Teaching **about** the goals: developing respect and understanding	• The learner understands local, national and global processes that both promote and hinder equality. • The learner knows different dimensions of inequality, their interrelations and applicable statistics. • The learner knows that inequality is a major driver of individual and collective dissatisfaction. • The learner understands ethical principles regarding inequality & is aware of the psychological processes that foster discrimination.
Socio-emotional learning objectives Teaching **for** the goals enhancing empathy and love **Behavioural Learning Objectives** Teaching **through** the goals Promoting advocacy and activism	• The learner is able to raise awareness about inequalities. • The learner is able to show solidarity with people who experience inequality. • The learner is able to maintain a vision of a just world. • The learner is able to plan, implement and evaluate strategies to reduce inequality. • The learner is able to identify and analyse different drivers of inequality. • The learner is able to identify inequalities in their local area in terms of quantity and quality.

Case studies for exploring equality and inequality

In this section readers will learn about two different groups – the Halaf community of Meso-potamia, and the Zapatistas of Mexico. After reading an introduction to each cultural com-munity there will be a set of suggestions for follow-up classroom activities.

Case study 13.2 The Halaf culture

(Information sheet to be distributed to students)

The Halaf culture, represented above, existed between about 6100 BC and 5100 BC. Its people lived in what is present day Turkey, Syria and northern Iraq. Archaeological investigation suggests that the Halaf developed a mode of living that was dedicated to equality (Frangipane, 2007). In this regard, it differed from many other cultures of the same period. This means that the Halaf were making very conscious decisions about fairness and choosing equality over inequality.

Dwellings in the Halaf villages were all quite similar. Houses were circular in shape and no house was bigger than another. Buildings were not constructed to signal a per-son's importance or hierarchy.

Halaf villages had communal public buildings used for public functions or for com-munity storage purposes. Goods like grains and foods were not managed or owned pri-vately, but instead were collectively farmed and distributed by the entire community. No hoarding or appropriation of the goods was permitted in the Halaf system. For the Halaf, cooperation prevailed over competition.

As well as fairly distributing food and goods, the Halaf community also maintained tight social cohesion. Their celebrations took the form of feasts, in which everyone was invited to participate and celebrate. Likewise, the funeral customs of the Halaf were designed to reassert equality. In other cultures, it was common to give 'important' families a prominent burial spot and to surround the body with valuable offerings like gold, grains and sacrificed animals. The Halaf did not develop this custom. Instead, everyone was treated fairly in death, as in life, and given the same sort of burial with the same sort of offerings.

Decision-making in the Halaf culture was carefully organised to ensure maximum participation. To maintain fair representation, meetings were organised across the vast territories of the Halaf culture. Often, different tribes of the Halaf would gather together for each others' ceremonies and feasts. This helped to maintain a sense of unity across the Halaf lands.

Follow-up classroom activity: design your own egalitarian community

Age of students 11–14 years
Learning Objectives:

- The learner is able to maintain a vision of a just world
- The learner is able to plan, implement and evaluate strategies to reduce inequality
- The learner is able to identify and analyse different drivers of inequality
- The learner understands local, national and global processes that both promote and hinder equality

Required Resources:

- Large sheets of white poster paper
- Pencils
- Ruler and compass
- Flash cards to create labels for buildings
- Images of the local physical environment that evoke signs of social inequality
- Photocopies of the Halaf culture narrative (Case study 13.2)
- Note: A 3D version of the village can also be constructed. If choosing this route ask students to bring in shoeboxes to represent buildings.

Step one: Introduction

Write the following question on the whiteboard/blackboard: 'What signs of inequality can we see in our local community?' If necessary, you can prompt students with images from the local built environment that evoke inequality e.g. pictures of expensive cars alongside packed buses/large gated houses and homeless shelters/derelict public buildings/private vs public schools.

Step two: Paired reading

In pairs, students will read the narrative about the Halaf community (Case study 13.2) (note: it may be necessary to carry out a pre-read vocabulary session with students, depending on differentiated literacy needs). Encourage students to underline any words that they do not understand. In pairs, students will orally answer the following questions:

- Why did the Halaf design houses and burial sites to be the same size and shape?
- Halaf feasts and ceremonies were careful to include everybody in the community. Do you think that the celebrations you attend (e.g. birthday parties/sports events are accessible to everyone in the community?)
- Would you like to have lived in the Halaf culture? Why/Why not?

Step three: Designing an egalitarian village

Break students into groups of five. Explain that they are now going to design their own egalitarian village. Brainstorm with students the types of places and buildings that their map might include e.g.

Public plazas/gardens/squares
Public Housing (encourage students to think carefully about the location and the size of houses)

Cycle Lanes

Libraries

Museums

Schools (public or private?)

Stores for food distribution

Bicycle lanes

Pedestrianised streets (encourage students to think about access for children, old people and physically impaired people)

Public hospitals

Community theatre/arts space

Communal vegetable gardens

Public water sources (e.g. free water dispensers in public squares)

For each building included, the students must justify the extent to which it promotes equality for all. The teacher might choose to model what a completed map will look like on the whiteboard, so that students have plenty of ideas and scaffolds before approaching the activity.

Note: The map design should ideally take an iterative approach. Students should be encouraged to engage in 2–3 design attempts before completing the full scale reconstruction of their egalitarian village.

During the design stage, there is also an opportunity to consider sustainable and renewable energy sources (as discussed in Chapter 10).

Step four: Presentation and discussion of maps

During presentations students will address the following areas:

- How have we promoted equality on our town (e.g. free access to libraries and public transport)
- Items that we have banned from our design e.g. 'No trespassing' or 'private property' signs/ private clubs/advertisements for luxury items that not everyone can afford
- The parts of the design process that we found most challenging
- How does our design compare/contrast against our local community (e.g. number of public buildings/presence of public parks and walking lanes/availability of public transport)
- What kind of energy sources have we considered for our egalitarian town/village?

Step five: Writing exercise

For the last part of the lesson, students will be encouraged to write a letter to a local councillor, asking for specific adjustments to be made to their local town to promote more equality. Letter writing should follow a pre-draft, draft and editing process, guided by peer support and teacher support. The completed letters should be displayed on walls around the mapped posters under the poster heading 'Our Equality Village'.

Further information about the Halaf community is available from multiple web sites such as https://www.metmuseum.org/toah/hd/half/hd_half.htm When discussing SDG 16 Peace and Justice in the context of civil war in Syria and the Israeli–Palestinian conflict, it is important to highlight how shared collective memories and identities including stories about the Halaf community can be obliterated through the destruction of cultural heritage.

Case Study 13.3 EZLN (The Zapatistas)

(Information sheet to be distributed to students)

In much of today's world, governments have not given fair treatment to their indigenous populations. This was especially the case for indigenous living in Chiapas, Mexico. During the 1950s and 1960s, the Mexican government forcibly relocated thousands of these indigenous people to the Lacondan Jungle. They did this so that elite agricultural producers could take over their valuable indigenous land, and thus increase their already vast wealth. Thousands of peasants, unable to find suitable land, had to abandon agriculture altogether and instead work as seasonal labourers for the wealthy land owners that had appropriated their native lands.

In 1991, in protest against this inequality, a group known as the Zapatistas rose in revolt. The Zapatistas took control of six towns in Chiapas and embarked on a long walking march to Mexico city, to highlight injustice against Chiapas' indigenous. They asked the Mexican government to bring in laws that would protect the rights of these people and that would ensure their access to their native land. However, the government refused. As a result, the Zapatistas set up an autonomous system of government in Chiapas to manage and govern their lands independently. These systems were called *caracoles*. *Caracoles* operate their own schools, health care clinics and subsistence farms, independent of the Mexican government. It also practices a horizontal organisational structure called the Good Government. Members serve for three years on a rotating basis in shifts as short as a few weeks, ensuring a completely inclusive form of direct democracy. Although life is still difficult for Chiapas' indigenous, the Zapatista movement showed them that through collaboration and community, a more equal way of living was indeed possible.

Classroom-based activities based on Case Study 13.3

Age of students 11–14 years
Lesson Objectives:

- The learner is able to identify and analyse different drivers of inequality.
- The learner understands local, national and global processes that both promote and hinder equality.

- The learner knows that inequality is a major driver of individual and collective dissatisfaction.
- The learner is able to plan, implement and evaluate strategies to reduce inequality.

Resources:

- Photocopies of Case study 13.2
- Digital device (e.g. I-Pad) with global map application (E.g. google maps) or atlas featuring map of Mexico and internet access (for project work)
- Project Book (e.g. scrap book or poster paper)
- Blank map of Mexico
- Reading Resources for student projects:
- Burton, Tony. 'Did You Know? Oaxaca Is the Most Culturally Diverse State in Mexico': Mexico Culture & Arts. Mexconnect, 24 Sept. 2007. Web. 13 July 2014. https://www.mexconnect.com/articles/1165-did-you-know-oaxaca-is-the-most-culturally-diverse-state-in-mexico/
- 'History of the EZLN'. EZLN: History. Mount Holyoke College, Web. 15 July 2014 https://www.internationalaffairs.org.au/news-item/the-zapatista-movement-the-fight-for-indigenous-rights-in-mexico/

Step one: Introduction

Divide student into pairs. Provide each pair with a copy of Case study 13.3. Orally, students should respond to the following questions as/after they read:

- In what country did the Zapatista movement occur?
- Why did the Zapatistas decide to revolt against the government?
- What steps did they take to bring about change in their communities?
- Using a digital device to help you can you calculate the time and distance from Chiapas to Mexico city?

Step two: Group-based project work

Inform students that in groups they are going to complete a multi-modal project about the Zapatistas. Projects should include images, texts and videos, if available e.g. An Introduction to Zapatista Education: https://www.youtube.com/watch?v=MiANjdbMPp4). In preparing to present the project students should be prepared to address the following themes:

- Descriptions of local activities organised by the Zapatistas to ensure equality (these may be related to agricultural practices; local government practices; education practices)
- Analysis of the effectiveness of the Zapatista strategies. For this, students will need to evaluate whether the steps taken by the Zapatistas were positive and effective in promoting equality.

Step three: Making a more egalitarian classroom

One of the goals of the Zapatista movement is to promote education through grass roots participation. With your students you will now think about ways that they can have greater autonomy in their learning. As a whole class group, brainstorm some ways of improving equality in the classroom. Some strategies might include:

Student-led curriculum design sessions
Self-study sessions built into the school timetable
Open access libraries
Replacement of tests and nightly homework with open ended, project-based activities
Weekly community and family collaboration events

After writing these suggestions on the board, divide students into pairs or groups of three (it may be a good idea to support students in joining their preferred groups, following the principles of grass roots collaboration). In their groups, students will add further strategies that will enable them to have more say in their education. Student groups will present their ideas to the class. At the end of presentations, students will **vote** on the three strategies that they would like to adopt for their classroom learning. The teacher will oversee the counting of votes and write the highest elected strategies on the board as a reminder of the students' voice and the democratic process they engaged in to reach consensus.

Links between SDG 10 and other goals

The 2030 Agenda calls for a 'just, equitable, tolerant, open and socially inclusive world in which the needs of the most vulnerable are met' (UN General Assembly, 2015). This call comes at a time when, despite important gains made since 2000 in lifting people out of poverty, inequalities and large disparities remain in income and wealth, and also in access to food, healthcare, education, land, clean water and other assets and resources essential for living a full and dignified life. Reducing inequalities is both a stand-alone SDG - SDG 10) and is intrinsically linked to the entire 2030 Agenda, and in particular the goals on ending poverty and hunger (SDG 1and SDG 2), good health and wellbeing (SDG 3), quality educa-tion (SDG 4) (gender equality (SDG 5), clean water and sanitation (SDG 6), affordable and clean energy (SDG 7), decent work and economic growth (SDG 8), resilient infrastructures and inclusive industrialisation (SDG 9) as well as more inclusive cities (SDG 11) and sustain-able ecosystems (SDG 15). Some of the links between SDG 10 and other SDGs are set out in Figure 13.3.

Conclusion - is equality possible?

Inequality is a loaded term. In reality, it is very difficult to ensure that everyone has precisely the same amount of goods or property as everyone else. In fact, the problem of inequality doesn't really come from some people having slightly more than others. The problem with inequality arises when the wealthy use their power to limit the freedoms of others. We saw this dynamic at play in Chiapas, when powerful Mexican landowners used their wealth to throw indigenous people off their lands. Inequality becomes unacceptable when it impedes on people's collective autonomy or ability to decide on the way of life that they would choose to live. If a homeless person has been forced out of their house because wealthy corporations

SDG 3

Health and Wellbeing

Health and wellbeing are determined by a wide range of social, economic and environmental factors. These are in turn shaped by wider forces: economics, social policies and politics including the distribution of money, power and resources. Level of inequality in the distribution of money, power and resources have a direct impact on the health and wellbeing of citizens locally, nationally and internationally.

SDG 2

Zero hunger

Food security is exacerbated by inequality. The fortunes of the world's richest 20 billionaires are greater than the entire GDP of Sub-Saharan Africa. This uneven distribution of hunger and malnutrition in all its forms is rooted in inequalities of social, political, and economic power. Therefore, the first step in tackling the inequalities of hunger is to understand how they are embedded in and magnified by the inequalities of power at work in the food system.

SDG 10 Reduced Inequalities

SDG 11

Sustainable Cities and Communities

As humanity becomes more urbanized, the urban environment is an ever more effective area in which to intervene in order to reduce inequality. Instead many urban policy interventions actually perpetuate inequality. Prioritizing policies which address inequality including free public transport for all will reap many environmental and socio-economic benefits.

SDG 1

No poverty

The reality of poverty perpetuates and fosters inequality, both at an individual and national level. Without financial, educational, social, political and cultural resources, it is very difficult to participate meaningfully and equally in a society with others who have access to such resources. Inequality in a society can lead to a 'culture of disparagement' towards those who are poor among those who are secure and safe.

SDG 13

Climate action

The widespread and unprecedented impacts of climate change are already disproportionately burdening the poorest, most vulnerable and marginalized groups, magnifying existing and overlapping inequalities. Recognising and addressing inequality is at the heart of climate justice.

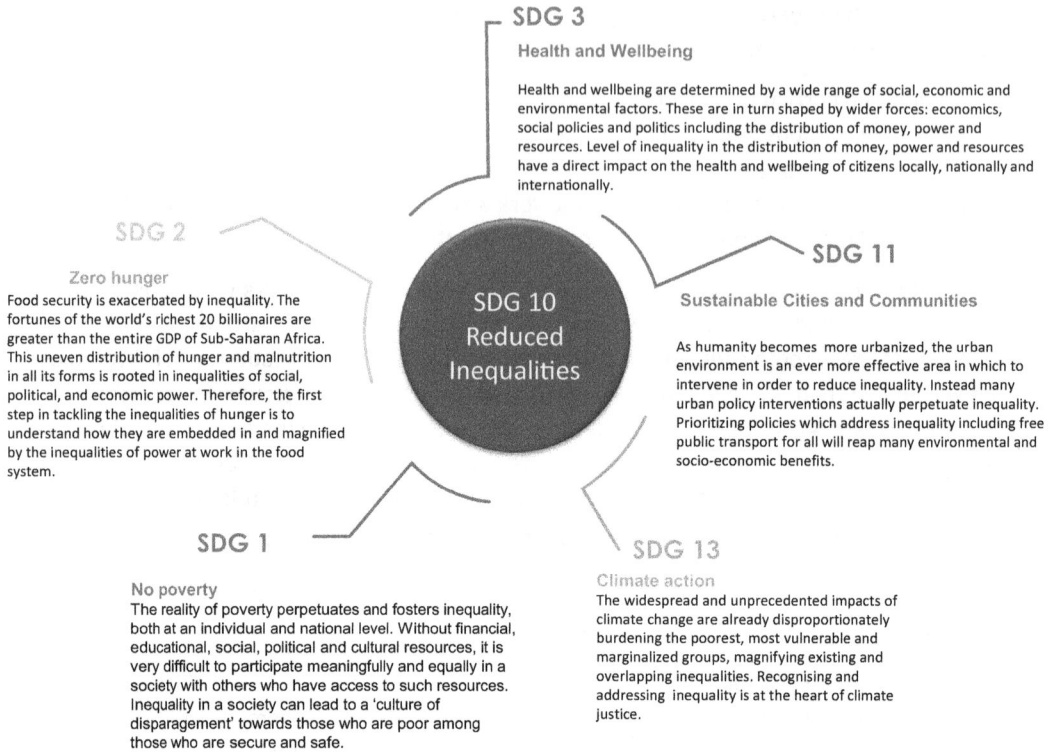

Figure 13.3 Links between SDG 10 and Some of the other SDGs.

or people have artificially inflated property prices, inequality is at work. This is the form of inequality that we must declare as unacceptable.

Throughout time, people have moved back and forth between different social possibilities. Slavery was abolished at a time when everyone thought it was a permanent fixture of human economies. In Early China, palaces were burned down by the people and replaced with non-hierarchical systems that were fairer for everyone. Even in large scale societies, people have come up with systems of management that are run by bottom up structures that ensured fairness and that rejected social hierarchies. Sometimes, we get stuck in a system, such as neoliberalism, which has led to unacceptable levels of inequality. However, this does not mean that other, more egalitarian systems are now unreachable. History teaches us that other options are always available, if we are brave enough to fight for them. It is up to us to explore alternatives and to collaborate actively in achieving them. Our job as teachers is to instil hope and possibility in the hearts of our students: to teach them that another, more equal way of living, is always possible.

Resources

An extensive list of resources, videos and case studies for SDG 10 is included in the SDG padlet accompanying this book: https://padlet.com/annedolan/o6rds38ylfy6a28h

Key dates

January 27th : Holocaust Memorial Day

February 21st: International Mother Language Day

March 8th: International Women's Day

March 21st: International Day for the Elimination of Racial Discrimination

2nd Tuesday in April: European Equal Pay Day

April 7th: World Health Day

April 7th: International Day of Reflection on the 1994 Genocide Against the Tutsi in Rwanda

April 8th: World Roma Day

May 8th: World Red Cross and Red Crescent Day

May 15th : International Day of Families

May 17th : The International Day Against Homophobia and Transphobia

May 21st: World Anti-Terrorism Day

May 21st: World Day for Cultural Diversity for Dialogue and Development

May 29th: International Day of United Nations Peacekeepers

June 20th: World Refugee Day

August 2nd: Roma and Sinti Genocide Remembrance Day

August 6th: Hiroshima Day

2nd Monday in October: Indigenous Peoples' Day.

August 23rd: International Day for the Remembrance of the Slave Trade and its Abolition

September 15th: International Day of Democracy

October 1st: International Day of Older Persons

October 11th: Indigenous Peoples Day

November 3rd: Men's World Day

November 4th: European Convention on Human Rights

November 9th: International Day Against Fascism and Antisemitism

November 20th: Universal Children's Day

November 25th: International Day for the Elimination of Violence against Women

November 29th: International Day of Solidarity with the Palestinian People

Dec 2nd: International Day for the Abolition of Slavery

December 3rd: International Day of Disabled Persons

December 10th: Human Rights Day

December 18th: International Migrants Day

Children's literature (SDG10)

Please note there is an extensive list of literature dealing with inequality as a result of poverty (SDG 1, Chapter 3), hunger (SDG 2, Chapter 4), lack of access to healthcare (SDG 3, Chapter 5), education (SDG 4, Chapter 6) and gender (SDG 5, Chapter 7),

Indigenous Children's Literature

Picture Books

Child, B.J. Thunder, J. (illus) and Jourdain, G. (Trans) (2018). *Bowwow Powwow* Minnesota Historical Society Press.

Elovitz Marshall, L. and Chavarri, E. (2016). *Rainbow Weaver / Tejedora del Arcoíris.* Children's Book Press.

Flett, J. (2021). *We All Play* Greystone Kids.

Flett, J. (2019). *Birdsong* Greystone Kids.

Florence, M. and Grimard, G. (2017). *Stolen Words* Second Story Press.

Gonzalez, X. and Garcia, A. (2017). *All Around Us* Cinco Puntos Press.

Greendeer, D. Perry, A. Bunten, A. and Meeches, G. (illus) (2022). *Keepunumuk: Weeâchumun's Thanksgiving Story* Charlesbridge.

Harjo, J. and Goade (Illus) (2023). *Remember* Random House Studio.

Noble Maillard, K. and Martinez-Neal, J. (illus) (2019). *Fry Bread: A Native American Family Story* Roaring Brook Press.

Saied Méndez, Y. and Kim, J. (illus) (2019). *Where Are You From?* HarperCollins.

Sainte-Marie, B. and Flett, J. (2022). *Sill This Love Goes On* Greystone Kids.

Sorell, T. and Lessac, F. (illus) (2021). *We Are Still Here: Native American Truths Everyone Should Know* Charlesbridge.

Sorell, T. and Lessac, F. (illus) (2018). *We Are Grateful Otsaliheliga* Charlesbridge.

Sorell, T. and Weshoyot (illus) (2018). *At the Mountain's Base* Kokila.

Thundercloud, R. and Fuller, K. J. (illus) (2022). *Finding My Dance* Penguin Workshop.

Novels

Boulley, A. (2023). *Warrior Girl Unearthed* Rock the Boat.

Durán, A. and Soler, S. (illlus) (2022). *Bruja* Oni Press.

Traditional Stories from Indigenous People

Cock-Starkey, C. and Bess Ross, H. (illus) (2023). *Lore of the Stars: Folklore & Wisdom From Above & Beyond* Wide Eyed Editions.

Keene, A. and Sana, C. (2021). *Notable Native People: 50 Indigenous Leaders, Dreamers and Change-makers from Past and Present* Ten Speed Press.

Mc Allister, A. and Baumert, O. (illus) (2023). *A World Full of Winter Stories: 50 Folk Tales and Legends from Around the World* Frances Lincoln.

Nelson, S.D. (2015). *Sitting Bull: Lakota Warrior and Defender of His People* Harry N. Abrams.

Pecore Weso, T. (2022). Native American Stories for Kids: 12 Traditional Stories from Indigenous Tribes Across North America.

Smith, C. (2022). *Ancestor Approved: Intertribal Stories for Kids* Heartdrum.

(Picture books)

Adeola, D. (2021). *Hey You! An Empowering Celebration of Growing Up* Black Puffin.

Akpojaro, J. and Leyhane, V. (2022). Questions and Answers About Racism Usbourne.

Brooks, F. and Ferrero, M. (illus) (2021). *All About Diversity* Usborne Publishing Ltd.

Cole, E. and Kamenshikova, J. (illus) (2021). *Our Diversity makes Us Stronger* Elizabeth Cole.

Davis, L. and Burobkina, M. (2022). *The Seeing: Inspiring Picture Book About Diversity, Frindship and Racism* Power of Yet.

Demetriou, A. and Mayers, A. (2022). *Me, in the Middle* Owlet Press.

Devenny, J. and Gordon, C. (2021). *Race Cars: A Children's Book About White Priviledge* Frances Lincoln.

Gear, T. L and Imamovic, M. (2022). *Just Like Grandpa Jazz* Owlet Press.

Gump, N.P. and Kushnerova, K. (2020). *The Story of the Lost Bear, Two Suns, The Way to Equality is Through The Heart* Independently Published.

Henry-Allain, L and Iwu, O. (2021). *My Skin, Your Skin: Let'sTalk About Race, Racism and Empowerment* Ladybird.

Memory, J. (2023). *A Kids Book About Racism* DK Children.

Oke, A. and Garrett, S. (2023). *Anti-Racism (The Kid's Guide)* Franklin Watts.

Spilsbury, L and Kai, H. (2018). Racism and Intolerance Wayland.

Thomas, C. and Laroche, J. (2020). Beautiful Skin: A Children's Book About Overcoming Racism Independently published.

Vinci, R. and Salameg, A. (illus) (2022) *Hope has a Dream.* Independent Publishing Network

(Information and Chapter books 9-12 years)

Abdel-Magied, Y a. and Namdhra, A. (2023). *Stand Up and Speak Out About Racism* Walker Books Cummings.

Quarry, M. Carter, N. A. and Magbadelo, D. (illus) (2021) *Grown: The Black Girld's Guide to Glowing Up* Andersen Press.

Evans, N. and Evans, N. (2023). *Everyday Action Everyday Change: Stay Positive and Motivated in the Fight Against Racism and Prejudice* Wren and Rook.

Ganeri, A. and Jeria, X. (2020). *Racism* Franklin Watts.

Heath, V. (2020). *Little Heroes, Big Hearts: An Anti-Racist Childrens' Story Book about Racism* Inequality and Learning to Respect Diversity and Differences Personal Development Publishing.

Jewell, T. and Durand, A. (2020). *This Book is Anti Racist: 20 lessons on how to wake up, take action and do the work* Francis Lincoln.

Jewell, T. and Miles, N. (2023). *The Antiracist Kid: A Book About Identity, Justice and Activism* Versify.

Lawrence, P. (2019). *Diver's Daughter A Tudor Story* Scholastic.

Nelson, Kadir. (2013). *Heart and Soul: The Story of America and African Americans* Balzer & Bray.

O' Neill, B. (2021). *The Great Book of Black Heroes: 30 Fearless and Inspirational Black Men and Women that Changed History* LAK Publishing.

Risbridger, E. (2021). *The Secret Detectives* Nosy Crow.

Shukla, N. and Heuchan, C. (2020). *What is Race? Who Are Racists? Wht Does Skin Colour Matter? And Other Big Questions?*

Wayland Thierry, J. (2020) *A Kid's Book About Sytemic Racism* A Kids Company About Inc.

Warga, J. (2023). *Other Words for Home* Balzer + Bray.

Young adult literature

Abdel-Fattah, R. (2017). *The Lines We Cross* Scholastic

Àbíké-Íyímídé, F. (2023). *Ace of Spades: How can you play the game when the cards are stacked against you* Usborne Publishing

Anyakwo, D. (2023). *My Life as a* Chameleon Atom Books

Blackman, M. (2001). *Noughts and Crosses* London: Penguin.

Blackman, M. (2004). *Knife Edge* London: Penguin.

Blackman, M. (2005). *Checkmate* London: Penguin.

Blackman, M. (2008). *Double Cross* London: Penguin.

Blackman, M. (2019). *Crossfire* London: Penguin.

Blackman, M. (2021). *Endgame* London: Penguin.

Choi, M.H.K. (2019). *Permanent Record* Atom Books

Diop, L. and Fitzsimons, B. (2023). *Black and Irish: Legends, Trailblazers, Everyday Heroes* Little Island Books.

Gibbons, A. (2017). *The Trap: Terrorism, Heroism and Everything in Between* Orion.

Jaigirdar, A. (2023). *The Dos and Donuts of Love: A Second Chance or a Recipe for Disaster* Hodder Children's Books.

Jewell, T. (2020). *This Book is Anti-Racist:20 Lessons on How to Wake Up* Frances Lincoln.

Khan, S. (2021). *Zara Hossain is Here* Scholastic.

Khan, M. (2018). I am Thunder: And I Won't Keep Quiet Macmillan Children's Books.
McKinney, L.L. (2021). *Nubia: Real One* DC Comics.
Omotoni, A. (2023). *Everyone's Thinking It* Scholastic.
Parker Rhodes, J. (2018). *Ghost Boys* Orion Children's Books.
Taylor, M. (2020). *All the Days Past, All the Days to Come* Viking Books for Young Readers.
Taylor, M. (2014). Roll of Thunder, Hear My Cry Penguin.
Taylor, M. (2003). Song of the Trees Puffin Books.
Thomas, A. (2020). *The Hate U Give*. Balzer + Bray.
Yang, K. (2021). *Parachutes* Katherine Tegan Books.

Books about Travellers

Picturebooks

DeBhairduin, O. and Anima, O. (illus) (2023). *The Slug and the Snail* Skein Press.
Dowd, S. and Shoard, E. (illustrator) (2017). *The Pavee and the Buffer Girl* The Bucket List.
Kelly, -Desmond, L. (2022). *The Horse, the Stars and the Road*. Little Island Books.
Kids' Own Publishing. (2005). *Fishing for Food and Mushrooms – A Collection of Stories, Poems and Pen Pictures by Traveller Children* Sligo: Kids' Own Publishing.
Kids' Own Publishing. (2008). *Can't Turn Back* Sligo: Kids' Own Publishing.
Kids' Own Publishing. (2019). *This Giant Tent – A Children's Celebration of Traveller Culture and Identity* Sligo: Kids' Own Publishing.
Kids' Own Publishing. (2021). (2nd Ed) *Can't Lose Cant* Sligo: Kids' Own Publishing.
O Neill, R. and Beautyman, K. (2019). *The Lost Homework* Child's Play (International) Ltd.
O'Neill, R. and Kang, C. (illus) (2022). *The Can Caravan* Child's Play (International) Ltd.
O'Neill, R. and Parker-Thomas, F. (illus) (2018). *Polonius The Pit Pony* Child's Play (International) Ltd.
O' Neill, R. Quarmby, K. and Tolson, H. (2016). *Ossiri and the Bala Mengro* Child's Play (International) Ltd.
O' Neill, R. Quarmby, K. and Nelissen, M. (illus) (2016). *Yokki and the Parno Gry* Child's Play (International) Ltd.

Young adult literature

DeBhairduin, O. and Mc Donagh, L. (illus) (2020). *Why the Moon Travels* Skein Press.
Dowd, S. and Shoard, E. (illus) (2019). *The Pavee and the Buffer Girl* Barrington Stoke.
Eliot, J. (2008). *Spokes: Stories from the Romani World* Five Leaves Publications.
James, K. (2015). *Gypsy Girl* Walker Books.
James, K. (2016). *Gypsy Girl Revenge* Walker Books.
McDonald, A. (2006). *Nothing but Trouble* A & C Black Publishers Ltd.
MC Donagh, R. (2021). *Unsettled* Skein Press.

References

Ahmed, N., Marriott, A., Dabi, N., Lowthers, M., Lawson, M. and Mugehera, L. (2022) *Inequality Kills: The Unparalleled Action Needed to Combat Unprecedented Inequality in the Wake of COVID-19*. GB: Oxfam. https://www.oxfam.org/en/research/inequality-kills
Ball, S.J. (2003) *Class Strategies and the Education Market Place*. London: Routledge.
Dolan, A.M. (2014) *You, Me and Diversity: Picturebooks for Teaching Development and Intercultural Education*. London: Trentham Books and IOE Press.
European Union Agency for Fundamental Rights. (2020) Roma and Travellers Survey: Europe Needs to Break the Vicious Circle of Poverty and Discrimination Against Roma and Travellers. https://fra.europa.eu/sites/default/files/fra_uploads/fra-2020-roma-travellers-six-countries_en.pdf
Gilbert, J..(2004) Still no place to go: nomadic peoples' territorial rights in Europe. *European Yearbook of Minority Issues* Leiden: Brill, 4(1), 141–159.

Government Publications. (2000) EQUAL STATUS ACT. Available at: www.irishstatutebook.ie/eli/2000/act/8/enacted/en/print

Hearne, R. (2020) *Housing Shock: The Irish Housing Crisis and How to Solve it*. Bristol: Policy Press.

IHRC and Pavee Point. (2008) Travellers Cultural Rights The Right to Respect for Traveller Culture and Way of Life. http://www.paveepoint.ie/wp-content/uploads/2015/04/Travellers-Cultural-Rights.pdf

Joyce, S. (2018) Mincéirs Siúladh: An Ethnographic Study of Young Travellers' Experiences of Racism in an Irish City, unpublished thesis (Ph.D.), University of Limerick. Available: https://ulir.ul.ie/handle/10344/7535.

Kenna, P. (2011) *Housing Rights, Law and Policy*. Dublin: Clarus.

Markovits, D. (2020) *The Meritocracy Trap*. New York: Penguin.

McDonagh, Michael. (1994). Nomadism in Irish Travellers' identity in McCann, M., O'Siochain, S. and Ruane, J. (1994) *Irish Travellers: Culture and* Ethnicity Dublin: Institute of Irish 95-109.

McGrath-Brookes, M., Hanley, J. and Higgins, M., 2021. A Fisher-eye lens on social work reform. *Journal of Social Work*, *21*(5), pp.1261-1277.

McVeigh, R. (2008) The 'final solution': Reformism, ethnicity denial and the politics of anti-travellerism in Ireland. *Social Policy and Society*, *7*(1), 91-102.

NCCA (2023) *Traveller Culture and History* https://ncca.ie/media/5959/traveller-culture-and-history-research-report_en.pdf

NCCA. (2019) *Traveller Culture and History in the Curriculum: A Curriculum Audit*. Dublin: NCCA. https://ncca.ie/media/4324/ncca_draftaudit_travellerculturehistory_0919.pdf

Ndahiro, Sandrine and Osikoya, Cathy. (2020) Unsilencing Black Voices. Accessed 25 June 2021. https://www.youtube.com/watch?v=iMNvmCDceb8

Obermeyer, Z., Powers, B., Vogeli, C. and Mullainathan, S. (2019) Dissecting racial bias in an algorithm used to manage the health of populations. *Science*, 366(6464), 447-453.

O'Broin, E. (2019) *Home: Why Public Housing Is the Answer*. Dublin: Merrion Press.

Putnam, Robert. (2015) *Our Kids : The American Dream in Crisis*. New York: Simon & Schuster.

Spence, E. (2016) Performing wealth and status: Observing super-yachts and the super-rich in Monaco. In Hay, I. and Beaverstock, J.V. eds., *Handbook on Wealth and the Super-Rich*. London: Edward Elgar Publishing. 287-301.

Stiglitz, J. (2016) *The Great Divide*. London: Penguin.

The Economist. (2021) The Pandemic's True Death Toll. Accessed 1 December 2021. https://www.economist.com/graphic-detail/coronavirus-excess-deaths-estimates

UNDP. (2018) *What Does it Mean to be Left Behind? A UNDP Discussion Paper and Framework for Implementation*. New York: UNDP.

UN General Assembly (2015) . Transforming our world: the 2030 Agenda for Sustainable Development, 21 October 2015, A/RES/70/1. https://sustainabledevelopment.un.org/post2015/transformingourworld

United Nations Development Programme (UNDO). (2022) Global Dashboard for Vaccine Equity. https://data.undp.org/vaccine-equity/

Vincent, C. and Ball, S. (2006) *Childcare, Choice and Class Practices: Middle Class Parents and their Children*. London: Routledge.

Watson, D., Kenny, O. and McGinnity, F. (2017) A social portrait of travellers in Ireland. *Research Series*, 56, 589-608.

Windle, J.A. (2016) *Making Sense of School Choice: Politics, Policies, and Practice Under Conditions of Cultural Diversity*. New York: Springer.

Wengrow, D. and Graeber, D., (2015) Farewell to the 'childhood of man': ritual, seasonality, and the origins of inequality. *Journal of the Royal Anthropological Institute, 21*(3) 597-619.

14 Learning to live sustainably

Lessons from sustainable communities (SDG 11)

Anne M. Dolan and Peadar Kirby

Introduction

SDG 11 seeks to make cities and communities more inclusive, safe, resilient and sustainable. This means guaranteeing access for all to adequate housing and basic services; assuring accessible and sustainable urbanisation and transport, and safeguarding the world's cultural and natural heritage, among other targets. Sustainable communities are resilient, as they recognise the nature of current and future shocks and plan accordingly. With a low ecological impact and low carbon emissions, sustainable communities have pleasant and healthy environments with clean air, parks and sustainable transport. The concept of meitheal (discussed in Chapter 1) has much to offer the business of establishing sustainable cities and communities as outlined in SDG 11. In the tradition of meitheal, a recognition of the rights, welfare, creativity and innovation of community members, is the foundation stone for sustainable communities. This chapter outlines the characteristics of sustainable communities, includes exemplars for teaching about sustainable planning with a focus on energy and food production. It also showcases one sustainable community in Cloughjordan, Co.Tipperary, Ireland.

Understanding the concept of sustainability and sustainable communities

The majority of the world's population live in cities. The ongoing growth of humanity in total and in urban settings in particular raises significant challenges and possibilities. For example, Goal 11 notes:

> Common urban challenges include congestion, lack of funds to provide basic services, a shortage of adequate housing and declining infrastructure. The challenges cities face can be overcome in ways that allow them to continue to thrive and grow, while improving resource use and reducing pollution and poverty. The future we want includes cities of opportunities for all, with access to basic services, energy, housing, transportation and more.
>
> (United Nations, 2015: np).

The concept of sustainability is holistic in nature, considering ecological, social and economic dimensions, recognising that all must be considered together in the interests of

DOI: 10.4324/9781003232001-17

environmental and human prosperity. A sustainable community/city is one that lives in accordance with sustainable development priorities, based on its unique social, economic and environmental conditions and perspective, and one that allows its citizens to enjoy a good quality of life in harmony with their surrounding nature. Sustainable communities do not simply emerge overnight. Forged by citizens committed to sustainability over a long period of time, sustainable communities have multiple benefits for their citizens (as illustrated in Case study (14.1).

Sustainable cities and communities

More and more of the world's people live in cities. Indeed, urbanisation is an unstoppable phenomenon (Habitat, 2018) (Figure 14.1). From 150 million people in 1900, by 2000 2.8 billion people were city dwellers. It is now recognised that more than 50% of the world's population is urban, a figure expected to grow to 60% by 2030. Most of this has happened in the Global South and today there are 25 megacities of more than ten million inhabitants (such

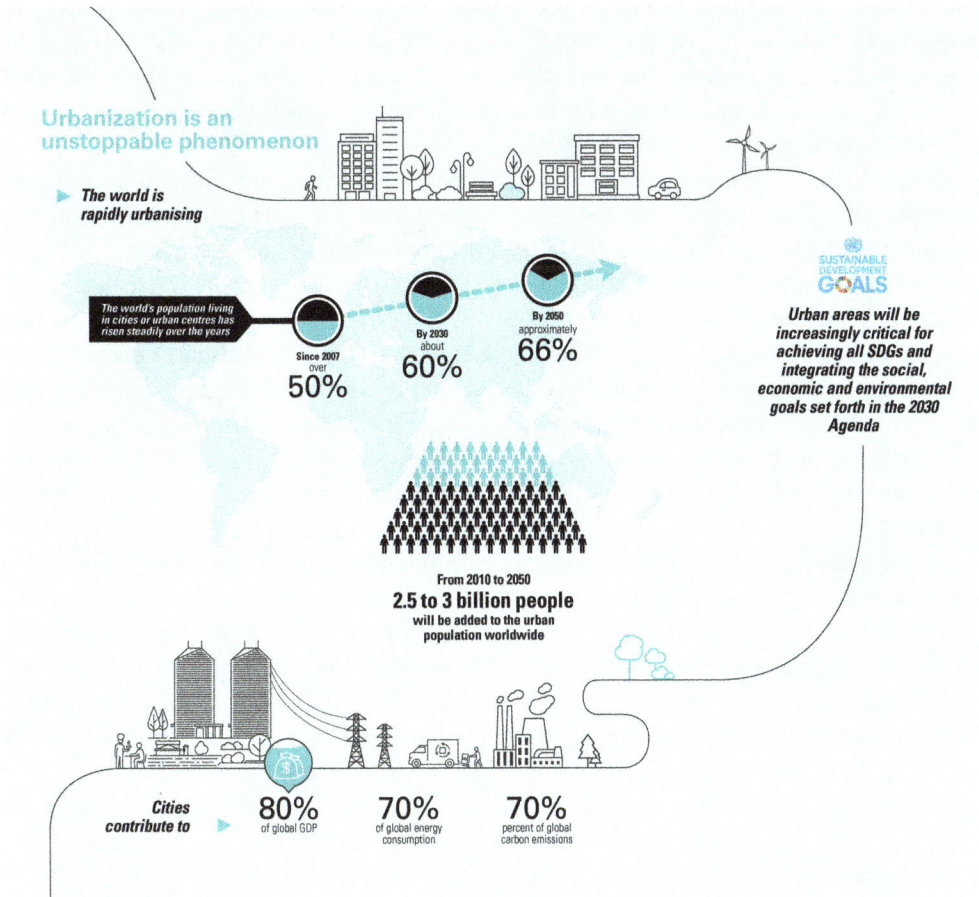

Figure 14.1 Urbanisation Is an Unstoppable Phenomenon. (Source Habitat, 2018: 6).

as Tokyo with 37.2 million, Saõ Paulo with 27.6 million, Shanghai with 24.2 million, Mexico City with 21.6 million and Mumbai with 20.7 million). Overall, 90% of expected urban growth is likely to occur in Africa and Asia, the only regions which still had a majority living in rural areas in 2014.

From the perspective of sustainability, this growth of urban settlements poses extreme challenges. On the one hand, these expanding cities are occupying farmland and natural habitats, often paving them over in the process. On the other, cities intensify demand for everything from energy and water, to food, clothing and fuel, all of which increase greenhouse gas emissions. For this reason, the Global Footprint Network has found that most cities' ecological footprints exceed those of their countries, indicating that city living places far more stress on natural resources and emits more greenhouse gases (GHGs). Overall, cities are estimated to be responsible for up to 80% of global emissions while the 100 highest-emitting urban areas account for 18% of the global carbon footprint (NASA Earth Observatory, 2019).

The reasons for the unsustainable nature of city living are much debated. Some analysts focus on socio-economic reasons, related to higher incomes and therefore more intense consumption patterns. Accordingly, urban dwellers spend more on heat and electricity, on property, on consumer goods and leisure services and goods, and on foreign travel than do semi-urban or rural dwellers. The only category on which the latter spend more is private driving since those living outside cities tend to have access to fewer transport options and have to travel greater distances.

Others take a more ecological view focusing more on waste, energy generation and consumption, the quality of buildings, city dwellers' diets, and transport options. This identifies a suite of issues that have contributed to high GHG emissions among urban dwellers. These include sending most waste to landfill, using fossil fuels to generate energy and to heat buildings, poor insulation and wasteful heating systems, high levels of meat consumption in urban diets as well as dependence on embodied food miles, and polluting transport options. Growing awareness of how these contribute to emissions has resulted in moving to more sustainable infrastructure and consumption options. Among these are the recycling of waste and composting, insulation and energy-saving in buildings, generating energy through sun and wind within urban areas, changes in consumption practices and low-polluting electric public transport.

This is what the Global Footprint Network calls the 'double dynamic' taking place in cities as they become the sites for developing more energy-saving modes of living, mobility and consumption, thus pioneering greater sustainability. In these ways cities, particularly larger ones, may be providing the key to stopping or slowing global warming through what has been called 'green urbanism' (Caradonna, 2014: 201). This needs to go much further than the current emphasis on greening existing energy, housing, transport and consumption practices. It should include a focus on living within ecological limits, on local self-sufficiency including locally produced energy and local food embedded in a strong local economy, on systems of circular metabolism that eliminate waste, on healthy lifestyles and strong community bonds.

Immense as these challenges are in the Global South, they become even more overwhelming for their cities where swift urbanisation tends to mirror the worst practices of polluting urban sprawl. As a result, some Chinese cities now have higher GHG emissions per capita than those in the USA. Furthermore, rudimentary energy, housing and transport infrastructure particularly in the huge slums that characterise some cities in the Global South, greatly limit the possibilities for fostering more sustainable lifestyles.

The third United Nations Conference on Housing and Sustainable Urban Development in 2016 adopted the New Urban Agenda as a global overarching framework for the development of cities over the next 20 years. This aims to promote international, national, subnational and local climate action and to support the efforts of cities to implement such action. It includes investing in low-emissions measures in buildings, energy efficiency, waste recycling and landfill gas capture, and shifts in transport options such as public transport and cycling.

SDG 11 goes further in setting the overall goal of making cities and human settlements inclusive, safe, resilient and sustainable. The targets it sets (Appendix 1) are extremely ambitious, not least because they seek to extend the benefits to everyone. So, for example, it aims to ensure, by 2030, access for all to adequate, safe and affordable housing and basic services and to upgrade slums. It seeks safe, affordable, accessible and sustainable transport systems for all, again by 2030. Other targets include protecting against the impact of disasters, protecting and safeguarding the natural and cultural heritage, and giving special attention to air quality and waste management. All SDG 11 targets are listed in Appendix1.

To achieve all this, it recognises the need for 'participatory, integrated and sustainable human settlement planning and management in all countries', a particularly ambitious target at a time when authoritarian governments are centralising power and neglecting the needs of the poor and marginalised (see Kirby, 2021: 21–29). Sustainable cities can only be achieved through sustainable and inclusive urban politics, something often forgotten when the focus is on technocratic solutions rather than on human ingenuity. Furthermore, the need to include the voice of children and young people is paramount. To date, the needs, interests and participation of children and young people often remain inferior to the design, planning and local politics of new urban communities (Christensen et al., (2017).

A final and very important dimension highlighted by SDG 11 is the need for 'universal access to safe, inclusive and accessible, green and public spaces' and special mention is made of access for women and children, and for the elderly and those with disabilities. One way of achieving this goal is to create 'positive economic, social and environmental links between urban, peri-urban and rural areas' as SDG 11 puts it, thus breaking down the divide between city and country that has been a marked feature of modern culture. One example from Ireland that seeks to break down this divide is Cloughjordan Ecovillage, Co. Tipperary (Case study 14.1).

Teaching the concept of sustainable cities and communities

Learning about sustainable living and sustainable communities is a key aspect of the SDGs. Key learning objectives are set out in Table 14.1. Living sustainably is built upon principles of

Table 14.1 Learning objectives for SDG 11 (Source UNESCO, 2017: 32)

Cognitive Learning Objectives Teaching ***about*** the goals: developing respect and understanding	1 The learner understands basic physical, social and psychological human needs and is able to identity how these needs are currently addressed in their own local rural and urban communities. 2 The learner is able to evaluate and compare the sustainability of their and other settlements systems in meeting the needs particularly in the areas food, energy, transport, water, safety, waste treatment, inclusion and accessibility, education, integration of green spaces and disaster risk reduction. 3 The learner understands the historical reasons for settlement patterns and while respecting cultural heritage, understands the need to find compromises to develop improved sustainable systems. 4 The learner knows the basic principles of sustainable planning and building, and can identify opportunities for making their own area more sustainable and inclusive. 5 The learner understands the role of local decision-makers and participatory governance and the importance of representing a sustainable voice in planning and policy for their area.
Socio-emotional learning objectives Teaching ***for*** the goals enhancing empathy and love	6 The learner is able to use his/her voice, to identify and use entry points for the public in the local planning systems, to call for the investment in sustainable infrastructure, buildings and parks in their area and to debate the merits of long-term planning. 7 The learner is able to connect with and help community groups locally and online in developing a future vision of their community. 8 The learner is able to reflect on their region in the development of their own identity, understand the roles that the natural, social and technical environments have had in building their identity and culture. 9 The learner is able to contextualise their needs within the needs of the greater surrounding ecosystems, both locally and globally, for more sustainable human settlements. 10 The learner is able to feel responsible for the environmental and social impacts of their own individual lifestyle.
Behavioural Learning Objectives Teaching ***through*** the goals Promoting advocacy and activism	11 The learner is able to plan, implement and evaluate community-based sustainability projects. 12 The learner is able to participate in and influence decision-making processes about their community. 13 The learner is able to speak against/for and to organise their voice against/for decisions made for their community. 14 The learner is able to co-create an inclusive, safe, resilient and sustainable community 15 The learner is able to promote low-carbon approaches at the local level.

respect for biodiversity and community members. Sustainable communities are characterised by resilience, hope and advocacy. Community resilience is a measure of the sustained ability of a community to respond to economic, social and environmental issues. It represents the ability and effort of communities to overcome challenges including climate change, food security and access to employment for stronger, more vibrant communities that also deliver positive economic, social and environmental impacts. By integrating access to sustainable energy, climate change adaptation, ecosystem management, these communities create resilient futures. Bringing students to a community making efforts to live sustainably (such as Cloughjordan Eco Village, Case Study 14.1) makes sustainability concepts more tangible. Here, students meet people living by the principles of sustainability in a manner that is community-led, mutually beneficial and hopeful.

Visits to eco village have a lasting legacy as illustrated in this reflection by a student teacher:

My visit to Cloughjordan has taught me that teaching about sustainability and climate change cannot be tackled through the school textbook alone. Our students must experience sustainable behaviours for themselves through hands on learning. It is vital that students are taught the skills necessary to deal with future dilemmas their generation will face at the hands of climate change. As a teacher inspired by the cooperative approach applied in Cloughjordan, I hope to promote more co-operative movements within the schools I teach in the future and spread the message of their initiative. I will instil the message in my students to the value of community and how working towards a common goal can positively affect the wellbeing of every person and the environment they live in.

Talking about sustainable living

One of the most important ways to teach about SDG 11 is to talk about living sustainably at individual, family, community, national and international levels. Key terminology for such discussion is set out in Table 14.2. Potential themes and topics are suggested in Tables 14.3

Table 14.2 Key terminology referring to sustainable communities

Key Terminology	
Community	a group of people with a common interest such as place of residence or participation in an interest group.
Community based development	an approach to implementing local development projects that advocates for community participation in decision-making and management, with a goal of using local knowledge and resources to run more effective projects.
Resilient	the ability to withstand adversity and bounce back from difficult life events
Resilient communities	The sustained ability of a community to use available resources including energy, food, transportation and communication to response to, withstand and recover from adverse situations including climate change and a financial crisis.
Sustainable communities	refers to communities planned, built, or modified to promote sustainable living. Sustainable communities tend to focus on environmental and economic sustainability, urban infrastructure, social equity, and municipal government

and 14.4. Ideally, core curricular areas of literacy and numeracy should include references to sustainable living. Indeed, there is an extensive list of children's literature listed at the end of this chapter. Activities such as designing an eco-friendly house (described in Chapter 10) and designing a sustainable village, town or city (Exemplar 14.1)., allow students to apply core concepts of sustainability to practical projects. One of the most effective ways to encourage students to talk about and think about sustainability is to bring them to community-based sustainability initiatives such as Cloughjordan Eco Village (Case Study 14.1).

Additional topics and approaches for teaching sustainable communities and cities are suggested in Tables 14.3 and 14.4.

Table 14.3 Suggested topics SDG 11 (Adapted from UNESCO, 2017: 33)

The need for shelter, safety and inclusiveness (human needs, contextualising our different individual and collective wants and needs according to gender, age, income and ability)
Inequality in housing provision from slum dwellers to mansion owners
Management and use of natural resources (renewables and non-renewables)
Sustainable energy (residential energy use, renewable energies, community energy schemes) and transportation
Sustainable food (agriculture, organic agriculture and permaculture, community supported agriculture, food processing, dietary choices and habits, waste generation
Urban ecology and how wildlife is adapting to humanities settlements
Sustainable planning, preventing unplanned urban sprawl, provision of basic services and infrastructure, planning in a way which respects local natural habitats
Sustainable resilient buildings and spatial planning (building materials, energy saving, planning processes)
Waste generation and management (prevention, reduction, recycling, reuse)
Communities and their dynamic (decision-making, governance, planning, conflict resolution, alternative communities, healthy communities, inclusive communities, eco villages transition towns)
Water cycle and restoring ground water through urban design (green roofs, rainwater harvesting, daylighting old river beds, sustainable urban drainage)
Disaster preparedness and resilience, urban vulnerability to disasters, resilience to weather problems and a culture of prevention and preparedness

Table 14.4 Suggested learning approaches and methods for SDG 11 (Source UNESCO, 2017: 33)

Excursions to ecovillages and other 'living laboratories', to waste treatment plants and other service centres to show current and best practice
Develop and run a (youth) action project on sustainable cities and communities
Invite older generations in to talk about how the settlement has changed over time. Ask them about their connection to the local area. Use art, literature and history to explore the settlement area and its changes
Build a community garden
Mapping projects: map the area to note where there is good use of public open space, human scale planning, areas where the needs of the community are addressed, green spaces, etc. This can also map the areas that need to be improved, such as areas most exposed to natural hazards
Develop a two-minute video clip on an example of a sustainable urban community
Develop an enquiry-based project: 'Would it be more sustainable if we all lived in cities?

Exemplar 14.1 Working as energy engineers: design a sustainable village, town or city

Resources: 20 cardboard boxes (different sizes) for each group.
General art material
Greenery from the garden
Development:
Before you begin creating your sustainable city or town, consider the factors which are important for you.

What mode of travel would you like to prioritise?

What source of energy will power your community?

How much green space will you create?

What facilities should be included for children and young people? Will there be space to play? Will there be spaces for teenagers to meet their friends?

What types of buildings are important?

In groups, students can decide what buildings and facilities should be prioritised. The boxes can be painted and set out in a plan to represent the students' ideas. Art material can be used for creating other features such as water sources, pathways and an access road. Greenery can be used for the green areas. Upon completion each group can present their sustainable communities, including a rationale for key decisions, to their class. Each community will be scored by the students according to factors such as energy sources, ingenuity and adherence to sustainability principles.

Exemplar 14.2 Working with Lego

Children's ability to design and dream is limited only by their imagination. Students are already conscious about the climate crisis, the decline of biodiversity and the importance of nature for our wellbeing. Armed with lego and their imagination, students can design amazing sustainable spaces. Using learning approaches (Table 14.4) and terminology (Table 14.2) teachers and students can explore themes/topics (Table 14.3) through lego construction, to achieve learning objectives (Table 14.1). Furthermore, the articulation of ideas and strategies for building a better physical space can help to alleviate eco-anxiety. Places of the future are the places we imagine today.

Traditionally, students have played with little red, yellow, green and blue blocks to build towers, bridges, houses or even cities, letting their imaginations fuel their design. There are opportunities to explore more complex designs and buildings through teaching students about renewable energy and net-zero homes (homes which produce more energy than that which they consume). To focus on solar energy students can design sustainable solar houses and villages. Certain features could include solar street lighting, solar robots, heat pumps, biodigesters, recycling centres, micro wind turbines, solar powered battery systems, enhanced use of natural lighting, cycling lanes for bicycles and maximum use of green spaces.

Educational Robotics is an interdisciplinary learning environment based on the use of robots and electronic components as the common thread to enhance the development of skills and competencies in students. Lego robotics also presents opportunities for students to work to address sustainability challenges through design and planning (Dolan, 2022). Robotics is an evolving industry along with a new generation of learning using lego robotics. Also known as Lego Mindstorms, lego robotics involves the use of robots for teaching coding and logical reasoning in schools. Through LEGO Robotics, students of all ages are introduced to engineering, mathematics and robotics principles. They are also given the opportunity to develop their critical thinking and problem-solving skills.

The FIRST LEGO League (FLL) is an international competition involving students (11 to 16 years) from over 90 countries. It involves a non-competitive global STEM challenge for teams of young people, to explore a real world theme, develop design and programming skills as well as teamwork, problem solving and communication skills all while having fun. FIRST is an acronym for 'For Inspiration and Recognition of Science and Technology', and the FIRST LEGO League encourages students to think like scientists and engineers, developing practical solutions to real-world issues. A First Leago League Junior version is available for younger students. Over several weeks, teams of up to six students research a real-world topic, display their ideas on a ShowMe poster and program a Lego model to bring their solution to life. Teams present and celebrate what they have discovered at a local or in school festival. Teacher guidelines are available (Butler et al., 2022).

Every year, *FIRST* LEGO League releases a new Challenge based on a real-world, scientific theme. Sustainability themes feature regularly. For *Climate Connections,* students were invited to focus on the Earth's past, present and future climates. Students researched a local climate problem, devised solutions and shared their results. For the challenge, *Food Factor,* students were invited to improve the quality of food by finding ways to prevent food contamination. Students have had the opportunity to explore awe inspiring storms, quakes, waves and natural disasters to address the theme *Nature's Fury.* Solutions for the waste problem were devised by students as part of the *Trash Trek* challenge. The transportation, use and disposal of water featured in the *Hydro Dynamics Challenge. Cargo Connect* dealt with the sorting, delivery and transportation of cargo including sustainable options. The theme of the 2019/2020 competition was *City Shaper,* which proposed the use of technology and robotics to solve real problems arising from urbanisation. Through the *City Shaper* project, students worked as architects. Addressing the concept of sustainable cities, students were invited to address the challenges facing cities including transportation, accessibility and even natural disasters.

Specific challenges from the *City Shaper* project included the following (Ruiz et al., 2020: 9696)

1   Expert in biodiversity and energy
    Challenge 1: Build a sustainable garden or orchard in a city (Sustainable roof).
    Challenge 2: Create an energy source that takes advantage of wind gusts (Wind Turbine).

2   Expert in mobility and energy
      Challenge 3: Build a marquee that reacts to traffic and emits light (Marquee).
      Challenge 4: Create an energy source that takes advantage of sunlight. (Photo-voltaic field).
3   Expert in efficiency and recycling
      Challenge 5: Create a lighting system that optimises and saves light (Urban lighting).
      Challenge 6. Make a building for recycling (waste separation).

In the *BOOMTOWN BUILD* module students has an opportunity to explore concepts in architecture including accessibility, environmentally friendliness and durability. In groups students were invited to construct a building for the fictional town of Boomtown that included at least one motorised part. Even if students are not participating in First Lego League, all of these challenges are applicable for design thinking using Lego. Once again in teams, the students can research their ideas, create a model and present their work to a wider audience.

Exemplar 14.3 Working with Minecraft

Created in 2011 by the Swedish company Mojang, Minecraft is a so-called open world game. Akin to a format of 'online Lego', Minecraft is a 3D computer game where players can literally build anything. Players interact with a keyboard and mouse in order to physically move in the world, via an avatar to gather, craft/edit and use *Minecraft* blocks. Players can create structures across different environments and terrains from houses to cities, and anything in between. Each player can create entire landscapes with unique architecture, flora and fauna. Some players re-create existing landmarks such as the Tower of London, or Dublin Castle while others create fantasy worlds. Blocks are the basic units of structure in Minecraft. There are over 100 different types of blocks each with their own characteristics and textures representing building materials of the physical world. Popular blocks include gravel, sand, wood, cobblestone and dirt. Others such as redstone, diamond ore and gold ore, are the foundation blocks for Minecraft's biomes which can be mined and used in different ways.

Microsoft launched *Minecraft: Education Edition* a special purpose game based learning platform with lesson plans for different subject area. The educational benefits of gaming including Minecraft have been well documented (Usher, and Moynihan, 2022; Lehane et al., 2021). Furthermore, the virtual world of Minecraft can be used for exploring aspects of sustainable living, from forestry to wastewater, recycling to clean energy, and more. *Minecraft Education Edition* contains a suite of lessons which deal with sustainability under the headings: Biodiversity; Climate futures; Rivercraft (dealing with a real world flood mitigation project); and Save the Oceans. It also features a set of lesson plans in a collection called Sustainability City. The seven lesson plans deal with the following themes:

Dependable Forests
It's Good to Be Green
Outflow Order
Sustainable Food Production
Sustainable Home
Alternative Energy
Radical Recycling

The Sustainability City world is a place for students to wander freely as they examine a wide range of issues, including the components of a sustainable home, managing waste products, clean electricity generation, and responsible forestry.

Microsoft Ireland and RTÉjr (a programme created by Ireland's National Television and Radio Broadcaster) have collaborated in a new national digital skills competition which challenges primary school students across the island of Ireland to use *Minecraft: Education Edition* to help shape Ireland's sustainable future. The students' work for this competition is truly inspirational and well worth viewing https://www.rte.ie/learn/irelands-future-is-mine/ Links to some individual entries are included in the padlet which accompanies this book. To prepare students to partake in Lego or Minecraft projects, a visit to a sustainable community is a good place to begin (Case study 14.1).

Case study 14.1 Cloughjordan Eco Village (CEV), Tipperary, Ireland

Founded in 1999, Ireland's first ecovillage now has a community of some 90 adults and 35 children living on a 67-acre site which backs on to the main street of Cloughjordan, Country Tipperary, Ireland. Its objective is to model sustainable living into the 21st century and to be an education, enterprise and research resource for the general public. Among its subsidiary objectives is to minimise pollution of the air, water and land, to demonstrate a new approach to rural regeneration, to facilitate the creation of local and sustainable livelihoods, and to provide for the cultural and non-material needs of the ecovillage and surrounding community. Among the reasons for choosing to locate in Cloughjordan was the rail link that services the town, thus allowing more sustainable travel. Cloughjordan Eco Village (CEV) therefore constitutes a model of a sustainable community, integrated into an existing urban settlement (Figure 14.2).

What distinguishes the ecovillage from any other Irish housing estate is its commitment to sustainability, understood not only as environmental sustainability but also as economic and social sustainability. Tipperary Energy Agency measured CEV's ecological footprint in 2014, using a methodology based on that of the Global Footprint Network. The ecological footprint is a composite measure of the impact of human activities on the planet in terms of the amount of land and water needed to produce goods as well as the capacity of the biosystem to assimilate the wastes generated, including carbon emissions. It is therefore a comprehensive measure of the pressure that human

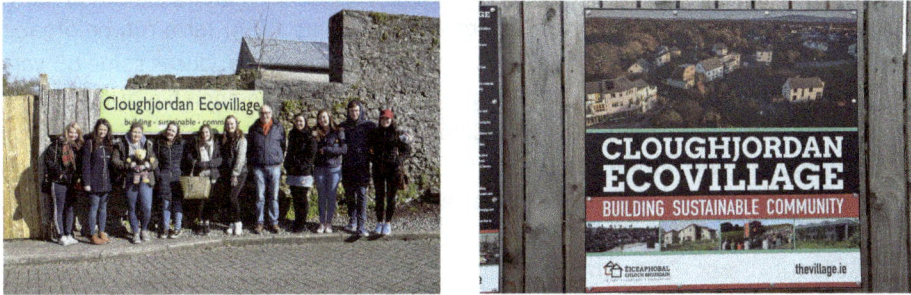

Figure 14.2 Cloughjordan Ecovillage.

lifestyles are putting on the Earth's resources clearly identifying the sources of unsustainability (see globalfootprintnetwork.net). Globally, it is estimated that the maximum footprint that allows each human to live within the planet's biocapacity is 1.8 global hectares (gHa). The average ecovillager's ecological footprint of 2 global hectares compares favourably to an ecological footprint of between 2.9 and 4.3 for other Irish towns and an ecological footprint of 5.0 for the average Irish person, as measured by the Global Footprint Network. This means that living as an average ecovillager requires 1.1 Earths whereas living as an average Irish person requires 3.14 Earths (www.globalfootprintnetwork.org).

Three key features help sustain this low ecological footprint

1 Building low-energy housing: While the ecovillage does not require any particular building designs, it has set out a range of standards and principles to which all buildings must adhere. These are contained in the Ecological Charter which sets targets for total heat input and exact specifications for insulation, as well as covering issues of air-tight construction, ventilation and maximising natural light and heat through facing buildings southwards. It recommends the use of non-toxic materials, regionally sourced and with low embodied energy. Guided by its Charter, CEV has pioneered the use of different building types such as passive timber-frame, Durisol blocks of chipped waste wood bonded with ecocement, cellulose, hemp-lime and cob. In 2017, 10 of the 55 houses in the ecovillage installed photovoltaic (PV) panels to generate energy.

2 Heating all houses in a carbon-neutral way: All homes depend on the district system for the supply of hot water and heating. The heating plant contains two 500-kilowatt wood-chip boilers backed up by 500m² of solar (thermal) panels. This system is the first of its kind in a private housing development in Ireland and is estimated to save some 113.5 tonnes annually of carbon emissions over what would be emitted by an equivalent-size development using conventional heating methods. The plant supplies hot water daily to all homes via a well-insulated network of piping and the water is stored in each house in an insulated storage tank supplying hot water and heating.

3   Local food production: The CEV food system is centred on Cloughjordan Commu-
    nity Farm (CCF), a Community-Supported Agriculture (CSA) farm run on organic
    principles. Based on around 10 acres of ecovillage land, it produces some 85 vari-
    eties of vegetables, salads, herbs and fruits to feed a membership of around 90
    people, supply the Middle Country Café co-operative, and to feed visiting educa-
    tion groups. The farm is run by two full-time farmers and also, as its ecologically
    sensitive methods are labour-intensive and there is minimal use of mechanical
    equipment, it relies on the manual labour of eight volunteers from the European
    Solidarity Corps (ESC), who each come for a year. CCF is committed to seed saving
    and currently about 60% of crops are grown from its own seeds. Over 2,500 trees
    were planted on the farm in 2020 adding Agroforestry as part of its practice for
    soil regeneration and sustainable cultivation. In response to the challenges of the
    Covid pandemic, the farm created an Open Food Hub in 2021. Located in the ecovil-
    lage's WeCreate Enterprise Centre, this initiative will develop sustainable ways of
    marketing the produce of small and medium-sized regional food producers via the
    virtual 'Tipperary Open Market', linking producers and consumers on-line. It will
    also provide digital training and mentoring to farmers, food producers, and other
    food hubs across Ireland.

A commitment to biodiversity characterises the way the whole ecovillage is maintained, using Permaculture principles. An example is the Sensory and Wildlife Garden,
with raised beds, willow structures, a composting area, a bug hotel, wildflower beds,
footpaths and a wildlife corridor. The ecovillage contains a wild woodland area in which
17,000 native varieties of trees were planted to help foster biodiversity. Two apiar-
ies are maintained, producing honey and recognising the importance of pollination to
our biodiversity. Plans are in train to undertake a full biodiversity audit as input to a
whole-site biodiversity plan to include the protection and promotion of biodiversity and
an education programme related to it. A Dark Sky bowl has been created for star gaz-
ing. This offers the possibility of identifying many of the constellations throughout the
seasons with a clear view of the milky way during the warmer months. It is planned to
apply for a dark-sky certificate from the international Dark-Sky Association and to promote astrotourism in the ecovillage, another contribution to creating local livelihoods.

To help foster livelihoods, the ecovillage has developed as a unique networked
hub of organisations, sometimes referred to as 'an ecosystem of innovation'. Among
these are Cloughjordan Community Farm, and Cloughjordan Community Arts, which
built an amphitheatre within the ecovillage, opened by President Michael D. Higgins
in April 2017. Cloughjordan Community Cooperative, founded in 2016, uses the food
produced by Cloughjordan Community Farm and the bread baked by Riot Rye bakery
in the ecovillage to produce wholesome meals in the co-op's Middle Country Café on
Cloughjordan's main street. Cloughjordan Co-Housing is another co-operative, planning a co-housing development within the ecovillage to offer low-cost and low-energy
homes with shared services. Among the micro-enterprises that flourish are Django's
Ecohostel, the WeCreate green enterprise centre which incorporates a fab lab, VINE

which provides internet services in the ecovillage, and Riot Rye bakery and baking school. These enterprises cooperate to enhance their businesses and model a form of resilient economic and social regeneration. As Covid has shown the possibilities for greater homeworking, the ecovillage sees this as an opportunity for further development of sustainable livelihoods contributing to a flourishing community. A new development plan is focused on providing more affordable and social housing options within the ecovillage while a project to recycle waste within the ecovillage aims to achieve a more circular and regenerative system of waste management.

Central to this flourishing community is a rich cultural life. The amphitheatre provides the basis for developing a programme of artistic events and festivals with a particular focus on how to live sustainably. The establishment of the ecovillage has drawn a wider group of artists to Cloughjordan - painters, sculptors, musicians, singers, writers, actors and playwrights, all contributing to a vibrant and busy cultural life. The ecovillage is committed to promoting the Irish language and all street names are in Irish only. Various activities through Irish, including a regular PopUp Gaeltacht, are a feature of the community's life. A labyrinth in the woodland area provides a space for meditative walking.

As a registered educational NGO, education is part of the DNA of the ecovillage with the aim of establishing itself as a leading national and international centre for education on sustainability, resilience, community living, and rural regeneration, rethinking and remodelling the society of the future. It offers a place-based learning experience of building a sustainable community which is unique to Ireland. This it does mainly through guided tours every Saturday and Sunday, and visits by schools, community groups and specialist professional groups from Ireland and abroad. Longer visits, particularly by groups of third-level students, permit a deeper immersion in the many aspects of the ecovillage. When Covid forced the cancellation of almost all formal education in 2020, the programme moved on-line with a virtual tour, a Deep Listening webinar series and modules on a range of topics related to sustainability (see www.thevillage.ie). A new area called Cuan Beo with a wooden cabin and a polytunnel with disability access has been developed to provide farm education.

In its 20 years of existence, the CEV community has learnt that building resilient community is its greatest challenge. All members pledge at least 100 hours voluntary labour a year so that the project can draw on an extensive range of skills and experience. Voluntary contributions from members are made towards the following: organising workshops for students and teachers; organic farming and seed saving; land management and forestry; low-energy building and renewable energy systems; urban drainage systems; waste disposal systems; cooking and nutrition; arts and crafts; health-care and wellbeing; psychotherapy and spirituality; communications and photography, and social media. Members step up to various roles, on various boards, on the office team, in looking after the land, and in varied educational activities. From the beginning, CEV adopted a consensus form of decision-making with the monthly members' meeting as the central forum for accountability and for making decisions. This has helped to make members feel they are driving the project. A complex governance system works to avoid the centralisation of power, managing to combine a rich culture of grassroots creativity with accountability to members for all that happens in the project. This takes careful management and a dedicated Process group organises all meetings and decision-making processes. These experiences have helped build skills of conflict resolution, facilitation, mediation and community building, with courses occasionally provided to train members in these skills. Visiting the ecovillage has a significant impact on visitors (14.2). The following comments from student teachers illustrate the impact of such visits.

> *My biggest takeaway from the visit was witnessing the ethos of the village and residents in terms of their community spirit and their outlook on the power of sustainable living and its impact on not just climate change but our own well-being and community spirit. Listening to the speakers from the cafe speak and the owner of the bread club talk about her reasoning for keeping their production levels low were the main ways in which I began to experience this ethos. It was enlightening and prompted me to think critically about their ideas and how we may incorporate them into my own town. Questioning the speakers about certain obstacles or limitations to their ethos was probably the most enriching aspect of the visit as they did not begrudge the criticism but rather embraced it and acknowledged it explaining that this is not a choice but rather a necessity for our well-being and community. They used this opportunity to inspire us in whatever way they could explaining the power and influence we can have on the next generation. I left the ecovillage with a whole new outlook and perspective on sustainability.*

> *It is without doubt an experience like none other for to understand the message encapsulated within the village one most walk the woodland paths and speak to the locals and witness the community ethos by walking through their farm, eating lunch in their cafe and walking through the food stalls in which they collect their fresh produce. Prior to ever visiting such a place one may begin to think of a radical society that is completely new and different to anything we've ever experienced. Whereas upon visiting you begin to discover that this way of living and the societal connection between the producers and consumers is based upon the values of a sustainable society as these business owners care about their locality rather than profiting from their product through market competition and expansion. It was refreshing to listen to the lady who worked in the cafe talk about how they would rather own a place where someone can sit for the day and talk to people rather than pressure them to buy a drink and lunch and leave when they have finished so as to make room for more customers. Although they may not be making a wage they know that the people living around them will not let them fail and will support them daily.*

Sustainable communities: a focus on food

In the Cloughjordan Eco Village, the benefits of community-based gardening and bakery projects extend beyond food security. Using biodynamic and organic farming methods, the farm aims to produce the highest quality, nutritionally dense vegetables, while also reducing the environmental impact of producing this food. The money gathered from members is used to pay farmers a salary and to purchase seeds and equipment. Everything that comes off the land then belongs to the members. Members have access to the most nutritionally complete vegetables and fruit possible creating sustainable links between the community and food sources.

As well as the provision of fresh vegetables and bread, these initiatives facilitate a sense of community well-being, resilience and pride. The eco village includes an award winning bakery (the Riot Rye Bakehouse), a 20, 000 tree biodiversity garden and personal allotments for growing vegetables. A community supported farm features 70 varieties of native Irish apples including Golden Spire, Honey Baw, White Moss, Cavan Wine, Red Stripe and Pig Snout among others. Féile na nÚll, an annual apple festival celebrates the yield of apples Those who tend to the tress and work the land are recognised during this annual celebration. Coinciding with the European Day of Sustainable Communities, the festival includes local food stalls, an apple bake competition, generation of juice from apple pressing and apple-based celebrations for the whole community.

The baker along with two farmers working on the village farm, operate a community-supported business model. This means villagers and others in the surrounding area commit to paying the baker for fresh bread three times a week, while others do the same with farm produce. This guarantees people's livelihoods while members receive locally produced fresh and seasonal food. Residents have the opportunity to eat vegetables that have been harvested the very same day.

Community gardens such as this have much to offer teachers and students involved in school and home gardens. An increased interest in gardening and local allotments was one of the positive trends to emerge during Covid 19, as the recreational, health, economic and environmental benefits of vegetable gardens were discovered (Sofo and Sofo, 2020). Evidence is emerging that, schools can be influential in the emerging agenda around the ecological, ethical and social aspects of food, diet and nutrition (Weitkamp et al., 2013). School growing programmes and garden based learning are becoming more popular as part of a Green Schools agenda. Popular crops include salads, soft fruits and vegetables. Growing, preparing and consuming food in school, teaches students the connection between growing plants and the food we eat, and the importance of eating healthily (Austin, 2021). Furthermore, many school gardens are designed with biodiversity in mind. Features such as insect hotels, bird feeders, ponds and bird watch hides, provide opportunities for students to observe and encounter flora and fauna within the school grounds. By engaging local volunteers, parents, and local organisations, school gardens can have a 'ripple effect' (Passy, 2014) throughout a school community and beyond. Ultimately, school gardens have the potential to be magnificent learning sites 'because they provide an arena for learning, space for pastoral care, a focus for school and community involvement and a source of pleasure for the school community (Austin, 2021: 1).

Links between SDG 11 and other sustainable development goals

According to Habitat (2018), SDG 11 is directly linked to targets and indicators in at least eleven other SDGs (Figure 14.3). In addition, about one third of the 234 indicators that are part of the global monitoring framework for SDGs can be measured at the local urban level, making the city an important unit for action and tracking progress towards sustainable development. Figure 14.3 sets out a detailed analysis of the various linkages between the urban targets under Goal 11 and targets in other goals.

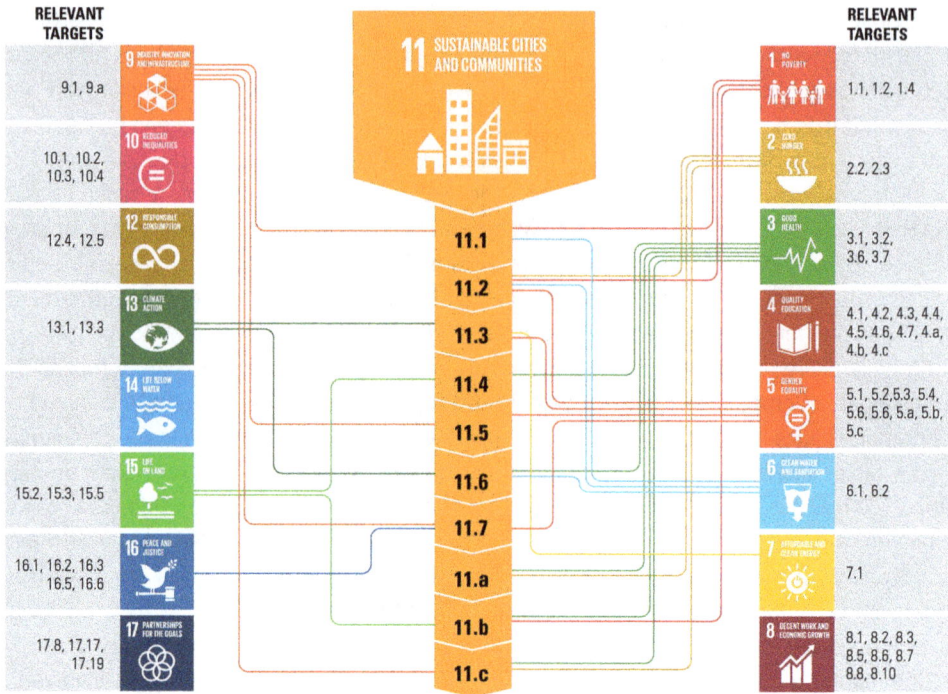

Figure 14.3 Interlinkages between SDG 11 and other SDGs. (Source Habitat, 2018: 10).

Students can be involved in drawing a web depicting the links between SDG 11 and other goals particularly in the context of population growth. Because of population growth in cities, there is the need to facilitate safe, regular and responsible migration and mobility of people (Target 10.7), since growing cities lead to increased waste production and emissions. For this reason, a change in production and consumption must also be achieved (Targets 12.3, 12.4 and 12.5) to reduce and even prevent cities becoming vulnerable to climate change and natural disasters. Investing in technology, research and innovation is important to achieve upgrades in infrastructures (Targets 9.1, 9.2, 9.3 and 9.4) such as sustainable transport systems (Target 11.2). Ensuring access to safe and affordable housing and basic services (Target 11.1) can increase security and safety, improve access to adequate sanitation and clean drinking water (Targets 6.1 and 6.2), reducing the impact of communicable diseases and maternal and children mortality (Targets 3.2 and 3.3).

The role of local government is vital as this is the layer of government closest to the people, and it often has significant decision-making and spending power. While SDG 11 is primarily focused on government action, the initiatives need community buy-in from individual citizens as well as community leaders. For example, individuals can take actions such as fixing up their local parks, creating rooftop gardens, or participating in community composting programmes to improve the quality of greenspaces and create additional ones in new spots. People can make small steps in their own neighbourhoods to support sustainable cities on a world-wide level. School based actions such as school gardens and walk to school schemes provide learning opportunities for action and reflection.

Conclusion

This chapter discusses the concept of sustainable cities and communities including practical activities which can be undertaken by students in schools. Sustainable communities are characterised by the spirit of 'meitheal' described in the introduction. Cloughjordan Ecovillage is one example of how a small community can together achieve a much higher level of sustainability than that of the average Irish person while living well with a vibrant social, cultural and economic life (see Kirby, 2020). It illustrates 'green urbanism' in practice, while echoing many of the issues covered by SDG 11. As is clear, the ecovillage is a project still developing, and has yet to achieve the ability to live comfortably within the limits of the ecosystem as its residents' lifestyles still require 1.1 Earths. However, it strives to show the ways that any urban community can, with foresight, commitment and planning, move decisively towards sustainability. As such, it represents a wake-up call about the crucial importance of local grassroots action to contribute to national and global actions if the goals of SDG 11 are to be achieved. Learning about sustainable communities such as Cloughjordan Eco Village will help students to understand the concept of sustainable living. More importantly, it provides them with the knowledge and understanding for making sustainable choices in their own lives now and in the future.

Resources

An extensive list of resources, videos and case studies for SDG 11 is included in the SDG padlet accompanying this book: https://padlet.com/annedolan/o6rds38ylfy6a28h

Web links

World The Bank provides a useful tool for exploring data on urbanisation: https://data.world-bank.org/indicator/SP.URB.TOTL.IN.ZS
Goal 11 Webpage: https://www.un.org/sustainabledevelopment/cities/
The Sustainable Living Podcast: https://sustainablelivingpodcast.com/blog/podcasts/
Cities: An interactive data visualization tool: The tool covers all cities with 500,000-plus inhabitants – illustrates the scale and speed of urban transformation that research by the International Institute of Environment and Development (IIED) has sought to document and describe: https://www.iied.org/cities-interactive-data-visual
Green Schools: Make a DIY city in a box: https://youtu.be/kp8xjAwdNOg

Key dates

March 21: International Day of Forests
April 22: Earth Day
May 22: International Day for Biological Diversity
June 5: World Environment Day
June 8: World Oceans Day
July 22: International Day for the Conservation of the Mangrove Ecosystem
Fourth Sunday in July: International Bog Day

September 21: Zero Emissions Day
December 11: International Mountain Day
Third Saturday in September: European Day of Sustainable Communities

Children's literature about co-operation and sustainable communities

Afzal, S. and Ghare, A. (illus) (2022). *Journey of the Midnight Sun* Orca Book Publishers.
Campoy, F. I., Howell, T. and López, R. (illus) (2016). *Maybe Something Beautiful: How Art Transformed a Neighborhood* HMH Books for Young Readers.
Claire, C. and Leng, Q. (illus) (2017). *Shelter* Kids Can Press.
Cumpiano, I. and Ramirez, J. (illus) (2009). *Quinito's Neighbourhood* Children's Book Press.
Drummond, A. (2011). Green City: *How One Community Survived a Tornado and Rebuilt for a Sustainable Future* Farrar, Straus and Giroux (BYR).
Drummond, A. (2016). *Energy Island: How One Community Harnessed the Wind and Changed Their World* Farrar, Straus and Giroux (BYR).
Drummond, A. (2017). Pedal Power: *How One Community Became the Bicycle of the World* Farrar, Straus and Giroux (BYR).
Drummond, A. (2020). *Solar Story: How One Community Lives Alongside the World's Biggest Solar Plant* Farrar, Straus and Giroux (BYR).
Durango, J. and Diaz, B. (illus) (2020). *The One Day House* Charlesbridge.
Fleischman, P. and Hawkes, K. (illus) (2002). *Weslandia* Candlewick.
Graham, K. and Paterson, W. (illus) (2016). *The Lemon Tree* Struik Lifestyle.
Krishnaswami, U. and Krishnaswamy, U. (illus) (2012). *Out of the Way! Out of the Way!* Groundwood Books.
Kurusa and Doppert, M. (illus) (2008). *The Streets Are Free* Annick Press.
Long, L. (2009). *Otis* Philomel Books.
McAllister, B. and Aardema, J. (illus) (2016) *Bicycles, Airships and Things That Go* Kids Future Press.
Nagara, I. (2015) *Counting on Community* Triangle Square.
Paratore, C. and Reed, M. (illus) (2008). *26 Big Things Small Hands Do* Free Spirit Publishing.
Penfold, A. and Kaufman, S. (illus) (2019) *All Are Welcome* Bloomsbury.
Richie, S. (2015) *Look Where We Live: A First Book of Community Building* Kids Can Press.
Robles, A. D. and Angel, C. (illus) (2006). *Lakas and the Makibaka Hotel* Children's Book Press.
Rodham, C. and Frazee, M. (illus) (2017). *It Takes a Village* Simon & Schuste.
Sís, P. (2020). *Madlenka* Square Fish.
Subramaniam. S. amd Prabhat, S. (illus) (2022). *Namaste is a Greeting* Walker Books.
Teckentrup, B. (2019). *We Are Together* Caterpillar Books.
Van Dongen, S. (2021). *The Neighbourhood Surprise* Tiny Owl Publishing.
Verde, S. and Parra, J. (illus) (2018). *Hey, Wall: A Story of Art and Community* Simon & Schuster/Paula Wiseman Books.

Children's literature about farming and community gardens

Picturebooks

Alary, L. and Reich, K. (illus) (2020). *What Grew in Larry's Garden* Kids Can Press.
Baker, J. (2008). *Belonging* Walker Books.
Booth, A. and Wilson, R. O. (illus) (2020) *Bloom: Hope in a Scary World* Tiny Owl Publishing Ltd.
Boughton, S. (2018). *The Extraordinary Gardener* Tate Publishing.
Briggs Martin, J. and Larkin, E. S. (illus) (2013). *Farmer Will Allen and the Growing Table* Readers to Eaters.
Brown, P. (2009). *The Curious Garden* Little Brown Books for Young Readers.
Brown, R. (2010). *Ten Seeds* Andersen Press.
Castaldo, N. and Hsu. G. (illus) (2020). *The Farm That Feeds Us: A Year in The Life Of An Oragnic Farm* Words and Pictures.

Clément, G. and Gavé, V. (illus) (2018). *A Big Garden* Prestel Publishing.

Colleen, M. and Oliver, A. (illus) (2020). *The Bear's Garden* Imprint.

Davies, N and Carlin, L. (illus) (2013). *The Promise* Walker Books.

Deenihan, J. L. B. and Rocha, L. (illus) (2019). *When Grandma Gives You a Lemon Tree* Sterling Children's Books.

DiSalvo-Ryan, D. (2019). *City Green* HarperCollins.

Dowding, C. (2023). *The No-Dig Children's Gardening Book Easy and Fun Family Gardening* Welbeck Children's

Dyer, H. (2012). *Potatoes on Rooftops: Farming in the City* Annick Press.

Fleischman, P. (2004). *Seedfolks* HarperTrophy.

Fullerton, A. (2019) *Community Soup* Pajama Press.

Grigsby, S. and Tadgell, N. (illus) (2010). *In the Garden with Dr. Carver* Albert Whitman & Company.

Hibbs, G. (2018). *Errol's Garden* Child's Play (International) Ltd.

Hillery, T. and Hartland, J. (2020). *Harlem Grown: How One Big Idea Transformed a Neighbourhood* Simon & Schuster/Paula Wiseman Books.

Ip, R. and Bray, A. (illus) (2021). *The Last Garden* Hodder Children's Books.

Lamba, M., Lamba, B. and Sanchez, S. (illus) (2017). *Green Green: A Community Gardening* Story Farrar, Straus and Giroux (BYR).

Lawston, R. (2021). *Finn's Garden Friends* Pikku Publishing.

Mangal, M. and Daley, K. (illus) (2021). *Jayden's Impossible Garden* Free Spirit Publishing.

Mortimer, H. and Cottle. K. (illus) (2021). *Omar, the Bees and Me* Owlet Press

McCanna, T. and Sicuro, A. (illus) (2020). *In a Garden* Simon & Schuster.

Guckin, I. (2023). *April's Garden* Graffeg.

Moore, T. and Van Dongen, S. (2020). *The Allotmenteers* Ragged Bears.

Pattou, E. (2007). *Mrs. Spitzer's Garden* HMH Books for Young Readers.

Paul, B. Paul, M. and Zunon, E. (illus) (2019). *I am a Farmer: Growing an Environmental Movement in Cameroon* The Millbrook Press Inc.

Peguignot, A. Shoemaker, T. and Fallahee, K. (illus) (2019). T*he Day the Farmers Quit* Independently published.

Pollak, B. (2006). *Our Community Garden* Beyond Words Publishing.

Sarah, L. and Lumbers, F. (illus) (2018). *Secret Sky Garden* Simon & Schuster.

Smit, N. (2020). In *The Garden* Little Island Books

Stewart, S. and Small, D. (illus) (2007). *The Gardiner* Square Fish.

Swann, R. and Hale, C. (illus) (2018). *Our School Garden* Readers to Eaters.

Tamaki, J. (2020). *Our Little Kitchen* Abrams Books for Young Readers.

Tree, I. and Tee, A. (illus) (2021). *When We Went Wild* Ivy Kids Eco.

Chapter Books

Moseley, E. (2020). *The Garden and the Glen: A Fable About Character and the Courage to Be Different* Lenox Street Press.

Yan Glaser, K. (2019). *The Vanderbeekers and the Hidden Garden* HMH Books for Young Readers.

References

Austin, S. (2021) The school garden in the primary school: Meeting the challenges and reaping the benefits. *Education, 3-13*, 1-15.

Butler, D., Broderick, N., Usher, J. and Moynihan, D. (2022) *First LEGO League Explore Cargo Connect Teacher Guide for Ireland*. Stevenage: The Institution of Engineering and Technology. www.dcu.ie/sites/default/files/staff/2022-04/Teacher_Guide_First_Lego_League_Explore_Cargo_Connect_v15.pdf

Caradonna, Jeremy L. (2014) *Sustainability: A History*. Oxford: Oxford University Press.

Christensen, P., Hadfield-Hill, S., Horton, J. and Kraftl, P. (2017) *Children Living in Sustainable Built Environments: New Urbanisms, New Citizens*. London: Routledge.

Dolan, A. M. (2022) Pedagogy of hope: Futures teaching for climate change. In Dolan, A. M. ed., *Teaching Climate Change in Primary Schools: An Interdisciplinary Approach*. London: Routledge, 284-304.

FIRST LEGO League. (2020) *What Is First Lego League*. https://www.firstlegoleague.org/about

Habitat, U. N. (2018) *Synthesis Report 2018: Tracking Progress Towards Inclusive, Safe, Resilient and Sustainable Cities and Human Settlements*. https://apo.org.au/sites/default/files/resource-files/2018-07/apo-nid182836.pdf

Kirby, Peadar. (2020) Cloughjordan ecovillage: Community-led transitioning to a low-carbon future. In Robbins, D. Torney, D. and Brereton, P. eds., *Ireland and the Climate Crisis*. Cham, Switzerland: Palgrave Macmillan, 287–303.

Kirby, Peadar. (2021) *Karl Polanyi and the Contemporary Political Crisis: Transforming Market Society in the Era of Climate Change*. London: Bloomsbury.

Lehane, P., Butler, D. and Marshall, K. (2021) *Building a New World in Education: Exploring Minecraft for Learning, Teaching and Assessment* (White paper). Dublin: Dublin City University. www.dcu.ie/sites/default/files/inline-files/m90135-minecraft-191121_web_singles.pdf

NASA Earth Observatory. (2019) *Sizing Up the Carbon Footprint of Cities*. https://earthobservatory.nasa.gov/images/144807/sizing-up-the-carbon-footprint-of-cities, downloaded 16th February 2021.

Passy, R. (2014) School gardens: Teaching and learning outside the front door. *Education 42*(1), 23–38.

Ruiz Vicente, F., Zapatera Llinares, A. and Montés Sánchez, N. (2020) "Sustainable city": A Steam project using robotics to bring the city of the future to primary education students. *Sustainability, 12*(22), 9696.

Sofo, A. and Sofo, A. (2020) Converting home spaces into food gardens at the time of Covid-19 quarantine: All the benefits of plants in this difficult and unprecedented period. *Human Ecology, 48*(2), 131–139.

UNESCO. (2017) *Education for Sustainable Development Goals-learning objectives*. https://unesdoc.unesco.org/ark:/48223/pf0000247444

United Nations. (2015) *Making Cities and Human Settlements Inclusive, Safe, Resilient and Sustainable*. https://sdgs.un.org/goals/goal11

United Nations (UN). (2020) *Sustainable Development Goal*. https://www.un.org/sustainabledevelopment/sustainable-development-goals/

Usher, J. and Moynihan, D. (2022) The future is mine: Geography education and minecraft education. *Primary Geography, 108*(2), 26–28.

Weitkamp, E., Jones, M., Salmon, D., Kimberlee, R. and Orme, J. (2013) Creating a learning environment to promote food sustainability issues in primary schools? Staff perceptions of implementing the food for life partnership programme. *Sustainability, 5*(3), 1128–1140.

15 Responsible consumption and production

Think before you buy (SDG 12)

Nicola Broderick and Joe Usher

Introduction

Our planet has provided us with an abundance of natural resources. Unfortunately, these resources have been used, abused and wasted causing many of the problems which the SDGs are designed to address. While consumers are more aware of the environmental impact of their purchases, over consumption continues to be one of the most significant challenges to sustainable development. Overconsumption means consuming resources that we cannot replenish or that cannot sustain themselves at the rate we are consuming them. Ecosystems are unable to cope with excessive resource extraction, resulting in biodiversity loss and the deterioration of the natural world. Every stage in the lifecycle of a product including production, transportation, consumption and disposal (including plastic packaging) generates physical waste and fossil fuel consumption. Consumption of flights and fast fashion together with marketing initiatives such as Black Friday and Cyber Monday, are fuelling our ecological crisis. Companies such as Shein promote a 'throwaway culture' by offering clothes so cheaply that they are often worn once before being discarded. Leonard (2011) describes the process of 'manufactured demand' wherby we as consumers are conditioned to think we need to spend money on something we don't actually need. An excellent example of this is bottled water whereby more than half a billion bottles of water are purchased every week in America, even though it already flows virtually free from the tap.

Aptly named books such as *There is no planet B* (Berners-Lee, 2021 and *The Day the World Stops Shopping* MacKinnon, (2021) urges us as consumers to consume less.

Sustainable Development Goal (SDG) 12 is concerned with responsible consumption and production. The official wording of SDG 12 is 'to ensure sustainable consumption and production patterns' (UN, 2017: 313). In order to achieve sustainable development patterns of production and consumption on both global and local levels, we urgently need to reduce our ecological footprint by changing the way goods and resources are produced and consumed. Encouraging corporations, industries, businesses and individual consumers to act more responsibly in this regard is equally as important. Understanding how individual behaviours and societal systems need to change to meet SDG targets is a fascinating way of bringing values, ethics and human rights into the classroom as well as integrating traditional disciplinary areas such as business, economics, science, geography and home economics. Through learning about SDG 12, students will recognise the economic interests of

DOI: 10.4324/9781003232001-18

multi-national corporations in sustaining high levels of consumption. By using the lens of the Four Hs Framework, students see how their role as consumers on a personal level (along with mass consumption promoted by the manufacturing sector) affects the environment. In doing so, the hope is that they will consume in a more ethical and responsible way. When students are able to visualise how their actions are benefiting the environment and community both locally and globally, they can develop a passion for sustainable living outside of the classroom and carry these ideals into the practices of their everyday lives both now and in the future.

Overview of chapter

This chapter begins by outlining the learning theory and a pedagogical framework underpinning the content and activities for the teaching of SDG 12. The chapter then focuses on the implementation of this pedagogical framework through the SDG 12 related topic of food (which links with the food and hunger activities detailed in chapter 5), and sustainable food production discussed in chapter 14 (SDG 11). Practical learning activities, discussion points and resources are detailed with references to appropriate case study examples from schools (Case studies 15.1, 15.2, 15.3, and 15.4).

Other SDG 12 topics including the clothing and tourism industries are highlighted. An overview of the SDG 12 targets can be seen in Appendix 1. Definitions of key terms, underlying the chapter are provided at the end of the chapter (see Table 15.8).

Learning theory

The learning theory underpinning the pedagogical framework and methods outlined in this chapter is very much centred on experiential and enquiry-based learning. This educational theory is inspired by the work of educationalist John Dewey (1938) who championed a move away from the rigid approach of passive learning towards a more participatory and democratic model with the student at the centre of the learning. Here learning is an active experience where students are encouraged and facilitated in becoming good active citizens (Aubrey and Riley, 2016). This philosophy emerged out of a concern that learning is often disconnected from everyday experience, alienating students as a result. Dewey saw education as a powerful force in peoples' lives and believed that learning is an active process and that tasks should be challenging and relate to real life, promoting learning through experiences and interactions. We argue that, in teaching about the SDGs, topics need to be relevant to students' everyday lives and that in order for the SDGs to be achieved, actions which have global consequences need to be taken at local and individual levels and embedded into the daily practices of ordinary, everyday life. This is also upheld by the Four Hs Framework which underpins this book. Indeed, Dewey suggests that students who are active and engaged within society can more readily bring their experiences to their learning. Here, teachers primarily act as facilitators of learning; aiding students to develop skills and competencies that enable them to 'thrive and contribute to a democratic society' (Aubrey and Riley, 2016: 9). Kolb (1984: 38) also highlights the importance of experience in education whereby knowledge acquisition is a process created 'through the transformation of experience' and whereby students are active in their own learning. Experiential learning promotes critical thinking, problem-solving and enquiry, and stresses the importance of connecting to students' real-world experiences. Ives and Obenchain (2006) outline three fundamental elements of experiential education, comprising: student-centred approaches, connections to the real world, and opportunities for reflection. These three elements are fundamental to an education that aims to attain societal change through the achievement of the SDGs. Contexts enable and restrict what students can do and come to know. This chapter purports the SDGs themselves to be an authentic context for learning, thus locating the SDGs within students' everyday real-world lived experiences. Inspired by experiential learning and the work of Dewey, the learning approaches presented thoughout this book are designed to facilitate students' learning and skill development through enhancing their capacity to take action in attaining the SDGs.

Enquiry-based learning comprises a student-centred, experiential, constructivist approach. Students are active in their learning and participate in the leading of investigations. Through posing questions and generating ideas, students actively create and collect data to help develop their understanding. Here, the learning begins with a problem or obstacle with which students can relate to; they analyse the situation; identify possible solutions; compare the implications of the different solutions and select the best course of action. They then implement this in practice. This involves the use of authentic, ill-defined, open-ended investigable questions or hypotheses formulated by students and teachers. Enquiries should be located in real-world contexts and align with student and societal interests. Students then follow an enquiry framework devising questions, investigating, collecting and interpreting evidence. Through adopting an enquiry based education framework, students design and conduct investigations that provide/gather the data necessary to arrive at conclusions, using the same systematic approach that scientists use (Lederman, 1992). In addition, aligning with Vygotsky's social constructivism, learning through enquiry-based learning requires collaboration to deal with complex, multi-faceted problems. Scaffolding is also a key feature of enquiry-based learning, whereby students are given appropriate support to help them learn and develop skills pertaining to the issue at hand.

Pedagogical framework.

The pedagogical framework guiding the approaches advocated in this chapter is informed by other enquiry and investigative frameworks for geography, science and citizenship education such as Levinson (2018), Sadler (2011), Hancock, Friedrichsen, Kinslow and Sadler (2019) and Roberts (2013) as outlined below (see Figure 15.1). While the framework is presented in a cyclical manner, there are instances where students will move forwards and backwards between phases as appropriate in conducting investigations, encountering new issues/additional complexities, gathering new/more data and undergoing further synthesis before deciding upon appropriate action(s).

Phase 1: encounter

This framework begins by introducing the students to a relevant topic relating to SDG 12. Through the *Encounter* phase, the students are made aware of the scientific, social and

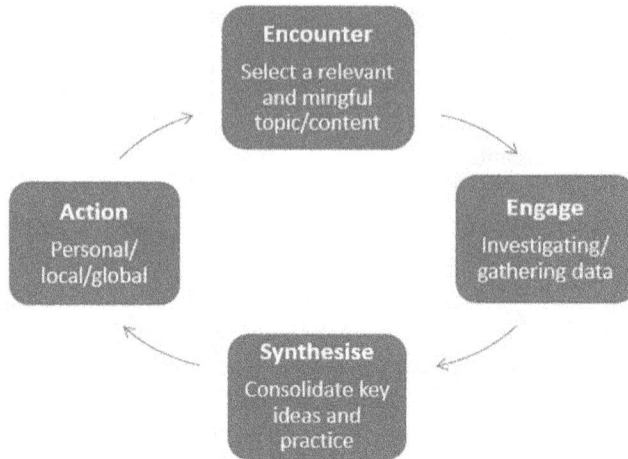

Figure 15.1 Pedagogical Framework Underpinning This Chapter.

cultural aspects which permeate the issue. This topic should be relevant to the students' everyday lives and complex in that there is no one 'correct' solution (Amos and Levinson, 2019). Students are provided with opportunities to ask enquiry questions regarding the topic, at a personal, social, local and global level, which will guide the teaching and learning. Here, the students hypothesise, speculate and generate ideas and questions for the investigation of a topic. Students draw on their existing knowledge, perceptions and everyday experiences. Teachers can facilitate students' engagement in a topic at the *Encounter* phase through the use of a stimulus such as photographs, videos, graphs, physical artefacts, newspaper articles and concept cartoons.

Phase 2: engage

The Engage phase involves the students actively carrying out investigations on the SDG 12 topic. Students use a range of resources to both create and collect data to develop their understanding of the issue. By analysing and interpreting the data related to their investigations, students reflect upon and modify their ideas and concepts as appropriate.

Phase 3: synthesise

In the *Synthesise* phase, students are provided with a culminating experience in which they attempt to synthesise key ideas and practices. Reasoning and opportunities to engage in discussion and debate are considered a central component of this framework. This is what students engage in as active participants in society, where they engage in discussion and debate about real-world everyday issues before they make informed decisions. These opportunities to engage in discourse, debate and argumentation within an educational environment provide students with opportunities to acquire increasingly sophisticated reasoning capacities and to develop empathy with various stakeholders.

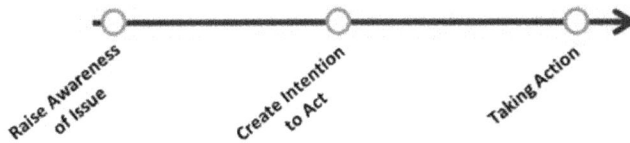

Figure 15.2 Continuum of Action. (Amos and Christodoulou, 2018).

Phase 4: action

The fourth and final phase, *Action,* empowers students to take action, where appropriate. This promotes citizenship education and involves the students making informed decisions which they can then enact at personal, individual, group and wider levels, thus contributing to a democratic society. Through this 'pedagogy of responsibility' (Martusewicz and Edmundson, 2005: 1), students develop an ecological and community identity that enables them to actively reflect upon their own lifestyles and consider their civic role and its impact on broader society, thus locating personal local actions within a global common cause (McInerney, Smyth, and Down, 2011; Smith and Sobel, 2014). This aligns with Amos and Christodoulou's (2018) continuum of 'taking action', as illustrated in Figure 15.2 where at one end of the continuum students raise awareness of the issue, at the middle students have an intention to act, and at the other side students take action in response to the issue. Through guidance from the teacher, it is crucial that this phase be student-led in that the actions agreed upon and taken by students individually and collectively are decided upon by the students themselves as they see fit.

Implementation of the pedagogical framework

'I shop, therefore I know that I am' is the basis of our consumer civilisation according to sociologist Colin Campbell (2004: 27) in commenting on human expression demonstrated through consumerism. Rates of consumption and production continue to increase exponentially. The pedagogical framework, *Encounter, Engage, Synthesis* and *Action* is implemented through specific topics associated with production and consumption, such as food and clothing, which apply to the universal classroom and human experience. The following sections will focus on the SDG 12 topic of food which links to Targets 12.2, 12.3, 12.5, 12.6 and 12A (Appendix 1). Connections to other topics and SDG 12 targets will be highlighted throughout.

SDG12 focus on food

The problems we are facing today require a profound change in the cultural fabric of our society. It is natural that the educational system, as one of the most powerful agencies of socialisation, be considered a key avenue through which such change can be spearheaded. We argue that the topic of food offers great opportunities to integrate knowledge and skills across disciplines, because it provides a palpable connection between humans and nature locally and globally. It is a topic enshrined within students' own everyday lives and exemplifies the global, far-reaching consequences of the most basic form of decision-making at local and individual levels. Learning about the production, transportation and disposal of food and the waste associated with food can bridge the growing divide between students and the origins of their food. Choosing to teach this topic addresses the need to reconnect students with the environment, linking urban and agricultural communities together, and providing hands-on learning and opportunities for students to reflect on their own everyday practices. By increasing food and sustainability literacies together in our educational practices, we can begin to overcome passivity, and the uncritical and dependent consumerism that characterises society's relationship with food. In doing so we can build capacity in our students to enact change, take action and make informed decisions. This topic also aligns with the targets of SDG 12, and the learning theory and pedagogical framework outlined above. Furthermore, explorations of the topic of food from the perspective of SDG 12 can also be linked with the activities about food and hunger discussed in chapter 5 (SDG 2).

Phase 1: encounter

Here, a class could be introduced to the topic of food and SDG 12 through various stimuli. In his 1967 Massey Lecture also known as his 'Christmas Sermon on Peace', Martin Luther King Jr (1967: np) said 'before you finish eating breakfast this morning you've depended on more than half the world'. Teachers can ask students to discuss what this means. The teacher encourages students to look through the contents of their own lunch boxes/food available in a school canteen and identify various food ingredients, stimulating a discussion pertaining to: where these food items originate from; how did they get here; how were they grown; and what jobs involve getting them 'from the land to my hand'?

Students generate ideas and questions around food production and consumption, such as the example depicted in Figure 15.3. The questions and observations that the students put forward could be recorded on the board and discussed as a class. The teacher

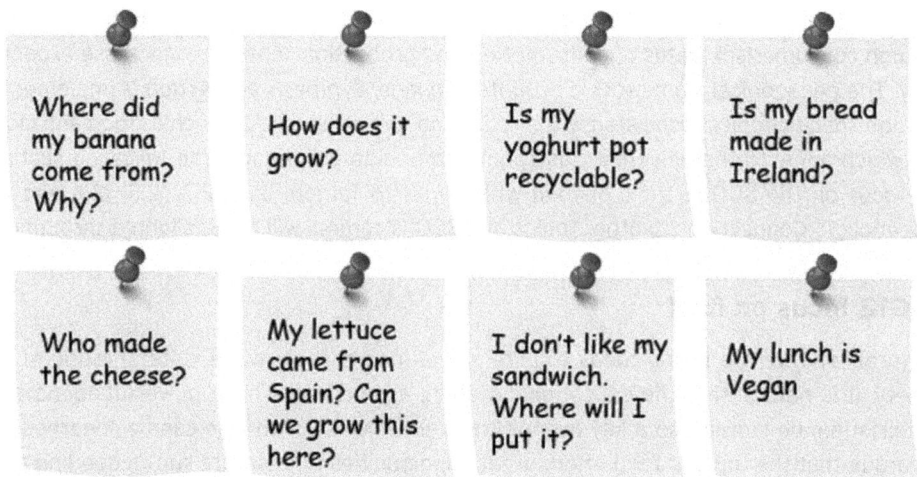

Figure 15.3 Sample Questions and Observations from a Senior Primary Class (Ages 10-12).

facilitates the categorisation of questions into investigable, open-ended 'big' questions. These questions are recorded on a poster or flipchart to guide investigations in later lessons. Further questions are added throughout the investigations and subsequent lessons. All questions are revisited at the end of the final phase, Action, to consolidate the students' learning. Further extensions of this topic for consideration are included in Tables 15.1, 15.2, 15.6 and 15.7.

Table 15.1 Some SDG 12 topics for consideration in the classroom

Fast Fashion (SDG 12 Targets 12.2; 12.5; 12.6; 12.8) could be introduced through a stimulating image with information on clothes production. For example 'Producing one new shirt produces more emissions than driving a car for 55 km'. Students could examine clothes labels and identify countries of origin and sources of the materials used. Reading newspaper articles (available on-line) such as *Stacey Dooley Investigates: Are your clothes wrecking the planet?* provide interesting contexts for the Encounter stage. The storybook *Where do clothes come from?* by Butterworth and Gaggiotti (2015) could be used to generate questions and stimulate thinking on this topic.

Sustainable tourism (SDG 12 Targets 12.2; SD12.8): Invite the students to consider a real-world scenario. For example Maya Bay in Thailand which is a very popular tourist destination encounters a number of issues:

(i) Uncontrolled development of tourist facilities such as a rapid growth of hotels along the coast line,

(ii) A damaged environment, both on the island and in the sea around it where the island has insufficient capacity to deal with the waste associated with the increased level of visitors to the bay,

(iii) Very large number of tourists.

Table 15.2 Some more SDG12 topics for consideration in the classroom

Fast Fashion (SDG 12 Targets 12.2; 12.5; 12.6; 12.8): Students could examine specific clothing items (such as a pair of jeans) in detail and identify the origin of each element, including fabric, buttons, zips, dye, design and threads. The journeys of these elements could be presented on a world map. Students could examine the working conditions of workers within the clothing trade, exploring case studies such as the 'Who Made My Clothes?' movement which emerged from the collapse of the Rana Plaza garment factory in Bangladesh and the OXFAM 'Clothes Line' Fairtrade clothes project.

Sustainable Tourism (SDG 12 Targets 12.2; 12.8): Students could engage in card sort activities, categorising facts about the positive and negative impacts of tourists in the Maya Bay area. These impacts could be categorised using the Development Compass Rose (see Figure 15.10 and Table 15.3). Students could observe images of the densely packed beaches and boats in Maya Bay and consider their own local areas and the impact (positive and negative) that such numbers of visitors would have on the area. Case studies of other tourist sites where visitor numbers were restricted or even banned outright such as Machu Picchu (Peru) or Croagh Patrick (Ireland) could be explored. Using https://www.airmilescalculator.com consideration should be given to flights to other tourist destinations and the environmental impact associated with such travel. Carbon-neutral hotels are also emerging in Ireland. Students could explore how such industries operate, for example Doolin Hotel (Ireland).

Table 15.3 Scenarios of the impacts of tourism in Maya Bay

Natural/Environmental	Economic	Social/Cultural	Who Decides?
Over tourism in Maya Bay with many boats has had a very harmful impact on the local natural environment: decimated corals, litter, sunscreen pollution as well as wildlife and habitat destruction.	The large tourist population in Maya Bay has led to increased prices for housing, rent, transport, food and other services, making them difficult to afford for local residents.	Many people from outside abroad have come to live in the Maya Bay area leading to the establishment of new English-speaking international private schools and increased infrastructure.	Environmental protection groups have called for a ban on tourists in the Maya Bay area to allow the natural environment to recover.
Thailand is one of the world's biggest contributors of ocean waste, most of which originates from the busy tourist beaches (such as cigarettes, plastic and sunscreen pollution).	Malee works as a hotel receptionist in the Maya Bay area. Her brother Somchai sells souvenirs in the local markets to tourists.	The local traditional fishing methods have been neglected with locals finding better jobs transporting tourists around Maya Bay.	The Phi Phi Tourist Association is against any reduction in the number of tourists.
An estimated 80% of coral reefs around Maya Bay have been destroyed by pollution from boats and littering from the beaches nearby.	Tourism makes up 12% of Thailand's economy. Over 5000 visitors on 200 boats visit Maya Bay every day.	Some local Maya Bay area residents have a negative attitude towards tourists who have changed their once quiet way of life.	The Thai government receives huge revenues from larger tourism receipts and taxes collected.

Table 15.4 Sample T chart

Claims	Evidence	Sources
Agriculture is the biggest contributor to greenhouse gas emissions in Ireland.	Agriculture was responsible for 35.4% of Ireland's greenhouse gas emissions in 2019. Of the 35.4%, Methane gas comprised over 50%.	Online-Environmental Protection Agency, Ireland.

Phase 2: engage

Informed by enquiry questions generated in the Encounter phase, this section is the main focus of teaching and learning. A sample of activities which focus on the life cycle of the food we eat, packaging associated with food and environmental consequences of our food choices are presented.

Table 15.5 Stakeholder perspectives

Different Stakeholders linked to the Irish beef industry	Beef farmers	Environmentalists	Meat Processing Plant owners/ workers	Consumers	Government
What is their role in the beef industry?	There are approximately 80,000 cattle beef farms in Ireland. There are seven million cattle (including calves, bulls, steers, heifers) of which one million beef cattle and 1.5 million dairy cattle. 90% of beef produced in Ireland is exported.	Environmental groups in Ireland such as An Taisce have been calling for at least a 50% reduction in the number of cows in Ireland. 33% of Ireland's greenhouse gas emissions comes from agriculture, 2/3 of which comes from livestock.	There are approximately 15,500 people employed in meat processing plants throughout Ireland.	On average, Irish people consume 19kg of beef per year. This is significantly higher than 16kg of seafood, 10kg of chicken, 10kg of pork, and 3.5kg of lamb per person consumed per year.	On average beef and sheep farms operate at a substantial loss. The government and EU subsidises these farms. Over 100% of beef and sheep farm income comes from subsidies.
Position on reducing beef production consumption?	Beef farmers and the Irish Farmers' Association (IFA) have argued to protect farmers' jobs and livelihoods and argue against a reduction in beef production ass consumption.	Environmentalists argue for a reduction in the production and consumption of beef in Ireland.	Workers and owners of meat processing plants and the Meat Industry Ireland (MII) argue to protect jobs in the beef industry and argue against a reduction in beef production and consumption.	Irish consumers continue to eat beef at a high level. Alternative options need to be communicated and marketed to convince consumers to change their behaviour and their recipes!	The Irish government has committed to a 51% reduction in greenhouse gas emissions by 2030.

Table 15.6 Some more SDG 12 topics for consideration in the classroom

Fast Fashion (SDG 12 Targets 12.2; 12.5; 12.6; 12.8)
Students could synthesise the main issues and concerns related to the clothing industry. Different stakeholder perspectives and experiences should be considered, facilitating the development of empathy with others. Opportunities to engage in discourse and debate pertaining to priorities and solutions to addressing the key issues should be provided, linking arguments to data and content from previous learning activities.

Sustainable Tourism (SDG12 Targets 12.2; SD12.8)
Students represent different stakeholders impacted by unsustainable tourism at Maya Bay. Each group must use evidence gathered in the Engage phase to support their claims. The teacher adopts the role of a chairperson and moderate the discussions. Students should be provided with opportunities to respond to other stakeholder group claims and opinions.

Table 15.7 Some more SDG 12 topics for consideration in the classroom

---

Fast Fashion (SDG 12 Targets 12.2; 12.5; 12.6; 12.8): Having explored both the environmental and socio-economic impacts of 'fast fashion', students devise appropriate actions informed by case study samples such as Depop and Freecycle movements which have both a local and global presence, focused on reducing waste. Students could participate in the sustainable fashion competition Junk Kouture (discussed in greater detail in chapter 20).

Sustainable Tourism (SDG 12 Targets 12.2; SD12.8): Students design a carbon neutral staycation in Ireland. Having considered the different stakeholder positions concerning the situation in Maya Bay, Thailand, students propose solutions and possible actions for local people, considering the impact it would have on the local community socially, economically as well as environmentally. Teachers should challenge students' proposals, encouraging them to strengthen their arguments with reference to facts and content knowledge.

Where does our food come from?

Consider bringing in shopping bags containing various food items (such as packaged mushrooms, grapes, butternut squash, carrots, bananas, peppers and pasta) and giving one bag to each group of students. Students observe, sort and classify food items and give reasons for their categories. Sample classification could include colour, shape, variety, grain, presumed age and packaging. Foods could also be classified in accordance with the food pyramid groupings. It is important that students work with real food items rather than printed generic food labels. Handling the real food and observing it up close, including packaging, can generate more targeted and interesting enquiry questions and investigations.

Students investigate each food item in their bag, observing and recording information from the packaging, labels or tags pertaining to the country of origin. They calculate the distance each food item has travelled to get to their classroom, and the carbon footprint of each item, mapping the origins of products and, using a website such as www.foodmiles.com (see Figure 15.4). This mapping activity can be completed digitally or on physical maps (see Figure 15.6).

Why do we import our fruit and vegetables?

Students then investigate why these food items are grown in these places. They use their atlases and climate maps to make inferences and informed observations as to why certain foods are grown in certain regions (e.g. bananas grown in the tropics). Questions and discussions regarding the sustainability of our food choice should emerge.

Who depends on the food industry?

The interdependence of people is examined by inviting the students to undertake a mind-mapping exercise on the various jobs involved in the production, transportation and sale of each food item. This can be completed with 'simple' single ingredient food items such as bananas or more complex food products such as a packet of crisps or sweets. These jobs could be categorised into primary, secondary and tertiary sectors (see Figure 15.7).

Figure 15.4 Calculating the Food Miles and Carbon Emissions for Transporting Food Items.

Case Study 15.1 Investigating Fairtrade chocolate

The students (aged eight to nine) in Mr Duffy's class in St Paul's National School, Ratoath, County Meath investigated the production of chocolate. After examining and mapping the tropical regions of the world where cacao is grown, students observed and sequenced the stages of chocolate production 'from the land to my hand'. The students tasted the chocolate at different stages of the production process, noting the bitter taste of cocoa powder in comparison to chocolate bars. They hypothesised and investigated ingredients listed on chocolate wrappers to find out what is added to make it sweet such as milk and sugar.

In their investigation of the various jobs that are interconnected and interdependent pertaining to the production and sale of chocolate, the students questioned the cost of a chocolate bar and what percentage of the total price each worker earns along the stages of production (such as cocoa farmers, transporters, factory workers, chocolate companies and shopkeepers). These investigations highlight how unfairness and injust processes are embedded into the production and consumption of chocolate. Students also learned about Fairtrade (see Figure 15.5) and undertook a survey of popular chocolate bars to identify which, if any, displayed a Fairtrade logo on the wrapper (See chapter 20 for more activites based on Fairtrade).

This study of chocolate further inspired the students to consider investigating other products that they consume including clothing and toys.

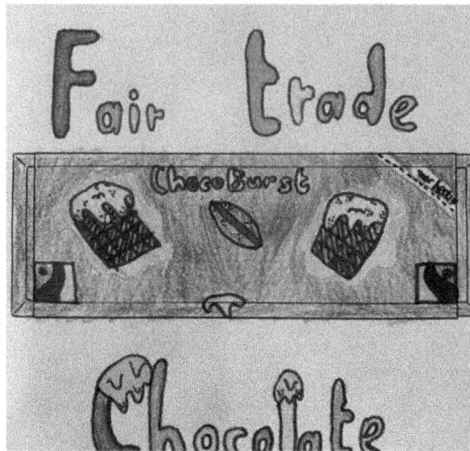

Figure 15.5 Sample of Students' (Aged 8-9) Poster on Fairtrade Chocolate.

Investigating the carbon footprint or sustainability cost of a food product.

Students can investigate the carbon footprint and/or sustainability cost of several food items. There are handbooks for teachers and student which can support this work. Gray (2023) invites us to consider food miles and the global impact of our meals in her book *Avocado Anxiety and other stories about where your food comes from*. We are all part of a complex food system. Trying to make sense of it, environmental journalist Louise Gray tracks the stories of our five-a-day and discovers the impact that growing fruits and vegetables has on the planet. Visiting farms, interviewing scientists and trying to grow her own, she asks important questions to dig up the dirt on familiar items in our shopping baskets. Are plant proteins as good for us as meat proteins? Why can we buy so-called 'seasonal' fruits like strawberries all year round? And is the symbol of clean eating, the avocado, fuelling the climate crisis? Students can virtually travel the journey of any food item or their favourite products 'from farm to fruit bowl' exploring production, consumption, potential waste and carbon footprint.

Take palm oil for instance. Palm oil is in everything from soap to lipstick and pizza to chocolate. It comes from the fruit or kernel of the Palm Oil Tree. Almost 50% of the packaged products in supermarkets contain palm oil, because it's such an adaptable ingredient that can be used in a huge variety of products. Its texture can help make things spreadable, it helps give products a longer shelf-life, and importantly, it has no odour or colour, so it doesn't affect the look or smell of the products it's used in. All these benefits make it very attractive to manufacturers. While oil palm trees are native to Africa, Indonesia and Malaysia now produce over

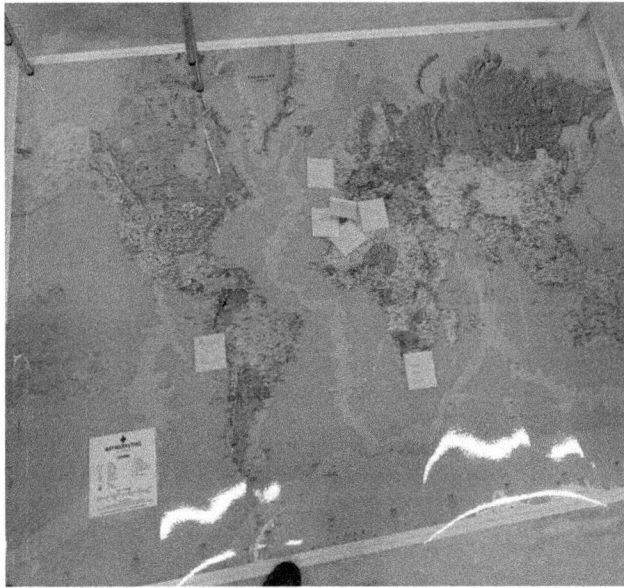

Figure 15.6 Mapping Product Origins on a World Map.

Interdependency of Jobs linked to My Product			
Product	**Primary**	**Secondary**	**Tertiary**
Carton of Milk (1 Ltr Avonmore) IRELAND	• farmer (milk from cows) • forestry worker (trees and wood to make cardboard carton) • Oil rig worker (oil for the plastic lid of carton)	• Creamery worker (treating the milk and checking quality) • Factory worker (making cartons) • factory worker (making plastic lids)	• Transporter (milk farm – creamery) • Transporter (milk to shops) • Transporter (wood from forest to factory) – oil to factory also • Shopkeeper (selling milk) • Designer (product design Carton)
Mange tout from GUATEMALA	• farmer/Labourer (working the land, planting seeds, weeding, fertilizing, harvesting) • Oil rig worker (oil to make plastic packaging)	• Factory worker (inspecting and weighing the food, packaging and labelling) • Factory worker (making the plastic packaging)	• Transporter (farm to factory for processing) • Transporter (from factory across the world to Irish shops) • Designer (design label, packaging) • Shopkeeper (display, stack and sell)
GRANOLA BAR (Nature Valley) – USA	• farmer (oats) • farmer/forestry (maple) • Beekeeper (honey) • farmer (sugar cane) • Oil rig worker (plastic wrapper)	• Factory worker (making wrapper) • factory worker (making sugar) • Baker/factory worker (for making the bar –mixing the ingredients)	• Shopkeeper (sells bar) • Transporter (raw materials from farm/forest to factory) • Transporter (bar from factory across Atlantic Ocean to Ireland) • Product designer (wrapper and shape of bar)

Figure 15.7 Student (Aged 12) Completion of Table Identifying Primary, Secondary and Tertiary Jobs Associated with a Product.

85% of the global supply of palm oil. As native forests are cut down to make way for palm oil plantations, large scale deforestation contributes to climate change and biodiversity loss. Palm oil can however be produced sustainability supporting small holders enabling them to manage the landscape and conserve rainforests. The Roundtable on Sustainable Palm Oil (RSPO) is a global organisation working to reform the industry. Look for the RSPO Certified Sustainable Palm Oil mark on products. Students can complete their own research on products such as palm oil, locating its presence in different products, investigating if it has been produced sustainably and communicating their findings to the manufacturer and to local press. Commodities such as palm oil and potential links with child labour are discussed in chapter 11.

Students can expand their product research to other household items. Shine's (2020), *How To Save Your Planet, One Object At A Time*, guides each of us to consider the sustainability of every item in our home. It aims to break down the environmental impacts of all the objects that surround us, from drills to teabags to running gear to TVs, and to offer simple advice on how to make the best choices on each. Berners-Lee (2022) reveals the carbon footprints of hundreds of elements in our lives, starting small: tap water, email, a paper bag, a nappy; then moving up to a roll of toilet paper, washing dishes, driving a mile, taking a bath, using a smartphone; and ending with the big stuff-making a ton of steel, a plane flight, space travel, wildfires, wars and deforestation.

What other factors are impacted by the production and consumption of food?

Often carbon emissions associated with food products are calculated only on the 'food miles' pertaining to the product in the life cycle and in different stages of the production process. Other considerations are necessary including food packaging, environmental impacts of food production and water usage. This BBC food calculator is a useful resource that the students could refer to: https://www.bbc.com/news/science-environment-46459714. Researchers Joseph Poore and Thomas Nemecek (2018) looked at the environmental impact of 40 major food products consumed globally. The researchers assessed the effect of these foods on climate-warming greenhouse gas emissions and the amount of land and fresh water used across all stages of their production, including processing, packaging, and transportation, but excluding the cooking process.

This connects with the 'circular economy', see Figure 15.8, which is geared towards the elimination of waste and the continual use of resources. In contrast to the 'take-make-waste' linear model, a circular economy is regenerative by design and aims to gradually decouple growth from the consumption of finite resources. Discussed in Chapter 12, the circular economy aims to keep products, equipment and infrastructure in use for longer, thus improving the longevity of these resources (Ellen MacArthur Foundation, 2013).

Waste materials and energy should become input for other processes: either a component or recovered resource for another industrial process (recycling or upcycling) or as regenerative resources for nature (e.g. compost).

As part of the circular economy, students examine food waste. When we waste food, we also waste all the energy and water it takes to grow, harvest, transport, and package it. If food waste goes to landfill, it rots and produces methane gas. Students could reflect on the level of food waste accruing to themselves or their household over the space of a week, documenting all food thrown out in a food waste diary. SDG 12 Target 12.3 is to reduce the level of food waste by 50%. To achieve this aim at a personal/community level, students could focus on reducing food waste in their school or household by 50%, outlining realistic actions and informed decisions to achieve this goal. Stop Food Waste is a programme funded by the National Waste Prevention Programme of the Environmental Protection Agency in

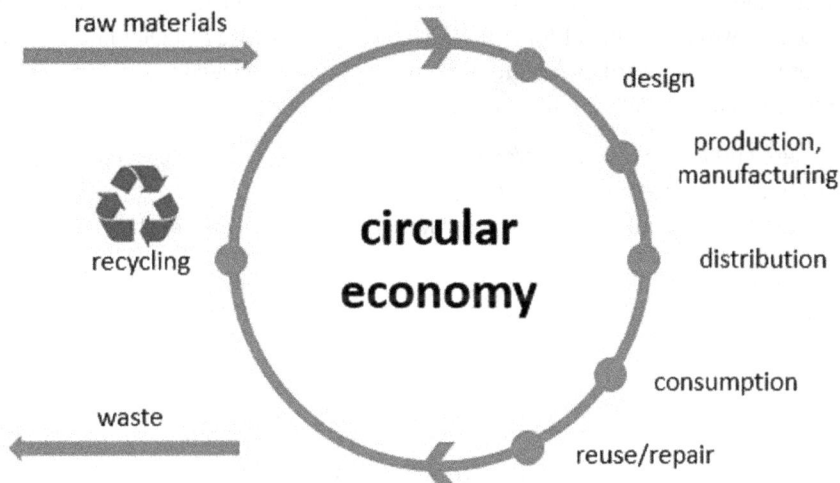

Figure 15.8 Circle Economy Diagram. (adapted from the Ellen MacArthur Foundation, 2013).

Ireland with numerous resources for schools and communities: https://stopfoodwaste.ie/resources-download/all/school/all/date

As part of the circular economy, students should be encouraged to consider reducing all waste (including food waste) by adopting the the 8 rs (detailed in chapter 12) as follows: Rethink; Repair; Reuse; Reduce; Refuse; Recycle; Recover; and Regift.

Where does the food packaging come from and where does it go?

The packaging in which our food is contained often has environmental implications alongside the production and transportation of food from place of origin to the consumer. Packaging is usually considered as an additional economic and environmental cost rather than an added value for waste reduction. It is a central element to food quality preservation during storage, prevents food safety issues (prevention of food-borne diseases and food chemical contamination) and extends food shelf-life. Packaging provides significant benefits in terms of reduction of food waste thanks to shelf life extension. A number of issues are worthy of examination here; for instance, when food items are thrown away the packing is also discarded. Examining whether the packaging can be recycled is fundamental in ascertaining the sustainability of the production and consumption of that particular food item. Single use plastic is widely used in packaging. Listed at the end of this chapter, is an extensive list of children's literature dealing with plastic.

Much attention has been paid to the potential of raw materials for replacing non-renewable oil resources used to produce single-use plastics. For example, bio-plastic packaging is produced using food resources such as corn or cane sugar. This contributes to increased food security concerns and pressure on agricultural land. Teachers could facilitate students in carrying out fair test investigations on the impact of different types of packaging on the preservation of food. Here, the students take a food item and wrap it in different types of material, for example plastic, tinfoil, beeswax wraps and sugar wrap (made from sugar cane). Students observe the food over a fixed period of time and record their findings.

It is also important to note that some sustainable wraps on the market, for example sugar cane wrap, corn wrap, are only fit for industrial composting. Along a similar line, compostable coffee cups were put forward as a solution to reduce single use plastic cups and are also only fit for industrial composting. Possible investigations include:

- Are there sufficient recycle bins/compostable bins available in your local area/town?
- Do all households have industrial compostable bins?
- How literate are people in your community regarding disposing waste?

Students could analyse recycling bins in the school and local area and record findings as to whether the bins were contaminated with non-recyclable waste, see case study 15.2:

Case Study 15.2: 'Where you *bin*?' Analysing Bins in Dublin Train Station

Student teachers undertaking the Geographical, Environmental and Outdoor Education major specialism at the Institute of Education, Dublin City University carried out a bin analysis at one of the largest train stations in Dublin. (see Figure 15.9). Recycling bins were the only type of bins available at platforms in Connolly Station. This left commuters with no options for disposing compostable and other non-recyclable waste, thus resulting in contaminated recycling bins and littering. Students also noted that all coffee shops in the train station used compostable coffee cups and lids but no compost waste disposal was available. This simple analysis demonstrated the broken chain in consumption and waste on a very local scale. The students wrote letters and emails to Irish Rail and local politicians to raise awareness about the issue. They also launched a campaign 'Where you bin?', making posters and presenting to their peers on campus, raising awareness of the contamination of recycling bins and lack of compost bins available.

Figure 15.9 Analysing Bin Provision.

What type of food should we eat?

Some 33% of Ireland's greenhouse gases are as a result of agriculture, with methane representing two thirds of these gases. In the E.U. approximately 10% of the contributions to greenhouse gases are as a result of agriculture. That places Ireland significantly above the E.U. average. Ruminant animals such as cattle and sheep are the main producers of methane, with 90-95% of agricultural methane emitted through eructation (burping) and only 5-10% through flatulence and slurry storage.

An Taisce, the national trust for Ireland concerning the environment and built heritage, have called for at least a 50% reduction of the national cattle herd in Ireland in order to reduce greenhouse gas emissions. Students should consider the impact of this, for example:

- Consider imports and exports associated with the food industry in Ireland.
- Three million hectares of land in Ireland are used to support the meat and dairy industries. Consider how a transition to a plant based food system would impact Ireland's imports and exports.
- Investigate if such a transition is feasible, considering weather and climate patterns and costs of infrastructure such as polytunnels and greenhouses.
- Examine case studies of other countries that have moved to a plant-based agricultural production system, for example the Netherlands, and the greenhouse technology involved.
- Investigate what jobs are dependent upon the Irish meat and dairy industries and if such jobs could be replaced.

Farming large animals puts a strain on our natural resources and creates polluting waste. Scientists are proposing eating insects to help solve this problem. Is the consumption of insects a viable alternative? Students could design alternative menus for their favourite restaurant or for the canteen comparing emissions produced by different meals, for example Chicken Burger V Cricket Kebab. Jones (2019) undertook a research project with Welsh primary students on edible insects and adapting their diets for climate change. The participating Welsh schools were involved in testing new products from Bug Farm Foods Ltd. The students acquired new knowledge on the issue of unsustainable food production and consumption, evaluated consumer feelings and questions about the potential for edible insects, researched answers to general concerns and explored potential action both individually and collectively. Links can be made with the activity *It bugs me* described in chapter 5, PP 113-114.

Phase 3: synthesise

During this phase students are given opportunities to share claims, evidence and data gathered from the *Engage Phase*. Here, students process information, communicate information, consider alternative perspectives and examine the validity and reliability of their findings and conclusions. It is important for students to discuss using evidence gathered *(Engage Phase)* and not simply opinion, belief or emotive convictions. Providing students with a space for social discourse with peers is an important context whereby students get an opportunity to wrestle with, negotiate and debate their ideas. This could take the form of oral debate, written debate, presentations, pictures, cartoons, drama role play, online

Natural impacts

These are impacts pertaining to the
environment -energy, air, soil, water, living
things- and their relationships to each other. It
includes the 'built' and 'natural' environment.

Who decides? Who benefits?
(Political Impacts)

These are impacts about power, who
makes choices about what is to happen,
who benefits and loses as a result of
these decisions, and at what cost.

Economic Impacts

These are impacts pertaining to jobs,
money, trading, aid, ownership, buying
and selling.

Social and Cultural Impacts

These are impacts pertaining to people,
their relationships, their traditions, culture,
and the way they live.

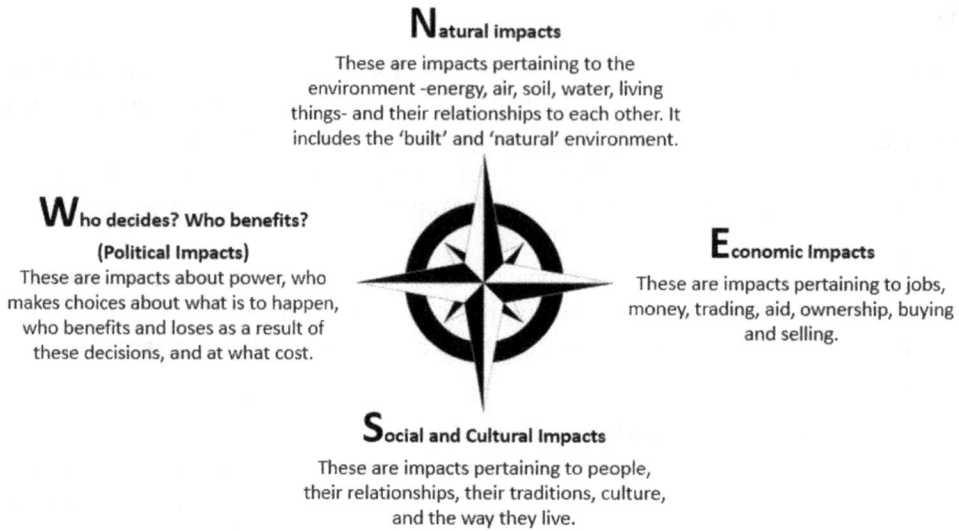

Figure 15.10 Development Compass Rose. (Source: TIDE tidegloballearning.net).

discussion boards and so forth. Teachers should challenge students during these discussions and debates, encouraging them to strengthen their arguments with reference to facts and content knowledge where appropriate.

Teachers could provide students with a framework to promote and support evidence based reasoning. T Charts can be used where students organise arguments in terms of *agree* and *disagree*. This emphasises the importance of supporting an argument with evidence and sources (see Table 15.4).

The views of different stakeholders should be considered (see Table 15.5). When presenting an issue, each group could take on a different perspective pertaining to relevant stakeholders.

The Development Compass Rose (see Figure 15.10) is used to encourage and facilitate students in considering various natural, economic, social and political impacts of the issue(s) at hand.

To create a supportive environment for discussion and debate teachers can encourage the use of sentence starters (e.g. I agree/disagree with; Our evidence was similar to....but we concluded...). Creating a safe classroom environment where student ideas and opinions are respected is imperative. This can be done through modelling active listening skills, highlighting the importance of challenging someone's idea rather than the person and discussing key questions in groups rather than asking individual students to respond. The OXFAM Education teachers' guide for teaching controversial issues (listed at the end of this chapter) provides excellent advice and practical suggestions for facilitating classroom discussions about controversial issues.

Phase 4: action

The teacher facilitates a student-led action or actions related to the lessons on the production and consumption of food. The students reflect upon what they have learned about food production and consumption and revisit their initial ideas and enquiry questions to see what they have learned and what other questions they could investigate.

Student decisions based upon individual/personal actions in the context of their own consumption habits is to be encouraged. They might also decide to grow their own vegetables in their home gardens or together, collaboratively in the school garden or community allotments. Other actions could be lobbying and campaigning for the provision of public allotments in their local areas, celebrating and promoting local food producers through local food markets, participating in or setting up sustainable recipe challenges whereby entrants must create delicious recipes using only locally sourced in-season ingredients. Students could also consider whether they should only be buying food produced locally and in season. The following case studies illustrate practical action taken by schools at personal, school level and community level.

Case Study 15.3: Action at class level: so you think you can recycle

Students from St. Augustine's National School, Clontuskert, Ballinasloe, Co Galway carried out research into waste management and recycling in Ireland. They surveyed items in their local supermarket, noting inconsistencies on the packaging indicating if materials were recyclable or not. Here they identified the 'Green Dot' as a problem in Ireland and across Europe as consumers often confuse it for a recycling symbol. The 'Green Dot' (see Figure 15.11) is a symbol used on packaging in some European countries and signifies that the producer has made a financial contribution towards the recovery and recycling of packaging in Europe. It does not necessarily mean that the packaging is recyclable. The students surveyed the adults in the local area and found 84% of respondents mistook the 'Green Dot' symbol for the recycling symbol. They created a website which includes videos and information to raise awareness and to report their findings (https://soyouthinkyoucanrecycle.com/). They also presented their work at the Galway Science and Technology Festival and the ESB Science Blast in Dublin. They continue to lobby and campaign for clarity and uniformity pertaining to the labelling of packaging and waste disposal.

Figure 15.11 Shows the 'Green Dot' symbol (left) and recycling symbol (right).

Case Study 15.4: Action at school community level

The students in Ard Rí Community National School in Navan, Co. Meath studied waste associated with food and lunches. As part of the 'Green Schools' initiative, they devised and implemented a 'Naked Lunch Boxes' campaign whereby all students in the school agreed to not use any plastic or foil packaging in their lunches (see Figure 15.12). They also developed 'Waste Free Wednesdays' whereby all bins were removed from the school for that day, thus highlighting to students the amount of waste produced in one day of school.

Ard Rí Community NS
@ArdRi_CNS

At @ArdRi_CNS we have #NakedLunchboxes. Now 90%+ of lunches have no foil, cling or freezer bags. Serious reduction of #waste in our bins. #reduce @GreenSchoolsIre

Figure 15.12 Sample of Whole School Action: Ard Rí Community NS Naked Lunches.

Links with other SDG goals

The SDGs are interdependent and integrated. They aim to impact all levels of society, reach across all sectors, embrace equity, inclusion, and universality. Progress on one goal can have a significant impact on progress in meeting others. SDG 12 is instrumental for reconciling

1 NO POVERTY — **Goal 1:** Encourage sustainable and ethical production and consumption patterns via Fair Trade.

6 CLEAN WATER AND SANITATION — **Goal 6:** Increase water quality be reducing pollution and plastic in the ocean.

14 LIFE BELOW WATER — **Goal 14:** Protect against overfishing and the exploitation of natural recourses below water.

8 DECENT WORK AND ECONOMIC GROWTH — **Goal 8:** Make explicit the implicit relationship between producer and consumer. Raise awareness of unjust work conditions

12 RESPONSIBLE CONSUMPTION AND PRODUCTION

3 GOOD HEALTH AND WELL-BEING — **Goal 3:** Promote healthy, locally produced food with a reduced carbon footprint.

2 ZERO HUNGER — **Goal 2:** Promote food security through reducing food waste and develop localised production and consumption cycles.

13 CLIMATE ACTION — **Goal 13:** Take immediate, individual and collective action through decision-making pertaining to consumption.

7 AFFORDABLE AND CLEAN ENERGY — **Goal 7:** Reduce food miles encouraging local production and consumption patterns.

Figure 15.13 Links to other SDG Goals.

economic, social and environmental objectives and decoupling greenhouse gas emissions from economic growth. Figure 15.13 demonstrates the connections SDG 12, and the material and activities covered in this chapter, have to other SDGs (SDGs 1, 2, 3, 6, 7, 8, 13 and 14).

Conclusion

SDG 12 is concerned with responsible consumption and production. In order to achieve sustainable development patterns of production and consumption on both global and local levels, we urgently need to reduce our ecological footprint by changing the way we produce and consume goods and resources. We also need to reduce the amount of waste produced in line with the circular economy. This chapter presents a number of different practical examples and case studies for inspiring teaching and learning about SDG 12 through the lens of the Four Hs Framework. The pedagogical framework underpinning the learning activities and resources advocated in this chapter lends itself to experiential learning and is informed by other investigative and enquiry frameworks. This framework comprises four phases; Encounter, Engage, Synthesise and Action, all of which focus on facilitating students in developing a deep understanding of SDG 12 and reflecting on their own personal roles and responsibilities in relation to responsible production and consumption. The framework enables and empowers students to investigate various current issues that are relevant to their lives both globally and locally and to take meaningful and appropriate action where possible. The chapter presents practical examples and inspiration for teaching topics relating to SDG 12 such as the fashion and sustainable tourism industries.

However, the main focus of the chapter is on the production and consumption of food. The topic of food is enshrined within students' own everyday lives and exemplifies the global, far-reaching consequences of the most basic form of decision-making at local and individual levels. Learning about the production, transportation and disposal of food and the waste associated with food can bridge the growing divide between students and the origins of their food. By increasing food and sustainability literacies together in our educational practices, we can begin to overcome passivity, and the uncritical and dependent consumerism that characterises society's relationship with food. In doing so, we can build capacity in our students to enact change, take action and make informed decisions. This topic aligns with the Four Hs Framework which underpins this book. Understanding how individual behaviours and societal systems need to change to meet SDG targets is a fascinating way of bringing values, ethics and human rights into the classroom. The learning activities included in this chapter align with the targets for SDG 12 as well as other SDGs and these links are clearly highlighted. If students see how their role as consumers on a personal level affects the environment, then they are more likely to consume in a more ethical and responsible way. By 'voting with their wallets', students as citizens have the power to encourage more ethical and responsible production practices.

Table 15.8 Key terminology for SDG 8

Agriculture: Agriculture is the science, art and practice of cultivating plants and livestock.

Carbon dioxide (CO2): Carbon dioxide (CO2) is an important heat-trapping (greenhouse) gas, which is released through human activities such as deforestation and burning fossil fuels, as well as natural processes such as respiration and volcanic eruptions.

Circular economy: Circular economy is an economic system aimed at eliminating waste and the continual use of resources.

Composting: Composting is a process that breaks down organic matter through the use of fungi, bacteria, insects, worms and other organisms to create a nutrient-dense 'compost'. This compost can then be used as a powerful fertiliser and soil.

Consumption: Consumption is defined as the purchasing of and use of goods and services by a household/individual.

Enquiry-based learning: Enquiry-based learning is a form of student-centred, active learning that starts by posing questions, problems or scenarios and involves student-led investigations, facilitated by teachers.

Experiential learning: Experiential learning is an engaged learning process involving hand-on, practical activities and investigations whereby students 'learn by doing' and by reflecting on the experience.

Fast fashion: Inexpensive clothing produced rapidly by mass-market retailers in response to the latest trends.

Fairtrade: an arrangement designed to help producers in growing countries achieve sustainable and equitable trade relationships.

Food miles: Food miles is the distance food is transported from the time of its making until it reaches the consumer. Food miles are one factor used when testing the environmental impact of food, such as the carbon footprint of the food. The distance can be measured in miles or kilometres.

Food waste: Food waste is food that is not eaten. The term also includes the energy and water it takes to grow, harvest, transport, and package food which is not eaten.

Greenhouse gases: Greenhouse gases are gases in Earth's atmosphere that trap heat. They let sunlight pass through the atmosphere, but they prevent the heat that the sunlight brings from leaving the atmosphere.

Interdependence: Interdependence refers to two or more things or people or organisations that impact and rely on each other.

Industrial composting: Industrial composting is a multi-step, closely monitored composting process done by a company. Here they use carefully measured inputs of water and air and keep the temperature at the right level. They optimise each step of the decomposition process, by controlling conditions like shredding material to the same size or controlling the temperature and oxygen levels. These measures ensure faster composting of materials. It is because of this controlled environment that bioplastics, meat and fish can be composted at industrial composting sites.

Methane gas (CH_4): Methane is a colourless, flammable, nontoxic gas with the chemical formula CH_4. This gas is formed naturally by the decomposition of organic matter. Wetlands, livestock and energy are the main sources of methane emissions to the atmosphere, where it acts as a greenhouse gas.

Natural resources: include things like plants, soil, sunshine, water, fossil fuels, air, wildlife, metals, and minerals.

Primary: Primary jobs involve extracting raw materials from the natural environment (e.g. mining, fishing, farming).

Production: The instruments or materials used to produce goods or services.

Recycle: Convert waste into reusable material.

Secondary: Secondary jobs involve making things (e.g. manufacturing).

(Continued)

Table 15.8 (Continued)

Single-use plastics: also referred to as disposable plastics are goods that are primarily made from fossil-fuel based chemicals. These are commonly used for plastic packaging and include plastic items intended to be used only once before being thrown away or recycled.

Sustainable tourism: Tourism that takes full account of its current and future environmental, social and economic impacts, addressing the needs of the environment, host communities, visitors and the industry.

Tertiary: Tertiary jobs involve providing a service (e.g. teaching, nursing, transportation).

Upcycling: Also known as creative reuse, is the process of transforming by-products, waste materials, useless, or unwanted products into new materials or products perceived to be of greater quality, such as artistic value or environmental value.

Resources

An extensive list of resources, videos and case studies for SDG 12 is included in the SDG padlet accompanying this book: https://padlet.com/annedolan/o6rds38ylfy6a28h

Key dates

March 22: World Water Day

April 19: World Banana Day

April (last week): Fast Fashion Revolution Week

May 14: World Fairtrade Day

June 7: World Chocolate Day

June 5: World Rainforest Day

July 28: World Nature Conservation Day

September 5: Amazon Rainforest Day

October 16: World Food Day

October (last week): Green Fashion Week

Sources of further information

Content knowledge, figures, infographics and other resources that would be useful in supporting learning SDG 12 are available on the following web pages:

CAFOD resources on the banana trade https://cafod.org.uk/Education/Primary-teaching-resources/Fairtrade/Banana-Fairtrade-game

Circular Economy: Explaining the Circular Economy https://www.mywaste.ie/the-circular-economy/

CONCERN resource Hunger, '1 in 8: Food and Our Place in the World' https://developmenteducation.ie/media/documents/One%20in%20Eight.pdf

Eco Eye Sustainable Food https://www.youtube.com/watch?v=1BdA7zcuigc

Further information Sustainable Development Goal 12 https://www.un.org/sustainable development/sustainable-consumption-production/

OXFAM Education: 'Clothes Line: fashion and clothing industry' resource https://fairtrade-wales.com/wp-content/uploads/8-lesson-plans-Clothes-Line-Oxfam.pdf

OXFAM Education 'Go Bananas' resource on banana trade https://www.oxfam.org.uk/education/resources/go-bananas

OXFAM Education Teaching Controversial Issues: a guide for teachers. https://oxfamlibrary.openrepository.com/bitstream/handle/10546/620473/gd-teaching-controversial-issues-290418-en.pdf?sequence=1&isAllowed=y

Practical Action https://practicalaction.org/schools/

The Story of Stuff: https://www.storyofstuff.org/

The Story of Stuff video: https://www.youtube.com/watch?v=9GorqroigqM

The Story of Bottled Water: https://www.youtube.com/watch?v=Se12y9hSOMO

The Story of Plastic: https://www.storyofstuff.org/movies/the-story-of-plastic-documentary-film/

Trócaire 'Exploring Fairtrade' https://www.trocaire.org/documents/exploring-fair-trade/

UNESCO Teacher Resources for SDG 12 https://en.unesco.org/sites/default/files/resources-sdg12.pdf

Children's Literature about Plastic and Plastic Pollution

Younger students

Augustin, J. (2022) *Let's Save Earth* Independently published.

Colon de Mejias, L. and Visco, T. (2018) *Pesky Plastic: An Environmental Story* Great Books 4 Kids.

Daynes, K. and Tremblay, M. (2020) *Questions and Answers about Plastic* Usborne Publishing Ltd.

Dorey, M. and Wesson, T. (illus) *Kids Fight Plastic: How to Be a #2minutesuperhero* Walker Books.

Eamer, C. and Edlund, B. (2017) *What a Waste: Where Does Garbage Go* Annick Press.

Inches, A. and Whitehead, P. (illus) (2009) *The Adventures of a Plastic Bottle: A Story about Recycling* New York: Little Green Books.

Jakeman, J. (2020) *The Adventures of Myrtle the Turtle: Teaching Kinds about Ocean Plastic Pollution and Recycling* Independently published.

Keck, Scott, S., Heffern, W. and Miasa, N. (illus) (2018) *Sip the Straw* Herndon, VA: Social Motion Publishing.

Kim, A and Li, J. (illus) *Plastic: Past, Present and Future* VIC, Australia: Scribe Publications.

Kooser, T. (2010) *Bag in the Wind* DK Children.

Layton, N. (2019) *A Planet Full of Plastic and How You Can Help* London: Wren and Rook.

Leonard, M.G. and Rieley, D. (2020) *The Tale of a Toothbrush: A Story of Plastic in Our Oceans.* London: Walker Books.

Lepetit, A. (2013) *Trash Magic: A Book About Recycling A Plastic Bottle* Capstone Press.

Love, S. and Duke, S. (2016) *My Little Plastic Bag* CreateSpace Independent Publishing Platform.

Meek, A. and Meek, E. (2020) *Be Plastic Clever* DK Children.

Mhin, M. (2019) *Earth Ninja: A Children's Book About Recycling, Reducing and Reusing* Grow Grit Press.

N.G.K., Fae, S. and Jannelle, D. (2019) *Harry Saves the Ocean! Teaching Children About Plastic Pollution and Recycling* NGK.

Owen, R. (2018) *Plastic Pollution on Land and in the Oceans: Let's Investigate* (Fundamental Science Key Stage 1) Ruby Tuesday Books Ltd.

Paul, M. (2015) *One Plastic Bag: Isatou Ceesay and the Recycling Women of Gambia* Minneapolis: Lerner Publishing Group.

Ritchie, S. (2019) *Join the No-Plastic Challenge! A First Book of Reducing Waste* Kids Can Press.

Salt, R. (2019) *The Plastic Problem* Firefly Books.

Simon, M. (2020) *You are Eating Plastic!: An Interactive Children's Book About Recycling, Sustainability and the Environment* Grivante Press.

Strong, J. and Smith, J. (2019) *Nellie Choc-Ice and the Plastic Island* Barrington Stoke.

Usupova, L. (2023) *Plastic Bag's Journey* Lola Usupova.

Older students

Andrus, A. (2021) *The Plastic Problem: 60 Small Ways to Reduce Waste and Help Save the Planet* Lonely Planet Kids.

Beer, J. (2020) *Kids Vs. Plastic: Ditch the Straw and Find the Pollution Salutation to Bottles, Bags and Other Single-Use Plastics* National Geographic Kids.

Dorey, M. and Wesson, T. (illus) (2019) *Kids Fight Plastic: How to Be a #2minutesupperhero* Walker Books.

Harvey, P. (2022) *The Plasticology Project: The Chilling Reality of Our Plastic Pollution Crisis and What We Can Do About It* Paul Harvey.

Mangun, C., Hope Allison, R. and Cosby, N. (2013) *I'm Not A Plastic Bag* Archaia Entertainment.

Poynter, D. (2019) *Plastic Sucks! How You Can Reduce Single-Use Plastic and Save Our Planet* Feiwel & Friends.

Seigle, L. (2018) *Turning the Tide on Plastic: How Humanity (And You) Can Make Our Globe Clean Again* Trapeze.

Thomas, I. and Paterson, A. (2018) *This Book is Not Rubbish:50 Ways to Ditch Plastic, Reduce Rubbish and Save the World* Wren & Rook.

Further books about plastic and the ocean are listed in Chapter 17.

Children's literature about consumption and production

Younger students

Beneba Carke, M. (2016) *The Patchwork Bike* Candlewick Press.

Bookless, E. and Deeptown, D. (2018) *Captain Green and the Plastic Scene* Marshall Cavendish International Asia Pte Ltd.

Butterworth, C. and Gaggiotti, L. (2015) *Where Do Clothes Come from?* London: Walker Books.

De la Bedoyere, C. (2019) *Curious Questions and Answers about Saving the Earth* Miles Kelly Publishing.

Eamer, C. and Edlund, B. (2017) *What a Waste? Where Does Garbage Go?* Annick's Press.

French, J. (2019) *What A Waste: Rubbish, Recycling, and Protecting Our Planet* London: DK

Children.

Gravett, E. (2020) *Too Much Stuff* Two Hoots.

Hawthorne, L. (2019) *Alba the Hundred Year Old Fish* Big Picture Press.

Hood, S. and Wern Comport, S. (illus) (2016) *Ada's Violin: The Story of the Recycled Orchestra of Paraguay* Simon & Schuster Books for Young Readers.

Jones, N. and Jones, J. (Ilus) *The Odd Fish* Farshore.

Kirk, E. (2011) *Human Footprint: Everything You Will Eat, Use, Wear, Buy, and Throw Out in Your Lifetime*. USA: National Geographic Kids.

Lord, M. and Blattman, J. (2020) *The Mess That We Made*, Flashlight Press.

Murray Whitaker, S. (2020) *Too Much Stuff* Independently published.

Oberman, R. and Farley, J. (illus) (2014) *Farid's Rickshaw Ride* Dublin: St Patricks College, Drumcondra.

Phoebe, S. (2019) *King Leonard's Teddy* Child's Play.

Roberts, S. and Peck, H. (illus) (2019) *Somebody Swallowed Stanley* London: Scholastic.

Seuss, Dr. (1971) *The Lorax* Random House Books for Young Readers.

Stahl, B, (2020) *Save the Scraps* Bethany Stahl.

Stevens, G. and Baker, T. (illus) *Finn the Fortunate Tiger Shark and his Fantastic Friends: Learn How to Protect Our Oceans with Finn* Be the change books.

Swann, K. and Padmacandra (illus) (2021) *The Tale of the Whale* Scallywag Press.

Trice, L. and Mitchell, H. (illus) (2016) *Kenya's Art* Charlesbridge.

Older students

Cole, S. and Vidal, O. (illus) (2019) *Tin Boy* Barrington Stoke.

Cole, S. and Vidal, O. (illus) (2021) *Welcome to Trashland* Barrington Stoke.

Cole, S. and Vidal, O. (illus) (2022) *Stitched-Up* Barrington Stoke.

Dumanoski, D. (2009) *The End of the Long Summer: Why We Must Remake Our Civilization on a Volatile Earth* London: Penguin.

Figueras, N. and Piccirrillo, E. (illus) (2019) *Lorac* Independently published.

Fowler, G. (2021) *City of Rust: An Out of This World Sci-Fi Adventure* Chicken House.

Johnson, M. (2021) *Pop! Fizzt Drinks. A Trillion Dollars. The Adventure That Ends With a Bang* Orion Children's Books.

Laird, E. (2018) *Song of the Dolphin Boy* Macmillan Children's Books.

Vandyke, A. (2018) *A Zero Waste Life in Thirty Days* Sydney: Random House Australia.

References

Amos, R. and Christodoulou, A. (2018) 'Really working scientifically: Strategies for engaging students with socio-scientific inquiry-based learning' (SSIBL). *School Science Review*, 100(371), 59–65.

Amos, R. and Levinson, R. (2019) 'Socio-scientific inquiry-based learning: An approach for engaging with the 2030 sustainable development goals through school science'. *International Journal of Development Education and Global Learning*, 11(1), 29–49.

Aubrey, K. and Riley, A. (2016) 'John Dewey: A democratic notion of learning'. In K. Aubrey and A. Riley (eds.), *Understanding and Using Educational Theories*. London: Sage. 7–26.

Berners-Lee, M. (2021) *There Is No Planet B: A Handbook for the Make Or Break Years-Updated Edition*. Cambridge: Cambridge University Press.

Berners-Lee, M., 2022. *The carbon footprint of everything*. Vancouver i Greystone Books Ltd.

Campbell, C. (2004) 'I shop, therefore I know that I am: The metaphysical basis of modern consumerism'. In K. M. Ekström, and H. Brembeck (eds.), *Elusive Consumption* (pp. 27–44). London: Routledge.

Dewey, J. (1938) *Experience and Education*. New York: Free Press.

Ellen MacArthur Foundation. (2013) *Towards the Circular Economy: Economic and Business Rationale for an Accelerated Transition*. Cowes: Ellen MacArthur Foundation.

Gray, L. (2023) *Avocado Anxiety and Other Stories About Where Your Food Comes From*. London: Bloomsbury.

Hancock, T. S., Friedrichsen, P. J., Kinslow, A. T. and Sadler, T. D. (2019) 'Selecting socio-scientific issues for teaching'. *Science & Education*, 28, 639–667.

Ives, B. and Obenchain, K. (2006) 'Experiential education in the classroom and academic outcomes: For those who want it all'. *Journal of Experiential Education*, 29(1), 61–77.

Jones, V. (2019) 'Adapting our diets for global climate change: Could eating bugs really be an answer?' *Teaching Geography*, 43(2), 1–75.

Kolb, D. A. (1984) *Experiential Learning: Experience as the Source of Learning and Development* (Vol. 1). Englewood Cliffs, NJ: Prentice-Hall.

Lederman, N. G. (1992). 'Students' and teachers' conceptions of the nature of science: A review of the research'. *Journal of Research in Science Teaching*, 29(4), 331–359.

Leonard, A. (2011) *The Story of Stuff: The Impact of Overconsumption on the Planet, Our Communities, and Our Health-And How We Can Make It Better*. New York: Free Press.

Levinson, R. (2018) 'Introducing socio-scientific inquiry-based learning' (SSIBL). *School Science Review*, 100(371), 31–36.

Luther King, M. (1967) *Massey Lecture 5* can be viewed. https://youtu.be/1jeyIAH3bUI

MacKinnon, J. B. (2021) *The Day the World Stops Shopping: How Ending Consumerism Gives Us a Better Life and a Greener World*. New York: Random House.

Martusewicz, R. and Edmundson, J. (2005) 'Social foundations as pedagogies of responsibility and eco-ethical commitment'. In D. W. Butin (ed.), *Teaching Social Foundations of Education: Contexts, Theories and Issues* (pp. 71–92). New Jersey: Lawrence Erlbaum Associates.

McInerney, P., Smyth, J. and Down, B. (2011) 'Coming to a place near you?' The politics and possibilities of a critical pedagogy of place-based education'. *Asia-Pacific Journal of Teacher Education*, 39(1), 3–16.

Poore, J. and Nemecek, T. (2018) 'Reducing food's environmental impacts through producers and consumers'. *Science*, 360(6392), 987–992.

Roberts, M. (2013) *Geography Through Enquiry: Approaches to Teaching and Learning in the Secondary School*. Sheffield: Geographical Association.

Sadler, T. D. (2011) *Socio-Scientific Issues in the Classroom: Teaching Learning and Research* (Vol. 39). New York: Springer.

Shine, T. (2020) *How to Save Your Planet: One Object At A Time*. New York: Simon and Schuster

Smith, G. A. and Sobel, D. (2014) *Place-and Community-Based Education in Schools*. New York: Routledge.

United Nations. (2017) Resolution adopted by the General Assembly on 6 July 2017, Work of the Statistical Commission pertaining to the 2030 Agenda for Sustainable Development (A/RES/71/313).

16 Teaching and learning about, through and for climate action and climate justice (SDG 13)

Anne M. Dolan

Introduction

Climate change is the defining crisis of our time. No corner of the globe is immune from the devastating consequences of climate change. Globally, we have emitted more industrial carbon since 1988 than in all of prior human history, utterly failing to flatten the Keeling curve, a graph (Figure 16.1) that shows the ongoing change in the concentration of carbon dioxide in the Earth's atmosphere. The results, which are now largely undisputed, are catastrophic. Rising sea levels, declining arctic sea ice, changes in precipitation patterns creating extreme flooding, droughts and more extreme weather events, such as heat waves, cyclones and tropical storms, are just some of the effects of changes to the global climate. Other impacts include increased acidification and warming of the oceans, decreased snow cover, glacial retreats and shrinking ice sheets. Each of these changes generate serious knock-on effects such as environmental degradation, economic disruption, increased poverty, food and water insecurity, homelessness, species extinction, conflict, terrorism and migration. Furthermore, impacts of climate change are more extreme for those with the lowest carbon footprint, those in the Global South. Business as usual is no longer an option. The time for bold brave collective action is now. This chapter discusses the challenge of climate change as a 'super wicked problem' (Levin et al., 2012) and the concept of climate justice. It discusses the importance of climate change education and it promotes the use of climate change games for facilitating deep learning in the classroom.

The challenge of climate change

The world has already warmed 1.1°C since the industrial revolution in the early 1800s. Only in 2015 was there a global commitment to address this problem. At the Paris Climate Conference (COP21) in December 2015, 195 countries adopted the first-ever universal, global climate deal. An agreement to maintain global warming below 2°C was the official outcome. If global warming exceeds 2°C, one or more major tipping points will occur, where the effects of climate change go from advancing gradually to changing rapidly, reshaping the planet. Indeed, research indicates that the climate crisis has already driven the world to the brink of multiple 'disastrous' tipping points (Armstrong McKay et al., 2022). According to this research, five dangerous tipping points may already have been passed, due to 1.1°C of global heating

DOI: 10.4324/9781003232001-19

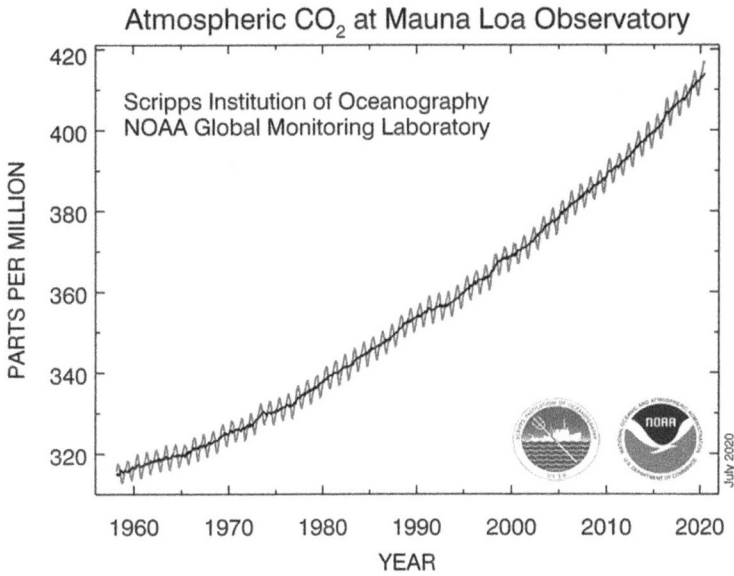

Figure 16.1 The Keeling Curve: A Graph Showing the Ongoing Change in the Concentration of Carbon Dioxide in the Earth's Atmosphere. (Source: https://www.esrl.noaa.gov/gmd/ccgg/trends/)

caused by humanity. These include a weakened Gulf Stream, the collapse of Greenland's ice cap and an abrupt melting of carbon rich permafrost. During a year of unprecedented climate impacts, 2021 brought us the sixth assessment report from the Intergovernmental Panel on Climate Change and COP26. This report by the Intergovernmental Panel on Climate Change (IPCC) found that climate change was rapid and intensifying. The UN Secretary General has called it a 'code red for humanity'. The IPCC (2021) report stated that without immediate, consistent, and massive reductions in greenhouse gas emissions, the Paris Agreement's objective of limiting global warming to 1.5°C above pre-industrial levels would be impossible to reach, but the window to keeping global warming to 1.5°C was still open. Responses to climate change include adaptation and mitigation measures. Adaptation involves taking appropriate actions to prevent or minimise the impacts of climate change. Such actions include large-scale infrastructure changes, such as building defences to protect against sea-level rise. Mitigation measures involve those which prevent or reduce the emission of greenhouse gases into the atmosphere. Such actions include increasing sources of renewable energy and ceasing the use of fossil fuels as a source of energy.

It is difficult to appreciate and articulate the current and potential catastrophic implications of climate change. Roubini (2022: 4) describes climate change as a 'megathreat', a severe problem which creates extensive damage and misery and cannot be solved easily or quickly. Climate change is recognised as a 'wicked problem' (Sweeney, 2020) and indeed a 'super wicked problem' (Levin et al., 2012). Wicked problems are social or cultural in nature. They are difficult to solve for many reasons including contradictory knowledge, the number of people and opinions involved, the potential economic burdens and the interconnected nature of these problems with other problems. Super wicked problems have four characteristics: (i) time is running out; (ii) those who accentuate the problem seek to define its solution; (iii) inadequate leadership; and (iv) the failure to recognise that short term costs will reap long term dividends.

Time is certainly running out. To preserve a liveable climate, greenhouse-gas emissions must be cut in half by 2030 and reduced to net zero by 2050 (UN, 2015). Those who accentuate the problem, the fossil fuel companies, continue to prosper while denying and delaying real action on the climate crisis. Since the 1970s fossil fuel companies including Exxon were fully aware of the links between fossil fuels and climate change (Supran et al. 2023). Despite this, they continued to cast doubt on climate science and lobby against action on global warming. Fossil fuel companies have confused the public and policymakers about the climate crisis and its solutions by harnessing a multibillion dollar propaganda and lobbying campaign to delay climate action. With political links and economic collateral, fossil fuel companies are extremely powerful. Interestingly, there were more delegates at COP 26 in Glasgow associated with the fossil fuel industry than from any single country. It is no coincidence that the UN COP26 climate conference adopted a final deal that at the last minute dropped wording calling for the 'phase out' of coal-fired power, replacing it with 'phase down'. In 2023, the United Arab Emirates one of the world's largest oil and gas producing countries, hosted Cop 28. The Chief Executive of the United Arab Emirates' national oil and gas company Adnoc, was the president of the COP 28 summit in Dubai. Bizarrely, while he was involved in co-ordinating a global deal to 'transition away' from fossil fuels, his company continued its plans to invest in oil and gas production. Ironically, COP 28 marked the first time in 30 years of climate talks, that a global resolution had been made addressing the future of all fossil fuels.

With some exceptions, there is a marked absence of leadership required for critical climate action at local, national and international levels. The 2015 Paris Climate Agreement represents an unprecedented international consensus on the need to transition from fossil fuels within the next few decades. Nevertheless, there remains a persistent reluctance to grasp the proverbial nettle of climate change. Declarations of climate emergency are not matched by a crisis appropriate response. While significant levels of global collaboration were mobilised in response to Covid 19, the same response has not been applied to the climate change crisis, the nature of which is ultimately far more serious. Under Donald Trump's administration, the US officially withdrew from the Paris Climate Agreement. While this decision was reversed just hours after Joe Biden was sworn in as President, it represents four years of lost time in the fight against climate change. Nonetheless, Joe Biden reneged on his own campaign promise to cease drilling for oil on federal lands as the US government subsequently gave approval for the Willow project, a major drilling initiative in Alaska. This kind of political dithering is an enormous obstacle to the immediate, rapid and large scale reductions in greenhouse gas emissions required to limit global warming to 1.5°C or 2°C (IPCC, 2021).

Finally, acting on climate change represents a trade-off between short-term and long-term benefits. Generally, people are motivated to avoid threats to their personal safety and well-being. However, many are overwhelmed by climate change and believe their actions will not matter in the long term. Others see climate change as an abstract concept which does not pose an immediate or potential risk. Some are not convinced that the current costs involved in reducing their carbon footprint are worthwhile in the short term. While building a climate-friendly, low-carbon society and economy is a big challenge, there are both short term and long term gains for all of us. The alternative is simply not an option.

Climate justice

A climate justice response recognises that people who have contributed least are most affected. While everyone is vulnerable, the impact is far greater on those in low income countries. Those who have contributed least to the problem, people in the Global South, face the worst consequences of climate change, as they struggle to cope with drought, storms and floods.

Climate change is further exacerbating poverty, migration, hunger and gender inequality. Furthermore, decades of progress have been eradicated because of Covid 19. In 2021, the UK's foreign aid budget was cut at a time when the need for humanitarian assistance has never been greater. By linking human rights and development, climate justice aims to achieve a human centred approach whereby the rights of the most vulnerable are safeguarded and the burden and benefits of climate change are shared by all. Climate justice begins at home, it begins with each decision we make in relation to energy, transport and lifestyle.

The transition to a low-carbon, climate-resilient economy has to be part of the solution as it makes economic, social, and environmental sense (Hicks, 2014). Political will and leadership are needed for this to happen. There is also a need to think inter-generationally. We need to imagine the world of 2050, 2060 and 2070 with an anticipated population of nine billion people, and take the right decisions now to ensure that our children and grandchildren inherit a liveable world (Tutu & Robinson, 2011).

Teaching about, through and for climate action and climate justice

The critical need for effective climate change education is well documented (Dolan, 2022; Mochizuki & Bryan, 2015). Indeed, climate change education should be firmly embedded in all national education agendas, an aspiration which is supported by the United Nations Sustainable Development Goals 4.7 (education for sustainable development) and SDG target 13.3 (education for climate protection and climate adaptation). As educators we have a moral duty to prepare students for a rapidly changing, uncertain, risky and possibly dangerous future. An aspiration for effective climate change education is powerfully articulated by Kagawa and Selby (2010: 4) whereby 'the learning moment can be seized to think about what really and profoundly matters, to collectively envision a better future, and then to become practical visionaries in realizing that future'. Teaching climate change education is conceptually challenging. It requires teachers to be knowledgeable about climate change, its causes and consequences. Yet, research indicates that educators have a limited understanding of climate change and climate action (Waldron et al., 2019). As a result, many young people believe that climate change education has not been adequately taught throughout formal education. This is borne out in a survey of 16–18 year olds by the University of Winchester (2020), which showed that although 54% see climate breakdown as the second biggest threat to the UK (after the quality of the NHS), less than half (46%) rated universities as doing a good job of addressing it. Nevertheless, well designed climate change education can have a significant impact. An analysis of climate change education studies revealed that climate change education programmes achieve a variety of positive outcomes. Most commonly, programmes increase climate knowledge, but they also can

Table 16.1 Suggested topics for climate change education, Adapted from UNESCO (2017: 37)

Carbon footprint
Greenhouse gases and their emissions
Adapting to climate change
Mitigation of climate change
Disaster risk reduction
Emission trading
Technological responses
Energy, agriculture and industry-related greenhouse gas emissions
Climate change-related hazards leading to disasters like drought, weather extremes, etc. and their unequal social and economic impact within households, communities and countries and between countries
Sea-level rise and its consequences for countries (e.g. small island states)
Migration and flight related to climate change
Prevention, mitigation and adaptation strategies and their connections with disaster response and disaster risk reduction.
Local, national and global institutions addressing the issue of climate change
Local, national and global policy strategies to protect the climate
Future scenarios (including alternative explanations for the global temperature rise)
Effects of and impacts on big eco-systems like forests, oceans, glaciers and biodiversity
Ethics and climate change

impact students' level of concern about climate change, their problem-solving skills, and behaviours (Monroe et al., 2019). Climate change education includes topics such as those listed in Table 16.1.

Understanding the complex nature of climate change through systems thinking

We live in a complex and dynamic world full of interconnected systems. An ocean is a system, and so too are trees, forests and other ecosystems. Each human being is a complex system. Systems are often embedded in larger systems, which are embedded in yet larger systems. The earth's climate is a system comprised of the subsystems of our atmosphere, our oceans, the land, and human society.

A systems thinking approach (discussed in Chapter 2) focuses on systems as a whole: how the parts interrelate and how interconnections create emerging patterns. A systems thinking approach takes a holistic, long-term perspective that focuses on relationships between interacting parts, and how those relationships generate behaviour over time. Systems thinking helps us to perceive phenomena as interconnected and dynamic. Systems thinking tools allow us to map and explore dynamic complexity. With a better understanding of systems, we can identify action points that lead to desired outcomes and avoid unintended consequences. Climate change is a complex systems problem. Take the Arctic for instance. The effects of a warming atmosphere on physical, chemical, biological, and human components of Arctic eco-systems are innumerable, far-reaching, and accelerating. Complex physical changes include direct effects such as the melting of sea-ice and sea level rise, to secondary effects such as decreased albedo (surface reflectivity) and coastal erosion, to tertiary effects such as the invasion of non-native species due to reduced temperatures. Indeed, research now claims that it is too late to save summer Arctic summer ice (Kim et al., 2023). Hence, preparations will need to be made for the subsequent increased extreme weather across the Northern Hemisphere.

A feedback loop is a cycle within a system that increases (positive) or decreases (negative) the effects on that system. Scientists are aware of a number of positive feedback loops in the climate system. In the Arctic, melting sea ice exposes more dark ocean (lower albedo), which, in turn, absorbs more heat and causes more ice to melt and so the cycle continues. Various other feedbacks – related to emissions from soils and permafrost, for example, and changes to ocean evaporation – are known or thought to exist. Feedback loops such as these are complex in themselves, and even more complex when considered as part of an integrated global climate system. Some are already at work, while others have yet to kick in. Others still, both positive and negative, may yet be discovered. Super wicked problems such as climate change require a whole systems approach through new consumer practices, well informed individual and collective responses, new technologies, new policy frameworks, and most importantly, new ways of engaging with each other. There is no one single 'silver bullet' solution for addressing climate change.

The complexity of climate change can be witnessed in the way we live our lives including short term and long term decisions we make. In our daily lives many activities are powered by fossil fuels or other sources of climate altering greenhouse gases. Every time we cook a meal, store data, heat our homes, these activities have an impact on the climate. Conversely, everything that sustains our very existence and enriches our lives is affected either directly or indirectly by climate change. Access to clean water, the price of our food, national security, the health of ourselves and our loved ones, economic opportunities for this generation and those to come, all are placed in jeopardy by climate change.

Systems thinking is important in an increasingly interconnected, interdependent, complex, volatile and uncertain world. (Mendler de Suarez, J., Suarez, P., & Bachofen, C., 2012). Due to the complexity of climate change and its constitution as a 'wicked problem' it is important to engage in systems thinking which involves collaborative problem-solving and innovation across multiple dimensions of environmental, social, economic, political and educational institutions and systems. According to Stevenson et al. (2017: 68) 'innovation depends on being able to learn collaboratively, adaptively, productively and quickly, as well as to act across different and often vast scales of both space and time.' However, simply learning about climate change is not sufficient as this presents climate change as an abstract entity far removed from daily living. Students should be able to understand the processes which contribute to climate change and discuss its impact on living things, people and the environment. It is important for students and teachers to think critically and creatively about approaches to climate change mitigation and adaptation whilst developing capacity for designing and adopting appropriate actions.

Learning approaches and methods

While learning about the science of climate change is important, cognitive comprehension is only part of an educational response. Teaching the facts of climate change is simply not sufficient. Furthermore, the persistent use of powerpoint slides with insufficient time for discussion and questions is widespread (Winn, 2003). Students need to understand the relationship between climate change and human action, specifically through the major weather events which are taking place in their world today. Equally, solutions to climate change will have to be generated by human responses. Students need to be able to pose solutions and take climate actions individually and collaboratively. Students need to learn *about, through,* and *for* climate action and climate justice. Suggested learning objectives are set out in Table16.2.

Table16.2 Teaching about, through and for climate action and climate justice: learning objectives (UNESCO, 2017: 36)

Cognitive learning objectives Teaching ***about*** the goals: developing respect and understanding	1	The learner understands the greenhouse effect as a natural phenomenon caused by an insulating layer of greenhouse gases.
	2	The learner understands the current climate change as an anthropogenic phenomenon resulting from increased greenhouse gas emissions
	3	The learner knows which human activities-on a global, national, local and individual level-contribute most to climate change
	4	The learner knows about the main ecological, social, cultural and economic consequences of climate change locally, nationally and globally and understands how these can themselves become catalysing, reinforcing factors for climate change.
	5	The learner knows about prevention, mitigation and adaptation strategies at different levels (global to individual) and for different contexts and their connections with disaster response and disaster risk reduction.
Socio-emotional learning objectives Teaching ***for*** the goals enhancing empathy and love	1	The learner is able to explain ecosystem dynamics and the environmental, social, economic and ethical impact of climate change.
	2	The leaner is able to encourage others to protect the climate.
	3	The learner is able to collaborate with others and to develop commonly agreed-upon strategies to deal with climate change
	4	The learner is able to recognize that their personal impact on the world's climate, from a local to a global perspective.
	5	The learner is able to recognize that the protection of the global climate is an essential task for everyone and that we need to completely re-evaluate our worldview and everyday behaviours in light of this.

(Continued)

Table 16.2 (Continued)

Behavioural learning objectives Teaching **through** the goals Promoting advocacy and activism	1 The learner is able to evaluate whether their private and job activities are climate friendly and -where not- to revise them. 2 The learner is able to act in favour of people threatened by climate change. 3 The learner is able to anticipate, estimate and assess the impact of personal, local and national decisions or activities on other people and world regions. 4 The learner is able to promote climate-protecting public policies. 5 The learner is able to support climate friendly economic activities.

Effective climate change education programmes are personally relevant and meaningful, use engaging teaching strategies, encourage deliberative discussion to explore and navigate disagreements and controversial issues, engage participants in the scientific process, address misconceptions, and/or incorporate school or community projects for participants to take action (Dolan, 2020). According to research, climate change is best taught with effective, well-tested education methods of experiential activities exploring the causes and impacts of climate change. In addition, effective climate change education can help build problem-solving skills by engaging students in classroom and community projects to increase awareness and support advocacy. Students learn more if they are prompted to assess their own ideas, talk through the evidence, and explain their thinking. Understanding and applying some or all of these strategies for climate change education can help educators improve their practice and deepen their students' learning (Monroe et al., 2019).

For educators, numerous resources exist for promoting climate change education in schools such as those listed in the padlet in the resource section of this chapter. Comprehensive approaches for teaching climate change in primary schools are discussed by Dolan (2022). An extensive list of children's and young adult literature dealing with climate change is also listed at the end of this chapter. Appropriate learning approaches for teaching climate change have been highlighted by UNESCO (Table 16.3).

The Greta Effect

Greta Thunberg's activism and speeches are inspiring to watch and have encouraged so many of us to stop, think and challenge the ongoing damage being done to our planet by huge organisations, and even on a smaller scale in our own homes. Greta Thunberg is the Swedish teenager who skipped school and inspired an international movement to fight climate change. In May 2018, aged 15, Greta won a climate change essay competition in a local newspaper. Three months later, she began protesting in front of the Swedish parliament building, vowing to continue until the Swedish government met the carbon emissions target agreed by world leaders in Paris, in 2015. She held a sign painted in black letters on a white background that read in Swedish 'Skolstrejk för klimatet', which means 'School Strike for Climate'.

Table 16.3 Learning approaches for teaching climate change Source, Adapted from UNESCO, 2017: 37

Performa role-play to estimate and feel the impact of climate change related phenomena from different perspectives

Analyse different climate change scenarios with regard to their assumptions, consequences and their preceding development paths

Develop and run an action project or campaign related to climate protection

Develop a web page or blog for group contributions related to climate change issues

Develop climate friendly biographies

Undertake a case study about how climate change could increase the risk of disasters in a local community

Develop and enquiry-based project investigating the statement 'Those who caused the most damage to the atmosphere should pay for it"

Greta began missing lessons to go on strike on Fridays, urging students around the world to join her. She has become a leading voice, inspiring millions to join protests around the world. Greta describes her Asperger's syndrome as a gift which affords her a superpower of being different. Her protests went viral on social media and as support for her cause grew, other strikes started around the world, spreading with the hashtag #FridaysForFuture. By December 2018, more than 20,000 students around the world had joined her in countries including Australia, the UK, Belgium, the US and Japan. She joined strikes around Europe, choosing to travel by train to limit her impact on the environment.

The teenager took the whole of 2019 off school to continue campaigning, to attend key climate conferences, and to join student protests around the world. Greta organised her first global day of action, the School Strike for Climate, in March 2019, and it exceeded all expectations. Among the 1.4 million students in 125 countries who spent the day striking for climate action, over 30,000 students walked out in Sydney, 10,000 rallied in London, England, and huge crowds gathered in New York, Toronto, Lisbon, San Francisco, and many other cities around the world. In September 2019, she travelled to New York to address a UN climate conference. Greta refuses to fly because of its environmental impact, so she made her way there on a racing yacht, in a journey that lasted two weeks. When she arrived, millions of people around the world took part in a climate strike, underlining the scale of her influence. Addressing the conference, she criticised politicians for relying on young people for answers to climate change.

> *This is all wrong. I shouldn't be up here. I should be back in school on the other side of the ocean. Yet you all come to us young people for hope? How dare you! You have stolen my dreams and my childhood with your empty words. And yet I'm one of the lucky ones. People are suffering. People are dying. Entire ecosystems are collapsing. We are in the beginning of a mass extinction. And all you can talk about is money and fairytales of eternal economic growth. How dare you!*
>
> Greta Thunberg, at the 2019 UN Climate Action Summit held in New York City

Named Time Magazine's Person of the Year in 2019, Greta continues to condemn our neoliberal obsession with growth and profit. Greta is both a heroine and a villain depending on one's perspective. She continues to irk climate deniers. Those who feel threatened by climate protests have objected to her message. However, her impact has been staggering. She has brought a much needed human dimension to the discussion. In a debate dominated by statistics, the measurement of emissions and projected future climate scenarios, Greta has delivered a simple message. Climate action is a moral issue. As a teenager she recognises that climate change will affect her future and that of every young person. She is not representing an organisation with a pre-determined political agenda. Her words are authentic, credible and trustworthy. Speaking about her own anguish and anger, she makes a connection with people on an emotional level. Greta Thunberg is working in solidarity with young people around the world including those from the Global South, those most affected by climate change.

Case study 16.1 Youth assembly on climate

The national broadcasting service Radio Teilifís Éireann (RTÉ) and the National Parliament (Houses of the Oireachtas) facilitated the country's first ever Youth Assembly on Climate in Leinster House, the home of the national parliament in 2019. This was a chance for young people to discuss what Ireland needs to do to tackle issues around the climate crisis. Students between the ages of 10 and 17 could apply, with a parent or guardian's permission. As part of the application, students included information about climate or environmental projects they have been involved in, as well as a one minute video pitch. Their videos outlined reasons for taking part and their opinions on climate issues. 157 applicants were selected. These students, from all over Ireland gathered in the Dáil to discuss the climate crisis and look at solutions. On Friday 15 November 2019, the Youth Assembly on Climate, called on adults and elected representatives to take action on their recommendations on climate change. Sitting in the seats of their TDs (*Teachta Dála* abbreviated as TD is a member of Dáil Éireann), the students focused on and debated climate disruption's growing impact on environment, economics, food and farming, energy and education. The event was chaired by Ceann Comhairle Seán Ó Fearghaíl (Chairperson of the Dáil) and broadcast live on national television in two sessions: the first setting the agenda, the second to ratify a climate proclamation – coinciding with the centenary of the first Dáil (first meeting of Irish parliament). An 11 year old girl from St. Augustine's NS, Clontuskert, Ballinasloe highlighted the global impacts of climate change, especially on the poorest people, and the need to end fossil fuel use, deforestation and biodiversity loss. The following is an outline of her speech:

My fellow Assembly Members, and citizens of Ireland, I am here to speak on behalf of the Environment Group. I ask for your attention. Our environment is critical to the air we breathe, the water we drink, the food we grow and the places we swim, play and walk. It is key to our health and well-being. Our environment also supports plants, animals, and ecosystems. Healthy ecosystems
and rich biodiversity are fundamental to life on our planet.
All this means that we need to look after our environment because we need it to

be able to look after us. The environment can be damaged by pollution and change caused by humans through how we make things, our choices and how we consume.

The more we don't care about the environment the more it will become polluted with contamination and waste that have harmful impacts. Climate change and the and the disruption it will cause is a worldwide threat. We need to work collectively both nationally and globally to act on climate change before it is too late. Global warming is leading to heating and acidification of the oceans, melting of the ice sheets, the destruction of soil, and alterations to our weather systems.

This is causing sea levels to rise as well as extreme weather events such as snow-storms, droughts, heat-waves and flooding. As climate change alters temperature and weather patterns it will also impact on animal life and plants.

What this all means is that the challenges will be different for both communities and biodiversity across Ireland and across the world. And sadly, some of the poorest and most vulnerable peoples and ecosystems will be worst affected.

Scientists have been warning us about climate change for over 30 years, … but no-one was listening. As the great environmental activist Greta Thunberg says, "We need to Unite Behind the Science" and get things done. There is no time left for deniers and those who put things off. There are a few areas we need to work on such as eliminating fossil fuel use, increasing waste prevention, as well as halting deforestation and biodiversity loss.

Fossil fuel use (including here in Ireland the harvesting and burning of peat) raises serious environmental concerns as it the single largest source of greenhouse gases globally. This can be reduced greatly by just switching to renewable energy in electricity, transport, heating and cooling. When we cut our bogs we destroy a globally important carbon store, and when we burn the peat from these bogs we release even more carbon. This must stop. Today the youth assembly is discussing climate change and the environment, and ways to bring about a positive change nationally and globally.

The environment group which I represent will be convening to debate positive change nationality and globally to decide on two key proposals for action.

We can all play a part and we all can make a difference. In fact I would say we all have to play a part and have to do things differently. It is not an option, as anything less than collective, determined and enduring action can only be regarded as short-sighted and reckless.

Thank You.

Delegates from the Youth Assembly on Climate issued this statement:

> *We, the youth of Ireland, call on our elected representatives and on adults to listen. We put forward our recommendations for action to stop climate breakdown. We are NOT experts. In our recommendations we offer ideas but we do NOT have answers. It is a starting point for adults and particularly for those elected to protect and progress our society. We call on you to listen to the science, to take on board our recommendations and to work on our behalf to ensure that we – and you – have a future.*

The 157 delegates of the RTÉ Youth Assembly issued these ten recommendations:

1   From your corner store to your supermarket, we call on the house to incentivise and obligate the installation of glass doors on open refrigerators.

2   For Ireland to ban the importation of fracked gas and invest solely in renewables.

3   Implementing measures that will allow that Irish goods be both eco-sustainable and affordable in todays' Irish Market.

4   Implement a tiered tax on emissions from large companies including those under capital Emissions Trading Scheme (ETS). This tax must be increased every year while threshold decreases, shifting the burden from individuals to corporations.

5   Investment in industrial hemp facilities to provide a viable, sustainable and alternative land use for farmers as well as employment in rural Ireland.

6   A labelling and pricing system showing the climate impact of food products based on criteria such as impact of packaging and distance travelled.

7   Ireland to outlaw acts of ecocide – the widespread and systematic loss of ecosystems, including climate and cultural damage.

8   Protect existing forests and make compulsory that at least 10% of all land owned for agricultural uses is dedicated to forestry.

9   A targeted nationwide information campaign to educate the population about the climate crisis regarding the causes, the effects and the solutions.

10 Mandatory 'sustainability' education from primary level to the workplace including a new compulsory Junior Cycle and optional Leaving Certificate subject.

While this youth assembly was noteworthy because of its coverage on national television, there has been a growing number of youth assemblies in Ireland and elsewhere. Following research and investigation each school can have its own climate assembly. Linking such an event to the Conference of the Parties (COP) is very worthwhile and allows students to make their own links to international debates.

Engaging in climate change education through games

Games and game-like elements have been used to educate, entertain and engage for thousands of years. Rapidly exploding in growth in recent years, games are now used in innovative ways, for teaching complex issues (Wu & Lee, 2015). Gamification is the application of game-design elements and game principles in non-game contexts. It can also be defined as a set of activities and processes to solve problems by using or applying the characteristics of game elements. 'Climate change games' are defined as games (including simulations) which explore some aspect of climate change as a central theme, focusing on processes, impacts, mitigation and adaption options and the role of human behaviour. Such games allow participants to vicariously experience some of the complexities associated with climate change and to consider options for future scenarios (Pfirman et al., 2021). Their potential for teaching other aspects of the SDGs feature in Chapter 7 (SDG 4) and Chapter 14 (SDG 11).

Games are popular tools for climate change education and engagement. Furthermore, they are uniquely suited to help students understand, care about and take action on climate issues (Wu & Lee, 2015). The increasing sophistication of climate games is reflected in the number of formats available. Climate change games are available as board games, card games, role-plays, or digital games (video games, online or offline computer games)

Reckien and Eisenack (2013). They also vary in terms of format, technical sophistication and scientific accuracy. Web based formats have increased significantly in the last decade. The 3D computer game *Minecraft* is discussed in greater detail in Chapter 14. There are many options available for participating in climate change games, including commercially available games, teacher designed games and student designed games. As we consider ways to broaden engagement with climate change education, we should include playful approaches and games in our portfolio of pedagogies.

Serious games

Serious games are designed to entertain and educate players, and to promote behavioural change. Devised to promote the transfer of skills and content from the game to the real world, they include the debriefing and explication of players' behaviours and cognitive skills while playing (Blumberg et al., 2013). Abt (1970) referred to serious games as combining the analytic and questioning concentration of the scientific viewpoint with the intuitive freedom and rewards of imaginative, artistic acts. Serious games have an explicit and carefully thought-out purpose. They are not intended to be played primarily for amusement, although this does not mean that serious games are not, or should not be, captivating and fun. One study reviewed the effectiveness of the 2030 SDGs Game (https://2030sdgsgame.com/) as a pedagogical tool for the promotion of interdisciplinary education (Andreoni and Richard, 2024:21). According to this research, the 2030 SDGs Game supports 'the co-creation of knowledge' and 'the development of problem-solving attitudes, soft skills and team-working abilities.'

Another study evaluated the effectiveness of the *EcoChains:Arctic Crisis*, a climate change card game. Research about this game was conducted whereby people were randomly assigned to either play the game or to read an article about the Arctic region (Pfirman et al., 2021). The game was found to be as effective as the article in teaching content of the impacts of climate change over the short-term, and was more effective than the article in long-term retention of new information. Furthermore, game players had higher levels of engagement and perceptions that they knew ways to help protect Arctic ecosystems. Players were also more likely to recommend the game to friends or family than those in the control group. The authors found that long term retention of key information was 'stickier' for those who played the game. The stickiness factor is a unique quality that causes the phenomenon to 'stick' in the minds of the public and influence their behaviour (Gladwell, 2000). Games are ideally placed for promoting transformative pedagogy through the Four Hs framework discussed in Chapter 2.

Three different kinds of games are showcased for illustrative purposes:

1   Commercially available climate change games: *The EcoChains: Arctic Crisis card game*
2   Teacher Designed Climate Change Games: The Climate Change Loop Card Game
3   Student designed climate change games: Climopoly

1. *The EcoChains: Arctic Crisis card game* (example of a commercially available climate change game)

The Arctic is a special place full of unique animals which depend on sea ice to live. It is also one of the fastest changing places on Earth due to climate change. *EcoChains* is a multiplayer card game about climate change dealing with the struggle for survival in a rapidly warming Arctic. The game is designed to increase players' knowledge of the Arctic marine ecosystem and to engage in considering mitigation options. Players build food chains as they learn about Arctic ecosystems and how humans impact the environment (e.g. how carbon pollution and diminishing sea ice can impact Arctic species). This game of strategy and survival gives players the opportunity to learn about the components of an Arctic marine food web, the reliance of some species on sea ice, and the potential impact of future changes on the ecosystem. The game was produced by Jogolabs and designed by a team of environmental scientists, educators and game designers.

Rules for playing are simple. (A link to detailed rules is available in the resources section of this chapter.) **Sea Ice cards** form the base of each player's food web. Each player builds food chains by connecting various **Arctic species cards** including the *polar bear, walrus, ringed seal and narwhal*. **Event cards** such as *carbon pollution*, triggers the melting of sea ice and causes some animals to migrate or die. Players can also play *Action cards* in order to help protect their food chains. The player who keeps the most animals alive wins. **Goal cards** also provide additional victory points. Discussions during the game and debriefing afterwards provides teachers with an opportunity to focus on the unique characteristics of the Arctic including its complex relationship with climate change. This discussion can also be supported by the Climate Change Loop Card Game discussed below.

2. The climate change loop card game (example of a teacher designed climate change game)

A game where all students have a card on which there is both a question and an answer. As a question is called out, each student works out the answer and if the answer is on their card, they call it out and read the question at the bottom of their card. Loop cards (Table 16.4) are constructed to ensure that all questions and answers are used and the sequence arrives back at the first question. Examples of climate change loop cards included in Appendix 4 can be edited in any way to suit student age, ability and numbers.

Loop cards

- provide a means to revise climate change vocabulary and concepts
- enhance students' listening and concentration skills
- provide an opportunity to enrich conceptual knowledge about climate change

A loop card game can be also be played on the table, akin to dominoes where each student links up the card containing the answer to follow the question card. The cards are shuffled

Table 16.4 Template for climate change loop card game discussed below. (See Appendix 4 for a sample loop card game).

I have	I have
....	....
Who has	Who has

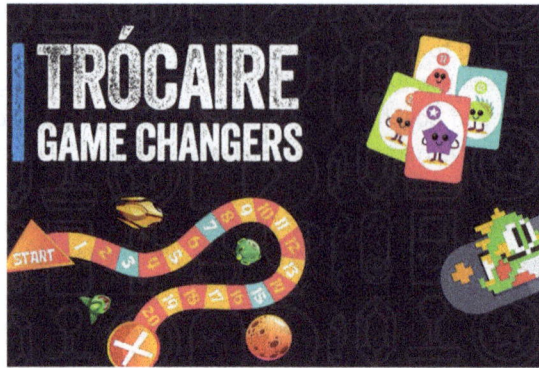

Figure 16.2 Game Changers. (Source: Trócaire).

and shared out between the students in the group. All students begin with their cards facing up. The first and last card can be placed in the middle. Every time a student has the correct answer – they say their answer and then read out their question and then turn their card over. The game ends when one student has all their cards turned over. Another way to use the loop cards is to work as a team and time the game from start to finish. The students can then try to beat their time.

3. Climopoly: an example of a student designed game

Making games is not a new idea in education (Walford, 2007). Indeed, learning can be more effective if students design their own games. Such games can include versions of Bingo (Appendix 3), Snakes and Ladders; Snap (with pictures and text describing the glossary of climate terms); Who Wants to be a Millionaire?; and Monopoly as illustrated in the game Climopoly below. However, according to Kafai (2006: 36), 'far fewer people have sought to turn the tables: by making games for learning instead of playing games for learning'. The Non-Governmental Organisation Trócaire has established an innovative game making competition. Game Changers (Figure 16.2) is a competition for young people who want to change the world and believe games are a way to do this. Using Games Based Learning (GBL) and game design, young people choose an issue of global justice related to the SDGs, and create a game that raises awareness of their chosen issue through the format of a game.

One group of prize winners decided to design a game called Climopoly based on the Monopoly game (Figure 16.3). Using the framework of the traditional Monopoly Game, every item on the board is linked to climate change. The aim of this game is to purchase a maximum amount of carbon credits. The gameboard itself and all associated resources are designed from recycled materials.

On the Climopoly board are 40 spaces. The four corners of the traditional Monopoly Board are maintained for clarity: called *GO*; *Free Parking*, *JAIL*, and *Go to Jail*. The traditional railway stations are replaced with local low carbon travel options e.g. the local bus station, train station, bike hire scheme and Park n'Ride. Along the sides of the board are climate friendly assets and resources. Climate resources include: local climate education initiatives (Forest

Figure 16.3 Climopoly (Student Created Climate Change Game).

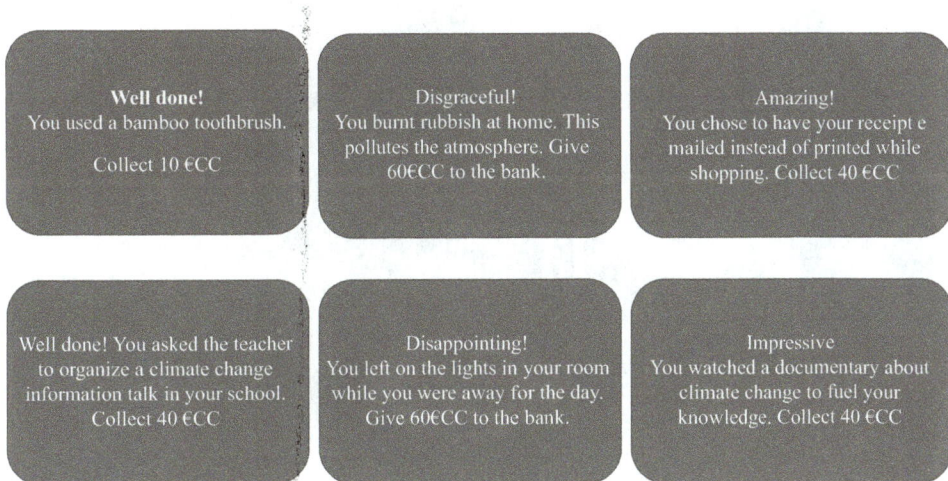

Well done!
You used a bamboo toothbrush.

Collect 10 €CC

Disgraceful!
You burnt rubbish at home. This pollutes the atmosphere. Give 60€CC to the bank.

Amazing!
You chose to have your receipt e mailed instead of printed while shopping. Collect 40 €CC

Well done! You asked the teacher to organize a climate change information talk in your school. Collect 40 €CC

Disappointing!
You left on the lights in your room while you were away for the day. Give 60€CC to the bank.

Impressive
You watched a documentary about climate change to fuel your knowledge. Collect 40 €CC

Figure 16.4 Examples of Chance Cards for Climopoly.

School, Galway Aquarium and Brigits' Garden); Bogs (Clara Bog and the Bog of Allen); natural amenities (River Shannon and Galway Bay); Climate Activists (Greta Thunberg, Saoirse Exton and Flossie Donnelly). Alternative sources of energy (carpooling, solar panels and wind turbines) also feature. The objective of the game is to acquire as many carbon credits (€CC) as possible and the playing rules are the same as the traditional monopoly game. Sample chance cards are listed in Figure 16.4. Students who designed Climopoly reflected on their learning in a positive manner as illustrated in Table 16.5.

Table 16.5 Responses from the design team

While doing the Gamechanger project for Trócaire, I learnt new things about climate change and sustainability. I learnt how to co-operate and work best as a team and how to keep things organized. Most of all I enjoyed being with my friends. We took a break from going on our phones to do something creative and educational. We also worked under pressure and learnt how to achieve our goal. We all had equally important jobs to do so no-one felt useless. Overall, I really enjoyed it. Working on 'Climopoly' was a great experience. We put a lot of hard work into the game. I learnt about everything climate related that is going on in our world today but I also learnt about the resources we have in Ireland that may help us to prevent or slow down climate change. I think that this exercise was a great way to promote sustainability and climate action. Since it was inspired by the much loved 'Monopoly' it might be more attractive to players. Each 'property' in the game is something related to sustainability or climate change, so that might give the player a little more insight on what is going on in this world. Overall, I really enjoyed spending time with my friends and working on this project and I hope that others learn and benefit from it.

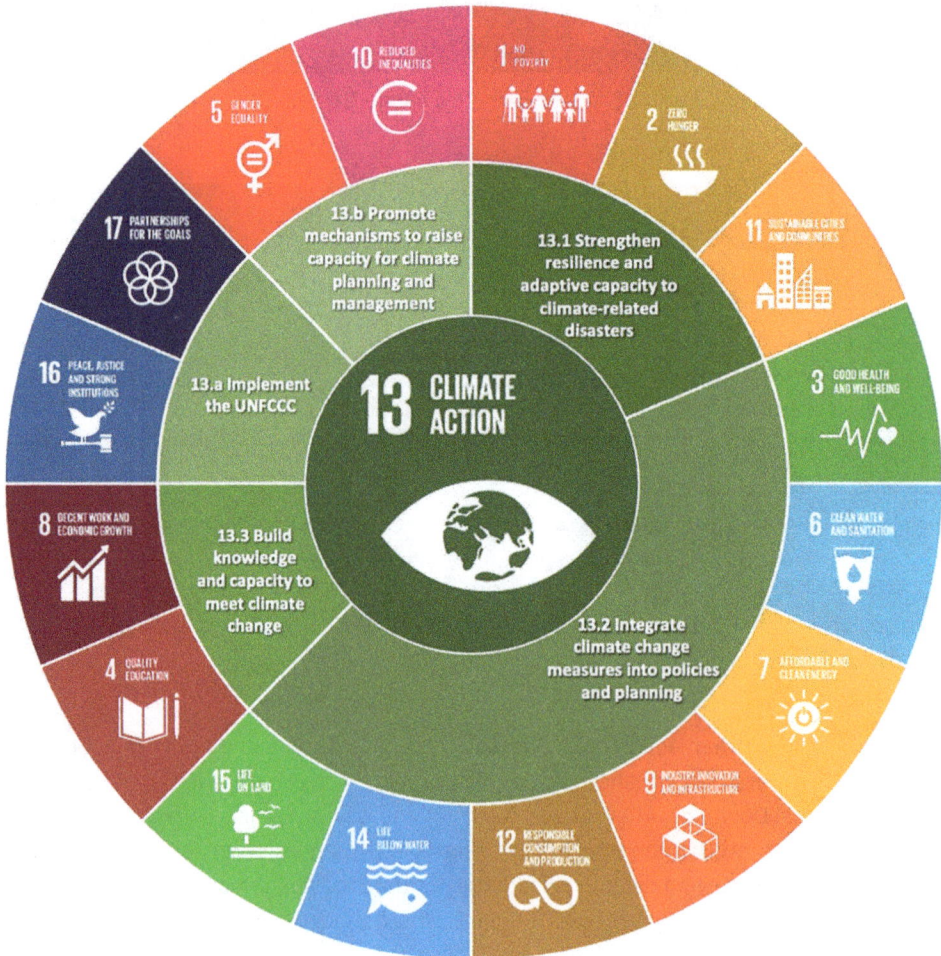

Figure 16.5 Relation among targets of Climate Action and the SDGs. (source Filho et al. 2023).

Links with other SDGs

Climate action has a central role in achieving all SDGs. Figure 16.5 illustrates the links between Climate Action targets and the other SDGs, links which are not well understood according to researchers (Filho et al, 2023). For instance, climate change measures need to be adopted into policies associated with all of the SDGs and SDGs 3,6,7,9,12,14, and 15 in particular. Not all of the SDGs have clear cross references to climate change or climate action efforts, yet all would benefit from such plans and policies. This cross sectoral thinking is essential to the success of the SDGs. While progress on climate action is essential for achieving other SDGs, the corollary is also true. The global climate challenge threatens to unravel decades of progress in all the other SDGs including health, poverty, hunger, life on land and below water and more. Climate change is a threat multiplier with the potential to worsen some of humanity's greatest challenges, including health, poverty and hunger. A warming climate will impact access to basic necessities including food, water and energy. Poorer nations will be more adversely affected. Furthermore, they will be least able to cope with associated social, economic and natural shocks. References to climate resilience and adaptation are interlaced throughout several goals. Games such as those highlighted in this chapter are well placed to help students understand how action to address climate change can reinforce or undermine other SDGs, and vice versa.

Conclusion

Climate change is a threat to local and global development with unprecedented potential consequences. Young people are currently affected by climate change albeit in differing ways depending on geographical, social and economic factors. They have a right to a comprehensive and robust climate change education, to ensure they become responsible decision makers now and in the future (Dolan, 2020). Education has a hugely important role to play in driving the transition to a sustainable future. By increasing the quality and accessibility of education and developing people's knowledge, attitudes and behaviours towards climate change, a just transition is possible. Climate change as a local and global challenge must be addressed though climate change education which includes a combination of local learning and action in addition to wider systematic mindset shifts. Simply teaching about climate change is not sufficient. Teaching about, through and for climate action and climate justice will empower students to take action and to advocate for action. Strategies outlined in this chapter and throughout this book, will assist teachers to facilitate deep learning, to build resilience and to develop hopeful citizens through action based learning.

Resources

An extensive list of resources, videos and case studies for SDG 13 is included in the SDG padlet accompanying this book: https://padlet.com/annedolan/o6rds38ylfy6a28h

Weblinks

https://padlet.com/annedolan/uir0u3bwz3octwz0 (primary)
https://padlet.com/annedolangalway/6u8blh9tocccx4sv (post-primary)
Trócaire game changers: https://www.trocaire.org/our-work/educate/game-changers/

Climate games

Eco Chains Arctic Crisis: Instructions for playing the game: https://ccnmtl.github.io/polarhub/
files/EcoChains-QuickStart-GamePlay_0.pdf

TheClimateCentre:https://www.climatecentre.org/priority_areas/innovation/innovation_tools/
climate-games/

Before the storm: https://www.climatecentre.org/games/2532/before-the-storm/

Climate Role Play: https://fn.se/wp-content/uploads/2016/08/climate_role_play.pdf

WorldClimateSimulation:https://www.climateinteractive.org/tools/world-climate-simulation/

Children's literature (SDG13)

(Picture books)

Aitken, S. (2011) *Fever at the Poles* Magic Wagon.

Bergen, L. (2008) *The Polar Bear's Home* Little Simon.

Bonsper, P. and Rink, D. (illus) (2015) *The Problem of the Hot World* Create Space Independent Publishing Platform.

Celano, M., Collins, M. and Madanasinghe, B. (illus) (2023) *Something Happened to Our Planet: Kids
Tackle the Climate Crisis* Magination Press.

Cole, J. and Degen, B. (illus) (2014) *The Magic School Bus and the Climate Challenge* Scholastic Press.

Dumas Roy, S. and Houssais, E. (illus) (2013) *Hot Air* Phoenix Yard Books.

French, L. and Gott, B. (illus) (2009) *Who Turned Up the Heat? Eco Pig Explains Global Warming* Looking
Glass Library.

Halls, S. and Okstad, E. (illus) (2020) *Elephant in My Kitchen* Egmont.

Hans, D.B. (2011) *Little Polar Bear* North South Books.

Herbert, M. and Mann, M.E. (2022) *The Tantrum that Saved the World* North Atlantic Books.

Jackson, E. and Calllwood, L. (illus) (2020) *Hunter's Icy Adventure: A True Story About the Global Problem of Climate Change* Ellie Jackson.

Kleiner, G. and Thompson, L. (illus) (2014) *Please Don't Paint Our Planet Pink: A Story for Children and
Their Adults* Cloudburst Creative.

Le, K. (2018) *The Lonely Polar Bear* Happy Fox Books.

Maclear, K. and Pak, K. (illus) (2017) *The Fog* Tundra.

O'Brien, O. and Finn-Kelcey, N. (2009) *Perry the Playful Polar Bear* BPR Publishers.

O'Brien, O. and Finn-Kelcey, N. (2010) *Perry the Polar Bear Goes Green: A Story about Global Warming*
BPR Publishers.

Okimoto, J.D. and Trammell, J. (2010) *Winston of Churchill: One Bear's Battle Against Global Warming*
Scholastic Canada, Limited.

Soontornvat, C. and Bell, R. J., (illus) (2022) *To Change a Planet* Scholastic Press

Teymorian, A. (2018) *There's Room For Everyone* Tiny Owl Publishing

Wortzel, J.D. and Champlin, L.(illus) (2021) *Coco's Fire: Changing Climate Anxiety Into Climate
Action* Future Perfect.Media LLC

Yun, D. and Oleynikov, I. (illus) (2023) *Where Can We Go? A Tale of Four Bears* Greystone Books

Informational picturebooks

Allen, T. (2020) *Sometimes People March* Balzer and Bray.

Artis, Z. and Greenspan, O. (2021) *A Kids Book About Climate Change* A Kids Company About Inc.

Barr, C. Williams, S. Husband, A. (illus) and Love, M. (illus) (2021) *The Story of Climate Change: a First
Book about How We Can Help Save Our Planet* (2021) Frances Lincoln Books.

Beer, S. (2021) *Change Starts With Us* Caterpillar Books.

Cooper, R. and Russell, H. (illus) (2022) *The Brainiac's Book of the Climate and Weather* Thames &
Hudson

Harmon, A. and Lozano, A. (Illus) (2021) *Climate Change and How We'll Fix it: The Real Problem and What We Can do to Fix it* Sterling Children's Books.

Jackson, T. and Kordic, D. (illus) (2021) *How Do We Stop Climate Change: Mind Mappers: Making Difficult Subjects Easy To Understand* Weldon Owen.

Jamieson, T. and Cai, R. (illus) (2022) *The Giant and the Sea* Lothian Children's Books.

Layton, N. (2020) *A Climate in Chaos: and How You Can Help* Wren & Rook.

Metcalf, L. H. and Bradley, J. (2023) *No World Too Big: Young People Fighting Climate Change Charlesbridge* Publishing.

Miles, D. (2020) *Climate Change, The Choice Is Ours: The Facts, Our Future and Why There's Hope* Global Publisher Services.

Minoglio, A. and Fanelli, L. (illus) (2021) *Our World Out of Balance: Understanding Climate Change and What We Can Do* Blue Dot Kids Press.

Nagara, I. (2013) *A is for Activist* Seven Stories Press.

Ralston, F. and Ralston, J. (Ilus) (2021) *What's the Weather?: Clouds, Climate and Global Warming* DK Children.

Roberts, S. and Lewin, H.J. (Ilus) (2022) *Somebody Woke Wilson: A Story About Carbon* Scholastic; 1st edition.

Saxby, C. and Racklyeft, J. (Ilus) (2021) *Iceberg* Allen & Unwin Children's Books.

Stevens, G. and Rewse, K. (illus) (2021) *Climate Action: The Future is in our Hands* 360 Degrees.

Taylor, A., Kirby, L. and Lirius. A. (illus). (2021) *Old Enough to Save the Planet* Magic Cat.

Chapter books and Informational Texts 9-12 years

Andreadis, E. and Koltsidopoulos, S. (illus) (2018) *Top Secret Mission Save the Planet* Zest Books.

Armour-Chelu, F. (2016) *Fenn Halfin and the Fearzero* Walker Books.

Chronicle Books. (2019) *We Are the Change: Words of Inspiration from Civil Rights Leaders* Chronicle Books.

Clinton, C. (2019) *She Persisted Around the World: 13 Women Who Changed History* Philomel Books.

Cole, S. and Vidal, O. (illus) (2020) *World Burn Down* Barrington Stoke.

Davies, N. (2021) *This is How Change Begins* Graffeg Limited.

David, L. and Gordon, C. (2007) *The Down-to-Earth Guide to Global Warming* Orchard Book.

De Fombelle, T. and Ardizzone, S. (2021) *Saving Celeste* Walker Books.

Dorey, M. and Wesson, T. (illus) (2021) *Kids Fight Climate Change: Act Now to Be a #2minutesuperhero* Walker Books.

Easton, E. and Chen, Z. (illus) *Enough! 20 Protestors who changed America* Crown Books for Young Readers.

Forde, C. and Lord, B. (illus) (2022) *Bright New World: How to Make a Happy Planet* Welbeck Editions.

Fountain, E. (2021) *Melt* Pushkin Children's Books.

Gold, H. and Pinfold, L. (illus) (2022) *The Last Bear* Harper Collins.

Gold, H. and Pinfold, L. (2023) *Finding Bear* Harper Collins.

Hall, J. and Lane, S. (illus) (2008) *A Hot Planet Needs Cool Kids: Understanding Climate Change and What You Can Do about It* Green Goat Books.

Harmon, A. and Lozano, A. (Illus) (2021) *Climate Change and How We'll Fix it: The Real Problem and What We Can do to Fix it Sterling* Children's Books.

Hawking, L. and Persico, Z. (2022) *Princess Olivia Investigates the Wrong Weather* Puffin.

Herman, G. (2018) *What Is Climate Change* Penguin.

Huddleston, T. (2019) *Flood World* Nosy Crow Ltd.

Huddleston, T. (2020) *Dust Road* Nosy Crow Ltd.

Huddleston, T. (2021) *Storm Tide* Nosy Crow Ltd.

Johnson, M. (2022) *Spark* Orion Children's Books

Jones, A. (2021) *Dear World Leaders: A Response to Children's Letters About Climate Change* Independently published.

Kennedy-Woodard, M., Kennedy Williams, P. and George, J. (illus) (2023) *You Are Unstoppable: How To Understand Your Feelings About Climate Change and Take Positive Action Together* Jessica Kingsley.

Leonard, M.G. and Neville-Lee, P. (illus) (2023) *The Ice Children* Macmillan Children's Books

Lerwill, B. (2020) *Climate Rebels* Puffin.

MacDibble, B. (2020) *How to Bee* Groundwood Books.

Penfold, N. (2020) *Where the World Turns Wild* Stripes Publishing.

Penfold, N. (2021) *Between Sea and Sky* Stripes Publishing.

Penfold, N. (2022) *Beyond the Frozen Horizon* Stripes Publishing.

Prentice, A., Reynolds, E. and Ramon, E.P. (illus) (2021) *Climate Crisis for Beginners: A Climate Change Book for Children* Usborne Publishing Ltd.

Ride, S., O'Shaughnessy, T. and Arnold, A. (illus) (2009) *Mission Save the Planet: Things You Can Do to Help Fight Global Warming* Flash Point.

Sandford, B. (2020) *Challenge Everything: An Extinction Rebellion Youth Guide to Saving the Planet* Pavilion Children's Books.

Saunders, K. and Leffler, D. (illus) (2023) *Bindi* Magabala Books.

Sedgwick, M. and Blow, P. (illus) (2022) *Wrath* Barrington Stoke.

Sima, A. and Miriam, J. (illus) (2023) *Climate: Our Changing World (Science in Action)* Albert Whitman & Company.

Stevenson, R. and Steinfeld, A. (illus) (2019) *Kid Activists: True Tales of Childhood from Champions of Change* Quirk Books.

Stevens, G. and Rewse, K. (illus) (2021) *Climate Action: The Future Is in our Hands* 360 Degrees.

Taylor, A., Kirby, L. and Lirius, A. (illus) (2021) *Old Enough to Save the Planet: Be Inspired by Real-Life Children Taking Action Against Climate Change* Magic Cat Publishing.

Ter Horst, M. and Panders, W. (illus) (2021) *Palm Trees at the North Pole: The Hot Truth About Climate Change* Greystone Kids.

Weiss-Tuider, K. and Schneider, C. (illus) (2023) *Mission Arctic: A Scientific Adventure to a Changing North Pole* Greystone Kids.

Chapter books and informational Texts (12 plus years)

Bradman, T. (2012) *Under the Weather: Stories about Climate Change* Frances Lincoln Children's Books.

Coffer, E., Donkin, A. and Rigano, G. (illus) (2023) *Global: A Graphic Novel Adventure about Hope in the Face of Climate Change* Hodder Children's Books.

Davenport, L. and Smith, J. (illus) (2021) *All the Feelings Under The Sun: How to Deal With Climate Change* Magination Press.

Dyu, L. (2019) *Earth Heroes: Twenty Inspiring Stories of People Saving Our World* Nosy Crow Ltd.

Grose, A. and Bohémier, L. (illus) (2024) *How to Manage Your Eco-Anxiety: An Empowering Guide for Young People (10 Steps to Change)* Harry N. Abrams

Heos, B. (2016) *Its Getting Hot in Here: The Past, Present and Future of Climate Change* Houghton Mifflin Harcourt.

Hooke, D. (2020) *Climate Emergency Atlas: What's Happening – What Can We Do* DK Children.

James, L. (ed.) (2024) *Future Hopes: Hopeful stories in a time of climate change* Walker Books.

Jeanes, R. and Kajfez, K. (illus) (2020) *Skyler and the Nature Net: An Action Packed Climate Change Story* Naturenet Books.

Nakate, V. (2021) *A Bigger Picture: My Fight To Bring a New African Voice to the Climate Crisis* One Boat.

Simmons, A. (2022) *Burning Sunlight* Andersen Press.

Thomas, I. and Paterson, A. (illus) (2020) *This Book Will (Help) Cool the Climate: 50 Ways to Cut Pollution Speak Up and Protect Our Planet!* Wren & Rook.

Books about Greta Thunberg

Picturebooks

Brookfield, E. (2020) *Go Green with Greta- No One Is Too Small to Save the Planet* Independently published.

Sanchez Vegara, M.I. and Weckmann, A. (2020) *Greta Tunberg Little People* BIG DREAMS.

Tucker, Z. and Persico, Z, (2019) *Greta and the Giants: Inspired by Greta Thunberg's Stand to Save the World* Frances Lincoln Children's Books.

Winter, J. (2019) *Our House Is On Fire: Greta Thunberg's Call to Save the Planet* Beach Lane Books.

Chapter books (9–12 years)

Camerini, V. and Carratello, V. (illus) (2019) *Greta's Story: The Schoolgirl Who Went On Strike to Save the Planet* Simon & Schuster Children's UK.

Chapman, A. (202) *Greta Thunberg and the Climate Crisis* Franklin Watts Ltd.

Giannella, V. and Marazzi, M. (2019) *We Are All Greta: Be Inspired by Greta Thunberg to Save the World* Laurence King Publishing.

Jina, D. and Braun, P. (illus) (2020) *The Extraordinary Life of Greta Thunberg* Puffin (Extraordinary Lives Series).

Leonard, A. (2020) *Who Is Greta Thunberg?* Penguin Workshop.

Part, M. (2019) *The Greta Thunberg; Being Different Is a Superpower* Sole Books.

Scholastic. (2020) *Planet Greta: How Greta Thunberg Wants You to Help Her Save Our Planet* Scholastic.

Chapter books and informational texts (12 plus years)

Blackwell, G. (2020) *I know This to be True Greta Thunberg: On Truth, Courage and Saving Our Planet* Chronicle Books.

Ernman, M., Thunberg, G., Ernman, B. and Thunberg, S. (2020) *Our House Is on Fire: Scenes of a Family and a Planet in Crisis* Penguin.

Rao, A. (2020) *One Earth: People of Colour Protecting Our Planet* Orca Book Publishers.

Thunberg, G. (2019) *No One Is Too Small to Make a Difference* Penguin.

Thunberg, G. (2022) *The Climate Book* Allen Lane.

Climate Sci Fi literature

Climate fiction, or cli-fi, is a form of speculative fiction that features a changed or changing climate as a major plot device. In recent years, climate fiction has been gaining a lot of steam, probably thanks in part to increased public awareness of the climate crisis.

Atwood, M. (2013a) *Oryx and Crake* Virago.

Atwood, M. (2013b) *The Year of the Flood* Virago.

Atwood, M. (2014) *Maddaddam* Virago.

Bacigalupi, P. (2009) *The Windup Girl* Night Shade Books.

Bacigalupi, P. (2016) *The Water Knife* Orbit.

Bertagna, J. (2017) (2nd ed.) *Exodus* Young Picador.

Block, F.L. (2014) *Love in the Time of Global Warming* Square Fish.

Boyle, T.C. (2019) *A Friend of the Earth* Bloomsbury Publishing.

Butler, O.E. (2019) *Parable of the Sower* Headline.

Cassidy, A. (2022) *The Drowning Day* UCLan Publishing.

Dimaline, C. (2019) *The Marrow Thieves* Jacaranda Books.

El Akkad, O. (2018) *American War* Picador.

Glass, J. *Vigil Harbor* Anchor Books.

Huddleston, T. (2019) *Flood World* Nosy Crow Ltd.

Kingsolver, B. (2013) *Flight Behaviour* Faber & Faber.

Landis, L. and Alessandra, N. (illus) (2019) *Chendell: A Natural Warrior* Waldo LLC.

Mbue, I. (2022) *How Beautiful We Were* Canongate Books.

Miller, S.J. (2019) *Blackfish City* Orbit.

Offill, J. (2021) *Weather* Granta Publications Ltd.

Olson, K. (2018) *The Sandcastle Empire* HarperTeen.

Onyebuchi, T. (2019) *War Girls* Razorbill.

Onyebuchi, T. (2020) *Rebel Sisters* Razorbill.

Robinson, K.S. (2005) *Forty Signs of Rain* Harper Collins.

Robinson, K.S. (2021) *The Ministry for the Future* Orbi.

Russell, K. (2020) *Orange World* Vintage.

Sedgwick, M. (2010) *Floodland* Orion Children's Books.

Simmons, K. (2018) *Pacifica* Tor Teen.

Smith, S.L. (2014) *Orleans* Penguin USA.

Sudbanthad, P. (2019) *Bangkok Wakes to Rain* Sceptre.

Suzan, L. (2023) *Giften* Pushkin Children's Books

Thompson, P. and Paganelli. E. (2023) *Greenwild: The World Behind the Door* Macmillan

Vaye Watkins, C. (2017) *Gold Fame Citrus* Riverrun.

Williamson, V. (2024) *War of the Wind* Neem Tree Press.

References

Abt, C. (1970) *Serious Games*. New York: Viking Press.

Andreoni, V. and Richard, A., 2024. Exploring the interconnected nature of the sustainable development goals: the 2030 SDGs Game as a pedagogical tool for interdisciplinary education. *International Journal of Sustainability in Higher Education*, 25(1), pp.21-42.

Armstrong McKay, D.I., Staal, A., Abrams, J.F., Winkelmann, R., Sakschewski, B., Loriani, S., Fetzer, I., Cornell, S.E., Rockström, J. and Lenton, T.M. (2022) Exceeding 1.5 C global warming could trigger multiple climate tipping points. *Science*, 377(6611), eabn7950.

Blumberg, F.C., Almonte, D.E., Anthony, J.S. and Hashimoto, N. (2013) Serious games: What are they? What do they do? Why should we play them in Dill, K.E. (Ed) *The Oxford Handbook of Media Psychology*, USA: Oxford University Press 334–351.

Dolan, A.M., 2020. *Powerful primary geography: a toolkit for 21st-century learning*. London Routledge.

Dolan, A.M. (Ed.) (2022) *Teaching Climate Change in Primary Schools: An Interdisciplinary Approach*. London: Routledge.

Filho, W.L., Wall, T., Salvia, A.L., Dinis, M.A.P. and Mifsud, M., (2023) The central role of climate action in achieving the United Nations' Sustainable Development Goals. *Scientific Reports*, 13(1), p.20582.

Gladwell, M. (2000) *The Tipping Point: How Little Things Can Make a Big Difference*. Boston:Little, Brown and Company.

Hicks, D. (2014) *Educating for Hope in Troubled Times*. London: IOE Press.

Kagawa, F., & Selby, D. (2010). *Education and climate change: Living and learning in interesting times*. New York: Routledge.

Kagawa, F. and Selby, D. (Eds.) (2010) *Education and climate change: Living and learning in interesting times* London:Routledge.

Kim, Y.H., Min, S.K. and Gillett, N.P., et al. (2023) Observationally-constrained projections of an ice-free Arctic even under a low emission scenario. *Nature Communications, 14*, 3139.

Levin, K., Cashore, B., Bernstein, S. and Auld, G. (2012) Overcoming the tragedy of super wicked problems: Constraining our future selves to ameliorate global climate change. *Policy Sciences, 45*, 123-152.

Mendler de Suarez, J., Suarez, P., Bachofen, C., Fortugno, N., Goentzel, J., Gonçalves, P., Grist, N., Macklin, C., Pfeifer, K., Schweizer, S., Van Aalst, M. and Virji, H. (2012) *Games for a New Climate: Experiencing the Complexity of Future Risks*. Pardee Center Task Force Report. Boston: The Frederick S. Pardee Center for the Study of the Longer-Range Future, Boston University. Retrieved from https://scienceimpact.mit.edu/sites/default/files/documents/%20Games%20for%20a%20New% 20Climate-%20Experiencing%20the%20Complexity%20of% 20Future%20Risks.pdf

Mochizuki, Y. and Bryan, A. (2015) Climate change education in the context of education for sustainable development: Rationale and principles. *Journal of Education for Sustainable Development, 9*(1), 4-26.

Monroe, M.C., Plate, R.R., Oxarart, A., Bowers, A. and Chaves, W.A. (2019) Identifying effective climate change education strategies: a systematic review of the research. *Environmental Education Research, 25*(6), 791-812.

Pfirman, S., O'Garra, T., Bachrach Simon, E., Brunacini, J., Reckien, D., Lee, J.J. and Lukasiewicz, E. (2021) "Stickier" learning through gameplay: An effective approach to climate change education. *Journal of Geoscience Education, 69*(2), 192-206.

Reckien, D. and Eisenack, K. (2013) Climate change gaming on board and screen: A review. *Simulation & Gaming, 44*(2-3), 253-271.

Stevenson, R.B., Nicholls, J. and Whitehouse, H. (2017) What is climate change education? *Curriculum Perspectives, 37*(1), 67-71.

Supran, G., Rahmstorf, S. and Oreskes, N., 2023. Assessing ExxonMobil's global warming projections. *Science*, *379*(6628), p.eabk0063.

Sweeney, J. (2020) Climate change in Ireland: Science, impacts and adaptation. In *Ireland and the Climate Crisis* (15-36). Cham: Palgrave Macmillan.

Tutu, D. and Robinson, M. (2011) Climate change is a matter of justice. *The Guardian*, December 5. http://www.guardian.co.uk/environment/2011/dec/05/climate-change-justice?intcmp=122.

UNESCO. (2017) Education for Sustainable Development Goals-Learning Objectives. https://unesdoc.unesco.org/ark:/48223/pf0000247444

UN General Assembly. (2015) Transforming Our World: the 2030 Agenda for Sustainable Development. Resolution adopted by the General Assembly on September 25, 2015. http://www.un.org/ga/search/view_doc.asp?symbol=A/RES/70/1&Lang=E

University of Winchester. (2020) The Value of a Degree. What Do Genz Expect from their University. https://www.winchester.ac.uk/media/content-assets/documents/The-value-of-a-degree-report-2020-(2).pdf

Walford, R. (2007) Using Games in School Geography, Cambridge: Chris Kington Publishing.

Waldron, F., Ruane, B., Oberman, R. and Morris, S. (2019) Geographical process or global injustice? Contrasting educational perspectives on climate change. *Environmental Education Research*, *25*(6), 895-911.

Winn, J. (2003) Avoiding death by PowerPoint. *Journal of Professional Issues in Engineering Education and Practice*, *129*(3), 115-118.

Wu, J.S. and Lee, J.J. (2015) Climate change games as tools for education and engagement. *Nature Climate Change*, *5*(5), 413-418.

17 Life under water (SDG 14)

Noirín Burke, Anna Quinn and
Padraic Creedon

Introduction

Sitting on the edge of the Atlantic, Ireland is surrounded by Ocean. To the east the narrow channel between Ireland and Great Britain, the Irish Sea provides a divide between two land masses. The Irish Sea is also a significant border in turns of geopolitics, where living things can pass from one territory to another. To the south the Celtic Sea is wider and wilder, full of life, with deep underwater features providing food and shelter for a diverse range of living things. To the West, are the wild waves of the Atlantic Ocean, shaping and sculpting our coastline, which influences the life that inhabits it. Our ocean and life under water has a direct impact on our daily lives, but we cannot think of it under just one heading; living things, as it is so much more. Wars have been fought over fishing grounds (Sverrir, 2016), nations can be divided on who rightly claims these marine territories (Irish Times, 2019), and all the while human development and population increases change our ocean environment on all levels, including the physical, biological and chemical (Gorick et al., 2016).

Located in the West of Ireland, Galway Atlantaquaria the National Aquarium of Ireland, is situated along the famous Salthill promenade, just a short distance from the heart of Galway City and overlooking Galway Bay. It is sheltered from the harshest Atlantic weather by the Aran Islands, which form a natural barrier across the mouth of the bay. Opened in 1999, the aquarium focuses on native Irish Species, both freshwater and marine, and the connection between humans and the natural world. Conservation Education is typically delivered through visitor engagement, signage, and formal education, though a range of online content is now also utilised.

Understanding the concept of sustainable oceans

The ocean is essential to life on Earth and may have given rise to life on our planet billions of years ago. Home to majestic sea life such as fish, turtles, colourful collar reefs and unique organisms, the ocean is an important ecosystem upon which our very survival is based. Healthy oceans and seas are essential to human existence and life on Earth. They cover 70% of the planet and provide food, energy and water. The ocean absorbs around one quarter of the world's annual carbon dioxide (CO2) emissions, thereby mitigating climate change and alleviating its impacts. Goal 14 is about conserving and sustainably using the oceans, seas and marine resources. Yet, human activity is endangering the oceans and seas, the planet's

DOI: 10.4324/9781003232001-20

largest ecosystem and affecting the livelihoods of billions of people. Indeed, approximately eight million metric tons of plastic are thrown into our oceans every year. In addition, millions of plastic microfibres litter the deep sea. Other threats to the ocean include over fishing, climate change and pollution. Steadily rising ocean temperatures are forcing fish to abandon their historic territories and move to cooler waters. Many commonly-eaten fish could face extinction as warming oceans due to climate change increase pressure on their survival while also hampering their ability to adapt. Research suggests that fish like sardines, pilchards and herring will struggle to keep pace with accelerating climate change as warmer waters reduce their size, and therefore their ability to relocate to more suitable environments (Avaria-Llautureo et al. 2021). As for Irish fisheries, we can likely expect more tropical and subtropical waters fish to move into our waters. Herring, cod, and mackerel are likely to move further north to the colder waters, which is already being witnessed by increased catches of these species off Norway and Iceland.

SDG 14 contains ten targets (listed in Appendix 1) for the conservation and sustainable use of our oceans.

Ocean ecosystems produce half the oxygen we breathe, they represent 95% of the planet's biosphere and soak up carbon dioxide, as the world's largest carbon sink. Yet until now, fragmented and loosely enforced rules governing the high seas have rendered ocean ecosystems susceptible to exploitation. The High Seas Treaty, an historic agreement to protect international waters and biodiversity in the oceans, was agreed at the UN on March 5th, 2023. This is a landmark agreement, a hopeful development. It is now imperative for citizens and governments to ensure that world leaders are held accountable and that commitments made under these international agreements are enforced. In order to protect our oceans all citizens, marine organisations and governments need to become ocean literate.

Teaching SDG 14: a focus on ocean literacy

To understand the complex nature of SDG 14, we must consider the relationships affecting marine living things and life under water. We need to appreciate the complex nature of the Ocean, and its role in shaping and supporting life, livelihoods, and a sustainable future for our planet. For this, we are going to introduce the concept of Ocean Literacy. Oceans form a critical part of our environment. Oceanography is the study of all aspects of the ocean. It includes marine life and its ecosystems, the movement of sediments, seafloor geology, tides, waves and coastal processes. While a study of the ocean or coastal life is geographical and scientific in nature, there are many other curricular aspects which need to be explored in the interest of an holistic understanding. Ocean literacy means 'understanding the ocean's influence on myself and my influence on the ocean' (Dromgool-Regan et al. 2017:2). An ocean literate person:

- Understands essential principles and fundamental concepts about the ocean
- Can communicate about the ocean in a meaningful way; and
- Is able to make informed and responsible decisions regarding the oceans and its resources.

Seven ocean literacy principles (Figure 17.1) have been developed by scientists and educators to help young people learn more about the ocean:

1   Earth has one big ocean with many features.
2   The ocean and life in the ocean shape the features of Earth.
3   The ocean is a major influence on weather and climate.
4   The ocean makes Earth habitable.
5   The ocean supports a great diversity of life and ecosystems.
6   The ocean and humans are inextricably interconnected.
7   The ocean is largely unexplored.

When we look at the learning objectives for teaching SDG 14, (UNESCO, 2017: 38) we can see the centrality of ocean literacy (Table 17.1).

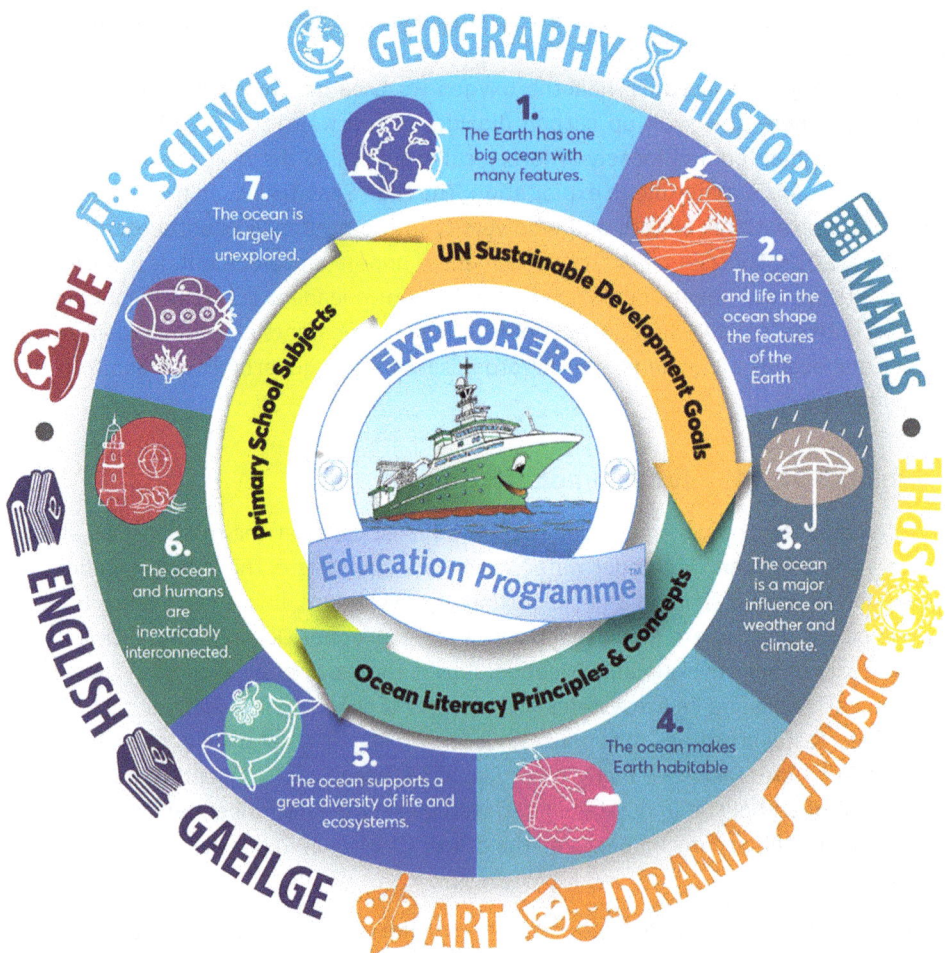

Figure 17.1 The Multi-Disciplinary and Cross-Curricular Features of Ocean Literacy. (Source: Explorers Education Programme https://www.marine.ie/site-area/areas-activity/education-outreach/explorers-education-programme).

Table 17.1 Learning objectives for SDG 14, Adapted from UNESCO (20017: 38)

Cognitive Learning Objectives Teaching ***about*** the goals: developing respect and understanding	For knowledge, individuals should understand the • Role of the ocean as a habitat, and the interconnections between marine living things. • Role of the ocean in our lives, but also the threats to the ocean and the link between climate and the ocean. • Opportunities for sustainable development of our ocean; through fisheries, aquaculture, seaweed production, renewable energy is another important aspect.
Socio-emotional learning objectives Teaching ***for*** the goals enhancing empathy and love	We must also consider the role of our attitude to the ocean, and how we value life under water. Do we consider how: • Our own actions impact the ocean and marine life. • We influence others in our community as a role model for values and attitudes. • We empathise with others, such as coastal/ fishing communities and people living in coastal and marine, who depend on life for sustainable futures. • We empathise with life under the water itself, how do we view marine life, their rights to the basic needs of living things such as food and shelter?
Behavioural learning objectives Teaching ***through*** the goals Promoting advocacy and activism	And finally, what actions and behaviours do we take for SDG 14 – life under water? • Do we support and communicate research and knowledge about the role of the ocean on life? • Do we influence others in the way we communicate about Ireland's connection to life under water? • Do we support a sustainable ocean and life under water by reducing our carbon footprint, eating local sustainable seafood? • Do we evaluate data on fisheries, consumption and material life cycles to make positive choices for life underwater? • Do we campaign for sustainable practices based on scientific evidence?

These components must be considered together, without knowledge or an appreciation for life under water we are unlikely to act, however without action, knowledge, and a positive attitude, our heretofore positive relationship with the oceans will be compromised.

Suggested topics and learning approaches for teaching SDG 14 are set out in Tables 17.2 and 17.3. This chapter adopts the transformative pedagogy of the Four Hs discussed in Chapter 2 (Figure 2.2).

SDG 14 activities for teaching action based ocean literacy

Human impact and the ocean (One small change workshop)

Our 'One Small Change' workshop focuses on what we as individuals can do in our daily lives to combat marine litter, reduce our carbon footprint and help conserve water, linking to its sister goal, SDG 6 'Clean water and sanitation'. Often, when dealing with topics considered quite 'heavy' such as marine litter and pollution, we can feel overwhelmed at the damage

Table 17.2 Suggested topics for SDG 14, adapted from UNESCO (2017: 39)

The hydrosphere: The water cycle, cloud formation, water as the great climate regulator

Management and use of marine resources (renewables and non-renewables): global commons and overfishing, quotas and how they are negotiated, aquaculture, seaweed, mineral resources

Sustainable marine energy (renewable energies, wind turbines and their controversy)

Marine ecology – the food web, predators and prey, competition, collapse

Coral reefs, coasts, mangroves and their ecological importance

Sea level rise and countries that will experience total or partial loss of land; climate refugees and what a loss of sovereignty will mean

The oceans and international law: international waters, territory disputes, flags of convenience and their related issues

Ocean pollutants: plastics, microbeads, sewage, nutrients and chemicals

The deep ocean and deep-sea creatures

Cultural relationships to the sea – the sea as a source of cultural ecosystem services such as recreation, inspiration and building of cultural identity

---

Table 17.3 Learning approaches for teaching about SDG 14 adapted from UNESCO (2017: 39)

Examples of learning approaches and methods for SDG 14 Life below Water

Develop and run a (youth) action project related to life below water

Undertake excursions to coastal sites

Debate sustainable use and management of fishery resources in school

Role-play islanders relocating from their country because of sea-level rise

Conduct a case study about cultural and subsistent relationships with the sea in different countries

Conduct lab experiments to provide students with evidence of ocean acidification

Develop an enquiry-based project: "Do we need the ocean or does the ocean need us?"

---

that has already been done to our planet, which leads us into a dangerous mind set of 'well, I'm only one person, my actions won't make a difference'. Young students can often feel a sense of 'eco-anxiety' as they are too young to take control and make positive changes. With our workshop we want to introduce the idea that every action we take has the potential to make a positive impact on the ocean, no matter what age we are. We also wanted to reiterate the importance of the ocean and why we need to make these changes.

To start the workshop, we often get the students' minds focused on the subject matter by carrying out a simple walking debate. Ensuring the students know there are no right answers to any of the statements is important, and after any discussion students may choose to change their mind if compelled by a fellow student's argument. Students must simply agree or disagree with the statements given to them. Encourage each student to have a reason for their stance.

An example of the statements used for junior students is as follows:

1   The world needs your help.
2   Turning off the lights in a room after you leave is good for the world.

3   We can never run out of water.
4   All of my rubbish should be put in one bin.
5   Animals love rubbish.
6   Helping our planet is easy.
7   Eating fish every day is ok.

For more senior groups the statements can become more complex.

1   The ocean is the most important thing in the world.
2   Ireland's coastal waters are not the cleanest in the world.
3   Ireland's fish stocks are slowly growing every year.
4   We can never run out of water.
5   The oceans' resources are vast and will never run out.
6   My actions do not impact on the ocean.
7   It's better to fix my broken phone rather than buying a new one.

After the walking debate, students will have touched on some of the socio-emotional learning objectives for SDG 14. During the debate the teacher should be ready to guide and provide background information when required. The themes of misinformation and fake news can be discussed in this context, particularly as students now face the much more difficult task of identifying falsehoods in the internet age.

As the discussion will likely have opened up a debate on water as a resource, we then carry out a follow-up activity of building a water filter which reinforces the strong link between SDG 14 and SDG 6, clean water and sanitation. This activity also presents the opportunity to tie in SDG 3 good health and well-being, as we all need water for good health. Meanwhile SDG 10 addresses reduced inequalities as we can investigate how our access to clean water compares to that of other countries.

Marine litter

Students are invited to examine several common materials which are used in daily life, such as plastic packaging, wet wipes and synthetic clothes and are asked to explore their life cycles from creation to end of life. An example of a wet wipes' life cycle is included (Figure 17.2), but research can be conducted on any material which may be more applicable to your students' daily lives.

Students are handed a shuffled deck of red cards (life cycle cards: Figure 17.2). They are then asked to arrange the cards in order of what comes first. When the students are happy with their order, the class discusses the material's life cycle. The more every day or common the items, the greater the personal impact the activity may have on the students. Remember that the goal is not to attack the students for their current choices but to simply encourage us all to challenge why we make the choices we do. Often the reasons why we make choices that could be considered environmentally damaging are rooted in common sense, cost is often a factor or ease of access. It is natural for us to seek out the most cost-efficient solution to problems or to find the easiest solution. Disposable wet wipes are cheaper and easier than

Source	Source	Processing	Processing
Crude Oil Extracted from the Ground.	Logging/harvesting natural raw materials, to produce fibres with good adsorption	Wood/Cotton is refined and made into a pulp	Plastic fibres blended with natural fibre pulp and cleaning chemicals added to create wet wipes with good adsorbing qualities while also being strong and elastic.

Plastic Production	Ocean Pollution	Landfill	Plastics in Ocean and Coasts
Strong plastic fibres formed.	"Flushable" Wet wipes which are non-biodegradable, enter the sewage system/ natural water systems when washed down drain.	Wet wipes enter landfills not decomposable. Natural fibres coated in antibacterial chemicals, which also kills the bacteria and enzymes required to break down natural fibres and solid waste in landfill sites.	Wet wipes enter the marine ecosystem. Causing a hazard to marine wildlife, plastic enters the food chain when plastic fibres are eaten by marine animals.

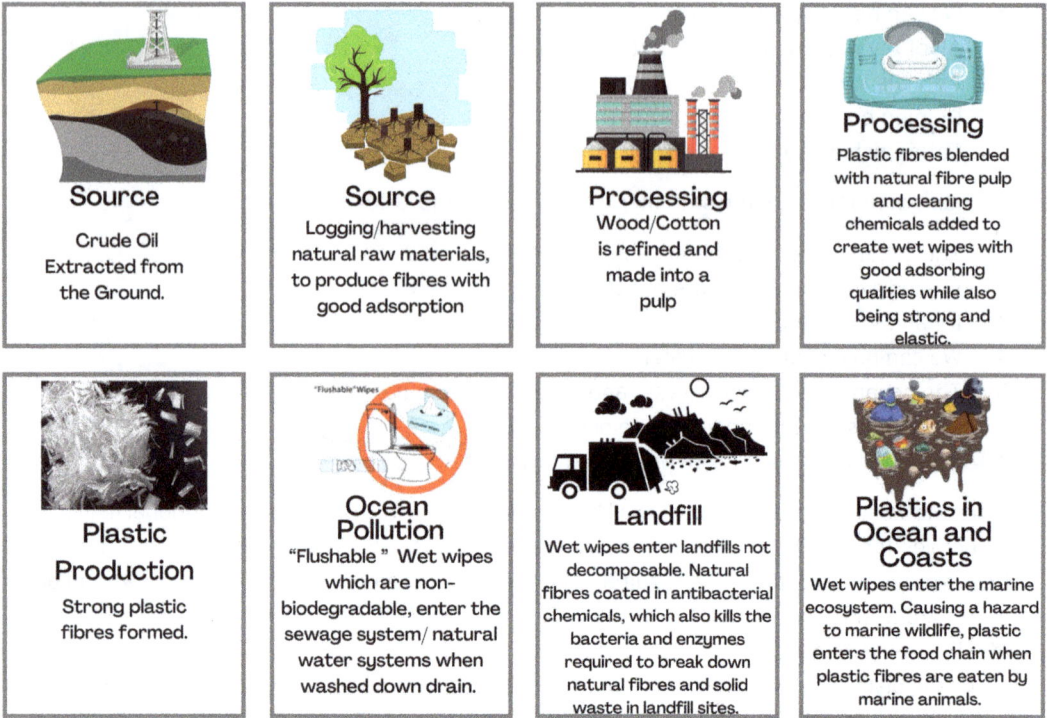

Figure 17.2 Wet Wipes Life Cycle Cards (Print these on red cards).

Table 17.4 Policy and action cards

Policy
Wet wipes containing plastic are banned.

Education
Public Relations Campaign is carried out to highlight the issue of wet wipes to the public. Promote the use of reusable cloth wipes or disposables made from natural materials such as cotton pads, bamboo wipes and paper towels.
Promote reducing consumption of single use plastic wipes.

New resources
Single use wet wipes replaced in the market by design made out of biodegradable materials such as bamboo while retaining the convenience of wet wipes.

Policy
A European Strategy for Plastics (2018)
New labelling requirements on wet wipes to inform consumers of environmental impact wet wipes pose and how to dispose of them properly. Producers to contribute to awareness, clean-up, collection and waste treatment of wet wipes.

Public consumer action
Refrain from buying wet wipes marketed as "flushable" to help reduce demand and selling power of environmentally damaging labelling.
Education
Irish Water and Clean Coasts will launch their annual *Think Before You Flush campaign.*

Community action
Individuals and communities support beach clean ups (e.g *Clean Coasts in Ireland*) to remove litter from our coasts.

more environmental alternatives; disposable nappies are much easier to deal with compared to reusable ones. Therefore, these items are so prevalent not because the people who buy them are uncaring or bad people.

The students are then presented with the green cards (policy and action cards: Table 17.4) and are asked to include them in the life cycle to interrupt or break the chain. Alternatives for using this product are then discussed. Students are asked how materials such as wet wipes affect out ocean. This discussion can branch off into a wide variety of marine issues such as:

Marine Litter:

- The Great Pacific Garbage Patch
- Marine litter being eaten by animals
- Microplastics in the ocean

Noise pollution

- 90% of global trade is carried out through shipping – cargo ships transport the bulk of these materials.
- Deep sea drilling for oil and other resource extraction used to create materials.

Finally, to conclude our workshop we ask the students to make a 'One Small Change' pledge for the ocean. Although one small action seems miniscule compared to the gravity of these ocean issues, collectively they have a significant impact. For example, if one student makes a pledge to bring a reusable water bottle to school for a year instead of buying a disposable one once a week, this would divest 36 bottles from landfill. If each student in a classroom makes this pledge, this would prevent 1,098 disposable bottles being thrown away per year. If the whole school (based on a school of eight classes, with 30 students per class) were to switch to reusable water bottles this would prevent 6,588 bottles being thrown away every year.

Armed with this knowledge, it is our hope that the student walks away from the workshop feeling empowered and inspired to make a positive change for our ocean. The workshop is designed to help students advocate for and spread awareness of the simple actions we can all do in our lives which collectively make a big impact. As part of our one small change initiative, we branched out into our local community to inspire positive change. As a result, the businesses directly connected to our aquarium pledged to use compostable materials when serving food. There are opportunities for the students, and the school to inspire positive change in their own community too. These changes do not have to be overwhelmingly big tasks. Simple achievable initiatives can help make a big difference. Organising a community clean up one Saturday a month for example, can make a huge difference, not only to the community but to the ocean too.

Extra activities/resources

Introduction to degradation and how long it takes for materials to break down can be found in the science category of the Explorers lesson plans section of the website (www.explorers.ie): https://oar.marine.ie/handle/10793/1100

Marlisco Marine litter video: https://www.youtube.com/watch?v=O17bBeXhYz4&t=2s
The Majestic Plastic Bag, a Mockumentary: https://www.youtube.com/watch?v=GLgh9h2ePYw

Empathy – marine biodiversity, marine food chains and webs and food production

SDG 14 is an absolute pleasure to teach as almost every student has some interest in the mysteries that exist below water. An alien world, rarely seen and barely explored, what person isn't somewhat intrigued by that? This is good, as it means before we even truly begin and with a few choice words we can stoke excitement on the topic. If you have the interest of your students from the get-go it is not difficult to hit the ground running.... or hit the sea swimming as it were.

The first learning objectives laid out for SDG 14 are the 'cognitive learning objectives'. Essentially, we need to ensure that the students have the 'foundational knowledge' needed to tackle the more difficult topics so that they can emotionally connect with the topic later. In our experience, there is no easier way to do this then to start with marine biology. Of course, we are biased as marine biologists but show us a student who does not have at least some interest in whales, dolphins, sharks, jellyfish or crabs and we will show you a liar. So, how do we tackle the learning objectives of SDG 14 in a simple, interesting, and most importantly, concise way? Our favourite method is by giving the students an utterly new and unique experience. Do that and they will remember it forever, along with a nice healthy dose of knowledge and ideas that otherwise may whither from their memories.

The experience we have mentioned is a focus on animal anatomy, specifically a squid dissection. Dissecting a squid is almost guaranteed to not only be something the students will never have done before, but highly likely something they will never have even considered. The initial reaction by the students, in our experience, is always strong. Often there is great excitement as well as revulsion (although we do believe the revulsion is mostly comical and put on for appearances). Either way, it is very unlikely you will be met with a 'meh' or 'that sounds boring'. Normally we would not just dive straight into a dissection. It is important to lay down that foundational knowledge and while we are at it, peak interest and allow the students to slowly and naturally open their minds to marine biology.

This first part is fairly easy, we find that seeing is better than hearing and feeling is better than seeing. So, passing around a selection of what we at Galway Atlantaquaria call 'bio facts', we can ignite the wonder and start the conversation. These bio facts can be remarkably simple and the opening questions that can accompany them can be seen below:

1   Seashells – Why do they look different from each other? What are they made of?
2   Mermaid's purse (shark and ray eggs) – Why are they called mermaids' purses?
3   Shark teeth – Why are they so easy to get? How many sharks live around Ireland?
4   Beach bones – What animals could this bone be from? Why does the bone wash up on the shore?

This blend of discussion, show and tell and tactile interaction is a perfect starter to SDG 14. The students will have physically interacted with the ocean; they will have questioned, wondered, and imagined all sorts of new things. This is where you want them, interested, with their minds open, and ready for more. Where bio-facts are not available, a slideshow of images of marine life can be used as a trigger for this activity.

Dissecting a squid

Now we come to the crux of our 'life below water' intro, the squid dissection (Figure 17.3). Before we begin our descent below the surface and into the shallows let me just lay out a brief description of how this activity plays out.

1   Discussion of the squid as an animal. What do we know and what do we think?
2   How has the squid adapted to life? Examine the outside of the squid's body and discuss the different body parts and their functions.
3   Open the squid up and examine the inside of the squid's body, then, discuss how the different internal organs function.

Carefully pack up the remains of each squid, dispose of materials, clean equipment, and summarise the experience with the group.

This one simple activity links to all of the cognitive learning objectives of SDG 14 (UNESCO, 2017: 38) as follows:

1   *The learner understands basic marine ecology, ecosystems, predator-prey relationships, etc.*
    ○   This one is simple; the very act of the dissection and the associated discussion hits this objective. The squid is highly adapted to its environment and thus understanding its anatomy leads to an understanding of greater marine ecology, the ecosystems it inhabits and its predator-prey relationships. Look no further than its tentacles and ink to see how it is adapted as both predator and prey.
2   *The learner understands the connection of many people to the sea and the life it holds, including the sea's role as a provider of food, jobs, and exciting opportunities.*
    ○   The students will lead you into this objective whether or not you bring it up. We have never been part of a squid dissection that did not have the questions 'are the squid dead?', 'did you kill them?' 'Where did you get them?' asked from very early on. The answers to these questions fit very neatly into learning objective two. The squid are caught by fishermen, that is their job. The squid we use are caught and sold as food to supermarkets and restaurants although we buy them as food for the animals in the aquarium. How do the fishermen find the squid? Amazing new technologies for fishing are constantly being developed. Fishing, marine biologists, educators, oceanographers and environmental consultants are just some of the career possibilities associated with the ocean.
3   *The learner knows the basic premise of climate change and the role of the oceans in moderating our climate.*
    ○   Here we meet our first challenge. The activity does not directly lend itself to a discussion on climate change, so as an educator you will likely need to loop this in yourself. Never fear though, as climate change is so significant and pervasive it can be easily linked to almost any topic. A link to this objective is as follows; these squid form part

of the diet required for the animals in the aquarium, those animals eat other animals too. While marine food is easily obtained now it may not always be. The waters around the world are warming due to climate change; the ocean has been acting as the earth's temperature regulator since long before humans ever existed. The ocean's ability to keep the earth cool by absorbing excess heat and CO_2 is not indefinite and we are seeing the effects of climate change through an increase in sea temperatures and an effect on Ocean pH. As the ocean warms, fish and marine species which can move across geographical areas will simply swim either further north or south, depending on the hemisphere they are in, thus, the natural balance of species ranges is being altered. Alarmingly, climate change is changing our oceans much faster and more drastically than it is changing our land. So, for now we can easily find the food we need to feed the animals of the aquarium, but this may not always be the case.

4   *The learner understands threats to ocean systems such as pollution and overfishing and recognizes and can explain the relative fragility of many ocean ecosystems including coral reefs and hypoxic dead zones.*

   ○   Threats to the ocean system can be identified through the following question: 'If fishermen are catching these squid, what will happen if all the squid run out?' This could be the first true moral conundrum we face during SDG 14 discussions. People need to make a living; fishing is an old, difficult but rewarding profession. However, if managed poorly the entire fish stock will be reduced and will eventually not be available for consumption. So, what of the squid we are currently dissecting, what of the other food we feed the animals in the aquarium? Where possible we source local and sustainable food supplies, but how do we assess what constitutes a sustainable fisheries or marine stock. What types of fish or animals are caught and how they are caught are the two most important factors in protecting the ocean from overfishing? Many fishermen understand the importance of these factors; unfortunately, there are some that do not. An ecosystem is like a table full of dominoes arranged in a line. If one species falls it can set off a chain reaction destroying the entire line. The ocean seems immensely powerful and indestructible but under that exterior lies a very fragile part of our planet that desperately needs help. Science provides a vital tool in this area, by monitoring and assessing stocks and working with fishing communities and governments to find a balance.

5   *The learner knows about opportunities for the sustainable use of living marine resources.*

   ○   Finally, we conclude our dissection by carefully packing away the remains of the squid. It does not get discarded, not only to protect the room from the smell of slowly decomposing marine life but to demonstrate the need to remove waste. The squid's purpose from our point of view was to keep the animals in the aquarium alive. Along the way we were able to learn about life in the oceans, how people live with and from the ocean and about how the oceans themselves struggle to survive while protecting the planet. The ocean is full of resources (like the squid we dissected) but this supply is not guaranteed to be infinite. They can be if we let them be. By learning what to use and what not to use, we can guarantee healthy oceans for thousands of years to come, we can guarantee that these squid can survive on Earth for as long as the Earth allows them to do so.

Our favourite way to end this session with the students is to send them a short video clip a day or two after the dissection. The video is a simple recording of their dissected squid remains being fed to the animals in the aquarium. Not only does it help prove that we practice what we preach but it shows the loop, such an important part of nature. The squid born from the ocean, survived on feeding from other life now returns to that cycle by feeding other ocean animals. It does not simply end up in a bin to slowly decompose but it loops back, as all things should.

Within a classroom it may not be possible to feed the squid you have dissected to your students or a classroom pet, but a nice extension to the activity is to get some fresh cooked squid and let your learners have a taste. You could also dissect a fish to compare its anatomy to that of a squid, as one is an invertebrate with no backbone, while the other, the fish has a backbone in its body.

This activity may seem like an odd one to choose when discussing empathy. But what is empathy? If we boil it down to its simplest definition, we would describe empathy as 'the ability to share and understand the feelings of others'. Is dissecting an animal not a complete contradiction to the idea of empathy? We don't believe so. Every animal in the world is different to us. It is difficult to understand exactly what these animals are feeling. Most of our understanding of 'feelings' are based on reading other people's voices, their body language and their movements. This is easier for animals that are closely related to us. In the case of chimpanzees, orangutans, gorillas, the similarities between ourselves and primates are clear. They act and move in ways that we understand. But a squid? It cannot speak, it's movements and body language are so alien to our own that to empathise with one is a very big ask. But, we need to empathise with nature if we are to protect it and thus protect ourselves. So the first step is understanding. If we can understand that squid see, eat, digest and have relationships with one another in ways that are similar to our own we can begin to empathise. They are not aliens, unknown beings we cannot hope to comprehend. They are just different living creatures. They want to find food to make sure they don't go hungry, they want to feel safe, they want to be healthy and they want to create lots of little tiny baby squid as well. If we can learn to empathise with nature even a little, by learning the anatomy of the squid it will be a step in the right direction for us all.

For further information on the steps to carrying out a squid dissection, see www. explorers.ie

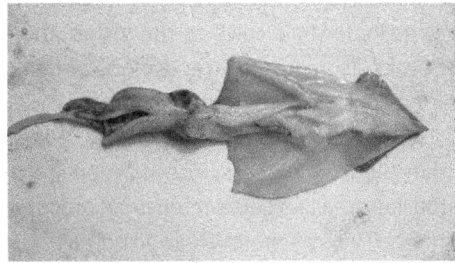

Figure 17.3 Squid External and Internal Features and a Dissection in Progress.

Hope – marine spatial planning and sustainable practices

The marine environment is highly complex, with a web of multiple aspects affecting life under water, and the ocean environment itself.

When we consider the marine environment as a habitat, we must first think about the basic needs of living things in water. These include water quality (though some living things prefer what we would consider poor water quality), food or access to an energy source, sunlight in the case of marine plants and hydrogen at hydrothermal vents, and shelter or somewhere to call home. Reproductive strategies abound in the ocean where we have fission, budding, eggs hatching externally, eggs hatching internally and live births. Some marine animals are born in freshwater, while others are born on land. Sexual reproduction can be external or internal. For example, all skates and whelks reproduce by laying egg cases. Many fish and invertebrates shed their eggs and sperm into the water column, an external method called broadcast spawning. Budding and fission, the division of one organism into two are examples of asexual reproduction. Asexual reproduction amongst starfish is through fission where the starfish's central disc is split into two pieces or autotomy (casting off of a part of the body) where one or more of the starfish's arms are lost.

For instance, certain starfish reproduce through fission either through the loss of an arm which then generates a new centre disc and new arms or through the splitting of the starfish in two, which results in the same growth of more arms and a complete disc. Budding occurs where seaweeds or animals break small pieces off themselves to create copies of themselves. The marine environment creates unique challenges to the cycle of life, some that have been met with amazing adaptability. Marine sex life is fascinating for students.

As mentioned earlier, water temperature, salinity, pH level, light intensity, substrate or surface type plus turbidity (measure of clarity of a liquid) can all influence marine living things' life processes and distribution.

With this in mind, we can reflect on how human developments and innovation can impact marine spaces. With increased activity in our coastal and marine environments over the last 200 years, the need for planning and protection has become more urgent. So too, has understanding the viewpoints of the many stakeholders which may cross paths within these spaces. We must also consider the connections between land and sea, and the impact of human behaviours on the ocean and coastal areas, even when people are not directly engaged with the ocean, or living or working by the shore.

Marine Spatial Planning (MSP) is the public process of analysing and allocating the spatial and temporal distribution of human activities in marine areas to achieve ecological and social objectives that have been specified through a political process. It allows stakeholders to contribute their voice to the vision and development plans within marine environments. It should also consider the ecological impacts of any changes, so that it can contribute to marine conservation plans.

The next activity is based on the students taking on the roles of different stakeholders within the MSP process. The location we used here is Galway Bay, however any coastal or estuarine area can be selected once maps can be downloaded or drawn for reference. The students carry out a pre-evaluation self-assessment (Table 17.5) to rate their level of knowledge of the subject content, attitude to the marine environment, and motivation to act for marine conservation. The students begin by reviewing maps of the marine area in question. In small groups, participants are invited to brainstorm the different layers to this area such as

- Seabed and coastal zones - the physical environment
- Biodiversity/habitat types - biological
- Protected Areas or areas of special conservation
- Human developments - nearby towns, transport links, islands
- Human activities - fisheries, tourism, seaweed farming, local communities, transport and shipping
- Weather patterns/climate
- Future of this area? Any issues with sea level rises, coastal erosion

Groups then share their ideas. Once this process is complete, the students are provided with role playing cards, introducing them to their role/character. The students are then introduced to a key scenario e.g. the installation of renewable ocean energy devices within the bay. However, different scenarios can be used depending on the geographical area selected, and topics could include:

- Sustainable seafood and aquaculture
- Marine Innovation
- Biodiversity and the protection of an endangered or threatened species
- Ecotourism
- Protection of local heritage
- Indigenous communities
- Shipping
- Coastal Protection

Students explore the relationship between people and energy by conducting a simple energy audit, based on some tasks common in everyday life. The aim of this task is to calculate the amount of energy consumed on a daily/monthly/annual basis. This helps students to appreciate the need for energy sources in general and renewable energy sources in particular.

Students are then asked to consider how wave and tidal energy devices work. This takes place through a series of simple water investigations. Tidal energy is influenced by the tidal cycle and range, which is influenced by the gravitational force of the moon and sun, and the shape of the surrounding seabed. Students can examine how waves are formed by wind, and how convection currents cause the movement of warm and cold water, from areas where the levels of heat from the sun is higher at the tropics, to the cooler areas at the earth's poles. This process providers students with some of the scientific knowledge needed to understand the concepts and devices being discussed in this activity.

Information cards are provided based on different energy devices and a list of criteria for where they could be located including ideal water depth, substrate (surface) type, and distance from shore. A set of Infomar maps (www.infomar.ie) is provided so the students can access areas within the bay to match these lists of criteria for each device. Student are asked to consider the sources of the data provided and how data can be evaluated. Once the students have all the background information, they are asked to provide any questions on post it cards or orally. They are then asked to review their stakeholder cards, and debate as a group if they should place renewable energy devices within the bay. For our activity, the following stakeholders include:

Local resident
Local public representative
Member of the local fishing community
Local Non Governmental Organisation (NGO)
A representative from the ocean energy device company
Local marine tour operator

Stakeholders could be changed to reflect different groups including

Youth groups
Academic scientists and researchers
Member of an international organisations
Government representatives, including local, regional and national
Local businesses including tourism, hospitality, producers, suppliers and commercial operations
Sports and recreation
Local artists, community groups, public organisations and consumers
Environmental non- governmental organisations.

Once students have time to review their role, they are asked to consider the feasibility of installing devices in the bay by voting, with the most votes forming the successful choice. The students are also asked to vote on the type of device, potential locations for the device and the number that would be installed. They are asked to consider the other aspects to life in the bay, which emerge during the brainstorming at the start of the activity. Once completed, groups are asked to share their choices including a rationale with the larger group.

The students are asked to view the Real Map of Ireland and consider this development on a larger scale. The Real Map of Ireland is available on https://www.marine.ie/site-area/ irelands-marine-resource/real-map-ireland-0 We call this 'The Real Map of Ireland' as you can see that Ireland's marine territory extends far beyond our coastline up to 220 million acres (approx. 880,000km2), an area more than ten times our land mass.

Further material for research is available for the students through the the Sustainable Energy Authority of Ireland (SEAI) video on test facilities in Ireland https://www.seai.ie/ sustainable-solutions/renewable-energy/ocean-energy/ocean-test-sites-in-ireland/ and the Atlantic Ocean Research Alliance (AORA) *Last Great Exploration Campaign on Earth* short video https://www.youtube.com/watch?v=uktwQre4O2M.

To complete the task, students consider their vision for the ocean in 30 years time?

- What would they like the bay to look like?
- What services would they see as part of the marine environment?
- How would they ensure sustainable practices within the bay?
- What is their hope for the ocean for the future?
- How does their vision of the local marine environment align with their hopes for the

wider ocean in the years to come?

- How might these hopes differ for different stakeholder groups?
- How can Marine Spatial Planning help us to work towards a sustainable ocean, which encompasses others' vision and hopes for their local areas and communities?

Finally, the students complete their self-assessment tool (Figure 17.4) to assess if there has been any change in knowledge, attitude or motivation.

Figure 17.4 Students Taking Part in Stakeholder Engagement.

Table 17.5 Ocean energy self evaluation tool

Before Score	Knowledge	After Score
	I know about how the ocean is important to Ireland	
	I know about the functions of Galway Bay – how people use it	
	I know about the renewable ocean energy	
	I know about marine spatial planning in Ireland	
	← Calculate Totals →	

0 = something you don't know anything about/never heard of
5= something you know a great deal

Before Score	Attitudes and Values	After Score
	I think the ocean is important to my daily life	
	I think Galway Bay is an important part of the county I live in	
	I believe we all have a responsibility to protect the ecosystems and life in Galway Bay	
	I think renewable ocean energy has an important role to play in the Irish Economy	
	→ Calculate Totals ←	

0 = something you strongly disagree with
5= something you strongly agree with

Before Score	Actions	After Score
	I can talk about the ocean around Ireland	
	I feel confident in discussing how people are connected to the ocean	
	I can share information about renewable energy in Ireland	
	I can list some simple functions of my local coastal area – Galway Bay	
	→ Calculate Totals ←	

0 = something you never think of or intend to do
5= something you always think of or intend to do

List 3 simple functions of Galway Bay (services it provides to people)

1.

2.

3.

Any other Suggestions:

Other ideas for incorporating SGD 14 into your classroom

Biodiversity challenge

Ask your student to consider types of marine biodiversity? Can they make an A-Z list of marine life? Or draw images? Using the students' ideas can you create an ocean wall display in your school? Once the names or drawings are completed can students think of links between any of the animals or plants? Do they live in the same place? Eat each other! Are any of them part of a human food web? Or used in a human product, like seaweed used in beer or ice-cream?

Citizen science project

Can your class collect any information for a citizen science project? The Irish Whale and Dolphin Group, Coastwatch, Bird Watch Ireland, the Purse Search Project and *Explore your Shore Project* from the National Biodiversity Centre, all have information to help guide students through collecting and recording data on species by the shore. The Explorers Education Programme, seashore guide workbook (https://oar.marine.ie/handle/10793/1592) can also be used to help identify coastal features and species and record data and information linked to the shore.

Water experiments

Do your students understand the links between the ocean and weather and climate? Can they look for patterns in how water and air absorb heat, or cool down? Can they explore earth observations, charts, and maps to examine ocean currents, wind patterns and weather systems? Can they investigate evaporation, condensation, precipitation, and accumulation by making a water cycle in a bag or a water cycle display? Can they explore convection currents, and how temperature affects the density of water? To learn about the physical properties of water, watch this video from Water Forum Ireland: *Magic of Water:Phenomenal Physics* (https://www.youtube.com/watch?v=vU7MSX2JzAk). More activities with water are discussed in chapter 9 (SDG 6).

Sustainable fisheries

Have students consider what fish they eat and where it comes from? Can they identify several Irish commercial fish or marine species? Do they understand the process of fish farming/aquaculture/seaweed farming? How do scientists assess fish stock levels and decide on minimum catch sizes and quotas for fisheries? Can students interview someone who works in the fishing community? Or visit a local fish shop? *STEM Series: Episode 1- Ocean Literacy* has a good section on food from the ocean: (https://www.youtube.com/watch?v=Xguwp3w9lB8).

Coastal communities

If your school is close to the ocean can you create a marine heritage book which looks at the history of the local area and its links to the sea? Are there any old ocean stories or folklore? If your school is away from the ocean can students explore ocean folklore from other parts of the world?

Exploring ocean hero's/role models

Do students know of any famous people who work with the ocean? Can they research a local ocean/national/international ocean hero? What would they classify as an ocean hero? What categories would they use?

Local communities
Authors
Scientist
Innovator
Film makers
Politicians
Sports people
Environmentalists
Photographers
Presenters
Business
School
Young person
Family
Educator/Teacher

Conclusion/summary

The interconnections between our ocean, life under and above water are extensive. The potential for using the ocean as a trigger with your class is endless. As a source of inspiration, reflection or as a platform for exploring sustainable living and innovation, we can use content across curriculum strands and strand units, across class and ability levels, focusing on knowledge and skills development. Through the concept of 'one ocean' which connects us all, we can use life under water and SDG 14 to create empathy within ourselves and our students for the world around us, the living things that sustain it and the diverse range of communities that inhabit it.

Resources

An extensive list of resources, videos and case studies for SDG 14 is included in the SDG padlet accompanying this book: https://padlet.com/annedolan/o6rds38ylfy6a28h

Key dates

April 3: World Aquatic Animal Day
May 2: World Tuna Day
May 22: International Day for Biological Diversity
May 22: World Seal Day

May 23: World Turtle Day
June 8: World Oceans Day
June 9: Coral Triangle Day
July 14: Shark Awareness Day
July 14: World Orca Day

In the USA the month of June is National Ocean Month

August 30: World Whale Shark Day
September 1: World Beach Day
October 8: World Octopus Day
October 17: World Sawfish Day
November 3: World Basking Shark Day
November 21: World Fisheries Day

Weblinks

Explorers Education Programme: www.explorers.ie
Ocean Literacy: The Essential Principles and Fundamental Concepts of Ocean Sciences for Learners of All Ages, Version 2: March 2013. Retrieved from: http://www.coexploration.org/oceanliteracy/documents/ OceanLitChart.pdf
Explorers planning guide for primary school teachers: ocean literacy and engagement. https://oar.marine.ie/handle/10793/1336
For more information on the Ocean Literacy (OL) principals visit www.oceanliteracy.net
EU Blue schools handbook: https://www.submariner-network.eu/images/projects/OceanLiteracy/PDF/220119_handbook_eueopean_blue_schools_220221.pdf
Ocean Literacy for all; A toolkit: https://unesdoc.unesco.org/ark:/48223/pf0000260721
An Tasice Cleancoasts run an annual Ocean Hero Award – https://cleancoasts.org/

Children's literature about life below water

Picturebooks

Atkinson, C. (2015) *To the Sea* Little, Brown Books for Young Readers.
Atkinson, C. (2018) *Off and Away* Little, Brown Books for Young Readers.
Bailey, E. (2020) *One Day on Our Blue Planet* Flying Eye Books.
Barr, C. and Kearney, B. (illus) (2021) *A Turtle's View of the Ocean Blue* Laurence King.
Barker, F. and Gray, H. (illus) (2021) *Setsuko and the Song of the Sea* Tiny Tree.
Barnard, B. (2017) *The New Ocean: The Fate of Life in a Changing Sea* Knopf Books for Young Readers.
Berne, J. and Puybaret, E. (illus) (2015) *Manfish: A Story of Jacques Cousteau* Chronicle Books.
Bland, N. (2021) *Walk of the Whales* Hardie Grant Children's Publishing.
Brewis, M. (2018) *Steve Terror of the Seas* Oxford University Press.
Brunellière, L. (2019) *Deep in the Ocean* Abrams Appleseed; Illustrated edition.
Burleigh, R. and Minor, W. (illus) (2018) *Trapped! A Whale's Rescue* Charlesbridge Publishing.
Butterfield, M. and Mineker, V. (illus) (2023) *The Secret Life of Oceans* Happy Yak.
Collier, G. and Lowman, S. (illus) (2023) *Dreaming of the Ocean* Collier Publishing LLC.
Conlon, D. and Izlesou, A. (illus) (2021) *Swim, Shark, Swim!* Graffeg Limited.
Cottle, K. (2020) *The Blue Giant* Pavilion Children's Books.
Cousteau, P. Hopkinson, D. and So, M. (illus) (2016) *Follow the Moon Home: A Tale of One Idea, Twenty Kids and a Hundred Sea Turtles* Chronicle Books.
Cusolito, M. and Wong, N. (illus) (2018) *Flying Deep: Climb Inside Deep-Sea Submersible Alvin* Charlesbridge.

Davies, N. and Cameron, A. (illus) (2016) *Into the Blue* Graffeg.

Davies, B. and Poh, J. (illus) (2020) *Little Turtle and the Changing Sea: A Story of Survival in Our Polluted Waters* Penguin Random House.

Davies, B. and Poh, J. (illus) (2021) *Little Turtle and the Sea* Little Tiger Press.

DiPucchio, K. and Figueroa, R. (illus) (2021) *Oona* Harper Collins Children's Books.

Dobell, D. and Thorns, B. (illus) (2020) *The World of Whales: Get to Know the Giants of the Ocean* Gestalten.

Elliott, D. and Meade, H. (illus) (2014) *In the Sea* Candlewick.

Fan, T. (2018) *Ocean Meets Sky* Simon & Schuster Books.

Ferrie, C. and Dale-Scott, L. (illus) (2020) *My First 100 Ocean Words* Sourcebooks Explore.

Ferry, B. and Martinez-Neal, J. (illus) (2020) *Swashby and the Sea* HMH Books for Young Readers.

Gray, C. and Triggs, L. (illus) (2020) *We used to Love Swimming- Children's Book About Turtles and Plastic Pollution* Independent Publishing Network.

Guendelsberger, E. and Leonard, D. (illus) (2020) *Inky the Octopus: The Official Story of One Brave Octopus' Daring Escape* Sourcebooks Wonderland.

Hanes, K. and Bonfield, C. (illus) (2017) *Seagrass Dreams* Seagrass Press.

Hart, Caryl. and Woolvin, B. (illus) (2021) *Meet the Oceans* Bloomsbury Children's Books.

Hawthorne, L. (2019) *Alba the Hundred Year Old Fish* Big Picture Press.

Howell, T. and Jones, R. (illus) (2018) *Whale in a Fishbowl* Schwartz & Wade.

James, J. (2020) *Marie's Ocean: Marie Tharp Maps the Mountains* Henry Holt and Co. (BYR).

Jenkins, S. (2016) *Down, Down, Down: A Journey to the Bottom of the Sea* HMH Books for Young Readers.

Keating, J. and Álvarez Miguéns, M. (illus) (2017) *Shark Lady: The True Story of How Eugenie Clark Became the Ocean's Most Fearless Scientist* Sourcebooks Explore.

Knapman, T. and Robins, W. (illus) (2019) *Let's Dive Into the Ocean* Silver Dolphin Books.

Knowles, L. and Webber, J. (illus) (2018) *The Coral Kingdom* words & pictures.

Krestovnikoff, M. (2020) *The Ocean: Exploring Our Blue Planet* Bloomsbury Children's Books.

Lambert, J. (2023) *Can You Share, Little Whale?* Little Tiger.

Lane Ferrari, S. and Vallicelli, G. (illus) (2019) *Clumsy Nelson* Serena Ferrari.

Lang, H. and Solano, J. (illus) (2016) *Swimming With Sharks: The Daring Discoveries of Eugenie* Albert Whitman & Company.

Le, X. and Marx, J. (2021) *Turtle Rescue: A Wild Adventure To Save Our Sea Life* Caterpillar Books.

Lebeuf, D. and Barron, A. (2020) *My Ocean Is Blue* Kids Can Press.

Lord, M. and Blattman (2020) *The Mess That We Made* Flashlight Press.

Macho, A. (2019) *The Whale, the Sea and the Stars* Floris Books.

Mc Donald, J. (2019) *Hello, World! Ocean Life* Pisces Books.

Mc Ginty, A.B. Havis, A.B. and Laberis, S. (illus) (2020) *The Sea Knows* Simon & Schuster/Paula Wiseman Books.

Messner, K. and Neal, C. (illus) (2022) *Over and Under the Waves* Chronicle Books.

Nivola, C. *Life in the Ocean: The Story of Oceanographer Sylvia Earle* Farrar, Straus and Giroux.

Pallotta, J. and Biedrzycki, D. (illus) (2006) *Dory Story* Charlesbridge.

Pallotta, J. and Leonard, T. (illus) (2012) *The Sea Mammal Alphabet Book* Bald Eagle Books.

Percival, T. (2019) *The Sea Saw* Simon & Schuster.

Portis, A. (2020) *Hey, Water* Scallywag Press.

Roberts, S. and Peck, H. (illus) (2019) *Somebody Swallowed Stanley* Scholastic.

Rosenstock, B. and Roy, K. (illus) (2018) *Otis and Will Discover the Deep: The Record-Setting Dive of the Bathysphere* Little, Brown Books for Young Readers.

Rossiter, J. (2019) *1,2,3 Who's Cleaning the Sea?* Independently published.

Seed, A. and East, N. (2021) *Interview with a Shark: and Other Ocean Giants Too* Welbeck Children's Books.

Sheneman, D. (2023) *The Deep End:Real Facts about the Ocean* HarperCollins.

Shurety, W. and Donnelly, P. (illus) (2021) *The Last Seaweed Pie* Storyhouse Publishing.

Smithers, A. and Aptsiauri, N. (illus) (2023) *Ocean Full of Wonder* Orange Lotus Publishing.

Stahl, B. (2019) *Save the Ocean* Bethany Stahl.

Stevens, G. and Baker, T. (illus) *Finn the Fortunate Tiger Shark and his Fantastic Friends: Learn How to Protect Our Oceans with Finn* Be the change books.

Stith, S. and Stith, S and Lechuga, M. (illus) (2023) *Black Beach: A Community, An Oil Spill and the Origin of Earth Day* Little Bee Books.

Swann, K. and Padmacandra (illus) (2021) *The Tale of the Whale* Scallywag Press.

Teckentrup, B. (2019a) *Fish Everywhere* Big Picture Press.

Teckentrup, B. (2019b) *Ocean: A Peek-Through Picturebook* Pisces Books.

Teckentrup, B. (2019c) *Ocean: A Peek-Through Picture Book* Pisces Books; Illustrated edition.

Todd-Stanton, J. (2017) *The Secret of Black Rock* Flying Eye Books.

Tyline King, H. and Holmes, E. (Illus) (2021) *Saving American Beach: The Biography of African Americam Environmentalist MaVynee Betsch* G.P. Putnam's Sons Books for Young Readers.

Watts, A. and Le, K. (illus) (2020) *Fish Who Found The Sea* Sounds True.

Williams, L. (2017) *If Sharks Disappeared* Roaring Brook Press.

Chapter books

Bethell, Z. (2021) *The Shark Caller* Usborne Publishing Ltd.

Davies, N. (2013a) *Whale Boy* Yearling.

Davies, N. (2013b) *Manatee Baby* Walker Books.

Davies, N. (2015) *The Whale Who Saved Us* Walker Books.

Davies, N. and Kinnear, N. (illus) (2018) *Ariki and the Giant Shark* Walker Books.

Farook, N. (2021) *The Boy Who Met A Whale* Nosy Crow Ltd.

Kurlansky, M. and Stockton, F. (2014) *World Without Fish* Workman Children's.

Laird, E. (2018) *Song of the Dolphin Boy* Macmillan Children's Books.

Ness, P. and Cal, R. (illus) *And the Ocean Was Our Sky* Walker Books.

Oxtra, C. and Ficorillu, F. (illus) (2020) *Tara and the Towering Wave: An Indian Ocean Tsunami* Stone Arch Books; Illustrated edition.

Reeve, P. (2021) *Utterly Dark and the Face of the Deep* David Fickling Books

Sedgwick, J. and Kutsuwada, C. (illus) (2021) *Tsunami Girl* Guppy Books.

Informational texts and chapter books

Alexander, H. and Lozano, A. (2018) *Life on Earth: Ocean with 100 Questions and 70 Lift-Flaps* Wide Eyed Editions.

Butterfield, M. (2019) *Blue Planet: Life on Our Oceans and Rivers* 360 Degrees.

Crane, C. (2020) *Protecting Earth's Waters* Children's Press.

Colón, E. (2020) *Ocean Animals and Their Ecosystems: A Nature Reference Book for Kids* Rockridge Press.

Crumpton, N. and Scott, G. (illus) (2023) *Everything You Know About Sharks Is Wrong!* Nosy Crow.

Cullis, M. and Luu, B. (illus) (2019) *Look Inside Seas and Oceans* Usborne Publishing Ltd.

Davies, N. (2004) *Oceans and Seas* Kingfisher Books Ltd.

Davies, N. and Croft, J. (illlus) (2015) *Surprising Sharks* Walker Books.

Davies, N. and Sutton, E. (illus) (2020) *A First Book of the Sea* Walker Books.

Druvert, H. (illus) and Grundmann, E. (2018) *Ocean* Thames and Hudson Ltd.

Hawkins, E. and Letherland, L. (2019) *Atlas of Ocean Adventures: A Collection of Natural Wonders, Marine Marvels and Undersea Antics from Across the Globe* Wide Eyed Editions.

Henriques, R. and Lertia, A. (illus) (2018) *Ocean: A Visual Miscellany* Chronicle Books.

Hestermann, B. and Hestermann, J. (2021) *Ocean Animals for Kids: A Junior Scientist's Guide to Whales, Sharks and Other Marine Life* Rockridge Press.

Hume, S. (2022) *An Anthology of Aquatic Life* DK Children.

Krestonvnikoff, M. and Calder, J. (illus) (2019) *The Sea: Exploring Our Blue Planet* Bloomsbury Children's Books.

Messner, K. and Forsythe, M. (2018) *The Brilliant Deep: Rebuilding the World's Coral Reefs* Chronicle Books.

Milner, C. (2019) *The Sea Book* DK Children.
Stewart-Sharpe, L. and Dove, E. (illus) (2020) *Blue Planet 11 BBC* Children's Books.
Trinick, L. and White, T. (illus) (2022) *Oceanarium: Welcome to the Museum* Big Picture Press.
Weiss, S. and De Amicis, G. (illus) (2019) *Ocean: Secrets of the Deep* What on Earth Books.
Zommer, Y. (2018) *The Big Book of the Blue* Thames and Hudson Ltd.

Picturebooks: plastic and the ocean

Brookes, D. and Simonovska, A. (illus) (2020) *Suki Seal and the Plastic Ring* Oakwood Publishing.
Byrd, J. and Meissner, A. (illus) (2023) *Marina: A Story About Plastic and the Planet* Paw Prints.
Carlisle, N. (2022) *Saving the Seas for the Purple and Green: A Story of Cleaning Up the Oceans* Sage Green Press.
Curtis, S. and Bean, I. (illus) (2020) *Turtle in a Tangle* Nielsen.
Gray, C. (2020) *We Used to Love Swimming- Children's Book About Turtles and Plastic Pollution* Independent Publishing Network.
Jackson, E. and Callwood, L. (illus) (2017) *Marli's Tangled Tale: A True Story About Environmental Problems Between Humans and Animals.* (Wild Tribe Heroes) London: Ellie Jackson.
Jackson, E. and Callwood, L. (illus) (2018) *Nelson's Dangerous Dive: A True Story About the Problems of Ghost Fishing Nets in Our Oceans* (Wild Tribe Heroes) London: Ellie Jackson.
Jackson, E. and Oldmeadow, L. (illus) (2017) *Duffy's Lucky Escape: A True Story about Plastic in Our Oceans* (Wild Tribe Heroes) London: Ellie Jackson.
Jones, N and Jones, J. (illus) (2022) *The Odd Fish: An Eco-Adventure Story About Plastic in the Ocean* Farshore.
Kearney, B. (2020) *Fish: A Tale About Ridding the Ocean of Plastic Pollution* DK Children.
Lane Ferrari, S. and Valliceli, G. (illus) (2019) *Saving Tally: An Adventure into the Great Pacific Plastic Patch* (Save The Planet Books) Serena Ferrari.
McCurdie, T. and Battistel, C. (illus) (2019) *Ocean's Plastic's Not Fantastic* Orangutan Books.
N.G.K., Fae, S. and Jannelle, D. (illus) (2019) *Harry Saves the Ocean! Teaching Children about Plastic Pollution and Recycling* NGK.
O'Connor, S. (2022) *The Whale Who Ate Plastic* Madra Rua Publishing.
Owen, R. (2018) *Plastic Pollution on Land and in the Oceans: Let's Investigate* (Fundamental Science Key Stage 1) Ruby Tuesday Books Ltd.
Owen, R. (2019) *The Problem with Plastic: Know Your Facts-Take Action-Save the Oceans* Ruby Tuesday Books Ltd.
Pego, A., Martins, I. and Carvalho, B.P. (illus) (2020) *Plasticus Maritimus: An Invasive Species* Greystone Books
Ravin Lodding, L, Pabari, D. and Machira Mwangi, M. (illus) (2023) *Flipflopi: How a Boat Made from Flip-Flops is Helping to Save the Ocean* Beaming Books
Wiesner, D. (2012) *Flotsam* Andersen Press.

More books about plastic and plastic pollution are listed in Chapter 15.

References

Avaria-Llautureo, J., Venditti, C., Rivadeneira, M.M., Inostroza-Michael, O., Rivera, R.J., Hernández, C.E. and Canales-Aguirre, C.B., 2021. Historical warming consistently decreased size, dispersal and speciation rate of fish. *Nature Climate Change*, 11(9), pp.787-793.
Dromgool-Regan, C., Burke, N. and Allard, B. (2017) *Explorers Planning Guide for Primary School Teachers: Ocean Literacy and Engagement* Galway, Marine Institute.
Gorick, Glynn, and the Flanders Marine Institute (VLIZ). (2016) Infographic produced in cooperation with the Oceans Past Initiative (OPI), for the EU-funded Sea Change project. Available at: https://www.marine.ie/Home/sites/default/files/MIFiles/Docs/EducationSupport/SDG%20500YEARS%20poster.pdf?language=en#Irish Times. (2019) *Who Owns Rockall? A History of Disputes Over a Tiny Atlantic Island*. Available at: https://www.irishtimes.com/news/politics/who-owns-rockall-a-history-of-disputes-over-a-tiny-atlantic-island-1.3919668

Kelly, Anna. (2017) "Eco-Anxiety at University: Student Experiences and Academic Perspectives on Cultivating Healthy Emotional Responses to the Climate Crisis" Independent Study Project (ISP) Collection. 2642. Available at: https://digitalcollections.sit.edu/isp_collection/2642)

Sverrir Steinsson. (2016) The cod wars: A re-analysis. *European Security,* 25:2, 256–275.

United Nations (UN). (2020) *Sustainable Development Goal.* Available at: https://www.un.org/sustainabledevelopment/sustainable-development-goals/

United Nations (UN). (2020) *Sustainable Development Goal.* Available at: https://www.un.org/sustainabledevelopment/sustainable-development-goals/UNESCO. (2017) *Education for Sustainable Development Goals-Learning Objectives.* https://unesdoc.unesco.org/ark:/48223/pf0000247444

18 Life on Land (SDG 15)

Miriam Hamilton

Introduction

Biodiversity is the living web of species and ecosystems that form the basis of life on Earth. While humanity itself is part of biodiversity, it is also a driver of biodiversity loss. There are five primary factors causing biodiversity loss: habitat loss, invasive alien species, overexploitation (extreme hunting and fishing pressure), pollution and climate change. As humans we are dependent on biodiversity for food, energy, medicine, economic security, and our overall well-being. Conversely, *Homo sapiens* are having a detrimental impact on many species and ecosystems. In reference to the famous fairytale, short term extractive thinking is literally killing the golden goose (ecosystems and habitats) which lays the golden eggs (biodiversity). Human activity (including growing population, consumption, poor management of natural resources and intensive farming) is responsible for a potential collapse of our biodiversity system. Ultimately, this threatens the survival of human civilisation and we are warned that we now have just a short window of time in which to act (Ceballos et al., 2017). SDG 15 seeks to protect, restore and promote the conservation and sustainable use of terrestrial ecosystems. This includes efforts to sustainably manage forests and halt deforestation, combat desertification, restore degraded land and soil, halt biodiversity loss and protect threatened species.

This chapter draws on SDG 15 learning objectives, proposing a whole class approach to raising respectful awareness, knowledge, skills and transformative beliefs among 10-16-year-olds using a **LIFE** (**L**isten, **I**nterpret, **F**ind out more and **E**volve) learning approach. This simple iterative cycle of learning connected to the word **'LIFE'** offers a framework for the teacher to facilitate the development of hope through knowledge and advocacy among the class, leading to an *evolution towards action*. It is proposed that you might consider the value of using a cooperative learning *'we sink or swim together'* approach (Johnson and Johnson, 1999), to navigate through the learning cycle with your class. This is an apt pedagogical approach given that the principles of cooperative learning are underpinned by the creation of interdependence among students. This concept of interdependence (as discussed in Chapter 1) connects deeply with the targets (Table 18.1) and learning objectives of SDG 15 (Table 18.2), where we acknowledge the importance of interdependence and mutual respect between all forms of life on Earth.

This chapter guides the reader through the four stages in this proposed iterative learning cycle, with suggestions for activities and advice on the whole class structuring of a range of cooperative learning approaches. It is important to consider emerging research, which

DOI: 10.4324/9781003232001-21

Table 18.1 List of targets for SDG 15: Life on land

15.1 Conserve and restore terrestrial and freshwater ecosystems
15.2 End deforestation and restore degraded forests
15.3 End desertification and restore degraded land
15.4 Ensure conservation of mountain ecosystems
15.5 Protect biodiversity and natural habitats
15.6 Promote access to genetic resources and fair sharing of the benefits
15.7 Eliminate poaching and trafficking of protected species
15.8 Prevent invasive alien species on land and in water ecosystems
15.9 Integrate ecosystem and biodiversity in governmental planning
15.A Increase financial resources to conserve and sustainably use ecosystem and biodiversity
15.B Finance and incentivize sustainable forest management
15.C Combat global poaching and trafficking

suggests that familiarity with collective success in the classroom, where the theoretical problems can be relatively simple to navigate, can foster the misconception that the achievement of collective action is usually easy (Spierre et al., 2013). Therefore, this chapter presents and explores an advocacy-based experiential game pedagogy with immense potential for teaching the sustainability goals ethically. Using a hybrid mix of active, cooperative and experiential learning opportunities, this chapter supports teachers with their facilitation of student learning and inspires whole class action, across SDG 15 targets and learning objectives. While this chapter focuses on SDG 15, the *LIFE* learning approach can be used for all SDGs. The four Hs model discussed at the outset of this book connects to the objectives and framing of the discussion on SDG 15, and exemplifies the concept of interdependence central to this chapter.

The Biodiversity Crisis: A Wake Up Call for Human Civilisation

As discussed in Chapter 1, life on land is facing an urgent crisis (Finn et al., 2023, WWF, 2022). The first Global Assessment of the Intergovernmental Science-Policy Platform on Biodiversity and Ecosystem Services (IPBES, 2019) found widespread, accelerating decline in Earth's biodiversity and associated benefits to people from nature. According to this report, at least a million species are at risk of extinction because of human actions. The abundance of native species in most major land habitats has fallen by a fifth since 1900. The decline in insect populations is another key example: where pollinators are not available, the cascading effects on ecosystems can quickly become catastrophic. Once these wild populations are eradicated or severely depleted, we have few ways to try to bring them backWe cannot replace the invaluable 'ecosystem services' of pollinating plants required for food production. What is now being termed a 'biological annihilation' is in our midst (Ceballos et al., 2017). Scientists have analysed both common and rare species and found alarming numbers of regional or local plants and animals have been lost to date. Much natural diversity has been lost in Ireland due to land use practices, invasive species, and so on. Take rhododendrons in Ireland for example. In Killarney National Park, rhododendrons are outcompeting many native species and are offering little habitat value to native fauna. Invasive alien species generally lack predators or competitors which would keep their population size in check. As a result, they can quickly become a dominant species, often with no benefit to the existing ecological community. Due to climate change, species continue to move away from warmer waters and lands. Such mass movements will cause different communities of species to encounter each other with unpredictable outcomes, with some winners and losers.

The United Nations Biodiversity Conference (COP15) ended in Montreal, Canada, on 19 December 2022 with a landmark agreement to guide global action on nature through to 2030. The plan includes concrete measures to halt and reverse nature loss, including putting 30% of the planet and 30% of degraded ecosystems under protection by 2030. Meanwhile the European Commission has published a long-awaited proposal for the EU Nature Restoration Law. Although passed by a narrow margin, this Law proposes to restore at least 20% of the EU's land and sea areas by 2030 and repair all ecosystems in need of restoration by 2050. These proposals are being resisted by powerful interest groups including farmers and businesses.

In January 2023, Ireland's *Citizens' Assembly on Biodiversity Loss* (2023) the first in the world, finalised its report and recommendations for the Irish government. This report calls for a referendum to constitutionally enshrine environmental human rights and the rights of nature. As part of the consultative process, Ireland held its first *Children and Young People's Assembly on Biodiversity Loss*. Designed with children and young people, the Assembly brought together 35 randomly selected Members aged 7–17 from across Ireland to explore, discuss and create calls to action on how to protect and restore biodiversity in Ireland (Figure 18.1). A youth assembly on biodiversity loss can be replicated in any education setting.

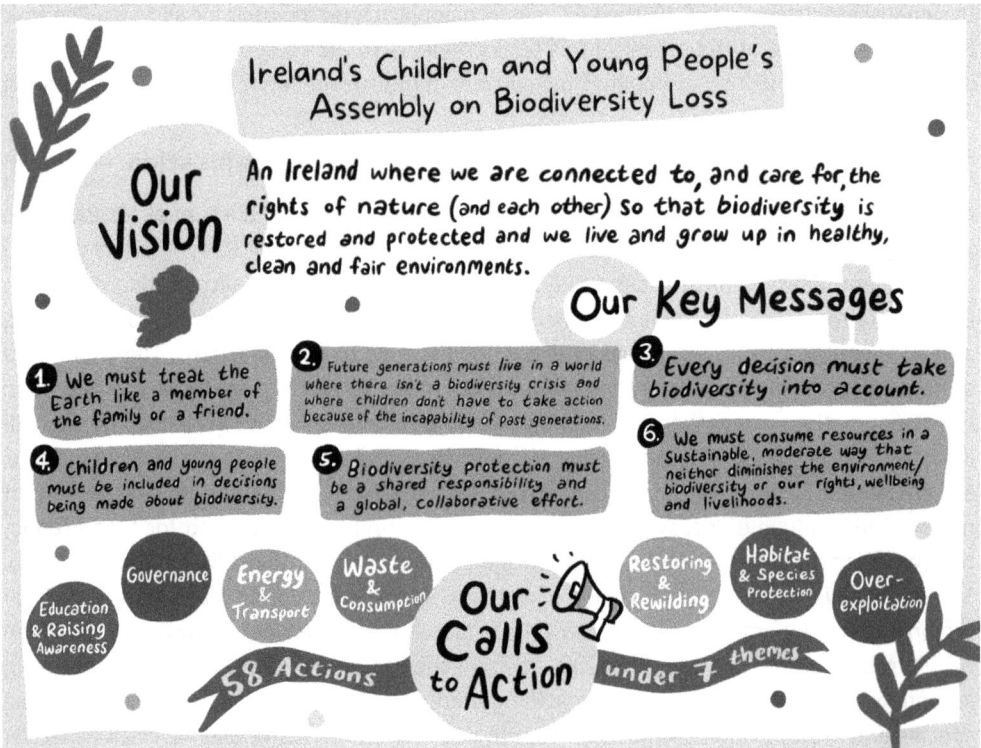

Figure 18.1 Key messages from Children and Young People's Assembly on Biodiversity Loss (2023) (Designed by graphic designer Hazel Hurley).

People depend on biodiversity in ways that are not always fully appreciated. Human health depends on ecosystem products, such as the availability of fresh water, food and fuel sources. Biodiversity loss can have significant and direct human health implications, while indirectly, changes in ecosystems affect livelihoods, incomes and local migration (W.H.O, 2020). However, hope is important and advocacy is promoted as an approach in this chapter to generate respect and empathy among our younger students so that together we can take action to reverse this trajectory.

In the 'Life on Land' Goal, we are asked to achieve 12 targets that *'Protect, restore and promote sustainable use of terrestrial ecosystems, sustainably manage forests, combat desertification, and halt and reverse land degradation and halt biodiversity loss'* (UN, 2020) (Table 18.1). UNESCO (2017) suggests cognitive, socio-emotional and behavioural objectives for each of the goals that are in keeping with the hope, advocacy and empathetic focus of this publication and the inherent aims of this chapter's focus on SDG 15. These objectives are mutually symbiotic as together they facilitate an interdependence between the development of knowledge of ecological processes, skills of argumentation that draw us to an emotional connection to life on land and the value of voice in advocating for a better way forward.

Why work cooperatively to achieve learning in Goal 15?

Groupwork is integral to facilitating enquiry approaches, as scientists from across a range of disciplines, work in teams and collaborate to solve scientific problems (Bass et al., 2009). Cooperative learning approaches have value as an alternative to didactic approaches. The approach can result in greater academic achievement, motivation and skill development due to increased interaction among adolescent students (Johnson and Johnson, 1999). Gillies and Nichols (2015) propose the use of cooperative learning strategies to facilitate a student led approach to problem solving, while Ahern-Rendell (1999) claims that cooperative learning strategies enhance critical thinking, which is conducive to learning about the sustainable development goals. Wolfenserberger and Canella (2015) cite effective groupwork as a key support to learning about the nature of scientific problems and incorporating cooperative learning principles enhances the development of personal and social skills (Altun, 2015). Similar to many educational jurisdictions, Ireland is currently embarking on significant reform of second level education with the implementation of new geography and science specifications. The overwhelming evidence in favour of student-led approaches in the upper primary/lower secondary level classroom is significant given the skills development focus in many specifications and curricula in Ireland and internationally. Despite the benefits of getting 10-16 years olds to work together, enquiry-based learning and cooperative groupwork are still very much on the periphery in many classrooms, where conventional methods still dominate (Meyer et al., 2013). This chapter provides a framework for teachers to begin to use, or expand their use of active and cooperative learning approaches, to facilitate effective student learning and action in Goal 15.

The life learning approach

This chapter proposes a whole class approach to achievement of meaningful learning in Goal 15 using a **LIFE** (**L**isten, **I**nterpret, **F**ind out more and **E**volve) learning approach. This simple and iterative cycle of learning offers a framework, to facilitate the development of respectful knowledge, skills and positive hopeful attitudes among the class, leading to an *evolution towards action*. The approach is designed to be flexible rather than prescriptive and teachers may choose to follow the approach or adapt it to their context and personal teaching style. The approach, as presented here, has been trialled and refined with a small group of students, with the generation of enhanced interest and knowledge of Goal 15. The time available to you will determine to some extent the pace at which you move through the learning cycle. Remember, this cycle can be used as an integrated approach within your teaching of discrete disciplines. For example, when teaching the characteristics of living things, or exploring ecology (in science or geography), some complementary work on SDG 15 could be introduced, as applied activities and learning. This would help the students make connections between the goals and their formal learning in other curricular subjects or disciplines. Once a learning unit is achieved, the cycle can be used to commence the next related learning unit. A suggested illustrative structure for addressing the targets within SDG15 is suggested using the LIFE learning approach in the following sections.

L. Listen and review the SDG mission

There are numerous resources available on the sustainable development goals (SDG) knowledge platform (UN, 2020) together with UNESCO (2017) learning objectives (Table 18.2). Here you will find general information on SDG 15 as well as the 12 important targets and objectives associated with this goal. Even if students have already completed some work on other goals, it may be a good idea to re-introduce the overall rationale and purpose of the goals. Activities discussed in chapter one may be useful to consider here. By facilitating an initial more general discussion, students will begin to think critically about our shared global plan to protect our planet and the respectful interdependence of all life. They will begin to appreciate the associated importance of ensuring safe environments to nurture and sustain life.

Focus on SDG 15

Numerous resources (including videos) for teaching about SDG 15 are detailed in the padlet to accompany this book. In order to embed comprehension and generate collaboration, it would be useful to discuss some of these resources with the class. The discussion can be supplemented with knowledge you have as the classroom teacher, and guided by the questions you feel will generate thinking and perhaps creative conflict. This is where constructive discussion among students opens up new perspectives and encourages student voice. Once a focus on SDG 15 has been established, the teacher is well positioned to audit how each of the stages, tasks and activities address the learning objectives associated with SDG 15. Indeed, with an older class it may be worthwhile conducting such an audit *with* the students following a learning phase, enhancing their ability to self-assess learning as it progresses. A digital or paper learning log with the objectives clearly outlined provides an opportunity for deep engagement with the objectives and heightens awareness of the importance of achieving learning across the cognitive, socio-emotional and behavioural domains.

I. Interpret the information inherent in SDG 15

Once some familiarity with SDG 15 is established, it may be worthwhile to examine the 12 discrete SDG15 targets (Appendix 1). There are a number of effective cooperative learning approaches, which facilitate the concurrent exploration of all 12 targets. Using active learning and an enquiry-based learning approach some of these approaches are suggested here. The use of a variety of tasks, activities and pedagogies enables the teacher to facilitate knowledge, skills, emotional responses and behavioural change among the students. This positions the learning objectives as key elements that underpin the targets supporting deep learning and promoting advocacy by careful use of a myriad of varied pedagogies and methodologies. This chapter provides examples of such pedagogies for use by the teacher as required. The 12 SDG 15 targets are included in Table 18.1 and Appendix 1 for reference, and the learning objectives for SDG 15 are listed in Table 18.2.

Table 18.2 Learning objectives of SDG 15 (Adapted from UNESCO, 2017: 40)

Cognitive learning objectives Teaching *about* the goals: developing respect and understanding	1	The learner understands basic ecology with reference to local and global ecosystems, identifying local species and understanding biodiversity.
	2	The learner understands the threats posed to biodiversity, including habitat loss, deforestation, fragmentation, overexploitation and invasive species, and can relate these threats to their local biodiversity.
	3	The learner is able to classify the ecosystem services of the local ecosystems including supporting, provisioning and regulating ecosystems.
	4	The learner understands the slow regeneration of soil and the multiple threats that are destroying and removing it much faster than it can replenish itself, such as poor farming or forestry practice.
	5	The learner understands that realistic conservation strategies work outside pure nature reserves to restore degraded habitats and soils, promote sustainable agriculture and forestry, and redress humanity's relationship to wildlife.
Socio-emotional learning objectives Teaching *for* the goals enhancing empathy and love	1	The learner is able to argue against destructive environmental practices that cause biodiversity loss.
	2	The learner is able to argue for the conservation of biodiversity on multiple grounds including ecosystems services and intrinsic value.
	3	The learner is able to connect with their local natural areas and feel empathy with nonhuman life on Earth.
	4	The learner is able to question the dualism of human/nature and realizes that we are a part of nature and not apart from nature.
	5	The learner is able to create a vision of a life in harmony with nature.
Behavioural learning objectives Teaching *through* the goals Promoting advocacy and activism	1	The learner is able to connect with local groups working toward biodiversity conservation in their area.
	2	The learner is able to use their voice effectively in decision-making processes to help urban and rural areas become more permeable to wildlife.
	3	The learner is able to work with policy-makers to improve legislation for biodiversity and nature conservation, and its implementation.
	4	The learner is able to highlight the importance of soil as our growing material for all food and the importance of remediating the erosion of our soils.
	5	The learner is able to campaign for international awareness of species exploitation.

Terminology and keywords

Prior to or during the activities, it may be worthwhile assessing the students' prior knowledge of the terminology of particular relevance to SDG 15. Table 18.3 highlights these terms and their meanings. These keywords may be useful to scaffold classroom discussion and support students in developing additional subject matter knowledge.

Table 18.3 SDG 15 terminology

Biodiversity- The variety and variability of life on Earth.

Biology- The study of life and living things.

Biome- The part of Earth where living things exist

Biome restricted species- Species that are largely or wholly confined to one biome.

Conservation- The wise use of our environment and resources.

Habitat- The place where an organism lives.

Endangered species- An endangered species is a species that is very likely to become extinct in the near future.

Deforestation- The permanent removal of trees to make room for something besides forest.

Desertification- The process by which fertile land becomes desert, typically as a result of drought, deforestation, or inappropriate agriculture.

Ecology- The study of living things in their environments.

Ecosystem- A biological community of interacting organisms and their physical environment.

Endangered- At risk of extinction.

Forest- An area covered chiefly with trees and undergrowth.

Freshwater- water found in ponds, lakes, rivers, streams, glaciers, icebergs, ice caps and sheets. It is a renewable and variable but finite natural resource.

Habitat destruction- The process by which a natural habitat becomes incapable of supporting its native species.

Habitat degradation- Processes of human origin that make habitats less suitable or less available for organisms to live in.

Habitat fragmentation- The process during which a large expanse of habitat is transformed into a number of smaller patches.

Landscape- All the visible features of an area of land,

Marine- Relating to or found in the sea.

Migration- The seasonal movement of animals from one region to another.

Migratory species- Species that move from one habitat to another during different times of the year, as they cannot live in the same environment all year.

Native species- A species that normally lives and thrives in a particular ecosystem.

Natural habitats- A natural habitat is an ecological or environmental area where a specific species lives.

Natural resources- Materials or substances occurring in nature which can be exploited for economic gain.

Ocean acidification- A reduction in the pH of the ocean over an extended period of time, caused primarily by uptake of carbon dioxide (CO_2) from the atmosphere.

Soil erosion- A gradual process of movement and transport of the upper layer of soil (topsoil) by different agents – particularly water, wind, and mass movement – causing its deterioration in the long term.

Cooperative approaches to learning about SDG 15

Remember to plan for (*in advance*) and audit (*following*), which SDG 15 learning objectives (Table 18.2) may be partially or fully achieved during each of the following suggested approaches. As a brief illustrative example, researching the meaning of and explaining key terminology such as, *deforestation* and *degradation*, may partially achieve cognitive learning objective 1, requiring that the student understands basic ecology with reference to local and global ecosystems. Read and explain pairs promote questioning (socio-emotional learning objective 4) and triads facilitate decision making (behavioural learning objective 2).

Jigsaw

This strategy is useful when the material to be discussed or learned can be divided into short segments, and where no one part must be taught before the other. Using the jigsaw approach, the class is divided into 'home groups' of 4 first and each student is numbered 1, 2, 3 or 4. The learning material is divided into 4 segments (e.g. Targets 15.1–15.4) and each student is given a different SDG 15 target (Table 18.1). Each student in the 'home' group reads their allocated SDG 15 target, before forming an 'expert group', with those from other home groups, with the same target as them. Each 'home group' splits, and all of the students with number 1 sit together (e.g. with Target 15.1), all students with number 2 sit together (e.g. with Target 15.2) etc. forming four 'expert groups'. The students in each 'expert group' come together and discuss the target agreeing on the main points of their material. They can prepare to teach their target before returning to their 'home group'. Suggested approaches for sharing their target information with their home group include using images, a graphic organiser, a summary or an oral presentation.

The teacher can provide advice and discuss potential expert group teaching options in advance of this jigsaw activity. Each student returns to their home group, and teaches the home group about the target that they studied. The teacher can set criteria to maximise learning. For example for target, *15.2-End Deforestation and Restore Degraded Forests* scaffolding for the expert group may include a request by the teacher to:

- Research the meaning of and explain key terminology such as, *deforestation* and *degradation*.
- Share three issues for living things associated with deforestation.
- Include at least two actions for addressing restoration of forest ecosystems.

This jigsaw technique is useful because it offers a structure to students engaging in self-directed active learning. It requires individual responsibility and stresses co-operation rather than competition. Differentiation is facilitated in the way the teacher can choose the level of scaffolding or the specific success criteria for the expert groups' learning. The teacher facilitates what knowledge and key learning may be generated, shared and presented to the home group. In order to discuss and learn about the 12 targets, home groups can be changed around after each selected group of targets are taught over a number of rotations of the jigsaw. This enables different students to work together developing both social skills and peer learning opportunities. There is no need to introduce all 12 of the targets at the same time nor at the same period of curricular learning. Follow on discussions through specific formal curricular areas such as science or geography can further consolidate the learning from this activity.

Read and explain pairs

This strategy is also useful for scaffolding learning of the targets in pairs. Students are arranged into pairs, as A and B. The 12 targets (or however many the teacher wants to explore in a given lesson), are placed in an envelope and given to the pair. Student A chooses a target and reads it silently first and then to their partner. For example Student A reads, *15.5 Protect Biodiversity and Natural Habitats requires us to: Take urgent and significant action to reduce the degradation of natural habitats, halt the loss of biodiversity and, by 2030, protect and prevent the extinction of threatened species.* Student A must then summarise the target to student B using a response stem such as...*What this is about for me is the importance of...* and the student elicits meaning and examples of what the target is related to. Student B is encouraged to ask clarifying questions or reiterate their understanding of the target and a discussion ensues as illustrated in Figure 18.2. When both students have a shared understanding of the basic content of the target they research anything that emerges in the discussion that would assist their further understanding of the target, and once the target is well explored they swop roles. Student B then reads and explains the next target with student A in the role of accuracy checker and questioner.

Questions can be scaffolded or suggested by the teacher if a pair require assistance or as groups become familiar with the approach. Alternatively, with a very capable class familiar with cooperative approaches, the students might select their own questions.

Suggested questions for Target 15.2 might include:

- What does *Biodiversity* mean?
- What is a *Natural Habitat*?
- How could *Biodiversity Loss* be halted?
- What is the difference between a *Threatened and Extinct Species*?
- Can we think of an example of a *Threatened Species*?

Short research activities could be completed, to find an example of a threatened species, or to read a more detailed description of a concept related to the target. Links to suggested reputable

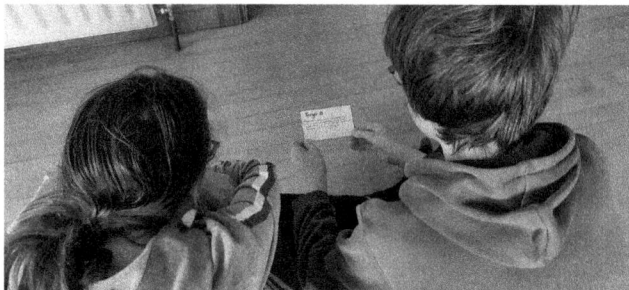

Figure 18.2 Students Engaging in Read and Explain Pairs.

pre-audited websites could be provided by the teacher during the lesson for this research phase. This paired approach is excellent for developing an enquiry stance among the students with the benefit of peer and teacher support. In order to maximise shared learning each pair could read and explain 2-3 targets and the whole class could listen to each pairs' feedback, understandings and suggestions. This could also assist the teacher as a form of assessment.

Triads

Introducing a third student to the group allows more scope for an additional supportive cooperative role and thus greater learning and perhaps the introduction of some practical experimental activities. If lesson time is available, each group of three receives a target and a related question/problem to be explored. For example, *15.3 End Desertification and Restore Degraded Land* lends itself very well to experimenting with soil types, drainage and mineral content of soil. The group can be provided with three soil types (clay, sandy, loam) in three beakers. Using the same volume of water, the students can plan and conduct a simple investigation to assess the ability of each type of the soil to allow water to drain, or be held between the particles.

Students in this triad can then discuss and later can extend the testing (by growing seedlings) thereby learning holistically about the implications for plant life trying to survive in each soil type. This can be investigated both in terms of anchorage/support to grow seedlings and discuss plant hydration. The presenter in each triad then shares the group's newly acquired knowledge based on their initial simple soil investigation and links this directly with their designated target. Time can then be given for each triad group to present their discrete investigation results and to make explicit the relationship of their results with their target, for the rest of the groups in rotation.

All three of these cooperative approaches have great scope in enabling the teacher to assume the role of facilitator of learning and to develop individual and group responsibility among the students. The approaches are interactive and promote questioning and discussion, which can be guided by the teacher, enabling achievement of many of the learning objectives associated with SDG 15. Pauses for the introduction of supplementary information or the dissemination of resources will break up the reporting style and facilitate applied learning opportunities during the learning, deepening the learning and achievement of the SDG objectives.

F. Find out more about SDG 15 targets

Simply introducing the main message of the targets within SDG 15 will not facilitate the critical thinking that will make a lasting impression on the students in the class. Use of the introductory strategies assists with framing the targets under SDG 15, but students should search out more information and maximise the depth of treatment on each of the targets they have begun to explore. For example, with Target *15.7 Eliminate Poaching and Trafficking of Protected Species* students could work in pairs to research additional information as a longer-term project idea. They must first understand what key concepts are embedded in the target such as, what *poaching* is, what the term *trafficking* refers to, identify the key issues for a named *protected species* and consider the potential individual and collective actions that could make a difference in achieving this target. This level of thought and planning will maximise achievement of the range of learning objectives associated with this goal.

A poster presentation, digital presentation, oral speech, role play, graphic organisation of the key points, video appeal or written report, are all pedagogies students could use to complete a small research piece on their target for dissemination to the rest of the class. Success criteria can be based on the achievement of one or more of the SDG 15 learning objectives. Target presentations can be incorporated into relevant curricular teaching to avoid presentation fatigue, (which may occur if all 12 were conducted on the same day). Students could choose their own presentation style or the teacher can negotiate a group's presentation mode from a range of options, to structure a variety of presentation types and expand knowledge and skill development among the class groups. This structuring of learning where the students act as researchers offers huge value in terms of student autonomy to manage data and information, assess and validate sources of information and to develop confidence in presenting information and communicating ideas, all key skills for life. It also differentiates the class in terms of the achievement of varied SDG 15 leaning objectives. The ability and age of the class will determine the level of scaffolding and self-directed learning appropriate and feasible to maximise learning.

E. Evolve into SDG 15 active citizens

It would be a shame if the students did not get the opportunity to decide on individual and group actions that may address some of the targets within SDG 15 that they have explored so far using the LIFE learning cycle. Spierre et al. (2013:1323), suggest an experiential approach called 'experiential game theoretic pedagogy' as an innovative pedagogy for sustainability ethics that; 'moves the learning experience from passive to active, apathetic to emotionally invested, narratively closed to experimentally open, and from predictable to surprising'. This pedagogy is structured as a series of games where players must make decisions that may adversely affect their classmates, in order to identify a gap between their moral aspirations and moral actions. This is an ideal approach to develop hope and advocacy.

While the *read, write, investigate and discuss* approaches used in the learning cycle in this chapter thus far facilitate knowledge development of SDG 15, it is important to move students into a more challenging phase of learning. Making a shift to experiential approaches at this stage is valuable, so that students can be situated in realistic scenarios that require moral reflection and judgements to be made, using evidence and experimentation (Spierre et al., 2013). There are many examples of such experiential games available online and the 'The Pisces Game' (*see link to game pedagogy below*) which explores consumption and limited resources is modified here for the upper primary/lower secondary age-group. This game is ordinarily used with older students but has value when simplified for younger classes. This modified version of the *'Pisces Game'* acts as a conceptual exemplar to illustrate the approach providing an insight into the value of game based pedagogies. Games are useful for exploring some of the more abstract targets of SDG 15, especially those targets requiring an understanding of the role of individual choice in the sustainability of life and limited resources. There are several references to games throughout this book with chapter 16 (SDG13) discussing games as a means of communicating the complexity of climate change. Games researched, designed or conceptualised by the students with discussion positioned as a central pedagogy throughout, could be particularly suitable to elicit knowledge and understanding of the SDG targets, with the achievement of inherent learning objectives related to each target. These targets may otherwise be taught in a very theoretical and content heavy way, leading to less meaningful engagement among the students.

The following modified method is suggested for teachers choosing to structure the Pisces Game with 10-16 year olds. It still has useful connections to targets 15.9, 15A, 15B and 15C. To extend learning and understanding of sustainability ethics, teachers could experiment with modifying aspects of the game further for their class to vary the sustainability focus. For example, introduce a rule allowing one team to steal (poach) from another (15-C) or facilitate the acquisition of a reward (grant) system for good conservation choices (15-B). The following method is suggested but not prescriptive:

1   Students are divided by their individual zodiac sign. This determines the teams or groups.
2   Each zodiac group represents a different village of fishermen, but all the villages are fishing for survival from a shared common lake.
3   The lake is represented by a large table or set of tables positioned in the centre of the classroom with the lake enclosed by a hulahoop as illustrated in Figure 18.3.
4   Each village has a small single fishing boat (scoop or ladle) and on each turn, boats harvest fish (scattering of varied coloured beads, bottle tops or smartie sweets/skittles) from the common lake
5   Teams take their turn to access the lake to fish according to an alphabetical order of their team zodiac sign and record their catch as a numerical score.
6   Each village needs to try to harvest enough fish to survive (four fish per person or as decided by the teacher) each round. Extra fish, if caught, may be used to build a private village fishpond (smaller hoop or ringed area), where villages can stock this pond with fish, or villages can share their fish with other groups.
7   Teams may also opt to eat as many fish as they can and this helps them gain points towards their score for the game. This deliberately creates incentives for selfish decision-making.
8   Teams may be facilitated by the teacher to develop strategies or rules through consensus to manage the common lake or decide on communal actions that may help other teams survive. This can be structured before, during and discussed after the game.
9   The zodiac teams at the end of the fishing order (e.g., the Pisces team) are significantly disadvantaged due to a lack of available common resources.
10 Initially, the game can be played competitively where the winning team is the one who has caught and/or eaten the most fish. In subsequent games, the goal can be the survival of the greatest number of villages and/or having some fish left to reproduce.
11 Following discussion, teams realise if they are catching last, they cannot catch enough to survive and the value of sharing excesses and managing limited resources emerges. In addition, if the lake is left with no fish, through excess fishing/eating then everyone is at threat.

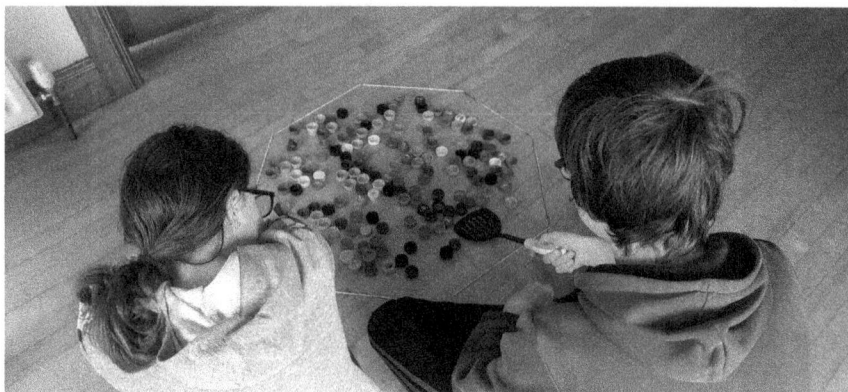

Figure 18.3 The Pisces Game in Action.

This game pedagogy has great potential to foster discussion and reflection on ethical, moral fair and respectful decision-making for the protection of life on our planet, where resources are limited and need time to replenish and recover. Research on the value of games (Spierre et al., 2013) indicated players experienced conflict, emotional investment, peer pressure, altruism and selfishness, but most importantly, these actions and experiences are explored during and after the experience. This helps students make sense of the decisions they make and helps them to realise that their actions may have short-term positive benefits for their team, but negative repercussions for others. The scope for achievement of a range of cognitive, socio-emotional and behavioural learning objectives associated with SDG 15 is significant in the effective use of this approach. Detailed descriptions of these sorts of experiential games are available online at the links provided below. *'Games4sustainability'* is a particularly useful resource as the games are aligned with the sustainable development goals and the search for a suitable game can be filtered by a specific goal. Other games use mobile app technology, which is especially appropriate for this age group of students. As with all resources, it is important that the teacher pilots the resource or trials it prior to introducing it in the classroom. Games are also discussed in chapter 7 (SDG 4) and chapter 16 (SDG 13).

Linking with other goals

It is important that the SDGs are taught with due regard to the interconnectedness of these goals. It is clear that SDGs 6, 12, 13, and 14 have particular links to SDG 15, (life on land) due to the interdependence of living things on environments and habitats that are clean and that support food chains and energy flow. This is clearly illustrated in Figure 18.4. Many connections between the SDGs can be identified and highlighted by teachers in science, geography and social or environmental education. Generating connections signifies the goals interdisciplinary relevance and value within and beyond formal subject or curricular knowledge. In addition, teaching a number of interconnecting SDGs together or exploring targets that overlap may suit an older class, who can still discern between the discrete goals. In the same way that linkage across the SDGs promotes a deeper appreciation of the challenge of sustainability, the achievement of learning objectives across the goals can be achieved through greater integration and reference to goals which have clear connections with others. Project or class work that recognises the interconnectedness of the SDGs is valuable and can be attempted concurrently or consecutively once a discrete goal is first introduced. Potentially, there can be a conflict of interest between industry, innovation and infrastructure (SDG 9) and life on land (SDG 15). When these conflicts arise use them as teaching opportunities in your classroom. The following scenario is an example of one such conflict.

In January 2024, according to Irish media, an Irish businessman has a unique proposal to solve the housing crisis in Dublin. He wants to see the conversion of some of the capital's green space into property.

He is proposing that 450 acres (10%) of Dublin's parklands would be used to build housing. The houses would then be offered to frontline workers - such as guards, nurses and firefighters. Dublin's biodiverse parks such as Marlay Park and the Phoenix Park would be involved in the conversion.

On the one hand such a proposal would greatly alleviate the housing crisis. On the other hand, the cost in terms of biodiversity would be enormous.

This scenario provides great potential for debate, research, cost analysis and role play. Perspectives from nurses, teachers, renters, park rangers and biodiversity experts could be explored. The class could be invited to make a final decision for this proposal giving reasons for their answer.

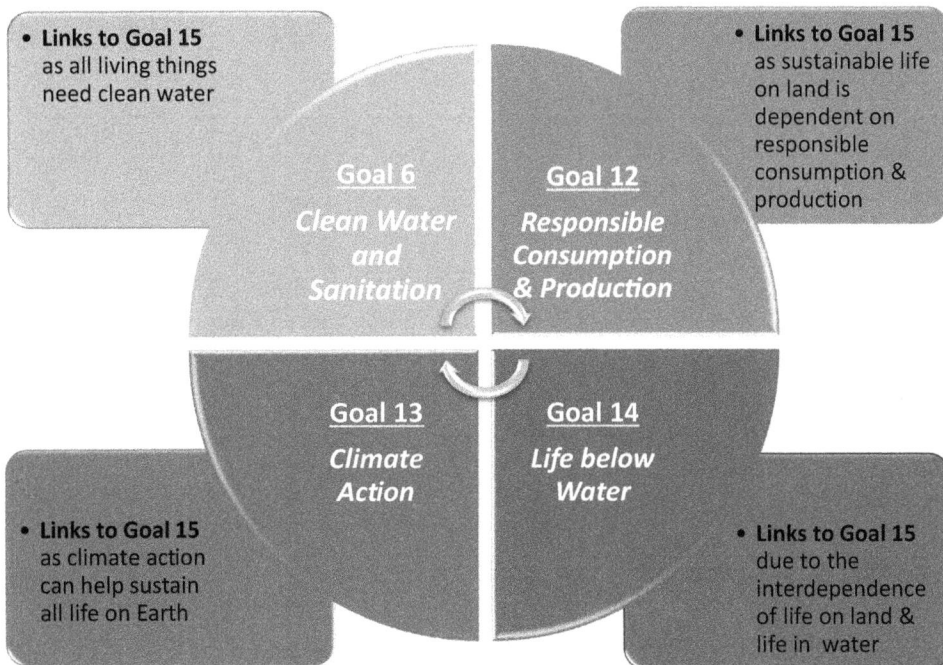

- **Links to Goal 15** as all living things need clean water

- **Links to Goal 15** as sustainable life on land is dependent on responsible consumption & production

Goal 6
Clean Water and Sanitation

Goal 12
Responsible Consumption & Production

Goal 13
Climate Action

Goal 14
Life below Water

- **Links to Goal 15** as climate action can help sustain all life on Earth

- **Links to Goal 15** due to the interdependence of life on land & life in water

Figure 18.4 Links between Goal 15 and other SDGs.

Conclusion

SDG 15 has huge scope for exploration between the upper primary and lower secondary age range. The connection we have as humans with other living things, where we share the same environments becomes less abstract for older students. The LIFE cycle in conjunction with cooperative and experiential game pedagogies, offers a range of pathways for the teacher to explore SDG 15 and achieve the learning objectives inherent in this goal with their students. Approaches shared in other chapters may also be useful for SDG 15, and it is important that the teacher formulates their own hybrid pedagogy; an overall approach they feel will work best with their classes. More importantly still, is that while we all engage and think about these SDGs, in doing so we are developing awareness and promoting positive action towards the kind of change necessary for a healthy and sustainable future.

Key dates

Feb 2: World Wetlands Day
Feb 27: International Polar Bear Day
Mar 3: World Wildlife Day
Mar 21: International Day of Forests
March 20: World Frog Day
March 20: World Sparrow Day
April 17: Bat Appreciation Day
April 22: Earth Day
Second Saturday of May: World Migratory Day
Third Friday of May: Endangered Species Day
May 8th: World Donkey Day
May 20: World Bee Day
May 22: World Biodiversity Day
June 5: World Environment Day
June 21: World Giraffe Day
June 22: World Camel Day
June 22: World Rainforest Day
July 28: World Nature Conservation Day
August 10: World Lion Day
August 12: World Elephant Day
August 19: World Orangutan Day
September 5: Amazon Rainforest Day
September 22: World Rhino Day
First Monday of October: World Habitat Day
Last Friday of October: World Lemur Day
Oct 4: World Animal Day
Fourth Wednesday of October: Sustainability Day
November 29: World Jaguar Day
December 4: World Cheetah Day
Dec 5: World Soil Day

December 14: Monkey Day
December 21: World Robin Day

Children's literature

There are countless examples of children's literature dealing with various aspects of bio-diversity including the superb work of Nicola Davies as listed below. Nicola Davies started her career as a Zoologist before working for the BBC Natural History Unit for ten years as a researcher and presenter for a number of natural history programmes including The Really Wild Show. For any teacher nervous about teaching biodiversity just select one of Nicola Davies' book and begin with a story.

Picturebooks

Davies, N. (2020) *Lost* Tiny Owl Publishing Ltd.
Davies, N. and Braun,S. (illus) (2018) *Brave and the Fox* Scholastic.
Davies, N. and Byrne, M. (illus) (2019) *Butterflies for Grandpa Joe* Barrington Stoke.
Davies, N. and Carlin, L. (illus) (2013)*The Promise* Walker Books.
Davies, N. and Carlin, L. (illus) (2018) *King of the Sky* Walker Books.
Davies, N. and Desmond, J. (illus) (2020) *My Butterfly Bouquet* Wren & Rook.
Davies, N. and Desmond, J. (illus) (2022) *One World: 24 Hours on Planet Earth* Walker Books.
Davies, N. and Fisher, C. (illus) (2017) *The Pond* Graffeg Limited.
Davies, N. and Foreman, M (illus) (2015) *White Owl, Barn Owl* Walker Books.
Davies, N. and Lozano, L. (illus) *I (Don't) Like Snakes* Walker Books.
Davies, N. and Ray, J.(illus) (2020) *Hummingbird* Wren & Rook.
Davies, N. and Rayner, C. (illus) (2023) *Protecting the Planet: Emperor of the Ice* Walker Books.
Davies, N. and Rubbino, S. (illus) (2017) *Just Ducks* Walker Books.
Davies, N. and Rubbino, S. (illus) (2021) *I (Don't) Ride the Wind* Walker Books.
Davies, N. and Sutton, E. (illus) (2022) *Protecting the Planet: The Season of Giraffes* Walker Books.

Picturebooks (9-12 years)

Davies, N. and Holland, B.(illus) (2020) *The Eel Question* Graffeg Limited.
Davies, N. and Izlesou, A. (illus) (2016) *The White Hare* Graffeg Limited.
Davies, N. and Jenkins, C. (illus) (2020) *The Selkie's Mate* Graffeg Limited.
Davies, N. and Low, M. (illus) (2018) *Bee Boy and the Moon Flowers* Graffeg Limited.
Davies, N. and Shum, F. (illus) (2017) *Elias Martin* Graffeg Limited.
Davies, N. and Uhren, A. (illus) (2016) *Mother Carey's Butter Knife* Graffeg Limited.

Chapter books

Davies, N (2016) *Walking the Bear* Walker Books.
Davies, N. (2019) *Ariki and the Island* of Wonders Walker Books.
Davies, N. (2021) *The Song that Sings Us* Firefly Press Ltd.
Davies, N. and Stower, A. (illus) (2017) *Animals Behaving Badly* Walker Books.
Davies, N. and Wright, A. (illus) (2013) *The Elephant Road* Walker Books.

Informational texts

Davies, N. (2014) *The Lion who Stole My Arm* Candlewick Press.
Davies, N. and Blythe, G. (illus) (2015) *Ice Bear* Walker Books.
Davies, N. and Boutavant, M. (illus) (2012) *Who's Like Me* Walker Books.

Davies, N. and Cameron, A. (illus) (2016a) *The Word Bird* Graffeg Limited.
Davies, N. and Cameron, A. (illus) (2016b) *Into the Blue (Animal Surprises)* Graffeg Limited.
Davies, N. and Cameron, A. (illus) (2017) *Animal Surprises: How to Draw* Graffeg Limited.
Davies, N. and Cameron, A. (illus) (2016) *The Secret of the Egg* Graffeg Limited.
Davies, N. and Cameron, A. (illus) (2018) *The Word Bird: How to Draw* Graffeg Limited.
Davies, N. and Cameron, A. (illus) (2022a) *Invertebrates Are Cool* Graffeg Limited.
Davies, N. and Cameron, A. (illus) (2022b) *Animal Surprises* Graffeg Limited.
Davies, N. and Cameron, A. (illus) (2023) *The Versatile Reptile* Graffeg Limited.
Davies, N., Carter, J., Conlon, D. and Catchpole, D. (illus) (2023) *Out There in the Wild: Poems on Nature* Macmillan Children's Books.
Davies, N. and Chapman, J. (2015) (illus) (2015) *One Tiny Turtle* Walker Book.
Davies, N. and Croft, J.(illus) (2015) *Surprising Sharks* Walker Books.
Davies, N. and Fisher, C. (illus) (2018) *Flying Free* Graffeg Limited; novel.
Davies, N. and Fisher, C. (illus) (2021) *The Mountain Lamb* Graffeg Limited;novel.
Davies, N. and Fox-Davies, S (illus) (2015) *Bat Loves the Night* Walker Books.
Davies, N. and Granström, B. (illus) (2017) *Dolphin Baby* Walker Books.
Davies, N. and Hearld, M. (illus) (2012) *A First Book of Nature* Walker Books.
Davies, N. and Hearld, M. (illus) (2019a) *Nature Poems, Give Me Instead of a Card* Walker Books.
Davies, N. and Hearld, M. (illus) (2019b) *Animal Poems, Give Me Instead of a Card* Walker Books.
Davies, N. and Horacek, P. (illus) (2019) *A First Book of Animals Walker* Books.
Davies, N. and Horáček, P (illus) (2023) *The Star Whale Otter* Barry Books Limited.
Davies, N. and Layton, N. (illus) (2007a) *Extreme Animals: The Toughest Creatures on Earth* Walker Books.
Davies, N. and Layton, N. (illus) (2007b) *What's Eating? Parasites—The Inside Story You* Walker Books.
Davies, N. and Layton, N. (illus) (2014a) *Survivors: The Toughest Creatures on Earth* Books Walker Books.
Davies, N. and Layton, N. (illus) (2014b) *Poo: A Natural History of the Unmentionable* Candlewick Press.
Davies, N. and Layton, N. (illus) (2014c) *Deadly: The Truth About the Most Dangerous Creatures on Earth* Walker Books.
Davies, N. and Layton, N. (illus) (2014d) *Talk Talk Squawk! How and Why Animals Communicate* Books Walker Books.
Davies, N. and Maland, N. (illus) (2015) *Big Blue Whale* Walker Books.
Davies, N. and Scobie, L. (illus) (2017) *The Variety of Life* Hodder Children's Books.
Davies, N. and Scobie, L. (illus) (2019) *The Wonder of Trees* Hodder Children's Books.
Davies, N. and Scobie, L. (illus) (2022) *The Magic of Flight* Hodder Children's Books.
Davies, N. and Sutton, E.(illus) (2018) *Lots* Walker Books.
Davies, N. and Sutton, E.(illus) (2021a) *Grow: Secrets of our DNA* Walker Books.
Davies, N. and Sutton, E.(illus) (2021b) *Tiny: The Invisible World of Microbes* Walker Books.
Davies, N. and Sutton, E. (illus) (2024) *Green: The Story of Plant Life on Our Planet* Walker Books.
Davies, N. and Wright, A. (illus) (2015) *The Leopard's Tale* Walker Books.

Sources of further information

A variety of facts, figures, infographics and other resources that would be useful in supporting learning about life on earth are available on the following web pages:

- Children and Young People's Assembly on Biodiversity Loss: https://cyp-biodiversity.ie/
- General Goal Videos-https://www.un.org/sustainabledevelopment/sustainable-development-goals/
- Goal 15 Videos-https://www.un.org/sustainabledevelopment/blog/category/life-on-land/
- UNESCO-Education for Sustainable Development Goals–Learning Objectives-https://www.

unesco.de/sites/default/files/2018-08/unesco_education_for_sustainable_development_
goals.pdf.

- Game ideas for Sustainability Ethics-http://resources4rethinking.ca/en/resource/serious-
game
- Games specifically addressing the Sustainable Development Goals- https://games
4sustainability.org/gamepedia/
- The Pisces Game- https://pdfs.semanticscholar.org/c1b2/4dd34232187ece6648d73a68
052c2c659bb2.pdf
- Extinction: The Facts (presented by Sir David Attenborough https://www.dailymotion.
com/video/x7w7wxr

References

Ahern-Rindell, A. (1999) Applying inquiry-based and cooperative group learning strategies to promote critical thinking. *Journal of College Science Teaching, 28*(3), 203-207.

Altun, S. (2015) The effect of cooperative learning on students' achievement and views on the science and technology course. *International Electronic Journal of Elementary Education, 7*(3), 451-467.

Bass, J., Contant, T. and Carin, A. (2009) *Teaching Science as Inquiry.* New York: Pearson.

Ceballos, G., Ehrlich, P. and Rodolfo, D. (2017) Biological annihilation via the ongoing sixth mass extinction signaled by vertebrate population losses and declines. *Proceedings of the National Academy of Sciences, 114*(30), 6089-6096.

Children and Young People's Assembly on Biodiversity Loss. (2023) *Children and Young People's Assembly on Biodiversity Loss.* Final Report. Available at: https://cyp-biodiversity.ie/

Citizens's Assembly on Biodiversity Loss. (2023) *Report of the Citizens's Assembly on Biodiversity Loss.* Available at: https://citizensassembly.ie/wp-content/uploads/Report-on-Biodiversity-Loss_mid-res.pdf

Finn, C., Grattarola, F. and Pincheira-Donoso, D. (2023) More losers than winners: Investigating anthropocene defaunation through the diversity of population trends. *Biological Reviews 98*(5), 1732-1748.

Gillies, R. and Nichols, K. (2015) How to support primary teachers' implementation of inquiry: Teachers' reflections on teaching cooperative inquiry-based science. *Research in Science Education, 45*(2), 171-191.

IPBES (2019): Global assessment report on biodiversity and ecosystem services of the Intergovernmental Science-Policy Platform on Biodiversity and Ecosystem Services. E. S. Brondizio, J. Settele, S. Díaz, and H. T. Ngo (editors). IPBES secretariat, Bonn, Germany. 1148 pages. https://doi.org/10.5281/zenodo.3831673

Johnson, D.W. and Johnson, R. (1999) *Learning Together and Alone: Cooperative, Competitive and Individualistic Learning.* 5th ed. Englewood Cliffs, NJ: Prentice-Hall.

Meyer, D.Z., Meyer, A.A., Nabb, K.A., Connell, M.G. and Avery, L.M. (2013) Theoretical and empirical exploration of intrinsic problems in designing inquiry activities. *Research in Science Education, 43*(3), 57-76.

Spierre, S., Sadowski, J., Berardy, A., McClintock, S., Augustin, S., Hohman, S. and Banna, Jay. (2013) An experiential, game-theoretic pedagogy for sustainability ethics. *Science and Engineering Ethics, 19*(3), 1323-1339.

UNESCO. (2017) *Education for Sustainable Development Goals - Learning Objectives.* Available at: https://www.unesco.de/sites/default/files/2018-08/unesco_education_for_sustainable_development_goals.pdf. (Accessed: 20 January 2021).

United Nations (UN). (2020) *Sustainable Development Goal.* Available at: https://www.un.org/sustainabledevelopment/sustainable-development-goals/ (Accessed: 20 May 2020).

Wolfenserberger, B. and Canella, C. (2015) Cooperative Learning about nature of science with a case from the history of science. *International Journal of Environmental & Science Education, 10*(6), 865-889.

World Health Organisation. (2020) Available at: https://www.who.int/globalchange/ecosystems/biodiversity/ (Accessed: 30 June 2020).

World, Wide Fund (WWF). (2022) *Living Planet Report.* Available at: https://livingplanet.panda.org/en-GB/

19 Peace, justice and strong institutions

Envisioning alternative pathways (SDG 16)

Fiona Dineen and Anne M. Dolan

Introduction

Issues of peace and justice permeate all aspects of society at a local, national and global level. The number of displaced people, fleeing war, persecution, conflict and human rights violations remains at a critically high level (United Nations, 2021). Exploring issues of justice and peace can be challenging and complex. Understanding and interpreting the root causes of conflict can uncover many contentious areas. Yet, it is important to create an awareness of basic human rights and freedoms for all people along with associated violation. While knowledge and understanding are key initial steps, it is also important to consider appropriate responses in these complex situations. Education plays a crucial role in developing solutions at a local, national and global level.

Promoting a culture of positive peace requires an appreciation of the interdependent relationship between peace and justice. For there to be peace, we need to work for justice and human rights. There are many perspectives that inform an understanding of justice, taking cognisance of relationships; retribution; fair-play; the promotion of equality and the upholding of human rights. World religions emphasise the importance of values and ethical standards in society in both relationships with others and our relationship with the natural world. Justice involves: recognising and respecting the inherent dignity in each person; taking social responsibility for building the common good; and showing solidarity and compassion to the most vulnerable and marginalised in society. Systems for legislation and governance at a local, national and international level have been developed to organise social relations in a way that recognises and respects human rights. As discussed in Chapter 3, the Universal Declaration of Human Rights (UDHR) is an internationally agreed list of basic rights and freedoms that are entitled to all people The UDHR was adopted by the United Nations in 1948. Through teaching about peace, it is important to remember that no child was ever born to hate. Therefore, we need to understand the deeply embedded root causes of conflict, prejudice, war and oppression. Aggressive behaviour is often linked to experiences of unfairness, racism, historical injustice, abuse of human rights and a basic lack of respect.

This chapter explores the building of peaceful, just and inclusive societies and the responsibilities of individuals, communities, institutions, and governments in challenging the structures that foster conflict, violence, oppression, poverty and all types of discrimination.

DOI: 10.4324/9781003232001-22

Examining economic, political, cultural and social structures assists in understanding how resources, power, values and relationships impact on human rights and the creation of just societies. It highlights the power that strong institutions and good governance have in challenging mindsets and leading to positive change.

Why is SDG 16 important?

The aim of SDG 16 is to promote peaceful and inclusive societies for sustainable development based on respect for human rights, protection of the most vulnerable and provision of access to justice for all. It envisions the building of effective, accountable and inclusive institutions, demonstrating good governance at all levels. This broadly entails the promotion of non-discriminatory laws and policies; combating corruption, bribery and organised crime; and the prevention of violence and terrorism. While this is the aim, progress reports for SDG16 continue to demonstrate that millions of people globally live in fragile and conflict-afflicted States (UN STATS, 2021). Billions of dollars have been spent supporting war in conflict affected areas, money which could have been more fruitfully used for the promotion of peace.

A New Agenda for Peace (UN, 2023) launched on July 20, 2023 represents the UN Secretary-General António Guterres' ideas for member states to prevent conflict and advance peace. The document sets out both a comprehensive diagnosis of the challenges we face and an extensive set of recommendations to address them, including a call for a recommitment to peace as follows:

> 'Nonetheless, peace remains an elusive promise for many around the world. Conflicts continue to wreak destruction, while their causes have become more complex and difficult to resolve. This may make the pursuit of peace appear a hopeless undertaking. However, in reality, it is the political decisions and actions of human beings that can either sustain or crush hopes for peace. War is always a choice: to resort to arms instead of dialogue, coercion instead of negotiation, imposition instead of persuasion. Therein lies our greatest prospect, for if war is a choice, peace can be too' (UN, 2023:3)

Education is crucial to achieving SDG 16. It ensures that citizens are aware of their fundamental rights and understand how they are represented and impacted by local and national governance systems. The importance of education is highlighted by the activist and Nobel Peace Laureate Malala Yousafzai (featured in chapter 8). In her address to the United Nations Youth Assembly, she called on everyone

> To wage a global struggle against illiteracy, poverty and terrorism and let us pick up our books and pens. They are our most powerful weapons. One child, one teacher, one pen and one book can change the world. Education is the only solution. Education first.
>
> (Yousafzai, 2013: np)

This chapter addresses learning objectives set out in Table 19.1. A list of targets for SDG 16 is available in Appendix 1. From the early years, it is important for students to foster an understanding and mutual respect towards diversity and difference. Students develop an appreciation of and can engage with the different sources of wisdom on issues of justice and peace. It

Table 19.1 Learning objectives for SDG 1 (Source UNESCO, 2017: 42)

Cognitive learning objectives Teaching **about** the goals: developing respect and understanding	1	The learner understands concepts of justice, inclusion and peace and their relationship to law.
	2	The learner understands their local and national legislative and governance systems and that they can be abused through corruption.
	3	The learner understands the importance of individuals and groups in upholding justice, inclusion and peace and supporting strong institutions in their country and globally.
	4	The learner understands the importance of the international human rights framework.
Socio-emotional learning objectives Teaching **for** the goals enhancing empathy and love	1	The learner is able to connect with others who can help them in facilitating peace, justice, inclusion and strong institutions in their country.
	2	The learner is able to debate local and global issues of peace, justice, inclusion and strong institutions.
	3	The learner is able to show empathy with and solidarity for those suffering from injustice in their own country as well as in other countries.
	4	The learner is able to reflect on their role in issues of peace, justice, inclusion and strong institutions.
Behavioural learning objectives Teaching **through** the goals Promoting advocacy and activism	1	The learner is able to critically assess issues of peace, justice, inclusion and strong institutions in their region, nationally and globally.
	2	The learner is able to publicly demand and support the development of policies promoting peace, justice, inclusion and strong institutions.
	3	The learner is able to become an agent of change in local decision-making, speaking up against injustice.
	4	The learner is able to contribute to conflict resolution at the local and national level.

is also important that they are encouraged to reflect on and debate their social responsibility in the world today. It is hoped that students will develop an aptitude for dialogue and participate positively and responsibly in a diverse global society.

Exploring the concept of peace

Peace has been a long cherished dream of humanity throughout the ages. Peaceful societies are fundamental to sustainable development. The word 'peace' is laden with meaning across the spectrum of human experience. Peace is multi-layered – beginning with the 'inner peace' of an individual and spanning levels of social, global and universal peace. Indeed, peace is the essence of all religions, the reason Being that the objectives of religion cannot be achieved without peace. In the bible, peace is translated from the Hebrew word *Shalom* – a greeting for well-being, health and prosperity. The Arabic greeting adopted by Muslims, *As-salamm 'alykum* means 'peace be upon you'.

Peace can be conceptualised in two ways: negative peace and positive peace. Negative peace is the absence of war and direct violence. Positive peace refers to the conditions or presence of just and non-exploitative relationships, as well as human and ecological well-being, in order to diminish the root causes of conflict and injustice (Navarro Castro & Nairo-Galace, 2019: 19). Peacebuilding organisations strive to promote a culture of 'positive peace'. Creating a culture of peace requires an understanding of the factors that contribute to peace and recognising the roots of conflict. A careful critical analysis of war, conflict and political violence is required in deciding a basis for action and resolving key issues.

According to International Alert (2022) positive peace is when:

- Everyone lives in safety, without fear or threat of violence, and no form of violence is tolerated in law or in practice;
- Everyone is equal before the law, the systems for justice are trusted, and fair and effective laws protect people's rights;
- Everyone is able to participate in shaping political decisions and the government is accountable to the people.
- Everyone has fair and equal access to the basic needs for their wellbeing – such as food, clean water, shelter, education, healthcare and a decent living environment;
- Everyone has an equal opportunity to work and make a living, regardless of gender, ethnicity or any other aspect of identity.

  Table 19.2 includes a list of some key terms that may be helpful to explore with the students prior to engaging in the activities for SDG 16. A discussion around each of these terms will elicit the students' prior knowledge and understanding in relation to conflict, peace and justice. This list is not exhaustive, rather a signpost of some of the concepts that will be discussed and elaborated on in the activities that follow later in the chapter.

Table 19.2 Key terms for SDG 16: peace, justice and strong institutions

Basic needs: Water, sanitation and food.

Climate justice: Refers to the efforts that are being made to improve the situation of those most badly affected by climate change. Often the people worst affected by climate change are the poorest people on the planet.

Conflict: A struggle or clash between opposing forces; a state of opposition between ideas, interests, etc.; disagreement or controversy.

Emergency response: A range of emergency supports to crisis-affected communities.

Global perspective: A global perspective is when someone can think about a situation as it relates to the rest of the world.

Healthcare: Basic healthcare, maternal healthcare, nutrition and hygiene.

Human rights: Internationally agreed list of basic rights and freedoms that all human beings are entitled to. The Universal Declaration of Human Rights was drawn up by the United Nations in 1948.

Justice: Is the concept that individuals are to be treated in a manner that is equitable and fair.

Long-term Aid: Providing local communities with education and skills for sustainable development.

Migrant: A person who moves from one place to another to seek a better life.

(Continued)

Table 19.2 (Continued)

Peace: More than freedom from war, conflict and violence, also ensuring conditions for wellbeing, so that people can live secure lives and have access to justice.

Persecute: To treat someone badly because of who they are or what they believe.

Restorative justice: A theory of justice that emphasises repairing the harm caused by criminal or damaging behaviour. The fundamental belief underpinning Restorative Justice is the assumption that that the perpetrator has a conscience, can recognise the effect of their actions, and feel sorry for the victim.

Refugee: A person who has been forced to leave their country in order to escape war, persecution, or a natural disaster.

Shelter: Shelter and camps for people forced from their homes.

Society: The larger community in which we live, as distinct from the smaller communities of neighbourhood to which we belong.

Social Justice: When a society is fair and just in its treatment of people, we say that social justice exists in that society.

Social injustice: When a society is unfair and unjust in its treatment of people, we say that there is social injustice in that society.

Unjust discrimination: Unfair or unjust treatment of a person or group of people because of their race, religion, age, nationality, ethnicity, gender or other personal traits. We say that people are discriminated against when they are treated unfairly for such reasons.

Values: Values are the things that you believe are important in the way you live and work.

Investigating and understanding contemporary conflicts

While many schools teach the history of the First and Second World Wars, there is less focus on current armed conflicts. Encouraging students to bring news stories about international events can open a dialogue about war and peace. At the time of writing this chapter, the explosion of violence in the Middle East along with the invasion of Ukraine and civil war in Sudan featured in news coverage about war.

The conflict between Israel and Hamas in the Gaza Strip has resulted in a humanitarian catastrophe that threatens the lives and well-being of millions of people. The violence, which began on October 7, 2023, after Hamas launched a series of attacks in Israel, has killed more than 33,000 Palestinians and 1,400 Israelis (at the time of writing). The majority of the casualties in Gaza are women and children, who have been subjected to indiscriminate and disproportionate airstrikes by the Israeli military. The bombing campaign has also destroyed vital infrastructure, such as hospitals, schools, water and sanitation facilities, and power plants, leaving the population without access to basic services and humanitarian aid. The situation in Gaza is not only a grave violation of international humanitarian and human rights law, but also of the Sustainable Development Goals (SDGs).

On 24 February 2022, after weeks of warnings from Western intelligence officials, the Russian president ordered a full-scale invasion of its Eastern European neighbour. This decision triggered the largest European conflict since the Second World War in the 1940s. Almost one year later on April 15th 2023, war erupted in Sudan, when violence broke out between the country's army and a paramilitary group called the Rapid Support Forces. Hundreds of civilians were killed and thousands injured, including women and children. The crisis also resulted in hundreds of thousands of people being forcibly displaced from their homes in search of safety. Reports indicated that civilians of all ages experienced various human rights abuses, including sexual assault and gender-based violence, as well as looting and shortages of food, water, and other basic goods and services, and collapse in communication channels. At the time of writing, the continued fighting in Sudan poses a humanitarian risk for residents who were already experiencing food insecurity as a direct result of climate change.

For teachers, the challenges of teaching about these harrowing contemporary issues, are immense. Those of us who have been in the classroom during other times of invasion and war know how difficult it can be to try to help students make sense of a conflict that we ourselves may not understand. The need to re-assure students while answering questions honestly requires skills of diplomacy, sensitivity and empathy. The challenge of distinguishing factual narrative from fake news cannot be overestimated as social media plays out scenes of indescribable suffering.

Ongoing conflicts in the Middle East, Ukraine and Sudan along with the associated humanitarian responses together with the emerging economic, social and cultural ramifications have raised significant challenges for the achievement of SDG 16. According to data from UNHCR, the speed of the exodus from Ukraine is significantly larger than the migration crisis of 2015, when 1.3 million asylum seekers from Syria, Iraq, Afghanistan and Africa, fleeing poverty and wars, entered Europe. At the time of writing, 8.4 million refugees have left Ukraine, while an estimated eight million people have been displaced within the country. Some 90% of Ukrainian refugees are women and children. In Africa, it is estimated that 100,000 people have left Sudan mainly to neighbouring Egypt, South Sudan, Chad and Central African Republic. These figures can be updated using UN data.

The humanitarian situation in Afghanistan has deteriorated since August 2021 when the Taliban took over the capital Kabul and took control of Afghanistan. After decades of conflict, the situation in Afghanistan is highly complex. Before the withdrawal of foreign troops triggered an escalation in fighting between the Taliban and former government forces, the country was already grappling with multiple crises. By the time the Taliban took power in August 2021, some half a million people had been newly displaced. The suspension of foreign aid and the freezing of government assets, combined with a prolonged drought, plunged the country into a severe economic crisis causing widespread hunger and poverty.

It is important to note that some wars and conflicts get more attention than others. Russia's invasion of Ukraine has captured the public's attention in the Global North in a way that other recent wars like those in Sudan, Afghanistan, Yemen or Ethiopia simply haven't. Furthermore, the Middle East War has also confirmed the worst fears of many in the region, that countries in the Global North are far less likely to empathise with Palestinian suffering, compared with that of Ukrainians or Israelis. There is a perception that the Global North cares more about Ukrainian refugees, than those who are suffering in Yemen, Gaza, South Sudan, and Syria. Furthermore, coverage of war by media in the Global North tends to omit context which is essential for understanding the underlying reasons for war. Regardless of the causes of conflict, invasion and war, every single life matters. The mass murder of civilians in the Middle East in both Gaza and Israel (especially women and children) represents an intolerable level of inhumanity. Both governments which provide military assistance and civil society which remains largely silent are complicit. Evil triumphs when good people remain silent, while the narrative of war becomes reductionist, binary and hateful. As George Orwell (1989:207) famously observed 'one of the most horrible features of war is that all the war-propaganda, all the screaming and lies and hatred, comes invariably from people who are not fighting.' Hence, for many the Global North's championing of human rights has become empty rhetoric.

Engaging students in an analysis of the reasons for poor coverage of conflicts in Africa and Asia promotes critical thinking and a more engaged understanding. Reasons for the intense coverage of the war in Ukraine in European media include geographical proximity, involvement of superpowers and access to economic resources including gas. However, ethnicity is also a reason, as Ukrainians are white. In some parts of Europe, Ukrainian migrants are treated better than migrants from the Global South. Media coverage not only creates awareness, it also promotes international humanitarian responses. Implicitly, it controls the narrative by suggesting some conflicts matter more than others. The lack of media coverage of conflicts in the Global South contributes to the further dehumanisation of non-white, non-European people. In the midst of war and devastation, there are moments of solidarity and beauty. These moments should be seized by teachers in a spirit of hope.

Activities for teachers and students

Teaching about war as it evolves is challenging. Here are some guidelines for supporting primary teachers in this difficult task.

Teach about peace

Peace cannot be taken for granted, hence the need to teach about peace initiatives and peace makers. There are no winners in war. As educators we need to re-focus on the importance of collaboration and conflict resolution. An intercultural approach based on critical thinking, dialogue and openness to recognise and engage with different narratives can help students to consider an issue such as war from multiple perspectives. Consider how the targets for Goal 16 to promote peaceful and inclusive societies can assist in creating a culture of positive peace.

Activities to explore peace

Ask students to reflect on their understanding of Peace with the following questions:

* What is Peace?
* How would you describe Peace?
* Research some Peaceful Activists, for example, Malala Yousafzai; Nelson Mandela, Mahatma Ghandi; Desmond Tutu; Karim Wasfi; Martin Luther King Junior; Jane Addams; Pope Francis
* Create a class 'Peace' contract...

- Pope Francis (2021) called on people to become 'artisans of peace'. Explore how young people can become peacemakers. What attitudes, values and skills are helpful in crafting peace and navigating peaceful pathways?
- Research greetings for peace in different languages
- Explore the Global Peace Index. Research the countries ranked highest and lowest on the Index. Consider the factors that contribute to peace and/or impede peace in the selected countries.
- Peace can be explored as a cross curricular theme. Take music for instance. Students can investigate how music is being used for positive change. Examples include the Recycled Orchestra of Cateura in Paraguay, which plays instruments made from materials recovered from landfill; the West-Eastern Divan Orchestra, which encourages peace by bringing together Israeli, Palestinian and other Arab musicians; the work of artist Pedro Reyes to transform decommissioned weapons into musical instruments and the Cross Border Orchestra in Ireland. Several schools in Ireland participate in Peace Proms. This programme promotes *'peace through music'* and engages almost 35,000 children from 600 schools giving them the opportunity to sing in a large-scale production with a choir of up to 3,000 and a full symphony youth orchestra.

Children's literature about war and peace

Understanding the causes and impact of conflict is complex and multi-layered. The use of story and literature provides a powerful insight into the lived reality of the human lives at the centre of these situations, and the many motivations and tensions that exist. Indeed, these contemporary sites of conflict are the 'living books' of our time and education plays a critical role in how we respond (McGettrick, 2014). Stories can illuminate issues from around the world and impact on how students think, feel and act in relation to the variety of perspectives encountered. Stories are particularly helpful for making the issues at the core of SDG 16 accessible to students and enabling a holistic response, deepening understanding, respect and empathy, while fostering advocacy and engagement. An extensive selection of books that explore issues of justice and peace is listed at the end of this chapter. This list is not exhaustive or prescriptive, however, it may be helpful to consider how such texts can provide a different lens of analysis for students.

Tell stories about the impact of war

From the Mediterranean to the Andaman Sea and the English Channel, refugees and migrants continued to lose their lives attempting dangerous sea crossings. By late 2021, nearly 1,600 had perished in the Mediterranean alone, most of them during attempts to cross from Libya and Tunisia to Italy. Non Governmental Organisations' (NGOs) rescue vessels brought many to safety while others were returned to Libya. The Office of the United Nations High Commissioner for Refugees (UNHCR) called for enhanced State-led search-and-rescue operations. The refugees and migrants who embark on these treacherous journeys are fleeing conflict and violence.

Alan Kurdi was a three-year-old Syrian toddler. His lifeless body was found on a Turkish beach in September 2015 (Figure 19.1). Alan's image focused international efforts on trying to

Figure 19.1 Image of Alan Kurdi by Yante Ismail on the Second Anniversary of his Death (©UNHRC/Yante Ismail).

resolve conflicts that forced people to flee. In the year after Alan's death 4,176 others died or went missing attempting similar journeys. The heartbreaking stories of people escaping war torn areas, has inspired many authors and illustrators to write fictional and information texts about this issue. The beautiful book *Sea Prayer* written by Khaled Hosseini and illustrated by Dan Williams was inspired by the story of Alan Kurdi. Dedicated to the thousands of refugees who have perished at sea fleeing war and persecution, *Sea Prayer* is composed in the form of a letter, from a father to his son, on the eve of their journey. Watching over his sleeping son, the father reflects on the dangerous sea-crossing that lies before them. It is also a vivid portrait of their life in Homs, Syria, before the war, and of that city's swift transformation from a home into a deadly war zone.

Tell stories about peacekeepers and peace accords

Since 1901, the Nobel Peace Prize (np) has been awarded to the person who had done most for 'fraternity between nations, for the abolition or reduction of standing armies and for the holding and promotion of peace congresses' The Nobel Peace Prize is a highly regarded award given to someone who is nominated for their work to promote peace. After an in-depth review process, the Norwegian Nobel Committee selects a Nobel Laureate to receive the prestigious award. Named after Alfred Nobel, a Swedish inventor and weapons maker, the Nobel Peace Award is considered to be the world's most prestigious award. To date the award has been given to over 100 people and over 20 organisations. Some famous winners include Malala Yousafzai, the 14th Dalai Lama, and Mother Teresa. A few United States Presidents have also won the prize, including Jimmy Carter and Barack Obama. Other well-known winners include Martin Luther King, Jr. and Nelson Mandela. Interestingly while nominated several times, Mahatma Gandhi was never awarded the Nobel Peace Prize. Students can research the origins and process of the Nobel Peace Prize. (Resources for teachers are available on https://www.nobelprize.org/education-network-nobel-prize-lessons/)

Students can read and write about peacekeepers in their locality, country or in other countries. While the list of Nobel Peace Prize Winners is a good place to start, attention should be paid to local and national peace activists who do not make it to official records.

Answer students' questions

Students have different questions about a contemporary war or invasion. It is important for these questions to be answered honestly in an age appropriate manner to ensure that students do not catastrophise in private. Try to avoid the use of graphic images. However, if students have seen something upsetting, provide a space for them to voice their concerns. It is also important to tailor the nature of your information and the level of detail to the temperament of the student. Those with an anxious disposition will need less information. On the other hand, more clarification may be required for students who lack empathy.

In the age of social media students have access to multiple sources of information about contemporary conflicts. This includes misinformation and disinformation shared on social media apps such as TikTok and Snapchat. It is critical for parents and teachers to keep students informed about war in the news based on reliable information from reputable sources, and to provide opportunities for students to ask questions.

Acknowledge feelings

How a teacher approaches difficult and potentially traumatic topics will always depend on the age, emotional readiness, and background of the student in the classroom. Open honest dialogue will help students verbalise how they feel. One way to start the conversation is to ask students what they already know. It's important to acknowledge students' feelings by giving them the time and space to express their emotions. Feeling angry, sad, and worried is normal, and time should be given to for students to talk about their emotional responses. You can tell students in your class that you feel sad too as do other people. Such discussions are important for helping students to clarify their feelings and for providing reassurance. If students find it difficult to explain how they're feeling then you could suggest writing or drawing instead. If they feel angry, taking some physical exercise can help.

Explore the geography and history of war zones

Using a globe and a world map, show students where regions in conflict are located. For instance, in the case of the Russian invasion of Ukraine, ask students to describe the location of Russia, Ukraine, and surrounding countries. Discuss the location of cities, towns and physical features which are mentioned in the news e.g. (Kyiv, Lviv, Mariupol, Odessa, the Drieper River and the separatist areas of Donetsk and Luhansk). Examine contemporary and historical maps of the region and discuss comparisons between these maps. For three and a half centuries, Ukraine has struggled to attain and maintain independence through struggles with empires as diverse as the Russian Empire, the Ottoman Empire and the Hungarian Empire. Russia and Ukraine were part of the 15 Soviet republics that made up the Union of Soviet Socialist Republics (USSR). Following the collapse of the Soviet Union in 1991, Ukraine declared independence on August 24.

Palestine is sometimes called the Holy Land. It is a sacred place for three major religions; Judaism, Christianity and Islam. Palestine is important to Jews because the ancient kingdom of Israel was located there. Jews believe that God promised the land to them. It is important to Christians because Jesus lived and worked there. Palestine also has several sites that are holy to Muslims. Situated in the so called Middle East, Palestine is located between the Jordan River and the Mediterranean Sea. Eurocentric Western Europeans, especially the British, gave the region the name Middle East distinguishing between the Far East', which meant China, Japan, Southeast Asia and the Near East which meant Turkey, Egypt and South West Europe. Palestine includes two regions, the West Bank (including East Jerusalem) and the Gaza Strip. Palestinian territories have been illegally occupied by Israel since 1967.

Many different peoples have lived in Palestine over thousands of years. The Ottomans ruled in Palestine for 401 years. After World War 1, Britain took control. The land was inhabited by a Jewish minority and Arab majority. Tensions between the two peoples grew when the international community gave Britain the task of establishing a 'national home' in Palestine for Jewish people. For Jews, it was their ancestral home, but Palestinian Arabs also claimed the land and opposed the move. On November 29, 1947 the United Nations adopted Resolution 181 (also known as the Partition Resolution) that would divide Great Britain's former Palestinian Mandate into Jewish and Arab states. In 1948 when the State of Israel was established, many Holocaust survivors welcomed the new state as a homeland where they would no longer be a vulnerable minority. However, the State of Israel has never been recognised by several Arab States. Meanwhile, investigations conducted by Amnesty International (2022) indicate that Israel has imposed a system of oppression and domination against Palestinians across all areas under its control. Since 1947, the region has experienced bitter fighting between Palestinian Arabs, who are mostly Muslims, and Israelis, who are mostly Jews. While much blame is attributed to both sides, this conflict arose due to decisions taken by colonial powers and failure to take decisive action when it was required. A two-state solution calls for establishing an independent state for Palestinians alongside that of Israel. War in the Middle East needs to be understood within its complex historical origins.

Teach about organisations and institutions promoting peace

The aim of SDG 16 is to significantly reduce all forms of violence, and work with governments and communities to end conflict and insecurity. Promoting the rule of law and human rights is key to this process, as is reducing the flow of illicit arms and strengthening the participation of countries in the Global South in global governance. This requires a critical look at institutions and their norms. As stated by the American poet and activist Amanda Gorman (2021: np) *'We've learned that quiet isn't always peace. And the norms and notions of 'what just is' isn't always justice.'* Freedom to express views, in private and in public, must be guaranteed. Ironically, Amanda Gorman's (2021) book *The Hill We Climb,* was removed from an elementary library section in one school in Florida following one parental complaint.

People must be able to contribute to decisions that affect their lives. Laws and policies must be applied without any form of discrimination. Disputes need to be resolved through functioning political and justice systems. National and local institutions must be accountable and need to be in place to deliver basic services to families and communities equitably and without the need for bribes (Duffy & Lowry, 2017).

Lack of access to justice means that conflicts remain unresolved and people cannot obtain protection and redress. Strong institutions are required to protect human rights and deliver justice to everyone. Governments have a responsibility to ensure people's rights are not abused.

Ask students to discuss institutions involved in peacekeeping either on a local or an international level. Consider why these institutions might be important for peace and justice. Encourage thinking from local to the global:

* Institutions in their own live, for example, guards/police
* Institutions on a national level e.g. government
* Institutions on an international level: the UN

Examples of relevant international bodies are: World Health Organisation (WHO); World Bank; International Monetary Fund (IMF); World Trade Organisation (WTO); United Nations High Commissioner for Refugees (UNHCR); United Nations High Commissioner for Human Rights (UNCHR); Organisation for Economic Co-operation and Development (OECD); United Nations Childrens' Fund (UNICEF); World Food Programme (WFP); United Nations Educational, Scientific and Cultural Organization (UNESCO); United Nations Office for Disaster Risk Reduction (UNISDR); UN Peacekeeping; and Médecins Sans Frontières.

ROLE OF UNITED NATIONS

The UN (United Nations) is an international organisation of countries set up in 1945, in succession to the League of Nations, to promote international peace, security, and cooperation. Since its founding after the Second World War the United Nations has sought to act as a forum for resolution in matters of international conflict. UN Peacekeeping helps countries navigate the difficult path between conflict and peace. It is responsible for promoting and protecting human rights.

Ideas about human rights have evolved over many centuries. But they achieved strong international support following the Holocaust and the Second World War. To protect future generations from a repeat of these horrors, the United Nations adopted the *Universal*

Declaration of Human Rights (UDHR) in 1948 and invited states to sign and ratify it. For the first time, the Universal Declaration set out the fundamental rights and freedoms shared by all human beings. In 1947, the UN established the Human Rights Commission to draft the UDHR. Representatives from a range of countries were involved in the drafting process. On 10 December 1948 the Declaration was adopted by the UN. The preamble to the UDHR sets out the aims of the Declaration, namely to contribute to 'freedom, justice and peace in the world', to be achieved by universal recognition and respect for human rights. These rights are then defined in 30 articles which include civil, political, economic, social and cultural rights.

In class, students can investigate the role and function of the UN. How did it come into being? How do its members make decisions? Do all nations have an equal say? Role play can be used to debate global issues by taking part in a Model UN.

UNITED NATIONS SECURITY COUNCIL

The United Nations Security Council (UNSC) has responsibility for maintaining international peace and security. There are five permanent countries that are always part of this Council: China, France, Russian Federation, United Kingdom and the United States of America. There are also ten non-permanent countries that are part of the UNSC, elected for two-year terms.

THE WORLD HEALTH ORGANIZATION (WHO)

The WHO is an example of one of the institutions necessary for creating a more just world. The role of the WHO is to direct and coordinate international health within the United Nations. WHO works worldwide to promote health, keep the world safe, and serve the vulnerable.

CONFLICT RESOLUTION

In any conflict situation, it is inevitable that efforts at conflict resolution and peace-making will take place. In specific scenarios, there will be many protagonists and duty-bearers involved in negotiations for peace. Ask the young people to choose one conflict situations. Possible conflict locations include Northern Ireland, Israel/Palestine, Former Yugoslavia (Bosnia/Kosovo), Democratic Republic of Congo (DRC), Rwanda, and South Sudan. For instance, the *Belfast Agreement,* also known as the *Good Friday Agreement*, was signed on 10 April 1998. It underpins Northern Ireland's constitutional settlement, and its institutions.

In small groups research the effort at conflict resolution in each situation, based on the following questions. Then create a mind map to illustrate what they know and a summary of their research.

- What caused the conflict?
- Who was involved?
- How long did the conflict last (conflict may still be ongoing)?
- Who has been involved in conflict resolution efforts in each context (local, national, international)? Has there been any significant peace agreement signed?
- In your opinion, have the efforts at peace been successful? Explain your answer with examples.
- Was the United Nations involved?

Further Discussion:

- What can leaders do to make a difference in the lives of young people and empower them to become responsible global citizens?
- Why is it so important for institutions and organisations to include young people in decision-making processes?
- What role does economic empowerment and education play in protecting vulnerable youth?
- How do you see the link between empowering young people and creating more peaceful and just societies?

Invite students to become peace advocates

Issues of justice and peace are complex and contentious. While media ensures a global awareness of the devastating impact of conflict on human rights, many may question how individual efforts can contribute to the achieving the targets of SDG 16. Each person has the capacity to become a peace advocate as follows:

- Consider how you can advocate for SDG 16 in your local area.
- Keep informed about global efforts for justice and peace.
- Contact local politicians re issues of human rights.
- Generate conversations about peace.
- Identify people/organisations at a local, national and global level campaigning for justice and peace.
- Research the work of solidarity groups e.g. the Irish Palestinian Solidarity Campaign (IPSC).
- Organise a peace campaign in your school.
- Find out more about activists such as Malala Yousafzai demonstrating the importance of taking-action against injustice (more information about Malala is available in chapter 8).

Linking SDG 16 with other SDGs

SDG 16 is fundamental to sustainable development. The potential achievement of all the goals is premised on creating the conditions for fair and just societies in the first instance. In many situations, armed conflict leads to food insecurity while the reverse is also the case. Indeed, conflict remains a key driver of poverty, food insecurity, hunger and malnutrition. It represents a significant barrier for the fulfilment of no poverty (SDG1) and zero hunger (SDG 2).

Conflict can cause food shortages and the severe disruption of economic activities, threatening the means of survival of entire populations. Additionally, wars commonly trigger the displacement of huge numbers of people, cutting them off from their food supplies and livelihoods. For instance, the entire population of Gaza faced unprecedented levels of hunger as starvation was used as a method of warfare. Food insecurity can precipitate political conflict. Resource scarcity including food insecurity and water stress will lead to further conflict, unless there is urgent intervention to build resilience and positive peace (Institute for Economics and Peace, 2020).

Climate change continues to both drive displacement and make life even more precarious for those already forced to flee. From drought in Afghanistan, to flooding in South Sudan, to

SDG 3

Good health and well-being

Millions of people continue to live in fragile and conflict-afflicted States. This impacts on their health and well-being. People are forcibly displaced, exploited and face discrimination on a daily basis. The structural causes of injustice at every level need to be addressed to ensure that people have fair and equal access to their basic needs for their well-being.

SDG 2

Zero hunger

The roots and causes of conflict are complex. Resource scarcity often augments conflict, leading to corruption, bribery and violence.

SDG 16 Peace, Justice and Strong Institutions

SDG 4

Quality Education

Education is critical for deepening an understanding of the contentious area of conflict. It ensures that citizens are aware of their fundamental rights and understand how they are represented and impacted by local and national governance systems. It also empowers people to advocate and work towards a more just and peaceful society.

SDG 13

Climate Change

Climate change poses serious challenges to sustainable development and peacefulness. Currently, more than one billion people live in countries that are unlikely to have the ability to mitigate and adapt to new ecological threats. Resource scarcity including food insecurity and water stress will lead to further conflict.

SDG 5

Gender Equality

During times of conflict, women can suffer disproportionately from human rights violations, sexual exploitation, and reduced access to education.

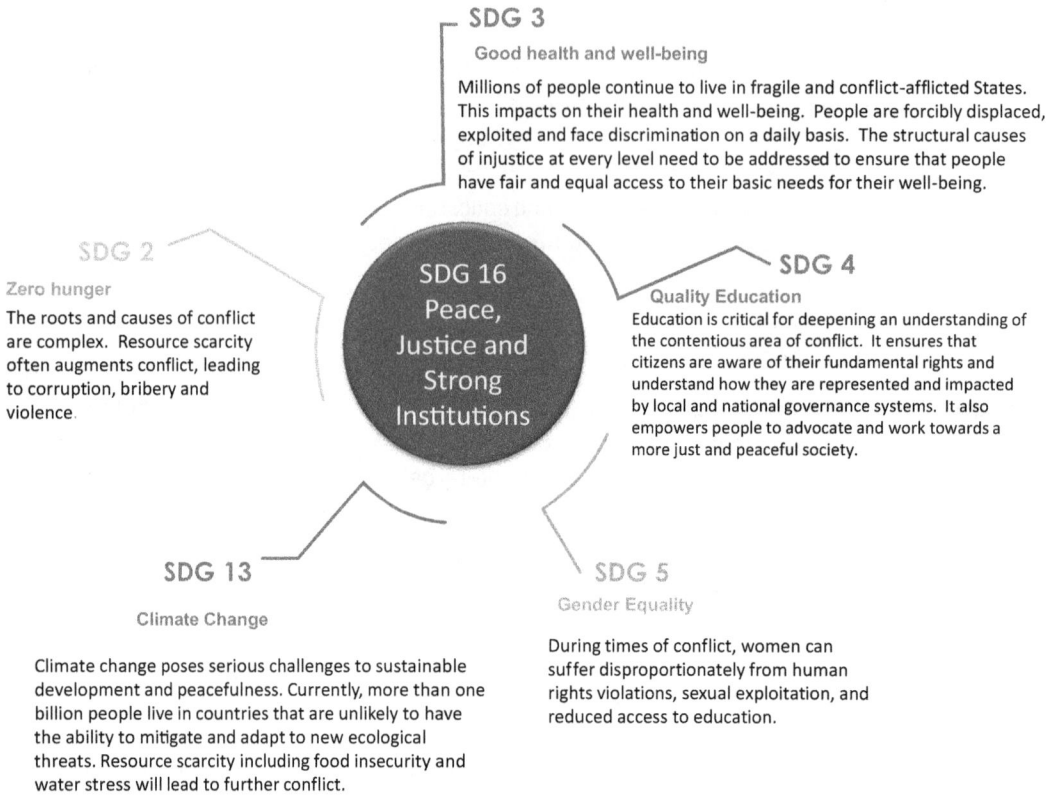

Figure 19.2 Linking SGD 16 to the other SDGs.

intercommunal fighting over dwindling water resources in Cameroon, climate change contributes to increased poverty, instability, conflict and human movement. Figure19.2 illustrates further links between SDG 16 and other SDGs.

Conclusion

In conclusion, this chapter provides students with an opportunity to explore the targets of SDG 16 and begin to understand the concepts of peace and justice. It highlights individual and collective responsibilities, entailed in the vision for society based on respect, solidarity, dialogue, openness and inclusive environmental protection, as outlined in SDG 16 at a local, national and global level. Through case studies on education, health care and displacement, it provides practical examples of inequalities faced by some cultures around the world and the need for justice to bring peace to all. As noted at the beginning of this chapter, this is a broad, complex and often contentious area. Students will require a sustained and multi-faceted engagement with issues of justice and peace to continue to develop and evolve their understanding and responsibility in this area. Education is key.

Alongside the horror and despair of conflict and war, there are stories of hope and humanity, as citizens around the world respond though multiple acts of solidarity. For teachers, it is important to focus on stories of kindness, solidarity and hope and to remember that no child was ever born to hate.

Resources

An extensive list of resources, videos and case studies for SDG 16 is included in the SDG pad-let accompanying this book: https://padlet.com/annedolan/o6rds38ylfy6a28h

A variety of facts, figures, info graphics and other resources that would be useful in sup-porting learning about issues of peace and justice are available on the following web pages:

- **Concern:** https://www.concern.net/schools-and-youth/educational-resources
- **Council on Foreign Relations:** Global Conflict Tracker: http://www.cfr.org/global-conflict-tracker/?category=us
- **Goal:** http://globalgoal.wpengine.com/wp-content/uploads/2019/10/Secondary-Exploring-Conflict.pdf
- **Institute for Economics and Peace:** Global Peace Index https://www.visionofhumanity.org/maps/#/
- **Trócaire:** http://www.trocaire.org/our-work/educate/peaceandjustice/
- **UNESCO:** https://en.unesco.org/themes/education/sdgs/material/16
- **United Nations:** http://www.un.org/sustainabledevelopment/peace-justice/
- **UN Refugee Agency:** https://www.unhcr.org
- **World Wise Global Schools:** http://www.worldwiseschools.ie/resource-item/goal-16-peace-justice/

Tracking peace in the world

- There are online resources available for teachers and students to keep abreast of cur-rent developments in global conflicts.
- **The Global Conflict Tracker** (https://www.cfr.org/global-conflict-tracker) is an interactive guide containing data, resources, and information about ongoing conflicts around the world. Currently the Tracker map displays almost 30 active conflicts due to civil war, criminal vio-lence, political instability, territorial disputes, transnational terrorism and sectarianism. Many conflicts are connected with increasing independence or social, political and economic power.
- **The Global Peace Index** (https://www.visionofhumanity.org/peace-academy/) is the world's leading measure of global peacefulness (Institute for Economics and Peace, 2021). It measures Peace across three areas: the level of Societal Safety and Security; the extent of Ongoing Domestic and International Conflict and the degree of Militari-sation. The 2021 Report found that The Middle East and North Africa (MENA) region remained the world's least peaceful region. It is home to three of the five least peaceful countries in the world. However, it recorded the largest regional improvement over the past year. Europe remains the most peaceful region in the world. The region is home to eight of the ten most peaceful countries. The situation in Ukraine, however, demon-strates the fragility of peace and the critical importance of globally striving to achieve the targets of SDG16 for stability in the most conflict afflicted areas.
- **Crises Watch** (https://www.crisisgroup.org/crisiswatch) a global conflict tracker, is a tool designed to help decision-makers prevent deadly violence by keeping them up-to-date with developments in over 70 conflicts and crises, identifying trends and alerting them to risks of escalation and opportunities to advance peace.

Key dates for justice and peace

- **January 1:** World Day of Peace
- **January 27:** Holocaust Memorial Day
- **February 20:** World Day of Social Justice
- **March 21:** International Day for the Elimination of Racial Discrimination
- **April 6:** International Day of Sport for Development and Peace
- **April 7:** International Day of Reflection on the 1994 Genocide Against the Tutsi in Rwanda
- **April 8:** World Roma Day
- **May 8:** World Red Cross and Red Crescent Day
- **May 16:** International Day of Living Together in Peace
- **May 17:** The International Day Against Homophobia and Transphobia
- **May 21:** World Anti-Terrorism Day
- **May 21:** World Day for Cultural Diversity for Dialogue and Development
- **May 29:** International Day of United Nations Peacekeepers
- **June 20:** World Refugee Day
- **August 2:** Roma and Sinti Genocide Remembrance Day
- **August 6:** Hiroshima Day
- **August 9:** International Day of Indigenous People
- **August 23:** International Day for the Remembrance of the Slave Trade and its Abolition
- **September 15:** International Day of Democracy
- **September 21:** International Day of Peace
- **October 24:** United Nations Day
- **November 4:** European Convention on Human Rights
- **November 6:** International Week of Science and Peace
- **November 9:** International Day Against Fascism and Antisemitism
- **November 20:** Universal Children's Day
- **November 25:** International Day for the Elimination of Violence against Women
- **November 29:** International Day of Solidarity with the Palestinian People
- **Dec 2:** International Day for the Abolition of Slavery
- **December 10)** Human Rights Day
- **December 18:** International Migrants Day

Picture books

Agee, J. (2019) *The Wall in the Middle of the Book* Scallywag Press.
Akinteye, P. (2020) *The War of Soaps and Sponges* TUEMS Children's Books.
Amnesty International. (2016) *We Are All Born Free: The Universal Declaration of Human Rights in Pictures* London: Amnesty International.
Anderson, Halperin, W. (2013) *Peace* Atheneum Books for Young Readers.
Anthony, S. (2016) *Green Lizards and Red Rectangles: A Story About War and Peace* Hodder Children's Books.
Brooks, J. and Daly, J. (illus) (2009) *Let There Be Peace: Prayers from Around the World* Lincoln Children's Books.
Cali, D. and Bloch, D. (illus) (2009) *The Enemy: A Book About Peace* Schwartz & Wade Books.
Davies, N. and Cobb, R. (illus) (2018) The Day War Came Candlewick.

De Fombelle, T. and Arsenault, I. (illus) (2019) Captain Rosalie Candlewick

DeLisa, J. (2010) *The Children's Peace Book: Children Around the World Share Their Dreams of Peace in Words and Pictures* Blue Point Books.

Donaldson, J. and Scheffler, A. (illus) (2020) *The Smeds and Smoos* Alison Green Books.

Gandhi, A., Hegedus, B. and Turk, E. (illus) (2014) *Grandfather Ghandi* Atheneum Books for Young Readers.

Gandhi, A. Hegedus, B. and Turk, E. (2016) *Be the Change: A Grandfather Ghandi Story* Atheneum Books for Young Readers.

Ghanameh, A. (2023) *These Olive Trees* Viking Books for Young Readers

Halls, S., Prasadam-Halls and Starling, T. (illus) (2020) *The Little Island* Andersen Press Ltd.

Hennessey, B.G. and Nakata, H. (illus) (2005) *Because Of You: A Book of Kindness* Candlewick Press.

Katz, K. (2006) *Can You Say Peace?* Scholastic.

Kobayashi, Y. (2018) *The Most Beautiful Village in the World* Museyon.

Kobayashi, Y. (2019) *The Circus Comes to the Village in the World* Museyon.

Kobayashi, Y. (2019) *Return to Most Beautiful Village in the World* Museyon.

Laurel Carter, A. and Duzakin, A. (illus) (2021) *What the Kite Saw* Groundwood Books.

Leaf, M. and Lawson, R. (illus) (2011) *The Story of Ferdinand* Grosset & Dunlap.

LeBox, A. (2015) *Peace Is An Offering* Dial Books for Young Readers.

Mattar, M. (2024) *Sitti's Bird: A Gaza Story* Crocodile Books.

McLaughlin, T. (2018) *Along Came a Different* Bloomsbury.

Meng, C. and Shi, E. (illus) (2017) *World Pizza* Union Square Kids.

Misra, N. (205) *The Peace Stick* Castlebridge Books.

Morpurgo, M. and Clohosy, C. (illus) (2020) *War Horse* Egmont.

Morpurgo, M. and Foreman, M. (illus) (2018) *Poppy Field* Scholastic.

Moushabeck, H. and Madooh, R. (illus) (2023) *Homeland: My Father Dreams of Palestine* Chronicle Books.

Newman, L. and Gal, S. (2020) *Welcoming Elijah: A Passover Tale with a Tail* Charlesbridge Publishing.

Newman, L. and Gal, S. (2022) *Here is the World: A Year of Jewish Holidays* Abrams Books for Young Readers.

Noor Khan, H. and Chamberlain, L. (2020) *The Little War Cat* Pan Macmillan.

Otoshi, K. (2008) *One* KO Kids Books.

O' Meara, K. and Torres, Q. (illus) (2022) *The Rare Tiny Flower* Tra Publishing

Parr, T. (2004) *The Peace Book*. Little Brown and Company.

Paul, M., Paul, B. and Meza, E. (2021) *Peace* North South Books.

Potter, A. and Tavares, M. (2014) *Jubilee: One Man's Big Bold and Very Loud Celebration of Peace* Candlewick.

Preus, M. and Takahashi, H. (illus) (2008) *The Peace Bell* Henry Holt and Co. (BYR).

Proimos, J. (2009) *Paulie Pastrami Achieves World Peace* Little, Brown Books for Young Readers.

Popov, N. (2005) *Why?* North-South Books.

Radunsky, V. (2004) *What Does Peace Feel Like?* Simon and Schuster.

Robinson, H. and Impey, M. (illus) (2014) *Where the Poppies Now Grow* Strauss House Productions.

Robinson, H. and Impey, M. (illus) (2016) *Flo of the Somme* Strauss House Productions.

Robinson, H. and Impey, M. (illus) (2018) *Peace Lily: The Battlefield Nurse* Strauss House Productions.

Ross, T. (2018) *Anti-War Story* Andersen Press.

Shamsi-Basha, K. Latham. I ad Shimizu, Y. (illus) (2020) *The Cat Man of Aleppo* G.P. Putnam's Sons Books for Young Readers

Shapiro, N. and Morgan, P. (illus) (2022) *An ABC of Democracy* Frances Lincoln.

Stelson, C. and Kusaka, A. (illus) (2020) *A Bowl Full of Peace: A True Story* Carolrhoda Books.

Stiefel, C and Gal, S. (illus) (2022) *The Tower Of Life: How Yaffa Eliach Rebuilt Her Town in Stories and Photographs* Scholastic Press.

Thompson, L. and Hale. C. (illus) (2012) *The Forgiveness Garden* Feiwel & Friends.

Vaugelade, A. (2002) *The War* Lerner Publishing Group.

Verde, S. and Reynolds, P.H. (illus) (2017) *I Am Peace: A Book of Mindfulness* Abrams Books for Young Readers.

Williams, S. and Moriuchi, M. (illus) (2005) *Talk Peace* Hodder Children's Books.

Winter, J. (2008) *Wangari's Trees of Peace: A True Story of Africa* Harcourt Books.

Information Books and Picturebooks for 8-12 year olds

Laird, E. and Amini, M. (illus) (2022) *Peace and Kindness for a Better World* Otter-Barry Books.

Mirza, S. (2018) *People of Peace 40 Inspiring Icons* Wide Eyed Editions.

Winter, A. and El Fathi, M. (illus) (2021) *Peace and Me: Inspired by the Lives of Nobel Peace Prize Laureates* Lantana Publishing; Illustrated edition.

Chapter books

Abouzeid, R. (2020) *Sisters of the War: Two Remarkable True Stories of Survival and Hope in Syria* Scholastic.

Allan, A. (2017) *Charlie's Promise* Cranachan Publishing Limited.

Bawden, N. (2017) *Carrie's War* Virago.

Blackwell, G. (2021) *The Blitz Bus* Zoetrope Books.

Booth, A. (2018) *Across the Divide* Catnip.

Boyne, J. (2007) *The Boy in the Striped Pyjamas* Vintage Publishing.

Boyne, J. (2015) *Stay Where You Are and Then Leave* Penguin Random House Children's UK.

Brady, J. and Aggs, P. (illus) *No Country: A Nation at War. Millions Displaced. One Family Trying to Survive.* David Fickling Books.

Brubaker Badley, K. (2015) *The War that Saved My Life* Dial Books.

Brubaker Badley, K. (2016) *The War I Finally Won* Dial Books.

Bsharat, A. Admedzai Kemp, R. and Copeland, S. (2019) *Trees for the Absentees* Neem Tree Press Ltd.

Caldecott, E. (2021) *The Short Knife* Andersen Press.

Carroll, E. (2017) *Letters From The Lighthouse* Faber & Faber.

Carroll, E. (2019) *When We Were Warriors* Faber & Faber.

Dassu, A.M. *Boy, Everywhere* Old Barn Books.

Devin, S. (2021) *Guard Your Heart* Pan Macmillan.

Diaz Gonzalez, C. (2013) *A Thunderous Whisper, In War Even an Insignificant Girl Can Be a Hero* Yearling.

Drewery, K. and Seki, N. (2020) *The Last Paper Crane* Hot Key Books.

Fargher, A. and Usher, S. (illlus) (2019) *The Umbrella Mouse* Pan Macmillan.

Fargher, A. and Usher, S. (illus) (2020) *Umbrella Mouse to the Rescue* Pan Macmillan.

Finder, R. and Greene, J.M. (2019) *My Survival: A Girl on Schindler's List* Scholastic.

Frank, A. (2007) *The Diary of a Young Girl* Penguin.

Gibbons, A. (2016) *The Trap: Terrorism, Heroism and Everything in Between* Hachette Children's Group.

Goldstyn, J. (2018) The Eleventh Hour Owlkids

Grant, M. (2019) *Purple Hearts* Egmont UK Ltd.

Gratz, A. (2019a) *Grenade* Scholastic.

Gratz, A. (2019b) *Allies* Scholastic.

Gratz, A. (2021) *Ground Zero: A Novel of 9/11* Scholastic.

Halahmy, M. (2016) *The Emergency Zoo* Alma Books Ltd.

Henderson, B. (2020) *The Siege of Caerlaverock* Cranachan Publishing.

Hiranandani, V. (2019) *The Night Diary* Penguin Putnam Inc.

Holland, S. (2020) *Havanfall* Bloomsbury

Holland, J. (2012a) *Duty Calls: Battle of Britain: World War 2 Fiction* Penguin Random House.

Holland, J. (2012b) *Duty Calls: Dunkirk World War 2 Fiction* Penguin Random House.

House, R. (2018) *The Goose Road* Walker Books.

Killeen, M. (2019) *Orphan, Monster Spy* Usborne Publishing Ltd.

Laird, E. (2006) *A Little Piece of Ground* Pan Macmillan.

Laird, E. (2008) *Kiss the Dust* Pan Macmillan.

Laird, E. (2017) *Welcome to Nowhere* Pan Macmillan.

Laird, E. (2021) *A House Without Walls* Pan Macmillan.

Magorian, M. (2014a) *Goodnight Mister Tom* Puffin.

Magorian, M. (2014b) *Back Home* Puffin.

Marsh, K. (2020) *The Nowhere Boy* Square Fish.

McKay, H. (2021) *The Swallows' Flight* Pan Macmillan.

McKay, H. and Green, R. (2019) *The Skylark's War* Margaret K. McElderry Books.

Merrill, J. and Solbert, R. (2015) *The Pushcart War* The New York Review of Books, Inc.
Morgan, G. (2015) *Poems from the Second World War* Pan Macmillan.
Morpurgo, M. (1997) *Waiting for Anya* Harper Collins.
Morpurgo, M. (2011) *Shadow* Harper Collins.
Morpurgo, M. (2015) *Listen to the Moon* Harper Collins.
Morpurgo, M. (2016a) *Only Remembered* Corgi Childrens.
Morpurgo, M. (2016b) *Private Peaceful* Harper Collins.
Morpurgo, M. (2017a) *Why the Whales Came* Egmont.
Morpurgo, M. (2017b) *War Horse* Egmont.
Morpurgo, M. (2017c) *Friend or Foe* Egmont.
Morpurgo, M. (2018) *Flamingo Boy* Harper Collins.
Morpurgo, M. (Ed.) (2020a) *War Stories* Macmillan Children's Books.
Morpurgo, M. (2020b) *The Day the World Stopped Turning* Square Fish Harper Collins.
Morpurgo, M. and Barroux (illus) (2019) *In the Mouth of the Wolf* Harper Collins.
Morris, H. (2018) *The Tattooist of Auschwitz* Hot Key Books.
Morris, H. (2020) *Citka's Journey* Zaffre.
Mozes Kor, E. and Rojany Buccieri, L. (2020) *The Twins of Auschwitz: The Inspiring True Story of a Young Girl Surviving Mengele's Hell* Monoray.
Palacio, R.J. (2019) *White Bird* Penguin Random House Children's UK.
Palmer, T. (2018) *Armistice Runner Two Lives Connected by Memory* Barrington Stoke.
Palmer, T. (2019) *D Day Dog* Barrington Stoke.
Palmer, T. (2020a) *Over the Line* Barrington Stoke.
Palmer, T. (2020b) *After the War: From Auschwitz to Ambleside* Barrington Stoke.
Parker Rhodes, J. (2018) *Towers Falling* Little Brown and Company.
Parr, L. (2021) *The Valley of Lost Secrets* Bloomsbury Children's Books.
Pollard, J. (2019) *Evacuee-a Real Life World War Two Story* Scholastic.
Prins, M. and Henk Steenhuis, P. (2015) *Hidden: True Stories of Children who Survived World War II* Scholastic.
Rai, B. (2019) *Now or Never: A Dunkirk Story* Scholastic.Sasaki, M. and DiCicco, S. (2020) *The Complete Story of Sadako Sasaki: and the Thousand Paper Cranes* Tuttle Publishing.
Saunders, K. (2015) *Five Children on the Western Front* Faber and Faber.
Savit, G. (2017) *Anna and the Swallow Man* Penguin Random House Children's UK.
Serraillier, I. (2003) *The Silver Sword* Red Fox.
Simons, M. (2010) *Let Me Whisper You My Story* Harper Collins.
Smith, D. (2013) *My Friend the Enemy* Chicken House Ltd.
Solakovic, M. (2018) *The Boy who Said Nothing – A Child's Story of Fleeing Conflict* John Blake.
Stevens, R. (in press) *The Ministry of Unladylike* Penguin Random House.
Watts, H. and Thomas, T. (2014) *The Ghost of the Trenches and other Stories* Bloomsbury Publishing PLC.
Weiss, H. (2014) *Helga's Diary: A Young Girl's Account of Life in a Concentration Camp* Penguin.
Westall, R. (2015a) *The Machine Gunners* Macmillan Children's Books.
Westall, R. (2015b) *Blitzcat* Macmillan Children's Books.
Wilkinson, S. *Name Upon Name* Little Island.
Young, N. (2021) (3rd Ed.) *Time School: We Will Remember* Them Nielson.
Zullo, A. (2016) *Survivors: True Stories of Children in the Holocaust* Non-Basic Stock Line.

References

Amnesty International (2022) *Israel's Apartheid Against Palestinians: Cruel System of Domination and Crime Against Humanity*. https://www.amnesty.org/en/documents/mde15/5141/2022/en/
Centre for Preventative Action, Council on Foreign Relations. (2021) *Global Conflict Tracker*. Available at: https://www.cfr.org/global-conflict-tracker/?category=us
Duffy, V. and Lowry, E. (eds) (2017) *Peace and Justice: It's Up to Youth*. Dublin: National Youth Council of Ireland.
Eurostat. (2021) *Sustainable Development Indicators: SDG 16*. Available at: https://ec.europa.eu/eurostat/web/sdi/peace-justice-and-strong-institutions

Goal. (2015) *Exploring Conflict: A Workshop Resource for Post-Primary Teachers and Students*. Dublin: Goal.

Gorman, A. (2021) The hill we climb. In Gorman, A. and Winfrey, O. eds. *The Hill We Climb: An Inaugural Poem for the Country*. New York: Viking.

Institute for Economics and Peace. (2021) *Global Peace Index*. Available at: https://www.visionof humanity.org/

Institute for Economics & Peace. Ecological Threat Register 2020: Understanding Ecological Threats, Resilience and Peace, Sydney, September 2020. Available at: http://visionofhumanity.org/reports

International Alert. (2022) *What Is Peacebuilding*? Available at: http://international-alert.org/about/what-is-peacebuilding/

McGettrick, B. (2014) *Reflections on Education in Palestine*, Address for Catholic Schools Week 2014, Woodlands Hotel, Adare, 27 January 2014.

Navarro Castro, L. and Nairo-Galace, J. (2019) *Peace Education: A Pathway to a Culture of Peace* (3rd Ed.). Miriam College: Centre for Peace Education.

Nobel Peace Prize. https://www.nobelprize.org/

Orwell, G. (1989) *Homage to Catalonia* London: Penguin Books

Pope Francis. (2021) Message for the Celebration of the 55th World Day of Peace, *Dialogue Between Generations, Education and Work: Tools for Building Lasting Peace.* Available at: https://www.vatican.va/content/francesco/en/messages/peace/documents/20211208-messaggio-55giornatamondiale-pace2022.html

Trócaire. (2021a) *Kindness: Explore SDG 16 through the Stories of Two Families in South Sudan.* Available at: https://www.trocaire.org/wp-content/uploads/2021/01/Education-Post-Primary-Kindness-Lent-2021.pdf?type=edu

Trócaire. (2021b) *Peace-ing it Together: Exploring SDG 16 through the Stories of Two Families in South Sudan*, available at: https://www.trocaire.org/wp-content/uploads/2021/01/Education-Youth-Resource-Lent-2021

UNESCO. (2020) *Education for Sustainable Development Goals: Learning Objectives*. Available at: https://unesdoc.unesco.org/ark:/48223/pf0000247444

UNESCO. (2021) *SDG Resources for Educators - Peace, Justice and Strong Institutions*. Available at: http://en.unesco.org/themes/education/sdgs/material/16

UNHCR. (2021) *On the Frontlines of the Global Displacement Crisis*. Available at: https://www.unhcr.org

UNICEF. (2021a) *Research and Reports*. Available at: http://www.unicef.org/research-and-reports

UNICEF. (2021b) *Strengthening Child Protection Systems: Every Child Has the Right to Access Vital Social Services and Fair Social Justice Systems*. Available at: https://www.unicef.org/protection/strengthening-child-protection-systems

UN (2023) *A New Agenda for Peace* https://dppa.un.org/en/a-new-agenda-for-peace

United Nations (UN). (2020) *Sustainable Development Goal*. Available at: https://www.un.org/sustainabledevelopment/sustainable-development-goals/

United Nations. (2021a) *Goal 16: Promote Just, Peaceful and Inclusive Societies*. Available at: http://www.un.org/sustainabledevelopment/peace-justice/

United Nations (UN). (2021b) *Peace, Justice and Strong Institutions: Why They Matter*. Available at: https://www.un.org/sustainabledevelopment/wp-content/uploads/2017/01/1600055p_Why_it_Matters_Goal16_Peace_new_text_Oct26.pdf

United Nations Development Programme (UNDO). (2022) *Global Dashboard for Vaccine Equity*. Available at: https://data.undp.org/vaccine-equity/

United Nations Department of Economics and Social Affairs. (2021) *SDG 16 2020 Progress Report*. Available at: https://sdgs.un.org/goals/goal16

Yousafzai, M. (2013) *Address to the United Nations Youth Assembly*, 12 July 2013. Available at: https://malala.org/newsroom/archive/malala-un-speech

20 Partnerships for transformation, making connections beyond the classroom (SDG 17)

Anne M. Dolan and Paula Galvin

Introduction

Partnership is not a new concept in the environmental/global citizenship discourse. It was endorsed as a key approach for achieving environmental and developmental change at the 1992 UN Earth Summit in Rio de Janeiro. SDG 17 Partnership for the Goals aims to strengthen the means of implementation and revitalise global partnership(s) for sustainable development. This transversal goal aims to strengthen the means of implementing all of the SDGs through partnerships (Stott and Murphy, 2020).

The United Nations (2015) stresses that partnerships are essential for the achievement of the Sustainable Development Goals. In an increasingly interconnected world, the SDGs can only be realised with strong global partnerships and cooperation. A successful development agenda requires inclusive partnerships at global, regional, national and local levels. Such partnerships should be established on a basis of a shared vision and clearly articulated principles and values, placing people and the planet at the centre. Strong international cooperation is needed now more than ever to ensure that all countries can achieve the Sustainable Development Goals.

This chapter discusses the importance of teaching about, for and through SDG 17; it highlights the example of Fairtrade as a model of partnership adopted by one primary school in Dublin; it illustrates models of partnership exercised by some schools and it concludes with a call for all teachers to teach the SDGs.

Partnership

Partnership is a term which evokes much sensitivity with its implicit connotations of sharing and trust. The Oxford Dictionary defines partnership in terms of a relationship between people or organisations. Other associated words include *association, cooperation, collaboration, participation, joint decision making* and *long-term relationship*. Yet, there exists a lack of clarity surrounding what exactly is meant by partnership, and the principles which underlie a partnership approach.

DOI: 10.4324/9781003232001-23

While traditional notions of aid and charity may imply an unequal relationship based on a donor and a recipient, the term 'partnership' suggests equality, respect, reciprocity and ownership (Bailey and Dolan, 2011). Still, some partnerships can be abusive and unequal in practice, and the term continues to mean different things to different people, sectors and institutions.

At a conceptual level partnership is generally understood as a positive attribute. Mohiddin (1998: 5) refers to partnership as the 'highest stage of working relationship between different people brought together by commitment to common objectives, bonded by long experience of working together, and sustained by subscription to common visions'. Typically, 'authentic' partnership is associated with the following characteristics; long-term shared responsibility, reciprocal obligation, equality, mutuality and balance of power (Fowler, 2000). Core principles of reciprocity, accountability, joint decision making, respect, trust, transparency, sustainability and mutual interests have been highlighted in the literature (Wanni, 2010; Dochas, 2010; Crawford, 2003).

Developing an agreed set of values and principles is important for fostering collaborative, robust and successful partnerships. In line with SDG 17, the Irish Government (2019) seeks to support partnership and collaborative efforts at all levels and between all stakeholders. Hence, a set of clearly stated values (Table 20.1) and principles (Table 20.2) for statutory/community partnerships is now part of government policy (Government of Ireland, 2022). (Figure 20.1).

Table 20.1 Sustainable, inclusive and empowered communities: shared values

Values	Meaning
Active participation	A commitment to active participation of all stakeholders, including citizens and noncitizens. Participation is rooted in the belief that communities have the right to identify their own needs and interests and the outcomes required to meet them. Building active participation involves a recognition that policies and programmes targeted at communities and groups will not and cannot be effective without the meaningful participation of those communities in their design, implementation and monitoring
Sustainable development	A commitment to sustainable development, including promoting cultural, environmental, economic and socially sustainable policies and practices.
Social justice	A commitment to social justice, including promoting policies and practices that challenge injustice and value diversity.
Social inclusion	A commitment to social inclusion. Prioritising the needs of communities experiencing social or economic exclusion, including rural isolation, and recognising that promoting social and economic inclusion requires us to recognise and seek to address the root causes of exclusion as well as developing strategies and mechanisms to promote and ensure inclusion.

(Continued)

Table 20.1 (Continued)

Values	Meaning
Human rights, equality and anti-discrimination	A commitment to human rights, equality and anti-discrimination, involving promoting human rights and equality in society and committing to addressing the multiple forms of discrimination experienced by many groups. Specifically, recognising the experiences of people in relation to gender-based issues and, in particular, the impact of gender inequality on women (including women from marginalised communities and minority groups) and on society as a whole. In accordance with the Public Sector Duty, we are committed to eliminating discrimination, promoting equality and protecting human rights
Collectivity	A commitment to collectivity. A collective approach requires a focus on the potential benefits for communities rather than focusing only on benefits for individuals. It recognises the rights of communities and groups, including funded organisations, to work autonomously and maintain a critical voice. It involves seeking collective outcomes in pursuit of a just and equal society.
Empowering communities	A commitment to empowering communities, increasing their knowledge, skills, consciousness and confidence to become critical, creative and active participants. It leads people and communities to be resilient, organised, included and influential.

(*Source*: Government of Ireland, 2019: 11, 37)

Table 20.2 Sustainable, inclusive and empowered communities: shared principles

Principles	Meaning
Respect	Respect the diversity of knowledge, skills, views and experience brought to the process by all stakeholders and will seek to maximise the potential this diversity brings while managing any conflict or disagreements that may arise in a positive and inclusive way.
Subsidiarity	Develop approaches that safeguard the ability of communities, whether communities of interest or geographic communities, to influence and, where possible, take decisions and actions, promoting power sharing and the exercise of power as close to communities as possible.
Harmonisation	Secure consistency with existing strategies and implement agreed objectives and actions relevant to community development and local development. We will develop approaches promoting harmonisation and common standards of good practice in community development and local development programmes, policies and processes throughout the country.
Value for money	Develop strategies and approaches that promote and ensure best value for money, underpinned by a collaborative, partnership and whole-of-government ethos that prioritises societal value and community need.
Implementation	Leverage the structures already in place, locally and nationally, and seek to maximise their potential.
Collaboration	Work collaboratively, engaging with a broad a range of stakeholders to ensure excellence of service.

(Government of Ireland, 2019: 12, 38)

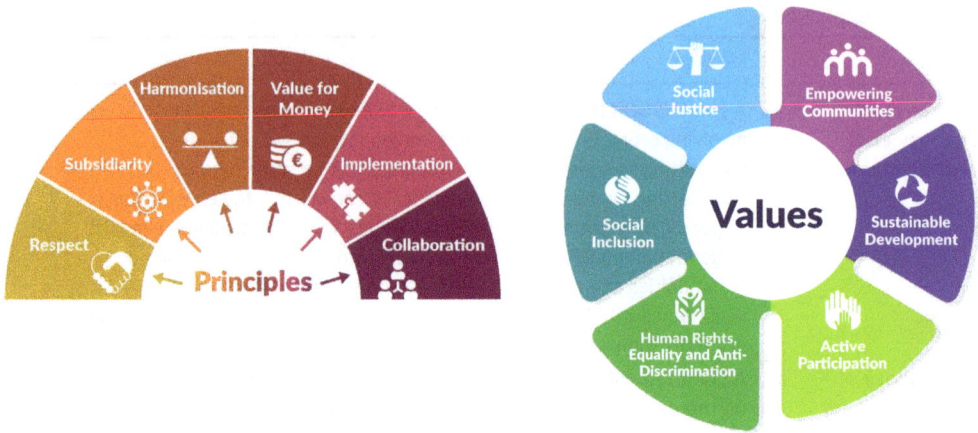

Figure 20.1 Values and Principles for collaborative partnership

There are many benefits to working in a partnership including solidarity, access to a broader platform of knowledge and skills, diversity of approaches and cost efficiency. Nonetheless, there are also potential pitfalls including loss of independence, funding challenges, poor articulation of a shared vision and divestment of core resources for supporting the partnership (IDEA, nd). It is important to note that partnership is not a neutral term and partnerships which are poorly conceptualised and badly managed end up promoting dependency, ultimately doing more harm than good. While benefits have generated an improvement in human and infrastructural capacity as well as a greater voice for Global Southern partners, partnerships have been criticised for the one-way flow of capacity from the Global North and the absence of genuine sharing (Nakabugo et al., 2010). In order to move beyond the often hollow rhetoric of 'partnership', it is imperative that partners openly address the issue of power in terms of ownership, decision-making, funding, planning and evaluation (Bailey and Dolan, 2011).

Sample learning objectives for teaching SDG 17 are listed in Table 20.3. Suggested topics are set out in Table 20.4 while some learning approaches and methods are listed in Table 20.5. Perhaps the most effective way to teach about partnership, is to give students several positive examples of participating in initiatives which demand elements of team work, collaboration and partnership. Benefits of collaborative work include promotion of social interaction, development of self-confidence and improvement in collaborative skills, as well as improvement in student decision-making skills. When used in combination with individual learning assignments, cooperative learning can enhance classroom instruction and make learning more social and fun for students. Not only is learning how to be an effective team member an important part of school life, it also determines the quality of one's participation in current and future partnership initiatives. Learning to work as part of a team helps students develop social skills, such as patience, empathy, communication, respect for others, compromise and tolerance. It also promotes self confidence and an ability to trust others.

Table 20.3 Learning objectives for SDG 17

Cognitive learning objectives Teaching *about* the goals: developing respect and understanding	1. The learner understands global issues, such as trade and Fairtrade and the interconnectedness and interdependency of different countries and populations. 2. The learner understands the importance of local and global partnerships and the shared accountability for sustainable development and knows examples of networks, institutions, campaigns of global partnerships such as local Fairtrade organisations. 3. The learner knows the concepts of global governance and global citizenship. 4. The learner recognizes the importance of cooperation, collaboration and partnership in the context of Fairtrade. 5. The learner knows concepts for measuring progress on sustainable development.
Socio-emotional learning objectives Teaching *for* the goals enhancing empathy and love	1. The learner is able to raise awareness about the importance of global partnerships for sustainable development. 2. The learner is able to work with others to promote global partnerships for sustainable development and demand governments' accountability for the SDGs. 3. The learner is able to take ownership of the SDGs. 4. The learner is able to create a vision for a sustainable global society. 5. The learner is able to experience a sense of belonging to a common humanity, sharing values and responsibilities, based on human rights.
Behavioural learning objectives Teaching **through** the goals Promoting advocacy and activism	1. The learner is able to become a change agent to realize the SDGs and to take on their role as an active, critical and global and sustainability citizen. 2. The learner is able to contribute to facilitating and implementing local, national and global partnerships for sustainable development. 3. The learner is able to publicly demand and support the development of policies promoting global partnerships for sustainable development. 4. The learner is able to support development cooperation activities. 5. The learner is able to influence companies to become part of global partnerships for sustainable development.

(*Source:* UNESCO, 2017: 44)

Table 20.4 Suggested topics for teaching SDG 17 (Source: UNESCO, 2017: 45)

Global partnerships between governments, the private sector and civil society for sustainable development, their shared accountability and possible conflicts between the different actors
Local, national and global systems, structures and power dynamics
Global governance and policies and the global market and trading system in the light of sustainable development
Global citizenship and citizens as change agents for sustainable development
Cooperation on and access to science, technology and innovation, and knowledge sharing
Global distribution of access to the internet
Development cooperation, development assistance, and additional financial resources for developing countries from multiple sources
Capacity-building to support national plans to implement all the SDGs
Measurements of progress on sustainable development

Table 20.5 Suggested learning approaches and methods for teaching SDG 17 (Source: UNESCO, 2017: 45)

Develop partnerships or global web-based distance education experiences between schools, universities or other institutions in different regions of the world (South and North; South and South)
Analyse the development and implementation of global policies on climate change, biodiversity, etc.
Analyse the progress in implementing the SDGs globally and at the national level, and determine who is accountable for progress or lack thereof
Plan and implement an SDGs awareness campaign
Perform simulation games related to global conference negotiations (e.g. National Model United Nations)
Plan and run a (youth) action project on the SDGs and their importance
Develop an enquiry-based project: Together we can....Explore this commonly used phrase and how it applies to the SDGs

Partnerships for sustainability and global citizenship: connections beyond the classroom

School community partnerships provide students with an opportunity to learn outside the classroom, 'thus strengthening academic and social development in a rapidly changing and diversifying world' (Shaw, 2018: 21). Partnerships can serve to strengthen, support, and even transform individual partners, resulting in improved programme quality, more efficient use of resources, and better alignment of goals and curricula (Harvard Family Research Project, 2010). An example of an innovative approach to partnership is detailed in Case study 20.1. whereby one teacher had an idea and established an award-winning partnership for change.

Case study 20.2 outlines a powerful partnership between a primary school and a community in Ireland which succeeded in obtaining the Fairtrade Town status for Clondalkin. This is the kind of partnership which is inspirational, hopeful and effective, based on student action, teacher inspiration, school support and community buy in. While all partnerships are challenging, four criteria support the generation of successful collaborations (Berrone et al., 2019): the need for a clear and mutually agreed purpose; the importance of the generation of effective processes and practices; the need to bring long term complementarity and mutual respect; and the need to be able to demonstrate achievement and impact. Each school community partnership is unique with its own set of opportunities and challenges. Learning to deal with challenges can generate unexpected and valuable learning opportunities. Further opportunities for engaging in community-based partnerships are available in the Transition Year (TY) Programme described in Case study 20.3.

Case study 20.1 The Irish Schools Sustainability Network (ISSN)

The Irish Schools Sustainability Network (ISSN) is a grassroots movement of teachers and students from schools across Ireland working together to accelerate climate and ecological action and support schools to deliver on education for sustainable development. The network brings teachers and students from primary and secondary sectors together once a month to provide a platform for discussion, training, and action on the climate emergency and biodiversity loss and to prioritise advocacy for sustainability education within the Irish Education System (NCCA, 2022).

The ISSN was founded in March 2021 in response to an observation that teachers were talking about important issues such as COVID19 and the war in Ukraine, but the twin climate and biodiversity crises were not part of daily discourse. Students, teachers, and senior management teams were unaware of the magnitude and scale of the emergency and urgent need for action. Education for sustainable development was largely left to the good will of individual champions as opposed to a strategic whole school approach. In November 2021 and again in November 2022, ISSN organised an online *Climate and Nature Summit* which brought together participants from over 2000 schools. The summit aimed to provide teachers with up to-date information about the interlinked issues of biodiversity and climate change, through the provison of resources and training for teaching these issues in the classroom.

The ISSN is trying to change the education system from within, identifying deficits and working together to address them. Another example of this is *Bitesize Biodiversity*. Teaching students about nature is challenging as teachers can be as disconnected from nature as students are and it is difficult to navigate how this education can be meaningfully incorporated into an already packed curriculum. To address this ISSN holds *Bitesize Biodiversity* virtual training sessions every Monday at 4pm for 15mins. Teachers in the network share information, resources, and activities about one living thing and participants are encouraged to use these materials in their classes before the next online session.

Partnerships are a crucial part of the ethos of the ISSN. One such partnership is with Education Support Centre Ireland (ESCI). The network works in partnership with ESCI's Climate Action Group, liaising with Waterford Education Support Centre that chairs this group. ISSN is supported by the Government of Ireland through its WorldWise Global Schools Programme and the Education for Sustainable Development Fund.

According to its website ISSN sees its mission as one of reimagining the Irish education system and fostering a culture of agency and empowerment steering away from a culture of apathy and acceptance. The network proposes that working together can create a community that sees nature as something with its own inherent value rather than a resource to be exploited. It asserts that education should inspire critical thinking and active democracy ensuring that everyone feels that they have a role to play in shaping a better future.

The activities of the network are led by a core group which has been together since the establishment of ISSN. In addition to their monthly meetings, the Climate and Nature Summit and Bitesize Biodiversity, their other activities include 5 Minutes of Sustainability video series; an Environmental Influencer Course; the Plant a Planet Campaign; and the delivery of teacher and student training programmes.

The ISSN was the brainchild of one secondary science teacher Dr Patrick Kirwan. For more information see https://www.issn.ie

Fairtrade: a model of partnership

The SDGs cannot be achieved without universal collaboration and co-operation. Thus, partnership is essential for the eventual realisation of all the goals. Introducing students to the concept of Fairtrade as a model of partnership makes this ambiguous concept more accessible to students. Fairtrade is a system of certification that aims to ensure a set of standards are met in the production and supply of a product or ingredient. For farmers and workers, Fairtrade means that their rights as workers are acknowledged, they are guaranteed a fair price for their products and they are entitled to health and safety practices in the workplace.

For shoppers it means high quality, ethically produced products. FLOCERT, an independent organisation, checks that the Fairtrade Standards have been met by the farmers, workers and companies that are part of the product supply chains. In order to reassure consumers that this has happened, the use of the Fairtrade Mark on products and packaging is licensed to indicate that rigorous standards have been met. (Figure 20.2). Fairtrade is an alternative approach to conventional trade. It offers consumers a powerful way to reduce poverty through everyday shopping. Based on a partnership between some of the most disadvantaged farmers and workers in the Global South, purchasing Fairtrade products allows people to support ethical trading through their consumer practices. Furthermore, Fairtrade provides farmers with a better deal and opportunity to improve their lives and plan for their future.

Figure 20.2 Fairtrade Logo.

Supporting farmers in the Global South by buying their products is a very real and tangible means to engage students with the knowledge, skills, and values to learn about fair and unfair trade. Learning about Fairtrade helps students to be empathetic towards those who endure harsh working conditions. Through learning about Fairtrade, supporting Fairtrade practices and producers, and highlighting awareness about Fairtrade, students learn the importance of working in solidarity with other people and their communities. It is also an example of a social justice project in which the links between local, national, and global citizenship are explored, evaluated, and enacted in a very real and powerful way. Fairtrade initiatives allow us as teachers to become agents of change by educating ourselves and our students about Fairtrade, by investigating the impact Fairtrade has had on some of the poorest farming communities in the world and by examining our role as consumers in the world.

Currently more than 86% of the value of a supply chain is absorbed by corporate brands and traders. Farmers and workers are part of this chain, but many still live below the poverty line. Fairtrade works with lots of different partners and stakeholders including producer organisations, businesses, trade unions and civil societies. Fairtrade cannot tackle poverty on its own. Inequality is deeply embedded in our society and has become more evident since the pandemic. Inequality in its many manifestations can be felt in education, in health, and particularly among those who are already weakened by poverty, vulnerability and dispossession.

However, Fairtrade does impact powerfully and significantly on the lives of hundreds of thousands of farmers and workers worldwide. The popularity and ubiquity of Fairtrade products continue to rise with sales of Fairtrade products in Ireland totalling 342 million euro in 2017 and 8.5 billion euro across 150 countries internationally. In the Global North, consumers can purchase more socially and environmentally responsible products and know that their purchase impacts in a very real way on the life of a worker in the Global South. The 17th SDG recognises multiple stakeholder partnerships as important vehicles for mobilising and sharing knowledge, expertise, technologies and financial resources to support the achievement of the SDGs in all countries, particularly those in the Global South.

Fairtrade as an approach for teaching the SDGS

The Sustainable Development Goals aim to end 'poverty in all its forms everywhere' while leaving no one behind. This ambition is central to Fairtrade's mission. The three pillars of Fairtrade are economic, environmental and social. Fairtrade is uniquely positioned to be able to contribute in a very powerful way to many issues at once. Fairtrade touches on all the United Nations SDGs to end poverty, protect the planet and ensure prosperity for all by 2030, but there are a few goals where Fairtrade has an exceptional impact. Through Community Development Premiums, additional funds that are directed back to farmers and workers with the sale of each Fairtrade product, producers can invest in their communities and undertake initiatives and projects that contribute to many of the issues at the heart of the SDGs. Indeed, supporting Fairtrade at local, national and global levels can do much to achieve the SDGs (Fairtrade, 2015).

Fairtrade's approach is holistic. It addresses many issues which have become increasingly important in our globalised world ranging from climate change to gender equality, from quality education to sustainable cities and communities. All 169 targets are related directly or indirectly to food and farming and Fairtrade impacts on all 17 of the SDGs. Teaching students about Fairtrade introduces them to easily understandable ideas about fairness and unfairness in the world. Teaching about supply chains and agricultural practices in the world has the potential to enable students to problem solve, to think critically about world issues, to raise awareness and to advocate for change. These lifelong learning skills also lead to a sense of empowerment and can combat feelings of helplessness and hopelessness amid reports of global warming, irreversible climate change, refugee crises and political instability.

Fairtrade has been a significant feature of the Irish global citizenship education landscape for more than 30 years. It is a testament to educators at all levels, that the distinctive blue, green, black and white of the Fairtrade logo (Figure 20.2) is recognised by more than 84% of the Irish population. Fairtrade products in our shops and supermarkets include chocolate, bananas, tea, coffee and hot chocolate. It is also an accessible approach with which we can engage young students (Gallwey, 2009). Although some of the global justice issues relating to food and hunger are complex, with appropriate methodologies, younger students (4-7 years) can be led to develop their understanding of justice and fairness (Dillon, Ruane and Kavanagh, 2010). There are many ways to engage students in learning about Fairtrade through learning about: where food comes from; the inequities in trading systems; and case studies of Fairtrade producers, farmers and workers. Students can conduct surveys in local shops to see which Fairtrade products are in stock and they can promote the purchase of such products. Table 20.6 illustrates how Fairtrade is linked to all SDGs. Case study 20.2 illustrates one school's partnership approach to Fairtrade.

Case study 20.2 On becoming a Fairtrade town: Clondalkin the 51st Fairtrade town in Ireland. (A reflection from Paula)

As a teacher with a passionate interest in global citizenship education for its ability to engage students in understanding issues of global justice, I had participated in the Irish Aid Our World awards since 2008. As part of one of these projects, we learned about Fairtrade and as a consequence of that we became a Fairtrade school in 2011. Following discussions with the students about how they might learn more about this issue, they suggested that we might look at the possibility of Fairtrade status being conferred on Clondalkin, our local town. While being somewhat awed by what I saw as their laudable ambition (or naiveté) we decided to investigate further. Their previous project had been entitled, 'A Better Future is in Our Hands' so it seemed that they really would emerge as true global citizens with a vested interest not only in their own futures but also in the futures of other global citizens.

First, we had to establish if the people of Clondalkin would be interested in having Fairtrade town status conferred. On a blustery Saturday morning in February 2013, we petitioned people at our local shopping centre to gauge the level of interest in this issue. We were overwhelmed by the support and managed to get more than 1,000 signatures in the course of the day. This was a testament to the persuasive powers of my fifth class (11-12 years) who managed to convince the citizens of Clondalkin that supporting Fairtrade was a good idea at local level as well as having an impact on farmers and workers in the Global South.

Buoyed up by optimism, our next mission was to have a motion passed by South Dublin County Council expressing their support for Clondalkin [becoming] a Fairtrade Town.

The students wrote to councillors, local TDs (Teachta Dála members of the Irish Parliament) and ministers and could not believe it when emails and letters were answered.

"I thought we were too small for people to listen to us!" This was what one of my students thought but when replies came, their confidence in their abilities grew.

The motion was duly passed. We had to set up a Fairtrade steering committee with students, teachers, parents and a local councillor. Students voted on who would best represent them on the committee and we also invited Councillor Francis Timmons (an independent councillor) to participate. Meetings were to be held monthly to discuss progress and possible other directions for the steering committee. Part of the process was to raise awareness of Fairtrade throughout the community of Clondalkin and to identify restaurants, cafes and shops who might be willing to support us. We also wanted to enlist the help and support of community groups.

A visit from our community guard, Sergeant Stephen Lydon revealed his willingness to persuade the Banghardaí (female members of the police force) and the gardai at his station to drink Fairtrade tea and coffee in their canteen. Our post office stationmaster, Stephen Coughlan, was hugely supportive in doing the same in the local post office. Clondalkin Tidy Towns also came on board and one of their members became a member of our steering committee.

We were invited to participate in local radio stations, Newstalk, Liffey Sound and WDAR (West Dublin Access Radio) and tell them about our campaign. Our story featured in our local paper, The Echo. We used a Facebook page 'Make Clondalkin a Fairtrade Town' to generate further interest and support. We ran competitions and raffles. As our support grew, we awarded hampers of Fairtrade goods to our supporters.

While this was going on in the community, we also organised awareness raising sessions among the pupils of our school. The fifth class students acted as peer educators for the younger classes Fairtrade telling them about Fairtrade products, the work of Fairtrade farmers and explained some of the processes involved in the production/trade of Fairtrade bananas, tea and chocolate. We organised bakery competitions, design a bookmark competition and Art competitions to spread the message of what we were trying to do.

At the Fairtrade Town and Supporters conference in Dublin Castle in 2013, two of my students ably represented Clondalkin as part of the campaign to become a Fairtrade town. The students networked with other representatives of towns all over Ireland and heard about creative ways in which they might further their cause.

As 2013 ended, we endeavoured to spread our message, advising people to buy Fairtrade goods for Christmas, trying to convince small businesses to buy Fairtrade goods where possible and continued our social media campaign.

In early 2014, we learned from Fairtrade Ireland that our campaign had been successful and that Clondalkin would become the 51st Fairtrade town in Ireland during Fairtrade Fortnight. We were to be conferred with this status on the 8th of March 2014, at a ceremony which would be attended by representatives of Fairtrade Ireland, two Fairtrade producers from Belize and Costa Rica, as well as the Lord Mayor of SDCC (South Dublin County Council), Dermot Looney, Minister Frances Fitzgerald, Councillors Francis Timmons, Kenneth Egan, parents and the entire school community.

We were presented with our certificate at a wonderful celebration filled with singing, drumming and cheers. It was an amazing day and we were so proud of our achievements.

Following this, we were invited by the Lord Mayor of SDCC, Dermot Looney to speak in the chamber of SDCC in Tallaght about our campaign. Fifth class students sat in the chamber and explained to the members of the council the motivation behind our campaign and how we had achieved Fairtrade status. This was a wonderful chance for the students to experience what it might be like to be a public representative.

The campaign to have Fairtrade status conferred on Clondalkin began in February 2013. The process, once initiated, took 12 months. Fairtrade Town status was conferred in 2014. As an active Fairtrade Town we raise awareness of Fairtrade, encourage businesses and schools in the town to promote/use Fairtrade products, speak to students from local primary and secondary schools and continue to attend Fairtrade Town and Supporters' Conferences.

Practical approaches to Fairtrade: establishing and maintaining partnerships

Our campaign to get Fairtrade status conferred on Clondalkin involved a range of activities. This included:

- A letter writing campaign with clear achievable results aimed at businesses and politicians involved in our local community
- Active student involvement
- Community involvement (inside the school and outside of the school)
- Petition/survey people in area/school to gauge interest
- Involve local councillor/minister/TD on board
- Inform Fairtrade Ireland of our plan/campaign
- Liaise with other Fairtrade schools/towns
- Use social media
- Inform local press
- Ask local banks/businesses for sponsorship (corporate social responsibility). They can be useful in providing prizes for events/activities during Fairtrade Fortnight
- Get involved in advocacy perhaps looking to get 100% Fairtrade bananas in local supermarkets, ask for Fairtrade spices to be provided in shops,
- Say 'thank you' to supermarkets on social media when they do sell Fairtrade products

Involving students in the design, delivery, and public engagement work of the project, included:

- Students feeling empowered
- Students acting as peer educators
- Students educating parents and family members
- Students developing confidence in engaging people
- Students developing skills and confidence in speaking on radio and to reporters

Successes and challenges of the campaign

- Clondalkin became the 51st Fairtrade Town in 2014. It is the only town in Ireland in which the campaign was led by primary school students.
- Students from primary schools continue to sit on Fairtrade Town Committee
- Students represent our school and our town at annual Fairtrade Towns and Supporters' Conferences
- Getting people interested and maintaining their interest
- Staying motivated can be challenging, beyond the 'fortnight' drive of Fairtrade Fortnight

One of the great aspects of Fairtrade Fortnight is meeting with farmers from Fairtrade co-operatives and listening to their stories, the impact and 'the power of you' can really be understood. It was very rewarding to welcome them into our communities.

For the past six years we have welcomed Fairtrade managers of co-operatives from Ghana, Costa Rica, Belize, Columbia, Grenada and Guatemala to our community. For the students who have been learning about Fairtrade and its impact on lives far away, this is a wonderful opportunity to share stories and make real connections with lived experiences.

For me, the most powerful statement came from one fifth class student involved in the campaign who said

Even though we are young, we can change the world.

We are currently campaigning to have Fairtrade status conferred on the whole of South Dublin County Council.

Table 20.6 Linking Fairtrade to other SDGs (Fairtrade, 2015)

Goal 1 : No poverty

Fairtrade seeks to ensure that farmers and workers make strong progress towards a living income and living wages

Goal 2: Zero hunger

Small-scale farmers continue to provide a large percentage of the world's population with food. Building robust livelihoods is crucial for achieving this goal. In addition, farmers and workers earning a dignified income or wage will be able to better provide for their own families.

(Continued)

Table 20.6 (Continued)

Goal 4: Quality education

Equitable access to training and informal education for adults and youth will increase future opportunities available to all. Fairtrade farmers and workers choose to spend a portion of their Fairtrade premium funds on children's education, while the three Fairtrade producer invest significantly in training and leaning opportunities for producers.

Goal 5: Gender equality

60–80% of the world's food is grown by women. However, this fact is not reflected in ownership of land or in the profits accrued from production. Fairtrade works to address this inequality through a number of initiatives which support women to participate equally in agriculture, earn better wages and diversify their income and opportunities.

Fairtrade standards are specifically designed to prevent gender inequality, increase female participation and empower women and girls to access the benefits of Fairtrade. This is achieved through increasing women's roles in Fairtrade producer organisations.

Fairtrade Women's School of Leadership is a year-long programme embedding ideas of human rights, personal development, entrepreneurship and financial management, which began in Latin America and is now being rolled out in Cote d'Ivoire.

Goal 8: Decent work and economic growth

Fairtrade, in line with the UN International Labour Organisation seeks to enable all workers to earn a decent wage for their work, to negotiate for better working conditions, to end forced and slave labour on Fairtrade plantations and to enable young people in conjunction with producer organisation, governments and communities to address the root causes of inequality.

Goal 9: Industry, innovation and infrastructure

Fairtrade standards and Fairtrade premiums ensure that farmers and workers can make decisions about investments in their communities and in their businesses. Fairtrade aims to ensure transparency in supply chains so that producers can make informed decisions about their businesses and develop sustainable relationships with their trade partners.

Goal 10: Reduced inequalities

Collective action and trade policies which will be beneficial for all farmers and workers are supported by Fairtrade. Living wage and living income strategies as well as Fairtrade prices and premiums provide pathways towards decent livelihoods for more people. Appropriate economic interventions and efforts will lead to gender equality, increased opportunities for young people and a reduction in discrimination

Goal 11: Sustainable cities and communities

Producer organisations are leaders and pillars of their communities. Fairtrade premiums are invested to improve infrastructure and services and to build resilience to offset the effects of climate change.

Goal 12: Responsible Consumption and Production

Fairtrade is considered the leading ethical label worldwide. Through campaigns and advocacy, thousands of communities and millions of citizens are brought together to demand social, economic and climate justice for all.

Goal 13: Climate action

Small scale farmers in the poorest areas of the world are feeling the devastating consequences of a changing climate. Fairtrade works with climate experts and producer organisations to build farmers' resilience to climate disasters and to employ environmentally sustainable practices.

Goal 15: Life on land

Fairtrade standards will reduce pressure on protected areas and forests and reduce loss of biodiversity.

Goal 17: Partnerships for the goals.

Fairtrade works with multiple partners; producer organisations, businesses, trade unions, civil society, governments and other multi-stakeholder bodies, to create new pathways towards realising the goals.

Case study 20.3 Transition Year (TY)

In Ireland, the Transition Year (TY) is a one year programme that forms the first year of a three year senior education cycle. Aimed at those in the 15-16 age group, TY has a strong focus on personal and social development and on education for active citizenship. While the vast majority of secondary schools offer a TY programme to their students, the programme is optional for students in most schools. Each school designs its own TY to suit the needs and interests of its students. The programme offers opportunities for schools and students to form long term and robust partnerships with the local community through work placements, volunteering opportunities and project work. The introduction of this programme represented a radical change to curriculum practice in Ireland with its focus on 'holistic, student-centred, active learning view of schooling' (Jeffers, 2011: 70). While collaboration on SDG issues can prove challenging for schools in the context of timetables and exam pressures, TY offers a unique opportunity for schools, students and the community to work together to address local issues. Each TY student has an opportunity to complete work placements in different business, cultural or voluntary settings. In the literature 'situated learning' or 'service learning' refers to learning in collaboration with local people in the community. Billing and Furco (2002: 23) define 'service learning' as

> Experiential pedagogy in which education is delivered by engaging students in community service that is integrated with an organised school curriculum. Service learning is premised on providing students with contextualised learning experiences that are based on authentic, real-time situations in their communities.

This kind of service learning can emerge from creative collaborations between schools and community partners. As discussed in Chapter 2 transformative education is required to address the challenges set out by the SDGs. Involving students in real life community issues is an excellent way for students to engage with the SDGs in a local setting. Through locally based school community partnerships, schools gain a practical laboratory for their projects and enquiry based learning whereas for local communities, the enthusiasm of young people is unleashed, a resource which will inevitably assist communities in the short and long term.

Kinsale Community College (which is discussed in greater detail in Case study 20.5) offers a dynamic and innovative TY programme. Students participate in a range of community based, national and international projects with a range of partners. Students from Kinsale Community College also won awards for their project 'Kinsale Cookbook' (Figure 20.3). Based on a collaboration with local food suppliers, the students created a cookery book with many locally sourced recipes. This project served to highlight the impact of food miles on our environment. This book is on sale locally for €10 with the proceeds being donated to the Irish Seed Savers Association.

Junk Kouture was created in 2010 by entrepreneurs Elizabeth Curran and Troy Armour to encourage students to create art from pieces of rubbish. Based on a

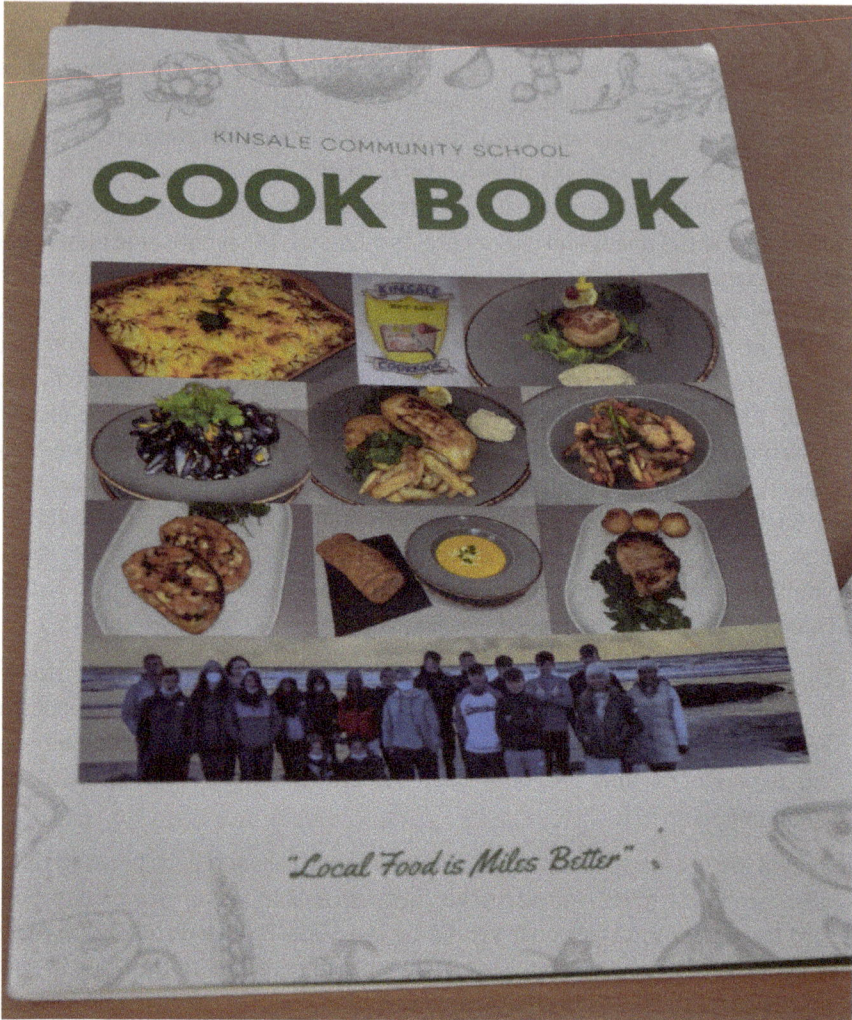

Figure 20.3 Kinsale Cook Book

simple, innovative idea, Junk Kouture encourages young designers in second level education to create striking couture designs and impressive works of wearable art from everyday junk that would normally find its way into the bin. This competition aims to inspire and ignite passion while at the same time educating people about the importance of recycling and reusing waste. But the platform is more than a design

Figure 20.4 Examples of Junk Kouture from kinsale Community School.

competition: it's a way to engage today's youth in climate action, to change the way we look at fashion and waste, and to come up with creative solutions to tackle the climate crisis. Junk Kouture is a popular TY project in many schools. At a time when the whole world seems hell-bent on disposal, the pioneering souls behind Junk Kouture are doing the opposite. The now global youth sustainability fashion competition challenges young people to design, create and model high end couture from everyday junk.

TY students are invited to create wearable art and outrageous couture trash fashion. The challenge is to rework 'junk' milk cartons, plastic bottles, orange peels and old CDs crafting them into eye-catching bespoke designs. Using only recycled materials, students embark on a nine-month programme of innovation and creation, with the grand hope of qualifying for a spot on the Junk Kouture stage.

In Ireland, where the competition started, over half of the secondary schools in the country including students from Kinsale Community College take part in the contests, which has become an everyday part of school life. TY students from Kinsale found that after participating in this competition (Figure 20.4) they had acquired new skills such as sewing and mending clothes. In line with SDG 12 (discussed in Chapter 15) the students also learnt about fast fashion and its impact on the environment. Through this initiative students also learn about the circular economy discussed in chapters 11 (SDG 9) and 15 (SDG 12).

Case study 20.4 St. Augustine's National School Clontuskert, Galway

https://clontuskert.scoilnet.ie/blog/

St. Augustine's National School (NS), a small three teacher primary school is located in a rural community in East Galway, Ireland. Although small in size its impact in national and international sustainability projects has been outstanding. St. Augustine's NS has a very active Parents' Association and Board of Management and has forged strong links with the local community. The school holds seven Green Flags for Waste Management, Energy Conservation, Water Conservation as well as Travel and Biodiversity. It holds seventeen Discover Primary Science and Mathematics Excellence Awards and has been awarded the British Science Council Crest Award for participation in the FIRST LEGO® League. Teaching and learning approaches are innovative and transformative with students being active collaborators in the learning process.

St. Augustine's National School, is the first Climate Action School of Excellence in Ireland and in 2022 it was accepted as an international Climate Action School. 3.4 million students across 148 countries joined the international Climate Action Project (https://climate-action.info/). In the past six years of involvement in this international project, St. Augustine's NS has been a leading ambassador and collaborator. The students have lobbied for and achieved national change with the Irish waste management system and the use of recycling symbols (discussed in Chapter 15). Students even received a letter from President Michael D. Higgins praising their commitment to Climate Action.

In 2022, students worked on the *Fierce Close* podcast with CURO (short for curiosity) University of Galway, Galway Library Services and Galway Based Company Soundtrack and Podcast to become critical thinkers and activists on Climate Change. The project takes its title from an Irish idiom for a humid day (*Fierce Close)*, one where a storm is imminent. Through sessions that build their philosophical skills through a creative outcome that can be shared with their communities, this project gives voice to young people's perspectives on climate change while building their critical thinking skills and debating literacy. The students were supported by professional philosophers to create and perform new monologues through skills-building workshops and guidance in podcast creation from the company Soundtrack and Podcast. This project responds to the scale of change expected in Galway City Council's Climate Strategy by allowing young people to meaningfully explore possible solutions together.

Both Kinsale Community School, Cork (Case study 20.5) and St Augustine's National School Clontuskert, Ballinasloe, Co Galway were inaugural winners of the Schools Sustainability Project in 2022, an SSE (Scottish and Southern Energy) Airtricity and Microsoft Ireland initiative which aims to create awareness among primary and post-primary students about renewable energy, sustainability and biodiversity, and technology and innovation. The Schools Sustainability Project competition is the most recent project SSE Airtricity and Microsoft Ireland have partnered on as part of their Solar for Schools programme. Launched in 2020, the renewable energy programme enables schools to power classrooms using energy generated from their own roof, helping them to reduce their carbon footprint, and their energy costs. A key objective of the partnership is to show students first-hand how they can play a part in combatting climate change.

Case study 20.5 Kinsale Community College, Cork https://www.kinsalecommunityschool.ie/

Located in West Cork Kinsale Community School a large post primary school, is an integral part of the Kinsale 'brand' and of its wider community. Sustainability in general and the SDGs in particular are central to the school's ethos. Sustainable development themes are now part and parcel of every subject right across the curriculum. The school has an active green school team which pioneers several innovate student-led projects. Before the annual international climate change COP Conference of the Parties, the school hosts ten local primary schools to share their knowledge and school based environmental actions.

Through numerous partnerships with local, national and international agencies, the school has enjoyed incredible success in its mission for sustainability. For their award winning Schools Sustainability Project in 2022, students undertook a *Save the Bees* initiative, planting a biodiversity orchard and a hedge row in their school to provide food for bees and other pollinators, and fruit for birds. They also provided local organic food for the school's Home Economics department and raised awareness of the importance of biodiversity and the climate crisis within and beyond the school community.

The school has appointed a Sustainability Chaplain whose role is to teach sustainability and to promote a whole school ethos of sustainability through engagement with students, teachers, parents and the Board of Management. The role also entails facilitating a Sustainability Advisory Board which will steer the school towards reducing its overall carbon footprint, teaching students about organic food growing in the newly constructed greenhouse and planting hedgerows as wildlife corridors and wild flower patches for pollinators around the school campus. This integrated approach to sustainability is detailed in the school's green map (Figure 20.5). The Sustainability Chaplain liaises with members of staff to visit their classes and give talks on best sustainable practices and what changes can be made to the school's our carbon footprint. Links to local community groups such as Transition Town Kinsale and Kinsale Tidy Towns are also organised. This new role is ground breaking for a post primary school and it could be seen as a very positive and important step in the direction towards having sustainability as a core subject at all levels of post primary education.

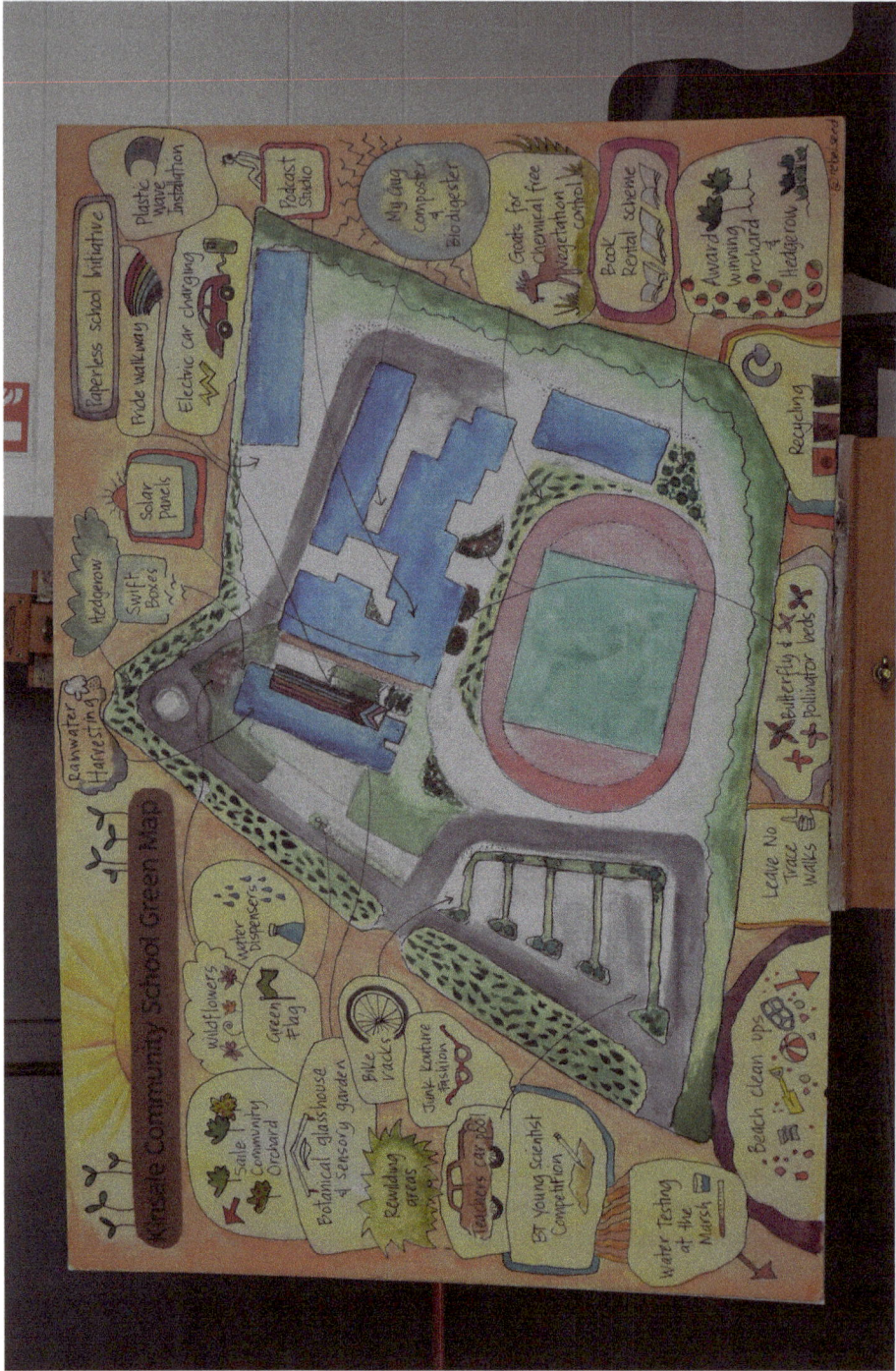

Figure 20.5 Kinsale Community School's Green Map.

Figure 20.6 Collaboration and Partnerships for Sustainability-Connections Beyond the Classroom.

Kinsale Community School hosted a two-day EU Council of Ministries Conference in collaboration with the Department of Education aimed at exploring Sustainable Education Strategies. The event, held on May 3rd and 4th, 2023 brought together educationalists and representatives from 13 different countries, as part of the European Education Area Strategic Framework, to discuss the need for collaboration across educational systems within Europe to address issues relating to sustainability, climate change, and biodiversity.

The highlight of the event was a panel discussion with students from Kinsale Community School, who shared their experiences in the Young Scientist Exhibition, Young Environmentalist, and Young Social Innovators programs. Fergal McCarthy, School Principal of Kinsale Community School and Vice President of the European Federation of Education Employers, said, *"this was a wonderful opportunity for our students to be given active agency in respect of a global concern which is very real and very urgent."* He commended the students for keeping these issues at the top of the agenda.

During the conference, visitors had the opportunity to witness first hand Kinsale Community School's commitment to sustainability through their various sustainable practices such as solar panels for energy generation, water harvesting for conservation, and the creation of an outdoor learning space where students cultivate plants and food. They also had a chance to see the MyGug, a locally produced invention that produces biogas for the Home Economics room and fertiliser from food waste generated in the school canteen and staffroom.

The Department of Education's conference held at Kinsale Community School marked a significant milestone in addressing the challenges posed by climate change, biodiversity loss, and sustainability, highlighting the vital role of education in creating a sustainable future. The school's unwavering commitment to sustainable practices through fostering a positive learning environment for students was evident throughout the event and served as a source of inspiration for educators and communities across Europe. The conference was a resounding success, emphasising the importance of Education for Sustainability and the need for collaborative partnerships to achieve a sustainable future. A record of this historic event is available in Figure 20.6. Through showcasing innovative and sustainable practices, Kinsale Community School is clearly a leader in sustainable education practices in Europe, emphasising the need for connections beyond the classroom.

Partnerships for transformation

In 2021, on the occasion of the seventy-fifth anniversary of the United Nations, Member States agreed that our challenges are interconnected, across borders and all other divides. These challenges can only be addressed by an equally interconnected response, through reinvigorated multilateralism with the United Nations at the centre of our efforts. The Secretary-General responded with Our Common Agenda (UN, 2021), calling for solidarity between people, countries and generations, and a corresponding renewal of the multilateral system to accelerate implementation of existing commitments and fill gaps in global governance that have emerged since 2015. The proposals in Our Common Agenda aim to turbocharge the 2030 Agenda including a proposal for a *Summit of the Future* as a once-in-a-generation opportunity to take these steps. During this summit Member States will consider ways to lay the foundations for more effective global cooperation and partnerships that can deal with today's challenges as well as new threats in the future.

Partnership is a core element of the SDGs and the Agenda 2030 programme. Partnerships can occur: on a micro level within and between schools; on a meso level between education institutions and community based or sectoral organisations (as described in case studies 20.1 and 20.2); and on a macro level between national and international institutes and organisations.

As demonstrated in the case studies above, schools have a vital role to play through local collaborations. While the first step is often taken by an innovative teacher or an inspirational school leader, support is needed for all partners engaged in this process. The partnerships described in the case studies are long term, robust and firmly supported by local and professional communities.

This book proposes a transformative approach to education based on the Four Hs: Head, Heart, Hands and Hope, built upon a pedagogy of hope respect, empathy and action as follows:

> A pedagogy of hope (A holistic framework for teaching and learning: Hope)
> A pedagogy of respect and understanding (Cognitive Learning: Head): Teaching *about* the Goals
> A pedagogy of empathy and love (Socio-emotional learning: Heart): Teaching *for* the Goals
> A pedagogy of advocacy and action (Behavioural Learning: Hands) Teaching *through* the goals

Within this framework the three interrelated dimensions of learning: the cognitive; social and emotional; and behavioural are seen as essential and interlinked components of Education for Sustainable Development and Global Citizenship Education (UNESCO, 2019).

Each chapter addresses aspects of this transformative pedagogy. Given the nature of the challenges facing our world today it is imperative for educators *to teach about, for and through* the SDGs. Working in partnerships within and beyond schools will provide opportunities for student agency, 'real life learning' and experiences of success, impact and hope.

Powerful pedagogies outlined in this book take learning outside the classroom and allow students to become designers and innovators of change. Children's literature listed at the end of every chapter provide useful entry points for students of all ages and abilities. The padlet which accompanies this book includes multiples resources, stories and activities for teachers. Sample planning templates for action are provided in Figure 2.4 (Chapter 2) and in Figure 20.7. Rather than feeling overwhelmed and powerless in light of the challenges facing the world today, take the first step: adopt a pedagogy of hope, teach about for and through the SDGs and see what happens. Together we can shape our future world.

Figure 20.7 Addressing the SDGs: A Framework for Action. (Source: Worldwise Global Schools).

Conclusion

At the midway point of the 2030 Agenda, the Sustainable Development Goals are significantly off-track worldwide. This is in partly due to the combined impacts of COVID-19, global instability and conflict, including wars in Ukraine and the Middle East, all in the context of the interlinked crises of climate change and biodiversity loss. Every SDG has been affected: the eradication of poverty has slowed significantly; food security is under immense pressure; the pandemic has set back health and education; and there is evidence of a pushback against gender equality. To put the world on a pathway to a sustainable present and future, a fundamental shift is required in commitment, solidarity, financing and action. As UN Secretary, Antonio Guterres (UN, 2023:2), put it, unless we act now, the 2030 Agenda could become an epitaph for a world that might have been.' However, it is important to remember that global problems can only be solved through collective action. For instance, there is enormous potential for net-zero initiatives that restore nature and improve the lives of people and communities. Although the task ahead is daunting, it is not impossible. While the challenges facing our world today are serious, there are multiple examples of action and advocacy which are making a difference. The multiple global crises facing our world today were caused by humanity and can be solved by humanity. Even though Agenda 2030 is not perfect, the SDGs goals are a much needed reminder that international cooperation and consensus is possible.

The principles of partnership, collaboration and co-operation are at the heart of the Goals. A partnership can be as small as two people working together or as large as a UN multilateral agreement. Goal 17 states explicitly that global partnership for sustainable development must be strengthened and revitalised. While this chapter highlights the example of Fairtrade as a fulcrum for teaching SDG 17, the same approaches can be applied to all SDG topics and themes. The approach to education advocated in this book recognises that the goals of global citizenship and sustainable development education overlap and converge over many issues and in their methodologies. As discussed in Chapters 1 and 2 conventional approaches to teaching and learning are not sufficient to meet the socio-environmental challenges of our time. Moving towards a more sustainable world will require that we relinquish some of our traditional approaches and ways of living. We need to seek out ways of teaching and learning which allow us to re-establish meaningful relationships with people and place, ultimately leading to the wisdom we need for living more fulfilling, sustainable and responsible lives. There are many fabulous examples of transformative learning for sustainability occurring in our schools. This book aims to share this practice and to inspire all teachers to teach about for and through the SDGs.

Resources

An extensive list of resources, videos and case studies for SDG 17 is included in the SDG padlet accompanying this book: https://padlet.com/annedolan/o6rds38zylfy6a28h

Further resources for teachers

Christian Aid: The Trading Game: https://www.christianaid.org.uk/sites/default/files/2017-08/trading-game-intro-to-the-game.pdf

Fairtrade Institute: https://www.fairtrade-institute.org/resources/
Fairtrade Ireland: https://www.fairtrade.ie/
Fairtrade schools (Ireland) https://www.fairtrade.ie/get-involved/fairtrade-schools/
Fairtrade UK https://www.fairtrade.org.uk/Buying-Fairtrade/
Fairtrade schools (UK) https://schools.fairtrade.org.uk/
Oxfam https://www.oxfamfairtrade.be/en/
Oxfam: Find your way through trade: Learn about food and global trade (a resource for 7–11 year olds): https://policy-practice.oxfam.org/resources/find-your-way-through-trade-learn-about-food-and-global-trade-620724/
Oxfam: Explore Fairtrade: help learners explore the need for a fairer global food system (a resource for 8–15 year olds). https://policy-practice.oxfam.org/resources/explore-fairtrade-help-learners-explore-the-need-for-a-fairer-global-food-syste-620719/
Sustainable Learning: https://www.sustainablelearning.com/resource/fairtrade-resources
Resources from multiple organisations: https://schools.fairtrade.org.uk/teaching-resources/resources-from-other-organisations/

Videos

What is Fairtrade: Made by Fairtrade Ireland: https://www.youtube.com/watch?v=g8LC3PJ-7r4&t=18s
The Fairtrade Story: https://www.youtube.com/watch?v=o6pcJxFen8Y
The difference that Fairtrade makes: informative case studies: https://www.youtube.com/watch?v=yKfvCJj4B5o
A visit to a banana plantation: https://www.youtube.com/watch?v=vOYXIOxmUGw&t=11s
Chocolate: the bitter truth. Child labour and the chocolate trade. BBC Panorama: https://www.dailymotion.com/video/x2mo7g4

Other useful websites

Irish Schools Sustainability Network (ISSN) https://www.issn.ie/what-we-do
Worldwise Global Schools' Programme: https://www.worldwiseschools.ie/
Global Village: https://globalvillageschools.ie/

Children's literature

Picturebooks

Ahmadi, A. and Abdollahi, E. (illus) (2015) *When I Coloured in the World* Tiny Owl Publishing Ltd.
Allepuz, A. (2019) *That Fruit Is Mine* Walker Books.
Amnesty International Lennon, J., Lennon, O. and Jullien, J. (illus) (2017) *Imagine* Francis Lincoln Publishers.
Anthony, S. (2020) *Green Lizards vs Red Rectangles and the Blue Ball* Hodder Children's Books.
Barasch, L. (2013) *First Came the Zebra* Lee & Low Books.
Beer, S. (2021) *Change Starts With Us* Caterpillar Books.
Belloni, G. and Trevisan, M. (2013) *Anything Is Possible* Owlkids.
Berrebi, D. Warsame, H. Bidnyak, D. (illus) and Hong, R. (illus) (2023) *Ally and Bibi: Back to the Jungle: A Story about the Sustainable Development Goals*. Independently Published.
Blake, Q. (2020) *The Weed* Tate Publishing.
Cronin, D. and Lewin, B. (illus) (2000) *Click Clack Moo Cows That Type* Atheneum Books for Young Readers.
Durango, J. and Diaz, B. (illus) (2017) *The One Day House* Charlesbridge.
Fan, T., Fan, E. and Fan, D. (2020) *The Barnabus Project* Tundra Books.
Gaines, J. and Swaney, J. (2020) *The World Needs Who You Were Made To Be* Thomas Nelson Gift Books.

Garcia, G. and Jimenez Osorio, N. (illus) (2022) *We Are All Connected: Taking Care of Each Other and the Earth* Skinned Knee Publishing.

Gorman, A. and Long, L. (illus) (2021) *Change Sings: A Children's Anthem* Viking Books.

Harris, M. and Ramírez González, A. (illus) (2020) *Kamala and Maya's Big Idea* Balzer + Bray.

Illustrajo, M. (2022) *Flooded* Frances Lincoln Children's Books.

Jones, N. and Jones, J. (illus) (2021) *The Perfect Fit* Oxford, OUP.

Kelsey, E. and Kim, S. (illus) *You Are Stardust: Our Amazing Connections with Planet* Earth Wayland.

Muth, J.J. (2003) *Stone Soup* Scholastic Press.

Orenstein-Cardona, A. and Moreno, J.M (illus) (2022) *The Tree of Hope: The Miraculous Rescue of Puerto Rico's Beloved Banyan* Beaming Books.

Otter, I. and Robin, C. (illus) (2019) *Together Animal Partnerships in the Wild* Caterpillar Books

Otter, I. and Anganuzzi, C. (illus) (2020) *Dear Earth* Caterpillar Books.

Quattrone, D. and Agnite, A. (illus) (2020) *In The Year 2020* Independently published.

Rex, A. and Park, L. (illus) (2020) *Unstopppable* Chronicle Books.

Shevah, E. (2021) *How to Save the World with a Chicken and an Egg* Chicken House.

Sinek, S. (2016) *Together Is Better: A Little Book of Inspiration* Portfolio Penguin.

Singh, R. and Ferrer, M. (illus) (2020) *111 Trees: How One Village Celebrates the Birth of Every Girl* Kids Can Press.

Tillman, N. (2017) *You're Here for a Reason* Feiwel & Friends.

Tillman, N. (2018) *You and Me and the Wishing Tree* Feiwel & Friends.

Timmers, L. (2022) *Elephant Island* Gecko Press.

Van Dongen, S. (2021) *The Neighbourhood Surprise* Tiny Owl Publishing Ltd.

Wheeler, L. and Long, L (illus) (2021) *Someone Builds the Dream* Crown Books for Young Readers.

Zandere, I. and Petraškevi, J. (illus) *One House For All* (2017) Book Island

Informational picturebooks and chapter books

Bauer, S.C. and Ntamack, E. (illus) (2022) Champions for Change Hop Off the Press, LLC.

Bauer, S.C. and Ntamack, E. (illus) (2022) Dream Chasers Hop Off the Press, LLC.

Bauer, S.C. and Ntamack, E. (illus) (2022) Inspiring OthersHop Off the Press, LLC.

Bauer, S.C. and Ntamack, E. (illus) (2021) Making a Difference Hop Off the Press, LLC.

Bauer, S.C. and Ntamack, E. (illus) (2021) Compassionate Kids Hop Off the Press, LLC.

Castillo, L. (2020) *Our Friend Hedgehog: The Story of Us* Knopf Books for Young Readers.

Ganeri, A. (2013) *Chocolate from Bean to Bar* Collins Educational.

Hess, I. (2010) *Think Fair Trade First* Global Gifts Inc.

Powell, J. (2014). *Fairtrade* Wayland; UK Collins Educational. Edition.

Raúf, O.Q. (2020) *The Night Bus Hero* Orion Children's Books.

Salyer, H. (2020) *Packs: Strength in Numbers* Clarion Books.

Schiller, R, and Beer, S. (illus) (2022) *Amazing Activists Who Are Changing Our World* Walker Books.

Shapiro, N. and Morgan, P. (2022) *An ABC of Democracy* Frances Lincoln.

Sirdeshpande, R. and Hayes, A. (IllIus) (2021) Good News: Why the World is Not as Bad as You Think Wren & Rook.

Sirdeshpande, R. and Tempest, A. (illus) (2021) *How To Change The World* Puffin.

Sirdeshpande, R. and Tempest, A. (illus) (2019) *How To Be Extraordinary* Puffin.

Sperring, M. and Quek, N, (illus) (2023) *If I Were the World* Bloomsbury Children's Books.

Spilsbury, L. (2020) *17 Ways to Save The World* Franklin Watts.

Stewart-Sharpe, L. and Hill, L. (2021) *What a Wonderful World: Be Inspired to Care For Our Planet With 35 Real-Life Stories and Green Tips* Templar Publishing.

Soontornvat, C. (2020) *All Thirteen: The Incredible Cave Rescue of the Thai Boys' Soccer Team* Candlewick.

Weintraub, A. and Hortonm L. (illus) (2018) *Never Too Young! 50 Unstoppable Kids Who Made a Difference* Sterling Children's Books.

Winfield Martin, E. *The Wonderful Things You Will Be* Puffin.

Children's literature about community gardens is listed in Chapter 14.

References

Bailey, F. and Dolan, A (2011) 'The meaning of partnership in development: Lessons in development education', *Policy and Practice: A Development Education Review*, 13, Autumn, 30-48.

Berrone, P., Ricart, J.E., Duch, A.I., Bernardo, V., Salvador, J., Piedra Peña, J. and Rodríguez Planas, M. (2019) 'EASIER: An evaluation model for public-private partnerships contributing to the sustainable development goals', *Sustainability*, 11(8), 2339.

Crawford, G. (2003) 'Partnership or power? Deconstructing the "partnership for governance reform" in Indonesia', *Third World Quarterly*, 24(1), 139-159.

Dochas (2010) *Partnership in Practice; A Kenyan Perspective on the Nature of Relationships with Irish NGOs*. Dublin: Dochas. Available: http://www.dochas.ie/Shared/Files/4/Partnership_in_Practice_Dochas_Kenya_research_report.pdf.

Fairtrade. (2015) *Sustainable Development Goals and Fairtrade: The Case for Partnership*. Available: https://www.fairtrade.ie/wp-content/uploads/2015/01/15-10_Sustainable_Development_Report.pdf

Fowler, A. (2000) 'Beyond partnership: Getting real about NGO relationships in the aid system', *IDS Bulletin*, 31(3), 1-13.

Furco, A. and Billig, S.H. eds. (2002) *Service Learning: The Essence of the Pedagogy*. Bristol: IAP.

Gallwey, S. (2009) 'Teaching about fairtrade', *Policy and Practice: A Development Education Review*, 9, Autumn, 59-66.

Government of Ireland/Department of Rural and Community Development. (2019a) *Sustainable, Inclusive and Empowered Communities: A Five- Year Strategy to Support the Community and Voluntary Sector in Ireland 2019-2024*. Available: https:// www.gov.ie/en/publication/d8fa3a-sustainableinclusive- and-empowered-communities-a-fiveyear-strategy/

Government of Ireland/Department of Rural and Community Development. (2019b) *Values and Principles for Collaboration and Partnership: Working with the Community and Voluntary Sector*. Available: https://www.gov.ie/en/publication/d4445-values-and-principles-for-collaboration-and-partnership-working/

Harvard Family Research Project. (2010) *Partnerships for Learning: Promising Practices in Integrating School and Out-of-School Time Program Supports*. Available: http://www.hfrp.org/publications-resources/browse-our-publications/partn...

IDEA (Irish Development Education Association). (nd) *Stronger Together: A Toolkit for Partnerships in and Beyond Development Education*. Available: https://irp-cdn.multiscreensite.com/9e15ba29/files/uploaded/IDEA_Working_in_Partnership_Toolkit.pdf

Jeffers, G. (2011) 'The transition year programme in Ireland. Embracing and resisting a curriculum innovation', *The Curriculum Journal*, 22(1), 61-76.

Mohiddin, A. (1998) 'Partnership: A new buzz-word or realistic relationship?' *Development*, 41(4), 5-12.

Nakabugo, M., Barrett, E., McEvoy, P. and Munck, R. (2010) 'Best practice in North-South research relationships in higher education: The Irish African partnership model', *Policy & Practice: A Development Education Review*, 10, Spring, 89-98.

Shaw, E. (2018) 'School-community partnerships: A vehicle for student success in an evolving world', *Journal of Initial Teacher Inquiry*, 4, 21-25.

Stott, L. and Murphy, D.F. (2020) 'An inclusive approach to partnerships for the SDGs: Using a relationship lens to explore the potential for transformational collaboration', *Sustainability*, 12(19), 7905.

UN, 2023 *The Sustainable Development Goals Report 2023: Special Edition. Towards a Rescue Plan for People and Planet*. https://unstats.un.org/sdgs/report/2023/

UN, (2021) Our Common Agenda Report of the Secretary General https://www.un.org/en/common-agenda

United Nations (UN). (2015) 'Sustainable development goals', available: https://www.un.org/sustainabledevelopment/sustainable-development-goals/(accessed 10 October 2021).

Wanni, N., Hinz, A. and Day, R. (2010) *Good Practices in Educational Partnerships Guide: UK-Africa Higher and Further Education Partnerships*, The Africa Unit, UK/Africa Partnerships in HE/FE. Available: http://www.hea.ie/files/Good_Practice_Guide-1.pdf

Appendix 1

Targets for the sustainable development goals

The 17 Sustainable Development Goals are defined in a list of 169 SDG Targets. Progress towards these Targets is agreed to be tracked by 232 unique Indicators. A full list of targets and indicators is available on the SDG Tracker website: (https://sdg-tracker.org/). The SDG Tracker presents data across all available indicators from the Our World in Data database, using official statistics from the UN and other international organizations. It is a free, open-access publication that tracks global progress towards the SDGs and allows people around the world to hold their governments accountable to achieving the agreed goals.

Goal 1: End poverty in all its forms everywhere

1.1   Eradicate extreme poverty
1.2   Reduce poverty by at least 50%
1.3   Implement nationally appropriate social protection systems
1.4   Equal rights to ownership, basic services, technology and economic resources
1.5   Build resilience to environmental, economic and social disasters
1.a   Mobilization of resources to end poverty
1.b   Establishment of poverty eradication policy frameworks at all levels

Goal 2: Zero hunger

2.1   Universal access to safe and nutritious food
2.2   End all forms of malnutrition
2.3   Double the productivity and incomes of small-scale food producers
2.4   Sustainable food production and resilient agricultural practices
2.5   Maintain the genetic diversity in food production
2.a   Invest in rural infrastructure, agricultural research, technology and gene banks
2.b   Prevent agricultural trade restrictions, market distortions and export subsidies
2.c   Ensure stable food commodity markets and timely access to information

Appendix 1

Goal 3: health and well-being

3.1 Reduce maternal mortality
3.2 End all preventable deaths under age five
3.3 End the epidemics associated with communicable diseases
3.4 Reduce mortality from non-communicable diseases and promote mental health
3.5 Prevent and treat substance abuse
3.6 Reduce road injuries and deaths
3.7 Ensure universal access to sexual and reproductive health-care services
3.8 Achieve universal health coverage
3.9 Reduce the number of deaths from hazardous chemicals and pollution
3.a Strengthen the implementation of WHO framework on tobacco control
3.b Support research and development and universal access to affordable vaccines and medicines
3.c Substantially increase health financing and the recruitment of the health workforce in developing countries
3.d Strengthen early warning systems for global health risks

Goal 4: quality education

4.1 Free primary and secondary education
4.2 Equal access to quality pre-primary education
4.3 Equal access to affordable technical, vocational and higher education
4.4 Increase the number of people with relevant skills for financial success
4.5 Eliminate all discrimination in education
4.6 Universal literacy and numeracy
4.7 Education for sustainable development and global citizenship
4a Build and upgrade inclusive and safe schools
4b Expand higher education scholarships for developing countries
4c Increase the supply of qualified teachers in developing countries

Goal 5: gender equality

5.1 End discrimination against women and girls
5.2 End all violence against and exploitation of women and girls
5.3 Eliminate forced marriages and genital mutilation
5.4 Value unpaid care and promote shared domestic responsibilities
5.5 Ensure full participation in leadership and decision making
5.6 Universal access to reproductive rights and health
5a Equal rights to economic resources, property ownership and financial services
5b Promote empowerment of women through technology
5c Adopt and strengthen policies and enforceable legislation for gender equality

Goal 6: clean water and sanitation

6.1 Safe and affordable drinking water
6.2 End open defecation and provide access to sanitation and hygiene
6.3 Improve water quality, wastewater treatment and safe reuse
6.4 Increase water-use efficiency and ensure freshwater supplies
6.5 Ensure full participation in leadership and decision making
6.6 Implement integrated water resource management at all levels
6a Expand water and sanitation support to developing countries
6b Support local engagement in water and sanitation management

Goal 7: affordable and clean energy

7.1 Universal access to modern energy
7.2 Increase global percentage of renewable energy
7.3 Double the improvement in energy efficiency
7a Promote access to research, technology and investments in clean energy
7b Expand and upgrade energy services for developing countries

Goal 8: decent work and economic growth

8.1 Sustainable economic growth
8.2 Diversify, innovate and upgrade for economic productivity
8.3 Promote policies to support job creation and growing enterprises
8.4 Improve resource efficiency in consumption and production
8.5 Full employment and decent work with equal pay
8.6 Promote youth employment, education and training
8.7 End modern slavery, trafficking and child labour
8.8 Protect labour rights and promote safe working environments
8.9 Promote beneficial and sustainable tourism
8.10 Universal access to banking, insurance and financial services
8a Increase aid for trade support

Goal 9: industry, innovation and infrastructure

9.1 Develop sustainable, resilient and inclusive infrastructures
9.2 Promote inclusive and sustainable industrialization
9.3 Increase access to financial services and markets
9.4 Upgrade all industries and infrastructure for sustainability
9.5 Enhance research and upgrade industrial technologies
9 a Facilitate sustainable infrastructure development and industrial diversification
9.b Support domestic technology development and industrial diversification
9.c Universal access to information and communications technology

Goal 10: reduced inequalities

10.1 Reduce income inequalities
10.2 Promote universal social, economic and political inclusion
10.3 Ensure equal opportunities and end discrimination
10.4 Adapt fiscal and social policies that promotes equality
10.5 Improved regulation of global financial markets and institutions
10.6 Enhanced representation for developing countries in financial institutions
10.7 Responsible and well-managed migration policies
10a Special and differential treatment for developing countries
10b Encourage development assistance and investment in least developed countries
10c Reduce transaction costs for migrant remittances

Goal 11: sustainable cities and communities

11.1 Safe and affordable housing
11.2 Affordable and sustainable transport systems
11.3 Inclusive and sustainable urbanization
11.4 Protect the world's cultural and natural heritage
11.5 Reduce the adverse effects of natural disasters
11.6 Reduce the environmental impacts of cities
11.7 Provide access to safe and inclusive green and public spaces
11a Strong national and regional development planning
11b Implement policies for inclusion, resource efficiency and disaster risk reduction

Goal 12: responsible consumption and production

12.1 Implement the ten year sustainable consumption and production framework
12.2 Sustainable management and use of natural resources
12.3 Halve global per capita food waste
12.4 Responsible managements of chemicals and waste
12.5 Substantially reduce waste generation
12.6 Encourage companies to adopt sustainable practices and sustainability reporting
12.7 Promote sustainable public procurement practices
12.8 Promote universal understanding of sustainable lifestyles
12a Support developing countries' scientific and technological capacity for sustainable con-sumption and production
12b Develop and implement tools to monitor sustainable tourism
12c Remove market distortions that encourage wasteful consumption

Goal 13: climate action

13.1 Strengthen resilience and adaptive capacity to climate-related disasters
13.2 Integrate climate change measures into policy and planning
13.3 Build knowledge and capacity to meet climate change

13a Implement the UN Framework Convention on Climate Change
13b Promote mechanisms to raise capacity for planning and management

Goal 14: sustainable cities and communities

14.1 Reduce marine pollution
14.2 Protect and restore ecosystems
14.3 Reduce ocean acidification
14.4 Sustainable fishing
14.5 Conserve coastal and marine areas
14.6 End subsidies contributing to overfishing
14.7 Increase the economic benefits from sustainable use of marine resources
14a   Increase scientific knowledge, research and technology for ocean health
14b   Support small scale fishers
14c   Implement and enforce international sea law

Goal 15: sustainable cities and communities

15.1 Conserve and restore terrestrial and freshwater ecosystems
15.2 End deforestation and restore degraded forests
15.3 End desertification and restore degraded land
15.4 Ensure conservation of mountain ecosystems
15.5 Protect biodiversity and natural habitats
15.6 Promote access to genetic resources and fair sharing of the benefits
15.7 Eliminate poaching and trafficking of protected species
15.8 Prevent invasive alien species on land and in water ecosystems
15.9 Integrate ecosystem and biodiversity in governmental planning
15a   Increase financial resources to conserve and sustainably use ecosystem and biodiversity
15b   Finance and incentivize sustainable forest management
15c   Combat global poaching and trafficking

Goal 16:

16.1 Reduce violence everywhere
16.2 Protect children from abuse, exploitation, trafficking and violence
16.3 Promote the rule of law and ensure equal access to justice
16.4 Combat organized crime and illicit financial and arms flows
16.5 Substantially reduce corruption and bribery
16.6 Develop effective, accountable and transparent institutions
16.7 Ensure responsive, inclusive and representative decision-making
16.8 Strengthen the participation in global governance
16.9 Provide universal legal identity
16.10 Ensure public access to information and protect fundamental freedoms
16a   Strengthen national institutions to prevent violence and combat crime and terrorism
16b   Promote and enforce non-discriminatory laws and policies

Appendix 1

Goal 17 partnerships for the goals

17.1   Mobilize resources to improve domestic revenue collection
17.2   Implement all development assistance commitments
17.3   Mobilize financial resources for developing countries
17.4   Assist developing countries in attaining debt sustainability
17.5   Invest in least-developed countries
17.6   Knowledge sharing and co-operation for access to science, technology and innovation
17.7   Promote sustainable technologies to developing countries
17.8   Strengthen the science, technology and innovation capacity for least developed countries
17.9   Enhanced SDG capacity in developing countries
17.10 Promote a universal trading system under the WTO
17.11 Increase the exports of developing countries
17.12 Remove trade barriers for least developing countries
17.13 Enhance global macroeconomic stability
17.14 Enhance policy coherence for sustainable development
17.15 Respect national leadership to implement policies for the sustainable development goals
17.16 Enhance the global partnership for sustainable development
17.17 Encourage effective partnerships
17.18 Enhance availability of reliable data
17.19 Further develop measurements of progress

Appendix 2

Cards for the *Web of Life* game

Web of Life Compiled by the Learning about Forests (Leaf) programme (https://leafireland.org/)

Cards with images are available to download on the following link: https://leafireland.org/resources/page/5/

Bat (e.g. Lesser horseshoe) native rare and endangered
I am a flying mammal.
I live in old houses or caves nearby forests I use echolocation to hunt my prey.
I eat beetles, spiders and flies.
I am eaten by (predators) domestic cats and bigger birds such as sparrow hawk.

Heron (e.g. Grey Heron) native and common
I am a flying mammal.
I live in old houses or caves nearby forests I use echolocation to hunt my prey.
I eat beetles, spiders and flies.
I am eaten by (predators) domestic cats and bigger birds such as sparrow hawk.

Salmon native and endangered
When I am young I live in the river and then in the Atlantic Ocean to mature.
I eat larvae, insects, worms, shellfish and other fish.
I am eaten by other fish or birds such as heron.

Ash (Fraxinus excelsior) common and native
Ireland's tallest deciduous tree.
My seeds grow in a bunch and are commonly known as the 'key bunch', they are a favourite snack for squirrels, birds and mice.
I produce timber that is strong and flexible so it is used for furniture making and also for items such as walking sticks, snooker cues and hurls.

Otter (Eurasian Otter) native and protected
I am a nocturnal, carnivorous mammal.
I live in a holt. My favourite home will be by any water environment, beside a forest.

I eat fish such as salmon, eel, frogs, crab and also some birds.

The destruction of my habitat through human disturbance and low water quality are a threat to the Irish Otter.

European Holly (Ilex aquifolium) native and protected

I am a small evergreen tree.

Separate male and female trees, only female trees have berries.

My berries are a food source for many birds.

I provide shelter from predators throughout the year, because of evergreen spiky leaves.

People praise me as a very special tree, there are many superstitions connected to me population.

Spider

I produce a special kind of silk to build my web and catch my prey

I can live almost anywhere

I eat insects such as fly, wasps or bee and other smaller spiders

I am eaten by birds and frogs

Fly

I like to eat everything!

I am eaten by birds, frogs, spiders and small mammals.

Soil

I am a living system, there are more microorganisms in a handful of soil than there are people on earth.

I act as an underground water filter.

I store carbon dioxide (app. 10%).

I am a great source of nutrients for plants.

Soil composition is 50% air and water and 50% minerals and organic matter.

Woodlouse

I eat dead or decaying plant matter – I am an 'ultimate recycler!'

I live in dark, humid places.

I am eaten by birds, small mammals or spiders.

Red Squirrel (Native and protected)

I am an omnivorous rodent.

My home is a drey, which is a nest made of twigs located on the tree.

I eat very ripe acorns, pine cones, and hazelnuts.

I am eaten by bigger birds (e.g. owls) foxes and pine martins.

I am threatened by the introduced grey squirrels, that eat the acorns before I am able to digest them (unripe).

Pine Martin (Native and protected)

I am a nocturnal mammal.

I am rare.

I like to live in woodlands.

I was hunted for fur and almost became extinct I am eaten by eagles and foxes.

I am omnivorous, I eat plants and animals such as squirrels, frogs, beetles, earthworms, berries and mushrooms.

Robin (Common, also known as redbreast)

I am territorial and will attack other birds (also same species) in order to protect my area.

I am eaten by other bigger birds and small mammals, such as pine marten.

I am omnivorous, I eat plants and animals such as insects and berries.

My nest is built in a well-concealed hollow in a wall or bank.

Bluebell (Hyacinthoides non-scripta) native and protected

I am a bulbous perennial plant. My flower looks like a bell.

My flowers in the spring create a purple carpet in the woods.

My nectar is nutritious for bees, butterflies and other insects.

Beetle (Coleoptera) native and common

I can live almost anywhere.

I am eaten by wasps, spiders, mice, birds (e.g. robin).

I like to eat plant parts such as leaves, seeds or fruits, or fungus and dung, and sometimes smaller insects.

Bee (there are 97 bee species in Ireland. Some species of bees are common some are endangered)

I am super important, I am a pollinator!

I live in a hive, in the hollow of a tree, or in a manmade beehive.

I am eaten by birds and some mammals and wasps.

Wren (Common resident throughout Ireland)

I live in a nest in the hollow of a tree or in a nesting box.

I eat insects such as beetles, flies and spiders.

I am eaten by mammals such as pine marten or red fox.

Chaffinch (Common resident throughout Ireland)

My nest is made out of moss and dried grass - often camouflaged with lichens and cobwebs.

I am eaten by bigger birds and mammals such as squirrels.

I like to eat mainly seeds, split grain or beechnuts My young feed on insects.

Rain (water is essential for life)

I fall from the clouds in the form of droplets, depending on the temperature I reach the earth as rain, hail, sleet or snow. This is called precipitation.

I can help generate electricity through hydropower.

River

I am a natural flowing watercourse that moves towards the ocean, sea, lake or other river.

Smaller rivers are called streams, creeks or brooks.
Sometimes I flow underground beneath the surface
World's longest river is the Nile, 6,650km Ireland's longest river is the Shannon 360.5km

Oak

I am known as the 'King of the Forest'.
I provide a habitat for over 400 different species.
I produce nuts called acorns, which are eaten by squirrels and other animals.
You can find Pedunculate Oak and Sessile Oak in Ireland - sessile means that the acorns have no stalk and pedunculate oak hang from long stalks.

Snowdrop

I appear in the Spring.
I prefer to grow in shady woodland areas, near streams or other damp areas.
My flowers and blubs are poisonous if eaten by humans.

Frog (Rana temporaria) native and protected

I am an amphibian and like to live on land and in the water
I hibernate during winter
My young are called tadpoles and feed on algae and small aquatic insects
I eat slugs and insects such as flies, mosquitos, moths and dragonflies
I use my sticky tongue to catch my prey I am eaten by otters, foxes and herons

Human 1

I am cutting down trees for paper production and not replanting.
Some human activities can be destructive. Can you think of ways we could change?

Human 2

I am polluting the rivers and making it difficult for species to live in them.
Some human activities can be destructive. Can you think of ways we could change?

Human 3

I am planting trees in my local area and taking part in community clean ups.
Some human activities can be constructive. Can you think of any ways we can help?

Note about the leaf programme (https://leafireland.org/)

The Learning about Forests (LEAF) programme is designed for schools and encourages environmental education through awareness raising among students, teachers and the wider community. The programme looks at all the functions of forests, ecological, social, economical and cultural.

The overall aims of the programme are to see an increased level of awareness and knowledge about the key role forests play for sustainable life on our planet and to stimulate activities that will help students achieve an increased level of environmental maturity irrespective of age and previous knowledge.

Appendix 3

Go Bingo (Taking action for change)

Instructions

Preparation

Prepare 10 to 20 "Find Someone Who" statements using vocabulary or concepts that relate to climate change. For example find someone who is able to draw the carbon cycle. Further examples are provided in Table 1. Create a variety of statements so that it will be easy to find a person with some characteristics but not so easy to find others. Each set of statements can be tailor made to suit examples of activism in your locality/region/country.

Directions

Announce that the class is going to do a brief interview activity in which students will ask each other questions relating to climate change. The goal is for each student to complete their sheet of statements/or one line of statements, matching each statement with a named student. Instruct students to find someone who can answer one of their questions or say "yes" to one of the descriptions. They should write that person's name on their checklist sheet and move on to the next question with another person. **Important:** A student can write a person's name only once.

Complete the chart

Ask everyone to stand up and begin the activity for a set amount of time. The goal of the activity may be to complete the entire chart or to tick five in a row.

Extension work

To review this exercise the teacher can discuss each item and ask children to discuss the definitions /concepts and to physically draw and label the carbon cycle.

Appendix 3

Find someone who

Table 1 Statements for climate change Go Bingo (NB these should be adapted in line with local social, economic and cultural factors

Volunteered with a local charity or development group Name_____	Read a book about an environmental or social justice issue Name_____	Had a difficult conversation with a person with whom you disagreed Name_____	Listening to a friend as s(he) described a problem and his/her emotional response
Sign an online petition Name_____	Adopted the role of group leader in a recent project Name_____	Has heard or read about climate change in the news Name_____	Has had a recent conversation with family members about climate change Name_____
Wrote a letter to a local or national newspaper Name_____	Has ever planted a flower or a tree Name_____	Has taken an action to address climate change (please note the kind of action taken) Name_____	Has considered running for a seat in local or national government Name_____
Stopped an act of prejudice or injustice Name_____	Learned about the SDGs Name_____	Knows the name of the government minister with the environment/climate change portfolio Name_____	Watched a TV documentary about an issue of local/global justice. Name_____
Include an action related to a local issue here. Name_____	Include an action related to a local issue here. Name_____	Has been on the Green School Committee at one time Name_____	Name_____

Appendix 4

Loop cards for climate change game

I have….
The name **'Arctic'** originates from the word 'arktos' which is a Greek word for bear.

Who has…….. Little Bear

I have….
Astronomers usually call the **'Little Bear'** constellation Ursa Minor (Latin for 'little bear'). In North America, the shape is called the Little Dipper. By far the most important and famous star in Ursa Minor is the North or Pole Star, known as Polaris. This is the star at the very end of the bear's long tail, hence the name Arctic.

Who has…….. Arctic Circle

I have….
This northernmost region of Earth, is located within the **'Arctic Circle'**, a line of latitude about 66.5° north of the Equator. Within this circle are the Arctic ocean basin and the northern parts of Scandinavia, Russia, Canada, Greenland, and the U.S. state of Alaska.

Who has…….. Sea Ice

I have….
The Arctic is almost entirely covered by water, much of it frozen. Each summer, the area of **'sea ice'** coverage decreases and grows again in winter.

Who has…….. Global Warming

I have….
As a result of **'global warming',** the overall area of the Arctic Ocean covered by sea ice has reduced rapidly over the past few decades. This means that the Arctic region is shrinking.

Who has………
Habitat for polar bears and seals

I have….
The sea ice cover is a hunting ground and 'habitat for polar bears and seals' and keeps the Arctic cool by reflecting sunlight.

Who has………
A wetter Arctic

I have….
A warmer Arctic will be **'a wetter Arctic'.** The movement from a frozen region towards a warmer, wetter Arctic will be due to the capacity of a warmer atmosphere to hold more moisture, by increased rates of evaporation from ice-free oceans, and by the jet stream relaxing.

Who has………
Ice dependent species

I have….
'Ice dependent species' such as narwhals, polar bears and walruses are at increasing risk with shrinking sea ice cover

Who has………
What happens in the Arctic
does not stay in the Arctic

I have….
'What happens in the Arctic does not stay in the Arctic'. Without urgent action to reduce greenhouse gas emissions, the world will continue to feel the effects of a warming Arctic: rising sea levels, changes in climate and precipitation patterns, increasing severe weather events, and loss of fish stocks, birds and marine mammals.

Who has………
The temperature is rising in the Arctic

I have….
'The temperature is rising in the Arctic'. The average temperature of the Arctic has increased 2.3degrees C since the 1970s. This is twice the global average

Who has………
The albedo effect

I have….
'The albedo effect' is refers to the ability of surfaces to reflect sunlight (heat from the sun). Light-coloured surfaces such as ice return a large part of the sunrays back to the atmosphere (high albedo). Dark surfaces such as bare rock and water absorb the rays from the sun (low albedo). As the Arctic loses snow and ice, bare rock and water absorb more and more of the sun's energy, making it even warmer. This is called the albedo effect.

Who has………
Feedback loop

I have….
In climate change, a **'feedback loop'** is the equivalent of a vicious circle – something that increases or decreases a warming pattern. A positive feedback loop increases temperature rise. The absorption of heat energy at the Earth's surface further warms the atmosphere, which causes more ice and snow to melt in an increasingly rapid cycle. This whole sequence is an example of a positive feedback loop– global warming is melting ice, thus reinforcing global warming, which further increases ice loss.

Who has………
Offshore oil production in the Arctic

I have….
Reduced ice cover is making it possible for more companies to explore possibilities for **'offshore oil production'** in the Arctic' which will further increase global warming.

Who has………
Sea level rise

I have….
The continual melting of the world's glaciers is fuelling **'sea level rise',** threatening coastal cities with flooding.

Who has………
Jet Stream

I have….
Strong rivers of westerly winds, known as jet streams, are driven primarily by temperature differences between low and high latitudes as well as the rotation of the Earth. As the Arctic warms, changes in the jet stream would have potential implications for the frequency of extreme weather in a future, warmer climate. This means an increase in the severity of heatwaves, intense rains, floods and fires.

Who has………
Gulf Stream

I have….
'The Gulf Stream', a strong ocean current brings water towards western Europe, with the result that air temperatures over the UK and Ireland are a few degrees higher that they would otherwise be.

Who has………
Freshwater

I have….
Some frozen features, such as glaciers and icebergs, are frozen **'freshwater'**.
Fresh water is vital to life and yet it is a finite resource. Of all the water on Earth, just 3% is fresh water. Fresh water is found in glaciers, lakes, reservoirs, ponds, rivers, streams, wetlands and even groundwater.

Who has………
As cold as Toronto

I have….
The glaciers and icebergs in the Arctic make up about 20% of Earth's supply of freshwater. If the melting of the polar ice caps releases large amounts of freshwater into the world's oceans, climate scientists fear that this could reduce the effect of the Gulf Stream meaning that Ireland and the UK could be '**as cold as Toronto**' during the winter months.

Who has………
Permafrost

I have….
'Permafrost' is any ground that **remains completely frozen**–32°F (0°C) or colder–for at least two years straight. These permanently frozen grounds are most common in regions with high mountains and in Earth's higher latitudes–near the North and South Poles.

Who has………
Thawing permafrost

I have....
The Arctic is warming more that twice as fast as the rest of the world, and some scientists believe that 'thawing permafrost', ground frozen since the last ice age, is about to release enormous amounts of climate warming emissions.

Who has.........
Tundra

I have....
A biome is a large area characterized by its vegetation, soil, climate, and wildlife. The Arctic is a **'tundra'** biome. This is a cold, dry desert environment with few plants on the surface, other than shrubs and mosses. Underneath there are hidden treasures in the permafrost (a layer of soil and water mixed and frozen together). One key element is peat, thousands-of-years-old semi-decomposed organic matter rich in carbon, which is highly flammable when it dries out.

Who has.........
Lightning

I have....
As the Arctic has warmed and the ice that keeps the poles cold has melted, warmer water temperatures have heated the air just enough to form storm clouds and discharge **'lightning'**. This provides the spark which causes several wildfires.

Who has.........
Boreal Forests

I have....
'Boreal forests' are still full of life that's adapted to withstand frigid temperatures year-round, such as caribou reindeer, or animals that can migrate long distances every winter. Full of deciduous trees and conifers, Boreal forests cover vast expanses in Canada, Alaska, and Russia. Boreal forests are also an important carbon sink. Like all forests they absorb carbon dioxide –a main contributor to global warming and climate change–removing it from the atmosphere and helping to keep the entire planet healthy.

Who has.........
Arctic

Please note: the cards for this game are available to download from the padlet (under the Games Section) https://padlet.com/annedolan/teaching-the-global-goals-o6rds38ylfy6a28h

Index

Note: **Bold** page numbers refer to tables and *italic* page numbers refer to figures.

For Product Safety Concerns and Information please contact our EU
representative GPSR@taylorandfrancis.com
Taylor & Francis Verlag GmbH, Kaufingerstraße 24, 80331 München, Germany

www.ingramcontent.com/pod-product-compliance
Lightning Source LLC
Chambersburg PA
CBHW061738210326
41599CB00034B/6723

9 781032 140285